Best Practices in the Behavioral Management of Health from Preconception to Adolescence

Volume III

Edited by Jodie A. Trafton, Ph.D. and William P. Gordon, Ph.D.
Institute for Disease Management

Published by Institute for Brain Potential

We would like to acknowledge the editorial assistance of Genevieve Tregor, M.S.

Jodie A. Trafton, Ph.D. and William P. Gordon, Ph.D., Editors

All guidelines and discussions are presented as examples or generalized information only and should never be used as the basis for a legal document. They are intended as resources that can be selectively used and adapted with the advice of legal and medical resources to meet state, local and individual hospital, and specific departmental needs and requirements.

The editors have made every effort to ensure the accuracy of the information herein, particularly with regard to drug selection, dose and behavioral treatments. However, appropriate information sources should be consulted, especially for new or unfamiliar drugs or procedures. It is the responsibility of every practitioner to evaluate the appropriateness of a particular opinion in the context of actual clinical situations and with due consideration to new developments. Authors, editors and the publisher cannot be held responsible for typographical or content errors found in this publication.

Orders: 866-992-9399
Customer Service: 650-960-3536

Library of Congress Cataloging-in-Publication Data

Best Practices in the Behavioral Management of Chronic Disease
Volume I: Neuropsychiatric Disorders
ISBN 978-1-932745-15-3   Library of Congress Control Number: 2007932255

Best Practices in the Behavioral Management of Chronic Disease
Volume II: Other Medical Disorders
ISBN 978-1-932745-32-0   Library of Congress Control Number: 2007932255

Best Practices in the Behavioral Management of Health from Preconception to Adolescence
Volume III
ISBN 978-1-932745-46-7   Library of Congress Control Number: 2007941663

IBP is a non-profit organization dedicated to providing advances in Behavioral Medicine through publications and conferences. IBP is a 501 (c) (3) organization (tax identification number 77-0026830) founded in 1984 as Institute for Cortext Research and Development. The Institute has trained over one million health professionals in the neurobehavioral sciences and has published books in the fields of Neuropsychology and Behavioral Medicine.

Printed in the United States of America

Volume III: PRECONCEPTION TO ADOLESCENCE

Contact Information and Additional Grant Support

Chapter 1: PRECONCEPTION CARE: IMPROVING BIRTH OUTCOMES THROUGH CARE BEFORE PREGNANCY
Brian Jack, M.D.
Department of Family Medicine
Boston University School of Medicine
Dowling 5
1 Boston Medical Center Place
Boston, MA 02118
Brian.Jack@bmc.org

Chapter 2: BEHAVIORAL INTERVENTIONS TO DECREASE THE BURDENS OF LOW BIRTHWEIGHT, LARGE FOR GESTATIONAL AGE, AND BIRTH DEFECTS
Jodie A. Trafton, Ph.D.[1] and Jennifer M. Singler, M.D.[2]
[1]Institute for Disease Management
P.O. Box J
Los Altos, CA
In4brain@mindspring.com
[2]University of California at Davis Medical School
Jmsingler@aol.com

Chapter 3: PREVENTING MOTHER-TO-CHILD TRANSMISSION OF HIV
Claire Thorn, MSc, Ph.D[1] and Marie-Louise Newell, M.B, MSc, Ph.D.[2]
MRC Centre of Epidemiology for Child Health
Institute of Child Health
University College London
30 Guilford Street
London, WC1N 1EH, UK
[1]c.thorne@ich.ucl.ac.uk
[2]m.newell@ich.ucl.ac.uk

Chapter 4: BIRTH: CARE OF INFANT AND MOTHER: TIME-SENSITIVE ISSUES
Maria Blois, M.D.
mgblois@aol.com

Chapter 5: INTERVENTIONS TO INCREASE CHILDHOOD VACCINATION RATES
James A. Taylor, M.D.
Child Health Institute
University of Washington
Box 354920
Seattle, WA 98195-4920
uncjat@u.washington.edu

Chapter 6: BEHAVIORAL INTERVENTIONS FOR PEDIATRIC ASTHMA

Ellen F. Crain, M.D., Ph.D.[1] and William Crain, Ph.D.[2]

[1]Jacobi Medical Center, Albert Einstein College of Medicine

1B25, Bldg.6, Jacobi Hospital

1400 Pelham Parkway

Bronx, NY 10461

ellen.crain@nbhn.net

[2] The City College of the City University of New York

NA 7/303

138th Street and Convent Avenue

New York, NY 10031

wcrain@ccny.cuny.edu

Chapter 7: BEHAVIORAL INTERVENTIONS FOR AUTISM SPECTRUM CONDITIONS

Gina Owens[1], Rosanna Kate Gordon, Ph.D.[2] and Simon Baron-Cohen, Ph.D.[1]

[1]Autism Research Centre

University of Cambridge, Douglas House

18b Trumpington Road,

Cambridge, CB2 8AH, UK

Gao20@medschl.cam.ac.uk

[2]Royal College of Psychiatrists' Research and Training Unit

Standon House

21 Mansell Street

London, E18AA, UK

kgordon@cru.rcpsych.ac.uk

Chapter 8: BEHAVIORAL INTERVENTIONS FOR EATING DISORDERS

Phillipa J. Hay, Ph.D.

School of Medicine Building 3,

Campbelltown Campus University of Western Sydney

2570 NSW, Australia

p.hay@uws.edu.au

Chapter 9: PRIMARY PREVENTION OF OBESITY

Nancy Sherwood, Ph.D[1], Robert Jeffery, Ph.D.[2]

[1]HealthPartners Research Foundation

8100 34th Avenue South

Post Office Box 1524

Minneapolis MN 55440-1524

Nancy.E.Sherwood@HealthPartners.com

[2]University of Minnesota Twin Cities

Department of Epidemiology, Room 300 WBOB 7525

1300 South 2nd St

Minneapolis MN 55454

Jeffery@epi.umn.edu

Chapter 10: LONG-TERM OUTCOMES OF TREATMENT FOR ATTENTION-DEFICIT/HYPERACTIVITY DISORDER

Jonathan D. Schmidt, Bradley H. Smith, Ph.D.
Department of Psychology, University of South Carolina
Columbia, SC 29208
smithb@gwm.sc.edu
Jonathandeanschmidt@yahoo.com

Chapter 11: EMPIRICALLY SUPPORTED TREATMENTS FOR CONDUCT DISORDERS IN CHILDREN AND ADOLESCENTS

Dustin A. Pardini, Ph.D.
Department of Psychiatry, University of Pittsburgh Medical Center
201 N. Craig St., Suite 408
Pittsburgh, PA 15213
dap38@pitt.edu

Chapter 12: PREVENTION OF YOUTH SMOKING

Raymond Niaura, Ph.D[1], Alessandra N. Kazura, M.D.[2]
Department of Psychiatry & Human Behavior
Centers for Behavioral & Preventive Medicine, The Miriam Hospital
Coro Center, Suite 500
One Hoppin Street
Providence, RI 02903
[1]Raymond_Niaura@brown.edu
[2]Akazura@lifespan.org

Chapter 13: ALCOHOL AND DRUG USE AMONG YOUTH: ADVANCES IN PREVENTION

Elizabeth J. D'Amico, Ph.D., and Stefanie A. Stern, M.A.
RAND
1776 Main Street
Santa Monica, CA 90401-3208
damico@rand.org
stern@rand.org

Chapter 14: INTERVENTIONS TO REDUCE RISKY SEXUAL BEHAVIOR, PREGNANCY AND SEXUALLY TRANSMITTED DISEASE IN TEENS

Douglas Kirby, Ph.D., and B.A. Laris
ETR Associates
4 Carbonero Way,
Scotts Valley, CA 95066
dougk@etr.org
Acknowledgement: This chapter is based on Emerging Answers 2007: Research Findings on Programs to Reduce Teen Pregnancy and Sexually Transmitted Diseases, Washington, D.C. National Campaign to Prevent Teen and Unplanned Pregnancy, 2007.

Chapter 15: BEHAVIORAL INTERVENTIONS TO REDUCE YOUTH EXPOSURE TO UNHEALTHFUL MEDIA
Leonard A. Jason, Ph.D. and William T. O'Donnell, Jr.
DePaul University, Center for Community Research
990 W. Fullerton Ave., Suite 3100
Chicago, Il. 60614
ljason@depaul.edu

Chapter 16: PREVENTION OF SCHOOL VIOLENCE
Catherine N. Dulmus, Ph.D.,[1] Eugene Maguin, Ph.D.,[1] Amy R. Manning, LMSW[2]
University at Buffalo, School of Social Work
[1]Buffalo Center for Social Research
221 Parker Hall
Buffalo, NY 14214-8004
cdulmus@buffalo.edu
emaguin@buffalo.edu
[2]685 Baldy Hall
Buffalo, NY 14260
amanning@buffalo.edu

Chapter 17: PREVENTION OF CHILDREN & YOUTHS' ACCESS TO AND OPERATION OF FIREARMS: A REVIEW OF INTERVENTIONS
Renee M. Johnson, Ph.D., MPH, David Hemenway, Ph.D.
Harvard School of Public Health
677 Huntington Avenue, Kresge Building Room 309
Boston, MA 02115
hemenway@hsph.harvard.edu
rejohnso@hsph.harvard.edu

Chapter 18: BEHAVIORAL INTERVENTIONS TO REDUCE INTIMATE PARTNER VIOLENCE AGAINST WOMEN
Gene Feder, Ph.D.[1], Marianne Hester, Ph.D.[2], Emma Williamson, Ph.D.[2] and Danielle Dunne[1]
[1]Centre for Human Sciences, Barts and the London
Queen Mary's School of Medicine and Dentistry
2 Newark Street
Whitechapel, London, E1 2AT
g.s.feder@qmul.ac.uk
d.e.dunne@qmul.ac.uk
[2]University of Bristol,
School for Policy Studies,
8 Priory Road,
Bristol, BS8 1TZ.
Marianne.Hester@bristol.ac.uk
E.Williamson@bristol.ac.uk

Preface

This new text is the first of its kind to bring together evidence-based reviews concerning behavioral interventions during the period from preconception, through infancy, childhood and adolescence. The topics include:

Preconception and Perinatal Development
There is now convincing evidence that behavioral interventions significantly reduce the risk of birth complications such as low birth weight, birth defects such as neural tube defects, and pediatric HIV.

Infancy Through Early Childhood
Modifiable environmental factors can greatly reduce the severity of asthma and there are effective ways to promote vaccination during childhood. Early diagnosis and treatment can lessen the lifelong problems arising from autism spectrum disorders.

Childhood Through Adolescence
There is also compelling evidence that early behavioral interventions can ameliorate attention deficits/hyperactivity disorders and the lifelong problems that can follow conduct disorders and antisocial behavior.

Eating disorders often develop in childhood. Primary prevention of obesity can be achieved through careful behavioral intervention. Guidelines for educators, parents and health professionals can be effectively implemented to reduce the likelihood of playing with firearms, use of illicit drugs and of smoking.

There are effective behavioral interventions that reduce the likelihood that youth will engage in risky sexual behavior, acquire sexually transmitted disease and have an unwanted pregnancy. Behavioral methods can also prevent violence at school and protect against intimate partner violence.

Conclusions
1. The most cost-effective and health-effective interventions begin at the earliest points in the life cycle, from preventing unwanted pregnancy, fetal abnormalities, and infant mortality, to acquiring life-long habits that make children and teens resistant to obesity, smoking, use of illicit drugs, antisocial behavior, and intimate partner violence.
2. The burden of health-related problems acquired by one generation is carried by the next generation, so that the lifetime costs in health and productivity are of a huge magnitude.
3. Unhealthful behaviors acquired before adulthood are more persistent and resistant to change, as is documented in Volumes I and II in this series.
4. Primary prevention is not only possible but should be a high priority for parents, educators, health professionals, and policy-makers.

We hope you enjoy this text. You will read state-of-the art findings that can be of immediate benefit to health professionals, educators, students, community and governmental organizations, and parents.

About The Best Practice Series:

Volumes I and II in the Best Practice Series review techniques for addressing chronic neuropsychiatric and medical disorders in adults. With the 2008 publication of Volume III, we now make available key research on changing unhealthful behavior throughout the lifespan.

The third volume extends our *Best Practices in Behavioral Management* series to include evidence-based interventions to optimize the health and functioning of youth. This three volume set provides the most comprehensive review of evidence-based research on interventions to promote health behavior change.

Written by national and international experts in the prevention and management of unhealthful behavior and chronic disease, *Best Practices* is divided into three volumes. In each volume, the chapters are organized to review the best controlled trials, focusing on long-term, randomized samples. The results are summarized in helpful tables. Authors present key insights, important advances, practice recommendations, and limitations of current knowledge. Volume I presents advances in preventing and managing chronic neuropsychiatric disorders and Volume II presents advances in preventing and managing other chronic medical disorders.

Volume III identifies effective clinical, community and public health interventions for preventing and managing conditions that start before adulthood. It is a valuable resource for health professionals, educators, policy and decision makers, researchers, students and informed parents. We believe you will find this work helpful in your efforts to insure children and youth receive a healthy start to life and develop lifelong habits that improve health and wellbeing.

PRECONCEPTION CARE: IMPROVING BIRTH OUTCOMES THROUGH CARE BEFORE PREGNANCY

Brian Jack, MD

INTRODUCTION

Preconception Care is widely recognized as an important component of health care for women of reproductive age (Institute of Medicine, 1985; Moos and Cefalo, 1987; Public Health Service, 1989; Committee on Perinatal Health, 1992; Jack and Culpepper, 1990; Cefalo and Moos, 1995; American College of Obstetricians and Gynecologists, 2003; Misra et al., 2003; Bernstein et al., 2000; Allaire and Cefalo, 1998; Moos, 2004). The overarching goal of preconception care is to provide health promotion, screening, and interventions to women of reproductive age to reduce risk factors that might affect future pregnancies (Fowler and Jack, 2003; Jack and Culpepper, 1991; Reynolds, 1998). Preconception care is part of a larger health care paradigm that leads to healthier women, infants and families (Weisman, 1997; Clancy and Maission, 1992). Recently, the CDC defined preconception care as:

> Preconception care is comprised of interventions that aim to identify and modify biomedical, behavioral, and social risks to a woman's health or pregnancy outcome through prevention and management, emphasizing those factors which must be acted on before conception or early in pregnancy to have maximal impact. Thus, it is more than a single visit and less than all well-woman care. It includes care before a first pregnancy or between pregnancies (commonly known as interconception care) (Centers for Disease Control and Prevention, 2006).

Preconception health promotion, counseling and risk assessment implies addressing potential precursors to adverse pregnancy outcomes before becoming pregnant. This suggests that providers will identify and address medical and psychosocial issues even before reproductive age. For example, the parent of a child with an inherited disorder would be counseled on the potential risk this would have on their offspring during their childbearing years. A sedentary teen might be counseled on her risk for obesity and its impact on future pregnancies and outcomes. Preconception guidelines should incorporate practical tools to address contraception and birth spacing, health education literacy and promotion, nutrition and weight management, tobacco and substance abuse, environmental exposures, medication benefits and risk, risky sexual behaviors, infection risks, optimal management of medical problems, stress reduction, and identification of skilled trained healthcare teams to address issues before becoming pregnant.

Preconception care is important because, for some conditions, treatment before pregnancy is essential. For example, there is substantial evidence that for optimal impact on reducing the risk of neural tube defects folic acid supplementation should start at least three months before conception. For other conditions, preconception care is important because many of the risk behaviors and exposures that impact fetal development and subsequent outcomes have their greatest impact during organogenesis, the first 48 to 52 days of pregnancy, before women enter prenatal care or even before they know they are pregnant.

Preconception care is not a new concept. William Dewee in 1825 in the first American textbook of Pediatrics wrote:

> "Physical treatment of children should begin as far as may be practicable, with the earliest formation of the

embryo; it will, therefore, necessarily involve the conduct of the mother, even before her marriage, as well as during her pregnancy."

Preconception care was first described in the modern era by Chamberlain in 1980 as a specialty service for women who had a previous poor reproductive outcome (Chamberlain, 1980; Chamberlain, 1981; Chamberlain and Lumley, 1986). It was then described by the US Public Health Service in the landmark publication "Preventing Low Birth Weight (Institute of Medicine, 1985) and later by Moos and Cephalo at the University of North Carolina (Moos and Cefalo, 1987). The concept was adopted by the US Public Health Service's Expert Panel on the Content of Prenatal Care (Public Health Service, 1991; Jack and Culpepper, 1990) who defined its components and emphasized that it is most effectively delivered as part of primary care services. Development of the concept was identified as a priority for the 1990s by the U.S. Public Health Service who included a recommendation to increase the proportion of primary care providers who offer age-appropriate preconception care and counseling to at least 60%, among their health promotion and disease prevention objectives for the year 2000 (US Public Health Service, 1991; US Public Health Service, 2000). Healthy People 2010 includes many objectives that address preconception health.

The importance of preconception care as a concept was articulated over the next decade in family medicine (Committee on Perinatal Health, 1993; Gjerdingen and Fontaine, 1991; Frey, 2002; Jack, 1995), obstetrics and gynecology (American College of Obstetricians and Gynecologists, 1995; American College of Obstetricians and Gynegologists, 2005; American College of Obstetricians and Gynecologists, 2003), nurse midwifery (Reynolds, 1998), nursing (Moos, 2002; Moos, 2003; Moos, 2004), and public health (Misra et al., 2003). The "Guidelines for

Perinatal Care" jointly issued by the AAP and ACOG recommends that "All health encounters during a woman's reproductive years, particularly those that are a part of preconception care should include counseling on appropriate medical care and behavior to optimize pregnancy outcomes" (American College of Obstetricians and Gynecologists, 2002; American Academy of Pediatrics, 2002; American College of Obstetricians and Gynecologists, 2005). In 2002, the March of Dimes suggested that "as the key physician/ primary care provider, the obstetrician/ gynecologist must take advantage of every health encounter to provide preconception care and risk reduction before and between conceptions – the time when it really can make a difference". The American Diabetes Association (2004), the American Academy of Neurology (Report of the Quality Standards Subcommittee of the American Academy of Neurology, 1998) and the American Heart Association/American College of Cardiologists (Hirsh et al., 2003) promulgated recommendations on preconception care in their specialties.

Despite this interest, there are only modest number of reports showing progress in implementing these concepts into clinical practice and very little research in this area. In 2006, the CDC re-energized the area of preconception care by convening a Select Panel on Preconception Care who made a series of recommendations aimed at achieving four goals to (1) improve the knowledge, attitudes and behaviors of men and women related to preconception health; (2) assure that all women of childbearing age in the United States receive preconception care services that will enable them to enter pregnancy in optimal health; (3) reduce risks indicated by a previous adverse pregnancy outcome through interventions during the interconception period and (4) reduce the disparities in adverse pregnancy outcomes (Centers for Disease Control and Prevention, 2006). The

CDC initiative led to workgroups to study and make recommendations for moving the concept of preconception care forward in the areas of clinical care, pubic health and consumer awareness (see section VII. "Next Steps and The Research Agenda").

COMPONENTS OF PRECONCEPTION CARE

Preconception care includes the provision of health education individualized to a woman's or couple's needs (health promotion), a thorough and systematic identification of risks (risk assessment), and the initiation of actions to address those risks (interventions). Each of these three components will be discussed below.

Preconception Heath Promotion

Health promotion that applies to all women of childbearing age is an important component of preconception care and consists of counseling and education to support healthful behavior about pregnancy and parenting. In family practice, education about pregnancy, birth, and parenting occurs throughout the parenting years. The preconception visit is an opportunity for more intensive involvement. Table 1 shows the content of the health promotion component of preconception care.

Table 1: Content of Preconception Care: Health Promotion by Education and Counseling (from Jack and Culpepper, 1990)

1. Pregnancy, birth, and parenting
2. Good dietary habits and optimal weight
3. Adverse health behaviors including tobacco, alcohol, and illicit drugs
4. Environmental exposures
5. Medications
6. Safe sexual practices
7. Exercise programs
8. Pregnancy planning, pregnancy spacing, and contraception
9. Prevention of unwanted pregnancy including imparting knowledge, influencing attitudes, providing contraception, and enhancing life options
10. Importance of early prenatal care
11. Counseling about the availability of social, financial, and vocational assistance programs
12. Arrangements for ongoing primary care

Pregnancy Readiness

An objective of preconception care is to assess a woman's readiness for pregnancy. Unwanted and unintended pregnancy is a major problem in the United States, where nearly half of all pregnancies are unintended. Unintended pregnancy is associated with delays in the initiation of prenatal care and behaviors that increase the risk for adverse birth outcomes. Interventions to prevent unwanted pregnancy obviously must occur before conception. Preconception health promotion supports the idea that women can choose whether to become pregnant. Preconception health promotion provides the opportunity to provide counseling about pregnancy planning, spacing, and contraception. These visits offer opportunities for reproductive education about such topics as sexuality, information sources on pregnancy and parenting, pregnancy planning, and readiness for pregnancy, including the option of delaying or not having children. For many women, the recognition that they can take control and direct the course of their own lives, rather than being at the mercy of external forces, is a necessary component of adopting control of their reproductive potential. Counseling can be offered about the availability of social programs, including vocational training, which might be considered an alternative to pregnancy (see Chapter 14). However, the effectiveness of such counseling during the preconception period has not been tested in controlled trials.

Family Planning

Family planning, education, and social services needed to provide these interventions should be considered part of preconception care. Because approximately half of pregnancies in the US are unintended many have suggested that health risks and behaviors need to be addressed at any encounter with the health care system (Institute of Medicine, 1995; Henshaw, 1998). There is some evidence that provision of preconception care can increase pregnancy planning and intention. In a sample of 1378 pregnant women presenting for prenatal care at a local health department, those who were previously exposed to a family planning preconception program (n= 456) were 51.8% more likely to identify their pregnancy as planned than those who attended the clinic prior to pregnancy but were not exposed to the preconception program (n=309) (Moos et al., 1996). This finding is important because research has consistently shown that planned pregnancies generally have better outcomes for both the women and infant. In addition, women who have benefited from preconception preventive interventions and experience unintended pregnancies may have fewer risk factors and adverse outcomes.

The interventions available include imparting knowledge, influencing attitudes, providing access to contraceptives, and enhancing life options. If a woman and her partner opt to delay pregnancy, the preconception visit offers the family physician an opportunity to discuss methods of contraception. Careful,

consistent use of contraception and conscientiously planning pregnancy can improve fetal outcome, reduce the number of abortions, have an impact on child abuse and neglect, and reduce health care costs. Since up to 50 percent of pregnancies are unplanned, contraceptive counseling is very important to decrease unwanted pregnancies and poor perinatal outcomes. Every woman of reproductive age should receive counseling and information about contraception options from abstinence to permanent sterilization. Unplanned pregnancies are associated with fetal anomalies caused by antibiotics (Yaris, 2004), higher rates of abortion, emotional distress, and low birth weight, higher rates of medical problems before and during the index pregnancy, later prenatal care entrance (Bitto et al., 1997) and parental neglect. Many opportunities exist for contraception counseling. However, if counseling is not initiated or insufficiently completed prior to the index pregnancy, providers should take the opportunity to discuss the link between short interval pregnancy and poor perinatal outcomes in the subsequent pregnancy before the woman is discharged from the hospital postpartum. Patients should be counseled that pregnancy intervals less than 27 months are associated with adverse perinatal and maternal outcomes. Risks associated with short interval pregnancies include low birth weight, prematurity, schizophrenia (Smits et al., 2004), SIDS, and neonatal death (USAID, 2002).

Choosing Healthy Behaviors

Counseling to promote and support healthful behavior should foster the idea that the woman can choose healthful behaviors. The preconception visit offers an opportunity to discuss many health options. Examples include a discussion of exercise programs, dietary habits, and optimal weight. Health promotion topics include helping women with smoking cessation, discussing risk associated with alcohol and drug use, and identifying resources for assistance with substance abuse and risky behaviors. Counseling about avoiding teratogenic medications or choosing alternative regimens is also important before pregnancy. Notably, however, counseling and other interventions to reduce use of teratogenic medications before pregnancy have not been tested in controlled trials, so the efficacy of such interventions for reducing birth defects is not known (see Chapter 2). The preconception visit offers an opportunity to provide information on avoidance of occupational hazards and exposure to environmental toxins. Working mothers can be counseled about work place hazards, legal rights of pregnant workers, and childcare options. Counseling about safe sexual practices and ways to prevent sexually transmitted diseases (STDs) including human immunodeficiency virus (HIV) is important before pregnancy.

Ongoing Primary Care

Preconception care should stress the value of early enrollment for prenatal care. Knowledge about publicly funded prenatal programs, eligibility requirements, and application processes may help low income women plan for risk reduction visits before and during pregnancy. This information may encourage women to enroll early for prenatal care once pregnant. Women should be encouraged to maintain an accurate menstruation calendar along with a record of the discontinuation of oral contraceptives and of any non-menstrual bleeding. It might allow more accurate dating of conception, which can better identify those women who are truly postdates and require intervention and can reduce the number of women erroneously considered postmature.

Preconception Risk Assessment

Preconception risk assessment identifies potential risk to future pregnancy and addresses those risks before conception. Risk assessment includes inquiring about general health status of both potential parents, physical examination and limited laboratory testing. Factors listed as part of preconception risk assessment were chosen based upon similar principles as outlined in the Report of the US Preventive Services Task Force, Guide of Clinical Preventive Services (US Preventive Services Task Force, 1996). Briefly, the following were used to select conditions included in the package of preconception services.

- The burden of suffering of the target condition;
- The condition presents in clinical care, either in primary or specialty settings;
- The accuracy of the screening tests available to detect the condition;
- The potential effectiveness and efficacy of the interventions available;
- The intervention had to be more effective if the condition was identified and addressed before pregnancy than if the screening for and treatment of the condition was equally efficacious during pregnancy. For example, there is no evidence that screening for and treating asymptomatic bacteruria before pregnancy offers any advantage to screening and treatment during pregnancy. Similarly, group B streptococcus screening and treatment is not included as part of the preconception care recommendations.

The evidence for the effectiveness identifying and intervening for each of the conditions listed is variable. Table 2 shows the fourteen preconception interventions identified by the CDC that provide clear, evidence-based effectiveness in improving pregnancy outcomes (Centers for Disease Control and Prvention, 2006). For some of the other conditions listed, there is expert consensus that common sense dictates that this activity be included (e.g., genetic counseling before pregnancy rather than during pregnancy, family planning, among others).

Table 2: Preconception Interventions That Show Clear, Evidence-Based Effectiveness in Improving Pregnancy Outcomes (from Centers for Disease Control and Prevention, 2006)

Preconception Risk Factor	Comment
Folic Acid Supplements	Daily use of vitamin supplements containing folic acid has been shown to reduce the occurrence of neural tube defects by two/thirds.
Rubella Sero-Negativity	Rubella immunization provides protective seropositivity and prevents the occurrence of the congenital rubella syndrome
Diabetes (Preconception)	The 3-fold increase in the prevalence of birth defects among infants of women with type 1 and type 2 diabetes is substantially reduced through proper management of diabetes.
Hypothyroidism	Levothyroxine® requirement for the treatment of hypothyroidism increases in early pregnancy. The dosage of Levothyroxine® needs to be adjusted for proper neurological development.
HIV/AIDS	Identification of HIV infection prior to conception allows timely treatment and provides women (or couples) additional information which can influence the timing of the onset of pregnancy.
Maternal PKU	Women diagnosed with Phenyketonurea as infants have infants with mental retardation; this adverse outcome is prevented when mothers are on a low Phenylalanine diet starting before conception and continued throughout pregnancy.
Oral Anticoagulant use	Warfarin (used for the control of blood clotting) has been shown to be a teratogen. To avoid exposure to warfarin in early pregnancy, medications can be switched to a non-teratogenic anti-coagulant before the onset of pregnancy.
Anti-Epileptic Drugs (AEDs)	Some anti-epileptic drugs are known teratogens. Women contemplating pregnancy should have teratogenic seizure control drugs changed to a less teratogenic treatment regimen prior to conception.
Accutane® Use	Use of Accutane® in pregnancy to treat acne results in miscarriage and birth defects. Effective pregnancy prevention should be implemented to avoid unintended pregnancies among women with childbearing potential who use the medication.
Smoking	Preterm birth, low birth weight, and other adverse perinatal outcomes associated with maternal smoking in pregnancy can be prevented if women stop smoking in early pregnancy. Since only 20% of women successfully control tobacco dependence during pregnancy, it is recommended that smoking cessation be completed before pregnancy begins.
Alcohol Misuse	Fetal alcohol syndrome and other alcohol-related birth defects can be prevented if alcohol binge drinking and/or frequent drinking behavior is controlled before pregnancy begins.
Obesity	Adverse perinatal outcomes associated with maternal obesity include neural tube defects, preterm delivery, diabetes, cesarean section, hypertensive and thromboembolic disease. Weight loss prior to pregnancy reduces these risks.

Using the above criteria and the evidence available, 10 categories of risks were identified. Each of these categories and specific conditions that were determined to be part of preconception risk assessment are listed in Table 3 and reviewed below.

Table 3: Content of Preconception Care: Risk Assessment (from Jack and Culpepper, 1990)
(Examples of important conditions, behaviors, or exposure are listed after each category.)

History
1. *Reproductive history:* menstrual, sexual, contraceptive, obstetric, breast-feeding
2. *Infectious disease history:* human immunodeficiency virus, hepatitis B, toxoplasmosis, rubella, varicella, bacterial vaginosis
3. *Exposure to teratogens:* occupational exposures (heavy metals, organic solvents), medications (gold, lithium, isotretinoin, folic acid antagonists, valproic acid, warfarin)
4. *Medical history:* cardiovascular disease, diabetes mellitus, seizure disorder, thyroid disease, immune thrombocytopenia, pulmonary embolism
5. *Family and genetic history:* Tay-Sachs disease, b-thalassemia, a-thalassemia, sickle cell anemia, cystic fibrosis, advanced maternal age, family history of genetic disease, previously affected pregnancy
6. *Nutrition:* food habits, attitudes, use of vitamins and minerals, food allergies, availability of food, bulimia, anorexia, pica, phenylketonuria
7. *Psychosocial risks:* lack of adequate financial resources, inadequate housing, inadequate medical insurance, communication difficulties, barriers to medical care, inadequate pregnancy readiness, lack of personal support, deficient coping skills, living in an abusive situation, psychiatric conditions, extremes of work or exercise
8. *High risk behaviors:* smoking, alcohol, substance abuse

Physical examination
1. general physical examination including blood pressure and pulse, height, weight, pelvic and breast examinations

Laboratory testing
1. *Offered to all women:* urine dipstick for protein and glucose, hemoglobin or hematocrit determination, hepatitis B and HIV testing, Papanicolaou smear
2. *Offered to high-risk women:* screening for gonorrhea, syphilis, Chlamydia, bacterial vaginosis, hemoglobinopathies, Tay-Sachs disease, abnormal parental karyotype; PPD; toxoplasmosis, herpes simplex and cytomegalovirus titers; toxicology testing for illicit drugs.

Infectious Diseases

There are several infectious diseases that adversely effect perinatal outcomes and for which there is evidence that the effect can be impacted by preconception care.

HIV

Worldwide there are more than 1900 infant lives lost to HIV daily and more than 700,000 lost annually. Perinatal HIV transmission still accounts for more than 90 percent of pediatric AIDS cases in the US. Additionally, 40 percent of these infants are born to mothers unaware of their HIV status. Preconception prevention of perinatal HIV transmission requires a multifaceted approach (see Chapter 3). Primary prevention includes early education to both men and women about risky sexual behavior such as unprotected intercourse and multiple partners, intravenous drug use, transfusions prior to 1985, and the benefit of identifying HIV positive men and women prior to conception. Couples should be counseled that transmission can occur during pregnancy, during labor, and post-natally through breastfeeding. They should be fully informed of risks. Treatment of women with antiretrovirals beginning in the first trimester through the labor period followed by treatment of the infant for 6 months reduces HIV transmission from a rate of 25 percent to 4 to 10 percent (US Public Health Service Task Force, 2002). Studies confirm that treating HIV positive mothers with anti-retrovirals can reduce perinatal transmission to 2 percent or less in women with a low viral load who do not breastfeed (Ioannidis et al., 2001). The Centers for Disease Control recommend HIV screening for all women who are pregnant. Evaluation of two programs, the opt-in and opt-out approach, assessed the frequency of HIV testing. The opt-in approach included informing women of their risk of HIV transmission to their newborn and offering them the HIV test. The opt-out approach included informing women that HIV testing was a part of the standard lab testing unless they declined being tested. Women given the opt-out approach tend to test more often, which may improve screening rates and subsequently reduce perinatal transmission (Centers for Disease Control and Prevention, 2004). For women of reproductive age, knowing HIV status prior to pregnancy allows for treatment and reduction of viral load, which will decrease transmission rates. Preconception prevention should include encouraging men and women to know their HIV status before pregnancy, reducing barriers to screening, instituting global education about risk and HIV transmission, treatment options, effective follow-up strategies for HIV positive women and discussion of further risk reduction in treated HIV positive women.

Hepatitis B

The CDC estimates that about 40,000 pregnant women per year (about 1% of pregnancies) are infected with Hepatitis B. Hepatitis B infection is declining due to routine vaccination in children and the mandate in some states for vaccination in middle school children prior to school enrollment (see Chapter 5). In 1997, the advisory committee on immunization prac-tices recommended vaccination of all children ages 0-18. The majority of these children are now of reproductive age and protected against hepatitis B infection. Therefore preconception prevention of transmission begins in childhood at birth or at the time of complete vaccination. Children between the ages of 0-18 who have not been vaccinated and adults who have high risk behavior should be offered vaccination during routine office visits prior to conception and during the peripartum period. Hepatitis B is predominantly a sexually transmitted disease in the US (Centers for Disease Control and Prevention, 2002). Causes of hepatitis B transmission include blood transfusions and lower transmissions through semen, infected wounds, and vaginal secretions. Others at high risk for hepatitis B include men who have sex with men, IV drug users, and those multiple sex partners. The USPTF does not recommend routine screening of the general population for hepatitis B. Studies have not shown a decrease risk in long-term outcomes when the general population is screened. However, all pregnant women should be screened for hepatitis B. Routine screening for hepatitis B surface antigen is protocol for prenatal care. If a woman is negative for hepatitis B and she is considered high risk because of her occupation, sexual partner, or lifestyle practices, she should be offered vaccination. Vaccination is safe both during pregnancy and the breastfeeding period. Reduction of long-term sequellae to hepatitis B is prevented by administration of immuno-prophylaxis at birth to infants with seropositive mothers. However, infants exposed to acute infection in utero have additional risks including low birth weight (Shepard, 1998) and prematurity (Hieber et al., 1977). All men and women who have hepatitis B should be told of the risks of transmission to the mother and subsequent risk to the infant if infected. Almost 25 percent of sexual contacts of a seropositive partner will become infected. If the woman develops an acute hepatitis B infection during pregnancy the risks of neonatal transmission range from 10 percent in the first trimester to 90 percent in the third trimester (American College of Obstetricians and Gynecologists, 1998). Chronic infection occurs in more than 90 percent of infected infants. Chronic infection poses a risk of cirrhosis and hepatocellualr carcinoma. Women who are chronic carriers are counseled on the importance of informing the pediatrician or family physician at birth. The infant will receive the hepatitis B immune globulin within 12 hours of delivery and hepatitis B vaccination at birth, 1, and 6 months respectively.

Hepatitis C

Hepatitis C is becoming a silent epidemic in the US. Many patients are unaware that they are carriers. Nearly 4 million Americans are infected with hepatitis C. Hepatitis C is transmitted through contaminated blood and blood products. Methods of transmission include blood transfusion, use of infected instruments during surgical procedures or body piercing, perinatal transmission during childbirth, hemodialysis, sharing of infected instruments in barber shops or nail salons, sharing of snorting straws among cocaine users, and IV drug use. Sporadic transmission has been reported in 5 percent of acute hepatitis cases and approximately 30 percent of chronic hepatitis C cases. Women testing positive for anti-HCV antibody in pregnancy range from 0.1 to 4.5 percent (Reinus et al., 1992; Moriya et al., 1995; Bohman et al.,

1992). Women testing positive should be counseled on the risk of transmission to others and possible risk to the newborn. The neonatal transmission in pregnancy is about 5 percent. Hepatitis C is not transmitted through breastfeeding. The risk increases in HIV positive women and in proportion to the maternal viral load. Currently, we do not have treatment for mother or infant or a means to decrease perinatal transmission therefore, routine preconception screening is not recommended (Zanetti et al., 1999). Women who are positive for hepatitis C and desire pregnancy should be counseled regarding uncertain infectivity, the link between viral load and neonatal transmission, the importance of avoiding hepatotoxic drugs, and the risk of chronic liver disease.

Varicella

Varicella (i.e. chickenpox) is a highly contagious disease. In children, varicella is usually mild but can be severe in adults and fatal in neonates and the immunocompro-mised. Since varicella vaccination is becoming widely implemented, women receiving the vaccine should be counseled not to become pregnant for at least 1 month after being vaccinated. Women with active disease during the first trimester or early second trimester are at risk for fetal problems including limb atrophy, scarring of the skin of the extremities, central nervous system abnormalities, and eye problems. The risk of congenital varicella from perinatal transmis-sion during first and second trimester ranges from 0.4 to 2.0 percent. The risk of congenital disease from vaccination should be very low.

Rubella

Preventing congenital rubella is important since it can affect all organ systems. Deafness is the most common sequelae of congenital rubella syndrome. Parents should be counseled on the importance of immuniza-tion. Routine screening should be offered to all women of reproductive age who have not been vaccinated. Women should be counseled not to become pregnant for 3 months after receiving vaccination due to a theoretical risk of transmission. But a woman that does become pregnant can be reassured that no documented cases have been reported. A woman with rubella in early gestation is at risk for premature birth, spontaneous abortion, and fetal death. Neonatal infections are rare when maternal infection occurs after 20 weeks. However, in women who are infected in the first trimester, 85 percent will have an infected fetus or infant. Women should be counseled that infants with congenital rubella are highly contagious and care-takers who are not immunized are at risk for infection.

Tuberculosis

Worldwide, tuberculosis (TB) is the infectious disease that kills the most people. The CDC reported more than 15,000 cases of TB in 2001 and 10-15 million latent infections. Tuberculosis affects all parts of the body including the pulmonary systems, skeletal system, gastrointestinal system, genitourinary system, and skin. The case fatality rate approaches 50% in untreated patients, areas of multidrug resistance, and infants with congenital disease. Tuberculosis in pregnancy is a risk factor for low birth weight and subsequently poor perinatal outcomes. Screening for TB prior to pregnancy allows for prophylaxis completion and the opportunity to reduce these risks. TB reduction includes first identifying those at risk for disease. High risk groups include persons with active TB within 2 years, those with personal contact with someone with active TB, illicit drug users, foreign-born persons in the US less than 5 years from high risk countries, elderly, children less than 4 exposed to high-risk adults, and persons with chronic medical conditions such as HIV, diabetes, organ transplant, end-stage renal disease, cancer, chronic steroid use,

underweight, health care workers, persons incarcerated, and those working in correction institutions (Jerant et al., 2000). Opportunity to screen is available at routine visits and annual exams for any stating that they desire pregnancy in the future and are among the high-risk groups above.

Sexually Transmitted Infections

Some women engage in high-risk sexual behavior, potentially exposing themselves to Sexually Transmitted Diseases (STDs) and HIV (Centers for Disease Control and Prevention, 2001). Men and women being treated for sexually transmitted diseases should be counseled on the risk of infertility imposed by having STDs. Untreated STDs can affect all parts of the reproductive tract for men and women.

Gonorrhea

According to the CDC, Gonorrhea occurs in about 125 per 100,000 persons, and complicates about 40,000 pregnancies per year in the US (i.e. about 1% of US pregnancies). It is the most common cause of pelvic inflammatory disease (PID). Women with PID are at risk for internal infections, chronic pelvic pain, and damage to fallopian tubes. In men, gonorrhea can block the tubes that carry sperm. If a woman has gonorrhea when she delivers she can pass the infection to her baby causing blindness, joint infections, or blood infections.

Chlamydia

Chlamydia has similar effects as gonorrhea in untreated women and men. The CDC estimates that 200,000 pregnant women per year (about 5% of pregnancies) in the US are infected with Chlamydia. An untreated pregnant woman is at increased risk of preterm delivery and can pass the infection to her baby during vaginal delivery leading to conjunctivitis or pneumonia.

Syphilis

The World Health Organization estimates 12 million new cases of syphilis annually. In 2002, the CDC reported 32,000 cases of syphilis, with an estimated 8,000 in pregnant women (i.e. about 0.2% of pregnancies). Syphilis has declined in both women and neonates. Women planning pregnancy should inquire thoroughly about sexual practices in their partner since the incidence of syphilis is increasing in men having sex with men and overall the rate of disease in men is 3.5 times that of women. Preconception screening for syphilis is high risk populations is an important step in reduction of neonatal syphilis. Persons at risk for syphilis include men having sex with men, persons in correctional facilities, commercial sex workers, those who trade sex for money, those having sex with high-risk individuals, and persons diagnosed with other sexually transmitted diseases. Additionally, the US Preventive Services Task Force recommends screening all pregnant women for syphilis in the first trimester. Understanding the importance of avoiding syphilis transmission, many states require syphilis screening as a part of their pre-marital screening. Syphilis can be cured if treated in its early stages. However, treatment does not prevent re-infection. Even if adequate treatment is established, repeat testing should occur during pregnancy during the first and third trimester. A woman with syphilis should be counseled about the risk to the unborn if untreated. Studies show that majority of stillbirths due to syphilis occur around thirty weeks gestation. Therefore, even in unplanned pregnancies, treatment of syphilis immediately might decrease risk of stillbirth and other perinatal morbidities. Perinatal morbidity and mortality is as high as 40 percent in women who are untreated. Additional risks include prematurity, neonatal death, developmental delay, blindness, deafness, bone and teeth abnormalities, and seizures.

Herpes

Genital herpes is common in the US. Five percent of all women of child-bearing age report a history of genital herpes infection and approximately 2 percent of women acquire genital herpes during pregnancy (Fischer, 2006). Women with herpes should be counseled on the risk to the fetus and newborn child. It is important to teach couples about the appearance of herpetic lesions since they may be asymptomatic. Women with active lesions at delivery should be offered cesarean section to avoid perinatal transmission.

Medical Conditions

There are several medical conditions that could have an adverse effect on pregnancy outcomes, leading to pregnancy loss, infant death, birth defects, or other complications for mothers and infants and for which there is evidence that the effect can be impacted by preconception care. For example in 2002, 6.1% of women of reproductive age had asthma, 5% were obese, 3.4% had cardiac disease, 3% were hypertensive, 9.3% were diabetic and 1.4% had thyroid disorder and treatment of these disorders can reduce complications (US Department of Health and Human Resources, 2002; Stephenson et al., 2004).

Diabetes

One percent of women of childbearing age have diabetes. Uncontrolled diabetes is associated with many adverse effects during the perinatal period (see chapter 2). These include both maternal and fetal morbidities. Maternal complications include congenital anomalies, fetal loss, and birth complications due to macrosomia. Fetal complications include abnormalities of the spine, skeleton, cardiovascular system and renal system. Every woman of childbearing age should be counseled on the effects of poorly controlled diabetes to herself and the unborn child.

Counseling should include importance of diabetes control before considering pregnancy. Important counseling topics include maintaining optimal weight control, maximizing diabetes control, self-glucose monitoring, a regular exercise program, and tobacco, alcohol, and drug cessation and social support to assist during the pregnancy. Women with diabetes are rarely discouraged from becoming pregnant except if they have renal complications, heart problems or vision complications associated with their uncontrolled diabetes. Detailed history and physical is important to ascertain the risk to mother and risk to fetus. In addition to routine history, the diabetic mother should be asked about current management of her disease, age at diagnosis, most recent hemoglobin A1C level, nutritional assessment, any complications associated with diabetes, smoking history, medications, and any other co-morbidity.

Hypertension

Hypertension in pregnancy is associated with many adverse outcomes for both mother and fetus. Twenty percent of women of childbearing age have a diagnosis of chronic hypertension. Women with chronic hypertension tend to have better outcomes when blood pressure is controlled than women with preeclampsia, a pregnancy-related condition characterized by high blood pressure and protein in the urine. However, super-imposed preeclampsia in women with hypertension and renal hypertension are both associated with significant adverse perinatal outcomes (Brown and Buddle, 1996). Providers should assess medication regimen, evidence of co-morbid conditions such as diabetes and heart disease, and renal function. Baseline proteinuria and uric acid is important since changes in pregnancy may indicate worsening disease. Hyperuricemia and proteinuria in gestational hypertension is significantly associated with maternal complications and lower birth weight babies when compared to women with

normal plasma uric acid levels (Roberts et al., 2005). Women with chronic hypertension should be counseled on the importance of blood pressure control, change in medications needed when close to conception time (discontinuation of diuretics and ace inhibitors), and the risk associated with hypertension in pregnancy for both mother and baby.

Lupus

Women with Lupus require and may seek information before conceiving. The perinatal outcome will depend on the stability of the disease. They should be counseled that only 50 percent of conceptions in patients with lupus will result in a normal pregnancy and 25 percent will result in preterm birth, the remaining 25 percent will result in spontaneous abortion. All lupus pregnancies should be considered high-risk and managed with involvement of a high-risk perinatal team. Women should wait at least 6 months after remission before conceiving. This "wait interval' will decrease the risk of flaring during pregnancy. Concerns about medication use should be reviewed. Most medications taken by lupus patients are safe during pregnancy. Cytoxan should be avoided during the first trimester. The greatest risk is that of prematurity and the sequelae that result from preterm delivery. Approximately 10 percent of women with lupus and anti-Ro antibodies with have a baby with neonatal lupus. Parents should be told that this is not Systemic Lupus Erythematosus and the baby can have a normal life. Although neonatal lupus is sometimes complicated by a heart problem, termed heart block, this can generally be corrected and the baby will have a normal life.

Seizures

Preconception counseling is important in women with seizure disorders. Complications associated with seizure disorder include an increased frequency of seizure, fetal malformations associated with medication use, miscarriage, and perinatal death. Medications have been associated with cleft lip and palate, cardiac anomalies, facial abnormalities, intra-uterine growth restriction, skeletal abnormalities, and low IQ. The patient and her partner should be counseled on the most opportune time for conception. The best time to conceive is after being seizure free and off anti-seizure medications for two years. It is not known which anticonvulsant medication is the least toxic. Thus, the single most clinically appropriate anticonvulsant for the woman's epilepsy should be initiated before pregnancy and the medication adjusted frequently to keep serum levels in the lowest effective range (Tayse, 1998; Delgado-Escueta and Janz, 1992).

Anemia

Anemia in pregnancy can cause poor fetal growth, preterm delivery, and low birth weight. Women planning pregnancy should be counseled on eating foods rich in iron, folate and vitamin B12. Providers should recommend a well balanced diet rich in lean meats, leafy green vegetables and legumes, wheat bread, and other iron rich foods. Women who eat limited fruits and vegetables may require supplementation prior to becoming pregnant.

Parental Behavior

There are several maternal and paternal behaviors that adversely effect perinatal outcomes and for which there is evidence that the effect can be impacted by preconception care. A substantial proportion of women who become pregnant engage in high risk behaviors proven to contribute to adverse pregnancy outcomes: in 2003, 10.7% of pregnant women smoked during pregnancy, a risk factor for low birth weight; while in 2002, 10.1% of pregnant women and 54.9% of women at risk of getting pregnant consumed alcohol, a risk for fetal alcohol

syndrome (Centers for Disease Control and Prevention, 2004). Although a smaller proportion of women use illicit drugs they are at extremely high risk for adverse outcomes.

Tobacco

Smoking is a major contributor to poor perinatal outcomes, accounting for one third of low birth weight babies. Low birth weight is a known indicator for infant morbidity and mortality (American College of Obstetricians and Gynecologists, 2001; US Preventive Services Task Force, 2003). Of the 120 million women who give birth each year, 11-12 percent report smoking with the highest percentage among women in their late teens (Martin et al., 2003). Smoking during pregnancy can be harmful to the unborn fetus and mother. Fetal effects include intrauterine growth retardation, prematurity and low birth weight. Secondary exposure is associated with respiratory illnesses such as asthma and bronchitis, ear infections, and sudden infant death syndrome. Maternal complications include placental abruption and preterm labor. Families desiring pregnancy should be counseled on the benefits of not smoking before, during, and after the pregnancy, and be educated about the risks of second smoke for everyone living in the household (see Chapter 2).

Cocaine

Substance use during pregnancy is associated with morbidity to both mother and infant. Cocaine use is associated with preterm delivery, placental abruption, low birth weight, poor growth, poor feeding, developmental delay, cerebral infarction, poor bonding, and Sudden Infant Death Syndromes. Parents should be counseled on the risks and offered information on programs that support abstaining and rehabilitation (see Chapter 2).

Heroin

Heroin use during pregnancy is associated

with similar outcomes as women who use cocaine. Heroin use increases risk for preterm delivery, miscarriage, intrauterine growth restriction, placenta abruption, stillbirth and neonatal withdrawal syndromes. Women should be directed to a program that can offer weaning from heroin use or methadone maintenance. They should not stop abruptly. The provider should recommend delaying pregnancy until they are abstinent from illicit drug use (see Chapter 2).

Alcohol

Fetal alcohol syndrome is the most common cause of preventable mental retardation. Every couple should be given accurate information about alcohol and its effect on pregnancy. Alcohol use during pregnancy causes fetal wastage, growth retardation, organ anomalies, neurosensory problems, and mental retardation. Currently we are unable to say this is a dose dependant relationship. Therefore, avoiding alcohol during pregnancy is the best instruction. Preconception instructions include review of associated risk, identification of programs that would help in cessation and long-term abstinence, and offering support during the treatment program (see Chapter 2). Effective brief interventions to encourage reductions in drinking have been developed for use in primary care clinics.

Family and Genetic History

The ideal time for genetic investigation and counseling is before a couple attempts to conceive (Wille et al., 2004). The identification of genetic risk can be accomplished by a careful genetic history. Patients with a specific indication such as advanced maternal age, a family history of genetic disease, or a previously affected pregnancy should be offered preconception genetic counseling. Carrier screening to determine if the parents are heterozygous for certain genetic conditions and therefore at increased risk for conceiving offspring with these disorders is of special significance because it allows relevant counseling before the first affected pregnancy. Common disorders for which genetic screening is recommended include Tay-Sachs disease for people of Eastern European or French Canadian ancestry; ß-thalassemia for those of Mediterranean, Southwest Asian, Indian Pakistani, or African ancestry; α-thalassemia for people of Southeast Asian ancestry; sickle cell anemia for people of African descent (American College of Obstetricians and Gynecologists, 1987) and cystic fibrosis for those with a family history of the disease (Lemne et al., 1990). The family history also might reveal other risks for genetic diseases, such as fragile X disease or Down syndrome. If either member of a couple is affected by genetic disease or has an affected relative, the couple should be referred for genetic counseling and possible genetic testing. Genetic counseling allows the couple to understand their risk and, if necessary, to arrange for diagnostic tests such as chorionic villous sampling or amniocentesis early in pregnancy. Such determinations could influence a couple's decision to conceive or adopt and could alter the clinical management of the pregnancy and newborn. Preconception screening not only provides a couple more time to consider their options and make plans; it also adds to the number of options available. For couples identified to be at risk during pregnancy, confirmatory testing only provides the option of induced abortion. When testing is done before conception, additional options include not bearing children, artificial insemination, in vitro fertilization, surrogate pregnancy, and adoption.

Nutrition

A women's nutritional status at conception can have profound effects on reproductive outcome. At the preconception visit a complete dietary history includes a history of food habits, attitudes, use of vitamins and mineral supplements, food allergies, knowledge about proper nutrition, and the availability of food. Lactose intolerance should be identified and the adequacy of dietary calcium assessed. Women who are at nutritional risk should be provided an individualized dietary intervention, possibly with the aid of a nutritionist. Women with low incomes, once pregnant, should be assisted to obtain additional food from such sources as the Aid to Families with Dependent Children (AFDC) food stamp program and to enroll in nutrition supplementation programs such as the WIC (Women's, Infants', and Children's) program as soon as possible. In some instances, the use of food pantries, soup kitchens, and similar facilities may need to be recommended.

Prevention of Neural Tube Defects

The preconception visit should include nutritional counseling to ensure that the diets of all women who might bear children contain an adequate amount of folic acid. It has been well demonstrated that a large portion of spina bifida and anencephaly can be prevented by supplementing dietary folic acid before conception and through the first trimester of pregnancy. In 1991, a large randomized trial of women who had had a previous child with a neural tube defect (NTD) conclusively demonstrated that 4 mg doses of folic acid before and during early pregnancy resulted in a 71% reduction of recurrence of NTDs (MRC Vitamin Study Research Group, 1991). This study did not address the possible benefit of lower doses of folic acid, although other studies have suggested that lower doses might result in comparable reductions. Additionally, there appear to be excellent prospects for substantially reducing the number of NTDs among US women who have not had a prior NTD-affected pregnancy through use of folic acid (Czizel andDudas, 1992). The U.S. Public Health Service now recommends that all women of childbearing age who are capable of becoming pregnant should consume 0.4 mg of folic acid per day for the purpose of reducing

their risk of having a pregnancy affected with spina bifida or other NTD. Because the effects of higher intakes are not well known but include complicating the diagnosis of vitamin B_{12} deficiency, care should be taken to keep the total folate consumption at less than 1 mg per day (US Department of Health and Human Services Public Health Service Centers for Disease Control, 1992). Implementing these recom-mendations might provide the opportunity for primary prevention of as many as 60% of these serious birth defects (Werler et al., 1993). A woman's risk of having a child with a NTD was found to be associated with early pregnancy red blood cell folate levels in a continuous dose-response relation. This find-ing suggests that it might be possible to identify and supplement women with low folic acid levels and thereby prevent NTDs (Daly et al., 1995). Data regarding the cost and benefits has also been published (de Weerd et al., 2004). Trials of interventions that have focused on encouraging use of supplements to reduce birth defects are reviewed in Chapter 2.

Underweight

Preconception assessment of nutrition status should identify women who are underweight and subsequently gain little weight (e.g. less than 25 pounds) during pregnancy as they are at high risk of fetal and neonatal morbidity and mortality (Naeye, 1979). Assessment should be done for conditions such as bulimia, anorexia, pica and once identified, nutritional counseling and in some cases treatment of an underlying emotional condition should be initiated.

Overweight

At the other extreme, marked obesity, specifically a body mass index of greater than 25, is associated with gestational diabetes, NTDs, hypertension, macrosomic infants, and resultant prolonged labor and shoulder dystocia (Johnson et al., 1987, see chapter 2 for more information). Thus treatment for both underweight and obese women is recommended before pregnancy.

Calcium

There is some evidence to demonstrate that supplementary dietary calcium reduces blood pressure and preeclampsia during pregnancy (Bucher et al., 1996). The current daily calcium intake recommendation for pregnant women and adolescent females is 1200 to 1500 mg, but the reported median daily intake is 600 to 700mg, which is insufficient to ensure optimal gestational blood pressure regulation. There is now adequate evidence to recommend that every woman of reproductive age should be advised to consume the current recommended level of calcium (McCarron and Haffon, 1996).

Vitamin A

The recommended dietary allowance for women is 2700 IU of vitamin A per day. Currently, about 1% to 2% of women average more than 10,000 IU of vitamin A from supplements. Evidence in humans suggests that more than 10,000 IU of vitamin A per day is teratogenic, resulting in cranial/neural crest defects (Rothman et al., 1995). Women in the reproductive age group are advised to avoid consuming vitamin A at these levels and should consume liver products only in moderation, as they contain large amounts of vitamin A. Women with a history of a previous pregnancy resulting in a fetus with an NTD should be advised not to attempt to achieve high doses of folic acid (i.e., 4 mg) by taking multivitamins because of the possibility of ingesting harmful levels of vitamin A.

Phenylketonuria

Infants born to women with classic phenylketonuria (PKU) and a maternal blood phenylalanine level of more than 20 mg/dl are likely to have microcephaly and mental retardation and are at increased risk of congenital heart disease and intrauterine growth

restriction. Dietary restrictions that result in lowered levels of maternal phenylalanine during the earliest weeks of gestation reduce the risk of fetal malformation (Drogari et al. 1987; Platt et al., 1992).

Environmental Exposures

Routine assessment of hobbies, habits, and home and employment environments might identify exposures associated with adverse reproductive consequences that can be minimized during the preconception period. The effects on human pregnancy of most of the chemicals in occupational use are unknown; but several, such as heavy metals and organic solvents, have been implicated in a variety of reproductive disorders. It is prudent to educate women for whom pregnancy is a possibility about such hazards and to provide them with the facts available about the teratogenic potential of any chemical or environmental agent to which they are exposed.

Mercury

Measures of mercury exposure in women of childbearing age generally fall below levels of concern. However, approximately 8% of women had concentrations higher that the US Environmental Protection Agency's recommended reference dose (5.8 µg/L), below which exposures are considered to be without adverse effects (Schober et al., 2003). Methylmercury is of particular concern because it is a well-established human neurotoxin and the developing fetus is most sensitive to its adverse effects (US Environmental Protection Agency, 1997; Agency for Toxic Substances and Disease Registries, 1999; National Academy of Sciences, 2000). Methylmercury bioaccumulates through the food chain so that concentrations are highest in large predatory fish. Exposure occurs primarily through consumption of seafood, freshwater fish, and shellfish (Mahaffey 1999; World Health Organization, 1990; Toffleson and Cordle, 1986). The US Food and Drug

Administration provides advice to pregnant women and women of childbearing age who may become pregnant to avoid consumption of shark, swordfish, King mackerel and tile fish (US Department of Health and Human Services and Environmental Protection Agency, 2004). Many state government agencies issue fish advisories and bans relating to mercury concentration in locally caught fish (MA Department of Public Health, 2004).

Psychosocial Risks

Preconception risk assessment provides an opportunity to identify risks related to personal, social, and psychological characteristics.

Psychological Risks

Psychological risks that can be identified by a sensitive interview include inadequate pregnancy readiness, lack of personal support, deficient coping skills, high stress and anxiety, and psychiatric conditions. Extremes of physical work, exercise, and other activity should be assessed (Culpepper and Thompson, 1990). The health status of poor and minority women contributes to persistent, disparities in birth outcomes. Lower physical functioning, emotional health, and overall health status of low income women in the month prior to pregnancy has been associated with an increaseed risk of preterm labor. Socio-economic status directly and indirectly influences three major determinants of health: health care access, environmental exposure, and health behavior (Adler and Newman, 2002). Racial inequalities and unequal treatment likewise influence these determinants (Salganicoff et al., 2002).

Physical, Sexual, and Emotional Abuse

Victims of domestic violence should be identified preconceptionally, as they are likely to be abused during pregnancy. Up to 25% of obstetric patients are physically abused while pregnant. Such assaults can result in placental separation; antepartum hemorrhage; fetal fractures; rupture of the uterus, liver, or spleen; and preterm labor. Information about available community, social and legal resources, and a plan for dealing with the abusive partner should be made available to abused women (Gazamarian et al., 1996).

Access to Care

Implementing a comprehensive preconception care program for many women includes addressing barriers to access to medical care. Real or perceived barriers to family planning or early prenatal care enrollment can be detected by preconception risk assessment. After these barriers are identified, advice, counseling, education, and developing a personal relationship with a family physician before pregnancy might successfully address some of these impediments. Good social support around the time of childbirth is important to the mental and physical health of the new mother (Thompson, 1990). Preconception evaluation should include an assessment of social support and family function. The family physician can assess social supports available to help identify potential problems such as domestic violence, parenting difficulties, and other stresses that may affect pregnancy or child rearing.

FATHERS

The fatherless family has many long-term effects on the mother, the child, and the social fabric of our society. Lone mothers are more likely to be stressed, depressed, have psychological problems, have difficulty bonding with their children and have more medical problems (O'Niell, 2002). All of these factors are known risk factors for poor perinatal outcomes. Guidelines for risk assessment should include inquiry about maternal health and social well-being, paternal health and well-being, family history, family structure, social history, mental health history, and environmental exposures before, during, and after pregnancy.

DELIVERY OF PRECONCEPTION CARE

The Expert Panel on the Content of Prenatal Care recommended that preconception care be embedded in the process of primary and preventive care, rather than an isolated visit (Public Health Service, 1989). While a pre-pregnancy planning visit in the months before conception has been recommended (Chamberlain, 1980; American College of Obstetricians and Gynecologists, 2005) improving preconception health will require a larger shift in the process of care for women of childbearing age.

As all women of reproductive age and potential presenting for continuing care in the primary care setting are candidates for preconception care, the essential and critical role of primary care physicians in the provision of preconception care is apparent; however, preconception care needs to be tailored to meet needs of the individual woman. Given that preconception care needs to take place across the lifespan and is a not just one visit, some recommendations will be more relevant to women at different stages in their lives and with varying levels of risk. Health promotion, risk screening, and interventions would be different for a young woman who has never experienced pregnancy than for a 35-year-old woman who has had three children. Women with chronic diseases, prior pregnancy complications, or behavioral risk factors may need more intensive interventions. At the clinical level, interventions for an individual need to be tailored to the specific needs of the woman. Such variations also place constraints on how interventions can and should be bundled or prepackaged.

The context of the CDC recommendations (Centers for Disease Control and Prevention, 2006) is that preconception care is not a single visit but a process of care designed to meet the needs of a woman during the different stages of her reproductive life. The purpose is to promote the health throughout the life span for women, children and families. Preconception care offers health services, that allow women to maintain optimal health for themselves, choose the number and spacing of their pregnancies and, when desired, to prepare for a healthy baby.

INTERVENTIONS AVALABLE AND THEIR EMPIRICAL SUPPORT

Examples of interventions that are available for preconception risks are listed in Table 4. Based on the available evidence, there currently is a relative short list of core interventions for which there is substantial evidence of efficacy when applied in the preconception period (see Table 2). The best evidence for the effectiveness of most components of preconception care has been documented when the focus of delivery was on a single risk behavior and accompanying intervention. Interventions that address multiple pregnancy-related risk behaviors simultaneously (e.g., the "package of preconception services") have not been well studied. For example, the effectiveness of interventions related to smoking, alcohol misuse, and obesity are based on studies of interventions delivered in primary care and not specifically delivered as part of preconception care.

Korenbrot in a 2002 systematic review showed that only a small number of studies have tested approaches for increasing preconception screening, counseling, and intervention (Korenbrot et al., 2002). These showed some degree of effectiveness.

The approach in one randomized clinical trial was to address preconception risk factors at the time of a negative pregnancy test. An average of nine risks per woman was identified; however, notifying women and their clinicians of identified preconception risks did not improve intervention rates (Jack et al., 1998). Another study using didactic lectures and chart cues resulted in significant increases in risk screening for medical risk factors (from 15 percent to 44 percent), for

Table 4: Content of Preconception Care: Interventions (from Jack and Culpepper, 1990)

1.	Treatment with 0.4 mg of folic acid per day; women with a prior neural tube defect-affected pregnancy should take an additional 4.0 mg of folic acid for 1 month before pregnancy.
2.	Treatment of medical disease; women with diabetes mellitus should enter a program for intensive control of their blood glucose.
3.	Modification of chronic disease medications to decrease maternal or fetal risk during pregnancy.
4.	Vaccination for rubella, hepatitis B, and varicella.
5.	Counseling, education, and testing for HIV, hepatitis B, bacterial vaginosis, and other infections.
6.	Nutrition counseling or referral; women of reproductive age should consume 1200–1500 mg of calcium per day.
7.	Substance abuse counseling or referral to treatment programs.
8.	Home visitation to treat psychosocial risks.
9.	Referral to social service agencies for services and support.
10.	Initiation of treatment or referral for psychiatric conditions.
11.	Provision of contraception and family planning services.
12.	Provision of safe shelters.
13.	Financial assistance and planning including medical assistance.
14.	Vocational training

medications (from 10 percent to 30 percent), for domestic violence (from 10 percent to 57 percent) and nutrition (from 9 percent to 50 percent). Yet levels of appropriate intervention and provider attitudes toward preconception care did not change significantly (Bernstein et al., 2000).

A prospective study of the impact of preconception health promotion on intendedness of pregnancy found that women who received the intervention during routine family planning visits were more likely to report intended pregnancies than those patients in the same clinic not exposed to the intervention (Moos et al., 1996).

Data from the Pregnancy Risk Assessment and Monitoring System (PRAMS) showed that 38 percent of mothers who planned pregnancies and an additional 30 percent with unplanned pregnancies had one or more indications for preconception counseling. Indicators of risk identified in PRAMS data include use of tobacco or alcohol, being underweight, or delayed initiation of prenatal care (Adams et al., 1993).

THE RESEARCH AGENDA AND NEXT STEPS

The greatest potential for further improvement in pregnancy outcomes lies in prevention strategies that, to be effective, must be implemented before conception. Preconception care articulates concepts of primary prevention of poor obstetric outcomes for mother, infant and family. This is a young field with great potential for improving population health. Some have likened the stage of development to cardiovascular research in the 1950-60s when the key risk factors for cardiovascular disease were elucidated and interventions were being conceived.

The slow growth of preconception care results from the many challenges faced in providing this care. The barriers to delivering preconception care as part of clinical services that were described in 1990 are as relevant today as they where then (see Table 5) (Jack and Culpepper, 1990). For preconception care to be fully realized there must be fundamental changes in how we provide care. For it to be

Table 5: Barriers to Delivery of Preconception Care as part of Clinical Services (from Jack and Culpepper, 1990b)

1. Those most in need of services are those least likely to receive them.
2. Provision of services is often badly fragmented.
3. There is a lack of available treatment services for high-risk behaviors.
4. Reimbursement for risk assessment and health promotion activities in inadequate.
5. Health promotion messages are not effective unless received by a motivated couple.
6. For only a few conditions are there data that intervention prior to conception is better that intervention early in pregnancy.
7. Many clinical training programs do not emphasize risk assessment and health promotion skills.

successful, there must be a shift from delivering procedure-based, acute care to counseling-based preventive care. For this to occur there must be fundamental changes in the financing of medical care and the education of trainees in the primary care specialties.

The CDC noted that improving preconception health among the 62 million women of childbearing age will require multi-strategic, action-oriented initiatives (Centers for Disease Control and Prevention, 2006). The CDC organized an interagency work group and a Select Panel on Preconception Care to advance the agenda of preconception care. These groups identified 10 recommendations and specific action steps (see Table 6) that can be used by persons, communities, public health and clinical providers, and governments to improve the health of women, their children and their families.

Table 6: Recommendations and Specific Action Steps Proposed by the CDC (from Centers for Disease Control and Prevention, 2006)

1. Individual Responsibility Across the Lifespan <ul><li>Develop, evaluate and disseminate reproductive life planning tools for women and men in their childbearing years, respecting variations in age; literacy, including health literacy; and cultural/linguistic contexts.</li><li>Conduct research leading to development, dissemination, and evaluation of individual health education materials for women and men regarding preconception risk factors, including materials related to biomedical, behavioral, and social risks known to affect pregnancy outcomes.</li></ul>
2. Consumer Awareness <ul><li>Develop, evaluate, and disseminate age-appropriate educational curricula and modules for use in school health education programs.</li><li>Integrate reproductive health messages into existing health promotion campaigns (e.g., campaigns to reduce obesity and smoking).</li><li>Conduct consumer-focused research to identify terms that the public understands and develop messages to promote preconception health and reproductive awareness.</li><li>Design and conduct social marketing campaigns necessary to develop messages for promoting preconception health knowledge and attitudes, and behaviors among men and women of childbearing age.</li><li>Engage media partners to assist in depicting positive role models for lifestyles that promote reproductive health (e.g., delaying initiation of sexual activity, abstaining from unprotected sexual intercourse, and avoiding use of alcohol and drugs)</li></ul>

3. Preventive Visits
   - Increase health provider (including primary and specialty care providers) awareness regarding the importance of addressing preconception health among all women of childbearing age.
   - Develop and implement curricula on preconception care for use in clinical education at graduate, postgraduate, and continuing education levels.
   - Consolidate and disseminate existing professional guidelines to develop a recommended screening and health promotion package.
   - Develop, evaluate, and disseminate practical screening tools for primary care settings, with emphasis on the 10 areas for preconception risk assessment (e.g., reproductive history, genetic and environmental risk factors).
   - Develop, evaluate, and disseminate evidence-based models for integrating components of preconception care to facilitate delivery of and demand for prevention and intervention services.
   - Apply quality improvement techniques (e.g., rapid improvement cycles, establish benchmarks and brief provider training, use practice self-audits, and participate in quality improvement collaborative groups) to improve provider knowledge and attitudes, and practices and to reduce missed opportunities for screening and health promotion.
   - Use the federally funded collaboratives for community health centers and other Federally Qualified Health Centers to improve the quality of preconception risk assessment, health promotion, and interventions provided through primary care.
   - Develop fiscal incentives for screening and health promotion.

4. Interventions for identified Risks
   - Increase health provider (including primary and specialty care providers) awareness concerning the importance of ongoing care for chronic conditions and intervention for identified risk factors.
   - Develop and implement modules on preconception care for specific clinical conditions for use in clinical education at graduate, postgraduate, and continuing education levels.
   - Consolidate and disseminate existing guidelines related to evidence-based interventions for the conditions and risk factors.
   - Disseminate existing evidence-based interventions that address risk factors that can used in primary care settings (i.e., isotretinoins, alcohol misuse, antiepileptic drugs, diabetes [preconception], folic acid deficiency, hepatitis B, HIV/AIDS, hypothyroidism, maternal phenylketonurea [PKU], rubella seronegativity, obesity, oral anticoagulant, STD, and smoking).
   - Develop fiscal incentives (e.g., pay for performance) for risk management, particularly in managed care settings.
   - Apply quality improvement techniques and tools (e.g., conduct rapid improvement cycles, establish benchmarks, use practice self-audits, and participate in quality improvement collaborative groups).

5. Interconception Care
   - Monitor the percentage of women who complete postpartum visits (e.g., using the Health Employer Data and Information Set measures for managed care plans and Title V Maternal Child Health Block Grant state measures), and use these data to

	identify communities of women at risk and opportunities to improve provider follow-up.
	• Develop, evaluate and replicate intensive evidence-based interconception care and care coordination models for women at high social and medical risk.
	• Enhance the content of postpartum visits to promote interconception health.
	• Use existing public health programs serving women in the postpartum period to provide or link to interventions (e.g., family planning, home visiting, and the Special Supplemental Nutrition Program for Women, Infants, and Children).
	• Encourage additional states to develop preconception health improvement projects with funds from the Title V maternal Child Health Block Grant, Prevention Block Grant, and similar public health programs.
6.	Prepregnancy Checkup • Consolidate existing professional guidelines to develop the recommended content and approach for such a visit. • Modify third party payer rules to permit payment for one prepregnancy visit per pregnancy, including development of billing and payment mechanisms. • Educate women and couples regarding the value and availability of prepregnancy planning visits.
7.	Health Insurance Coverage for Women with Low Incomes • Improve the design of family planning waivers by permitting states (by federal waiver or by creating a new state option) to offer interconception risk assessment, counseling, and interventions along with family planning services. Such policy developments would create new opportunities to finance interconception care. • Increase health coverage among women who have low incomes and are of childbearing age by using federal options and waivers under public and private health insurance systems and the State Children's Health Insurance Program. • Increase access to health-care services through policies and reimbursement levels for public and private health insurance systems to include a full range of clinicians who care for women.
8.	Public Health Programs and Strategies • Use federal and state agency support to encourage more integrated preconception health practices in clinics and programs. • Provide support for CDC programs to develop, evaluate, and disseminate integrated approaches to promote preconception health. • Analyze and evaluate the preconception care activities used under the federal Healthy Start program, and support replication projects. • Convene or use local task forces, coalitions, or committees to discuss opportunities for promotion and prevention in preconception health at the community level. • Develop and support public health practice collaborative groups to promote shared learning and dissemination of approaches for increasing preconception health. • Include content related to preconception care in educational curricula of schools of public health and other training facilities for public health professionals
9.	Research • Prepare an updated evidence-based systematic review of all published reports on science, programs, and policy (e.g., through the Agency for Healthcare Research and Quality).

- Encourage and support evaluation of model programs and projects, including integrated service delivery and community health promotion projects.
- Conduct quantitative and qualitative studies to advance knowledge of preconception risks and clinical and public health interventions, including knowledge of more integrated practice strategies and interconception approaches.
- Design and conduct analyses of cost-benefit and cost effectiveness as part of the study of preconception interventions.
- Conduct health services research to explore barriers to evidence-based and guidelines-based practice.
- Conduct studies to examine the factors that result in variations in individual use of preconception care (i.e., barriers and motivators that affect health-care use).

10. Monitoring Improvements
- Apply public health surveillance strategies to monitor selected preconception health indicators (e.g., folic acid supplementation, smoking cessation, alcohol misuse, diabetes, and obesity).
- Expand data systems and survey (e.g., the Pregnancy Risk Assessment and Monitoring System and the National Survey of Family Growth) to monitor individual experiences related to preconception care.
- Use geographic information system techniques to target preconception health programs and interventions to areas where high rates of poor health outcomes exist for women of reproductive age and their infants.
- Use analytic tools (e.g., Perinatal Periods of Risk) to measure and monitor the proportion of risk attributable to the health of women before pregnancy.
- Include preconception, interconception, and health status measures in population-based performance monitoring systems (e.g., in national and state Title V programs).
- Include a measure of the delivery of preconception care services in the Healthy People 2020 objectives.
- Develop and implement indicator quality improvement measures for all aspects of preconception care. For example, use the Health Employer Data and Information Set measures to monitor the percentage of women who complete preconception care and postpartum visits or pay for performance measures.

In the clinical arena, there is a need to build tools that clinicians can use such as (1) practice-based guidelines; (2) practical screening instruments; and (3) menus of ways in which interventions can be initiated that are flexible and fit with the skills, motivation and practice setting of various providers.

There is also a great need to organize a public health effort to integrate the concepts of preconception care into public health programs at the local, state and national levels. Finally, all the above will be more effective if done in conjunction with consumer awareness campaigns designed to begin to change the public perceptions of the importance of these concepts.

There is a need for more research in (1) how to best screen for risks and provide the most effective interventions; (2) how to adapt and apply the science of behavior change developed over the past two decades to preconception care; and (3) how to organize and carry out a series of research studies about how best to deliver the package of preconception services at the practice, health plan and community level.

As of this writing, the CDC is supporting interdisciplinary work groups to advance preconception health in the areas of consumer knowledge, clinical practice, public health programs, health care financing, and data and research activities. A NIH sponsored conference designed to develop the research agenda in preconception care is being planned for 2007.

REFERENCES

Adams MM, Bruce FC, Shulman HB, Kendrick JS, Brogan DJ. (1993) Pregnancy planning and preconception counseling: The PRAMS Working Group. Obstet Gynecol 82:955-959.

Adler NE, Newman K. (2002) Socioeconomic disparities in health: Pathways and policies. Health Affairs 21(2): 60-76.

Agency for Toxic Substances and Disease Registries. (1999) Toxicological Profile for Mercury. Atlanta, GA: Agency for Toxic Substances and Disease Registries, US Dept of Health and Human Services.

Allaire AD, Cefalo RC. (1998) Preconceptional health care model. Eur J Obstet Gynecol Reprod Biol 78:163-8.

American Academy of Pediatrics, American College of Obstetricians and Gynecologists. (2002) *Guidelines for Perinatal Care*. Gilstrap LC, Oh W, eds. 5th ed. Elk Grove Village, IL: American Academy of Pediatrics.

American College of Obstetricians and Gynecologists, (2003) Access to women's health care. ACOG Statement of Policy. Washington, DC: American College of Obstetricians and Gynecologists.

American College of Obstetricians and Gynecologists. (1998) ACOG educational bulletin. Viral hepatitis in pregnancy. Number 248, July 1998. Int J Gynaecol Obstet. ;63:195-202.

American College of Obstetricians and Gynecologists (1995) ACOG Technical Bulletin. Preconceptional care. Number 205. Washington DC.

American College of Obstetricians and Gynecologists. (2005) The importance of preconception care in the continuum of women's health care. ACOG Committee Opinion No 313. Obstet Gynecol 106:665-6.

American College of Obstetricians and Gynecologists. (2001) American College of Obstetricians and Gynecologists (ACOG) educational bulletin. Smoking cessation during pregnancy. Number 260, September 2000. Int J Gynaecol Obstet. 75:345-8

American College of Obstetricians and Gynecologists. (2002) Guildelines for women's health care. 2nd ed. Washington, DC: American College of Obstetricians and Gynecologists.

American College of Obstetricians and Gynecologists, Preconception Work Group. (2005) The importance of preconception care in the continuum of women's health care. (ACOG Committee Opinion) OB/GYN. 106(3):665-666.

American College of Obstetricians and Gynecologists. (1987) Antenatal diagnosis of genetic disorders. Technical Bulletin No. 108. Washington, DC.

American Diabetes Association. (2004) Preconceptional care of women with diabetes. Diabetes Care. 27: S76-S78.

Bernstein PS, Sanghvi T, Merkatz IR. (2000) Improving preconception care. J Reprod Med 45:546-52.

Bitto A, Gray RH, Simpson JL, Queenan JT, Kambic RT, Perez A, Mena P, Barbato M, Li C, Jennings V. (1997) A Prospective Study Among Planned and Unplanned Pregnancies in Natural Family Planning Users. Am J Public Health 87(3): 338-43.

Bohman VR, Stettler W, Little BB, et al. (1992) Seroprevalence and risk factors for hepatitis C virus antibody in pregnancy. Obstet Gynecol 80:609-13.

Brown MA, Buddle ML. (1996) Hypertension in pregnancy: maternal and fetal outcomes according to laboratory and clinical features. *MJA* 165: 360-365.

Bucher HC, Guyatt G, Cook RJ, et al. (1996) Effect of calcium supplementation on pregnancy induced hypertension and preeclampsia: a meta-analysis of randomized controlled trials. JAMA 275:1113–7.

Cefalo RC, Moos MK. (1995) Preconceptional health promotion. In: Cefalo RC, Moos MK, eds. Preconceptional health care: a practical guide. 2nd Ed. St Louis: Mosby.

Centers for Disease Control and Prevention. (2006) Recommendations for improving preconception health and health care – United States: a report of the CC/ATSDR Preconception Care Workgroup and the Select Panel on Preconception Care. MMWR 55(No. RR-6): 1-23.

Centers for Disease Control and Prevention (2004) Reducing HIV Transmission from Mother to Child: An Opt out Approach to HIV Screening at Childbirth.

Centers for Disease Control and Prevention. (2004) Alcohol consumption among women who are pregnant or who might become pregnant – United States, 2002. MMWR 53(50):1178-81.

Centers for Disease Control and Prevention. (2001) Revised guidelines for HIV counseling, testing, and referral. Revised recommendations for HIV screening of pregnant women. MMWR 50;RR-19: 1-14.

Centers for Disease Control and Prevention (2002) Sexually Transmitted Diseases Treatment Guidelines --- 2002 .MMWR 51(RR06);1-80.

Chamberlain G. (1980) The pre-pregnancy Clinic. *Br Med* J 281:29-30.

Chamberlain G. (1981) The use of the pre-pregnancy clinic. Matern Child Health. 6:314-316.

Chamberlain G, Lumley J eds. (1986) Prepregnancy Care: A Manual for Practice. Chichester: Wiley.

Clancy CM, Massion CT. (1992) American women's healthcare: A patchwork quilt with gaps. JAMA 268:1918-20.

Committee on Perinatal Health. (1993) *Toward Improving the Outcome of Pregnancy (TIOP II): The 90s and Beyond.* White Plains, NY: March of Dimes, National Foundation.

Culpepper L, Thompson JE. Work during pregnancy. In: Merkatz IR, Thompson JE, Mullen PD, Goldenberg R, editors. New perspectives on prenatal care. New York: Elsevier, 1990:211–34.

Czeizel AE, Dudas I. (1992) Prevention of the first occurrence of neural-tube defects by periconceptional vitamin supplementation. N Engl J Med 327:1832–5.

Daly LE, Peadar NK, Molloy A, Weir DG, Scott JM. (1995) Folate levels and neural tube defects: implications for prevention. JAMA 274:1698–702.

Delgado-Escueta AV, Janz D. (1992) Consensus guideline: preconception counseling, management, and care of the pregnant women with epilepsy. Neurology 42:149–60.

de Weerd S, Polder JJ, Cohen-Overbeek, TE, Zimmermann LJ, Steegers EA. (2004) Preconception care: preliminary estimates of costs and effects of smoking cessation and folic acid supplementation. *J Reproductive Med* 49: 338-44.

Drogari E, Smith I, Beasley M, Lloyd JK. (1987) Timing of strict diet in relation to fetal damage in maternal phenylketonuria. Lancet 2:927–30.

Fischer R. (2006) Genital Herpes in Pregnancy. Available at: http://www.emedicine.com/med/topic3554.htm; accessed on October 11, 2007.

Fowler JR, Jack BS. (2003) Preconception Care. In: Taylor RB, David AK, Fields SA, Phillips DM, Scherger JE, editors. *Family Medicine Principles and Practice.* 6th Edition. New York: Springer; pp.85-94.

Frey KA. (2002) Preconcepton care by the

non-obstetrical provider. Mayo Clin Proc 77:469-73.

Gazamarian JA, Lazoricks S, Spitz AM, et al. Prevalence of violence against pregnant women. JAMA 1996;275:1915-20.

Gjerdingen DK, Fontaine P. (1991) Preconception health care: a critical task for family physicians. J Am Board Fam Pract 4:237–50.

Henshaw SK. (1998) Unintended Pregnancy in the United States. Family Planning Perspectives 30:24-2.

Hieber JP, Dalton D, Shorey J, Combes B.(1977) Hepatitis and pregnancy. J Pediatr. 91(4):545-9.

Hirsh J, Fuster V, Ansell J, Halperin JL. (2003) American Heart Association; American College of Cardiology Foundation. American Heart Association/ American College of Cardiology Foundation guide to warfarin therapy. Circulation 107(12):1692-711.

Hobbins D. (2001) Prepping for healthy moms and babies. Making the case for preconception care and counseling. AWHONN Lifelines 5:49-54.

Institute of Medicine. (1985) Committee to Study the Prevention of Low Birth Weight. Preventing low birth weight. Washington DC: National Academy Press.

Institute of Medicine. (1995) Best Intentions. Unintended pregnancy and the well-being of children and families. Washington DC. National Academy Press.

Ioannidis JP, Abrams EJ, Ammann A, et al. (2001) Perinatal transmission of human immunodeficiency virus type 1 by pregnant women with RNA virus loads <1000 copies/ml. J Infect Dis 183:539-545.

Jack B. (1995) Preconception care (or how all family physicians "do" OB). Am Fam Physician 51:1807–8.

Jack BW, Culpepper L, Babcock J, Kogan M, Wesimiller D. (1998) How effectively are interventions initiated after preconception risk assessment at the time of a negative pregnancy test? A randomized controlled trial. J Fam Pract 47:33-38.

Jack B, Culpepper L. (1990a) Preconception care. In: Merkatz IR, Thompson JE, Mullen PD, Goldenberg RL, editors. New perspectives on prenatal care. New York: Elsevier, pp. 69–88.

Jack BW, Culpepper L. (1990b) Preconception care: risk reduction and health promotion in preparation for pregnancy. JAMA. 264:1147-1149.

Jack BW, Culpepper L. (1991) Preconception care. J Fam Prac 32:306-315.

Jerant JF, Bannon M, and Rittenhouse S. (2000) Identification and Management of Tuberculosis. Am Fam Physician 61: 2667-78, 2681-2.

Johnson SR, Kolberg BH, Varner MWS, Railsback LD. (1987) Maternal obesity and pregnancy. Surg Gynecol Obstet 164: 431–7.

Korenbrot CC, Steinberg A, Bender C, Newberry S. (2002) Preconception care: a systematic review. Matern Child Health J 6:75-88.

Lemna WK, Feldman GL, Kerem B-S, et al. (1990) Mutation analysis for heterozygote detection and the prenatal diagnosis of cystic fibrosis. N Engl J Med 322:291–6.

Mahaffey KR, (1999) Methylmercury: a new look at the risk. Public Health Rep 114:397-413.

March of Dimes Birth Defects Foundation. (2002) March of Dimes Updates: Is early prenatal care too late? Contemporary Ob/Gyn 12:54-72.

Martin JA, Hamilton BE, Sutton PD, Ventura SJ, Menacker F, Munson ML. (2003) Births: final data for 2002. Natl Vital Stat Rep 52(10):1-113.

Massachusetts Department of Public Health. A guide to eating fish safely in Massachusetts. Massachusetts Department of Public Health, Center for Environmental Health –Bureau of Environmental Health

Assessment. Boston MA: August 2004.

McCarron DA, Hatton D. (1996) Dietary calcium and lower blood pressure: we can all benefit [editorial]. JAMA 275: 1128–9.

Misra DP, Guyer B, Allston A. (2003) Integrated perinatal health framework. A multiple determinants model with a life span approach. Am J Prev Med 25:65-75.

Moos MK, Bangdiwala SI, Meibohm AR, Cefalo RC. (1996) The impact of a preconceptional health promotion program on intendedness of pregnancy. Am J Perinatol 13:103-8.

Moos MK. (2004) Preconceptional health promotion: progress in changing a prevention paradigm. J Perinat Neonatal Nurs 18:2-13.

Moos MK, Cefalo RC. (1987) Preconceptual health promotion: a focus for obstetric care. Am J Perinatol. 47:63-67.

Moos MK. (2002) Preconceptional health promotion: opportunities abound. Matern Child Health J 6:71-3.

Moos MK. (2003) Preconceptional wellness as a routine objective for women's health care: an integrative strategy. J Obstet Gynecol Neonatal Nurs 32:550-6.

Moriya T, Sasaki F, Mizui M. (1995) Transmission of hepatitis C virus from mothers to infants: Its frequency and risk factors revisited. Biomed Pharmacother 49:59-64.

MRC Vitamin Study Research Group. (1991) Prevention of neural tube defects: results of the Medical Research Council Vitamin Study. Lancet 338:131–7.

Naeye RL. (1979) Weight gain and the outcomes of pregnancy. Am J Obstet Gynecol 135:3–9.

National Academy of Sciences. (2000) Toxicological Effects of Methylmercury. Washington, DC: National Research Council.

O'Neill R. Experiments in Living: the Fatherless Family. Civitas. The Institute for the Study of Civil Society. September 2002.

Platt LD, Koch R, Azen C, et al. (1992) Maternal phenylketonuria collaborative study, obstetric aspects and outcome: the first 6 years. Am J Obstet Gynecol 166:1150–62.

Public Health Service. (1989) Caring for our future: the content of prenatal care -- a report of the Public Health Service Expert Panel on the Content of Prenatal Care. Washington, DC: US Department of Health and Human Services, Public Health Service.

Public Health Service Task Force. (2002) Recommendations for use of antiretroviral drugs in pregnant HIV-1-infected women for maternal health and interventions to reduce perinatal HIV-1 transmission in the United States.

Reinus JF, Leikin EL, Alter HJ, et al. (1992) Failure to detect vertical transmission of hepatitis C virus. Ann Intern Med 117: 881-6.

Report of the Quality Standards Subcommittee of the American Academy of Neurology. (1998) Practice parameter: management issues for women with epilepsy. Neurology 51:944-8.

Reynolds HD. (1998) Preconception Care: An integral part of primary care for women. J Nurse Midwifery 43(6):445-458.

Roberts JM, Bodnar LM, Lain KM, Hubel CA, Markovic N, Ness RB and Pwers RN. (2005) Uric Acid is as Important as proteinuria in Fetal Risk in Women with Gestational Hypertension. Hypertension *46:1263.*

Rothman KJ, Moore LL, Singer MR, et al. (1995) Teratogenicity of high vitamin A intake. N Engl J Med 333:1369–73.

Salganicoff et al. Women's Health in the United States: Health Coverage and Access to Care: Kaiser Women's Health Survey, 2002.

Schober SE, Sinks TH, Jones RL, Bolger PM, McDowell M, Osterloh J, Garrett ES,

Canady RA, Dillon CF, Sun Y, Joseph CB, Mahaffey KR. (2003) Blood Mercury Levels in US Children and Women of Childbearing Age, 1999-2000. JAMA 289:1667-1674.

Shepard TH. (1998) Catalog of Teratogenic Agents pp 1309. 9th ed.Baltimore, MD: Johns Hopkins University Press, .p1309.

Smits L, Pedersen C, Mortensen P, Van Os J. (2004) Association between short birth intervals and schizophrenia in the off-spring. Schizophr. Res 1;70(1):49-56.

Stephenson MD, Ballem PJ, Tsang P, Purkiss S, Ensworth S, Houlihan E, Ensom MH. (2004) Treatment of antiphospholipic antibody syndrome in pregnancy: a randomized pilot trial comparing low molecular weight heparin to unfraction-ated heparin. J Obstet Gynaecol Canada 26: 729-34.

Taysi K. (1998) Preconceptional counseling. Obstet Gynecol Clin North Am 15:167–78.

Thompson JE. Maternal stress, anxiety, and social support during pregnancy: possible direction for prenatal intervention. In: Merkatz IR, Thompson JE, Mullen PD, Goldenberg R, eds. New perspectives on prenatal care. New York: Elsevier, 1990; 319-35.

Toffleson L, Cordle F. (1986) Methyl-mercury in fish: a review of residual levels, fish consumption, and regulatory action in the United States. Environ Health Perspec 68:203-208.

USAID. (2002) Birth Spacing Update. US Department of Health and Human Services, Health Resources and Services Administration, Maternal and Child Health Bureau. (2002) *Women's Health USA 2002*. Rockville, Maryland: US Department of Health and Human Services.

US Department of Health and Human Services Public Health Service Centers for Disease Control (1992) Recommendations for the use of folic acid to reduce the number of cases of spina bifida and other neural tube defects. MMWR 41:1–8.

US Department of Health and Human Services and US Environmental Protec-tion Agency. What you need to know about mercury in fish and shellfish. EPA-823-r-04-005; March 2004. Available at: http://www.cfsan.fda.gov/~dms/admehg3.html. Accessed on October 23, 2006.

US Environmental Protection Agency. (1997) Mercury Study Report to Congress, Volume I: Executive Summary. Washing-ton, DC: Environmental Protection Agency. Publication EPA-452/R-97-003

US Public Health Service. (1991) Healthy People 2000: National health promotion and disease prevention objectives. (DHHS Pub. No. 91-502212.) Washington DC: US Department of Health and Human Services.

US Public Health Service. (2000) Healthy People 2000: midcourse review and 1995 revisions. Washington DC: US Depart-ment of Health and Human Services.

US Preventive Services Task Force (1996). Guide to clinical preventive services, 2nd ed. Baltimore: Williams and Wilkins.

US Preventive Services Task Force. (2003) Counseling: Tobacco use. Guide to Preventive Services, Third Edition, Periodic Updates. AHRQ website, viewed 12/2003.

Weisman CS. (1997) Changing definitions of women's health: Implications for health care and policy. Matern Child Health J 1:179-189.

Werler MM, Shapiro S, Mitchell AA. (1993) Periconceptional folic acid exposure and risk of occurrent neural tube defects. JAMA 269:1257–61.

Wille MC, Weitz B, Kerper, P, Frazier S. (2004) Advances in preconception genetic counseling. J Perinatal Neonatal Nurs 18: 28-40.

World Health Organization. (1990) Environmental Health Criteria 101: Methyl-mercury. Geneva, Switzerland: World Health Organization.

Yaris F. (2004) Inadvertent Fetal Exposures to Antibiotics during Unplanned Pregnancies. 17th World Conference of Family Doctors: Abstract 3687. Presented Oct. 14, 2004.

Zanetti AR, Tanzi E, Newell ML. (1999) Mother-to-infant transmission of hepatitis C virus. J Hepatol 31 Suppl 1:96-100.

BEHAVIORAL INTERVENTIONS TO DECREASE THE BURDENS OF LOW BIRTHWEIGHT, MACROSOMIA, AND BIRTH DEFECTS

Jodie A. Trafton and Jennifer M. Singler

INTRODUCTION

In spite of considerable improvements in prenatal and neonatal care in the United States over the past several decades, infant morbidity and mortality remain a problem, especially in economically disadvantaged communities and among ethnic minorities. In 2007, the United States ranked 41st out of 221 countries in infant mortality, with a rate that is over 2.5 times higher than that of the 1st ranked country. Although overall infant mortality has decreased, a Centers for Disease Control and Prevention report found that the black-white gap for infant mortality has widened over the past two decades (Centers for Disease Control and Prevention, 2002). In most of the developing world, prenatal care and subsequent birth outcomes have improved but remain poor, exacerbated by political unrest, economic instability, inadequate health care, and poor baseline maternal nutrition.

Although many factors contribute to poor fetal development, there are two main modifiable categories of birth complications that have been addressed by the medical establishment over the past century: birth defects and extremes of birth weight, including: low birthweight (LBW, 1500–2499g), very low birthweight (VLBW, less than 1500g), and macrosomia/large for gestational age (defined as birth weight greater than 4000g, or greater than 90th percentile).

The causes of some birth defects have been easier to determine and modify than birth weight. For example, the decrease in children born with a neural tube defect (NTD) in the United States since the mid-1990s can be directly attributed to the public campaign to increase the amount of folic acid consumed both by pregnant women and the U.S. population as a whole (Mathews, 2006). This chapter will review randomized controlled studies in the USA and internationally that have attempted to utilize behavioral interventions to modify the risk factors for poor birth outcomes associated with extremes of birth weight and birth defects.

Low and Very Low Birthweight

The problem of LBW infants is significant; in 2005, 8.2% of all infants born in the United States weighed less than 2500g, and 1.5% weighed less than 1500g (Hamilton et al., 2007). Worldwide, about 16% of all live births are LBW infants, an estimated 18 million every year (UNICEF, 2004). The majority of LBW infants are born in developing countries. However, since the mid-1980s the percentage of LBW infants in the U.S. has increased slowly but steadily by more than 20% over a span of two decades, from a low of 6.7% in 1984 (Martin et al., 2006). Some of this increase, especially in whites, is due to increases in delivery before the fetus is full-term (i.e. preterm delivery), changing obstetrical practices, and increased rates of multiple gestations. Nevertheless, blacks continue to have a two- to threefold higher risk than whites for LBW and VLBW infants (Centers for Disease Control and Prevention, 2002).

LBW and VLBW infants are at increased risk for congenital malformations, infections, perinatal death, disorders of metabolism (hypothermia, hypoglycemia), and impaired postnatal growth. LBW infants have a 40-fold greater chance of dying in the neonatal period and a 50% greater chance of developing serious developmental problems (UNICEF, 2002). They have a higher rate of long-term developmental and neurological outcomes, including attention-deficit disorder, learning disabilities, poor school performance, and chronic health conditions such as chronic lung disease.

As adults, LBW infants are at increased risk for chronic diseases such as hypertension, diabetes, and cardiovascular disease (Stein et al., 2006; Fall et al., 2003; Godfrey and Barker, 2000). Starting at birth and extending into their adult years, they represent a significant cost to the U.S. healthcare system. A study conducted in California examining the costs of births by gestational age and birthweight found that the hospital costs for LBW infants in that state alone approached $700,000,000, or nearly $34,000 per LBW infant, in 2000 (Schmitt et al., 2006).

Low birthweight has two main causes: 1) being born too early, which is referred to as preterm delivery and defined as delivery before 37 weeks gestation, or 2) not growing at the normal rate during gestation, which is referred to as intrauterine growth retardation (IUGR), and defined as birth weight below the 10th percentile for gestational age. Preterm delivery accounts for the majority of cases of LBW in the U.S., whereas IUGR accounts for the majority of cases of LBW infants in developing countries (Fall et al., 2003). In the U.S. major risk factors for preterm delivery include maternal and fetal stress, infections, and violence; smoking accounts for 20-30% of all cases of IUGR. In the developing world, poor maternal nutrition, low prepregnancy body-mass index (BMI), and inadequate weight gain are key risk factors for IUGR/LBW, as are infections such as malaria, which leads to chronic anemia (Kramer, 1987; see also Table 1). Other, less quantifiable risk factors for LBW include indicators of low socioeconomic status such as education, income, and stress (Ricketts et al., 2005). Most behavioral interventions to prevent LBW have focused on improved pre-natal care, with an emphasis on maternal nutrition including protein intake, micronutrient supplementation and smoking cessation.

Table 1. Determinants of preterm birth and IUGR in developing country settings, in decreasing order of importance (from Kramer, 2003)

Preterm birth	IUGR
Genital tract infection	Low energy intake, low gestational weight gain
Multiple births	Low prepregnancy Body Mass Index
Pregnancy-induced hypertension	Short stature
Low prepregnancy Body Mass Index	Malaria
Incompetent cervix	Cigarette smoking
Prior preterm birth	Primiparity
Abruptio placenta	Pregnancy-induced hypertension
Heavy work	Congenital anomalies
Cigarette smoking	Other genetic factors

Macrosomia and Large For Gestational Age

Macrosomia is also associated with birth complications and occurs in more than 10% of pregnancies in the U.S. (Zamorski and Biggs, 2001). A study of 146,526 births in Northern California found that mothers of macrosomic infants had higher rates of complications and medical intervention. These included a greater chance of cesarean birth, chorioamnionitis (an infection of the placenta and amniotic fluid), shoulder dystocia (an obstetrical emergency where the infants' shoulders get stuck after the head is delivered), fourth-degree perineal lacerations (tears that extend through the anal sphincter and the tissue underneath), postpartum hemorrhages, and prolonged hospital stay (Stotland et al., 2004). Based on an analysis of all births in the U.S. between 1995 and 1997, fetal mortality was greater when birth weights were greater than 4250 in nondiabetic mother or greater than 4000g in diabetic mothers, and maternal diabetes doubled the relative risk of fetal mortality (Mondestin,

2002). Macrosomia is associated with shoulder dystocia, which occurs in 5-9% of deliveries of macrosomic infants as compared to 0.6-1.4% of deliveries of non-macrosomic infants (Baxley and Gobbo, 2004). Shoulder dystocia results in injury to the infant in 20% of shoulder dystocia deliveries, most commonly nerve damage (i.e. brachial plexus lesions), broken clavicles or humeri, contusions and lacerations, and birth asphyxia. Mothers may suffer excessive blood loss and vaginal and vulvar lacerations (Lerner, 2007).

The greatest risk factor for macrosomia is maternal hyperglycemia during pregnancy, either resulting from preexisting type I or II diabetes in the mother or from gestational diabetes during the pregnancy. Maternal diabetes doubles the risk of macrosomia (Zamorski and Biggs, 2001). Maternal obesity has also been associated with risk for macrosomia, and elevates risk of type II and gestational diabetes. In all types of diabetes and possibly with maternal obesity, maternal hyperglycemia directly increases fetal risk. Maternal hyperglycemia during pregnancy has also been associated with risk of shoulder dystocia, birth injuries such as bone fractures and nerve palsies, and hypoglycemia during the perinatal period.

A 2002 survey in the U.S. found that 26% of non-pregnant women between 20-39 years of age were overweight and an additional 29% were obese (Hedley et al., 2004). Rates of pre-existing diabetes in pregnant women have increased in association with the increased incidence of obesity. Thus, more than half of the women of child-bearing age in the U.S. are at elevated risk for complications related to diabetes and macrosomia.

Gestational diabetes occurs in 2-5% of pregnancies, and is hypothesized to result from an insufficient compensatory growth of pancreatic islet cells in combination with insulin resistance produced by high levels of progesterone and other hormones during pregnancy (Branisteanu and Mathieu, 2003).

Generally, gestational diabetes does not occur until the second half of pregnancy when hormone levels are higher, and thus risks associated with diabetes during the first trimester (e.g., miscarriage, major congenital abnormalities, stillbirth (Yang et al., 2006, Casson et al., 1997, Dunne et al., 2003)) are not present in women with gestational diabetes.

Risk of macrosomia is also associated with longer length of gestation, male gender of the fetus, and self-identification as black or Hispanic (Okun et al., 1997; Dooley et al., 1991).

Congenital Anomalies

Although rare compared to birthweight extremes and often underreported, congenital anomalies, also known as birth defects, are the leading cause of infant mortality in the United States. They are also a significant contributor to childhood morbidity, causing metabolic disorders and disability. Approximately 3-5% newborns in the U.S. have a structural birth defect. In the majority of cases, the cause is unknown, making prevention efforts difficult. The most common anomalies reported on U.S. birth certificates include, in order of frequency: cleft lip/palate, Down syndrome, omphalocele/gastroschisis (in which abdominal organs stick out of the navel or abdominal wall), meningomyelocele/spina bifida, (in which the meninges and spinal cord protrude through a defect in the vertebral column) and anencephaly (in which much of the brain does not develop) (Martin et al., 2006). An estimate of the lifetime cost of 18 common birth defects (22% of babies with a birth defect have one of these 18) for all affected births in 1992 was $8 billion in 1992 dollars, with costs ranging from $75,000 to $503,000 per new case (Waitzman et al., 1995).

In this chapter, we focus on those anomalies whose prevention has been amenable to behavioral or public health interventions, specifically those related to vitamin deficiency, alcohol, tobacco and illicit drug use, and use of potentially teratogenic medications. Vitamin deficiencies have been associated with neural tube defects (spina bifida, encephalocoele, and anencephaly), maternal alcohol use with fetal alcohol syndrome, cocaine use with urinary tract defects, and tobacco use with cleft lip/palate.

We note that public health interventions have successfully targeted other causes of birth defects. For example, infection with rubella, a mild childhood illness, during the first trimester of pregnancy causes a syndrome of birth defects, including eye defects, hearing loss, heart defects, mental retardation and movement disorders, in 25% of affected pregnancies. Immunization programs have virtually eliminated rubella-related birth defects in the U.S. (Centers for Disease Control, 2005), however, this infection remains a preventable cause of birth defects in developing countries. In these developing countries, interventions to increase rubella vaccination rates should be considered. However, such interventions are not needed in the U.S. and have not been tested in randomized controlled trials (RCTs).

INTERVENTIONS TO PREVENT LBW
Nutritional Supplements

Observational studies have suggested a strong association between prepregancy weight, gestational weight gain and positive fetal growth, and publicly-funded Women, Infants and Children (WIC: Special Supplementation Food Program for Women, Infants, and Children, implemented in 1975) programs to improve maternal health are a staple in many inner-city clinics (Kotelchuck et al., 1984; Kowaleski-Jones and Duncan, 2002). However, the overall evidence from RCTs supporting the effectiveness of nutritional supplementation is not strong. A 2003 Cochrane Review of twenty-five RCTs involving over 8,000 women concluded that,

although dietary advice and supplementation effectively increased a pregnant woman's energy intake and modestly improved fetal growth and survival, the interventions were "unlikely to confer major benefits on infant or maternal health" (Kramer and Kakuma, 2003). Moreover, they concluded that high protein supplementation, in which protein accounted for more than 25% of total energy consumed, was not beneficial and possibly even harmful to the developing fetus. The Cochrane Review did conclude that supplementation, especially high-energy supplements, did appear to reduce the risk of stillbirth and neonatal death, although data were limited and the biological mechanism for this reduction was unclear. An independent review of the evidence from RCTs (Merialdi et al., 2003) of more than 4000 women concurred with the Cochrane Review. The authors concluded that a balanced energy-protein supplementation reduced the risk of small-for-gestational-age (SGA) by 30% (95% Confidence Interval (CI): 20% - 43%) in developing countries with high rates of undernutrition. The overall methodological quality of the RCTs was highly variable, including non-blinded observers measuring dietary intake, variable reporting of treatment allocation procedures, and inadequate reporting of exclusion of participants. Only one trial reported a double-blind design. All trials were hampered by the innate difficulty in ensuring compliance with the dietary supplement and assessing for possible changes to the normal diet in treatment and/or control groups. Studies reported variable improvements in birthweight and rates of prematurity, although neither factor seemed to be associated with long-term benefits for child growth and development. We will discuss the results of some of these trials (summarized in Table 2) by type of intervention: nutritional counseling, balanced energy/protein supplementation, and high-protein supplementation.

Nutritional Counseling

An RCT of over 500 pregnant women in rural Greece (Kafatos et al., 1989) randomized the participants by clinic to receive either bimonthly at-home nutrition counseling in addition to standard prenatal care, or standard prenatal care alone. The study region has high rates of perinatal and infant morbidity and mortality. Analysis of nutritional intake in a subset of 70% of study participants at time of intake showed that the women were adequately nourished, although total intake was lower than the recommended daily value of 2300-2400 kcal per day. Bimonthly nutrition counseling starting at around 27 weeks gestation was associated with improved dietary intake (as demonstrated by monthly dietary recall and food-weighing inventory) and a statistically significant increase in maternal weight gain ($p<0.05$). No differences were found in mean birthweight (3391g in intervention group vs. 3376g in control group), LBW (4.5% vs. 3.9%), or SGA (6.0% in both groups). The number of premature infants was less in the intervention group: 3.7% vs. 8.3%, which was statistically significant ($p<0.04$). The authors concluded that, although the decrease in prematurity was encouraging and education was associated with the study goal of increasing caloric intake during pregnancy, the effect of this intervention on improving pregnancy outcomes in an already adequately nourished population was indeterminate.

Balanced Energy/Protein Supplementation

A study evaluated the efficacy of the WIC program in preventing low birth weight in 400 at-risk low-income women in the U.S. (Metcoff et al., 1985). After controlling for maternal weight at enrollment, the authors concluded that WIC food voucher supplementation starting in mid-pregnancy had a statistically significant effect only for those women who smoked during pregnancy; their babies were significantly heavier by +168g ($p=0.017$) compared to smokers who did not receive WIC assistance. The lack of improvement in birth weight in non-smokers occurred despite documented improvement in nutritional status (per biochemical plasma markers) in all WIC-supplemented mothers when compared to controls ($p=0.009$).

Of the several RCTs reviewed that analyzed the effects of providing a balanced nutritional supplement (<25% of total energy from protein) to pregnant women, the most striking results occurred in a large trial of over 1400 women in rural Gambia (Ceesay et al., 1997). This trial of chronically undernourished women was notable for its use of a much higher energy supplement than that used in other trials, as well as its use of a locally-made supplement that is more feasible for use in a rural healthcare system. Women were recruited into the study at 20-24 weeks' gestation, and received supplements for an average of 82 days during the second half of pregnancy. The authors found statistically significant reductions not only in low birthweight babies (Odds Ratio (OR)=0.61 in supplemented group), but in rates of stillbirth and perinatal death (OR=0.47 and 0.54, respectively). The improvement in birthweight varied by season of the year (reflecting crop harvests and baseline nutritional intake), with the greatest improvement seen during the "hungry season." Birthweights increased by an average of 201g ($p<0.001$) in the supplemented group.

The Bacon Chow study randomized a group of 300 well-nourished pregnant women in rural Taiwan to receive a high calorie, high nutrient liquid supplement or a low calorie liquid placebo. The Bacon Chow study is the, only double-blind trial of nutritional supplementation conducted to date. No differences in birthweight or fetal deaths were observed (McDonald et al., 1981). The trial followed the women from the birth of one child through the birth of a second, and did find that the birthweight of the second infant in the

Table 2. Nutrition supplement trials

Trial	Participants	Intervention	Results
Nutritional Counseling			
Kafatos et al., 1989	568 pregnant women in rural area of Greece <27 wks gestation; 20 local clinics randomized to intervention or control via computer-generated random numbers; of note, this population was not nutritionally at risk	1: Intervention group received bimonthly nutrition counseling at home by a study nurse from the clinic 2: Control group received no counseling	Although maternal weight gain in intervention group was significantly greater (p<0.05), there were no significant differences between the groups for **LBW, mean birthweight, SGA** **Percent premature:** 1: 3.7% 2: 8.3% (p<0.04)
Balanced Energy/Protein Supplementation			
Ceesay et al., 1997	5-year controlled trial of 1460 chronically undernourished pregnant women from 28 villages in rural Gambia	Women in those villages randomized to intervention received daily supplementation (mean 82 +/- 31 days) with locally-made high-energy groundnut biscuits (1027 kcal/day, 22g protein) starting about 20-24 wks gestation; women in control-group villages received the supplement after delivery	**Birth weight** increased by 201g (p<0.001) in the hungry season, by 94g (p<0.01) in the harvest season, and by 136g (p<0.001) over the whole year **Low birthweight** was less frequent in supplemented women, OR 0.61 (95%CI 0.47-0.79, p<0.001) **Stillbirths** decreased in supplement group, OR=0.47 (0.23-0.99, p<0.05). **Death in first week of life** in supplement group, OR=0.54 (0.35-0.85, p<0.01)
Kardjati et al., 1988	747 'nutritionally-vulnerable' pregnant women at 26-28 weeks gestation in three villages in rural East Java	1: Intervention group received 'high-energy' supplement providing 465 kcal energy and 7.1g protein 2: control group supplement contained 52 kcal energy and 6.2g protein ('low-energy'); trained fieldworkers observed daily home consumption of supplement	No difference found between 2 groups in **mean birthweight** or **% LBW** Hypothesized that most gains seen in those women with lowest home dietary intake and/or low prepregnancy weight

Trial	Participants	Intervention	Results
Metcoff et al., 1985	410 women in Oklahoma enrolled at mid-pregnancy	1: 238 women received WIC food supplementation vouchers 2: 172 did not	WIC supplemented women who smoked had significantly heavier infants than unsupplemented smokers (+168g, p=0.017)
McDonald et al., 1981 (Bacon Chow study)	294 well-nourished pregnant women in rural Taiwan with 'marginal' diets, a population termed to be 'nutritionally at risk' and low SES. Subjects enrolled in the final trimester of one pregnancy and were followed to the end of lactation after a second pregnancy.	Three weeks after birth of the first infant, 1: intervention-group women received twice-daily nutrient-rich liquid supplement (daily total of 800 kcal, 40g protein); 2: control group received placebo that was low in calories and nutrients (total 80 kcal)	No significant differences between intervention and control group infants for **birth weight, number LBW, fetal deaths** In supplement group, **birth weight of second** infant was statistically higher that first infant (+161.4g, p<0.05)
High protein supplementation			
Mardones et al., 1988	597 low-income Chilean women <20 weeks gestation with low weight-for-height at first visit	1: Intervention group received high-protein (22% of energy content), high iron, nutrient-fortified powdered milk supplement; 2: control group received normal-protein (12%), minimally-fortified powdered milk supplement. Both formulas provided 500kcal per serving and were distributed at monthly clinic visits for home consumption.	**Mean birthweight** in intervention group was 73g higher than in controls 1: 3178g 2: 3105g (p<0.05) No significant difference in **% of LBW** infants <2501g **Birthweight <3001g:** 1: 19.92% 2: 27.27% (p<0.05) **IUGR infants** 1: 9.96% 2: 26.89% (p<0.05)
Mora et al., 1979	433 women in Columbia in 3rd trimester of pregnancy considered at high risk of malnutrition based on survey of previous children	1: Received weekly food supplements for entire family of bread, milk, vegetable oil, and a vitamin/mineral supplement (total 856 kcal and 38.4g protein); 2: normal unsupplemented diet	1: increased birth weight of full-term males (+95g, p<0.05). Birthweight was associated with duration of supplementation and parallel effects on maternal weight gain.

Trial	Participants	Intervention	Results
Rush et al., 1980	1051 low-income black women in New York City ≤ 30 weeks gestation deemed at high risk for having LBW infants; 768 singleton live births included in study results	Three groups: 1: Supplement group: high-protein beverage containing 470 kcal, 40g protein, vitamins/minerals 2: Complement group: balanced energy/protein beverage of 322 kcal, 6g protein, vitamin 3: Control group: vitamin per routine prenatal care	– No statistically significant differences between the three groups for **birth weight** of infants – In 1: significant decrease in **LBW** of infants in those mothers who smoked heavily (p value not given), likely due to increased gestation length and accelerated fetal growth – 1: resulted in an *increase* of **very early premature births, neonatal deaths** (Relative Risk (RR)=2.78, 95% CI 0.75-10.36), and significant **growth retardation** up to 37 weeks gestation

intervention group was 161g higher than the first infant (p<0.05).

A study of over 700 women in East Java also randomized to a high- or low-energy supplement found no evidence of any benefit of nutritional supplementation on fetal growth, although it was hypothesized that any detectable differences were masked by the overall improved home diet that may have occurred during the study (Kardjati et al., 1988). Another reasonably well-executed study by Mora and colleagues (1979) in Columbia found that only male infants had increased birth weight. This difference was small but statistically significant (+95g, p<0.05) and was associated with duration of supplementation and positive maternal weight gain.

High protein supplementation

One trial examined the results of isocaloric protein supplementation in 600 low-income Chilean women considered at risk for LBW infants based on being underweight at their first prenatal visit (Mardones et al., 1988). Both the intervention and control groups received a powdered milk supplement, but the intervention group received one that was high in protein, iron, and other nutrients. Mean birthweight in the intervention group was 73g higher than the control group (p<0.05), although there was no detectable difference in proportion of LBW infants between the two groups. There was a significant difference in percentage of IUGR infants and infants weighing less than 3001g between the two groups, with more in the control group.

A well-done large study of 1000 poor black women in New York City raised several key points (Rush et al., 1980). This study had three arms: the "supplement group" received a high-protein (>25% of total energy from protein) beverage totaling 470kcal and 40g protein, another (the "complement group") a balanced energy/protein beverage of 322 kcal and 6g protein, and a control group that received normal prenatal care including vitamins and minerals. Like in the WIC study done by Metcoff and colleagues, they found a significant decrease in the number of LBW infants born to women smokers; this result was felt to be secondary to increased gestation length and accelerated fetal growth in those receiving the high-protein supplement. In the study as a whole they did not find any significant differences in birthweight across the three groups, although the group of women receiving the balanced supplement had almost-significant improvements in length of gestation, mean birth weight (+41g), and percentage of LBW infants. The high-protein supplementation actually resulted in a borderline significant increase in premature births, neonatal deaths, and IUGR.

In sum, these studies suggest that nutritional supplementation may modestly increase birthweight in at risk populations. Greatest improvements have been observed in the highest risk populations: undernourished women in developing countries, and low-income smokers in the United States.

Micronutrient Supplementation

Micronutrients, vitamins and minerals required in minute amounts by the human body for normal functioning, are important factors in pregnancy outcomes: both in inadequate and excess amounts. Poor women in the U.S. and worldwide often consume insufficient amounts of micronutrients due to diets lacking in fruits, vegetables, animal protein, and fortified foods. These baseline deficiencies are exacerbated during pregnancy due to the competing demands from the developing fetus. There are a host of micro-nutrient deficiencies that pose serious health risks to the mother and fetus; deficiencies of Vitamins A, B6, and B12, iodine, zinc, iron, calcium, magnesium, copper, and selenium have all been linked with complications of pregnancy, childbirth, or fetal development. However, the link between maternal and fetal nutrition is indirect and poorly understood. IUGR can be replicated in experimental

animals by reducing protein and energy in the maternal diet, but interventions of energy and protein supplements in humans, as discussed in the previous section, are less convincing (Fall et al., 2003). IUGR as a consequence of poor maternal nutrition should, in theory, be preventable; thus, a focus on micronutrient status as an alternative to macronutrient intake has gained in popularity. Micronutrient supplementation is also appealing because it is a very feasible intervention. Providing pregnant women with vitamin and mineral supplements is cheaper and easier to imple-ment than increasing total energy intake, especially since standard prenatal care already includes iron and folate supplementation. In the U.S., multivitamin tablets are so routinely prescribed prior to and during pregnancy that RCTs are considered by some to be unethical (Scholl et al., 1997).

An observational study of urban pregnant teenagers in the U.S. (Scholl et al., 1997) and a RCT of HIV-positive women in Tanzania (Fawzi et al., 1998) both concluded that multivitamin and mineral supplementation reduced the risks of LBW and preterm delivery. Another prospective observational study, this one among nearly 800 women in rural India, concluded that a diet low in micronutrient-rich foods such a green leafy vegetables, fruits, and dairy products has an adverse affect on fetal growth, especially in low-BMI women. Women with high intakes of green-leafy vegetables had infants that were nearly 200g heavier than those women who never consumed them (p<0.005) (Rao et al., 2001). In 1999, the UNICEF/UNU/WHO released recommendations for a multimicro-nutrient supplement containing the recom-mended daily allowance (RDA) of 15 micro-nutrients (including folic acid and iron) for pregnant and lactating women in developing countries (UNICEF/WHO/UNU, 1999; see Table 3). Over $3.3 million in UNICEF-sponsored pilot programs to improve birth-weight through micronutrient supplementation are on-going in developing countries (UNICEF, 2002).

Table 3: Composition of UNICEF/UNU/ WHO daily multi-micronutrient supplement for pregnant women in developing countries (UNICEF/UNU/WHO, 1999)

Vitamin A	800 mcg
Vitamin D	200 IU
Vitamin E	10 mg
Vitamin C	70 mg
Vitamin B1	1.4 mg
Vitamin B2	1.4 mg
Niacin	18 mg
Vitamin B6	1.9 mg
Vitamin B12	2.6 mcg
Folic Acid	400 mcg
Iron	30 mg
Zinc	15 mg
Copper	2 mg
Selenium	65 mcg
Iodine	150 mcg

Despite the strong push to improve micronutrient status during pregnancy, evidence from RCTs is inadequate to conclude that there are benefits to women and infants. A 2003 overview of nutrition interventions to prevent or treat IUGR found a striking lack of evidence from RCTs and systematic reviews that single micronutrient supplementation decreased SGA or LBW (Merialdi et al., 2003). The one exception was magnesium supplementation, which showed a 33% decrease in risk of LBW in a pooled result of 4 trials. A similar meta-analysis of interventions to increase birthweight also failed to find evidence of single-micronutrient supplementation on rates of preterm delivery (Villar et al., 2003). Most studies have examined the short-term effects of single micronutrient supplements on maternal micronutrient status and fetal growth, but under-nutrition is most commonly linked to chronic deficiencies in multiple micronutrients (Fall et al., 2003). Furthermore, the detrimental effects of

chronic, decades-long micronutrient deficiencies on reproductive health are unlikely to be improved in only a few months of supplementation (Villar et al., 2003). Those trials that have shown the most convincing data are those that focused on increasing energy intake and thus provided micronutrients incidentally; the well-known Bacon Chow study in Taiwan and a large trial in The Gambia (both reviewed in the previous section) are two examples.

A 2006 Cochrane review evaluating data from nine prospective RCTs of supplementation of three or more micronutrients, including over 15,000 women, concluded that there was insufficient evidence to recommend replacement of iron and folate supplements with a multi-micronutrient supplement (Haider and Bhutta, 2006). The pooled data showed that, when compared with supplementation with less than three micronutrients, no supplementation, or placebo, multi-micronutrient supplementation reduced the risk of LBW (RR=0.83, 95% CI: 0.76-0.91) and SGA (RR=0.92, 95% CI: 0.86-0.99). However, the data were not statistically significant when multi-micronutrient supplementation was compared with iron/folic acid alone. The authors noted that while providing a single multi-micronutrient supplement is economically and logistically attractive, controversy remains over the possible dangerous interactions between micronutrients when taken concurrently. For example, one nutrient may impair the absorption of another, leading to dangerously high levels of one and negligible levels of another. They concluded by echoing other recent meta-analyses that further research is needed to determine both benefits and possible negative effects of multi-micronutrient supplementation in pregnant women and their fetuses.

We reviewed the results of eight RCTs of multi-micronutrient supplementation published from 1994-2007, all but one of which were a double-blind design (Table 4). Most trials enrolled women in developing countries; one notable exception was a 2005 study in France (Hininger et al., 2004). Three of the trials were placebo-controlled, although only one (Hininger et al., 2004) had a control arm receiving a true placebo and no supplemental iron/folic acid. Women were enrolled at varying gestational ages, ranging from peri-conceptionally to late (35 weeks) gestation. Most trials used an intention-to-treat analysis and were of sound methodological quality, reporting good randomization and adequate blinding of participants. Loss to follow-up was variable, ranging from over 20% in three trials to less than 5% in others. Major outcomes reviewed were mean birthweight and LBW. Results were marginal at best, with some reporting incremental improvements, others no difference at all in mean birthweight or percentage of LBW infants, as well as one concerning finding of increased perinatal mortality.

Three trials, one small and two large, compared a multi-micronutrient supplement to placebo. A small trial conducted in France of 100 well-nourished pregnant women, who were recruited around 14 weeks gestation, compared daily multi-micronutrient supplement (without iron) to placebo (Hininger et al., 2004). This trial is notable for its hypothesis that even "apparently healthy pregnant women" in a developed country have poor micronutrient status and would therefore benefit from supplementation. It also differs from all other trials in that the placebo arm did not specifically receive iron and folic acid as part of routine care. The supplemented group had significantly higher plasma levels of some micronutrients and a 10% improvement (250g) in mean birth-weight compared to placebo (3300g vs. 3049g, p=0.03). The number of LBW infants (defined in this study as <2700g) was significantly less in the intervention group (2 vs. 9, p=0.02), although how many were less than the international standard for LBW of

2500g was not recorded. Notably, there were problems in execution of the trial: only 65 of the original 100 women were in the final cohort, a loss of nearly 35%.

The next placebo-controlled trial was conducted in Zimbabwe, recruiting over 1000 pregnant women at 22-35 weeks gestation (Friis et al., 2004). Two facts about the study population should be noted: the background percentage of LBW was only 10%, a relatively good outcome in the developing world, and 30% of participants were HIV-positive. All women received standard pre-natal care including iron and folic acid supplements. The intervention group took a daily supplement similar to that advocated by UNICEF and the control group was given a placebo. The study was powered to detect an 80g difference in birth weight with an allowance for 20% loss to follow-up; only 66% of women completed the study, although loss to follow-up was evenly distributed across the two groups and across study variables. Although supplementation was associated with an increase in birth weight of almost 50g, this was not statistically significant (p=0.08). Micronutrient supple-mentation was not associated with a significant decrease in LBW, IUGR-LBW, or preterm delivery (RR 0.84, 0.71, and 0.82, respectively; p≥0.15).

The largest of the three placebo-controlled trials randomized 8468 HIV-negative preg-nant women in urban Tanzania to daily multivitamins or placebo (Fawzi et al., 2007). Following on their success in treating pregnant HIV-positive women (RCT men-tioned above, Fawzi et al., 1998), the authors assessed the same primary outcomes in an HIV-negative population: LBW (<2500g), prematurity, and fetal death. All women received standard prenatal care that included daily iron and folic acid as well as malaria prophylaxis at 20 and 30 weeks of gestation. Women were recruited at 12 to 27 weeks gestation and received daily multi-vitamins or placebo until 6 weeks after delivery. Supplementation consisted of 6-10 times the RDA of several B vitamins and vitamin C and twice the RDA of vitamin E, and omitted zinc and vitamin A (and thus differing from the standard UNICEF supplement and that used in most other studies). Of the primary outcomes, multi-vitamin supplementation reduced only the incidence of LBW, from 9.4% to 7.8%, a relative risk of 0.82 (95% CI: 0.70 to 0.95, p=0.01). Supplementation had no significant effect on fetal mortality or prematurity. There was a modest increase in mean birthweight of 67g in the supplemented group (p<0.001), similar to that seen in other trials. Multivitamins reduced the risk of births that were small for gestational age (<10th percentile) from 13.6% in the placebo group to 10.7% in the supplemented group, a relative risk of 0.77 (p<0.0001), and resulted in a small but significant decrease in the risk of maternal anemia (p=0.01). The authors concluded that, given the benefits and the low cost of providing supplementation, prenatal multivitamin supplementation could be a cost-effective strategy for improving birth outcomes in the developing world.

A large trial of 1200 women in Nepal analyzed whether second and third trimester supplementation with one RDA of 15 vitamins and minerals would increase birth weight and prolong gestation when compared to routine iron and folic acid supplements (Osrin et al., 2005). This nutritionally-at-risk population had documented high rates of LBW, ranging from 27% in hospitals to 40% in some rural regions. The intervention group had a statistically significant increase in mean birthweight of 77g (2810g versus 2733g, p=0.004) and a 25% relative decrease in proportion of LBW infants (OR for LBW was 0.69, p=0.014). There was no effect on length of gestation. The authors concluded that given the, at best, modest effects observed, more research was needed before supplementation could be advocated as a public-health priority.

Another trial in rural Nepal of nearly 5000 newly-pregnant women also failed to show that a multi-micronutrient supplement was significantly better than standard prenatal iron and folic acid in improving birth weight (Christian et al., 2003). This trial utilized five different micronutrient supplements: folic acid, folic acid-iron, folic-acid-iron-zinc, a multi-micronutrient supplement containing one RDA of 15 vitamins and minerals (per UNICEF recommendations except for increased iron and zinc to account for the excess anemia in the population at baseline), and Vitamin A alone as the control. The trial attained a high level of compliance with supplementation (median 88%) and a small (5%) loss to follow-up. As in the previous study, the population had poor baseline nutrition (mean maternal weight was low, only 43kg) and a high level of LBW infants at baseline: 43% of infants in the control group weighed less than 2500g. Mean birthweight was only modestly improved by multi-micro-nutrient supplementation, an increase of 64g; folic acid-iron increased birthweight by 37g, and folic-acid-iron-zinc and folic acid alone showed no improvement over controls. Multi-micro-nutrient supplementation was no better than folic acid-iron at preventing LBW, decreasing the risk by 14% compared to 16%. The authors estimated that this translated into a number-needed-to-treat of 11-12 women to prevent one LBW baby. Also of note was the beneficial effect of adding iron to the folic acid, likely due to its treatment of maternal anemia.

The two previous studies from Nepal pooled their data after initial publication and reported a paradoxical increase in perinatal mortality after micronutrient supplementation (Christian et al, 2005). Although this was noted in each trial separately, these findings did not attain statistical significance until the data were combined. Among 2700 live births, the relative risk of perinatal death (within 7 days) was 1.36 (95% CI, 1.02-1.81) and of neonatal death (within 28 days) was 1.52 (1.03-2.25). The authors suggested that the higher birthweight from multivitamin supplementation could lead to difficulties during labor in this population of short and chronically undernourished South Asian women. Although hesitating to generalize that supplementation was detrimental, they advised caution in implementing prenatal multivitamin supplementation uniformly across populations.

A trial conducted in semirural Mexico concurred with the finding that iron alone improves birthweight without the addition of other vitamins and minerals (Ramakrishnan et al., 2003). Over 800 women, nearly one-third of whom were overweight (BMI>25), were recruited early in pregnancy and given a multi-micronutrient or iron-only (control) supplement by a trained health worker at home six days a week. Even after adjusting for confounding variables (higher percentage of overweight women in iron-only group and 25% loss to follow-up), no difference was found between the two groups for mean birthweight, LBW, IUGR, or preterm delivery.

A trial of 2100 women in semi-urban Guinea-Bissau tested the hypothesis that a supplement with twice the RDA of micronutrients would result in proportionately increasing birthweights and decreased perinatal mortality compared to a supplement with the standard one RDA (Kæstel et al., 2005). Mean gestational age at recruitment was 22±7 weeks and data were available for 1100 births. Women were divided into three groups: control (folic acid and 60mg iron), supplement with one RDA micronutrients (with 30mg iron), and supplement with two RDA micronutrients (iron remained at 30mg). Doubling the amount of micronutrients resulted in an almost doubling of the mean increase in birthweight, suggesting a dose-response effect of supplementation: one RDA resulted in a 53g increase (p=0.15) in

birthweight and two RDA in a 95g increase (p=0.009) when each was compared to the control group. The linear trend remained statistically significant when adjustments were made for anemia, malaria parasitemia, infant sex, and season of birth (p=0.014), as well as with the addition of gestational duration (p=0.055). The difference in proportion of LBW infants was not significant between the three groups. However, the percentage of infants weighing less than 3000g did attain statistical significance, with an adjusted OR=0.63 (p=0.002) for LBW in mothers receiving twice the RDA of micronutrients when compared with controls. Perhaps the most important finding of this study was the effect of a doubled micronutrient supplement on pregnancy outcomes in anemic women, about 30% of participants. Birthweight increased by 218 grams in the two-RDA group compared to controls (p=0.005). The amount of iron in the supplement was only half that given to the control group (30mg versus 60mg), suggesting that the observed effects was due to the micronutrients. The authors also noted that women were enrolled into the study as late as 3 weeks before expected delivery, and concluded that supplementation in late pregnancy can have a positive impact on birthweight.

The final study is a large trial of 5500 well-nourished women in Hungary that differs from the other trials in that a multi-micronutrient supplement or trace-element placebo tablet was given periconceptionally until week 12 of pregnancy, instead of throughout gestation (Czeizel et al., 1994). This trial was also key for establishing the efficacy of folic acid in prevention of neural tube defects and will be discussed in the next section on birth defects. There was no difference in mean birthweight or percentage of LBW infants between the two groups. One confounding variable not taken into account in the analysis was the cross-over effect after women left the study at the end of their first trimester: about 60% of the women in both groups took multivitamins during the remainder of their pregnancy, which, as other studies have suggested, may increase birthweight.

In summary, although iron and folic acid supplementation clearly improve birth outcomes, the benefits of additional micronutrient supplementation are equivocal. Although some studies suggest a beneficial effect of additional micronutrients, some found no improvement, and some suggested a possible detrimental effect on birth outcomes.

Table 4. Multi-micronutrient supplement trials

Trial	Participants	Intervention	Results
Hininger et al., 2004	100 apparently healthy pregnant French women 14±2weeks gestation followed monthly to delivery (65 completed study)	Daily consumption of 1: micronutrient supplement (iron-free) 2: placebo. Not specified if women took folic acid and iron as standard of care at baseline.	**Birthweight:** 1: 3300g 2: 3049g (p=0.03); **LBW <2700g:** 1: 2% 2: 9% , (p=0.02)
Friis et al., 2004	1669 pregnant Zimbabwean women 22-35 weeks gestation (mean 29 weeks); 360 (33%) HIV-positive; 1106 (66%) completed study	1: Daily micronutrient supplement containing RDA of 11 micro-nutrients plus 3000μg Vitamin A 2: placebo; supple-mental iron and folic acid part of antenatal care. Termed "effectiveness trial" because all tablets given at enrollment with no follow-up visits; 85% estimated daily adherence at 50%	Analysis was intention-to-treat. **Birthweight** in supplemented group 49g higher than control group (p=0.08); **gestational length** 0.3weeks longer (p=0.06). RR of **preterm delivery, birthweight <2500g, IUGR-LBW ranged** 0.71-0.84 (p≥0.15). In HIV-positive women, effect on birthweight appeared to be greater (but not statistically significant).
Fawzi et al, 2007	8468 pregnant Tanzanian women 12-27 weeks gestation (mean 21 weeks); 7866 live births; all HIV-negative	1: Daily multivitamin (including multiples of the RDA of B vitamins, vitamins C and E; vitamin A and zinc were omitted) 2: placebo; all received folic acid and iron, and malaria prophylaxis at 20 and 30 weeks of gestation Pills given at monthly visits, no adherence values stated.	Analysis was intention-to-treat. **Mean birthweight** 1: 3148g, 2: 3083g difference of 67g (p<0.001) **LBW <2500g** 1: 7.8%, 2: 9.4% RR=0.82 (95%CI 0.70-0.95, p=0.01) **Small for gestational age** 1: 10.7%, 2: 13.6% RR=0.77, 95% CI 0.68-0.87, p<0.001)

Trial	Participants	Intervention	Results
Osrin et al., 2005	1200 pregnant Nepalese women with singleton pregnancies up to 20weeks gestation; 5% loss to follow-up	1: Daily micronutrient supplement (RDA of 15 vitamins & minerals) 2: routine folic acid and iron supplement	Analysis was intention-to-treat. **Mean birthweight** 1: 2810g +/- 453 2: 2733g +/- 422 mean difference of 77g (95% CI 24-130, p=0.004). 25% relative decrease in proportion of **LBW**; OR=0.69, (95% CI 0.52-0.93, p=0.014) no difference in duration of gestation, head circumference, infant length
Kæstel et al., 2005	2100 pregnant women 22±7 weeks gestation at enrollment in urban Guinea-Bissau; 1670 (79.5%) completed trial; birthweight for 1100 infants	Participants received: 1: supplement with one RDA of 15 micronutrients, 2: supplement with 2 RDA; 3: daily iron and folic acid (control) only group 3 received 60mg iron, 1, 2: contained 30mg iron	Analysis was intention-to-treat. **Mean birthweight** 1: 3055g (p=0.15), 2: 3097g (p=0.009), 3: 3002g **LBW<3000g:** 2: 35.6% 3: 46.7% (adjusted OR=0.63, p=0.002) – no reduction in perinatal mortality or LBW<2500g
Christian et al., 2003	4926 pregnant women in rural Nepal enrolled in 1st trimester, 4130 live births; 5% loss to follow-up	Women received one of five daily supplements: 1: folic acid, 2: folic acid-iron, 3: folic acid-iron-zinc, 4: multi-micronutrients (RDA of 15 vitamins & minerals except for higher iron and zinc), 5: vitamin A (control). "Cluster" randomiza-tion = randomization done in blocks of five within each village	Analysis was intention-to-treat. 2: Folic acid-iron increased **mean birthweight** 37g (p=0.001) and reduced **% LBW** infants from 43% to 34% (RR=0.84, 95% CI 0.72-0.99, p=0.01) 4: multi-micronutrients increased **mean birthweight** 64g (p=0.0014) and reduced **% LBW** infants from 43% to 35% (RR=0.86, 95% CI 0.74-0.99, p=0.01) 1, 3: Folic acid alone and folic acid-iron-zinc had no effect on birthweight compared to control
Czeizel et al., 1994	5502 Hungarian women recruited periconceptionally, pregnancy outcomes for 5453 participants (99%)	1: Multivitamin 2: trace element daily for at least 1 month prior to planned conception through week 12 of gestation	Analysis was intention-to-treat. No significant differences in mean birthweight, LBW between the groups

Trial	Participants	Intervention	Results
Ramakrish nan et al., 2003	873 pregnant women in semirural Mexico recruited before 13weeks gestation; notable for 1/3 participants being overweight; 25% loss to follow-up (656 pregnancy outcomes, equal numbers in each group)	1: Micronutrients (1 to 1.5 times RDA) with iron 2: iron supplements alone (control), 6 days/week, directly-observed therapy at home. 60mg iron (as ferrous sulfate) was 200% RDA, standard of care in Mexico.	Analysis was intention-to-treat. No significant differences: **Mean Birthweight**: 1: 2981g, 2: 2977g **LBW**: 1: 8.49%, 2: 8.89% **IUGR**: 1:10.09%, 2: 11.78%

Smoking

Smoking is estimated to be responsible for 20-30% of low birth weight cases and 15% of preterm birth and is associated with an 150% increase in perinatal mortality (Andres and Day, 2000). The strong associations between smoking and poor birth outcomes make smoking cessation during pregnancy an obvious target for behavioral intervention to reduce birth complications. Interventions to encourage smoking cessation have been studied extensively in the population as a whole and in pregnant women. Results of these numerous trials have been summarized in practice guidelines (Fiore, 2000) and updated in our chapter on smoking cessation (Volume 1, Chapter 11). Before reviewing the literature on the effectiveness of smoking cessation interventions on birth outcomes, we will briefly summarize smoking cessation recommendations for pregnant women.

Guideline recommendations for smoking cessation in pregnant women

As described in Volume 1, Chapter 11, studies of smoking cessation during pregnancy have shown that interventions that provide more intensive counseling than minimal advice, self-help materials and referral to a smoking cessation program produce significantly higher smoking cessation rates than usual care. These should be offered to all pregnant smokers. Because quitting smoking at any point during pregnancy may provide benefits to both fetus and mother, treatment should be offered throughout the course of pregnancy. Enhancing social and financial support during pregnancy may also improve smoking cessation success. Pharmacological therapies have been insufficiently studied in pregnant women, and thus the safety of pharmaco-therapy during pregnancy is not known. Nevertheless, pharmacotherapy for smoking cessation should be considered as a second line treatment for pregnant women unable to quit with intensive psychosocial intervention when the potential benefits of quitting outweigh the risks of pharmacotherapy.

Review of trials to prevent LBW

Fewer trials have examined the effect of smoking cessation interventions on birth weight. Most of these have been under-powered to detect effects on birth outcomes, however, meta-analysis of the results of these trials has attempted to overcome this limitation.

A 2004 meta-analysis of all randomized controlled trials to date examined the effectiveness of smoking cessation programs during pregnancy on birth outcomes (Lumley et al., 2004). We summarize the results of this meta-analysis and discuss the interventions that produced the largest effects in the included trials. Lumley and colleagues identified 16 randomized controlled trials that measured the effect of a smoking cessation program on birth outcomes. Results of these trials were pooled to investigate the overall efficacy of these programs (Table 5). Across trials, smoking cessation programs during pregnancy significantly increased mean birthweight by 33g, and significantly reduced the risk of low birth weight, and preterm birth. This meta-analysis did not observe a significant effect of smoking cessation programs on very low birthweight or neonatal death, however, only 3 trials examined these outcomes, and thus the analyses were underpowered to detect such effects.

Table 5: Effect of smoking cessation programs during pregnancy on birth outcomes (from Lumley et al., 2004)

Variable	# of trials	Pooled participants	Outcome [95% confidence interval]
Mean birthweight	16	6892 treatment 6276 control	Weighted mean difference: 33.03g [95% CI: 11.32-54.74], p=0.003
Low birthweight	13	4515 treatment 4415 control	Relative risk: 0.82 [0.70, 0.95] p=0.007
Very low birthweight	3	2379 treatment 2386 controls	Relative risk: 1.26 [0.69, 2.32], not significant
Preterm birth	11	5529 treatment 5403 control	Relative risk: 0.84 [0.72,0.98], p=0.002
Neonatal death	3	2065 treatment 2078 controls	Relative risk: 1.17 [0.34, 4.01], not significant

Among the 16 trials reviewed by Lumley and colleagues, only 3 reported significant effects of the intervention on birthweight within the individual trial. These 3 trials are reviewed in more detail below (Table 6). Notably, in 2 of these 3 trials, the intervention reduced rates of low birth weight without increasing smoking cessation rates, and one of these interventions included pharmacological treatment (Panjari et al., 1999; Wisborg et al., 2000).

The first trial to report an effect of a smoking cessation intervention on birth outcomes was conducted in 1984 (Sexton and Hebel, 1984). Nine hundred and thirty-five women who were less than 18 weeks pregnant and smoked greater than 10 cigarettes per day were randomized to receive a smoking cessation intervention or a no contact control. The smoking cessation intervention consisted of at least one personal visit and often more, supplemented by monthly telephone calls and biweekly mail contacts. The women received information about smoking risks and quitting tips from two women with master's level training in pregnancy counseling and smoking cessation. The visits provided information, support, practical guidance and behavioral strategies. At follow-up at the 8th month of pregnancy, 43% of the treated women had quit smoking, as compared to 20% of control women, and the greater reduction in smoking in treated women was biochemically verified by testing of salivary thiocyanate. There was no difference in infant mortality between groups, and gestational age was nearly identical. However, birthweight was significantly different between groups. Birthweight of infants of treated women was on average 92g greater than infants of control women (mean birthweight: 3278 +/- 627g versus 3186 +/- 566g). Thus, this study suggested that an effective smoking cessation intervention could increase birthweight by increasing intrauterine growth rather than by reducing preterm birth.

Panjari and colleagues (1999) investigated the effects of four smoking cessation counseling visits by a midwife plus a smoking cessation pamphlet versus the pamphlet alone in pregnant women smokers who were still smoking by their first antenatal visit. Three hundred and thirty-nine women received the intervention and 393 received the pamphlet alone. Counseling visits were personalized, informal, non-judgmental and provided standard cognitive-behavioral content and support to encourage smoking cessation. Women were well-matched on all measured variables at baseline, including smoking history, frequency and quantity. Smoking cessation was assessed in late pregnancy by self-report and urinary cotinine measurement. No differences in smoking cessation rates between groups were detected by either method (11.9% in counseled women versus 9.8% of controls). However, women who received the intervention reported smoking fewer cigarettes in late pregnancy than control women (mean self-reported cigarettes/day: 8.7 +/- 7.6 in counseled women versus 11.5 +/- 9.7 in controls). This difference was not detected in urinary cotinine values, and thus could indicate a tendency for counseled women to underreport use at follow-up. Despite similar smoking cessation outcomes, women receiving the counseling intervention had significantly heavier babies (mean birthweight: 3,250 +/- 526g for intervention versus 3,166 +/- 589g for controls, an 84g difference). This difference was related to a trend towards preterm delivery in the control group (Rate of preterm delivery: 5.3% of intervention, 8.7% of control, p=0.07). This study concluded that either a reduction in the number of cigarettes smoked per day was sufficient to increase birth weight, or additional contact with a midwife had a beneficial effect for increasing birthweight and/or reducing preterm birth by improving health in some other manner.

Wisborg and colleagues (2000) investigated the effects of providing nicotine patches to women who smoked 10 or more cigarettes per day after the first trimester. Two hundred fifty pregnant women were provided with 4 sessions of smoking cessation counseling by a midwife. The first was 45-60 minutes long and consisted of an assessment of smoking habits and previous quit attempts, education about the pharmacology and psychological effects of smoking and effects of smoking during pregnancy, and development of a plan to stop smoking. At this visit, women were randomized to receive either nicotine (n=124) or placebo (n=126) patches. The women in the nicotine patch group received 15 mg patches for 8 weeks and 10 mg patches for 3 weeks. Additional counseling visits were 15-20 minutes long and scheduled 8 and 11 weeks after the initial visit, plus 4 weeks before the expected delivery date. The study found no difference in smoking cessation among women randomized to nicotine versus placebo patches with continuous abstinence rates of 21% in the nicotine patch group versus 19% in the placebo group. Despite the lack of effect on smoking cessation, women receiving the nicotine patch had higher mean birthweights (mean difference 186 g [95% CI: 35, 336]) and lower rates of low birthweight (3% versus 9%) than those receiving the placebo patch, with no difference in the rate of preterm delivery. Moreover, mean birthweight increased with greater adherence to nicotine patch use (mean difference from placebo based upon actual weeks of nicotine patch use: 244 for 2 weeks, 345 g for 4 weeks, 494g for 9 weeks). The reasons for the increased birthweight in patients randomized to receive nicotine patches are unknown, and further research is needed to confirm this effect.

Thus, although an overall beneficial effect of smoking cessation interventions on birth outcomes has been demonstrated, the mechanism underlying these effects is not clear and may not be consistent across all interventions. Some of the strongest effects on birthweight were observed in the absence of an effect on smoking cessation, and trials differed in whether improvements in birth weight was associated with reductions in preterm birth or increased intrauterine growth rates. It is conceivable that some of these interventions may have improved birth outcomes by altering other factors (e.g., reducing stress or increasing social support). Further study is needed, not only to improve the effect of these interventions on smoking outcomes, but also to determine how they improve birth outcomes.

Since the 2004 meta-analysis, two additional trials have examined the effect of smoking cessation interventions on birth outcomes. Both studies investigated the impact of home counseling visits by midwives.

Polanska and colleagues (2004) randomly selected clinics from the 33 maternity units in a district of Poland based upon clinic patient volume to provide or not provide a program of midwife delivered home visits of intensive individual anti-smoking counseling. The intervention consisted of four home midwife visits: the first assessed smoking dependence and discussed the benefits of smoking cessation, the second assessed desire to quit, determined a quit date and obtained agreement to a "delaration to quit smoking," the third assessed whether the quit attempt was successful, and the fourth counseled the woman about how to avoid smoking and maintain abstinence. Women who did not quit during the initial visits were offered an additional 5 visits if desired. Controls received standard written information about smoking cessation. Intervention participants were similar to controls on most measures, but had higher levels of nicotine dependence. Women receiving the intervention were more likely to quit smoking (44% quit rate versus 17% in controls). When

including women who refused to participate in the home visits, women at intervention clinics were still more likely to quit than those at control clincs (48% versus 34%). Although the difference in mean birthweight between groups was not reported, women who spontaneously quit smoking or quit smoking during the intervention had significantly higher birthweight babies than those who continued to smoke. The high rates of smoking cessation in this trial were attributed to the prevalence of light smokers in the Polish population.

Tappin and colleagues (2005) investigated a similar intervention using motivational interviewing during home midwife visits in clinics in Scotland. Pregnant women smokers at less than 24 weeks gestation were stratified by their level of smoking and amount they had cut down thus far during pregnancy and randomized to either a motivational interviewing intervention or the control group. Midwives received extensive training in motivational interviewing and offered all women standard health promotion including information on smoking and pregnancy. Women in the intervention group were also offered two to five 30-minute home visits of motivational interviewing to reduce smoking from the same midwife. Although the study was well powered, and the midwives provided high quality motivational interviews of approximately one hour per woman in the intervention group, there was no change in smoking behavior based upon self-report, or biochemical assays. Mean birthweight also did not significantly differ between groups, suggesting that in this population high quality motivational interviewing does not improve smoking cessation rates during pregnancy or birth outcomes for those women who do not spontaneously quit by 24 weeks of gestation.

In summary, research to date suggests that when women successfully quit smoking during pregnancy, mean birthweight is increased, and risk of low birthweight and

Table 6: Smoking cessation during pregnancy interventions that examined birth outcomes after Lumley et al., 2004.

Trial	Participants	Intervention	Outcomes
Tappin et al., 2005	7622 pregnant smokers at antenatal booking 1: 351 2: 411	1: Motivational interviewing at home by specially trained midwives 2: control All women received standard health promotion information.	**Smoking Cessation rate:** 1: 4.8%, 2: 4.6%, not significant **Birth weight (in grams):** 1: 3078, 2: 3048, not significant
Polanska et al., 2004	Pregnant women from maternity centers in Poland 1: 149 current smokers and 56 spontaneous quitters 2: 144 current smokers and 37 spontaneous quitters	1: 4 midwife visits during pregnancy and one after delivery 2: standard written information about the health risk from maternal smoking to the fetus	**Smoking cessation rate** was significantly higher in the intervention group (OR=2.5 (95% CI 1.8-3.7)). The difference in **mean birth-weight** between quitters and non-quitters after controlling for sociodemographic factors expected to contribute to birth weight: 1: 182.8 g (p=.02) 2: 92.4 g (p=.4).

preterm birth is lowered. Many women spontaneously quit smoking during pregnancy and smoking cessation interventions overall improve quit rates and birth outcomes. However, women who quit during pregnancy either spontaneously or after intervention tend to be lighter smokers. No intervention has been shown to reliably encourage smoking cessation among highly dependent smokers, or women resistant to low level smoking cessation interventions. Additional research to develop effective methods to reach the population of heavy smokers is needed to reduce the rate of birth complications related to tobacco use.

Caffeine consumption

Observational studies have suggested that caffeine consumption may be associated with increased risk of spontaneous abortion, low birth weight, and fetal death. For example, a study of 88,482 pregnant women in Denmark found that coffee consumption significantly increased risk of fetal death in a dose dependent manner; the relative risk compared to women who did not drink coffee was 1.33 times greater for those drinking 4-7 cups per day and 1.59 times greater for those drinking 8 or greater cups per day (Bech et al., 2005). These studies suggest that reducing caffeine consumption in women who are pregnant or trying to conceive may reduce risk of fetal death, spontaneous abortion and low birth weight. However, because caffeine consumption is associated with tobacco and alcohol use in most populations, it has been difficult to definitively determine the individual effect of caffeine use on birth outcomes in observational studies. RCTs are needed to demonstrate that reduction or elimination of caffeine consumption during or before pregnancy can reduce birth complications.

To date, only one RCT has examined a behavioral intervention to reduce caffeine consumption in pregnant women (Bech et al., 2007; Table 7). This study recruited pregnant women who were drinking at least 3 cups of coffee per day and randomized them to receive either regular instant coffee or decaffeinated instant coffee. They were told to use this coffee in place of their regular coffee, but were not told to avoid other caffeinated beverages or refuse coffee provided by others. The intervention successfully reduced, but did not eliminate caffeine consumption in pregnant women during the second half of the pregnancy. Participants used similar amounts of alcohol and tobacco in each group. There was no difference between groups in birthweight, or other measured birth outcomes, suggesting that reducing caffeine intake in the second half of

pregnancy does not have a significant impact on birthweight. However, they did find a difference in birthweight of 263g between groups in the subpopulation of 297 women that smoked more than 10 cigarettes per day, with women smokers drinking caffeinated coffee having lower birthweight babies. The authors hypothesized that this difference might be related to induction of CYP1A2, an enzyme that metabolizes caffeine and other substances in smokers, as CYP1A2 activity has been associated with altered fetal growth. Further research is needed to confirm this effect in smokers, determine whether complete elimination of caffeine effects birthweight, examine the effects of caffeine reduction in the first half of pregnancy, and examine the effect of reducing caffeine intake on miscarriage and fertility.

Table 7: RCTs of interventions to reduce caffeine consumption in pregnancy

Trial	Participants	Intervention	Outcome
Bech et al., 2007	1207 Pregnant women drinking at least 3 cups of coffee per day and less than 20 weeks pregnant. 1153 women with a liveborn singleton were included in the analysis	Women were provided: 1) Instant coffee 2) Decaffeinated instant coffee Women were told to replace their normal coffee with the provided coffee, but were not told to avoid regular coffee provided by others or other caffeinated beverages.	**Caffeine intake** 1: 317 mg/day 2: 117 mg/day **Birth weight** 1: 3539 +/- 604 g 2: 3519 +/- 607 g, not significant No significant differences in born preterm, small for gestational age, and low Apgar score.

ADDITIONAL UNDERSTUDIED MODIFIABLE BEHAVIORAL RISK FACTORS

Partner Violence

Partner violence during pregnancy is associated with low birthweight babies, with an odds ratio of 1.4 in a meta-analysis (Murphy et al., 2001), and with premature birth, with an odds ratio of 1.6 in a study of over 3000 pregnant women in Alabama

(Neggers et al, 2004). Thus, effective interventions to reduce partner violence during pregnancy would be hypothesized to reduce birth complications. This has not been specifically studied in trials to date. Partner violence is covered in depth in chapter 18.

Illicit Drug Use

Substance use during pregnancy has been associated with increased risk for preterm birth, small for gestational age, low birth-weight, birth defects, stillbirth, and fetal, maternal and neonatal death (Kennare et al., 2005; Wolfe et al., 2005; Fuddy et al., 2003; Ludlow et al., 2004). Because maternal use of illicit drugs often co-exists with other risk factors for poor birth outcomes (e.g. domestic abuse, poor nutrition, tobacco and alcohol use, infectious disease), it is not known the extent to which these elevated risks for poor birth outcomes are due to the substance use itself as opposed to other risk factors. Nevertheless, effective interventions to reduce illicit drug use also tend to reduce related psychosocial problems. Given these associations, interventions to prevent or reduce illicit drug use in pregnant women are hypothesized to reduce birth complications, and use of behavioral treatments for substance use disorders is recommended. Behavioral treatments for substance use disorders are covered in depth in Volume I, Chapter 9. The effectiveness of such interventions for preventing poor birth outcomes, however, is not known. We were unable to identify any randomized controlled trials that investigated the effects of behavioral interventions to reduce illicit substance use on birthweight, birth defects or other birth outcomes. This remains an obvious area for future research on methods to reduce birth complications.

Several randomized controlled trials of general interventions have addressed domestic violence issues and illicit drug use as part of more comprehensive perinatal health programs for high-risk women (Table 8). Olds and colleagues (2004) conducted a three arm randomized trial of home visitation for low income women during their first pregnancy and the subsequent first two years of the child's life. Women received either regular home visits from a paraprofessional, regular home visits from a nurse or assessment of child development alone with referral for detected problems. Primary outcomes focused on child development and health of the mother, but birth outcomes were also examined. Although birth outcomes of the original pregnancy were not significantly improved, follow-up analysis at 4 years found that rates of low birthweight babies in subsequent pregnancies were significantly lower in the group receiving paraprofessional home visits, and non-significantly lower in the nurse visit group as compared to assessment and referral controls. While reasons for this improvement were not completely determinable, the home visits seemed to have beneficial effects for reducing domestic violence risk in the nurse home visit group, and improving mother's mental health in the paraprofessional group. These effects may have improved subsequent birth outcomes by reducing maternal stress.

Heins and colleagues (1990) investigated whether birth outcomes for pregnant women at high risk for LBW could be improved by replacing standard obstetric management with midwife management focusing on health behavior and detection and management of preterm labor symptoms. This randomized trial found no difference in rates of LBW and VLBW between groups, suggesting that while midwife management did not improve outcomes, it was at least as effective as current standard high-risk obstetric management. Interestingly, the authors noted a trend towards better outcomes with midwife management among black women but better outcomes with standard obstetric care among white women. Although these differences were not significant, they suggest that there may be racial differences in health care needs during pregnancy. Given the substantially higher rates of LBW in African-American women, determining optimal health care needs of this population is a priority, and additional research to determine whether behavioral health counseling and education is particularly beneficial for this population is warranted.

Table 8: Trials of general perinatal behavioral health care interventions

Study	Participants	Intervention	Outcomes
Olds et al., 2004	735 low income women recruited during pregnancy of their first child	1: free developmental screening and referral for their children at 6, 12, 15, 21 and 24 months of age 2: 1 plus paraprofessional home visiting during pregnancy and the child's first two years of life 3: 1 plus nurse home visits during pregnancy and the child's first two years of life.	Outcomes reported for women's subsequent pregnancies 4 years later. **LBW during later pregnancy**: 1: 7.7%, 2: 2.8%, 3: 5.9%, p=0.03 for 1 versus 2 comparison, not significant 1 versus 3 No differences between groups in **substance us**e at follow-up, but significant reductions in **domestic violence in last 6 months** in 3. 1: 13.6%, 2: 14.2%, 3: 6.9%
Heins et al., 1990	1458 women at high risk of low birth-weight outcomes	1: Prenatal interventions by nurse-midwives and nurses. Initial 1 hour visit with assessment and counseling on behavioral risks including nutrition, substance use, stress, activity and social support, and instruction on detecting signs of preterm labor, was followed with 20-30 minute visits every 1-2 weeks with review. 2: standard high-risk prenatal care by obstetricians. Initial visit including medical and obstetric history with less emphasis on behavioral risk plus physical. Patients had regular but less frequent and shorter visits with the MD throughout their pregnancy which focused on monitoring weight and encouraging rest.	Birth outcomes by race: **LBW** White: 1: 12.3%, 2: 10.8%, OR 1.20 (95% CI: 0.8 - 1.9) Black: 1: 18.4%, 2: 20.5%, OR 0.80 (95% CI: 0.6 - 1.1) **VLBW** White: 1: 3.5%, 2: 2.6% OR 1.36 (95% CI: 0.5 - 3.4) Black: 1: 3.4%, 2: 5.4% OR 0.63 (95% CI: 0.5 - 1.3) No significant difference between groups in birth outcomes. No difference in **smoking cessation rates** between groups (1: 17%, 2: 15%) **Fetal deaths** excluded from analysis: 1: 3 deaths, 2: 10 deaths

CONCLUSIONS FROM INTERVENTIONS TO REDUCE LBW

1) All women should take an iron supplement (in addition to folic acid, reviewed later), ideally prior to becoming pregnant. The current literature does not provide convincing evidence from RCTs to recommend multi-micronutrient or specific nutrient supplements during pregnancy, although physicians should consider each woman's nutritional status on

an individual basis.

2) Balanced protein-energy supplementation, especially among high-risk women and those in developing countries, can be recommended to increase pre-gestational weight/BMI and improve maternal nutrition. This intervention cannot be recommended for low-risk women, given the lack of clear benefit in the current literature.

3) All women should be encouraged to quit smoking and offered smoking cessation aids, including intensive counseling interventions. Interventions to increase social and financial support should be provided to women having difficulty quitting. Use of nicotine patches in pregnant smokers may reduce risk of LBW even without increasing smoking cessation rates.

4) Caffeine consumption may increase risk of spontaneous abortion, low birthweight, and neonatal mortality, and limiting or eliminating caffeine consumption during preconception and pregnancy is recommended. However, reducing caffeine consumption in the second half of pregnancy did not reduce the risk of LBW in non-smokers.

5) Domestic violence and illicit substance use may also increase risk of low birthweight and neonatal mortality, and these problems should be addressed. However, the effectiveness of existing interventions for drug use and domestic violence for reducing risk of poor birth outcomes has not been adequately studied.

INTERVENTIONS TO PREVENT MACROSOMIA/LARGE FOR GESTATIONAL AGE AND OTHER DIABETES-RELATED COMPLICATIONS

Because other risk factors for macrosomia, abnormally high birthweight, are either non-modifiable (e.g. race), or not reliably prevented by available behavioral interventions (e.g. maternal obesity), interventions to reduce risk of macrosomia have focused on controlling maternal hyperglycemia. Medical interventions (i.e. c-section or induction of labor when macrosomia is suspected) to prevent birth complications from macrosomia have been attempted. The practicality of these medical interventions is limited by difficulties in reliably identifying macrosomic fetuses in utero and relatively low rates of permanent injury in macrosomic babies; cost-effectiveness analyses do not favor these medical interventions over expectant treatment under current conditions (Rouse et al., 1996; Herbst, 2005). It has been estimated that to prevent a single case of permanent brachial plexus injury, 3,700 women with an estimated fetal weight of 4,500g would need to have an elective c-section (Rouse et al., 1996).

Randomized clinical trials of behavioral interventions to date have focused primarily on identifying optimal criteria for identification of women at risk for fetal macrosomia and optimal treatment for women with gestational diabetes. These trials are presented in table 9 and summarized below.

Screening

Griffin and colleagues (2000) demonstrated that universal screening of pregnant women with a 50g glucose challenge test at 26-28 weeks improved detection of gestational diabetes and reduced rates of macrosomia, c-section, prematurity, pre-eclampsia and admission to the neonatal intensive care unit as compared to risk factor-based screening at 32 weeks. This large, and well-executed study utilized a broad definition of risk factors in the comparison group, and thus suggests that risk factors are not adequate predictors of gestational diabetes to optimally reduce maternal and fetal harm related to diabetes. Based upon this study, universal glucose screening of pregnant women for gestational diabetes is recommended to reduce complications related to hyperglycemia. A glucose challenge test should be administered and followed-up with a formal glucose tolerance test if elevated glucose levels one hour later are detected.

Comprehensive diabetes care: Diet, home glucose monitoring and insulin

The large and influential ACHOIS trial (Crowther et al., 2005) examined whether comprehensive diabetes care (including dietary counseling, blood glucose monitoring and insulin therapy when needed) improved birth outcomes over standard prenatal care. This trial followed 1000 women with gestational diabetes randomized to receive diabetes care or standard care alone and found that addition of diabetes care reduced rates of macrosomia and large for gestational age. In conjunction with these main effects, diabetes care significantly reduced birth complications including need for induction of labor, shoulder dystocia, admission to the neonatal intensive care unit and all serious perinatal complications.

Insulin

The additional benefit of treatment with insulin in patients receiving dietary management of gestational diabetes has been examined in a number of small trials. These were summarized by Giufrrida and colleagues (2003) in a metaanalysis of the 6 existing randomized controlled trials. Although trial results were not consistent, the meta-analysis found a small statistically significant beneficial effect of insulin, with treatment of 11 women needed in order to prevent one case of macrosomia.

Glucose monitoring

Several trials have tried to determine the optimal method of monitoring of glycemic control in women with gestational diabetes. A small underpowered study by Homko and colleagues (2002) compared women randomized to monitoring their blood glucose levels with a home monitor versus having their blood glucose monitored in weekly clinic

visits. This study did not detect a significant beneficial effect of home glucose monitoring on birth complications.

In another small study, de Veciana and colleagues (1995) compared comprehensive diabetes care with management based upon home glucose testing of pre-meal glucose levels (with a goal of 60-105 mg/dl) to the same care based upon 1 hour post-meal testing (with a goal of less than 140 mg/dl). This study found that women in the post-meal testing group received more insulin and had reduced birth complications including lower birth weight, reduced rates of macrosomia, large for gestational age, neonatal hyperglycemia and shoulder dystocia. Thus, management of blood glucose levels based upon post-meal home monitoring of glucose levels is recommended.

Exercise

The benefit of adding an exercise program to the treatment of gestational diabetes has not been tested in a large, appropriately powered trial. However, there have been 4 small trials of adding high intensity exercise programs to treatment of gestational diabetes and these were summarized in a metaanalysis by Ceysens and colleagues (2006). This meta-analysis found no effects of exercise on rates of macrosomia or any other birth outcomes. Thus, there is not evidence to recommend addition of an exercise program to gestational diabetes care regimens, but because this treatment has not been adequately tested in trials, this is a valid area for future research.

Ultrasound Monitoring

Several trials investigated whether the addition of fetal ultrasound monitoring to predict macrosomia in the fetus could reduce the need for intensive management of gestational diabetes, and need for insulin treatment. Kjos and colleagues (2001) examined whether need for management with insulin could be reduced by screening fetal abdominal circumference by ultrasound. Pregnant women with elevated fasting plasma glucose were randomized to receive one of two treatments: either 1) management with long-acting insulin plus standard insulin before breakfast and dinner with capillary glucose targets of less than 90 mg/dl before meals and less than 120 mg/dl at 2 hours after meals or 2) management with insulin if fetal abdominal circumference was greater than 70th percentile and/or if venous fasting plasma glucose was greater than 120 mg/dl. Women in the second group who met criteria for insulin management received the same treatment with stricter capillary glucose targets of less than 80 mg/dl before meals and less than 100 mg/dl 2 hours after meals. Results of this study were equivocal. Women receiving standard insulin management had lower glucose levels, and lower rates of c-section than women receiving ultrasound screening. However, there was no difference between groups in birthweight, large for gestational age or neonatal morbidity. Schaefer-Graf and colleagues (2004) revisited this question with a second trial comparing standard criteria for use of insulin to a combination of fetal abdominal circumference criteria and less strict capillary glucose cut-offs. They found that these alternate criteria did not reduce the percentage of women who received insulin, however they did alter who received insulin, as one-third of the women in the ultrasound group received a different treatment strategy than they would have in the control group. There was no difference between groups in birth complications including large for gestational age, c-section rate, prematurity, infant hypoglycemia after birth, or admission to the neonatal intensive care unit. This suggests that use of these ultrasound criteria is a valid alternative to standard practices and may reduce the need for capillary glucose monitoring.

Bonomo and colleagues (2004) investigated whether use of ultrasound monitoring to modify glycemic targets when fetuses were found to have high fetal abdominal circumference would improve pregnancy outcomes. Women with gestational diabetes were randomized at 30 weeks to either conventional management with diet, self-monitoring of blood glucose and insulin if necessary to meet a glycemic target of 90 mg/dl fasting and 120 mg/dl after meals or management with glycemic targets based upon fetal abdominal circumference. When fetal abdominal circumference was less than 75th percentile, women were treated with less stringent glycemic targets of 100mg/dl fasting and 140 mg/dl after meals. If fetal abdominal circumference was greater than 75th percentile, glycemic targets were made more strict at 80 mg/dl fasting and 100 mg/dl after meals. Women in the ultrasound monitoring group received greater management with insulin and had fewer macrosomic or large for gestational age infants than those in the control group. This suggests that use of ultrasound monitoring in combination with intensified glycemic control in high-risk women may reduce rates of macrosomia beyond that of screening and standard management.

Treatment of borderline gestational diabetes

Another randomized trial by Bomono and colleagues (2005) investigated whether treatment of women with borderline gestational diabetes, defined as having an elevated 50g glucose challenge test followed by a normal 100g glucose tolerance test, improved neonatal outcomes. To determine whether borderline gestational diabetes was associated with birth complications, an additional matched control group with normal results on the 50g glucose challenge test was included. Randomized women with borderline gestational diabetes received either standard pregnancy management with no special diabetes care, or initial dietary counseling plus outpatient visits every 2 weeks with additional dietary counseling and laboratory monitoring of fasting and 2 hour post-meal glucose, HbA1c and frucosamine, weight and blood pressure. Compared to matched controls, women with borderline gestational diabetes in standard care had infants with abnormal fetal growth as measured by the neonatal ponderal index (i.e, they were heavy for their volume) and higher rates of large for gestational age. In women with borderline gestational diabetes, dietary counseling and glucose monitoring at clinic visits reduced

rates of large for gestational age and the neonatal ponderal index to equivalent or lower levels than the matched control population. The trial found no difference between the three groups in birth complications, however. This study suggests that even borderline gestational diabetes can increase risk of large for gestational age infants, and dietary counseling and monitoring and eliminate this risk. However, the clinical benefit and cost-effectiveness of management of women with borderline gestational diabetes is debatable.

Table 9: RCTs of interventions to reduce rates of macrosomia/large for gestational age

Study	Participants	Intervention	Results
Screening Interventions			
Griffin et al., 2000	Pregnant women attending outpatient obstetric clinics 1: 1299 2: 1853	1) Universal Screening: all patients received a 50g glucose challenge test at 26-28 weeks and if their plasma glucose at 1 hour was >=7.8 mmol/l then a formal 3 hour 100g oral glucose tolerance test was performed. If a patient had any risk factor, they received a repeat 50g glucose challenge test at 32 weeks if they tested negative at 26-28 weeks. 2) Risk-factor based screening: if patients had any risk factor for GD they received a formal 3 hour 100g oral glucose tolerance test at 32 weeks. Risk factors included: first degree relative with diabetes, gained >100 kg in current pregnancy, had a previous baby >4.5 kg, previous unexplained still-birth/ intra-uterine death, previous major malformation, previous GD, glycosuria in 2nd fasting urine sample, macrosomia or polyhydramnios in current pregnancy	**Detected prevalence of GD:** 1: 2.70%, 2: 1.45%, p<.03 **Gestational age at diagnosis:** 1: 30 +/- 2.6, 2: 33 +/- 3.7 weeks, p<.05 In 2, the development of a risk factor during pregnancy was associated with a very low rate of **spontaneous vaginal delivery** (2: 22%, 1: 76%) and a high rate of **large for gestational age** (2: 78%, 1: 9.5%), **prematurity** (2: 33%, 1: 4.8%) and **c-section** (2: 33%, 1: 9.5%). In 1, the presence or absence of a risk factor did not influence outcome.

Study	Participants	Intervention	Results
Management based upon glycemia alone versus ultrasound			
Schaefer-Graf et al., 2004	199 low risk (no medical conditions, no tobacco, alcohol or drug abuse) Caucasian women with gestational diabetes who attained fasting capillary glucose (CG) <120 mg/dl and 2 hour postprandial CG<200 after one week of diet. Diet consisted of a 30 kcal/kg/day diet with caloric restriction for overweight women (25 kcal/kg/day). Women were advised to exercise after meals and self-monitor CG 6 times/day (before and 2 hours after each of 3 meals).	1) Management based upon maternal glycemia alone: insulin initiated if fasting CG was repeatedly >90 mg/dl or 2-hour CG >120 mg/dl 2) Management based upon maternal glycemia plus ultrasound: insulin was initiated if fasting CG>120 mg/dl or 2h-CG>200 mg/dl, or if fetal abdominal circumference > 75th percentile	No difference in % assigned to insulin treatment (1: 30%, 2: 40%) or mean duration of insulin treatment (1: 8.3 weeks, 2: 8.1 weeks), however 34% of women in the ultrasound group received a different treatment strategy than they would have if in group 1. All women in 2 who received insulin, met ultrasound criteria for insulin treatment. No differences in birth complications **C-section rate:** 1: 19%, 2: 18.2%, NS **Age at delivery:** 1: 39.3, 2: 39.0 weeks, NS **Large for gestational age (>90th percentile):** 1: 10.0%, 2: 12.1%, NS **Small for gestational age (<10th percentile):** 13.0%, 12.1%, NS **Hypoglycemia (<40 mg/dl) at birth** 1: 16.0, 17.0%, NS **Admission to NICU** 1: 15.0%, 14.1%, NS
Bonomo et al., 2004	229 pregnant women with gestational diabetes, diagnosed before the 28th week, and treated for 2 weeks with diet and self-monitoring of blood glucose before randomization 1: 78, 2: 151	1: Conventional management with a glycemic target of 90 fasting/120 post-prandial 2: Modified management with ultrasound monitoring. Glycemic target varied based upon fetal abdominal circumference (AC). If AC > 75 %ile, target = 80 fasting/100 post-prandial, if <75 %ile, target = 100 fasting, 140 post-prandial	Greater use of insulin in 2 **Large for gestational age (>90th percentile):** 1: 17.9%, 2: 7.9%, p<.05 **Small for gestational age (<10th percentile):** 1: 9.0%, 2: 6.0%, NS **Macrosomia:** 1: 11.5%, 2: 3.3%, p<.05

Study	Participants	Intervention	Results
Kjos et al., 2001	98 women with fasting plasma glucose of 105-120 mg/dl All women received education in diabetes self-care including self-monitoring of blood glucose 4-7 times per day, techniques for self-administration of insulin, diet prescription of 30 kcal/kg/day for women <120% of ideal weight and 25 kcal/kg/day for others, and exercise advice to walk 3 times/day for 20-30 minutes after each meal.	1) Management with insulin NPH plus standard insulin before breakfast and dinner, target CG <90 preprandial and <120 2-hours post-prandial 2) Management with insulin if fetal abdominal circumference >=70th percentile and/or if any venous fasting plasma glucose was > 120 mg/dl Insulin management was as in 1 with stricter CG targets of <80 mg/dl preprandial and <110 mg/dl 2 hours postprandial.	During the management phase, women in 1 had lower fasting plasma glucose and capillary glucose levels. Birth outcomes: **Birth weight** 1: 3271 +/- 458 g, 2: 3369 +;- 461 g, NS **Large for gestational age (>90th percentile):** 1: 6.3%, 2: 8.3%, NS **Neonatal morbidity:** 1: 25%, 2: 25%, NS **C-section rate:** 1: 14.6%, 2: 33%, p=.03 In 2, women who did not receive insulin had lower birth weights than those that did receive insulin.
Intensity of Care			
Garner et al., 1997	300 pregnant women with GD Women in 2 with persistant fasting >140 mg/dl or 1 hour post-prandial >200 mg/dl were treated as in 1, but analysed as in 2	1. Strict glycemic control and tertiary level obstetric care including dietary counseling for a 35 kcal/kg ideal body weight diet, home glucose monitoring with a target of fasting <80 mg/dl, and 1 hour postprandial <140 mg/dl, with insulin if needed, bi weekly visits with ultrasound of fetal growth 2: routine care with an unrestricted diet, two measurements of glucose per week for study purposes.	No difference between **birth weights, macrosomia rates, birth trauma, neonatal hypoglycemia or other metabolic complications** in this pilot study.
Bonomo et al., 2005	300 Caucasian pregnant women with Borderline Gestational	1: standard management, no special care 2: dietary treatment and regular monitoring: Dietary	Women in 2 showed reduced fasting and 2 hour post-prandial plasma glucose associated with

Study	Participants	Intervention	Results
Bonomo et al., 2005 cont.	Glucose Intolerance, defined by an elevated 50-g glucose challenge test (> 7.8 mmol/l at 1 hour) followed by a normal 100g oral glucose tolerance test, were randomized to group 1 or 2. A control group of 150 randomly selected, age- and body mass index-matched pregnant women with normal screening test results were followed as controls. Testing was completed between 24-28 weeks, and repeated between 30-34 weeks if normal.	advice included providing 24-30 kcal/kg/day based upon prepregnancy body weight with calories divided into 3 meals plus 2-3 snacks of 50-55% carbohydrate, 25-30% protein, and 20-25% fat. Regular monitoring included outpatient visits every 2 weeks with weight, blood pressure, fasting (target < 5 mmol/l) and 2 hour postprandial blood glucose (target (<6.7 mmol/l), HbA1c, and frucosamine measurement, and discussion of dietary habits and dietary compliance. Urine was tested every morning at home for ketones. 3: control, standard management, no Borderline Gestational Glucose Intolerance	treatment **Macrosomia (>= 4000g):** 1: 10.7%, 2: 5.3%, 8.0%, NS **Large for gestational age (>90th percentile):** 1: 14%, 2: 6.0%, 3: 9.1%, p<.05 **Small for gesational age (<10th percentile):** 1: 6.0%, 2: 8.7%, 3: 5.3%, NS **neonatal Ponderal Index (g X 100 cm^3):** 1: 2.73 +/- .35, 2: 2.64 +/- .24, 3: 2.64 +/- .30, p=.03 No difference in **c-section rate, maternal weight gain, gestational week at birth, birth weight or length, apgar at 5 min, hypoglycemia at birth, or admission to NICU.**
Giuffrida et al., 2003	1281 pregnant women with gestational diabetes 1: 637 2: 644	Meta-analysis of 6 RCTs comparing 1: diet alone 2: diet plus insulin	**Macrosomia** RR -0.098 (95% CI: -0.168 - -0.028), Number necessary to treat with insulin to prevent one case of macrosomia: 11 (95% CI 6 -36) Suggests a potential benefit of insulin, but evidence is weak and trials are heterogenous.
Gonen et al., 1997	273 pregnant women at term with an ultrasonic fetal weight estimation of 4000-4500 g 1: 134 2: 139	1: induction of labor 2: expectant management	**Birth weight** 1: 4062 +/- 306.9, 2: 4132 +/- 347, p.024 **C-section rate:** 1: 19.4%, 2: 21.6%, NS No difference in **shoulder dystocia,** or **overall neonatal morbidity**

Study	Participants	Intervention	Results
Homko et al., 2002	58 pregnant women with gestational diabetes <+33 weeks gestation and a fasting blood glucose <95 mg/dl 1: 31 2: 27	1: Glucose self-monitoring 4 times daily (fasting and 1 hour after meals) with a reflectance meter with memory 2: Periodic monitoring of metabolic status at prenatal visits (fasting and 1 hour after 1 meal) Both groups received care from a diabetes educator, nutritionist and maternal-fetal medicine sub-specialists, including individualized counseling on management of GD with goals of fasting blood glucose <95 mg/dl and 1-hour post-prandial glucose <120 mg/dl	No significant difference in any maternal outcomes, including: **Maternal complications** (Polyhydramnios, preeclampsia, hemmorage, placental abruption), diabetes self-efficacy, blood glucose control, or dietary compliance No difference in fetal outcomes: **Macrosomia rate (>90th percentile):** 1: 16.1%, 2: 22.2%, NS **c-Section rate:** 1: 35.5%, 2: 18.5%, NS **Birth trauma rate:** 1: 3.1%, 2: 3.7%, NS Also **birth weight, gestational age at delivery, apgar score, neonatal hypo glycemia and NICU admission** were not different,
Crowther et al., 2005 ACHOIS trial	1000 Pregnant women between 24 and 34 weeks gestation with GD 1: 490 2: 510	1: Dietary advice, blood glucose monitoring, and insulin therapy as needed 2: Routine care	**Any serious perinatal complication:** 1: 1%, 2: 4%, p=.01 **Shoulder dystocia:** 1: 1%, 2: 16%, p=.08 **Admission to NICU:** 1: 71%, 2: 61%, p=.01 **Induction of labor:** 1: 39%, 2: 29%, p<.0001 **C-section rate:** 1: 31%, 2: 32%, NS **Birth weight (g):** 1: 3335 +/- 551, 2: 3482 +/- 660, p<.001 **large for gestational age:** 1: 13%, 2: 22%, p<.001 **Macrosomia (>=4kg):** 1: 10%, 2: 21%, p<.0001

Study	Participants	Intervention	Results
de Veciana et al., 1995	66 pregnant women with gestational diabetes who required insulin therapy at 30 weeks or earlier	1: Management based upon preprandial monitoring. Target: 60-105 mg/dl. Tested fasting, preprandial and bedtime blood glucose daily. 2: Management based upon 1- hour postprandial monitoring. Target: <140 mg/dl. Tested fasting, and 1 hour after each meal. All evaluated weekly by the perinatal-diabetes team. Diet prescribed of 30-35 kcal/kg ideal body weight, as 3 meals plus 1-3 snacks with 40-45% of calories as carbohydrate. Insulin therapy included split dosed short-acting and intermediate-acting (NPH) human insulin to reach targets.	No difference in maternal weight gain, gestational age at delivery, or overall rate of c-section. Women in 2 received more insulin per day. **Birth weight (g):** 1: 3848 +/- 434, 2: 3469 +- 668, p=.01 **Large for Gestational Age:** 1: 42%, 2: 12%, p=.01 **Macrosomia (>4000g):** 1: 36%, 2: 9%, p=.01 **Neonatal hyperglycemia:** 1: 21%, 2: 3%, p=.05 **Shoulder dystocia** 1: 18%, 2: 3%, p=0.10
Exercise			
Ceysens et al., 2006 Cochrane Review of 1: Avery, 1997 2: Bung, 1991 3:Jovanovic-Peterson, 1989 4:Brankston, 2004	114 pregnant women with gestational diabetes randomized into trials of high intensity exercise	1: 3-4 times/week cycling on an ergometer at 70% VO2 max for 30 minutes compared to no exercise 2: Cycling for 45 minutes 3 times/week at 50% VO2 max compared to insulin treatment 3: 20 minutes training on an arm ergometer 3 times/week compared to no exercise 4: 30 minutes circuit type resistance training 3 times/week compared to no exercise	No difference in need for insulin in 1, 3 and 4 (RR 0.98, 95% CI 0.51-1.87) No difference in **macrosomia rates** reported in any trial (i.e. exercise versus no exercise or exercise versus insulin). No difference in all outcomes evaluated. Studies are underpowered to assess the effect of high-intensity exercise on GD outcomes.

CONCLUSIONS OF INTERVENTIONS TO REDUCE MACROSOMIA

Based upon research to date, universal screening of pregnant women for gestational diabetes followed by treatment of identified cases is recommended, with dietary counseling, blood glucose monitoring with a target of <140 mg/dl at one hour after meals, and insulin therapy as needed. Use of fetal ultrasound monitoring to identify cases with large fetal abdominal circumference for intensified management with lower glycemic targets may additionally improve outcomes. Providing women with borderline gestational diabetes with dietary counseling and blood glucose monitoring may reduce risk of large for gestational age in this population.

Suggestions for future research

Effective interventions to prevent or reduce obesity in women of child-bearing age are needed to reduce risk of macrosomia and large for gestational age directly, and by reducing risk of pre-existing type II diabetes and gestational diabetes. Existing research on interventions to prevent or reduce obesity are reviewed in Chapter 9 and Volume I, Chapter 18. As a large percentage of cases of macrosomia are not predicted by known variables, additional research to identify other modifiable factors that contribute to macrosomia is warranted.

INTERVENTIONS TO PREVENT BIRTH DEFECTS

Neural Tube Defects

Neural tube defects (NTDs) are congenital malformations that arise during development of the brain and spinal cord, a process that is complete within one month of fertilization (i.e., by week six after the last menstrual period, and thus often before a women realizes she is pregnant). NTDs include anencephaly, which is incompatible with life, spina bifida (which includes meningocele and meningomyelocele), and encephalocoele. The latter two NTDs have a high incidence of perinatal and infant mortality, and survivors often suffer severe morbidity, including learning disabilities, physical deformities, reduced mobility including paraplegia, and incontinence. In the U.S., spina bifida and anencephaly are the fourth and fifth most common birth defects, with rates in 2004 of 19.3 and 10.9 cases per 100,000 live births, respectively. The cost to the U.S. healthcare system is estimated to be $480 million annually (Bentley et al., 1999). Worldwide,

NTDs are one of the most common congenital malformations, with marked variability in incidence across geographic areas, ethnicity, and socioeconomic status; some of the highest incidences approach 120 per 100,000 live births in parts of Ireland, Egypt, and among Sikhs in India (IMPAC, 2006).

In 1992, after a seminal randomized trial in the U.K. confirmed years of suspicions that deficiencies in folic acid played a role in NTDs (MRC Vitamin Study Research Group, 1991), the U.S. Public Health Service recommended that all women capable of becoming pregnant consume 0.4 mg of folic acid daily and that those at high risk who already had a history of a NTD-pregnancy consume 4 mg daily (Centers for Disease Control and Prevention, 1992). This was followed in 1996 by optional, and in 1998 by mandatory, folic acid fortification of flour and other grain products to increase consumption by an average of 0.1 mg (Food and Drug Administration, 1996). A large public health campaign to increase awareness and educate young women was also begun, led by obstetricians, pediatricians, and the March of Dimes. A review of pre- and post-fortification birth data found that the incidence of NTDs had declined by more than 25%, and folic acid fortification was hailed as a public health success (Centers for Disease Control and Prevention, 2004). The direct relationship between folate and NTDs is a remarkable and unique example of an instance in which a specific birth defect can be substantially prevented easily and consistently on a large-scale level. It is also cheap: one cent per person per year in the United States, which translates into $1,000 per NTD prevented (Wald, 2004). It has been estimated that the proportion of NTDs that can be prevented by periconceptional folic acid is at least 50%, since genetic and environmental factors are also suspected to contribute to overall risk (Pitkin, 2007). Yet the likely public-health benefits of fortifying food stuffs with folic acid or eating foods naturally rich in folate is complex, a public health decision that remains unresolved outside of the U.S., most notably in Europe, where no country has yet mandated food fortification.

Multiple retrospective and prospective trials have examined the relationship between maternal folic acid intake and the occurrence of NTDs in offspring. Although greater than 90% of cases of NTDs occur spontaneously in women who have not had a previous NTD-affected pregnancy, most studies have been recurrence trials, involving women who have already had a NTD pregnancy. Logistically this allows for smaller trials, since the risk of recurrence is significantly higher, ranging from 2% to 10%, but it does limit the pertinence of the findings (Pitkin, 2007). Only one trial performed since 1980, a retrospective case-control trial, has failed to find a decrease in the incidence of NTD with periconceptional folic acid or multivitamin supplementation (Lumley, 2001). A 2001 Cochrane review analyzing the results of four RCTs of periconceptional folate supplementation involving over 6,000 women found a relative risk of 0.28 (95% CI: 0.13 – 0.58) of having a NTD with folic acid supplementation when compared to controls (Lumley, 2001).

We will discuss the results of these four RCTs and one information-dissemination RCT in Australia that looked at folate awareness after printed material was provided (Table 10). The four RCTs were of variable methodological quality, and only one included women who had no history of a NTD-affected pregnancy. Doses of folic acid in these trials ranged from 0.36 mg to 4 mg per day, and two of the trials compared the effectiveness of multivitamins alone versus folic acid in preventing NTDs.

One of the earliest published RCTs on folic acid supplementation was conducted in Wales, an area with historically high rates of NTDs (Laurence et al., 1981). One hundred-eleven women identified as having had a previous NTD pregnancy were randomized to receive 4 mg of folic acid daily versus placebo, starting from the time contraception was stopped through early pregnancy. Compliance was assessed through tablet history and serum folate concentrations measured at weeks 6-9 of pregnancy; 16 out of 60 (27%) of the women in the treatment group were classified as non-compliers. None of the 44 women in the treatment arm who were also compliant had a recurrence of a NTD, and six of the 67 women (9%) who were either in the placebo group (51) or non-compliers (16) had a recurrence (p=0.04). Thus, although the authors were able to show a beneficial biological effect of folic acid supplementation in early pregnancy on recurrence of NTDs, they also noted that they were unsuccessful "(a)s a trial of the methodology of preventing neural-tube defects by giving prophylactic folate": two of the 60 women in the treatment arm had a recurrence due to non-compliance.

The definitive trial that led to the change in U.S. public health policy was the Medical Research Council Vitamin Study, conducted in the U.K. and six other countries in the 1980s (MRC Vitamin Study Research Group, 1991). This double-blind prevention trial enrolled 1817 women, at least one month before conception, with a previous NTD-affected pregnancy and randomized them into four groups: 4 mg folic acid daily, folic acid and other vitamins daily, other vitamins daily, and a control capsule of iron and calcium (these were present in all four tablet formulations). Results were available for 1195 completed pregnancies; there were 6 NTDs among 593 supplemented women (the first two groups) and 21 among placebo-controlled women (latter two groups), a risk reduction of 72% (RR=0.28, 95% CI: 0.12-0.71). The other vitamins alone showed no significant protective effect (RR=0.80, 95% CI: 0.32-1.72).

Table 10. Folic Acid supplementation trials

Trial	Participants	Intervention	Results
Laurence et al., 1981	111 high-risk women in Wales with NTD in previous pregnancy	1: Twice daily 2mg folic acid 2: placebo starting from time contraception was stopped through early pregnancy; Compliance was assessed via tablet history and serum folate concentration at week 6-9 of pregnancy	No recurrences of **NTD** among the 44 compliant women, 2 recurrences among 16 non-compliers in intervention group, and 4 **NTD** among 51 women receiving placebo Thus, a total of 6 **NTD** out of 67 untreated cases (9%) vs none out of 44 treated cases (p=0.04)
MRC Vitamin Study Research Group, 1991	1817 high-risk women in 33 medical centers (17 in UK, 16 in six other countries) with NTD in previous pregnancy; 1195 had a completed pregnancy	Four supplementation groups: 1: folic acid, 2: other vitamins, 3: folic acid plus vitamins, 4: neither (control capsules contained ferrous sulfate and dicalcium phosphate), taken daily from date of randomization (begun $\geq$1 month before conception) until week 12 of pregnancy	RR of **NTD** in groups taking folic acid was 0.28 compared to control groups (95% CI 0.12-0.71); 72% of **NTD** were prevented No effect of multivitamins alone on risk of **NTD**; RR=0.80, 95% CI 0.32-1.72
Kirke et al., 1992	354 non-pregnant Irish women with NTD in previous pregnancy, resulting in 257 pregnancies and 261 infants; 106 already pregnant women served as non-randomized control group resulting in 103 infants	Three treatment groups: 1: folic acid only (0.12mg per tablet), 2: multivitamins without folic acid, 3: multivitamins plus folic acid; all taken 3x daily for at least 2 months before conception and until the date of the third missed menstrual period	Trial ended early prior to target number being reached due to decline in eligible participants. 1 **NTD** in 89 infants of women in group 2 (MV only), compared to none in 172 infants of women in the groups (1,3) randomized to receive folic acid 3 **NTD** in 103 infants in non-randomized control group recurrence rate of **NTD** between folic acid groups and non-randomized controls was significant (p=0.02)

Trial	Participants	Intervention	Results
Czeizel et al., 1992	7540 mostly nulliparous Hungarian women planning pregnancy, leading to 4753 confirmed pregnancies, and 4157 informative pregnancies (abortion after prenatal diagnosis of birth defects, stillbirth, or live birth)	1: Daily multi-vitamin containing 0.8mg folic acid 2: trace-element supplement, starting at least one month before conception until date of second missed menstrual period or later	No difference in rates of early or intermediate fetal death or abortion **Rate of congenital malformations:** 1: 13.3/1000 2: 22.9/1000, p=0.02 **NTDs:** 1: 0/2104 informative pregnancies 2: 6/2053 (p=0.029)
Watson et al., 1999	1197 women of child-bearing age (15-44 yrs) in Australia compromising 6 local government areas (divided into 3 pairs for purpose of randomization)	Printed information recommending folate intake to decrease risk of NTD provided to one randomly selected local government area in each of the 3 pairs	Primary outcome measure was folate awareness, assessed by association between folate and spina bifada. – 4% additional increase (p=0.04) due to the intervention over a significant baseline increase of 3.4% (p=0.02) in folate awareness owing to intervention (OR adjusted for cluster randomization 1.37, 95% CI 1.33-1.42, p=0.0001)

A double-blind trial in Ireland of 350 women used a significantly smaller dose of periconceptional folic acid and found a non-significant difference in recurrence of NTDs (Kirke et al., 1992). Women with a previous NTD-affected pregnancy were randomized to receive one of three treatments at least 2 months prior to conception: 0.36 mg folic acid daily, folic acid plus multivitamins, and multivitamins alone. A non-randomized control group of 106 already-pregnant women, also with a history of a NTD pregnancy, had 103 completed pregnancies, of which three had a NTD. In the randomized groups, there were 261 fetuses: no recurrences in the two folic-acid groups and one NTD in the multivitamins-only group, a difference that was not statistically significant given the small sample size and low rate of recurrence.

The difference between the folic acid groups and the non-randomized controls was statistically significant (p=0.02), although this failed to reach statistical significance when the multivitamin group was added to the non-randomized controls (p=0.06).

A large primary occurrence trial in Hungary is the only study that enrolled low-risk women planning pregnancy (Czeizel and Dudás, 1992). Seventy-five thousand forty mostly nulliparous women were randomized to receive either a daily multivitamin containing 0.8mg folic acid or a trace-element supplement, starting at least one month prior to conception and until the date of the second missed menstrual period. There were 4753 confirmed pregnancies. The prevalence of congential malformations was significantly lower in the group receiving the multivitamin with 13.3 per 1000 pregnancies as compared to 22.9 per 1000 in the trace-element supplement group (p=0.02). There were no NTDs in 2104 pregnancies in the multi-vitamin group and but 6 cases of NTDs among 2053 pregnancies in the trace-element group, a statistically significant difference (p=0.029).

One trial looked at the effectiveness of disseminating information about folic acid to women of child-bearing age in Australia (Watson et al., 1999). This was a community randomized trial involving six communities matched in pairs; printed information on dietary folate intake to reduce the risk of NTDs was disseminated to schools, clinics, and stores in three of the communities, chosen randomly, and pre- and post-surveys were conducted to determine women's knowledge about the association between folate and spina bifida. Approximately 12% of the 1197 women interviewed prior to the intervention were aware of the association between folate and NTDs, with great variability by age (younger women were less likely to know than older women, p<0.001). After the intervention there was a statistically significant background increase of 3.4% (p=0.02) in folate awareness since the pre-intervention survey in the control communities (n=603), as well as an additional increase of 4.0% (p=0.04) in the intervention communities (n=603; OR adjusted for cluster randomization 1.37, 95% CI: 1.33-1.42, p=0.0001). Only 70% of women who were aware knew the correct timing of the intervention. Thus, provision of educational material can increase awareness of the relationship between folate and NTDs, although how well this translates into birth outcomes was not assessed.

Alcohol

According to the 2002 US National Survey on Drug Use and Health, approximately 9% women in the U.S. continue to drink alcohol during their pregnancy (Substance Abuse and Mental Health Services Administration, 2004). Of pregnant women in the U.S., 3% reported binge alcohol use (more than 5 drinks per sitting), and 3% reported using illicit drugs in the past month. Rates of alcohol use in pregnancy quadrupled in the early 1990's and have been steady since.

Alcohol use during pregnancy has been associated with a variety of birth complications, birth defects, and developmental problems in children. Fetal Alcohol Spectrum Disorders (FASD) is a umbrella term that describes the range of problems that may occur in children when a mother drinks alcohol during pregnancy. FASD includes:
1: Fetal alcohol syndrome (FAS), which is characterized by brain damage, facial deformities (including small eyes, a thin upper lip and smooth skin in place of the normal groove between the nose and upper lip), and growth deficits (including small size without catch up growth and smaller brain size). Children with FAS often also have additional alcohol-related birth defects and alcohol-related neurodevelopmental disorder.
2: Alcohol related birth defects (ARBD) are physical conditions linked to prenatal alcohol exposure and commonly include heart, liver, and kidney, skeletal, ear and eye defects.
3: Alcohol-related neurodevelopmental disorders (ARND) are functional or cognitive impairments related to problems with brain development as a result of prenatal alcohol use. Common problems include reduced head size at birth, structural brain abnormalities, and a pattern of behavioral and mental problems such as difficulties with learning, memory, attention and problem solving.
4: Other conditions in alcohol-exposed individuals that do not meet full criteria for a FAS diagnosis.
FASD is estimated to occur in 1 in 100 live births, or roughly 40,000 infants per year in the United States (May and Gossage, 2001).

Additionally, alcohol use during pregnancy has been associated with increased rates of spontaneous abortion, and low birth weight. Numerous studies have documented a relationship between moderate or greater alcohol consumption and spontaneous abortion. For example, a study in Denmark followed 430 couples who were attempting to get pregnant for six menstrual cycles or until they became pregnant. The authors identified 186 pregnancies, which resulted in 131 births and 55 spontaneous abortions by collecting women's urine samples and men and women's alcohol consumption records daily. This study found that both male and female alcohol consumption during the week of conception increased the risk of spontaneous abortion; and that both male and female alcohol consumption increased risk of spontaneous abortion (increased relative risk by 2-3 times for women and 2-5 times for men depending on when alcohol was consumed and adjustment factors) although increases in risk were only significant at levels of 10 or more drinks per week (Henriksen et al., 2004). In a study of nearly 25,000 pregnancies, Kesmodel and colleagues (2002) concluded that female alcohol consumption of 5 or greater drinks per week increased risk for spontaneous abortion in the first trimester. Heavy alcohol consumption has consistently been associated with intrauterine growth retardation and low birth weight, and some studies have identified a similar effect of moderate alcohol consumption (e.g. Virji, 1991; Faden and Graubard, 1994).

Detrimental effects of paternal alcohol use on pregnancy outcomes, including increased risk of spontaneous abortion, low birth weight, congenital heart defects, and mild cognitive impairments, have been documented, but the causal mechanisms for these effects are not clear (Abel, 2004).

Studies investigating the relationship between the amount of alcohol consumed and risk of birth complications and defects have not conclusively identified a "safe" level of drinking. A recent systematic review of trials investigated the effect of low to moderate alcohol consumption (i.e. up to 10.4 standard drinks in United Kingdom units (83g) per week) as compared to no alcohol consumption. Although there was no evidence of a harmful effect of low to moderate alcohol consumption on miscarriage, stillbirth, intra-uterine growth restriction, prematurity, low birthweight or birth defects, weaknesses in study methodology did not allow for the conclusion that drinking at these levels during pregnancy is safe (Henderson et al., 2007).

The annual cost for treatment and care of individuals with FAS in the United States has been estimated in a number of studies. Due to differences in prevalence estimates used, and costs included in the analysis, there have been a wide range of results. A 2003 review of published studies corrected these estimates to reflect a standard prevalence rate of 2/1000 live births, and to include residential care for mentally retarded individuals with FAS (Lupton, 2003). They reported that estimates of annual cost of FAS in the United States ranged from $2.3 to 11.1 billion in 2002 dollars. When adjusted to 2002 dollars and changes in the medical services price index, the two well-documented estimates of lifetime cost per case of FAS range from $2.0 to 2.9 million. By all accounts, the cost of FAS is extremely high and justifies relatively intensive preventative interventions.

This work provides rationale for behavioral interventions targeting reducing risky alcohol use in a number of populations including pregnant women, women of reproductive age, and couples trying to conceive. Additionally, even broadly disseminated or intensive interventions may prove cost effective given the high value of offsetting even one case of FAS.

Review of RCTs to reduce risk of alcohol-related birth defects

No randomized trials of interventions to reduce alcohol use during pregnancy have documented reductions in the incidence of FASD in children, nor have any been powered to do so. To date, the only interventions to reduce alcohol use during pregnancy that have been studied in randomized trials have been assessment and brief interventions. These studies have examined alcohol use as an endpoint. The majority of these trials have been small and thus lack statistical power to fully assess treatment effects. Nevertheless, evidence to date suggests that these low intensity interventions are moderately effective for identifying and reducing alcohol use in pregnant women. These trials are described below (Table 11).

Gorensson and colleagues (2006) demonstrated that alcohol use is significantly more likely to be detected when midwives are taught to conduct assessments of alcohol use with two validated assessment instruments. One of these instruments was the Alcohol Use Disorder Identification Test (AUDIT), a brief screener that can be self-administered or administered by a clinician in less than 3 minutes. The second was the Time-line Follow-back interview (TLFB), a longer guided interview-based assessment of drinking on each day of a designated time period (e.g. every day of pregnancy). In this study, 10 mid-wives were randomized to receive or not receive a 1-day training course in the use of these assessment instruments. They were all provided structured notes where they could record patients' alcohol use; the mid-wives who did not receive training were provided with a 3 point frequency scale, while the trained mid-wives were provided a space to record AUDIT and TLFB scores. The medical records of 315 pregnant women seen by these 10 mid-wives after the start of the study were reviewed to determine how often alcohol use during pregnancy was detected and recorded by the mid-wives. Trained mid-wives detected and documented alcohol use in their pregnant patients' charts

at significantly higher rates than non-trained mid-wives, who detected alcohol use in only 1 out of 153 patients (compared to 36 out of 159 in the trained cohort). Although detection of alcohol use is not likely to be sufficient to reduce alcohol-related birth defects, it is a necessary first step if medical professionals hope to intervene with at risk-women. This study suggests that training mid-wife staff in validated alcohol use assessment techniques can improve detection of potentially risky alcohol use during pregnancy.

In two studies, Chang and colleagues (1999; 2000; 2005) compared the effects of assessment alone to assessment plus a brief intervention using motivational interviewing techniques. Both trials recruited women who had screened positive on a brief screening instrument designed to identify risky prenatal drinking, and in depth assessment interviews about alcohol use were administered on all participants. Women in the brief intervention groups received an additional motivational interview including feedback about assessment results, goal-setting, and discussion of possible life-style changes and practical strategies to implement them. One trial included the pregnant woman's partner in the interview session, the other did not. In both the assessment and assessment plus brief intervention conditions, pregnant women decreased alcohol use significantly. The addition of a brief intervention did not significantly improve overall alcohol use outcomes, but there were indications that adding the motivational interviewing component may help certain subpopulations. In the initial study, women who were abstinent before the assessment were significantly more likely to remain abstinent if they received the brief intervention.

Notably, alcohol use decreased to low levels with assessment only, which would have made it difficult to observe any additional benefit of a brief intervention. Also of note, the percentage of women who continued to drink after assessment and brief intervention is similar to the percentage of births with FASD complications.

A study by Handmaker and colleagues (1999) supports the findings of these two trials. In a small sample, Handmaker randomized pregnant women who screened positive for alcohol use to receive either a mailing about the risks of alcohol use or a brief motivational interview focusing on the risk of drinking to the developing fetus. At two month follow-up, the groups did not differ in abstinence rates or alcohol consumption, however this study was likely underpowered to detect anything but very large differences between groups. They did show, however, that the heaviest drinkers had better alcohol use outcomes if they received the motivational interview.

Because these studies have not assessed the impact of these interventions on FASD outcomes, it is possible that the reductions in alcohol use observed occurred only in the population of women who do not drink in a manner that would lead to FASD. There are no trials to date of more intensive interventions to treat women who do not respond to assessment and brief intervention alone. In our opinion, these women should be referred to standard evidence-based treatments for alcohol use disorders that have been validated in the general population of alcohol use disorder patients until more specific information is obtained. These treatments may include group or individual cognitive behavioral therapy, 12-step facilitation, motivational enhancement therapy, referral to mutual help groups, and contingency management interventions (see Volume 1, Chapter 9).

Ingersoll and colleagues (2005) also conducted a trial of motivational interviewing, however, they focused their intervention on preventing accidental pregnancy in college-age women who met criteria for risky drinking. Participants were randomized to receive either an information pamphlet on women's health or a 60-75 minute motivational interviewing session that included in-depth assessment of recent drinking and contraceptive use, personalized feedback on the risks from their behavior, and a discussion of ways to reduce risk and their ability to do so. One month after the intervention, the women in the motivational interviewing group had significantly better drinking outcomes than controls, drinking lower quantities per drinking episode and lowering their risk of having an alcohol-exposed pregnancy. This suggests that intervening on risky drinking before conception is a viable and potentially valuable strategy for reducing fetal alcohol exposure, however, longer-term follow-up is needed to determine if these effects persist over time.

Conclusions

To date, only relatively low-intensity interventions to reduce risk of FASD have been studied in randomized controlled trials. These studies suggest that assessment and motivational interviewing maybe helpful in reducing alcohol use in pregnancy, although the additional benefit of adding a motivational interviewing to an in-depth assessment is equivocal. One study has suggested that motivational interviewing may reduce the risk of women becoming pregnant while drinking in a risky manner. Targeting risky drinking women before they are pregnant may be a useful strategy for lowing FASD risk. Larger trials that assess and are powered to detect reductions in FASD incidence are needed to inform efforts to reduce these costly birth defects. Additionally, studies of higher intensity, or stepped-care interventions (i.e. initial low intensity interventions followed by higher intensity interventions for women who don't rapidly respond) are needed to address drinking in the population of women who continue to drink during pregnancy following detection and brief intervention.

Lastly, intensive public health campaigns

to reduce FASD should be considered and evaluated to reduce the cost of this health problem. These might include increased media attention to alcohol-related defects, and public health announcements about risks.

Table 11: RCTs to reduce alcohol use during pregnancy

Study	Participants	Intervention	Results
Handmaker et al., 1999	42 pregnant women who reported alcohol consumption were randomized. 34 were available at follow-up 1: 18 2: 16 Participants in each group had a 2:1 ratio of light/moderate: heavy drinkers	1: Participants received a mailing with written information about the risks related to alcohol use in pregnancy which referred them to their health care providers 2: Participants received a one hour motivational interview based on the method of Miller and Rollnick focusing on the health of the participant's unborn baby. The session included feedback on the severity of the subject's drinking, and examination of a chart of fetal development by gestational week.	At two month follow-up, there was no difference between groups in **total alcohol consumption or abstinent days**. There was a interaction effect between **peak blood alcohol levels** at baseline and treatment condition, where subjects with the highest peak blood alcohol levels showed larger decreases in peak blood alcohol if they were in 2. Effect sizes for change in alcohol use: **Consumption:** 1: 0.40, 2: 0.46 **Blood alcohol level:** 1: 0.46, 2: 0.77 **Abstinence:** 1: 0.20, 2: 0.69
Ingersoll et al., 2005	228 female students in an urban university who were at risk for an alcohol exposed pregnancy as defined by having sex with a man and used contraception ineffectively, and drinking at risk levels (at least 1 binge of 5 or more drinks or consuming 8 or more drinks per week on average) in the last 90 days	1: Participants received an informational pamphlet about women's health 2: Participants received a 60-75 minute motivational interview including the following structured activities: recording of 90 days of timeline followback on drinking and contraception use, personalized feedback on risk, exercises on decisional balance, temptation and confidence, and development of goals and change plans for drinking and contraception	At one month post-intervention, **Reduction in risky drinking rates:** 1: 15%, 2: 29% **Reduction in highest number of drinks per day:** 1: 0.4, 2: 2.2, p=.003 **Reduction in risk of an alcohol exposed pregnancy:** 1: 54.3%, 2: 73.9%, p=.005

Study	Participants	Intervention	Results
Goransson et al., 2006	315 women admitted to an antenatal clinic were seen by 10 midwives who had been randomized (5:5) to receive or not receive training 1: 153 2: 162	1: Midwives did not receive training (treatment as usual) 2: Midwives received a 1-day training in use of the AUDIT (alcohol use disorders identification test) and Timeline Followback (TLFB) method for identifying problem drinking, and about problems related to drinking in pregnancy In 1, patient record review was conducted. Records were structured and included a section where the midwife graded alcohol use as "seldom-never", "maximum 1/week", or ">once/week". In 2, AUDIT scores for the last year and TLFB during pregnancy were recorded.	**Patient report of alcohol use while pregnant:** With AUDIT alone: 1: 1/153, 2: 23/139, p<.0001 With TLFB alone: 1: 1/153, 2: 24/139, p<.0001 With both AUDIT and TLFB 1: 1/153, 2: 36/139, p<.0001
Chang et al., 2005	304 pregnant women and their partners. All women had positive alcohol use disorder screening results on the T-ACE.	1: control 2: Brief intervention with partner averaging 25 minutes consisting of knowledge assessment and feedback, goal setting and contracting, lifestyle changes with pregnancy, strategies to resist temptation and ways partner could help, with results printed and provided to couple All subjects received in depth research assessments about their drinking	Rates of **any alcohol consumption** decreased in both groups from nearly 30% at baseline to 1: 2.0% or 2: 1.9%. Similarly **number of drinks per episode** decreased in both groups to 1: 0.40 and 2: 0.39 drinks. Partner involvement increased effectiveness of the intervention in the heaviest drinking women.
Chang et al., 1999	250 women initiating prenatal care who screened positive on the T-ACE, an alcohol screen designed to detect prenatal risk	1: Comprehensive assessment (2 hours) of alcohol use plus a brief intervention 2: Comprehensive assessment only	From baseline to delivery, 1 and 2 had significant reductions in **alcohol use**. **Reduction in drinks per drinking day:** 1: 0.3, 2: 0.4, NS

Prescription teratogens

Reducing exposure of pregnant women to prescription teratogens, medications that increase the risk of fetal abnormalities, is another strategy with potential for decreasing rates of birth defects. A study of prescribing in eight Health Maintenance Organizations in the U.S. from 1996 to 2000 estimated that 1.1% of pregnancies were exposed to a known teratogenic medication, and 5.8% were exposed to a potentially teratogenic medication (Andrade et al., 2004). A study of ambulatory care prescribing in the U.S. from 1998 to 2000 found that the most commonly prescribed potential teratogens in women of child-bearing age are anxiolytics, anticonvulsants, antibiotics and statins. A list of known and possible teratogenic medications can be found at: http://www.emedicine.com/med/topic3242.htm#section~us_food_and_drug_administration_rating_of_teratogenic_effects_of_medications. Women of child-bearing potential received a prescription for a potential teratogen at 7.7% of all visits, but received counseling on contraception use at only 6.1% of visits in which one of these prescriptions were involved (Schwartz et al., 2005). Because it is generally difficult to determine the cause of a birth defect, the number of birth defects due to medication exposure is unknown. These studies suggest, however, that current prescribing practices expose a substantial number of pregnancies to this potential harm.

No randomized controlled trials of interventions to reduce use of potentially teratogenic medications in pregnant women were identified. Several programs have been developed, implemented and described that attempt to reduce exposure of pregnant women to known teratogenic medications, specifically thalidomide, a treatment for for multiple myeloma, AIDS-related complications and leprosy, and isoretonin (Accutane), a treatment for acne. The "System to Manage Accutane Related Teratogenicity™" requires physicians who prescribe Accutane to obtain a set of stickers to use to document appropriate prescribing practices in women of child-bearing potential. Physicians are required to read training documents and use stickers to indicate that they have: conducted appropriate pregnancy testing before prescribing, insured that women have selected and committed to use 2 forms of effective contraceptive while on the medication and at least 1 month before and after, and obtained patient signature on a information/consent form describing birth defects associated with Accutane use and inviting them to participate in the Accutance Survey. Evaluation studies have shown that physicians generally use the stickers (>90% compliance) and that rates of prescribing of Accutane decreased following implemenation of the system (Brinker et al., 2005, Mendelsohn et al., 2005). Despite these promising effects, it is unknown how often the physicians use the system correctly, or whether use of this system reduces rates of birth defects.

A similar system, the "System for Thalidomide Education and Prescribing Safety (S.T.E.P.S.)", is in place for use with thalidomide prescribing. This system has been used substantially (124,000 registered patients between 1998 and 2004) with only one documented pregnancy among registered patients, which ended in miscarriage (Uhl et al., 2006). These evaluations suggest that such systems are helpful, but further study is needed to determine their clinical and cost-effectiveness. This remains a promising area of research for improving efforts to reduce birth defects.

SUMMARY OF INTERVENTIONS TO PREVENT BIRTH DEFECTS

1) All women planning to become pregnant should take 0.4 mg folic acid daily to prevent NTDs. Women who have had a NTD-affected pregnancy should take 4 mg folic acid daily.

2) All pregnant women should be assessed for alcohol use during pregnancy using validated assessment tools and provided information on the effects of alcohol on the developing fetus. Brief motivational interviewing sessions may provide some additional reduction in drinking for subpopulations of women who drink during pregnancy. Non-pregnant women identified as drinking in a risky manner should be provided a motivational interviewing session to encourage reductions in drinking and risk of an alcohol-exposed pregnancy.

3) All women should be encouraged to quit smoking and illicit drug use and offered evidence-based smoking cessation and substance use disorder interventions, as described earlier in the chapter.

4) Although research on this topic is limited, women of child-bearing age should be warned of potential teratogenic effects of medications they are prescribed. Contraceptive counseling and pregnancy testing of women at risk before prescribing is recommended.

REFERENCES

Abel E. (2004) Paternal contribution to fetal alcohol syndrome. Addict Biol 9(2):127-133.

Andrade SE, Raebel MA, Morse AN, Davis RL, Chan KA, Finkelstein JA, Fortman KK, McPhillips H, Roblin D, Smith DH, Yood MU, Platt R, Gurwitz J. (2006) Use of prescription medications with a potential for fetal harm among pregnant women. Pharmacoepidemiol Drug Saf 15(8):546-554.

Andres RL, Day MC. (2000) Perinatal complications associated with maternal tobacco use. Semin Neonatol 5(3): 231-241.

Avery MD, Leon AS, Kopher RA. (1997) Effects of a partially home-based exercise program for women with gestational diabetes. Obstetr Gynecol 89(1):10–5.

Baxley EG, Gobbo RW. (2004) Shoulder dystocia. Am Fam Physician 69(7): 1707-1714.

Bentley JR, Ferrini RL, Hill LL. (1999) American College of Preventive Medicine public policy statement. Folic acid fortification of grain products in the U.S. to prevent neural tube defects. Am J Prev Med 16: 264-267.

Bech BH, Nohr EA, Vaeth M, Henriksen TB, Olsen J. (2005) Coffee and fetal death: a cohort study with prospective data. Am J Epidemiol 162(10): 983-990.

Bech BH, Obel C, Henriksen TB, Olsen J. (2007) Effect of reducing caffeine intake on birth weight and length of gestation: randomised controlled trial. BMJ 334 (7590): 409.

Bonomo M, Corica D, Mion E, Goncalves D, Motta G, Merati R, Ragusa A, Morabito A. (2005) Evaluating the therapeutic approach in pregnancies complicated by borderline glucose intolerance: a randomized clinical trial. Diabetes Med 22: 1536-1541.

Bonomo M, Cetin I, Pisoni MP, Faden D, Mion E, Taricco E, Nobile de Santis M, Radaelli T, Motta G, Costa M, Solerte L, Morabito A. (2004) Flexible treatment of gestational diabetes modulated on ultrasound evaluation of intrauterine growth: a controlled randomized clinical trial. Diabetes Metab 30(3):237-244.

Branisteanu DD, Mathieu C. (2003) Progesterone in gestational diabetes mellitus: guilty or not guilty? Trends Endocrinol Metab 14(2):54-56.

Brankston GN, Mitchell BF, Ryan EA, Okun NB. (2004) Resistance exercise decreases the need for insulin in overweight women with gestational diabetes mellitus. Am J Obstetr Gynecol 190(1):188–193.

Brinker A, Kornegay C, Nourjah P. (2005) Trends in adherence to a revised risk management program designed to decrease or eliminate isotretinoin-exposed pregnancies: evaluation of the accutane SMART program. Arch Dermatol 141(5): 563-569.

Bung P, Bung C, Artal R, Khodiguian N, Fallenstein F, Spatling L. (1991) Therapeutic exercise for insulin-requiring gestational diabetics: Effects on the fetus-results of a randomized prospective longitudinal study. J Perinatal Med 21(2): 125-137.

Casson IF, Clarke CA, Howard CV, McKendrick O, Pennycook S, Pharoah PO, Platt MJ, Stanisstreet M, van Velszen D, Walkinshaw S. (1997) Outcomes of pregnancy in insulin dependent diabetic women: results of a five year population cohort study. BMJ 315(7103): 275-278.

Ceesay SM, Prentice AM, Cole TJ, et al. (1997) Effects on birth weight and perinatal mortality of maternal dietary supplements in rural Gambia: 5 year randomised controlled trial. BMJ 315: 786-790.

Centers for Disease Control and Prevention. (1992) Recommendations for the use of folic acid to reduce the number of cases of spina bifida and other neural tube defects. MMWR 41(RR-14):1-7.

Centers for Disease Control and Prevention. (2002) Infant mortality and low birth weight among black and white infants – United States, 1980–2000. MMWR 51(27): 589-592.

Centers for Disease Control and Prevention. (2004) Spina bifida and anencephaly before and after folic acid mandate – United States, 1995-1996 and 1999-2000. MMWR 53: 362-365.

Centers for Disease Control and Prevention. (2005) Achievements in public health: elimination of rubella and congenital rubella syndrome – United States, 1969-2004. MMWR 54(11): 279-282.

Ceysens G, Rouiller D, Boulvain M. (2006) Exercise for diabetic pregnant women. Cochrane Database of Systematic Reviews CD004225.

Chang G, Goetz MA, Wilkins-Haug L, Berman S. (2000) A brief intervention for prenatal alcohol use: an in-depth look. J Subst Abuse Treat 18(4):365-369.

Chang G, Wilkins-Haug L, Berman S, Goetz MA. (1999) Brief intervention for alcohol use in pregnancy: a randomized trial. Addiction 94(10):1499-1508.

Chang G, McNamara TK, Orav EJ, Koby D, Lavigne A, Ludman B, Vincitorio NA, Wilkins-Haug L. (2005) Brief intervention for prenatal alcohol use: a randomized trial. Obstet Gynecol 105(5 Pt 1):991-998.

Charles DHM, Ness AR, Campbell D, et al. (2005) Folic acid supplements in pregnancy and birth outcome: re-analysis of a large randomized controlled trial and update of Cochrane review. Pediatric and Perinatal Epidemiology 19: 112-124.

Christian P, Khatry SK, Katz J, et al. (2003) Effects of alternative maternal micronutrient supplements on low birth weight in rural Nepal: double blind randomised community trial. BMJ 326: 571-576.

Christian P, Osrin D, Manandhar DS, et al. (2005) Antenatal micronutrient supplements in Nepal. BMJ 366: 711.

Crowther CA, Hiller JE, Moss JR, McPhee AJ, Jeffries WS, Robinson JS; Australian Carbohydrate Intolerance Study in Pregnant Women (ACHOIS) Trial Group. (2005) Effect of treatment of gestational diabetes mellitus on pregnancy outcomes. N Engl J Med 352(24): 2477-2486.

Czeizel AE and Dudás I. (1992) Prevention of the first occurrence of neural-tube defects by periconceptional vitamin supplementation. N Engl J Med 327:1832-1835.

Czeizel AE, Dudás I, Métneki J. (1994) Pregnancy outcomes in a randomised controlled trial of periconceptional multivitamin supplementation. Arch Gynecol Obstet 255: 131-139.

de Veciana M, Major CA, Morgan MA, Asrat T, Toohey JS, Lien JM, Evans AT. (1995) Postprandial versus preprandial blood glucose monitoring in women with gestational diabetes mellitus requiring insulin therapy. N Engl J Med 333(19):1237-1241.

Dooley SL, Metzger BE, Cho NH: Gestational diabetes mellitus. (1991) Influence of race on disease prevalence and perinatal outcome in a U.S. population. Diabetes 40 Suppl 2: 25-29.

Dunne F, Brydon P, Smith K, Gee H. (2003) Pregnancy in women with Type 2 diabetes: 12 years outcome data 1990-2002. Diabet Med 20: 734-738.

Faden VB, Graubard BI. (1994) Alcohol consumption during pregnancy and infant birth weight. Ann Epidemiol 4(4): 279-284.

Fall CHD, Yajnik CS, Davies AA, et al. (2003) Micronutrients and fetal growth. J Nutr 133: 1747S-1756S.

Fawzi WW, Msamanga GI, Spiegelman D, et al. (1998) Randomized trial of effects of vitamin supplements on pregnancy outcomes and T cell counts in HIV-1-infected women in Tanzania. Lancet 351: 1477-1482.

Fawzi WW, Msamanga GI, Urassa W, et al. (2007) Vitamins and perinatal outcomes among HIV-negative women in Tanzania. N Engl J Med 356:1423-1431.

Fiore MC. (2000) US public health service clinical practice guideline: treating tobacco use and dependence. Respir Care 45(10): 1200-1262.

Friis H, Gomo E, Nyazema N, et al. (2004) Effect of multimicronutrient supplementation on gestational length and birth size: a randomized, placebo-controlled, double-blind effectiveness trial in Zimbabwe. Am J Clin Nutr 80: 178-184.

Food and Drug Administration. (1996) Food standards: amendment of standards of identity for enriched grain products to require addition of folic acid. Federal Register 61: 8781-8797.

Fuddy LJ, Prince CB, Tang MC. (2003) Perinatal substance use among high risk women in Hawaii: patterns and impact on pregnancy outcomes. Asian Am Pac Isl J Health 10(1):50-57.

Garner P, Okun N, Keely E, Wells G, Perkins S, Sylvain J, Belcher J. (1997) A randomized controlled trial of strict glycemic control and tertiary level obstetric care versus routine obstetric care in the management of gestational diabetes: A pilot study. Am J Obstet Gynecol 177: 190-195.

Godfrey KM and Barker DJP. (2000) Fetal nutrition and adult disease. Am J Clin Nutr 71: 1344-1352.

Gonen O, Rosen DJ, Dolfin Z, Tepper R, Markov S, Fejgin MD. (1997) Induction of labor versus expectant management in macrosomia: a randomized study. Obstet Gynecol 89(6): 913-917.

Goransson M, Magnusson A, Heilig M. (2006) Identifying hazardous alcohol consumption during pregnancy: implementing a research-based model in real life. Acta Obstet Gynecol Scand 85(6): 657-662.

Griffin ME, Coffey M, Johnson H, Scanlon P, Foley M, Stronge J, O'Meara NM, Firth RG. (2000) Universal vs. risk factor-based screening for gestational diabetes mellitus: detection rates, gestation at diagnosis and outcome. Diabetic Medicine 17: 26-32.

Giuffrida FM, Castro AA, Atallah AN, Dib SA. (2003) Diet plus insulin compared to diet alone in the treatment of gestational diabetes mellitus: a systematic review. Braz J Med Biol Res 36(10):1297-1300.

Haider BA and Bhutta ZA. (2006) Multiple-micronutrient supplementation for women during pregnancy. Cochrane Database of Systematic Reviews Issue 4. Art. No.: CD004905.

Hamilton BE, Martin JA, and Ventura SJ. (2007) Births: preliminary data for 2005. National Vital Statistics Reports 55.

Hyattsville, MD: National Center for Health Statistics. Available at: http://0-www.cdc.gov.mill1.sjlibrary.org/nchs/products/pubs/pubd/hestats/prelimbirths05/prelimbirths05.htm (accessed 10/14/07).

Handmaker NS, Miller WR, Manicke M. (1999) Findings of a pilot study of motivational interviewing with pregnant drinkers. J Stud Alcohol 60(2):285-287.

Hedley AA, Ogden CL, Johnson CL, Carroll MD, Curtin LR, Flegal KM. (2004) Prevalence of overweight and obesity in the United States, 1999-2004. JAMA 291: 2847-2850.

Heins HC Jr, Nance NW, McCarthy BJ, Efird CM. (1990) A randomized trial of nurse-midwifery prenatal care to reduce low birth weight. Obstet Gynecol 75(3 Pt 1): 341-345.

Henderson J, Gray R, Brocklehurst P.(2007) Systematic review of effects of low-moderate prenatal alcohol exposure on pregnancy outcome. BJOG 114(3):243-252.

Henriksen TB, Hjollund NH, Jensen TK, Bonde JP, Andersson AM, Kolstad H, Ernst E, Giwercman A, Skakkebaek NE, Olsen J.(2004) Alcohol consumption at the time of conception and spontaneous abortion. Am J Epidemiol 160(7):661-667.

Herbst MA. (2005) Treatment of suspected fetal macrosomia: a cost-effectiveness analysis. Am J Obstet Gynecol 193: 1035-1039.

Hininger I, Favier M, Arnaud J, et al. (2004) Effects of a combined micronutrient supplementation on maternal biological status and newborn anthropomorphic measurements: a randomised double-blind, placebo-controlled trial in apparently healthy pregnant women. Eur J Clin Nutrition 58: 52-59.

Homko CJ, Sivan E, Reece EA. (2002) The impact of self-monitoring of blood glucose on self-efficacy and pregnancy outcomes in women with diet-controlled gestational diabetes. Diabetes Educ 28(3):435-443.

IMPAC. (2006) "Prevention of neural tube defects." In: Standards in Maternal and Neonatal Care. World Health Organization. Available at: http://www.who.int/making_pregnancy_safer/publications/Standards1.5N.pdf (accessed 2/13/07)

Ingersoll KS, Ceperich SD, Nettleman MD, Karanda K, Brocksen S, Johnson BA. (2005) Reducing alcohol-exposed pregnancy risk in college women: initial outcomes of a clinical trial of a motivational intervention. J Subst Abuse Treat 29(3):173-180.

Jovanovic-Peterson L, Durak EP, Peterson CM. (1989) Randomized trial of diet versus diet plus cardiovascular conditioning on glucose levels in gestational diabetes. Am J Obstetrics Gynecol 161:415–419.

Kæstel P, Michaelsen KF, Aaby P, et al. (2005) Effects of prenatal multimicronutrient supplements on birth weight and perinatal mortality: a randomised, controlled trial in Guinea-Bissau. Eur J Clin Nutrition 59: 1081-1089.

Kafatos AG, Vlachonikolis IG, Codrington CA. (1989) Nutrition during pregnancy: the effects of an educational intervention program in Greece. Am J Clin Nutr 50: 970-979.

Kardjati S, Kusin JA, De With C. (1988) Energy supplementation in the last trimester of pregnancy in East Java: I. Effect on birthweight. Brit J Obstetr Gynaecol 95: 783-794.

Kennare R, Heard A, Chan A. (2005) Substance use during pregnancy: risk factors and obstetric and perinatal outcomes in South Australia. Aust N Z J Obstet Gynaecol 45(3):220-225.

Kesmodel U, Wisborg K, Olsen SF, Henriksen TB, Secher NJ. (2002) Moderate alcohol intake in pregnancy and the risk of spontaneous abortion. Alcohol Alcohol 37(1): 87-92.

Kirke PN, Daly LE, Elwood JH, et al. (1992) A randomised trial of low dose folic acid to prevent neural tube defects. Arch Dis Child 67:1442-1446.

Kjos, SL, Schaefer-Graf U, Sardesi S, Peters RK, Buley A, Xiang AH, Bryne JD, Sutherland C, Montoro MN, Buchanan TA. (2001) A randomized controlled trial using glycemic plus fetal ultrasound parameters versus glycemic parameters to determine insulin therapy in gestational diabetes with fasting hyperglycemia. Diabetes Care 24: 1904-1910.

Kotelchuck M, Schwartz JB, Anderka MT, et al. (1984) WIC participation and pregnancy outcomes: Massachusetts state-wide evaluation project. Am J Public Health 74: 1086-1092.

Kowaleski-Jones L and Duncan GJ. (2002) Effects of participation in the WIC program on birthweight: evidence from the National Longitudinal Survey of Youth. Am J Public Health 92: 799-804.

Kramer MS. (1987) Intrauterine growth and gestational duration determinants. Pediatrics 80: 502-511.

Kramer MS. (2003) The epidemiology of adverse pregnancy outcomes. J Nutr 133: 1592S-1596S.

Kramer MS and Kakuma R. (2003) Energy and protein intake in pregnancy. Cochrane Database of Systematic Reviews Issue 4, Art. No.: CD00032.

Laurence KM, James N, Miller MH, et al. (1981) Double-blind randomised controlled trial of folate treatment before conception to prevent recurrence of neural-tube defects. BMJ 282: 1509-1511.

Lerner H. (2007) Shoulder Dystocia: Facts, evidence and conclusions. Available at: http://www.shoulderdystociainfo.com/. Accessed June 14, 2007.

Ludlow JP, Evans SF, Hulse G. (2004) Obstetric and perinatal outcomes in pregnancies associated with illicit substance abuse. Aust N Z J Obstet Gynaecol 44(4):302-306.

Lumley J, Watson L, Watson M, et al. (2001) Periconceptional supplementation with folate and/or multivitamins for preventing neural tube defects. Cochrane Database of Systematic Reviews 3:CD001056.

Lumley J, Oliver SS, Chamberlain C, Oakley L. (2004) Interventions for promoting smoking cessation during pregnancy. Cochrane Database of Systematic Reviews 4: CD001055

Lupton C. (2003) The financial impact of fetal alcohol syndrome. SAMHSA FASD Center for Excellence. Accessed at http://www.fascenter.samhsa.gov/publications/cost.cfm on 3/15/07.

Mardones-Santander F, Rosso P, Stekel A, et al. (1988) Effect of a milk-based food supplement on maternal nutritional status and fetal growth in underweight Chilean women. Am J Clin Nutr 47: 413-419.

Martin JA, Hamilton BE, Sutton PD, et al. (2006) Births: final data for 2004. National Vital Statistics Reports 55(1). Hyattsville, MD: National Center for Health Statistics. Available at: http://www.cdc.gov/nchs/data/nvsr/nvsr55/nvsr55_01.pdf (accessed 1/30/07)

Mathews TJ. (2006) Trends in spina bifida and anencephalus in the United States, 1991-2004. National Center for Health Statistics, Health E-Stats. Available at: http://www.cdc.gov/nchs/products/pubs/pubd/hestats/spine_anen.htm (accessed 2/13/07)

May PA, Gossage JP. (2001) Estimating the prevalence of fetal alcohol syndrome: a summary. Alcohol Research & Health 25(3): 159-167.

McDonald EC, Pollitt E, Mueller W, et al. (1981) The Bacon Chow Study: maternal nutritional supplementation and birth weight of offspring. Am J Clin Nutr 34: 2133-2144.

Mendelsohn AB, Governale L, Trontell A, Seligman P. (2005) Changes in isotretinoin prescribing before and after implementation of the System to Manage Accutane Related Teratogenicity (SMART) risk management program. Pharmacoepidemiol Drug Saf 14(9):615-618.

Merialdi M, Carroli G, Villar J, et al. (2003) Nutritional interventions during pregnancy for the prevention or treatment of impaired fetal growth: an overview of randomized controlled trials. J Nutr 133: 1626S-1631S.

Metcoff J, Costiloe P, Crosby WM, et al. (1985) Effect of food supplementation (WIC) during pregnancy on birth weight. Am J Clin Nutr 41: 933-947.

Mondestin MA, Ananth CV, Smulian JC, Vintzileos AM (2002) Birth weight and fetal death in the United States: the effect of maternal diabetes during pregnancy. Am J Obstet Gynecol 187(4): 922-926.

Mora JO, de Paredes B, de Navarro L, et al. (1979) Nutritional supplementation and the outcome of pregnancy. I. Birth weight. Am J Clin Nutr 32: 455-462.

MRC Vitamin Study Research Group. (1991) Prevention of neural tube defects: results of the Medical Research Council Vitamin Study. Lancet 338: 131-137.

Murphy CC, Schei B, Myhr TL, Du MJ. (2001) Abuse: a risk factor for low birth weight? A systematic review and meta-analysis. CMAJ 164(11): 1567-1572

Neggers Y, Goldenberg R, Cliver S, Hauth J. (2004) Effects of domestic violence on preterm birth and low birth weight. Acta Obstet Gynecol Scand 83(5): 455-460.

Okun N, Verma A, Mitchell BF, Flowerdew G (1997) Relative importance of maternal constitutional factors and glucose intolerance of pregnancy in the development of newborn macrosomia. J Matern Fetal Med 6(5): 285-290.

Olds DL, Robinson J, Pettitt L, Luckey DW, Holmberg J, Ng RK, Isacks K, Sheff K, Henderson CR Jr. (2004) Effects of home visits by paraprofessionals and by nurses: age 4 follow-up results of a randomized trial. Pediatrics 114(6):1560-1568.

Osrin D, Vaidya A, Shrestha Y, et al. (2005) Effects of antenatal multiple micronutrient supplementation on birthweight and gestational duration in Nepal: double-blind, randomised controlled trial. Lancet 365: 955-962.

Panjari M, Bell R, Bishop S, Astbury J, Rice G, Doery J. (1999) A randomized controlled trial of a smoking cessation intervention during pregnancy. Australia and New Zealand Journal of Obstetrics and Gynaecology 39(3): 312-317.

Pitkin RM. (2007) Folate and neural tube defects. Am J Clin Nutr 85: 285S-288S.

Polanska K, Hanke W, Sobala W, Lowe JB. (2004) Efficacy and effectiveness of the smoking cessation program for pregnant women. Int J Occup Med Environ Health 17(3):369-377.

Ramakrishnan U, González-Cossío T, Neufeld LM, et al. (2003) Multiple micronutrient supplementation during pregnancy does not lead to greater infant birth size than does iron-only supplementation: a randomized controlled trial in a semirural community in Mexico. Am J Clin Nutr 77: 720-725.

Rao S, Yajnik CS, Kanade A, et al. (2001) Intake of micronutrient-rich foods in rural Indian mothers is associated with the size of their babies at birth. Pune Maternal Nutrition Study. J Nutr 131: 1217-1224.

Ricketts SA, Murray EK, Schwalberg R. (2005) Reducing low birthweight by resolving risks: results from Colorado's Prenatal Plus program. Am J Public Health 95: 1952-1957.

Rouse DJ, Owen J, Goldenberg RL, Cliver SP. (1996) The effectiveness and costs of elective cesarean delivery for fetal macrosomia diagnosed by ultrasound. JAMA 276(18):1480-1486.

Rush D, Stein Z, Susser M. (1980) A randomized controlled trial of prenatal nutritional supplementation in New York City. Pediatrics 65: 683-697.

Schaefer-Graf UM, Kjos SL, Fauzan OH, Buhling KJ, Siebert G, Buhrer C, Ladendorf B, Dudenhausen JW, Vetter K. (2004) A randomized trial evaluating a predominantly fetal growth-based strategy to guide management of gestational diabetes in Cauasian women. Diabetes Care 27: 297-302.

Schmitt SK, Sneed L, Phibbs CS. (2006) Costs of newborn care in California: a population-based study. Pediatrics 117: 154-160.

Scholl TO, Hediger ML, Bendich A, et al. (1997) Use of multivitamin/mineral prenatal supplements: influence on the outcome of pregnancy. Am J Epidemiol 146: 134-141.

Schwarz EB, Maselli J, Norton M, Gonzales R. (2005) Prescription of teratogenic medications in United States ambulatory practices. Am J Med 118(11):1240-1249.

Sexton M, Hebel JR. (1984) A clinical trial of change in maternal smoking and its effect on birth weight. JAMA 251: 911-5.

Stotland NE, Caughey AB, Breed EM, Escobar GJ. (2004) Risk factors and obstetric complications associated with macrosomia. Int J Gynaecol Obstet 87(3): 220-226.

Substance Abuse and Mental Health Services Administration. (2004) National Survey on Drug Use and Health. Pregnancy and Substance Use. The NSDUH Report January 2, 2004.

Stein REK, Siegel MJ, Bauman LJ. (2006) Are children at moderately low birth weight at increased risk for poor health? A new look at an old question. Pediatrics 118: 217-223.

Tappin DM, Lumsden MA, Gilmour WH, Crawford F, McIntyre D, Stone DH, Webber R, MacIndoe S, Mohammed E. (2005) Randomised controlled trial of home based motivational interviewing by midwives to help pregnant smokers quit or cut down. BMJ 331(7513):373-377.

Uhl K, Cox E, Rogan R, Zeldis JB, Hixon D, Furlong LA, Singer S, Hollim T, Beyer J, Woolever W. (2006) Thalidomide use in the US: experience with pregnancy testing in the S.T.E.P.S. programme. Drug Saf. 29(4): 321-329.

UNICEF. (2002) Reduction of low birth weight: a South Asia priority. UNICEF – Regional Office for South Asia.

UNICEF. (2004) The state of the world's children 2005: childhood under threat. The United Nations Children's Fund (UNICEF). Available at: http://www.unicef.org/publications/files/SOWC_2005_(English).pdf (accessed 1/29/07)

UNICEF/WHO/UNU. (1999) Composition of a multi-micronutrient supplement to be used in pilot programmes among pregnant women in developing countries. New York: UNICEF/WHO/UNU.

Villar J, Merialdi M, Gülmezoglu AM, et al. (2003) Nutritional interventions during pregnancy for the prevention or treatment of maternal morbidity and preterm delivery: an overview of randomized controlled trials. J Nutr 133: 1606S-1625S.

Virji SK.(1991) The relationship between alcohol consumption during pregnancy and infant birthweight. An epidemiologic study. Acta Obstet Gynecol Scand 70(4-5):303-308.

Waitzman NJ, Romano PS, Scheffler RM, Harris JA. (1995) Economic costs of birth defects and cerebral palsy – United States, 1992. MMWR 44(37): 694-699.

Wald NJ. (2004) Folic acid and the prevention of neural-tube defects. NEJM 350: 101-103.

Watson MJ, Watson LF, Bell RJ, et al. (1999)

A randomized community intervention trial to increase awareness and knowledge of the role of periconceptional folate in women of child-bearing age. Health Expectations 2: 255-265.

Wisborg K, Henriksen TB, Jespersen LB, Secher NJ. (2000) Nicotine patches for pregnant smokers: a randomized contolled study. Obstet Gynecol 96(6): 967-971.

Wolfe EL, Davis T, Guydish J, Delucchi KL. (2005) Mortality risk associated with perinatal drug and alcohol use in California. J Pernatol 25(2):93-100.

Yang J, Cummings EA, O'connell C, Jangaard K. (2006) Fetal and neonatal outcomes of diabetic pregnancies. Obstet Gynecol 108:644-650.

Zamorski MS, Biggs WS. (2001) Management of Suspected Fetal Macrosomia. Am Fam Physician 63(2): 302-306.

PREVENTING MOTHER-TO-CHILD TRANSMISSION OF HIV

Claire Thorne and Marie-Louise Newell

INTRODUCTION

HIV infection can be transmitted vertically from mother to infant during pregnancy, around the time of delivery or postnatally, through breastfeeding. Mother-to-child transmission of HIV (MTCT) is the predominant mode of acquisition of infection among children globally and thus the epidemic among children mirrors that among pregnant women. Pediatric HIV infection is now regarded as a chronic disease of childhood in resource-rich settings, as a result of widespread availability and use of highly active antiretroviral therapy (HAART). However, in developing country settings where access to HAART remains limited, pediatric HIV infection contributes substantially to infant and child mortality.

Global Epidemiology

Since HIV was first identified in 1981, the HIV/AIDS epidemic has developed into a global pandemic. There were 38 million adults and 2.3 million children living with HIV/AIDS by the start of 2006 (UNAIDS, 2005). Each day, approximately 1800 infants acquire HIV infection vertically from their mothers and an estimated 700,000 children became newly infected with HIV in 2005 (UNAIDS, 2005). More than 90% of the children with HIV/AIDS are living in sub-Saharan Africa, which is home to 77% of the 17.5 million women estimated to be living with HIV; most of the remaining infected women live in those parts of the world where there are also generalized HIV epidemics, including South and South-East Asia and the Caribbean. Eastern Europe and Central Asia have the fastest growing HIV epidemic currently, fuelled by illicit injection drug use,

but with disturbing signs of maturing to a generalized epidemic with increasing heterosexual transmission in some countries, such as Russia, Moldova, Ukraine and Kazakhstan (Ostergren and Malyuta, 2006; UNAIDS and WHO, 2005). Antenatal HIV prevalence is highest in sub-Saharan Africa, although it varies by region, from around 30% in Southern Africa, to 13% in Eastern Africa (where there is a declining trend in some parts) and 4-7% in Central and Western Africa (UNAIDS, 2005).

The United Nations General Assembly incorporated a Declaration of Commitment on HIV/AIDS within their Millennium Goals in 2000 (UNAIDS, 2002). The targets within this declaration included a 25% reduction in the percentage of pregnant women aged 15-24 who are HIV infected by 2010 and a 20% reduction in infant HIV infection by 2005, and 50% by 2010. The need for such targets highlights the continued growth and acceleration of the HIV pandemic in many parts of the world, with a reversal of the declining trends in maternal, infant and child mortality that were achieved in the 1980s and early 1990s in parts of sub-Saharan Africa.

Vertical transmission: rates, timing, mechanisms and risk factors
Rates and timing

Much of our understanding of MTCT has come from epidemiological studies, particularly cohort studies with prospective follow-up of infants born to HIV-infected women from birth and clinical trials. Prior to the introduction of interventions to reduce MTCT, reported rates of transmission from cohort studies varied considerably and were 15-20% in Europe, 16-30% in the USA, 25-

40% in Africa and 13-48% in South and South East Asia (European Collaborative Study, 1996; Kumar et al., 1995; Working Group on Mother-to-Child Transmission of HIV, 1995; Matheson et al., 1996). Much of the variation was due to the different breastfeeding rates between study populations.

In non-breastfeeding populations, most transmission takes place in late pregnancy and around the time of delivery, with early *in utero* transmission likely to be rare in uneventful pregnancies (Mandelbrot et al., 1996; Newell, 1998; Magder et al., 2005). In breastfeeding populations, peri-partum (around delivery) transmissions make up about 40% of total transmissions, with post-natal transmissions accounting for a similar proportion of infections (de Cock et al., 2000; Simonon et al., 1994; de Cock et al., 2000; Bertolli et al., 1996).

Mechanisms

Intra-uterine transmission may occur as a result of fetal exposure to cell-free and/or cell-associated HIV in the amniotic fluid. HIV infection of the placental cells and/or disruption of the integrity of the placenta may also result in fetal exposure. During labor, uterine contractions may result in micro-transfusions between maternal and fetal blood circulation or HIV infection may ascend from the genital tract to amniotic fluid and the fetus once membranes have ruptured (Kwiek et al., 2006). However, much intrapartum infection is likely to be the result of direct contact between the infant and infectious maternal cervicovaginal secretions and blood as he or she passes through the birth canal. Presence of HIV RNA in the oropharyngeal aspirates of neonates at birth can be used as a marker of infant oral mucosal exposure to HIV in genital secretions during birth (Mandelbrot et al., 1999).

Postnatal transmission of HIV through breast milk is a major contributor to the overall likelihood of infection in infants in breastfeeding populations. Transmission of HIV through breastfeeding was recognized after cases of postnatal transmission by women who acquired infection after delivery and cases of infants infected through breast milk pooling or wet nursing (Van de Perre et al., 1991; Hira et al., 1990; Palasanthiran et al., 1993; Nduati et al., 1994). The risk of postnatal transmission remains for as long as breastfeeding continues, and prolonged breastfeeding (beyond age 12 months) is estimated to double the overall MTCT risk (John-Stewart et al., 2004; Richardson et al., 2003). With regard to timing of postnatal transmission, a distinction between early and late postnatal acquisition of infection through breastfeeding can be made. Late postnatal transmission (LPT) is usually defined as acquisition of HIV infection through breast-feeding in infants with a negative HIV test at or after a specific age (usually 4-6 weeks). In a large meta-analysis using data from 9 clinical trials in Africa, the estimated LPT rate was 8.9 per 100 child-years of breastfeeding (95% confidence interval (CI): 7.8-10.2) and LPT risk was roughly constant over time (Breastfeeding and HIV International Transmission Study (BHITS), 2004).

Risk factors

Maternal plasma HIV RNA level is the best individual predictor of MTCT risk (Garcia et al., 1999; Shaffer et al., 1999; Cooper et al., 2002; European Collaborative Study, 1999; European Collaborative Study, 2005) and clinical risk factors associated with transmission such as AIDS and primary HIV infection in pregnancy are themselves associated with high plasma viral loads. Viral load in the genital tract has also been shown to be an independent risk factor for MTCT (Chuachoowong et al., 2000; Tuomala et al., 2003). Factors associated with shedding of HIV in the genital tract include plasma RNA viral load, co-infection with sexually transmitted disease, CD4 count and viral subtype (John et al., 2001; Seck et al., 2001; Mofenson et al., 1999; John-Stewart et al., 2005). Documentation of MTCT even at very low plasma HIV viral loads reflects the likelihood that viral loads in the genital tract and in plasma are not necessarily concordant, and also highlights that additional risk factors are important. Obstetric and infant factors identified as increasing MTCT risk include vaginal delivery, prolonged duration of rupture of membranes, chorioamnionitis, prematurity, low birth weight and female gender (Kuhn et al., 1999; Fawzi et al., 2001; The European Mode of Delivery Collaboration, 1999; The International Perinatal HIV group, 2001; Mwanyumba et al., 2002b; Mofenson et al., 1999; Galli et al., 2005; European Collaborative Study, 2003; Magder et al., 2005).

Specific risk factors for postnatal transmission relate to breast health and the infectivity of breast milk, including breast milk viral load, clinical and sub-clinical mastitis, nipple lesions and mode of infant feeding (John-Stewart et al., 2004; John et al., 2001; Sterling et al., 2001). The limited information available on HIV RNA in breast milk suggests a moderate correlation between viral load in plasma and in breast milk, with RNA levels in breast milk generally lower than those in plasma (Willumsen et al., 2001; Willumsen et al., 2003; Rousseau et al., 2003). Non-exclusive breastfeeding (that is, the provision of water or other fluids, and foods to breastfeeding infants, which is common in most settings worldwide) is associated with a higher risk of postnatal acquisition of HIV (Coutsoudis et al., 2001; Iliff et al., 2005). It is postulated that while exclusive breastfeeding may promote intestinal microflora that may be beneficial in resisting infection and modulating infant's immunological responses, mixed feeding may result in exposure of the infant to dietary antigens and pathogens than may disrupt the integrity of the intestinal mucosal barrier to HIV (World Health Organization, 2001).

PREVENTION OF MOTHER TO CHILD TRANSMISSION INTERVENTIONS

A wide variety of approaches to prevent MTCT have been or are being evaluated, directed at all, some, or one of the three periods when transmission can take place (i.e. during pregnancy, around the time of delivery and the postnatal period). These include those that aim to reduce maternal viral load, to avoid or reduce exposure of the infant to the virus in maternal blood, cervical secretions and breast milk, or to boost the infant's ability to resist or clear the virus.

As maternal viral load is the pre-eminent risk factor for MTCT, the first intervention to be evaluated in a randomized controlled trial was pharmacological – the use of the antiretroviral drug, zidovudine (ZDV). ZDV, a nucleoside analogue reverse transcriptase inhibitor (NRTI) was the first antiretroviral drug, licensed in 1987 for use in treatment of HIV disease. In addition to the NRTIs, there are three other main classes of antiretroviral drugs – protease inhibitors (PIs), non-nucleoside reverse transcriptase inhibitors (NNRTIs) and fusion inhibitors. These reduce viral load by preventing viral replication through a variety of mechanisms including inhibition of the synthesis of HIV DNA and prevention of viral entry. The role of the different classes of antiretroviral drugs in PMTCT varies according to whether they can cross the placenta. For example, ZDV, 3TC and nevirapine (NVP) all easily cross the placenta (in the case of NVP, rapidly) (Mirochnick, 2000; Mandelbrot *et al.*, 2001) which allows a prophylactic effect for the infant as well as a reduction in maternal viral load. However, as PIs do not cross the placenta (Dorenbaum et al., 2002; Marzolini et al., 2002) their effect is limited to the impact on maternal viral load. A more recent approach to pharmacological intervention has been the use of antiretroviral drugs to reduce breastfeeding transmission, with both the use of antiretroviral drugs given to the mother (to reduce viral load in the breast milk) and antiretroviral prophylaxis given to the breastfeeding infant (Gaillard et al., 2004).

Avoidance of breastfeeding where this is safe, feasible, acceptable, affordable and sustainable is recommended by WHO and UNAIDS, as it effectively eliminates post-natal transmission of HIV infection. However, for most HIV-infected mothers, particularly those living in much of sub-Saharan Africa, avoidance of breastfeeding is not an option. Furthermore, in many African settings breastfeeding may normally continue until at least 12 months of age and often longer, with the introduction of other fluids and foods from a very early age. Thus, several other approaches have been or are being investigated with regard to reducing the exposure of breastfeeding infants to HIV, such as interventions to change breast-feeding practices, including early weaning and exclusive breastfeeding (Coutsoudis et al., 2001; Iliff et al., 2005; Thea et al., 2004; Becquet et al., 2005; Becquet and Leroy, 2005). Although the outcomes of such inter-ventions appear promising, the acceptability and feasibility of these interventions may provide barriers to their implementation.

Elective caesarean section (CS) before labour and before rupture of membranes was investigated as a potential intervention for preventing MTCT as a result of the epide-miological observations that vaginal delivery and long durations of ruptured membranes were associated with increased transmission risk (Moodley et al., 1994; European Collaborative Study, 1994; Shaffer et al., 1998; European Collaborative Study, 1999; Kind et al., 1998; Maguire et al., 1997). The effectiveness of elective CS in reducing MTCT risk compared with vaginal delivery (The European Mode of Delivery

Collaboration, 1999) resulted in a major change in the obstetric management of HIV-infected pregnant women in resource-rich settings. Another intervention aimed at reducing intra-partum risk of transmission is vaginal disinfection. Disinfection of the birth canal during labor with microbicides aims to reduce MTCT of HIV infection through limiting exposure of the infant to infective cervico-vaginal secretions. The theoretical advantages of such an intervention include its relatively low cost, which makes it suitable for use in resource-poor settings and its safety and ease of application. The antiseptic agents chlorhexidine and benzalkonium chloride both neutralize HIV and appear to be well tolerated (Burman et al., 1992; Wainberg et al., 1990); both have been investigated as potential interventions for PMTCT.

Other risk factors that have been targeted with specific interventions include maternal vitamin A deficiency (low serum retinol levels) (Semba et al., 1994; Greenberg et al., 1997; Nduati et al., 1995), addressed with maternal/neonatal vitamin A supplementation and chorioamnionitis or infection of the fetal membranes (Mofenson et al., 1999; Mwanyumba et al., 2002a), addressed with antibiotic prophylaxis.

The most effective strategy to prevent new pediatric HIV infections is to prevent their mothers from becoming infected in the first place. Primary prevention activities need to be appropriate for the setting in which they are to be applied, for example, in a setting where the epidemic is largely concentrated in risk groups such as injection drug users and sex workers, a focus is needed on prevention and harm reduction among these groups. However, in a setting with a generalized epidemic such as in sub-Saharan Africa, with heterosexual transmission the driving force behind the epidemic, a broader approach is needed, such as a national campaign like the "ABC" campaigns (Abstinence, Be faithful, Condoms) (Okware et al., 2005). A further important component of PMTCT is the prevention of unwanted pregnancies in HIV-infected women. For a woman with known HIV infection, access to effective contraception is required if she wishes to avoid pregnancy, which requires access to family planning services and integration between HIV services and reproductive health services in general.

RANDOMIZED CONTROLLED TRIALS OF PMTCT INTERVENTIONS

Antiretroviral prophylaxis

ZDV was investigated as a prophylactic regimen in pregnancy, intra-partum and post-partum for the infant in the AIDS Clinical Trials Group (ACTG) 076 trial, published in 1994 (Connor et al., 1994). Since this seminal trial, other antiretroviral prophylactic regimens have been investigated in clinical trials in various settings. Tables 1 and 2 summarize the results of these trials, in non-breastfeeding populations (mainly in developed countries, but also in Thailand where artificial feeding of infants born to HIV-infected women has been a feasible and successful strategy) and in breastfeeding or primarily breastfeeding populations, all in sub-Saharan Africa.

In 2005, the Ghent Group on HIV in Women and Children carried out an analysis on a pooled individual patient data set of mother-child pairs (around 3500) from clinical trials in African breastfeeding populations (DITRAME/ANRS049a, CDC-RETRO-CI, PETRA, HIVNET 012, SAINT and the Vitamin A trial) (Coutsoudis et al., 1999). The aim was to directly compare the 6 week peripartum efficacy of the different antiretroviral regimens, hitherto not directly comparable due to population differences, for example in maternal CD4 count. In adjusted analyses, compared with placebo the most efficacious regimen was ZDV+3TC (from 36 weeks gestation, intrapartum and for 7 days to the neonate), associated with a 77% reduced risk, versus a 51% reduction for ZDV+3TC

used intrapartum and postnatally only, 45% for short antenatal ZDV (from 36 weeks) and 40% for single dose NVP (sdNVP). The longer regimen of ZDV+3TC was the only regimen associated with a significantly decreased MTCT risk (by 61%) when sdNVP was taken as the baseline (Leroy et al., 2005). Results from the Thai trial – PHPT-2, in a non-breastfeeding population similarly provides evidence for the increased efficacy of using combinations of ARV drugs rather than monotherapy for PMTCT (Table 1) (Lallemant et al., 2004).

Nested studies within clinical trials have provided important information on the use of antiretroviral prophylaxis, including the findings regarding the use of sdNVP and the emergence of drug resistance. In the HIVNET 012 trial, 25% of women and 46% of the infected infants exposed to sdNVP had NVP resistance at 6-8 weeks post-partum (Eshlemann and et al., 2001); further sub-studies reported that 32% of women had NVP resistant mutations at 7 days and/or 6-8 weeks after delivery (Eshleman et al., 2004) and that infection with sub-type C virus was associated with a significantly higher resistance rate than sub-types A or D (Eshleman et al., 2005).

Timing of maternal and infant dosing of sdNVP was investigated in the HIVNET 012 trial, in which NVP was detected in the cord blood of 94% (244/259) of infants whose mothers reported taking NVP >1 hour before delivery and in 92% (12/13) of those whose mothers took the drug < 1 hour before delivery (Jackson et al., 2006). In the HIVNET 024 trial (on use of antibiotics to prevent chorioamnionitis-related MTCT - see later section), where use of sdNVP followed the HIVNET 012 protocol, no effect on MTCT by timing of either maternal or infant dose was apparent within "reasonable" proximity to delivery, i.e. within 48 hours and 72 hours of delivery for mothers and infants respectively (Chi et al., 2005).

Table 1 : Clinical trials of prophylactic ART for prevention of mother to child transmission: non-breastfeeding populations

Trial name Setting	Study design	Study drug(s)	Antenatal/ Intrapartum	Post-natal	Efficacy
PACTG 076/ ANRS 024 USA, France (Connor *et al.*, 1994)	Randomized, placebo-controlled trial	ZDV	Long (from 14-34 weeks) IP: intravenous	Infant: long (6 weeks)	VTR at 18 months: 8.3% in ZDV arm 25.5% in placebo arm (68% efficacy)
Bangkok CDC short-course ZDV trial Thailand (Shaffer *et al.*, 1999)	Randomized, placebo-controlled trial	ZDV	Short (from 36 weeks) IP: oral	None	VTR at 6 months: 9.4% in ZDV arm 18.9% in placebo arm (50.1% efficacy)
Thai Perinatal HIV Prevention Trial (PHPT-1) (Lallemant *et al.*, 2000)	Randomized trial, no placebo	ZDV	Long (from 28w) Short (from 36 w)	Infants: Long (for 6w) Short (for 3 days)	Short-Short arm was stopped. VTR at 6 months: 6.5% in long-long arm 4.7% in long-short arm 8.6% in the short-long arm
PACTG 316 trial (USA, Europe, Brazil, Bahamas) (Dorenbaum *et al.*, 2002)	Randomized, placebo-controlled trial	sdNVP in women already on ZDV or ZDV-containing HAART	Non-study ART antenatally . IP: sdNVP plus ZDV intravenously vs placebo	sdNVP within 72 hr of birth vs placebo plus non-study ART including ZDV	VTR 1.4% in sdNVP arm 1.6% in placebo arm
Thai PHPT-2 trial Thailand (Lallemant *et al.*, 2004)	Randomized trial	Antenatal ZDV boosted with sdNVP	Short ZDV (from 28 wks) IP: All ZDV plus Arm 1. sdNVP Arm 2. sdNVP Arm 3. placebo	All infants received 7 days ZDV plus: Arm 1. sdNVP Arm 2. placebo Arm 3. placebo	Enrollment in the placebo-placebo (i.e. ZDV only) arm was stopped at first interim analysis. VTR 1.9% for NVP-NVP arm and 2.8% in the NVP-placebo arm (not statistically significantly different)

A major challenge in many resource-poor settings where there may be very limited antenatal care coverage is the sufficiently early identification of HIV-infected pregnant women for the application of peripartum antiretroviral prophylaxis. Two trials have investigated the efficacy of post-exposure prophylaxis in infants born to women who did not receive any antenatal antiretroviral prophylaxis – the PEP trial in South Africa and the NVAZ trial in Malawi (Table 2).

Increasing information is available from trials investigating the use of antiretroviral therapy to prevent postnatal transmission. With regard to the use of monotherapy in breastfeeding infants, a postnatal transmission rate of 1% was reported among breastfeeding infants who were HIV negative at birth and given either NVP or 3TC for 6 months in the SIMBA trial (Table 1). Trials are currently ongoing with regard to the use of HAART to prevent postnatal transmission. The Kisumu trial is an ongoing open label phase II trial investigating safety, tolerability and efficacy of HAART (ZDV+3TC+NVP) from 34 weeks of pregnancy to 6 months post-partum in a breastfeeding population in Kenya. Women in the study are encouraged to breastfeed exclusively and wean rapidly at 6 months. Preliminary results suggest HAART is well tolerated by most pregnant or lactating women in the study (Thomas et al., 2005).

In the Mashi trial, HIV-infected mothers received ZDV antenatally from 34 weeks and were randomized to receive maternal and infant sdNVP or maternal and infant placebo, and also randomized to formula feed with 4 weeks ZDV, or breastfeed with 6 months of infant ZDV prophylaxis. Between March 2001 and October 2003, 1200 infected pregnant women were enrolled. The trial design was modified after publication of the PHTP-2 trial results(Lallemant et al., 2004): the infant sdNVP placebo arm was stopped mid-way through the trial, and there was a revised objective to assess whether maternal placebo + infant sdNVP was equivalent to sdNVP for mother and infant. In this revised phase, MTCT rates at 1 month were 4.3% and 3.7% in the NVP/NVP and the placebo/NVP arms respectively, showing no advantage of adding maternal SD NVP to infant SD NVP in the presence of maternal and infant ZDV prophylaxis (which contrasts with findings from DITRAME and PHPT-2 trials). HIV-free survival was 85.8% among the formula feeding arm and 84.4% in the breastfeeding/ ZDV prophylaxis arm at 18 months, a non significant difference (Shapiro et al., 2005).

Elective caesarean section

Results from the European mode of delivery randomized trial became available in early 1999 (The European Mode of Delivery Collaboration, 1999). The trial started in Italy in late 1993, extending to five other European countries in early 1995, with a total of 436 women randomized to either vaginal delivery or elective CS (i.e. before labor and before rupture of membranes). Vaginal delivery was found to be associated with a more than two-fold increased MTCT risk, independent of the use of prophylactic ART with zidovudine. The transmission rate was 1.8% in women allocated to elective CS versus 10.5% in those randomized to vaginal delivery, representing 80% efficacy.

Formula feeding

Evidence from a randomized clinical trial on the efficacy of formula feeding in PMTCT was not available until 2000, when Nduati and colleagues reported the results from their trial conducted in Kenya between 1992 and 1998 (Nduati et al., 2000). A total of 425 mother-child pairs (antiretroviral naïve) were enrolled, 212 were randomized to breast feeding and 213 to formula feeding. Compliance with the assigned mode of feeding was 96% in the breastfeeding arm and 70% in the formula arm. Median duration of breastfeeding was 17 months and

Table 2: Clinical trials of prophylactic antiretroviral therapy for prevention of mother to child HIV transmission: breastfeeding and breast- & formula-feeding populations

Trial name Setting	Details	Study drug(s)	Antenatal/ Intrapartum	Post-partum	Infant feeding	Efficacy
Ivory Coast CDC short-course ZDV trial Ivory Coast (Wiktor et al., 1999) (Leroy et al., 2002)	Randomized, placebo-controlled trial	ZDV	Short (from 36 weeks) IP: oral	None	BF	VTR at 3 months: 15.7% in intervention arm 24.9% in placebo (37% efficacy) VTR in pooled analysis with CDC trial at 24 months: 22.5% in intervention arm 30.2% in placebo (26% efficacy)
DITRAME / ANRS049a Trial Ivory Coast / Burkina Faso (Leroy et al., 2001)	Randomized, placebo-controlled trial	ZDV	Short (from 36 weeks) IP: oral	Mother: short (1 week)	BF	VTR at 6 months: 18.0% in intervention arm 27.5% in placebo (38% efficacy) VTR at 15 months: 21.5% in intervention arm 30.6% in placebo arm (30% efficacy) VTR in pooled analysis with CDC trial at 24 months: 22.5% in intervention arm 30.2% in placebo arm (26% efficacy)
PETRA trial South Africa, Uganda and Tanzania (The Petra study team, 2002)	Randomized, placebo-controlled trial	ZDV + 3TC	1. Short (from 36 w) + IP 2. IP only 3. As 2	1. Short (7 days) mother & infant 2. As 1 3. Placebo	BF	Placebo arm was stopped. VTR : 14.9% antenatal/intrapartum/ neonatal ZDV/3TC 18.1% intrapartum/neonatal ZDV/3TC only

Trial name Setting	Details	Study drug(s)	Antenatal/ Intrapartum	Post-partum	Infant feeding	Efficacy
HIVNET 012 trial Uganda (Guay et al., 1999; Jackson et al., 2003)	Randomized trial	NVP versus ZDV	No antenatal ART. IP: sdNVP versus oral ZDV	Infant: sdNVP within 72 hr of birth vs ZDV (7 days)	BF	Placebo arm was stopped. VTR at 18 months: 15.7% in NVP arm 25.8% in ZDV arm (41% efficacy)
SAINT trial South Africa (Moodley et al., 2003)	Randomized trial	NVP versus ZDV/3TC	No antenatal ART. Intrapartum: sdNVP 200mg versus ZDV plus 3TC	Mother & infant: sdNVP within 48 hrs of birth versus ZDV + 3TC (7 days)	BF & FF	VTR at 8 weeks: 12.3% in NVP arm 9.3% in ZDV/3TC arm (not statistically significant difference)
SIMBA trial Uganda, Randa (Vyankandondera et al., 2003)	Randomized trial	antenatal ZDV+ddI; NVP versus 3TC postnatally	Short ZDV+ddI (from 36 weeks)	Infant: sdNVP at birth, then NVP twice daily versus 3TC twice daily Mother: ZDV + ddI	BF	VTR at 6 months: 7.8% (VTR the same in the two arms, this was an equivalency trial). Postnatal transmission rate was 0.9% (6 weeks to 6 months).
NVAZ trial Malawi (Taha et al., 2004)	Randomized, open label trial.	PEP with sdNVP versus ZDV +sdNVP	None (trial evaluating PEP)	Infant: sdNVP immediately after birth versus sdNVP followed by ZDV twice daily for 7 days	BF	VRT at 6-8 weeks 20.9% for NVP only arm 15.3% for NVP+ZDV arm Excluding infants who were HIV positive at birth, the respective rates were 12.1% and 7.7% (36% efficacy)
PEP trial South Africa	Randomized, open-label trial	PEP with sdNVP versus 6 weeks ZDV	None (trial evaluating PEP)	Infant: sdNVP within 24 hours of birth versus	BF & FF	VTR at 12 weeks: 8% in NVP arm 13.1% in ZDV arm in infants not infected at birth.

transmission continued throughout the breastfeeding period (Richardson et al., 2003). The cumulative probability of MTCTrate at 24 months was 37% (95% CI: 29-44%) in the breastfeeding arm and 20% (95% CI :14-27%) in the formula-feeding arm. The estimated absolute rate of postnatal transmis-sion was 16% at 24 month follow-up. Mortality at 24 months was similar in the two arms, at 24% in the breastfeeding and 20% in the formula feeding arms (Nduati et al., 2000).

Vaginal disinfection

In the first trial to evaluate the effect of vaginal disinfection in PMTCT, conducted in Malawi in the mid 1990s, chlorhexidine was applied as a swab in the intervention group (Biggar et al., 1996). This intervention had no statistically significant effect on the MTCT rate, but in the sub-group of women with duration of rupture of membranes exceeding four hours use of chlorhexidine was associat-ed with a significantly reduced transmission risk (25% versus 39% in the non-intervention arm). This trial had several shortcomings including a lack of randomization (women were enrolled during blocks of time) and a high rate of loss of follow-up of infants before infection status could be determined.

Gaillard and colleagues conducted a randomized controlled trial in Kenya on 898 HIV-infected women in labour to determine the effectiveness of vaginal irrigation with 120 ml chlorhexidine (0.2% concentration at the beginning of the trial, rising to 0.4% during the last 11 months) compared with no intervention (Gaillard et al., 2001). There was no difference in infant HIV status at 6 and/or 14 weeks between arms. However, a trend towards decreased MTCT risk with the 0.4% concentration was apparent.

In a small placebo-controlled phase II trial in West Africa, Mandelbrot and colleagues investigated the safety and tolerability of benzalkonium chloride in vaginal disinfection

and neonatal washing (Mandelbrot et al., 2002). A total of 107 HIV-infected women were enrolled, and self-administered either benzalkonium chloride (1%) or placebo vaginal capsules from 36 weeks gestation. During labor, another capsule was administered and the infant was washed with either a solution of the disinfectant (1%) or a placebo within half an hour of delivery. On an intent-to-treat basis, the MTCT rate was similar between the two groups, at 23.5% in the intervention arm and 24.8% in the placebo arm. However, as a phase II trial, it was not powered to assess the efficacy of the intervention with regard to PMTCT.

Thus, there is currently no evidence of a protective effect of vaginal disinfection in PMTCT. Given the low cost of this intervention and its relative ease of use, there is a need for a large randomized controlled trial to address whether or not vaginal disinfection is of additional benefit in HIV-infected pregnant women receiving antiretro-viral prophylaxis (Wiysonge et al., 2005a).

Vitamin A supplementation

No clinical trial has provided results to support the use of vitamin A supplementation as a PMTCT intervention (Table 3). Indeed, the Tanzanian trial found that use of supplementation in pregnancy and intra-partum resulted in an increased risk of MTCT (Fawzi *et al.*, 2000). The Cochrane review of vitamin A supplementation, which as yet does not include the ZVITAMBO Study results, estimated the odds ratio comparing vitamin A supplementation with placebo to be 1.14 (95% CI: 0.93-1.38) (Wiysonge et al., 2005b); however, this review did report a significant increase in birth weight associated with supplementation.

The ZVITAMBO Study has been the largest study investigating the role of vitamin A supplementation to date, and is limited to its effect on postnatal transmission (Humphrey et al., 2006). Regarding mortality

Table 3 Trials investigating the efficacy of vitamin A supplementation in prevention of mother to child HIV transmission

Trial reference and setting	Study design	Intervention	Results
Durban, South Africa (Coutsoudis et al., 1999)	Randomized, placebo-controlled trial 728 women enrolled	Daily oral vitamin A (5000IU retinyl palmitate, 30mg beta-carotene) or placebo antenatally from third trimester; 200,000IU retinyl palmitate or placebo intrapartum	VTR rate at 3 months: 20.3% in intervention arm 22.3% in placebo arm. No significant effect of intervention
Dar es Salam, Tanzania (Fawzi et al., 2000)	Randomized, placebo-controlled trial 1078 women included	Daily oral vitamin A (5000 IU retinyl palmitate, 30mg beta-carotene), multivitamins plus vitamin A, multivitamins without vitamin A or placebo from 20 weeks gestation, continuing postnatally	Mother-child pairs in the vitamin A arm were at increased risk of MTCT (RR 1.28, 95% CI 1.09-1.76), whilst those in the multivitamin without vitamin A arm had a similar risk to those receiving placebo (RR 1.04 95% CI 0.82-1.32)
Blantyre, Malawi (Kumwenda et al., 2002)	Randomized, placebo-controlled trial 697 women enrolled	Daily oral vitamin A (3mg retinol equivalent) with daily iron and folate, versus iron and folate only from 18-28 weeks gestation to delivery	VTR at 6 weeks: 26.6% in the vitamin A arm 27.8% in the control arm 24 week rate: 27.7% in the vitamin A arm 32.8% in the control arm No significant effect of intervention.
ZVITAMBO Study Zimbabwe (Humphrey et al., 2006)	Randomized, placebo-controlled trial 14,110 mother-child pairs (4495 HIV-infected mothers)	Postnatal (within 96 hours of delivery) intervention: "Aa": maternal (400,000 IU) and infant (50,000 IU) vitamin A supplementation or "Ap": maternal supplementation and infant placebo or "Pa": maternal placebo and infant supplementation or "Pp": maternal and infant placebo	VTR at 6 weeks: Aa: 23.9%, Ap: 28.7%, Pa: 28.4%, Pp: 25.2% VTR among infants PCR negative at baseline at 24 months: Aa: 28.8%, Ap: 33.8%, Pa: 32.7%, Pp: 28.4% No significant effect of either maternal or neonatal supplementation on postnatal transmission.

of the children in the study, although no overall effect of vitamin A supplementation on mortality was apparent by age 2 years, the effect varied depending on the timing of infection of the infant. In infants presumed infected intrapartum, neonatal but not maternal supplementation was associated with a 28% reduction in mortality, but no effect was apparent on those infected in utero. However, among infants who were PCR negative at 6 weeks, supplementation to either mother or infant was associated with a doubling in the risk of death by age 2 years. The authors of the study concluded that although their results support the use of vitamin A supplementation in the care of HIV-infected children, their findings also suggest that caution is needed where programs of universal vitamin A supplementation for women and/or children are being considered, if there is a high background prevalence of HIV infection.

Antibiotics to prevent chorioamnionitis-associated MTCT

The main aim of the HPTN 024 trial was to try to reduce chorioamnionitis-associated MTCT with the use of antibiotics, with the secondary aim of reducing chorio-amnionitis-associated pre-term delivery (Goldenberg et al., 2006). The trial was conducted in Zambia, Malawi and Tanzania, with enrollment starting in 2001. However, the trial was stopped early in February 2003 with 2098 infected and 355 uninfected women (there was one uninfected woman enrolled per every five infected women) when interim analyses indicated a lack of effect of the intervention on chorioamnion-itis. This placebo-controlled trial involved enrollment at 20-24 weeks gestation, with women in the intervention group receiving two antibiotic courses, one prenatal (at enrollment, with metronidazole and erythro-mycin for 7 days) and one perinatal (with metronidazole and ampicillin) from onset of labor/premature rupture of

membranes). Although there was a reduced rate of bacterial vaginosis and trichomoniasis in the intervention arm four weeks after the initial course of antibiotics, there was no difference in the rate of histologic chorioamnionitis between arms.

EVIDENCE FROM LONGITUDINAL STUDIES ON PREVENTION OF MOTHER TO CHILD TRASMISSION INTERVENTIONS

Although randomized controlled trials are the gold standard with regard to evaluating the effectiveness of interven-tions, for some aspects of PMTCT trials are not possible or feasible, as a result of ethical concerns or where unfeasibly large numbers would be required to achieve adequate statistical power in populations of infected women receiving HAART, where the risk of transmission may be as low as 1-2%. Longitudinal studies have contributed substantially to our understanding of not only the epidemiology of MTCT, but also of the effectiveness of interventions in a non-trial setting.

Prophylactic antiretrovirals

An open-label intervention cohort study in Côte d'Ivoire, the ANRS 1201/1202 DITRAME Plus study, has reported one of the lowest MTCT rates to date from sub-Saharan Africa (ANRS 1201/1202 Ditrame-plus Study Group, 2005). In the study, the 6 week efficacy of two regimens was assessed: the first, antenatal ZDV from 36 weeks plus sdNVP for mother and infant, with 7 days of neonatal ZDV prophylaxis had a 6 week MTCT probability of 6.5% (95% CI: 3.9-9.1%) and the second, antenatal ZDV+3TC from 32 weeks, ZDV+3TC intrapartum boosted with sdNVP, and sdNVP and 7 days ZDV for the infant, had a 6 week probability of 4.7% (95% CI: 2.4-7.0%). These regimens were not significantly different from each other with regard to effectiveness but were significantly more effective than short-course

ZDV monotherapy in the same setting (ANRS 1201/1202 Ditrame-plus Study Group, 2005) (Table 1). In the Thai ZDV&3TC open label study, which was carried out in a non-breastfeeding population, antenatal ZDV+3TC was given from 34 weeks of pregnancy, with 4 weeks of neonatal ZDV, there was an 18 month MTCT rate of 2.8% (Chaisilwattana et al., 2002). Both studies reported good tolerance to the combination of ZDV and 3TC.

Longitudinal follow-up of the sub-group of women with low CD4 counts who had participated in the Thai PHPT-2 trial (Table 1) and postnatally received NNRTI-based regimens was carried out to investigate whether there were clinically significant consequences of exposure to sdNVP. Prevalence of NNRTI resistance mutations among those with NVP exposure was estimated to be 18%. Results showed that despite a worse virological response than those non-exposed, a clinically significant proportion of exposed women had undetectable viral loads after 6 months of therapy, including those with resistance mutations. Women with a greater delay (> 6 months) between delivery and initiation of the NNRTI-based regimens had a better virological response to treatment than those who started ART earlier (Jourdain et al., 2004).

The increasing use of HAART in pregnancy in developed country settings has resulted in a growing proportion of women achieving undetectable viral loads by the time of delivery, which has had a substantial impact on vertical transmission. MTCT rates are currently at their lowest ever levels, at around 1-2%, as evidenced by the results from cohort studies (Cooper et al., 2002; European Collaborative Study, 2006; Galli et al., 2005; Warszawski et al., 2005). In the PACTG 316 trial (Table 1) in which nearly half of the enrolled women received antenatal HAART, the MTCT rates in both arms were

less than 2% (Dorenbaum et al., 2002). In a recent analysis of the European Collaborative Study, use of antenatal HAART was associated with a 93% decreased risk of MTCT compared with no antenatal ART and a 75% decreased risk compared to mono- or dual therapy, independent of maternal CD4 count, mode of delivery and prematurity (European Collaborative Study, 2006).

With regard to the use of HAART in the postnatal period to prevent breastfeeding transmission, some recent findings have been reported from a cohort study in Botswana. Shapiro and colleagues compared breast milk HIV RNA and DNA viral loads between lactating women receiving HAART as a result of having CD4 counts <200 cells/ mm^3 or AIDS (for a minimum of 2 months before breast milk sampling) and those who were not receiving HAART. Receipt of HAART was strongly associated with suppression of breast milk HIV RNA (88% of those on HAART versus 36% without had undetectable levels), but had no effect on cell-associated viral load (HIV DNA levels) (Shapiro et al., 2005). Further research is needed, both on the pharmacokinetics of antiretroviral drugs in breast milk and the efficacy of HAART in preventing postnatal transmission (Bulterys et al., 2005).

Mode of delivery

There is a consistent body of evidence from observational studies and from a large international meta-analysis confirming the findings of the mode of delivery trial – that caesarean section approximately halves the risk of MTCT, independent of antiretroviral prophylaxis (The International Perinatal HIV group, 1999; Ioannidis et al., 2001; European Collaborative Study, 1996; Mandelbrot et al., 1996). However, the added benefit of elective CS as an intervention among women on successful HAART (i.e. with undetectable or very low viral loads) is uncertain. In the European Collaborative Study, a two-thirds reduction in MTCT risk associated with elective CS, independent of maternal viral load and CD4 count was found in the HAART era; however, although a significant effect of elective CS in reducing MTCT among women with undetectable viral loads at delivery was seen, the analysis did not adjust for HAART use (European Collaborative Study, 2005). A cohort collaboration and meta-analysis of observational data among women with undetectable viral loads and receiving antenatal HAART are required to answer the question of the added benefit of elective caesarean section.

Breastfeeding

A secondary objective of the ZVITAMBO trial of vitamin A supplementation was to investigate the role of infant feeding practices on postnatal transmission of HIV, with information collected on the feeding practices of mother-child pairs enrolled in the trial. Results showed that early (before 3 months of age) mixed feeding was associated with an increased risk of postnatal transmission (in infants with a negative HIV test at 6 weeks of age) compared with exclusive breastfeeding, declining from a four-fold increased risk at 6 months, to a two and a half fold-increased risk by 18 months (Iliff et al., 2005). The study also found that more than two-thirds of all breastfeeding transmission occurred after 6 months, consistent with results from other studies (Leroy et al., 2003; Coutsoudis et al., 2001;Fawzi et al., 2002). These findings not only support the potential of promoting exclusive breastfeeding as a PMTCT intervention in breastfeeding populations, but also early weaning. However, successful promotion of exclusive breastfeeding is likely to be a challenge, and requires adequate counseling and ongoing support for mothers (Morrow et al., 1999; Coutsoudis et al., 2002). In the DITRAME Plus (ANRS 1201/1202) Study in Côte d'Ivoire, the acceptability of exclusive breastfeeding was low, with only 10% probability of exclusive breastfeeding at 3 months; however, early cessation of breast-feeding by 6 months of age was more acceptable, with 63% of women completely stopping breastfeeding by this time (Becquet et al., 2005).

WHAT IS THE OPTIMUM APPROACH TO PREVENT MOTHER TO CHILD TRANSMISSION?

Developed country settings

Widespread use of HAART, often started before or early in pregnancy, has resulted in steep declines in the number of infants with HIV infection in developed country settings. For example, fewer than 200 children were estimated to have become newly infected with HIV in 2005 in Western and Central Europe (UNAIDS, 2006). As fewer than one or two in a hundred children born to HIV-infected women with access to a range of effective PMTCT interventions will become HIV infected in developed country settings, a public health goal of elimination of vertically-acquired HIV infection is now on the agenda (Mofenson, 1999). However, some vertical infections do still occur which could have been prevented, largely due to late identification of HIV infection in the mother and limited use of prophylaxis (European Collaborative Study, 2005; Mayaux et al., 2003; Peters et al., 2003), highlighting the need for effective screening programs and improved access to antenatal care for certain groups. In most developed country settings there is now a policy for universal antenatal HIV testing, in many countries with an opt-out approach whereby pregnant women are informed that they will be routinely tested for HIV unless they specifically decline. The debate regarding the effectiveness of elective CS among women on HAART is ongoing, reflected by policies and practices for mode of delivery varying within and between countries. Concerns exist that the potential side effects of CS delivery (i.e. post-partum complications) (Marcollet et al., 2002; Read et al., 2001; Read & Newell 2005) may outweigh the benefits of reduced MTCT risk exist, but it should be remembered that HIV-infected women are generally at increased risk of post-partum complications compared to uninfected women, regardless of mode of delivery (European HIV in Obstetrics Group, 2004), and that the side-effects are usually manageable in this setting.

With the theoretical elimination of vertically-acquired pediatric HIV infection, there has been a shift in focus towards the 99 children per hundred or so who are uninfected, yet exposed to antiretroviral drugs in utero and early neonatal life. There are concerns that such exposure may have adverse effects in the medium to long-term, with regard to immunological, hematological and mitochondrial functioning and potential genotoxicity, which require further long-term monitoring (European Collaborative Study, 2004; Le Chenadec et al., 2003; Tardieu et al., 2003; Blanche et al., 1999; Poirier et al., 2003; Oleske, 2003; Poirier et al., 2004). Nevertheless, the tremendous benefits of antiretroviral prophylaxis far outweigh the potential costs.

Less developed country settings

The vast majority of HIV-infected pregnant women live in resource-poor settings, where only 9% of pregnant women are covered by PMTCT programs and thus have access to antiretroviral prophylaxis (UNAIDS, 2006). Among this 9% of women accessing PMTCT, sdNVP is the most widely used antiretroviral prophylaxis - a reflection of its relative ease of use, low cost and efficacy. However, there are concerns regarding the emergence of drug resistance to NVP and the potentially detrimental effect this may have on the mother's future therapeutic management and health (Jourdain et al., 2004; McIntyre, 2006). However, there

is accumulating evidence to show that adding postnatal ZDV+3TC to peri-partum sdNVP for up to 1 week significantly reduces prevalence of NVP resistance (McIntyre et al., 2004;Chaix et al., 2005). The lowest MTCT rates ever have recently been reported in resource-poor settings with the use of ZDV+3TC+ sdNVP or ZDV+sdNVP (Tables 1 and 2) (ANRS 1201/1202 Ditrame-plus Study Group, 2005), but the applicability of these rates in a non-trial or research setting remains untested. The development of effective programs applying interventions identified as efficacious in clinical trials or longitudinal research studies on a population level is a challenge in many developing country settings, even in those where there is a high uptake of HIV testing (Temmerman et al., 2003;Stringer et al., 2003). Given the efficacy of combination regimens and their associated lower rates of drug resistance, PMTCT programs should consider introducing these more complex regimens where possible, as reflected in current WHO recommendations (see Resources section). However, the priority regarding prevention of new HIV infections in infants must be to increase coverage of PMTCT programs in settings where most HIV-infected women live, to include as many of the 91% of HIV infected women who currently have no access to antiretroviral prophylaxis as possible.

THE NEED FOR FURTHER RESEARCH

A key concern requiring additional research relates to the issue of infant feeding by HIV-infected women, most of whom live in settings where formula feeding is not an option (Rollins et al., 2004). This is highlighted by the fact that even with complete coverage of an effective peripartum antiretroviral prophylactic intervention, an estimated 300,000 children will acquire infection through breastfeeding every year. Unsurprisingly, new research initiatives investigating use of antiretroviral prophylaxis to prevent MTCT are now concentrating on the postnatal period with prophylaxis either to mothers or to their breastfeeding infants. There are many uncertainties with regard to the safety, feasibility and efficacy of HAART use to prevent postnatal transmission, which require investigation (Gaillard et al., 2004). The Kesho Bora clinical trial, ongoing in several African countries, should provide important information in this respect. In addition, the potential for adverse effects in uninfected infants exposed to antiretroviral drugs in breast milk over a relatively long periods and during an important time with regard to growth and development needs careful assessment (Bulterys et al., 2005). Another important issue requiring further research is the consequence of the emergence of viral resistance after sdNVP exposure on the future response to HAART in infected women and infants, particularly in the sub-Saharan African setting. Important information will be provided by the OCTANE (Optimal Combination Therapy After Nevirapine Exposure) clinical trial, which recently started in five African countries to compare effectiveness of protease-inhibitor-containing or NVP-containing HAART among women with and without prior exposure to sdNVP (www.clinicaltrials.gov/ct).

CONCLUSIONS

Scaling-up of PMTCT activities is urgently needed within the context of expanding access to antiretrovirals overall in resource-poor settings, to include improved access to antenatal care and voluntary counseling and testing. It is apparent that services to prevent HIV infections in infants have not been scaled up as rapidly as antiretroviral treatment programs (UNAIDS, 2006) as highlighted by the fewer than 10% of infected women worldwide who are estimated to benefit from PMTCT interventions currently. We are in the position of knowing what interventions are required to reduce MTCT rates to below 1-2% and the challenge now is to translate the evidence into practice, particularly in settings where most HIV-infected women live.

RESOURCES
World Health Organization resources:
 www.who.int

For monthly surveys of PMTCT publications and abstracts:
www.who.int/reproductive-health/rtis/mtct/monthly-publications/listing_mtct-reports.html
Scaling-up antiretroviral therapy in resource-limited settings: treatment guidelines for a public health approach. WHO: Geneva, 2004.
HIV transmission through breastfeeding. A review of available evidence. WHO: Geneva, 2004.

For "Antiretroviral drugs for treating pregnant women and preventing HIV infection in infants. Guidelines on care, treatment and support for women living with HIV/AIDS and their children in resource-constrained settings."
http://www.who.int/reproductive-health/rtis/docs/arvdrugsguidelines.pdf

World Health Organization: 3 by 5 initiative: www.who.int/3by5/about/en

Websites
Guidelines
www.aidsinfo.nih.gov/guidelines

For an exhaustive and frequently up-dated resource on safety of antiretrovirals in pregnancy:
PUBLIC HEALTH SERVICE TASK FORCE: Safety and toxicity of individual antiretroviral agents in pregnancy. *Supplement to PHSTF Recommendations for*

use of antiretroviral drugs in pregnant HIV-1 infected women for maternal health and interventions to reduce perinatal HIV-1 transmission in the United States (2004). http:\\aidsinfo.nih.gov

For general information and research updates try:
www.womenchildrenHIV.org

The Antiretroviral Pregnancy Registry (voluntary reports from clinicians of exposures to antiretroviral drugs in pregnancy, and pregnancy outcomes) www.apregistry.com

REFERENCES

ANRS 1201/1202 Ditrame-plus Study Group (2005) Field efficacy of zidovudine, lamivudine and single dose nevirapine to prevent peripartum HIV transmission. AIDS 19: 309-318.

Becquet R, Ekouevi DK, Viho I, Sakarovitch C, Toure H, Castetbon K, Coulibaly N, Timite-Konan M, Bequet L, Dabis F, Leroy V. (2005) Accept-ability of exclusive breast-feeding with early cessation to prevent HIV transmis-sion through breast milk, ANRS 1201/ 1202 Ditrame Plus, Abidjan, Cote d'Ivoire. J Acquir Immune Defic Syndr 40: 600-608.

Becquet R, Leroy V. (2005) HIV and infant feeding: a complex issue in resource-limited settings. AIDS 19:1717-1718.

Bertolli J, St Louis ME, Simonds RJ, Nieburg PI, Kamenga MC, Brown C, Tarande M, Quinn TC, Ou CY. (1996) Estimating the timing of mother-to-child transmission of human immunodeficien-cy virus in a breastfeeding population in Kinshasa, Zaire. J Infectious Dis 174: 722-726.

Biggar RJ, Miotti PG, Taha TE, Mtimavalye LAR, Justesen A, Yellin F, Liomba GN, Miley W, Waters D, Chiphangwi JD, Goedert JJ. (1996) Perinatal intervention trial in Africa: effect of a birth canal cleansing intervention to prevent HIV transmission. Lancet 347: 1647-1650.

Blanche S, Tardieu M, Rustin P, Stama A, Firtion G, Ciraru-Vigneron N, Lacroix C, Rouzioux C, Mandelbrot L, Desguerre I, Rotig A, Mayaux MJ, Delfraissy JF. (1999) Persistent mito-chondrial dysfunction and perinatal exposure to antiretroviral nucleoside analogues. Lancet 354: 1084-1089.

Breastfeeding and HIV International Transmission Study (BHITS). (2004) Late postnatal transmission of HIV-1 through breastfeeding: an individual patient data meta-analysis. J Infectious Dis 204: 2154-2166.

Bulterys M, Weidle PJ, Abrams EJ, Fowler MG. (2005) Combination antiretroviral therapy in african nursing mothers and drug exposure in their infants: new pharmacokinetic and virologic findings. J Infectious Diseases 192: 709-712.

Burman LG, Christensen P, Christensen K, Fryklund B, Helgesson AM, Svenning-sen MW, Tullus K, Swedish Chlorhexi-dine Study Group. (1992) Prevention of excess neonatal morbidity associated with group B streptococci by vaginal chlorhexidine disinfection during labour. Lancet 340: 65-69.

Chaisilwattana P, Chokephaibulkit K, Chalermchokcharoenkit A, Vanprapar N, Sirimai K, Chearskul S, Sutthent R, Opartkiattikul N. (2002) Short-course therapy with zidovudine plus lamivudine for prevention of mother-to-child trans-mission of human immunodeficiency virus type 1 in Thailand. Clin Infectious Dis 35: 1405-1413.

Chaix ML, Dabis F, Ekouevi DK, Rouet F, Tonwe-Gold B, Viho I, Bequet L, Peytavin G, Toure H, Menan H, Leroy V, Rouzioux C. (2005) Addition of 3 days of ZDV+3TC postpartum to short course ZDV+3TC and single dose nevirapine provides low rate of NVP resistance mutations and high efficacy in preventing peripartum HIV-1 transmis-sion: ANRS DITRAME Plus, Abidjan, Cote d'Ivoire. 12th Conference on Retroviruses and Opportunistic Infections, 22-25 February 2005, Boston, USA. Abstract 72LB.

Chi BH, Wang L, Read JS, Sherrif M, Fiscus SA, Brown ER, Taha TE, Valentine M, Goldenberg RL. (2005) Timing of maternal and neonatal dosing of nevirapine and the risk of mother-to-child transmission of HIV-1: HIVNET 024. AIDS 9: 1857-1864.

Chuachoowowng R, Shaffer N, Siriwasin W, Chaisilwattana P, Young NL, Mock PA, Chearskul S, Waranawat N, Chaowana-chan T, Karon JM, Simonds RJ, Mastro TD, for the Bangkok Collaborative Perinatal HIV Transmission Study Group. (2000) Short-course antenatal zidovudine reduces both cervicovaginal human immunodeficiency virus type 1 RNA levels and risk of perinatal transmission. J Infectious Dis 181: 99-106.

Connor EM, Sperling RS, Gelber RD, Kiselev P, Scott GB, O'Sullivan MJ, Van Dyke R, Bey M, Shearer WT, Jacobson RL, Jimenez E, O'Neill E, Bazin B, Delfraissy JF, Culnane M, Coombs RW, Elkins MM, Moye JJ, Stratton P, Balsey J. (1994) Reduction of maternal-infant transmission of human immunodeficiency virus type 1 with zidovudine treatment. New Engl J Medicine 331: 1173-1180.

Cooper ER, Charurat M, Mofenson L M, Hanson IC, Pitt J, Diaz C, Hayani K, Handelsman E, Smeriglio V, Hoff R, Blattner WA. (2002) Combination antiretroviral strategies for the treatment of pregnant HIV-1-infected women and prevention of perinatal HIV-1 transmission. J Acquir Immune Defic Syndr 29: 484-494.

Coutsoudis A, Goga AE, Rollins N, Coovadia HM. (2002) Free formula milk for infants of HIV-infected women: blessing or curse? Health Policy Plan. 17: 154-160.

Coutsoudis A, Pillay K, Kuhn L, Spooner E, Tsai WY, Coovadia HM, the South African Vitamin A, Study Group. (2001) Methods of feeding and transmission of HIV-1 from mothers to children by 15 months of age: prospective cohort study from Durban, South Africa. AIDS 15: 379-387.

Coutsoudis A, Pillay K, Spooner E, Kuhn L, Coovadia HM, For the South African Vitamin A Study Group. (1999) Randomized trial testing the effect of vitamin A supplementation on pregnan-cy outcomes and early mother-to-child HIV-1 transmission in Durban, South Africa. AIDS 13: 1517-1524.

de Cock KM, Fowler MG, Mercier E, de Vincenzi I, Saba J, Hoff E, Alnwick DJ, Rogers MF, Shaffer N. (2000) Prevention of Mother-to-Child HIV Transmission in Resource-Poor Countries - Translating Research into Policy and Practice. JAMA 283: 1175-1182.

Dorenbaum A, Cunningham CK, Gelber RD, Culnane M, Mofenson LM, Britto P, Rekacewicz C, Newell ML, Delfraissy JF, Cunningham-Schrader B, Mirochnick M, Sullivan JL, for the International PACTG316 Team. (2002) Two-dose intrapartum/newborn nevira-pine and standard antiretroviral therapy to reduce perinatal HIV transmission. A randomized trial. JAMA 288: 189-198.

Eshleman SH, Guay LA, Mwatha A, Cunningham SP, Brown ER, Musoke P, Mmiro F, Jackson JB. (2004) Compari-son of nevirapine (NVP) resistance in Ugandan women 7 days vs. 6-8 weeks after single-dose nvp prophylaxis: HIVNET 012. AIDS Res Hum Retroviruses 20: 595-599.

Eshleman SH, Hoover D, Chen S, Hudelson S, Guay L, Mwatha A, Brown E, Mmiro F, Musoke P, Jackson J, Kumwenda N,

Taha T. (2005) Comparison of nevira-pine resistance in women with subtype C compared with subtypes A and D after single dose NVP. 12th Conference on Retroviruses and Opportunistic Infections, 22-25 February 2005, Boston, USA. Abstract 799.

Eshlemann SH, et al. (2001) Selection and fading of resistance mutations in women and infants receiving nevirapine to prevent HIV-1 vertical transmission (HIVNET012). AIDS 15: 1951-1957.

European Collaborative Study. (1994) Caesarean section and risk of vertical transmission of HIV-1 infection. Lancet 343: 1464-1467.

European Collaborative Study. (1996) Vertical transmission of HIV-1: maternal immune status and obstetric factors. AIDS 10: 1675-1681.

European Collaborative Study (1999) Maternal viral load and vertical transmission of HIV-1: an important factor but not the only one. AIDS 13: 1377-1385.

European Collaborative Study. (2003) Are girls more at risk of intrauterine-acquired HIV infection than boys? AIDS 18: 344-347.

European Collaborative Study. (2004) Levels and patterns of neutrophil cell counts over the first 8 years of life in children of HIV-1 infected mothers. AIDS 18: 2009-2017.

European Collaborative Study. (2006) The mother-to-child HIV transmission epidemic in Europe: evolving in the East and established in the West. AIDS in press.

European Collaborative Study. (2005) Mother-to-child transmission of HIV Infection in the era of highly active antiretroviral therapy. Clin Infectious Dis 40: 458-465.

European HIV in Obstetrics Group. (2004) Higher rates of post-partum complications in HIV infected than in uninfected women irrespective of mode of delivery. AIDS 18: 933-938.

Fawzi WW, Msamanga GI, Hunter DJ, Renjifo B, Antelman G, Bang H, Manji K, Kapiga S, Mwakagile D, Essex M, Spiegelman D. (2002) Randomized trial of vitamin supplements in relation to transmission of HV-1 through breast-feeding and early child mortality. AIDS 16: 1935-1944.

Fawzi WW, Msamanga GI, Hunter DJ, Urassa E, Renjifo B, Mwakagile D, Hertzmark E, Coley J, Garland SM, Kapiga S, Antelman G, Essex M, Spiegelman D. (2000) Randomized trial of vitamin supplements in relation to vertical transmission of HIV-1 in Tanzania. J Acquir Immune Defic Syndr 23: 246-254.

Fawzi WW, Msamanga GI, Renjifo B, Spiegelman D, Urassa E, Hashemi L, Antelman G, Essex M, Hunter DJ. (2001) Predictors of intrauterine and intrapartum transmission of HIV-1 among Tanzanian women. AIDS 15: 1157-1165.

Gaillard P, Fowler MG, Dabis F, Coovadia HM, Van Der Horst CM, van Rompay K, Ruff AJ, Taha TE, Thomas T, de Vincenzi I, Newell ML, Ghent International Working Group on Mother-to-Child Transmission of HIV. (2004) Use of antiretroviral drugs to prevent HIV-1 transmission through breastfeeding: from animal studies to randomized clinical trials. J Acquir Immune Defic Syndr 35: 178-187.

Gaillard P, Mwanyumba FM, Verhofstede C, Claeys P, Chohan V, Goetghebeur E, Mandaliya K, Nydinya-Achola J, Temmerman M. (2001) Vaginal lavage with chlorhexidine during labour to reduce mother-to-child HIV transmission: clinical trial in Mombasa, Kenya. AIDS 15: 389-396.

Galli L, Puliti D, Chiappini E, Gabiano C, Tovo PA, Pezzotti P, de MM. (2005)

Lower mother-to-child HIV-1 transmission in boys is independent of type of delivery and antiretroviral prophylaxis: the Italian Register for HIV Infection in Children. J.Acquir.Immune.Defic.Syndr. 40: 479-485.

Garcia PM, Kalish LA, Pitt J, Minkoff HL, Quinn TC, Burchett SK, Kornegay J, Jackson JB, Moye JJ, Hanson C, Zorrilla C, Lew JF, Women and Infants Transmission Study. (1999) Maternal levels of plasma human immunodeficiency virus type 1 RNA and the risk of perinatal transmission. New Engl J Med 341: 394-402.

Goldenberg RL, Mwatha A, Read JS, iyi-Jones S, Sinkala M, Msmanga G, Martinson F, Hoffman I, Fawzi W, Valentine M, Emel L, Brown E, Mudenda V, Taha TE. (2006) The HPTN 024 Study: the efficacy of antibiotics to prevent chorioamnionitis and preterm birth. Am J Obstetrics Gynecol 194: 650-661.

Greenberg BL, Semba RD, Vink PE, Farley JJ, Sivapalsingam M, Steketee R, Thea DM, Schoenbaum EE. (1997) Vitamin A deficiency and maternal-infant transmission of HIV in two metroplitan areas in the United States. AIDS 11: 325-332.

Guay LA, Musoke P, Fleming TR, Bagenda D, Allen M, Nakabiito C, Sherman J, Bakak P, Ducar C, Deseywe, M, Emel L, Mirochnick M, Fowler, MG, Mofenson LM, Miotti PG, Dransfield K, Bray D, Mmiro F, Jackson JB. (1999) Intrapartum and neonatal single-dose nevirapine compared with zidovudine for prevention of mother-to-child trans-mission of HIV-1 in Kampala, Uganda: HIVNET 012 randomized trial. Lancet 354: 795-802.

Hira SK, Mangrola UG, Mwale C, Chintu C, Tembo G, Brady WE, Perine PL. (1990) Apparent vertical trans-mission of human immunodeficiency virus type 1 by breast-feeding in Zambia. J Pediatrics 117: 421-424.

Humphrey JH, Iliff PJ, Marinda E T, Mutasa K, Moulton LH, Chidawanyika H, Ward BJ, Nathoo KJ, Malaba LC, Zijenah LS, Zvandasara P, Ntozini R, Mzengeza F, Mahomva AI, Ruff AJ, Mbizvo MT, Zunguza CD. (2006) Effects of a single large dose of vitamin A, given during the postpartum period to HIV-positive women and their infants, on child HIV infection, HIV-free survival, and mortality. J Infectious Diseases 193: 860-871.

Iliff PJ, Piwoz EG, Tavengwa N V, Zunguza CD, Marinda ET, Nathoo KJ, Moulton LH, Ward BJ, Humphrey JH. (2005) Early exclusive breastfeeding reduces the risk of postnatal HIV-1 transmission and increases HIV-free survival. AIDS 19: 699-708.

Ioannidis JPA, Abrams EJ, Bulterys M, Goedert JJ, Gray L, Korber BT, Mayaux MJ, Mofenson LM, Newell ML, Shapiro DE, Teglas JP, Wilfert C. (2001) Perinatal Transsision of Human Immunodeficiency Virus Type 1 by Pregnant Women with RNA Virus Loads<1000 Copies/mL. J Infectious Dis 183: 539-545.

Jackson JB, Musoke P, Fleming T R, Guay LA, Bagenda D, Allen M, Nakabiito C, Sherman J, Bakaki P, Owor M, Ducar C, Deseywe M, Mwatha A, Emel L, Duefield C, Mirochnick M, Fowler JMG, Mofenson LM, Miotti PG, Gigliotti M. (2003) Intrapartum and neonatal single-dose nevirapine compared with zidovudine for prevention of mother to child transmission of HIV-1 in Kampala, Uganda: 18-month follow-up of the HIVNET 012 randomized trial. The Lancet 362: 859-867.

Jackson, J. B., Parsons, T., Musoke, P., Nakabiito, C., Donnell, D., Fleming, T., Mirochnick, M., Mofenson, L., Fowler, M. G., Mmiro, F., Guay, L. (2006) Association of cord blood nevirapine concentration with reported timing of dose and HIV-1 transmission. AIDS 20: 217-222.

John GC, Nduati RW, Mbori-Ngacha D, Richardson BA, Panteleef D, Mwahtha A, et al. (2001) Correlates of mother-to-child human immunodeficiency virus type 1 (HIV-1) transmission: association with maternal plasma HIV-1RNA load, genital HIV-1 DNA shedding and breast infections. In pp. 206-212.

John-Stewart GC, Mbori-Ngacha D, Ekpini ER, Janoff EN, Nkenganson J, Read JS, Van de Perre P, Newell ML, for the Ghent IAS Working Group on HIV in Women and Children. (2004) Breast-feeding and transmission of HIV-1. J Acquir Immune Defic Syndr 35: 196-202.

John-Stewart GC, Nduati RW, Rousseau CM, Mbori-Ngacha DA, Richardson BA, Rainwater S, Panteleeff DD, Overbaugh J. (2005) Subtype C Is associated with increased vaginal shed-ding of HIV-1. J Infectious Dis 192: 492-496.

Jourdain G, Ngo-Giang Huong N, Le Coeur S, Bowonwatanuwong C, Kantipong P, Leechanachai P, Ariyadej S, Leenasirimakul P, Hammer SM, Lallemant M, Perinatal HIV Prevention Trial Group. (2004) Intrapartum expo-sure to Nevirapine and subsequent maternal responses to Nevirapine-based antiretroviral therapy. New Engl J Med 351: 229-240.

Kind C, Rudin C, Siegrist CA, Wyler CA, Biedermann K, Lauper U, Irion O, Nadal D, Schupbach J, Swiss Neonatal HIV Study Group. (1998) Prevention of vertical HIV transmission: additive protective effect of elective Cesarean section and zidovudine prophylaxis. AIDS 12: 205-210.

Kuhn L, Steketee RW, Weedon J, Abrams EJ, Lambert G, Bamji M, Schoenbaum EE, Farley JJ, Nesheim SR, Palumbo PE, Simonds RJ, Thea DM, Perinatal AIDS Collaborative Transmission Study (1999) Distinct Risk Factors for Intra-uterine and Intrapartum Human Im-munodeficiency Virus Transmission and Consequences for Disease Progression in Infected Children. J Infectious Dis 179: 52-58.

Kumar RM, Uduman SA, Khurranna AK. (1995) A prospective study of mother-to-infant HIV transmission in tribal women from India. J Acquir Immune Defic Syndr 9: 238-242.

Kumwenda N, Miotti PG, Taha TE, Broadhead R, Biggar RJ, Jackson JB, Melikian G, Semba RD. (2002) Ante-natal vitamin A supplementation increases birth weight and decreases anemia among infants born to human immunodeficiency virus-infected wo-men in Malawi. Clin Infectious Dis 35: 618-624.

Kwiek J, Mwapasa V, Milner DA, Alker AP, Miller WC, Tadesse E, Molyneux ME, Rogerson SJ, Meshnick SR. (2006) Maternal-fetal microtransfusions and HIV-1 mother-to-child transmission in Malawi. PLoS Medicine 3: e10.

Lallemant M, Jourdain G, Le Coeur S, Kim S, Koetsawang S, Comeau AM, Phoolcharoen W, Essex M, McIntosh K, Vithayasai V. (2000) A trial of short-ened zidovudine regimens to prevent mother-to-child transmission of human immunodeficiency virus type 1. Peri-natal HIV Prevention Trial (Thailand) Investigators. N Engl J Med 343: 982-991.

Lallemant M, Jourdain G, Le Coeur S, Mary JY, Ngo-Giang Huong N, Pharm D, Koetsawang S, Kanshana S, McIntosh K, Thaineua V. (2004) Single-dose perinatal nevirapine plus standard zidou-vudine to prevent Mother-to-Child transmission of HIV-1 in Thailand. N Engl J Med 351: 217-228.

Le Chenadec J, Mayaux MJ, Guihenneuc-Jouyaux C, Blanche S. (2003) Perinatal antiretroviral treatment and hematopoiesis in HIV - uninfected infants. AIDS 17: 2053-2061.

Leroy V, Karon JM, Alioum A, Ekpini ER, Meda N, Greenberg AE, Msellati P, Hudgens M, Dabis F, Wiktor SZ. (2002) 24-month efficacy of a maternal short-course zidovudine regimen to prevent mother-to-child transmission of HIV-1 in West Africa. AIDS 16: 631-641.

Leroy V, Karon JM, Alioum A, Ekpini ER, Van de Perre P, Greenberg AE, Msellati P, Hudgens M, Dabis F, Wiktor SZ, for the West Africa PMTCT Study Group (2003) Postnatal transmission of HIV-1 after a maternal short-course zidovudine peripartum regimen in West Africa: a pooled analysis of two randomized clinical trials. AIDS 17: 1493-1501.

Leroy V, Montcho C, Manigart O, Van de Perre P, Dabis F, Msellati P, Meda N, Bruno You Simonon A, Rouzioux C, the Ditrame Study Group, A. 0. c. t. (2001) Maternal plasma viral load, zidovudine and mother-to-child transmission of HIV-1 in Africa: DITRAME ANRS 049a trial. AIDS 15: 517-522.

Leroy V, Sakarovitch C, Cortina-Borja M, McIntyre J, Coovadia H, Dabis F, Newell ML. (2005) Is there a difference in the efficacy of peripartum antiretroviral regimens in reducing mother-to-child transmission of HIV in Africa? AIDS 19: 1865-1875.

Magder LS, Mofenson L, Paul ME, Zorrilla CD, Blattner WA, Tuomala RE, LaRussa P, Landesman S, Rich KC. (2005) Risk factors for in utero and intrapartum transmission of HIV. J Acquir Immune Defic Syndr 38: 87-95.

Maguire A, Sanchez E, Fortuny C, Casabona J, Working Group on HIV-1 Vertical Transmission in Catalonia (1997) Potential risk factors for vertical HIV-1 transmission in Catalonia, Spain: the protective role of Caearean section. AIDS 11: 1851-1857.

Mandelbrot L, Burgard M, Teglas JP, Benifla JL, Khan C, Blot P, Vilmer E, Matheron S, Firtion G, Blanche S, Mayaux MJ, Rouzioux C. (1999) Frequent detection of HIV-1 in the gastric aspirates of neonates born to HIV-infected mothers. AIDS 13: 2143-2149.

Mandelbrot L, Mayaux MJ, Bongain A, Berrebi A, Moudoub-Jeanpetit Y, Benif-la JL, Ciraru-Vigneron N, Le Chenadec J, Blanche S, Delfraissy J F, Serogest, The French Pediatric HIV Infection Study Group (1996) Obstetric factors and mother-to-child transmission of human immunodeficiency virus type 1: The French perinatal cohorts. Am J Obstet Gynecol 175: 661-667.

Mandelbrot L, Msellati P, Meda N, Leroy V, Likikouet R, Van de Perre P, Dequae L, Sylla-Koko F, Ouangre A, Ouassa T, Ramon R, Gautier-Charpentier L, Cartoux M, Dosso M, Dabis F, Welffens-Ekra C. (2002) 15 Month follow up of African children following vaginal cleansing with benzalkonium chlorine of their HIV infected mothers during late pregnancy and delivery. Sex Transm Inf 78: 267-270.

Mandelbrot L, Peytavin G, Firtion G, Farinotti R. (2001) Maternal-fetal transfer and amniotic fluid accumulation of lamivudine in human immunodeficien-cy virus-infected pregnant women. Am J Obstet Gynecol 184: 153-158.

Marcollet A, Goffinet F, Firtion G, Pannnier E, Le Bret T, Brival M-L, Mandelbrot L. (2002) Differences in postpartum morbidity in women who are infected with the human immunodeficiency virus after elective cesarean delivery, emergency cesarean delivery, or vaginal delivery. Am J Obstet Gynecol 186: 784-789.

Marzolini C, Rudin C, Decosterd LA, Telenti A, Schreyer A, Biollaz J, Buclin T, The Swiss Mother and Child HIV Cohort

Study (2002) Transplacental passage of protease inhibitors at delivery. AIDS 16: 889-893.

Matheson PB, Thomas PA, Abrams EJ, Pliner V, Lambert G, Bamji M, Krasinski K, Steketee RW, Chiasson MA, Thea DM, New York City Perinatal HIV Transmission Collabor-ative Study Group (1996) Heterosexual behavious during pregnancy and peri-natal transmission of HIV-1. AIDS 10: 1249-1256.

Mayaux MJ, Teglas JP, Blanche S, French Pediatric HIV Infection Study Group (2003) Characteristics of HIV-infected women who do not receive preventive antiretroviral therapy in the French Perinatal Cohort. J Acquir Immune Defic Syndr 34: 338-343.

McIntyre JA. (2006) Controversies in the use of nevirapine for prevention of mother-to-child transmission of HIV. Expert Opin Pharmacother 7: 677-685.

McIntyre JA, Martinson N, Investigators for trial 1413, Boltz V, Palmer SJ, Coffin JM, Mellors JW, Hopley M, Kimura T, Robinson P, Mayers DL. (2004) Addition of short course combivir (CBV) to single dose viramune (sdNVP) for prevention of mother-to-child transmission (MTCT) of HIV-1 can significantly decrease the subsequent development of maternal NNRTI-resistant virus. XV International AIDS conference, Bangkok, Thailand, 11th-16th July 2004 .

Mirochnick M. (2000) Antiretroviral pharmacology in pregnant women and their newborns. Ann N Y Acad Sci 2000: 287-297.

Mofenson LM. (1999) Can perinatal HIV infection be eliminated in the United States? JAMA 282: 577-579.

Mofenson LM, Lambert JS, Stiehm ER, Bethel J, Meyer III WA, Whitehouse J, Moye JJ, Reichelderfer P, Harris DR, Fowler MG, Mathieson BJ, Nemo GJ, Pediatric AIDS Clinical Trials Group

Study 185 Team (1999) Risk factors for perinatal transmission of human immunodeficiency virus type 1 in women treated with zidovudine. N Engl J Med 341: 385-393.

Moodley D, Bobat RA, Coutsoudis A, Coovadia HM. (1994) Caesarean section and vertical transmission of HIV-1. Lancet 344: 338.

Moodley D, Moodley J, Coovadia HM, Gray GE, McIntyre JA, Hofmyer J, Nikodem C, Hall DB, Gigliotti M, Robinson PJ, Boshoff L, Sullivan JL. (2003) A Multicenter randomized con-trolled trial of Nevirapine versus a combination of Zidovudine and lami-vudine to reduce intrapartum and early postpartum Mother-to-Child transmis-sion of Human Immunodeficiency virus type 1. J Infectious Dis 187: 725-735.

Morrow AL, Guerrero ML, Shults J, Calva JJ, Lutter C, Bravo J, Ruiz-Palacios G, Morrow RC, Butterfoss FD. (1999) Efficacy of home-based peer counselling to promote exclusive breastfeeding: a randomized controlled trial. Lancet 353: 1226-1231.

Mwanyumba F, Gaillard P, Inion I, Verhofstede C, Claeys P, Chohan V, Vansteelandt S, Mandaliya K, Praet M, Temmerman M. (2002a) Placental inflammation and perinatal transmission of HIV-1. J Acquir Immune Defic Syndr 29: 262-269.

Mwanyumba FM, Gaillard P, Inion I, Verhofstede C, Claeys P, Chohan V, Vansteelandt S, Mandaliya K, Praet M, Temmerman M. (2002b) Placenta inflamation and perinatal transmission of HIV-1. J AIDS 29: 262-269.

Nduati RW, John GC, Kreiss JK. (1994) Postnatal transmission of HIV-1 through pooled breast milk. Lancet 344: 1432.

Nduati RW, John GC, Ngacha DA, Richard-son S, Overbaugh J, Mwath, , Achola J, Onyango F, Hughes JP, Kreiss JK. (2000)

Effect of Breastfeeding and Formula Feeding on Transmission of HIV-1: a Randomized Clinical Trial. JAMA 283: 1167-1174.

Nduati RW, John GC, Richardson BA, Overbaugh J, Welch M, Ndinya-Achola JO, Moses S, Holmes KK, Onyango F, Kreiss JK. (1995) Human immunodeficiency virus type 1-infected cells in breast milk: association with immuno-suppression and vitamin A deficiency. J Infectious Dis 172: 1461-1468.

Newell ML. (1998) Mechanisms and timing of mother-to-child transmission of HIV-1. AIDS 12: 831-837.

Okware S, Kinsman J, Onyango S, Opio A, Kaggwa P. (2005) Revisiting the ABC strategy: HIV prevention in Uganda in the era of antiretroviral therapy. Postgrad Med J 81: 625-628.

Oleske JM. (2003) Long-term outcomes in infants born to HIV-infected women. J Acquir Immune Defic Syndr 32: 353.

Ostergren M, Malyuta R. (2006) Elimina-tion of HIV infection in infants in Europe--challenges and demand for response. Semin Fetal Neonatal Med 11: 54-57.

Palasanthiran P, Ziegler JB, Stewart GJ, Stuckey M, Armstrong JA, Cooper DA, Penny R, Gold J. (1993) Breast-feeding during primary maternal human immunodeficiency virus infection and risk of transmission from mother to infant. J Infect Dis 167: 441-444.

Peters VB, Liu KL, Dominguez KL, Frederick T, Melville SK, Hsu HW, Ortiz IR, Rakusan TA, Gill B, Thomas P. (2003) Missed opportunities for perinatal HIV prevention among HIV-exposed infants born 1996-2000, pedia-tric spectrum of HIV disease cohort. Pediatrics 111: 1186-1191.

Poirier MC, Divi RL, Al Harthi L, Olivero OA, Nguyen V, Walker B, Landay AL, Walker VE, Charurat M, Blattner WA. (2003) Long-Term Mitochondrial Tox-icity in HIV-Uninfected Infants Born to HIV-Infected Mothers. J Acquir Immune Defic Syndr 33: 175-183.

Poirier MC, Olivero OA, Walker DM, Walker VE. (2004) Perinatal genotoxic-ity and carcinogenicity of anti-retroviral nucleoside analog drugs. Toxicol Appl Pharmacol 199: 151-161.

Read JS, Tuomala RE, Kpamegan E, Zorrilla C, Landesman SH, Brown G, Vajaranant M, Hammill HA, Thompson B. (2001) Mode of delivery and postpartum morbidity among HIV-infected women: the women and infants transmission study. J Acquir Immune Defic Syndr 26: 236-245.

Read JS, Newell M-L. (2005) Efficacy and safety of cesarean delivery for preven-tion of mother-to-child transmission of HIV-1. Cochrane Database Syst Rev. 19:CD005479.

Richardson BA, John-Stewart GC, Hughes JP, Nduati RW, Mbori-Ngacha D, Overbaugh J, Kreiss JK. (2003) Breast-Milk Infectivity in Human Immuno-deficiency Virus Type 1-Infected Mothers. J Infect Dis 187: 736-740.

Rollins N, Meda N, Becquet R, Coutsoudis A, Humphrey J, Jeffrey B, Kanshana S, Kuhn L, Leroy V, Mbori-Ngacha D, McIntyre JA, Newell ML, for the Ghent IAS Working Group on HIV in Women and Children (2004) Preventing post-natal transmisssion of HIV-1 through breast-feeding: modifying infant feeding practices. J Acquir Immune Defic Syndr 35: 188-195.

Rousseau CM, Nduati RW, Richardson BA, Steele MS, John-Stewart GC, Mbori-Ngacha D, Kreiss JK, Overbaugh J. (2003) Longitudinal Analysis of Human Immunodeficiency Virus Type 1 RNA in Breast Milk and of its Relationship to Infant Infection and Maternal Disease. J Infect Dis 187: 741-747.

Seck K, Samb N, Tempesta S, Mulanga-Kabeya C, Henzel D, Sow PS, Coll-Seck A, Mboup S, Ndoye I, Delaporte E. (2001) Prevalence and risk factors of cervicovaginal HIV shedding among HIV-1 and HIV-2 infected women in Dakar, Senegal. Sex Transm Infect 77: 190-193.

Semba RD, Miotti PG, Chiphangwi JD, Saah AJ, Canner JK, Dallabetta GA, Hoover DR. (1994) Maternal vitamin A deficiency and mother-to-child transmission of HIV-1. Lancet 343: 1593-1597.

Shaffer N, Chuachoowong R, Mock PA, Bhadrakom C, Siriwasin W, Young NL, Chotpitayasunondh T, Chearskul S, Roongpisuthipong A, Chinayon P, Karon JM, Masto TD, Simonds RJ, Bangkok Collaborative Perinatal HIV Transmission Study Group (1999) Short-course zidovudine for perinatal HIV-1 transmission in Bangkok, Thailand: a randomized controlled trial. Lancet 353: 773-780.

Shaffer N, Roongpisuthipon A, Siriwasin W, Chotpitayasunondh T, Chearskul S, Young NL, Parekh B S, Mock PA, Bhadrakom C, Chinayon P, Kalish ML, Phillips SK, Granade TC, Subbarao S, Weniger BG, Mastro TD, Bangkok Collaborative Perinatal HIV Transmission Study Group (1998) Maternal Viral Load and Perinatal Human Immuno-deficiency Virus Type 1 Subytpe E Transmission, Thailand. J Infect Dis 179: 590-599.

Shapiro RL, Ndung'u T, Lockman S, Smeaton L, Thior I, Wester C, Stevens L, Sebetso G, Gaseitsiwe S, Peter T, Essex M. (2005) Highly Active Anti-retroviral Therapy started during preg-nancy or postpartum suppresses HIV-1 RNA, but not DNA, in breastmilk. J Infect Dis 192: 713-719.

Simonon A, Lepage P, Karita E, Hitimana DG, Dabis F, Msellati P, Van Goethem C, Nsengumuremyi F, Bazubagira A, Van de Perre P. (1994) An assessment of the timing of mother-to-child transmission of human immunodefi-ciency virus type 1 by means of polymerase chain reaction. J Acquir Immune Defic Syndr 7: 952-957.

Sterling TR, Vlahov D, Astemborski J, Hoover DR, Margolick JB, Quinn TC. (2001) Initial plasma HIV-1 RNA levels and progression to AIDS in women and men. N Engl J Med 344: 720-725.

Stringer EM, Sinkala M, Stringer JSA, Mzyece E, Makuka I, Goldenberg RL, Kwape P, Chilufya M, Vermund S. (2003) Prevention of mother-to-child transmission of HIV in Africa: successes and challenges in scaling-up a nevirapine-based program in Lusaka, Zambia. AIDS 17: 1377-1382.

Taha TE, Kumwenda NI, Hoover DR, Fiscus SA, Kafulafula G, Nkhoma C, Nour S, Liomba GN, Miotti PG, Broadhead RL. (2004) Nevirapine and zidovudine at birth to reduce perinatal transmission of HIV in an African setting. JAMA 292: 202-209.

Tardieu M, Rustin P, Lacroix C, Chabrol B, Desguerre I, Dollfus C, Mayaux MJ, Blanche S. (2003) Persistent mtiochondrial dysfunction in HIV-1 exposed but uninfected infants: clinical screening in a large prospective cohort. AIDS 17: 1769-1785.

Temmerman M, Quaghabeur A, Mwan-yumba FM, Mandaliya K. (2003) Mother-to-child HIV transmission in resource poor settings: how to improve coverage? AIDS 17: 1239-1242.

The European Mode of Delivery Collaboration. (1999) Elective caesarean section versus vaginal delivery in preventing vertical HIV-1 transmission: a randomized clinical trial. Lancet 353: 1035-1039.

The International Perinatal HIV group. (1999) Mode of delivery and vertical transmission of HIV-1: a meta-analysis from fifteen prospective cohort studies. N

Engl J Med 340: 977-987.

The International Perinatal HIV group. (2001) Duration of ruptured membranes and vertical transmission of HIV-1: a meta-analysis from fifteen prospective cohort studies. AIDS 15: 357-368.

The Petra study team (2002) Efficacy of the three short-course regimens of zidovudine and lamivudine in preventing early and late transmission of HIV-1 from mother to child in Tanzania, South Africa and Uganda (Petra study): a randomized, double-blind, placebo-controlled trial. Lancet 359: 1178-1186.

Thea DM, Vwalika C, Kasonde P, Kankasa C, Sinkala M, Semrau K, Shutes E, Ayash C, Tsai WY, Aldrovandi G, Kuh L. (2004) Issues in the design of a clinical trial with a behavioral inter-vention--the Zambia exclusive breast-feeding study. Control Clin Trials 25: 353-365.

Thomas T, Amornkul P, Mwidau J, Masaba R, Slutsker L, Mwaengo D, Vulule J, de Cock K, Fowler M. (2005) Preliminary findings: incidence of serious adverse events attributable to nevirapine among women enrolled in an ongoing trial using HAART to prevent mother-to-child transmission. 12th Conference on Retroviruses and Opportunistic Infections, 22-25 February 2005, Boston, USA. Abstract 809.

Tuomala RE, O'Driscoll PT, Bremer JW, Jennings C, Xu C, Read JS, Matzen E, Landay AL, Zorrilla C, Charurat M, Anderson DJ. (2003) Cell-associated genital tract virus and vertical trans-mission of human immunodeficiency virus type 1 in antiretroviral-experienced women. J Infect Dis 187: 375-384.

UNAIDS. (2002) Implementing the Declar-ation of Commitment on HIV/AIDS. Action guide for United Nations Country Teams. UNAIDS, Geneva.

UNAIDS. (2005) AIDS epidemic update, December 2005. UNAIDS, Geneva.

UNAIDS, WHO. (2005) Eastern Europe and Central Asia Fact Sheet. In UNAIDS, Geneva.

UNAIDS. (2006) 2006 Report on the global HIV epidemic. UNAIDS, Geneva.

Van de Perre P, Simonon A, Msellati P, Hitimana DG, Vaira D, Bazubagira A, Van Goethem C, Stevens AM, Karita E, Sondag-Thull D, Dabis F, Lepage P. (1991) Postnatal transmission of human immunodeficiency virus type 1 from mother to infant: a prospective cohort study in Kigali, Rwanda. N Engl J Med 325: 593-598.

Vyankandondera J, Luchters S, Hassink E, Pakker N, Mmiro F, Okong P, Kituuka P, Ndugwa CM, Mukanka N, Beretta A, Imperiale M, Loeliger E, Guiliano M, Lange J. (2003) Reducing risk of HIV-1 transmission from mother to infant through breastfeeding using antiretro-viral prophylaxis in infants (SIMBA). In.

Wainberg MA, Spira B, Bleau G, Thomas R. (1990) Inactivation of Human Immunodeficiency Virus Type 1 in tissue culture fluid and in genital secre-tions by the spermicide Benzalkonium Chloride. J Clin Microbiol 28: 156-158.

Warszawski J, Tubiana R, Le Chenadec J, Blanche S, Teglas JP, et al (2005) Is intrapartum intravenous zidovudine still beneficial to prevent mother-to-child HIV-1 transmission? 12th Conference on Retroviruses and Opportunistic Infec-tions, 22-25 February 2005, Boston, USA. Abstract: 781.

Wiktor SZ, Ekpini ER, Karon JM, Nkenganson J, Maurice C, Severin ST, Roels TH, Kouassi MK, Lackritz EM, Coulibaly IM, Greenberg AE. (1999) Short-course oral zidovudine for preven-tion of mother-to-child transmission of HIV-1 in Abidjan, Cote d'Ivoire: a randomized trial. Lancet 353: 781-785.

Willumsen JF, Filteau SM, Coutsoudis A, Newell ML, Rollins N, Coovadia HM,

Tomkins AM. (2003) Breastmilk RNA viral load in HIV-infected South African women: effects of subclinical mastitis and infant feeding. AIDS 17: 407-414.

Willumsen JF, Newell ML, Filteau S M, Coutsoudis A, Dwarika S, York D, Tomkins AM, Coovadia HM. (2001) Variation in breastmilk HIV-1 viral load in left and right breasts during the first 3 months of lactation. AIDS 15: 1896-1897.

Wiysonge CS, Shey MS, Shang JD, Sterne JA, Brocklehurst P. (2005a) Vaginal disinfection for preventing mother-to-child transmission of HIV infection. Cochrane Database Syst Rev CD003651.

Wiysonge CS, Shey MS, Sterne JA, Brocklehurst P. (2005b) Vitamin A supplementation for reducing the risk of mother-to-child transmission of HIV infection. Cochrane Database Syst Rev CD003648.

World Health Organization. (2001) Breastfeeding and replacement feeding practices in the context of mother-to-child transmission of HIV. An assessment tool for research. WHO, Geneva.

Working Group on Mother-to-Child Transmission of HIV (1995) Rates of mother-to-child transmission of HIV-1 in Africa, America, and Europe: Results from 13 perinatal studies. J Acquir Immunodefic Syndr Human Retrovirol 8: 506-510.

BIRTH: CARE OF INFANT AND MOTHER: TIME-SENSITIVE ISSUES

Maria Blois

INTRODUCTION

Certain behavioral interventions in the peri-partum period are essential for ensuring a healthy birth and a good start to healthful behavior for both mother and baby. The time just before, during and after birth is a unique window of time in which healthy behaviors can be started and thus carried on, or a time where opportunity is lost. For example, the American Academy of Pediatrics argues that when newborns are restrained properly when riding for the first time, it establishes the pattern for continued compliance with a measure that can save their lives or prevent serious injury (AAP, 1999a). In a similar vein, mothers who do not successfully initiate breastfeeding in the peri-partum period may experience milk supply problems that may ultimately lead to breastfeeding failure. This review will present evidence primarily from randomized controlled trials in four major areas: choosing the birth environment; the promotion of exclusive breastfeeding; the importance of kangaroo care and essential physical contact between mother and baby; and the proper use of infant car safety seats. Each of these issues is time-sensitive and intervention is critical in the period immediately surrounding birth for optimal success. Key outcomes from randomized controlled trials will be presented in a table at the end of each section. The scope of this review includes only issues that apply to *the majority of* mothers, not issues that pertain to a small percentage of mothers. For this reason, some seemingly relevant issues (*e.g.* postpartum depression with an estimated incidence of 10-15% among new mothers) are not included (Freeman et al, 2006).

BIRTH ENVIRONMENT

In high and middle-income countries, hospitals, instead of the home, have become the birth setting for the majority of child-bearing women. The change to planned hospital birth for low risk pregnant women during this century was not supported by good evidence. Routine medical interventions have also increased over time, leading to questions about benefits, safety and risk for healthy, low-risk childbearing women. Given that there are a number of biological reasons why the birth process might be enhanced if the mother is supported in a quiet, secure and known environment, there is increasing interest in the impact of the environment on the outcomes of labor and birth (Olsen et al., 1998).

Birthing choices available to pregnant women today can include: 1) standard obstetric care in a hospital, 2) midwife care (with physician back-up) in a hospital or birth center, or 3) midwife care in a free standing birth center or at a planned home-birth. This section will review the available data on the effects of some of these choices. Randomized controlled trials (RCT) are detailed in Table 1.

Birth center versus conventional hospital care

Birth centers with home-like birth settings have been established in or near conventional hospitals for the care of pregnant women who prefer and require little or no medical intervention during labor and birth. A 2005 meta-analysis (Hodnett et al., 2005) of all randomized or quasi-randomized controlled trials that compared the effects of a home-like institutional birth environment to conventional hospital care included six trials involving 8677 women. Allocation to a home-like setting significantly increased the likelihood of:

- no intrapartum analgesia (4 trials;

n=6703; Relative Risk (RR) 1.19, 95% Confidence Interval (CI): 1.01 - 1.40),
• spontaneous vaginal birth (5 trials; n=8529, RR 1.03, 95% CI: 1.01 - 1.06)
• preference for same setting next time (1 trial, n=1230, RR 1.81, 95% CI: 1.65 - 1.98)
• satisfaction with intrapartum care (1 trial, n=2844, RR 1.14, 95% CI: 1.07 - 1.21)
• breastfeeding initiation (2 trials, n=1431, RR 1.05, 95% CI: 1.02 - 1.09)
• breastfeeding continuation to 6 to 8 weeks (2 trials, n=1431, RR 1.06, 95% CI: 1.02 - 1.10)
• avoiding an episiotomy (5 trials, n=8529, RR 0.85, 95% CI: 0.74 - 0.99)

Along with the modest benefits of the home-like setting, they also reported the following areas of caution for this maternity care choice:
• increased likelihood of vaginal perineal tears (4 trials; n=8415. RR 1.08, 95% CI: 1.03 - 1.13)
• trend towards higher perinatal mortality in the home-like setting (5 trials, n=8529, RR 1.83, 95% CI: 0.99 - 3.38)

The authors concluded that when compared to conventional institutional settings, home-like settings for childbirth were associated with modest benefits, including reduced medical interventions, increased maternal satisfaction and increased breastfeeding initiation and continuation rates. Because of the trend towards higher perinatal mortality in the home-like setting, caregivers and clients were cautioned to be vigilant for signs of complications.

It should be noted that between 29% and 67% of women allocated to home-like settings were transferred to standard care before or during labor.

Similarly in one RCT (Waldenstrom et al., 1994), 1,230 women interested in birth center care and meeting low-risk medical criteria in early pregnancy were randomized to two groups: standard obstetric care and birth center care. Women who were in the birth center care group used less pharmacological pain relief, experienced more support from the midwife, experienced greater freedom in expressing their feelings during the birth, were more satisfied with their own achievement and felt more involved in the birth process. The authors concluded that birth center care gave women interested in a natural childbirth, by avoiding pharmacological pain relief, greater opportunity to give birth according to their prenatal wishes, and contributed to a slightly more positive birth experience.

Another RCT (MacVicar et al., 1993) randomized 3510 women to two methods of maternity care: the first was consultant-led maternity care in delivery suite rooms with resuscitation equipment for both mothers and baby in evidence, monitors present and a delivery bed on which both anaesthetic and obstetric procedures could be easily and safely carried out; the second was midwife-led maternity care for both antenatal care and delivery taking place in rooms similar to those in one's own home to simulate a home delivery. This study found no difference in percentage of mothers and babies discharged home alive and well between the two groups, however, mothers in the midwife-led group showed higher levels of satisfaction with care antenatally and during labor and delivery.

Additionally, a pilot study (Woodward et al., 2004) for a RCT of water birth versus land birth found that a randomized controlled trial is feasible and demonstrated outcome measures which can be successfully collected in an average delivery suite.

Home birth versus hospital birth

A recent review (Olsen et al., 1998) comparing the effects of planned hospital birth with planned home birth backed up by a modern hospital system in case a transfer should turn out to be necessary found no strong evidence to favor either home or hospital birth for selected low-risk pregnant women. One small study (Dowswell et al., 1996) showed that randomizing women to home or hospital delivery was possible. The small trial was not launched in order to reach a definitive conclusion. The aim was rather to show that it is possible to get an informed consent from pregnant women to be randomized either to a planned home or a planned hospital birth. The trial was too small to draw any reliable conclusions, however there was one impressive difference: the majority of mothers in the hospital group were disappointed about the allocation.

Weaker evidence from observational studies suggests that planned home birth may lead to fewer interventions and fewer neonatal problems. A recently published meta analysis of the methodologically best, observational, comparative, original studies investigating the mortality related to planned home and

Table 1: Effects of Birth Environment (RCT)

Study	Participants	Intervention	Outcome
Waldenstrom et al., 1994	1,230 women interested in birth center care, meeting low-risk medical criteria in early pregnancy	Group 1: Standard obstetric care Group 2: Birth center care	Group 2 women used less pharmacological pain relief, experienced more support from the midwife, experienced greater freedom in expressing their feelings during the birth, were more satisfied with their own achievement and felt more involved in the birth process.
MacVicar et al., 1993	3510 women	Group 1: Consultant-led maternity care in delivery suite rooms with resuscitation equipment and monitors present. Group 2: Midwife-led maternity care in rooms similar to home to simulate home delivery	No difference in percentage of mothers and babies discharged home alive and well. Group 2: Showed higher levels of satisfaction with care antenatally and during labor and delivery.
Woodward et al., 2004	80 women between 36 and 40 weeks of gestation No pregnancy problems, no anticipated labor and delivery problems	Group 1: Standard delivery Group 2: Waterbirth Group 3: 20 women participated in non randomized 'preference arm'.	Group 2: Babies demonstrated a significantly lower umbilical artery pCO_2 (p=0.003). Women were willing to participate and randomization did not appear to alter satisfaction.

planned hospital births revealed no statistical difference in mortality between planned home and planned hospital birth; the confidence interval was not compatible with extreme excess risks in any of the groups (OR 0.87, 95% CI: 0.54 - 1.41) (Olsen, 1997). The principal difference in the outcome was a lower frequency of low Apgar Scores (OR 0.55, 95% CI: 0.41 - 0.74) and severe lacerations (OR 0.67, 95% CI: 0.54 - 0.83) in the home birth group. Fewer medical interventions occurred in the home birth group: induction (statistically significant ORs in the range 0.06 to 0.39), augmentations ((0.26 to 0.69) and episiotomy (0.02 to 0.39), operative vaginal birth (0.03 to 0.42) and cesarean section (0.05 to 0.31). There were no maternal deaths. The authors concluded that home birth is an acceptable alternative to hospital confinement for selected pregnant women, and leads to reduced medical interventions.

If mortality is a prime concern, an extremely large trial would be required to answer whether there is differential mortality risk between home and hospital birthing with sufficient power. With the data currently available one could argue that for low risk pregnancies both home and hospital births are sufficiently safe for safety to no longer be of overriding importance.

In sum, there is no strong evidence to favor either home or hospital birth for selected low-risk pregnant women. Weaker evidence from observational studies suggests that planned home birth may lead to fewer interventions and fewer neonatal problems. Home-like settings for childbirth were associated with modest benefits, including reduced medical interventions, increased maternal satisfaction and increased breast-feeding initiation and continuation rates. Mothers in midwife-led groups showed higher levels of satisfaction with care antenatally and during labor and delivery. Based on this evidence, in countries and areas where it is possible to establish a home birth service backed up by a modern hospital system, *all low-risk pregnant women should be offered the possibility of considering a planned home birth or care in a birth center and they should be informed about the quality of the available evidence to guide their choice.*

BREASTFEEDING

Human (breast) milk has a distinct and irreplaceable value to the human infant. Human babies, like all mammals, have evolved to be breastfed and evidence suggests that babies reach their maximum potential on human milk. The unique composition of human milk provides excellent nutrition for human brain growth in the first year of life. Although breastfeeding may not seem the best choice for each individual family, it is almost always recommended for baby. The World Health Organization recommends that all infants be fed exclusively human milk from birth to six months of age, with continued breastfeeding through the next two years and then for as long as is desired thereafter by mother and infant (WHO, 2002). A 2002 review looked at 29 independent studies and concluded that infants who are exclusively breastfed for six months experienced less morbidity from gastrointestinal infection than those who were mixed breastfed and no deficits were demonstrated in growth among infants who were exclusively breastfed for six months or longer (Kramer et al., 2002). Contraindications to breastfeeding include when mother is HIV positive in a developed country (see Chapter 3), HTLV-I positive, or if she is currently using antimetabolites, radiopharma-ceuticals at a therapeutic dose, or drugs of abuse (except cigarettes and alcohol) (Lawrence et al., 1999, p.225).

There is extensive evidence for short-term and long-term health benefits of breast-feeding. Babies who are not exclusively breastfed for the first three to four months are more likely to suffer health problems such as gastroenteritis (Howie et al., 1990), respiratory infection (Victoria et al., 1989), otitis media (Aniansson et al., 1994), urinary tract infections (Pisacane et al., 1992), necrotizing enterocolitis (Lucas et al., 1990), atopic disease if a family history of atopy is present (Saarinen et al., 1995) and diabetes mellitus (Karjalainen et al., 1992; Mayer et al., 1988). Breastfeeding has also been found to have an analgesic effect in term neonates (Carbajal et al., 2003). Breastfeeding is also beneficial to a mother's health. Women who do not breastfeed are significantly more likely to develop epithelial ovarian and breast cancer than women who breastfeed (Gwinn et al., 1990; Rosenblatt et al., 1993; Layde et al., 1989).

Unacceptably high levels of child mortality continue in low-income countries and poor areas of middle-income countries. It is estimated that if 90% of infants were exclusively breastfed at 0-5 months and continued to be breastfed from 6-11 months, worldwide child deaths would be reduced by about 13% (Coutinho et al., 2005). Little is known about which interventions to promote breastfeeding are most effective. In this review, promotion of breastfeeding will be considered from various and often overlapping perspectives which include providing institutional support, educating the physician, educating the mother, and providing peer support. Information from all designated randomized controlled trials (RCT) will be summarized in Table 4.

Providing institutional support

The WHO/UNICEF sponsored Baby-Friendly Hospital Initiative (BFHI) was developed to help make breastfeeding the norm in birthing environments and consists of specific recommendations for maternity care practices (Table 2).

Women in most countries encounter

Table 2: Toward becoming a Baby-Friendly Hospital: 10 steps to successful breastfeeding (WHO/UNICEF, 1989)

Every facility providing maternity services and care for newborn infants should:
1. Have a written breastfeeding policy that is routinely communicated to all health care staff.
2. Train all health care staff in skills necessary to implement this policy.
3. Inform all pregnant women about the benefits and management of breastfeeding.
4. Help mothers initiate breastfeeding within a half hour of birth.
5. Show mother how to breastfeed and how to maintain lactation even if they should be separated from their infants.
6. Give newborn infants no food or drink other than breast milk, unless medically indicated.
7. Practice rooming-in – allow mothers and infants to remain together – 24 hours a day.
8. Encourage breastfeeding on demand.
9. Give no artificial teats or pacifiers to breastfeeding infants.
10. Foster the establishment of breastfeeding support groups and refer mothers to them on discharge from the hospital or clinic.

From WHO/UNICEF: Protecting, promoting and supporting breastfeeding: the special role of maternity services, a joint WHO/UNICEF statement, Geneva 1989, World Health Organization

promotion of artificial feeding in various forms, a factor which has been implicated in women choosing to feed their babies on formula (WHO Data Bank, 1996). One RCT (Howard et al., 2000) found that women who received formula company packs were more likely to cease breastfeeding before hospital discharge and before 2 weeks. Similarly, another RCT (Frank, 1987) found that women who received a research discharge pack designed to be consistent with the WHO code of Marketing of Breastmilk Substitutes instead of the commercial discharge pack provided by formula companies were more likely to prolong exclusive breastfeeding (p=0.004, one-tailed), to be partially breast-feeding at 4 months postpartum (p=0.04, one tailed) and to delay the daily use of solid foods in the infants diet (p=0.017, one-tailed).

In order to protect and promote breastfeeding, through the provision of adequate information on appropriate infant feeding and the regulation of the marketing of breast milk substitutes, WHO adopted the International Code of Marketing of Breast-milk Substitutes in 1981 (WHO, 1981). The Code stipulates that there should be absolutely no promotion of breast milk substitutes, bottles and teats to the general public; that neither health facilities nor health professionals should have a role in promoting breast milk substitutes, and that free samples should not be provided to pregnant women, new mothers or families. This Code was endorsed by the US in 1994.

To be designated a Baby-Friendly Hospital, each hospital must meet the ten criteria and comply with International Code of Marketing of Breastmilk Substitutes. Since 1996, 27 hospitals have been certified Baby-Friendly in the US.

Several studies have demonstrated the effectiveness of the BFHI. A longitudinal mail study of 1085 women found that increased BFHI practices improved the chances of breastfeeding beyond 6 weeks (DiGirolamo et al., 2001). A 2003 study of the prevalence and duration of breastfeeding throughout Switzerland found that children born in a baby friendly health facility were more likely to be breastfed for a longer time (Merten et al., 2005). One RCT (Coutinho et al., 2005) made the point that although BFHI achieves high rates of exclusive breastfeeding in hospital, the rates fall rapidly thereafter. Follow up visits helped maintain these rates.

Their program of home visits was successful in this population at improving rates of exclusive breastfeeding during the first six months of life.

Promoting physician education

The greatest decline in the breastfeeding rate occurs during the first 4 postpartum weeks. Mothers who discontinue breast-feeding are more likely to report lack of confidence in their ability to breastfeed, problems with the infant latching or suckling, and *lack of individualized encouragement from their clinicians* in the early post discharge period (DiGiralamo et al., 2003). Mothers are looking to their physicians to help them get breastfeeding off to a good start. This is a two-part intervention: physicians must first be specifically educated about breastfeeding management (Table 3) and second, they must communicate this knowledge, confidently and enthusiastically. In fact, one study found that a perceived neutral attitude from the hospital staff is related to not breastfeeding beyond 6 weeks (DiGirolamo et al., 2003).

Several studies have demonstrated that educating primary care physicians about breastfeeding improves breastfeeding rates in their patients. In one RCT (Labarere et al., 2005), participating physicians received a five hour training program on breastfeeding. Intervention mothers were then invited to attend an outpatient visit in the office of one of the participating primary care physicians within 2 weeks after the birth. Mothers in the intervention group were more likely to report exclusive breastfeeding at four weeks, and longer breastfeeding duration. They were less likely to report any breastfeeding difficulties.

Similarly, a multivariate model (Taveras et al., 2004) found that mothers whose pediatric providers recommended formula supplemen-tation if an infant was not gaining enough weight (Odds Ratio (OR) 3.2, 95% CI: 1.04 - 9.7), or who considered their advice to

Table 3: Management of the mother-infant nursing couple (adapted from Lawrence et al., 1999)

- Even if the new mother does not ask to nurse her baby immediately after birth, the obstetrician and delivery room staff should suggest and facilitate it. Data confirms the view that delivery room protocols that intercept interaction and suckling between mother and infant also impact on long-term lactation success (Lindenberg et al., 1990, Righard 1990, Widstrom, 1990).

- The physician should see that patients are permitted to have their infants with them as much as they wish. Help the mother find a comfortable position. Help the infant to the breast. Ensure proper positioning: Ventral surface of the infant faces the mother. Wait until baby opens wide, then bring baby to mother. Baby should take most of the areola into his mouth, with his lips flared out. To release baby, insert small finger into the corner of his/her mouth to break the seal.

- Encourage skin-to-skin contact which as been shown in a RCT to extend the duration of exclusive breastfeeding (Vaidya et al., 2005).

- Milk production is influenced by the frequency, intensity and duration of suckling by the infant, especially in the early postpartum period. Infants should be nursed on demand around the clock and receive no other food or drink. Feedings should occur 8 – 12 times per 24 hour period. Successful breastfeeding is an infant-led process. Allow infant to nurse on the first side until satiated (falls asleep or releases breast) then offer the second side. Frequent small feedings will provide good stimulation to the breast without stressing the mother. The milk supply is best stimulated by suckling (Pollitt et al., 1981).

- Pediatric practitioners continue to debate whether or not to recommend supplement feeding a breastfed infant. For the normal full-term infant it is not necessary. No significant differences were found in serum bilirubins and weight loss between supplemented and unsupplemented breastfed infants (Herrara, 1984). Not only is it not necessary, it can jeopardize the nursing relationship. In that same study (Herrara, 1984) at age 3 months a significant number of supplemented infants were no longer breast-feeding (still breastfeeding, 81% unsupplemented versus 53% supplemented). In a similar study (Gray-Donald et al., 1985), mothers who requested formula in the hospital and requested a going-home formula package were more likely to discontinue breastfeeding.

- Many new mothers wonder if their baby is getting enough milk. One way to identify a failure to thrive situation before it becomes serious is to keep track of infant output. In the first week of life the pattern of an infant receiving adequate colostrum, which has a cathartic effect on the gut, is to have a stool with most feedings. 4-6 stools a day and 6-8 wet diapers a day is normal. Weight gain after the first week of life should be 15 to 30 g daily. Birth weight should be regained in 2 weeks. Fussing is not necessarily a sign of baby not getting enough milk. If output is within normal limits, express confidence that the baby is getting just what he needs. If the baby is not gaining weight, suggest more frequent nursings instead of supplementing with formula.

mothers on breastfeeding duration to be not very important (OR: 2.2, 95% CI: 1.2 - 3.9) were more likely to have discontinued exclusive breastfeeding by twelve weeks.

Encouraging parental education

Along with institutional support and physician education, parental education has been found to be an effective tool for promoting breastfeeding. A meta-analysis of five randomized controlled trials involving 582 women on low incomes in the USA showed breastfeeding education had a statistically significant effect on increasing initiation rates compared to routine care (RR 1.53, 95% CI:1.25-1.88) (Dyson et al., 2005). For example, one RCT (Ryser, 2004) found that exposure to the Best Start program significantly increased positive breastfeeding sentiment (p<.01), decreased negative breastfeeding sentiment (p<.01) and increased breastfeeding control (p<.01). The Best Start Program was developed using the concept of social marketing, and promotes breastfeeding by utilizing counseling strategies, educational materials, policies, and community–based activities (Bryant et al., 1992). Another RCT (Serwint et al., 1996) found that after attending a prenatal pediatric visit 45% of mothers changed their mind in favor of breastfeeding compared to 14% of mothers who did not attend the pediatric visit.

One interesting RCT highlighted the special importance of fathers as breastfeeding advocates (Wolfberg et al., 2004). Couples were recruited during the second trimester from a university obstetrics practice and 59 expectant fathers were randomized to two groups, either a two hour intervention class on infant care and breastfeeding promotion or a class on infant care only. Breastfeeding was initiated by 74% of the women whose partners attended the infant care plus breastfeeding promotion class as compared with 41% of women whose partners attended the infant care only class (p= 0.02). The authors concluded that expectant fathers can be influential advocates for breastfeeding, playing a critical role in encouraging a woman to breastfeed her newborn infant.

Providing peer support

The use of peer support as a method to promote breastfeeding is equivocal. In one RCT (Muirhead et al., 2006), 225 women at 28 weeks gestation were allocated to control or peer group. All peer support and control group mothers received normal professional breastfeeding support. Additionally, those in the peer support group still breastfeeding on return home from hospital had peer support until 16 weeks. Thirty-five of the 112 (31%) women in the peer support group were breastfeeding at 6 weeks compared to 33/113 (29%) in the control group, a difference of 2% (95% CI: -10% to 14%). These differences were not statistically significant. Peer support did not increase breastfeeding in this population by a statistically significant amount.

Table 4: Breastfeeding Promotion Randomized Controlled Trials (RCT)

Study	Participants	Intervention	Outcome
Howard et al., 2000	547 pregnant women	Group 1: Received specially designed educational packs about infant feeding at first prenatal visit.

Group 2: Received formula company pack. | Group 2 more likely to cease breastfeeding before hospital discharge (RR 5.80, 95% CI: 1.25-54.01), and before 2 weeks (OR 1.91, 95% CI: 1.02-3.55) |

Study	Participants	Intervention	Outcome
Frank et al., 1987	343 breastfeeding low-income urban women	Group 1: Received research breast-feeding bedside counseling by trained counselor Group 2: Routine breastfeeding counseling. Group 1b: Received research discharge packs designed to consistent with the WHO Code. Group 2b: Received commercial discharge packs provided by the formula company	Research counseling delayed the first introduction of solid foods (p=0.03) one tailed. Women who received the research discharge pack were more likely to prolong exclusive breastfeeding (p=0.004, one tailed) and to be partially breastfeeding at 4 months postpartum (p=0.04 one tailed) and to delay the daily use of solid foods in the infant's diet (p=0.017, one tailed).
Coutinho et al., 2005	350 mothers who just gave birth	Group 1: Baby-friendly hospital birth plus home visits Group 2: Baby-friendly hospital birth only	Exclusive breastfeeding at days 10-180: mean aggregated prevalence Group 1: 45%* vs. Group 2: 13% (p<0.0001)
Labarere et al., 2005	226 mothers of full term singleton infants who were breastfeeding on day of discharge	Group 1: Invited to attend an individual, routine, preventive, outpatient visit in the office of trained primary care physician within 2 weeks after birth Group 2: Usual predischarge and postdischarge support	Exclusive breastfeeding at 4 weeks: Group 1: 83.9%, Group 2: 71.9% (Hazard ratio: 1.17, 95% CI: 1.01-1.34) Breastfeeding duration: 1: median 18 weeks, 2: 13 weeks; (Hazard ratio: 1.09, 95% CI: 1.03-1.92) Breastfeeding difficulties: 1: 55.3%, 2: 72.8% (Hazard ratio: 0.76, 95% CI: 0.62-0.93)
Vaidya et al., 2005	92 lactating mother- infant pairs in the first 6 months of birth	Early postpartum mother-baby skin-to-skin contact	Longer duration of exclusive breastfeeding p<0.001
Ryser, 2004	54 low income women	Group 1: exposure to the Best Start program Group 2: control	Compared to control group, experimental group had significantly increased positive breastfeeding sentiment (p<.01), decreased negative breastfeeding sentiment (p<.01) and increased breast-feeding control (p<.01).

Study	Participants	Intervention	Outcome
Serwint et al., 1996	156 pregnant women	Group 1: Prenatal pediatric visit Group 2: No prenatal pediatric visit	Of mothers who breastfed, 45% in Group 1 changed their mind in favor of breastfeeding compared to 14% in Group 2.
Wolfberg et al., 2004	59 expectant fathers	Group 1: Attended a 2 hour intervention class on infant care and breastfeeding promotion led by a peer-educator Group 2: Attended a class on infant care only	Percent initiating breastfeeding: Group 1: 74%*, Group 2: 41% (p=0.02)
Muirhead et al., 2006	225 women at 28 weeks gestation	Group 1: Peer support group – normal professional breastfeeding support plus peer support until 16 weeks (if still breastfeeding on return home from the hospital) Group 2: Control group – normal professional breastfeeding support	Breastfeeding at 6 weeks: 1: 31%, 2: 29% (95% CI = -10% - 14%) Median breastfeeding duration: 1: 2 days , 2: 1 day (p=0.5) Median breastfeeding duration, primagravidae 1: 7 days, 2: 3 days Duration among women who started to breastfeed: 1: 72 days, 2: 56 days No statistically significant differences
Chapman et al., (2004)	165 pregnant women	Group 1: Intervention Breastfeeding peer counseling services included 1 prenatal visit, daily perinatal visits, 3 postpartum home visits, and telephone contact as needed Group 2: Standard care	Not initiating breastfeeding: Group 1: 9%*, Group 2: 23% (RR 0.39, 95% CI:0.18-0.86) Stopping breastfeeding at 1 month: 1: 36%, 2: 49% (RR 0.72, 95% CI: 0.50-1.05) At 3 months: 1: 56%, 2: 71% (RR 0.78, 95% CI: 0.61-1.00)
Dennis et al., 2002	256 breastfeeding mothers	Group 1: Peer support group (conventional care plus telephone-based support, initiated within 48 hours after hospital discharge from a woman experienced with breastfeeding who attended a 2.5 hour orientation session) Group 2: Conventional care	Continued breastfeeding at 3 months: Group 1: 81.1*%, Group 2: 66.9% (p=0.01)

The results of this study could have been affected because there was limited antenatal contact and no contact with women while in the hospital. The absence of peer support during the crucial first days prior to homecoming may have reduced the effect of peer support. The support and co-operation of health professionals is also required for peer supporters to function and some may have been unwilling to accept lay people being involved in the care of these women.

Alternatively, one RCT (Chapman et al., 2004) found that peer counselors significantly improved breastfeeding rates and had an impact on breastfeeding rates at 1 and 3 months postpartum. Similarly, another RCT (Dennis et al., 2002) found that telephone-based peer support intervention was effective in maintaining breast-feeding to 3 months post-partum and improving satisfaction with the infant feeding experience. There were no obvious differences in the patient populations in these three trials to account for the differences in outcomes.

Conclusions

Research to date supports the value of institutional support, provider and patient education for improving breastfeeding rates. Not promoting formula use or supplemental feeding, and enthusiastic promotion of breast-feeding appear to be important components of these interventions. The additional benefit of peer support networks for promoting breast-feeding are not clear, however, evidence suggests that they may be helpful for some populations and no negative effects have been noted.

HOLD ME CLOSE: ENCOURAGING ESSENTIAL MOTHER/BABY PHYSICAL CONTACT

It has been suggested that increased physical contact between a mother and her newborn (holding) promotes greater maternal responsiveness and more secure attachment between infant and mother, among other benefits. Current research has focused on three general types of physical contact, skin-to-skin contact (kangaroo care), in-arms holding and the use of a soft carrier to hold baby. Information from designated randomized controlled trials (RCT) will be detailed in Table 5.

Benefits of Kangaroo Care (KC)

The method of skin-to-skin contact between mother and baby (kangaroo care) is the normal mammalian post-natal condition (Ferber et al., 2004). Current research on kangaroo care has primarily focused on questions about the safety and effectiveness of this method.

Preterm infants

The benefits of skin-to-skin contact for *preterm* infants, those infants born at an estimated gestational age of less than 37 weeks, have been the most extensively studied. Historically, one of the initial motivations for promoting skin-to-skin contact between mother and premature baby was largely financial. Kangaroo Mother Intervention (KMI) started in 1978 in Colombia as a way of dealing with overcrowding and minimal resources in hospitals caring for premature babies. KMI is described as an alternative comprehensive care method to standard hospital care for Low birth weight (LBW) infants (Whitelaw, 1985). KMI has three components: 1) kangaroo position (baby is placed naked and prone upright against mother's chest), 2) kangaroo nutrition (exclusive or near exclusive breast milk), and, 3) kangaroo discharge (early dis-charge from the hospital).

In a RCT of KMI (Charpak et al., 2001), 746 infants who were born at <2000g were followed. Infants were randomly assigned to two groups. The first group was the KMI group. These infants were kept in an upright position in skin-to-skin contact, firmly attached to the mother's chest for 24 hours a day. Their temperature thus was maintained within the normal range by the mother's body heat. The infants were breastfed regularly and premature formula supplements were used to guarantee adequate weight gain as necessary. They were examined daily until they gained at least 20g per day. They remained in the kangaroo position until they no longer accepted it. The control inter-vention infants were kept in incubators until they could regulate their temperature and show appropriate weight gain. They were usually discharged when they weighed 1700g. The practice of the neonatal intensive unit was to severely restrict the parent's access to their infants. Infants who received KMI spent less time in the hospital, the severity of infections was less, and more of these infants were breastfed until three months of corrected age.

The term "Kangaroo Mother Care" (KMC) refers to the method of skin-to-skin contact between mother and baby done directly from birth. In this method, babies are fed breast milk exclusively (usually, no premature formula supplements are given) and support is given to the mother-infant dyad. Data from RCTs have found that KMC resulted in better physiological outcomes and stability than the same care provided in incubators (Bergman et al., 2004); that KMC managed babies had better weight gain, earlier hospital discharge and, higher exclusive breast-feeding rates (Ramanathan et al., 2001); and that KMC positively impacted a mother's sense of competence and facilitated the mother-infant attachment process (Tessier et al., 1998). A recent meta-analysis (Conde-Agudelo et al., 2003) of three studies involving 1362 low birthweight infants found that KMC was associated with the following reduced risks: nosocomial infection, severe illness, lower respiratory tract disease at 6 month follow-up,

and not exclusively breastfeeding at discharge. KMC infants had gained more weight per day by discharge. Concerns about the methodological quality of the included trials led the authors to conclude that although KMC appeared to reduce severe infant morbidity without any serious deleterious effect reported, there was still insufficient evidence to recommend its routine use in LBW infants.

The term "kangaroo care" (KC) simply refers to any amount of skin-to-skin contact and is used interchangeably with the term "skin-to-skin contact." The additional elements described in the previous methods (e.g. exclusive breast milk, early discharge) are not necessarily required. Kangaroo care improved state regulation in three RCTs. In the first trial, infants receiving KC had higher mean tympanic temperatures more quiet sleep and less crying than their counterparts (Chwo et al., 2002). A higher mean tympanic temperature (within the normal range) is a general indicator of improved neonate stability and shows their ability to maintain an appropriate body temperature. In the second trial, which was designed to study the safety of three continuous hours of KC for preterm infants (Ludington-Hoe et al., 2004), apnea, bradycardia, and periodic breathing were ab-sent during KC. Regular breathing increased for infants receiving KC compared to infants receiving standard NICU care. In the third trial of 28 preterm infants (Ludington-Hoe et al., 2006), arousals and rapid eye movement, two developmental milestones, were significantly lower for the group that experienced skin-to-skin contact. The patterns demonstrated by the skin-to-skin group were found to be analogous to more mature sleep organization.

KC has been found to help women breastfeed successfully, which is especially important for vulnerable premature babies as breastfeeding confers immunological and nutritional benefits to babies which cannot be duplicated with premature formulas. In a RCT of 50 infants (Bier et al., 1996), mothers in the skin-to-skin group were found to have more stable milk production and were more likely to still be breastfeeding at 1 month after discharge. In a prospective observational study of 119 mothers of very low birth weight infants, kangaroo care was one of the significant correlates that predicted successful lactation beyond 40 weeks corrected age (Furman et al., 2002).

Weaker evidence of the benefits of KC for preterm babies includes a review that found that heart rate and abdominal skin temperature rose with skin-to-skin contact and periodic breathing episodes dropped during KC (Ludington-Hoe et al., 1994). Similarly, a study of 73 KC infants who were compared with 73 matched controls, found that at term, KC infants showed more mature state distribution and more organized sleep-wake cyclicity. At 3 months, KC infants had higher thresholds to negative emotionality and more efficient arousal modulation (Feldman et al., 2002b). Another study followed 70 preterm infants, half of whom received kangaroo care, and found that KC accelerated autonomic and neurobehavioral maturation (Feldman et al., 2003). One group of researchers (Feldman et al., 2002a) found that at three months, mothers and fathers of KC infants were more sensitive and provided a better home environment. At six months, KC mothers were more sensitive and infants had higher mental and psychomotor development.

Term Infants

Only a few studies have reported the use of KC with *term* infants. One RCT (Ferber et al., 2004), which looked specifically at kangaroo care for term infants, included 47 healthy mother-infant pairs. Mothers were randomly assigned to KC shortly after delivery or the no-treatment standard care. KC began at 15 to 20 minutes after delivery and lasted for 1 hour. During a 1 hour long observation, starting at 4 hours postnatally, multivariate ANOVA revealed a significant difference between the profiles of the 2 groups (F[10,36] = 2.39; p=0.02): the KC infants slept longer; were mostly in a quiet sleep state; exhibited more flexor movements and postures; and showed less extensor movements. Authors concluded that KC improved state organization and motor system modulation of the term newborn infant shortly after delivery. Further evidence from RCTs found that KC had positive effects for extrauterine temperature adaptation in hypothermic term infants (Huang et al., 2006); and that KC had an analgesic effect for term infants during a standard heel lance procedure (in the skin-to-skin group, crying and grimacing were reduced by 82% and 65% respectively) (Gray et al., 2000).

A recent meta-analysis of KC (Anderson et al., 2003) found that KC after birth had a positive effect on long-term breastfeeding in term dyads, and that the temperature of the healthy, newly delivered infant remained in a safe range, provided ventral-to-ventral KC was uninterrupted and the infant was thoroughly dried and covered across the back. In another study, KC was found to significantly decrease crying 60 minutes post birth in term infants (Christensson et al., 1995). Studies have shown that maternal touch by massage rather than by holding in the postnatal period also was beneficial in terms of improved weight gain in preterm infants (Ferber et al., 2002a) and in maturation of circadian rhythms and melatonin secretion in term infants (Ferber et al., 2002b). In a case study of 3 mothers with full term infants with breastfeeding difficulties, infants were held in kangaroo care for one hour prior to breastfeeding. KC was found to be a worthwhile intervention to try when mother and full term infant are struggling to achieve breastfeeding success (Meyer et al., 1999).

Benefits of In-Arms Holding

Simple holding, even without the skin-to-skin contact, also has benefits including reduced crying and more secure attachment. In one RCT (Hunziker et al., 1986), 99 mother-infant pairs were randomly assigned to either the supplemental carrying group in which parents were asked to carry their baby for a minimum of three hours per day and infant carriers were provided, or to the traditional care group. At the time of peak crying (6 weeks old), infants who received supplemental carrying cried and fussed 43% less overall and 51% less in the evening hours (4 pm to midnight).

In an effort to treat excessive crying in newborns, one RCT (Barr et al., 1991) focused on KC as a therapy for colic. 66 mothers of infants 4 weeks of age or less who came to their pediatricians with complaints of crying problems were randomized to either standard pediatric advice plus the recommendation to increase supplemental carrying by 50% or standard pediatric advice alone. The supplemental group carried their infants 6.1 hours/day throughout the intervention period, an increase of 2.2 hours/day (56%) more than that provided by the standard group. There was no difference between groups in the duration or frequency of crying or fussing at any time throughout the intervention period. KC was not found to be an effective therapy for colic and the authors speculated that in marked contrast to healthy infants, this apparent resistance to increased carrying may indicate an important difference in state regulation and control in infants with colic.

Soft Baby Carriers Facilitate Holding

With the understanding that having access to a soft baby carrier can facilitate holding, one RCT specifically provided soft carriers to new moms to study the effect. In this trial (Anisfeld, 1990), 49 mothers of newborn infants were randomly assigned to either receive a soft baby carrier or a plastic infant seat. Subjects were asked to use their product daily. Using a transitional probability analysis of a play session at 3 ½ months, mothers in soft baby carrier group were more contingently responsive to their infants' vocalizations. When the infants were 13 months old, the Ainsworth Strange Situation was administered and more experimental than control infants were securely attached to their mothers. Authors concluded that mothers who were given soft carriers at birth were more responsive to their babies and the babies were more securely attached.

The safety of soft carriers was studied in a 3-period crossover trial in which 24 preterm and 12 term newborns were continually monitored while being carried horizontally or vertically in a sling or lying in a pram (Waltraud et al., 2002). The 90% confidence interval of oxygen saturation in both infant sling positions remained within a +/- 2% interval around the average oxygen saturation in the pram. Authors concluded that preterm and term infants who were carried in slings were not at risk of clinically relevant changes of oxygen saturation or heart rate.

Table 5: Effectiveness of mother/baby physical contact (RCT)

Study	Participants	Intervention	Outcome
Chwo et al., 2002	34 premature newborns	Group 1: KC Group 2: Standard premature baby care	Mean tympanic temperature: Group 1: 37.3 degrees C*, Group 2: 37 degrees C (p<0.001). More quiet sleep: 1: 62%*, 2: 22% (p<0.001) Crying: 1: 2%*, 2: 6% (p<.0.01)

Study	Participants	Intervention	Outcome
Charpak et al., 2001	746 premature newborns (<2000g)	Group 1: KMI – Skin-to-skin contact on the mother's chest 24 hours/day, nearly exclusive breastfeeding, and early discharge, with close ambulatory monitoring. Group 2: Traditional care – Infants remained in incubators until the usual discharge criteria were met.	Days spent in the hospital at term: (among infants <1200 g) Group 1: 5.8 days*, Group 2: 15.9 days Frequency of nosocomial infections: 1: 3.4%*, 2: 6.8% (rate ratio 2.01, 95% CI: 1.04-3.87) Breastfed at 3 months corrected age: 1: 81.7%*, 2: 75.3% (p=.05)
Bergman et al., 2004	34 premature newborns between 1200 and 2199g at birth	Group 1: KMC Group 2: Incubator care	Stabilization score (measured in terms of a set of pre-determined physiological parameters, and a composite cardio-respiratory stabilization score): Group 1: 77.11,* Group 2: 74.24, mean difference 2.88 (95% CI: 0.3-5.46, p=0.031) Stable in the sixth hour: 1: 18/18,* 2: 6/13
Ramanathan et al., 2001	28 premature newborns whose birth weight was less than 1500g	Group 1: KMC for at least four hours per day in not more than 3 sittings. KMC after shifting out of the NICU and at home Group 2: Standard care (incubator or open care system)	Weight gain after first week of life: Group 1: 15.9+/- 4.5g/d*, Group 2: 10.6+/-4.5g/d (p<0.05). Days in hospital: 1: 27.2*, 2: 34.6 (p<0.05). Exclusively breastfeeding at 6 weeks: 1: 12/14*, 2: 6/14 (p<.0.05).
Tessier et al., 1998	488 premature newborns weighing <2001g and their mothers	Group 1: KMC- Breast-milk and preterm formula. Infants monitored daily until gaining 20g/day. Group 2: Standard NICU care. Incubators until appropriate weight gain. Discharged after weight is 1700g.	"Bonding effect"- change in mother's perception of her child as being within normal limits was observed in Group 1 mothers. "Resilience effect"- In stressful situations Group 1 mothers felt more competent than Group 2 mothers.

Study	Participants	Intervention	Outcome
Ludington-Hoe et al., 2004	24 premature newborns (33-35 weeks gestation at birth) nearing discharge	Group 1: KC for 3 continuous hours Group 2: Standard NICU care	Group 1: Mean cardiorespiratory and temperature outcomes remained within clinically acceptable ranges. Group 1: Apnea, bradycardia, and periodic breathing were absent. Regular breathing increased.
Ludington-Hoe et al., 2006	28 premature newborns	Group 1: KC Group 2: Routine NICU care	Arousals and rapid eye movement were significantly lower for Group 1.
Huang et al., 2006	78 consecutive cesarean term newborns with hypothermia problems	Group 1: KC with their mothers in the post-operative room Group 2: Routine care under radiant warmers	Mean temperature: Group 1: 36.29 degrees C*, Group 2: 36.22 degrees C (p=0.044)
Bier et al., 1996	50 premature newborns with birthweights <1500g whose mothers planned to breast feed	Group 1: KC - infants were clothed in a diaper and held upright between mothers' breasts; both mother and infant were covered with a blanket Group 2: Standard contact-infants were clothed, wrapped in blankets, and held cradled in mother's arms.	Oxygen saturation readings of less than 90% during intervention: Group 1: 11%*, Group 2: 24% (p<0.001). More stable milk production in Group 1. Continued breastfeeding at 1 month after discharge: 1: 50%*, 2: 11% (p<0.01).
Ferber et al., 2004	47 term newborns and their mothers	Group 1: KC beginning at 15 to 20 minutes after delivery and lasting for 1 hour. Group 2: Standard care	During a 1 hour observation, starting 4 hours postnatally, Group 1 infants slept longer, were mostly in a quiet sleep state, exhibited more flexor movements and postures and showed less extensor movements. Multivariate ANOVA F[10,36] = 2.39* p=0.02
Gray et al., 2000	30 term newborns	During a standard heel lance procedure: Group 1: Held by their mothers in a whole body, skin-to-skin contact Group 2: Swaddled in crib	In Group 1: Crying was reduced by 82%* Grimacing was reduced by 65%* (p<0.0001 for both)

Study	Participants	Intervention	Outcome
Hunziker et al., 1986	99 term newborns	Group 1: Parents were asked to carry their baby for a minimum of three hours per day, and it was emphasized that carrying should occur throughout the day, not only in response to crying. Group 2: Traditional care	Group 1 at 6 weeks of age cried and fussed 43% less overall (1.23 v 2.16 hours/day) and 51% less during evening hours (4 pm to midnight) (0.63 v 1.28 hours). (p<0.001)
Barr et al., 1991	66 mothers of infants 4 weeks of age or less who came to their pediatricians with complaints of crying problems	Group 1: Standard pediatric advice plus the recommendation to increase supplemental carrying by 50% Group 2: Standard pediatric advice	No difference between groups in the duration or frequency of crying or fussing at any time throughout the intervention.
Anisfeld et al., 1990	49 mothers of term newborns	Group 1: Received soft baby carriers Group 2: Received plastic infant seats	Mothers mean responsivity score at 3 ½ months: Group 1: .56*, Group 2: .33 (p<0.02) Infants securely attached to mother at 13 months old (Ainsworth Strange Situation): 1: 83%*, 2: 38% (p=.019).

Conclusions

In sum, safety has been adequately demonstrated for all types of holding (kangaroo care, in-arms and in a sling). There is strong evidence to support the use of kangaroo care for *preterm* babies with benefits that include shortened hospital stay, decreased morbidity, higher exclusive breastfeeding rates/longer breastfeeding duration, increased weight gain, improved state regulation, and improved maternal sense of competence. Evidence-based benefits of KC for *term* babies include improved state organization and motor system modulation; improved extrauterine temperature adaptation; and an analgesic effect. No serious deleterious effects were reported. Simple holding, without the skin-to-skin contact, was found to reduce crying, and the provisions of soft carriers led to mothers who were more responsive to their babies and to babies who were more securely attached. Given the many benefits of physical contact between mother and baby, it appears reasonable to encourage this essential practice of holding – promoting skin-to-skin contact, in-arms holding, and holding in a soft baby carrier, as a matter of course in the care of new babies (both premature and term) and their parents.

PROMOTING CAR SEAT USE

In 1996, 653 children (newborns through 4 years of age) were killed as occupants in motor vehicles. Of these fatalities, 52% were unrestrained (US Dept of Transportation, 1997). Current legislation in all 50 states requires the use of car seats or child restraint systems (CRS) for infants and young children. Current guidelines recommend that until one year old *and* at least 20 pounds, infants should be in a rear-facing car seat that is tightly installed in the back seat, preferably in the center position. The car seat should never be used in a front seat where an air bag is present. The car seat should recline at approximately a 45-degree angle with the harness straps snug on the child at or below shoulder level. The harness clip should be at armpit level. From one to four years and at least 20 pounds to approximately 40 pounds, children should be in a forward-facing car seat or high back booster. From four to at least eight years old, or until they are 57 inches tall, children should ride in a belt-positioning booster (National Highway Traffic Safety Administration, 2006; American Academy of Pediatrics, 2006).

A study on restraint use for 5,527 children under 80 pounds found that 72.6 percent of 3,442 observed CRS displayed one or more critical misuses. The most common misuses were loose vehicle safety belt attachment to the CRS and loose harness straps securing the child to the CRS. 11.8 percent of the children observed in the study were not using any type of CRS or safety belt. Among children 60 to 79 pounds, almost one in four (24.2 percent) was unrestrained (National Highway Traffic Safety Administration, 2004).

Correctly used CRS are 71% effective in preventing fatalities attributable to car crashes and 67% effective in preventing injury that requires hospitalization. With 100% correct use, about 53,000 injuries and 500 deaths could be prevented each year in the United States among children from birth to 4 years of age (National Technical Information Service, 1986).

Despite the fact that car seat use has been shown to be effective in reducing injury and death to children under 4 years of age who are passengers in cars (Johnston et al., 1994),

many parents do not use car seats for their children or use them incorrectly. Research has focused on two possible reasons, lack of access to car seats (affordability) and lack of parent education (stressing the importance of car seats), or a combination of these two factors. This review covers interventions aimed at increasing car seat use for infants and young children. Randomized controlled trials (RCT) will be summarized in Table 6.

Arguing that assuring that newborns are restrained properly when riding for the first time establishes the pattern for continued compliance with a measure that can save their lives or prevent serious injury, the American Academy of Pediatrics recommends that admission orders for newborns include an order written by a physician for parent instruction about use of car seats. It also recommends that discharge policies for newborns include the following (AAP, 1999a):

- Determination of the most appropriate car seat for each newborn according to maturity and medical condition.
- Provision of information about correct use of car seats, with hands-on teaching (AAP, 1999b and 1998).
- For each infant born at <37 weeks gestation, a period of observation in a car seat before hospital discharge to monitor for possible apnea, bradycardia, or oxygen desaturation (AAP, 1996).
- Physicians should work for coverage of appropriate CRS as a benefit of health coverage. Until that time, hospitals are encouraged to have a giveaway or loan program for parents who cannot afford to purchase a car seat.

Loaner programs for infant car seats have contributed to increased use of car seats among the general population (Colletti, 1986). In one RCT (Christophersen et al., 1982), 30 mother infant pairs from obstetric unit were randomly assigned to two groups. A control group was discharged from the obstetrics unit with no particular emphasis on car safety and no loaner restraint seat available. An experimental group was offered a loaner restraint seat, instruction on how to carry the infant in the seat out to the car, and instruction on how to fasten the restraint in the automobile with the auto lap belt. Correct use of the loaner restraint seat on the first ride home was observed in 67% of the experimental mothers and in none (0%) of the control mothers. Mothers in the control group were expected to obtain a restraint seat through conventional means and apparently did not do so. Although this difference was no longer significant at four- to- six week follow-up this study points out the short-term impact that hospital staff can have on the parents' use of restraint seats.

In a follow-up to this initial study (Christophersen et al., 1985), 129 mother-newborn pairs were randomly assigned to two groups. All of the participants had their babies at a hospital that had an established car seat loaner program with strong support from the medical staff, the nursing staff, and the hospital administration; the hospital was in a state that had a law mandating child restraint usage. One group was exposed to the regular hospital program and the other group had, in addition, a demonstration for the mothers on the correct method of fastening the baby into the car seat and the car seat into the

automobile seat; written handouts of how to use a car seat with an infant; a physician's order for the demonstration; and a physician's order to be discharged in a car seat. Although there was no significant difference between the groups, both groups had correct usage rates above 90% at hospital discharge and maintained usage at better than 80% for one full year. Simply providing the car seat seemed to have had a powerful effect.

Car seat use has been found to decrease as children get older, and toddlers have been found to receive less protection from motor-vehicle-related injuries than infants (Johnston et al., 1994). One RCT looked at the impact of providing booster seats for 4-7 year olds (Gittelman et al., 2006) and found that education in a pediatric emergency department did not convince parents to purchase and use booster seats; however, the combination of education with installation markedly increased booster seat use in this population. Similarly, another RCT (Louis et al., 1997) concluded that distributing car seats for toddlers from inner city families resulted in long-term use among a currently low-use population.

Conclusion

In sum, CRS use has been shown to be effective in reducing injury and death to infants and children. Current research

Table 6: Interventions to Promote the Use of Car Safety Seats (RCT)

Study	Participants	Intervention	Outcome
Christophersen et al., 1982	30 mother infant pairs	Group 1: Standard discharge with no particular emphasis on car safety and no loaner car seat. Group 2: Offered a loaner restraint seat at discharge, with staff demo on how to put the infant into seat, carry infant in the seat out to the car and how to secure seat in car.	Correct use of loaner restraint seat on the first ride home: Group 1: 0%, Group 2: 67%*. Difference was no longer significant at four- to- six weeks follow-up.

Study	Participants	Intervention	Outcome
Christophersen et al., 1985	129 mother-newborn pairs	Group 1: Standard discharge regarding car seat use. Group 2: Standard discharge plus demonstrations, handouts, and physicians orders requiring car seat use.	No significant difference between two groups. Both groups: At hospital discharge: 90% correct usage rates; At one year: 80% correct usage rates.
Louis et al., 1997	53 families from low-income urban minority community	Group 1: Given car seat Group 2: Given car seat plus one hour education session on importance of using car restraints.	Groups 1 and 2: Car seat use increased markedly immediately after distribution (from 6% to 83%; p<0.0001) and remained high 1 year later (60%), regardless of education.
Gittelman et al., 2006	225 children aged 4 to 7 years, weighing 40 – 80 pounds presenting to emergency department (ED) without a booster seat, residing in lower socioeconomic communities	Group 1: Received standard discharge instructions Group 2: Received five-minute booster seat training. Group 3: Received five-minute booster seat training and free booster seat with installation.	Before randomization, 79.6% of parents reported that their child was usually positioned in the car with a lap/shoulder belt and 13.3% with a lap belt alone. 147 (65.3%) of parents were contacted for follow-up at one month. Purchased and used a booster seat after their ED visit: Group 1: 1 parent (1.3%), Group 2: 4 parents (5.3%). Used booster seat after ED visit: Group 3: 55 parents (98.2%)*; 42 (75%) of these parents reported using the seat 100% of the time.

suggests that access to car seats is the leading factor in car seat use. These results corroborate past findings on other safety-device giveaway programs (Shaw et al., 1988; Gorman et al., 1985) and indicate that provision of car seats is the intervention most likely to result in high use of car seats in a population not currently using them.

CONCLUSIONS

1. Home-like settings are as effective as hospital birth centers for selected low-risk pregnant women. Home-like settings for childbirth were associated with minor benefits, including reduced medical interventions, increased maternal satisfaction and increased breastfeeding initiation and continuation rates.

2. Institutional support, provider and patient education improve breastfeeding rates in randomized trials. Avoiding the promotion of formula or supplemental feeding, and enthusiastic promotion of breastfeeding appear to be valuable components of these interventions.

3. Safety has been adequately demonstrated for all types of holding (kangaroo care, in-arms and in a sling). *Kangaroo care for preterm babies is strongly supported with benefits that include shortened hospital stay, decreased morbidity, increased breastfeeding initiation and continuation rates, increased weight gain, improved state regulation, and improved maternal sense of competence.* Evidence-based benefits of KC for *term* babies include improved state organization, improved temperature regulation; and an analgesic effect. No serious negative effects were reported. Simple holding, without the skin-to-skin contact, was found to reduce crying, and the provisions of soft carriers led to mothers who were more responsive to their babies and to babies who were more securely attached.

4. *Child restraint use has been shown to be effective in reducing injury and death to infants and children. Evidence supports access to car seats as the leading factor in car seat use.*

REFERENCES

American Academy of Pediatrics. (1996) Committee on Injury and Poison Prevention and Committee on Fetus and Newborn Safe transportation of premature and low birth weight infants. Pediatrics 97:758-760.

American Academy of Pediatrics. (1998) Car Seat Shopping Guide for Children With Special Needs (brochure). Elk Grove Village, IL: American Academy of Pediatrics.

American Academy of Pediatrics. (1999a) Committee on Injury and Poison Prevention. Safe Transportation of Newborns at Hospital Discharge. Pediatrics 104:986-7.

American Academy of Pediatrics. (1999b) Family Shopping Guide to Car Seats (brochure). Elk Grove Village, IL: American Academy of Pediatrics.

American Academy of Pediatrics. (2006) Selecting and using the most appropriate car safety seats for growing children: guidelines for counseling parents. Available at: www.aap.org/policy/re0116.html. Accessed September 18, 2006.

Anderson GC, Moor E, Hepworth J, Bergman N. (2003) Early skin-to-skin contact for mothers and their healthy newborn infants. Cochrane Database Syst Rev.

Anisfeld E, Casper V, Nozyce M, Cunningham N. (1990) Does infant carrying promote attachment? An experimental study of the effects of increased physical contact on the development of attachment. Child Dev 61:1617-1627.

Aniansson G, Alm B, Andersson B, Hakansson A, Larsson P, Nylen O, et al. (1994) A prospective cohort study on breastfeeding and otitis media in Swedish infants. Pediatr Infect Dis J 13(3):183-8.

Barr RG, McMullan SJ, Spiess H. (1991) Carrying as colic therapy: a randomized controlled trial. Pediatrics 87:623-630.

Bergman NJ, Linely LL, Fawcus SR. (2004) Randomized controlled trial of skin-to-skin contact from birth versus conventional incubator for physiological stabilization in 1200- to 2199-gram newborns. Acta Paediatr 93(6):779-85.

Bier JA. Ferguson AE. Morales Y, Liebling JA, Archer D, Oh W, Vohr BR. (1996) Comparison of skin-to-skin contact with standard contact in low-birth weight infants who are breast fed. Arch Pediatr Adolesc Med. 150(12):1265-9.

Bryant CA, Coreil J, D'Angelo SL et al. (1992) A strategy for promoting breastfeeding among economically disadvantaged women and adloscents. NAACOGS Clin Issues Perinatal Women's Health Nurs 3:723.

Carbajal R, Veerapen S, Couderc S, et al. (2003) Analgesic effect of breast feeding in term neonates: randomised controlled trial. BJM 326(7379):13.

Charpak N, JG Ruiz-Palaez, Z Figueroa de

Calume, Y Charpak. (2001) A randomized, controlled trial of Kangaroo Mother Care: Results of follow-up at one year of corrected age. Pediatrics 108(5): 1072-9.

Christensson K, Cabrera T, Christensson E, Uvnas Moberg K, Winberg J. (1995) Separation distress call in the human neonate in the absence of maternal body contact. Acta Paediatr. 84: 468-473.

Christophersen ER, Sosland-Edelman D, LeClaire S. (1985) Evaluation of two comprehensive infant car seat loaner programs with 1 year follow-up. Pediatrics 76(1):36-42.

Christophersen ER, Sullivan MA. (1982) Increasing the protection of newborn infants in cars. Pediatrics 70(1):21-5.

Chwo MJ, Anderson GC, Good M, Dowling DA, Shiau SH, Chu DM. (2002) A randomized controlled trial of early kangaroo care for preterm infants: effects on temperature, weight, behavior, and acuity. J Nurs Res 10(2):129-42.

Colletti RB. (1986) Longitudinal evaluation of a state-wide network of hospital programs in improved child passenger safety. Pediatrics 77:523-9.

Conde-Agudelo A, JL Diaz-Rossello, JM Balizan. (2003) Kangaroo mother care to reduce morbidity and mortality in low birthweight infants. Cochrane Database Syst Rev (2):CD002771.

Coutinho PI, Cabral de Lira M, de Carvalho Lima and A Ashworth. (2005) Comparison of the effect of two systems for the promotion of exclusive breastfeeding. Lancet 366:1094-1100.

Dennis CL, Hodnett E, Gallop R, Chalmers B. (2002) The effect of peer support on breast-feeding duration among primiparous women: a randomized controlled trial. CMAJ 166(1):21-8.

DiGirolamo AM, Grummer-Strawn LM, Fein SB. (2003) Do perceived attitudes of physicians and hospital staff affect breast-feeding decisions? Birth 30(2):94-100.

DiGirolamo AM, Grummer-Strawn LM, Fein SG. (2001) Maternity care practices: implications for breastfeeding. Birth 28(2): 94-100.

Dowswell T, Thornton JG, Hewison J, Lilford RJL. (1996) Should there be a trial of home versus hospital delivery in the United Kingdom? Measuring outcomes other than safety is feasible. BMJ 321:753.

Dyson L, McCormick, E. Renfrew MJ. (2005) Interventions for promoting the initiation of breastfeeding. Cochrane Database of Systematic Reviews. Issue 2 CD001688.

Feldman R, AI Eidelman. (2003) Skin-to skin contact (Kangaroo Care) accelerates autonomic and neurobeharioural maturation in preterm infants. Dev Med Child Neurol 45(4): 274-81.

Feldman R, Eidelman AI, Sirota L, Weller A. (2002a) Comparison of skin-to-skin (kangaroo) and traditional care: Parenting outcomes and preterm infant development. Pediatrics 110:16-26.

Feldman R, Weller A, Sirota L, Eidelman AI. (2002b) Skin-to-skin contact (kangaroo care) promotes self-regulation in premature infants: sleep-wake cyclicity, arousal modulation, and sustained exploration. Dev Psychol 38:194 –207.

Ferber SG, Kuint J, Weller A, Feldman R, Dollberg S, Arbel E, Kohelet D. (2002a) Massage therapy by mothers and trained professionals enhances weight gain in preterm infants. Early Hum Dev 67:37-45.

Ferber SG, Laudon M, Kuint J, Weller A, Zisapel N. (2002b) Massage therapy by mothers enhances the adjustment of circadian rhythms to the nocturnal period in full-term infants. J Dev Behav Pediatr 23:410-415.

Ferber SG, Makhoul IR. (2004) The effect of skin-to-skin contact (kangaroo care) shortly after birth on the neurobehavioral responses of the term newborn: a randomized, controlled trial. Pediatrics

113(4):858-65.

Frank DA, Wirtz SJ, Sorenson JR, Heeren T. (1987) Commercial discharge packs and breast-feeding counseling: effects on infant-feeding practices in a randomized trial. Pediatrics 80(6):845-54.

Freeman MP, Hibbeln JR, Wisner KL et al. (2006) Randomized dose-ranging pilot trial of omega-3 fatty acids for postpartum depression. Acta Psychiatr Scand 113:31-5.

Furman L, N Minich, M Hack. (2002) Correlates of lactation in mothers of very low birth weight infants. Pediatrics 109(4): e57. (http://www.pediatrics.org/cgi/content/full/109/4/e57)

Gittelman MA, Pomerantz WJ, Laurence S. (2006) An emergency department intervention to increase booster seat use for lower socioeconomic families. Acad Emerg Med 13(4):396-400.

Gorman RL, Charney E, Holtzman NA, Roberts KB. (1985) A successful city-wide smoke detector giveaway program. Pediatrics 75:14-18.

Gray L, L Watt, E Blass. (2000) Skin-to-skin contact is analgesic in healthy newborns. Pediatrics 105(1):e14.

Gray-Donald k, Kramer MS Munday S et al. (1985) Effect of formula supplementation in the hospital on the duration of breastfeeding: a controlled clinical trial. Pediatrics 75:514.

Gwinn ML, Lee NC, Rhodes PH, Layde PM, Rubin GL. (1990) Pregnancy, breast-feeding and oral contraceptives and the risk of epithelial ovarian cancer. J Clin Epidemiol 43:559-68.

Herrara AJ. (1984) Supplemented versus unsupplemented breastfeeding. Perinatol Neonatol 8:70.

Hodnett ED, Downe S, Edwards N, Walsh D. (2005) Home-like versus conventional institutional settings for birth. Cochrane Database Syst Rev (1):CD000012.

Howard C, Howard F, Lawrence R, Andresen E, DeBlieck E, Weitzman M. (2000) Office prenatal formula advertising and its effect on breast-feeding patterns. Obstet Gynecol 95(2):296-303.

Howie PW, Forsyth JS, Ogston SA et al. (1990) Protective effect of breast feeding against infection. BJM 300:11-6.

Huang YY, Huang CY, Lin SM, Wu SC. (2006) Effect of very early kangaroo care on extrauterine temperature adaptation in newborn infants with hypothermia problems. Hu Li Za Zhi 53(4):41-8.

Hunziker UA, Garr RG. (1986) Increased carrying reduces infant crying: A randomized controlled trial. Pediatrics 77:641-648.

Johnston C, Rivara FP, Soderberg R. (1994) Children in car crashes. Analysis of data for injury and use of restraints. Pediatrics 93:960-5.

Karjalainen J, Martin JM, Knip M, Ilonen J, et al. (1992) A bovine albumin peptide as a possible trigger of insulin-dependent diabetes mellitus. NEJM 327(5):302-7.

Kramer MS, Kakuma R. (2002) Optimal duration of exclusive breastfeeding. Cochrane Database Syst. Rev (1): CD003517.

Labarere J, Gelbert-Baudino N, Ayral AS et al. (2005) Efficacy of breastfeeding support provided by trained clinicians during an early, routine, preventive visit: a prospective, randomized, open trial of 226 mother-infant pairs. Pediatrics 115(2): e139-46.

Lawrence, RA, Lawrence RM. (1999) *Breastfeeding: A Guide for the Medical Professional.* Fifth ed. St. Louis: Mosby.

Layde PM, Webster LA, Baughman AL et al. (1989) The independent associations of parity, age at first full term pregnancy and duration of breastfeeding with the risk of breast cancer. J Clinical Epid 42:963-73.

Lindenberg CS, Artola RC, Jimenez V. (1990) The effect of early postpartum mother-infant contact and breastfeeding promotion on the incidence and continuation of breastfeeding. Int J Nurs Stud 27: 179.

Louis B, Lewis M. (1997) Increasing car seat use for toddlers from inner-city families. Am J Public Health 87(6):1044-5.

Lucas A. Cole TJ. (1990) Breastmilk and neonatal necrotizing enterocolitis. Lancet 336(8730):1519-23.

Ludington-Hoe SM, Anderson GC, Swinth JY, Thompson C, Hadeed AJ. (2004) Randomized controlled trial of kangaroo care: cardiorespiratory and thermal effects on healthy preterm infants. Neonatal Netw 23(3):39-48.

Ludington-Hoe SM, Johnson MW, Morgan K, Lewis T, Gutman J, Wilson PD, Scher MS. (2006) Neurophysiologic assessment of neonatal sleep organization: preliminary results of a randomized controlled trial of skin contact with preterm infants. Pediatrics 117(5):e909-23.

Ludington-Hoe SM, Thompson C, Swinth J, Hadeed AJ, Anderson GC. (1994) Kangaroo care: Research results, and practice implications and guidelines. Neonatal Netw 13(1):19-27.

MacVicar J, Dobbie G, Owen-Johnstone L, Jagger C, Hopkins M, Kennedy J. (1993) Simulated home delivery in hospital: a randomised controlled trial. Br J Obstet Gynaecol 100(4):316-23.

Mayer EJ, Hamman RF, Gay EC, Lezotte DC, Savitz DA, Klingensmith GJ. (1988) Reduced risk of IDDM among breast fed children: the Colorado IDDM registry. Diabetes 37(12):1625-32.

Merten D, Dratva J, Ackermann-Liebrich U. (2005) Do baby-friendly hospitals influence breastfeeding duration on a national level? Pediatrics 116(5):e702-8.

Meyer K, Anderson GC. (1999) Using kangaroo care in a clinical setting with fullterm infants having breastfeeding difficulties. MCN Am J Matern Child Nurs 24(4):190-2.

National Highway Traffic Safety Administration. (2004) Misuse of Child Restraints. DOT HS 809 671, March 2004.

National Highway Traffic Safety Administration. (2006) Child passenger safety. Available at: www.nhtsa.dot.gov/people/ injury/ childps. Accessed Sept. 18, 2006.

National Technical Information Service. (1986) An Evaluation of Child Passenger Safety: The Effectiveness and Benefits of Safety Seats. Springfield, VA: DOT report DOT MS 806890.

Olsen O, Jewell MD. (1998) Home versus hospital birth. Cochrane Database System Rev Issue 3. CD000352.

Olsen O. (1997) Meta-analysis of the safety of home birth. Birth 24(1):4-13.

Pisacane A, Graxiano K, Mazzarella G, Scarpellino B, Zona G. (1992) Breastfeeding and urinary tract infection. J Pediatrics 120(1):87-9.

Pollitt E, Consolazio B, Goodkin F. (1981) Changes in nutritive sucking during a feed in two-day and thirty day old infants. Early Hum Dev 5:201.

Ramanathan K, Paul VK, Deorari AK, Taneja U, George G. (2001) Kangaroo Mother Care in very low birth weight infants. Indian J Pediatr 68(11):1019-23.

Righard L, Alade MO. (1990) Effect of delivery room routine on success of first breastfeed. Lancet 336:1105.

Rosenblatt KA, Thomas DB. (1993) WHO collaborative study of neoplasia and steroid contraceptives. Lactation and the risk of epithelial ovarian canter. Int J Epidemiol 22(2):192-7.

Saarinen UM, Kajosaari M. (1995) Breastfeeding as prophylaxis against atopic disease: prospective follow-up study until 17 years old. Lancet 346(8982):1065-9.

Shaw KN, McCormick MC, Kustra SL, Ruddy RM, Casey RD. (1988) Correlates of reported smoke detector usage in an inner-city population; participants in a smoke detector give-away program. Am J

Public Health. 78:650-3.

Sibley L and Ann Sipe T. (2004) What can a meta-analysis tell us about traditional birth attendant training and pregnancy outcomes? Midwifery 20(1):51-60.

Taveras EM, Li R, Grummer-Strawn L et al. (2004) Opinions and practices of clinicians associated with continuation of exclusive breastfeeding. Pediatrics 113(4): e283-90.

Tessier R, M Cristo, S Velez, M Giron, JG Ruiz-Palaez, Y Charpak and N Charpak. (1998) Kangaroo mother care and the bonding hypothesis. Pediatrics 102:e17.

US Department of Transportation, (1997) National Highway Traffic Safety Administration. Traffic Safety Facts 1996. A Compilation of Motor Vehicle Crash Data from the Fatal Accident Reporting System and the General Estimates System. Washington, DC: US Department of Transportation, National Highway Traffic Safety Administration.

Vaidya K, Sharma A, Dhungel S. (2005) Effect of early mother-baby close contact over the duration of exclusive breast-feeding. Nepal Med Coll J 7(2):138-40.

Victoria CG, Smith PG, Barros PC et al. (1989) Risk factors for deaths due to respiratory infections among Brazilian infants. Int J Epidemiol 18:918-25.

Waldenstrom U, Nilsson CA. (1994) Experience of childbirth in birth center care. A randomized controlled study. Acta Obstet Gynecol Scand 73(7):547-54.

Waltraud S, Nitsch P, Wassmer G, Roth B.

(2002) Cardiorespiratroy stability of premature and term infants carried in infant slings. Pediatrics 110:879-883.

Whitelaw A, Sleath K. (1985) Myth of the marsupial mother: home care of very low birth weight babies in Bogota, Colombia. Lancet 1(8439):1206 –1208.

Widstrom A-M, Wahlberg V, Matthiesen A-S et al. (1990) Short-term effects of early suckling and touch of the nipple on maternal behavior. Early Hum Dev 21:153.

WHO (1981) World Health Organizatin. Contemporary patterns of breast-feeding. In Report on the WHO Collaborative Study on Breast-feeding. Geneva, 1981, World Health Organization.

WHO (2002) World Health Organization. Infant and young child nutrition: global strategy for infant and young child feeding. WHO: Geneva, Executive Board paper 2002. Report No:EB 109/12 2002.

WHO Data Bank. (1996) WHO Global Data Bank on Breast-Feeding, Breast-feeding: the best start in life. Nutrition Unit. Geneva: World Health Organization, 1996.

Wolfberg AJ, Michels KB, Shields W et al. (2004) Dads as breastfeeding advocates: results from a randomized controlled trial of an educational intervention. Am J Obstet Gynecol 191(3):708-12.

Woodward J, Kelly SM. (2004) A pilot study for a randomized trial of waterbirth versus land birth. BJOG 111(6):537-45.

INTERVENTIONS TO INCREASE CHILDHOOD VACCINATION RATES

James Taylor

INTRODUCTION

Immunizations are perhaps the most effective treatment used in medicine to prevent disease. It has been said that immunization ranks after only clean water and sewage removal on its positive effect on the health of the people (Plotkin and Plotkin, 1994). Vaccination programs against small pox led to the world-wide eradication of this disease. In 1952 there were 21,269 cases of paralytic polio in the United States. After the beginning of routine polio vaccination this number fell dramatically; the last indigenous case of paralytic polio in the US was in 1979 (Strebel et al., 1992). Reported cases of diphtheria, measles, mumps, pertussis, rubella, congenital rubella syndrome, tetanus, and invasive haemophilus influenza type b disease all decreased by more than 90% after the introduction of routine immunization against these diseases (Orenstein et al., 1990).

There are several different types of vaccination programs including routine adult and adolescent immunizations and vaccines for children with particular conditions. However, routine immunizations programs for infants and preschool children have the greatest impact on the public health. Vaccination of preschool children is the focus of this chapter. As of 2006, the United States Centers for Disease Control and Prevention recommends the following immunizations for preschool children: Hepatitis B (HepB); Diptheria, Tetanus, Pertussis (DTP); Haemophilus influenze type b (Hib); Inactivated poliovirus (IPV); Measles, Mumps, Rubella (MMR); Varicella; Meningococcal (MPSV4); Pneumococcal (PCV); Influenza; Hepatitis A (HepA). The most recently updated schedule for recommended vaccines for children and adolescents is available at: http://www.cdc.gov/nip/recs/child-schedule.htm.

Perhaps because of the remarkable success of vaccination against diseases such as polio, measles, mumps and rubella, there was limited focus on the effectiveness of delivery of immunizations to preschool children until the early 1990's. Until then, most outbreaks of vaccine-preventable diseases, such as measles, were small and thought to be the result of unsuccessful immunization. However, the measles epidemic of 1989-1991 was a stark demonstration of the problem of underimmunization of infants and preschool children in the US. During these two years, there were over 55,000 cases of measles reported which represented an 800% annual increase when compared to the period 1980-1988. As many as 166 deaths occurred from measles during the epidemic. The main cause of this sudden outbreak was the failure to vaccinate substantial numbers of children 12-15 months of age against this preventable disease. Children living in disadvantaged areas of cities such as Chicago, Houston and Los Angeles accounted for a disproportionately large number of cases (Atkinson et al., 1992).

The measles epidemic served to highlight significant problems with the vaccine delivery system. Cognizant of these problems, the Centers for Disease Control and Prevention developed a set of 18 "Standards for Pediatric Immunization Practices" for use by vaccine providers in public health and practice settings (1993). In addition to vaccine management, the standards dealt with removing barriers to obtaining immunizations, effective education for parents, and a recommendation that providers periodically assess the immunization status of their patients.

When the Standards for Pediatric Immunization Practices were developed, there was little evidence that any, or all, of the individual components were associated with the immunization status of young children. Subsequently, Pierce et al. (1996) compared change in immunization rates among children vaccinated in 2 public health clinics in Albuquerque, NM. In one clinic there was a concerted effort to implement all 18 standards while the other served as a control. Prior to implementation of the standards, 57.5% of 12 month children were up-to-date for immunizations at the intervention site, rising to 80.4% after implementations. There was no change in immunization rates at the control site (Pierce et al., 1996). Although these results are impressive, the unique features of these clinics did not allow for an adequate assessment of the whole compliment of standards. At the control site, immunizations were only offered one day per week, and not as part of other comprehensive services such as a health supervision visit. Conversely, vaccinations were provided 6 days per week at the intervention clinic. This one intervention alone could have accounted for much of the observed differences. Evaluation of many of the individual standards, many of which are described in the following sections, suggests that effectiveness of these standard practices are mixed.

Subsequent to the development of the Standards for Pediatric Practices, at least 3 important changes have significantly altered the delivery of immunizations in the US. First, there has been a shift in the setting where children receive vaccinations. At the time of the measles epidemics it was estimated that half of all immunizations were administered in public health settings. By 1997, 73% of US children received some or all of their immunizations in a primary care practice (Santoli et al., 1999). This change highlighted the central role of the practitioner

in increasing the immunization status of young children. Second, there has been a substantial increase in the number of vaccines recommended for children less than 2 years old. To "fully immunize" a child in the first two years of life in 1988 required a total of 5 injections and three doses of oral poliovirus vaccine. By 2006, up to 18 separate injections were required for children less than 2 to receive all recommended vaccines. Finally, with the explosion of the internet and other forms of electronic communication, information on serious "adverse effects" and alleged adverse effects from immunizations is readily available. Although much of what is disseminated via these mechanisms is not scientifically valid, parental concern about side effects of immunization is likely to become an increasingly important for vaccine refusal. In a national survey of parents of young children conducted between 1998 and 2000, concerns about side effects was the single most commonly cited barrier to obtaining recommended vaccines (Taylor et al., 2002b). In this study, concerns about vaccine safety were not associated with immunization status, however, there are accumulating data that substantial numbers of children are exempted from school vaccination requirements because parents refuse to immunize their children because of safety concerns (Salmon et al., 2005). Because of the "herd immunity" phenomenon with immunizations, there is a paradox with vaccine refusals. Moderate community levels of immunization against some diseases provide a large degree of protection even for those children that are unimmunized (Clements et al., 2001). However, if the proportion of unimmunized children rises sufficiently the risk of vaccine-preventable disease may increase dramatically even among children who have, or are likely, to be fully immunized (Feikin et al., 2000; Omer et al., 2006).

It is against this backdrop that efforts to

increase the immunization status of preschool children are implemented and can by evaluated. The measles epidemic of the late 1980's and early 1990's provided dramatic evidence of the public health importance of maximizing preschool vaccinations; many of the recommendations in the Standards for Pediatric Immunization Practices required changes in the systems of health care delivery. With the shift in provision of immunizations from the public to private sector the role of the individual health care practitioner has become a key determinant of the overall immunization rate of a community. Finally, the increasing public concerns over vaccine safety have highlighted the role of parents in the immunization process. Interventions to increase the immunization status are designed to address one or more of these factors ("system", practitioner, parental). Methods to address system factors include vaccination requirement mandates, community-based public policy initiatives and removal of barriers to receipt of immunizations. In addition to assessing the importance of parental health beliefs regarding vaccines on immunization status, interventions designed to minimize the effects of family socioeconomic status on vaccination rates have been evaluated. However, because of the success of some of the programs aimed at "systems" factors, and because parents generally believe that immunizations are important for the health of their children (Taylor and Cufley, 1996; Taylor et al., 2002b), practitioner factors are probably now the single most important determinant of the immunization status of preschool children in the United States.

In this chapter we will review interventions to increase immunization rates for which there is published evidence of efficacy. Although there is much overlap, interventions are grouped into the three main categories of systems approaches, interventions aimed at parents, and practice- or practitioner-based

interventions.

Most of the studies of these interventions are limited by relatively weak research designs. There are few published randomized controlled trials of interventions to increase immunization. More commonly, investigators compare change in immunization status of a group of children (or comparable groups of patients) before and after an intervention is implemented. Although a group of "control' children may also be included in these studies, the length of observation needed to evaluate an intervention designed to increase immunization rates makes before and after assessments prone to bias from numerous secular trends.

Standard definitions of what constitutes a "fully immunized" preschool child are based on receipt of a certain set of vaccines prior to the age of 19 months, or 2 years. Thus, after a baseline assessment of immunization status on a group of children and implementation of an intervention, up to 2 years of observation is needed to assess the effects of the intervention on a new cohort of children. During this period a myriad of other influences such as new vaccines licensed, well publicized "scares" about the safety of one or more vaccines, shortages of immunizations or changes in financing for immunizations may significantly contaminate the assessment of the particular intervention implemented. Some researchers have sought to minimize the effects of a long observation period by measuring immunization status at earlier ages (e.g. 8 months), or using proxy outcomes such as delay in receiving vaccines.

Cross sectional studies of immunization rates of different groups of patients, such as those followed by different groups of providers, allow for more rapid results. Because there are significant differences in how immunizations are delivered by different providers, for example, it is possible to assess the effect of one or more particular immunization delivery practices on immunition status. The major limitation of this type of study is that there may be other differences besides the immunization practice being assessed that affect vaccination rates. Investigators attempt to adjust for known confounding variables; however, it may be difficult to adequately adjust for some variables, and some of the influences affecting immunization rates may be unknown.

Finally, over the past quarter century immunization delivery to preschool children has become increasingly politicized. Physician groups such as the American Academy of Pediatrics, local and state health departments and the Center for Disease Control (CDC) are highly invested in promoting immunizations. Drug companies invest billions of dollars in developing new vaccines in hopes of generating billions of dollars of profits. Conversely, lay groups, some scientists, and some public figures strongly oppose one or more vaccines because of concerns over safety. Within this milieu, interpretation of study results is difficult, particularly when there are few well done randomized controlled trials.

INTERVENTIONS
Systems Approaches
School/daycare mandates

Although school and daycare vaccination requirements are neither a dramatic nor an innovative intervention, they may be one of the most effective methods for increasing preschool immunization rates. Currently, all 50 states in the US require vaccination against diphtheria, tetanus, pertussis, measles, rubella and polio for school entry; $\geq 95\%$ of children are immunized against these diseases at the time of entry into kindergarten (Hinman et al., 2002). Most of the laws mandating vaccination against these illnesses have been in place for several decades; thus, most of the investigation of the effect of vaccination requirements for school and daycare entry has

been limited to more recently licensed vaccines. However, during the 1976-1977 school year the state of Alaska began strict enforcement of measles vaccination requirements. At the beginning of this period 8.3% of school children had no evidence of measles immunization. One month after strict enforcement was initiated, the percentage of those unvaccinated had dropped to 0.06% (Orenstein and Hinman, 1999). In 1999, California began mandating hepatitis B vaccination for entry into 7th grade. To assess the impact of this mandate data on a cohort of students entering 5th and 6th grade in San Diego in 1998 were reviewed. In 1998, 15.8% of these children were fully immunized against hepatitis B. By 1999, 70.6% of 7th graders (i.e. those who had been is 6th grade in the previous year) were immunized. In 2000, when students in the 5th grade in 1998 were entering 7th grade, the rate of hepatitis B vaccination among San Diego 7th graders was 89.9% (2000; 2001). Davis and Gaglia compared varicella vaccination status among children in states with and without a requirement for this immunization for school or daycare entry. Using data from the 2002 National Immunization survey, these investigators reported that 84.9% of children 19-35 months old who lived in states that required vaccination were immunized against varicella vs. 76.8% of those living in states without any mandates. This difference in varicella vaccination status was significantly different, even after adjusting for potentially confounding variables (Davis and Gaglia, 2005). Overall, in a review of published studies, school/daycare vaccination requirements were found to increase immunizations rates by a mean of 15% (Briss et al., 2000).

Public Policy Initiatives and removal of barriers to obtaining immunizations

Multi-component community-based interventions to increase the immunization status of preschool children, particularly for those in indigent areas, have been evaluated. The key components of a successful community-based intervention are thought to be culturally appropriate education for parents, removal of systemic barriers, and assistance for immunization providers. In a particularly well conducted study, Waterman and colleagues implemented a demonstration project in an inner-city Latino neighborhood in San Diego (Waterman et al., 1996). Free, walk-in immunization clinics were established with a computerized reminder/recall system. Vaccine outreach and education programs were offered at schools and churches. The immunization rate of 2 year-old children living in the zip code area in which the interventions occurred increased from a baseline of 37% to 50%. In contrast, in a demographically similar zip code area which served as a control, the immunization rate increased by one percent.

In 1993, United States Congress enacted the Vaccines for Children (VFC) program (Santoli et al., 1999). Under this program, vaccines are provided at no charge for children who are enrolled in Medicaid, those who are uninsured and some who are under-insured, and American Indian/Alaska Native children. In addition to eliminating a financial barrier to immunizations, a major goal of the program is to enhance the partnership between public health departments and private practitioners who provide vaccines. As part of the program, public health departments perform periodic immunization audits and provide feedback for these providers.

There is evidence that the VFC program is effective in raising immunization rates of young children. In a study of inner-city practices in New York, the immunization status of children vaccinated prior to, and after, the use of VFC vaccines were compared. During 1993, 17.9% of preschool children in the selected practices were fully immunized compared to 42.2% of those vaccinated after implementation of VFC ($p < .05$). This increase was much greater than the trends in immunization rates in New York during the study period, and was independent of practitioner participation in managed care plans (Fairbrother et al., 1997).

In addition to VFC, other programs that removed financial barriers to obtaining immunizations have been shown to be effective, particularly among less affluent populations. In a 1997 survey, 66% of responding pediatricians indicated that they would refer their uninsured patients to a public health provider for vaccinations; only 8% of this sample indicated that they would refer insured patients (Zimmerman et al., 1997). This fractured care, which almost certainly led to lower immunization status has been helped by programs to provide free vaccine in the private sector (such as VFC), and insurance coverage for disadvantaged families. Rodewald and colleagues studied the impact of providing Child Health Plus, an insurance program that provides ambulatory care and immunizations to New York children of families earning less the 222% of the poverty level (Rodewald et al., 1997). Before and after implementation assessments were done with study children to evaluate the impact of the program. Among 1730 children enrolled in the program, immunization rates rose by 7% (76% to 83%, $p = 0.03$). Visits to public health clinics for vaccines decreased significantly ($p = 0.009$); immunization visits by study children to their primary care provider increased significantly.

Not all programs to provide free vaccines to all children, regardless of socioeconomic status, have been as successful. Taylor and colleagues compared the immunization status of children in private practices using vaccines provided free by state health departments to that of children seen by practitioners in states without such programs (Taylor et al., 1997). A total of 15 practices from 11 states participated in the study; 7 of these practices used state supplied vaccines. Data were collected on 857, 2-3 year old children. After controlling for maternal education, size of geographical area and age of the child, there was no evidence that the free vaccine was associated with a greater likelihood of being fully immunized (Odds Ratio (OR) 1.08, 95% Confidence Interval (CI): 0.71 - 1.64). After including the individual practice in the regression model as a random effects term, the basic finding that there was no significant increase in immunization status associated with free vaccine continued to be supported (OR 1.29, 95% CI: 0.59 - 2.81). However, the individual practice that the child attended was statistically associated with the likelihood of being fully immunized (p <.001), highlighting the importance of the practice and practitioner in determining the immunization status of children. In this study, parents who said that they paid, at least partially for immunization out-of-pocket, had children that were as likely to be fully immunized as those of parents who indicated that they had no out-of pocket expenditures for vaccines. This study suggests that for more affluent families the financial costs of vaccines are not a limiting factor.

Parental factors

Socioeconomic factors and remedies

One of the most consistent findings of assessments of immunization status is that children from disadvantaged families are at significant risk for being underimmunized. Although there are undoubtedly several reasons for this, two of the most malleable potential causes for underimmunization among children from disadvantaged families are lack of access to a primary care provider and inadequate health insurance. However, access to a primary care provider by itself does not entirely eliminate the effects of socioeco-mics on immunization status. In a study of 13,520 children who were patients of primary care pediatricians from 42 states,

maternal education status, used a proxy for socioeconomic status, was significantly associated with immunization status (Taylor et al., 2001). The immunization rate of children whose mothers had at most graduated high school was 74.2%, compared to 79.9% for those whose mothers had some college education and 84.8% for children of mothers who were college graduates (p < 0.001). Ortega et al. (2000) surveyed a randomly selected sample of parents of children from Delaware regarding 5 measures designed to determine if the child had a "medical home" in which he/she received comprehensive primary care services. Overall, markers of a child having a medical home were not associated with immunization status at 3 months, 12 months and 24 months of age; family income was associated with immunization status at each point. However, there was a suggestion in this study that some of the individual characteristics of a medical home (or continuous access to a primary care provider) might be important. For example, parents who indicated that their children were without a regular doctor for some point in their lives were 2.6 (95% CI: 1.1 - 5.9) times more likely to be underimmunized at 24 months than those who had continuous care. Children who did not have a regular place for preventive or well-child care were more likely to be underimmunized at 12 months than those with this care (OR 3.1, 95% CI: 1.1 - 8.8).

A major reason for a child to be without a regular doctor or to not have a regular place for well-child care is lack of health insurance. Smith et al. (2006) reviewed data from the 2001 and 2002 National Immunization Survey. Among children who had no lapses in insurance coverage during the previous 12 months, 73.5% were fully immunized. This compares to 64.8% of those who had health insurance at the time of the survey, but who had some lapse in coverage during the prior 12 months. Among children who were uninsured at the time of the immunization assessment, 53.3% were up-to-date for vaccines; only 47.4% of those who had never had health insurance were fully immunized. The immunization rate for those who were continuously insured was statistically higher than that of each of the groups with less coverage. One of the more striking findings of this study was that the immunization rate of children who had Medicaid or State Child Health Insurance Program coverage at the time of the survey was 70.0%. While this was slightly lower than the rate for children with private insurance (75.6%), it was substantially higher than the immunization rate of children with no insurance at the time of the survey (52.6%). When considered collectively, these data suggest that having insurance coverage that provides regular access to a primary care provider may, in part, mitigate the deleterious effects of low socioeconomic status on the immunization status of preschool children.

There is also evidence that the use of community outreach workers can be used to improve the immunization status of disadvantaged children. Rodewald et al. (1997) conducted a randomized controlled trial in nine offices in Rochester, NY that provided care to a large proportion of lower socioeconomic status families. Patients were randomized to one of four groups: 1) a community outreach worker to track immunization status and help parents bring their children to the provider for vaccinations, 2) a system of prompting the child's provider at every visit regarding the need for one or more immunizations (reducing "missed opportunities" for vaccination), 3) both interventions, or 4) a control group. A total of 2741 children completed the study. Compared to the control group, the investigators found that the use of a community outreach worker increased the immunization rate of study children by 20 percent (p < 0.001). There was no statistically significant effect of prompting providers to reduce missed opportunities on immunization status.

Parental health beliefs

In 1992, a five component health belief model was developed to explain the decision process used by parents when considering immunization of their children. In this model, parents weighed the following components: (1) perceived susceptibility of the child to diseases prevented by vaccines; (2) the severity of those diseases; (3) the perceived benefits of immunizations in preventing disease; (4) barriers to obtaining immunizations; and (5) perceived self-efficacy, the perception that the parent is able to promote her/his child's health in spite of obstacles (Cutts et al., 1992). Using this model, Taylor and Cufley (1996) found that the health beliefs of parents of children seen by private pediatricians in the Seattle, WA area were largely positive. On a scale of 1 to 6, with 6 indicating strongly positive beliefs about vaccines, the mean parental health belief score was 4.6. There was no statistically significant difference in the overall health belief score between parents of children who were fully vaccinated and those of parents whose children were underimmunized. Health belief scores for the various components of the health belief model ranged from 4.1, for perceived barriers, to 5.8 for both perception of benefits of vaccines and perceived susceptibility to vaccine preventable diseases. The only difference in scores between parents of children who were fully immunized and those of parents of children who were underimmunized was for the self-efficacy component (mean scores 5.6 and 5.4, respectively, p = 0.019).

These findings were generally confirmed in a national survey of 13,520 parents of children followed by practicing pediatricians. When asked what was the most difficult barrier that they had to overcome to obtain immunizations for their child, 74% of parents responded, "nothing." The most commonly cited barrier was concerns about vaccine side effects, identified by 22.6% of parents. However, after controlling for potentially confounding variables such as race, ethnicity, and maternal education level, citing a concern about vaccine safety was not associated with the immunization status of the parents' children. Other possible barriers listed on the survey included concerns about the expense of vaccines, the confusing immunization schedule, the inconvenience of the vaccination process, having a child who was frequently too ill to receive needed immunizations, and religious barriers. While children of parents who cited one of these barriers were at statistically significant risk for under-immunization, each barrier was cited by less than 6% of respondents. Overall, one or more barrier to obtaining immunizations was identified by 13.7% of the parents; children of these parents were at risk for underimmunization (risk ratio 1.75, 95% CI: 1.59 - 1.92). However, the overall impact of parental perception of barriers to receiving immunization was minimal; nationally, the perception of one or more barriers to immunization by a parent was calculated to lead to a 1.6% decrease in the immunization rate of children at 8 months of age.

Although the vast majority of parents of US children have positive beliefs regarding vaccination, there is evidence that vaccine refusal is a growing phenomenon. In 48 states children entering school can be granted a non-medical or "personal" exemption from the requirement for full vaccination, in addition to medical exemptions. In 1991 the average state personal exemption rate was 0.99% of children entering school; by 2004 the rate had risen to 2.51%. Salmon and colleagues conducted a case-control study comparing the health beliefs of parents of children who claimed a non-medical exemption to school vaccination requirements to those of parents whose children were fully immunized (Salmon et al., 2005). The most

commonly cited reason for refusing vaccines was a concern about safety, identified by 68.6% of the 277 responding parents whose child claimed an exemption. Compared to parents of fully vaccinated children, those who refused one or more immunizations for their child had significantly less positive health beliefs about vaccine efficacy and vaccine safety, and were significantly less concerned about the severity of vaccine preventable diseases and the susceptibility of their child to these diseases.

While the proportion of children claiming a personal exemption to school vaccination requirements is small, it is likely indicative of a broader, community-wide, hesitancy regarding the immunization of preschool children. Areas with higher rates of students claiming personal exemptions have been shown to have higher rates of measles and pertussis (Salmon et al., 1999; Feikin et al., 2000; Omer et al., 2006). For example, Feikin et al. (2000) found that every 1% increase in the rate of students in a county claiming exemptions to immunization requirements was associated with a 1.6 fold increase in the incidence rate of measles in the county. This increased risk was greatest for children aged 3-10 years, presumably because of high levels of exposure to infected individuals at day care centers and schools.

Perhaps more importantly, in certain areas exemption rates are as high as 18%, leading to the possibility of more widespread outbreaks of vaccine preventable infections in these communities. The exact level of under-immunization in preschool children at which an outbreak of a vaccine preventable infection becomes likely is dependent on several factors such as the infectivity of the organism, degree of exposure and rate of immunity in older children and adults. However, a review of data from the measles outbreak of 1989-1991 suggests that the transmission of this disease among preschool children was negligible in census tracts in which 80% of more children were immunized by their second birthday, and 93% of individuals older than 6 years were immune. The incidence rate of measles was negatively and significantly associated with the measles immunization rate; in census tracts were the immunization rate was 40-59% the mean incidence of measles ranged from 13.6 to 30.8 cases/1000 population in children < 5 years old (Hutchins et al., 2004).

Practitioner-based interventions

As the delivery of immunizations has progressively moved out of public health settings and into private practices, the specific policies and procedures of individual providers have become an increasingly important determinant of the overall immunization rate of US preschool children. Many of the Standards for Pediatric Immunization Practices, published in 1993 were devoted to policies recommended for implementation in practice settings. Unfortunately, much of the evidence to date suggests that many of these recommended policies do not increase practice immunization rates (Koepke et al., 2001; Taylor et al., 2002a). One of the most touted policies, using all office visits to immunize children thereby reducing "missed opportunities," has not been found to be an effective method for increasing vaccination rates in either observational studies or randomized controlled trials. For example, in a randomized controlled trial that included almost 2000 patients, the medical records of young children were screened at every visit for needed vaccines, and providers notified when their patients were eligible for an immunization. Despite this concerted effort to reduce missed opportunities, the immunization rate of patients in the intervention and control groups were similar at the end of the trial (Szilagyi et al., 1996). In one observational study assessing practice immunization policies, vaccination rates were *negatively* associated with the use of acute- or chronic

illness visits for immunizations, while in another study of 112 practices in 40 states, no association between practice immunization rates and use of acute visits for vaccination was detected (Szilagyi et al., 1994; Taylor et al., 2002a). These various results indicate the need for evidence-based guidelines, rather than a reliance of expert consensus. There is some published evidence that the following interventions are associated with increased levels of fully immunized children in the practice setting: (1) Limiting contraindications to immunizations; (2) Reminder/recall systems; (3) Auditing practice immunization rates; and (4) maximizing the number of immunizations given at one visit. The evidence base for each of these interventions will be described.

There have been trials of specific practitioner-based interventions, most notably for reminder/recall systems. However, much of the published evidence on the efficacy of multiple practitioner policies or procedures on increasingly immunization rates is based on 3 observational studies. Koepke and colleagues (2001) surveyed immunization behaviors of 251 practicing physicians in Pennsylvania who provided vaccinations. Stated behaviors were compared to the practice immunization rate, with the primary outcome being up-to-date for recommended vaccines at 12 months of age. Zimmerman et al. (1999) conducted surveys of 29 immunization providers who were members of a group of multi-specialty practices in Minnesota. Twenty-five of the providers were family physicians. The practice immunization registry was used to collect data on the immunization status of patients followed by the study providers. Study outcomes were timely receipt of DTP #3, DTP #4, and MMR #1 defined as a child receiving the vaccine no sooner than recommended and no later than 1 month after the recommended age range. Data were analyzed at the patient level, assessing the influence of specific practitioner policies on a child's likelihood for receiving immunizations at the appropriated time. Finally, Taylor and colleagues (2002a) compared practice immunization rates with stated policies of primary care pediatricians who were members of a national practice-based research network. Data from 112 practices in 40 states were collected. The main study outcomes were practice immunization rates at 8 and 19 months determined by abstraction of vaccination data from medical records on at least 80 consecutively seen children in each practice. Potentially confounding variables such as type of practice and sociodemographic characteristics of the patients were included in the analyses.

Another large study comparing practice vaccination policies with immunization rates among 32 pediatric and 10 family medicine practices in Florida was conducted by Page and colleagues (2002). The investigators attempted to specifically assess the impact of following each of the Standards for Pediatric Immunization Practices. Unfortunately, the usefulness of the results of the project are somewhat limited by several factors such as lack of adjustment for important confounding variables, lack of variability in practice immunization policy for some of the evaluated standards, and method for determining practice policy. Despite these limitations, some of the findings in this project are helpful in assessing the efficacy of practice-based interventions in increasing immunization rates.

Limiting contraindications to immunization

One of the Standards for Pediatric Immunization Practice called for practitioners to only follow "true" contraindications to vaccination. The only absolute contraindication listed by the Advisory Committee on Immunization Practices (ACIP) of the CDC is a history of anaphylaxis to one of the constituents in a vaccine (Pediatrics, 2006b). ACIP advises "precaution" in vaccinating a

child with a moderate or severe illness. Thus, most investigators provide clinical scenarios describing a hypothetical patient with a particular set of conditions, and ask responding providers to indicate whether they would administer the hypothetical patient one or more particular vaccines. Frequently the conditions described do not contraindicate administration of the immunization (Pediatrics, 2006a).

Taylor et al. (2002a) provided a list of 13 clinical conditions in a hypothetical 4 month old infant being seen for a health supervision visit. The conditions described included: history of anaphylaxis to tetanus toxoid, gastroenteritis without dehydration, afebrile otitis media, family history of severe reaction to DTP, anaphylaxis to eggs, upper respiratory tract infection (URI) without fever, seizure disorder being treated with carbamazepine, bronchiolitis without fever, fever < 39° C, fever between 39° and 40°, fever > 40°, cerebral palsy and congenital immunodeficiency. Practitioners in each participating practice were asked to indicate which of these conditions would be a contraindication to administering a DTaP. The median number of contraindications chosen was 4.66; practices endorsing fewer contraindications to vaccinations had higher immunization rates at 8 months (p = 0.02) and 19 months (p=0.01). For each clinical condition that was not judged to be a contraindication, the practice immunization increased by 2.0 percent at 8 months and 2.6 percent at 19 months. These results confirmed the findings of a smaller study conducted by this group of researchers. In the previous project, 15 pediatricians from 12 states were provided a similar list of contraindications. The mean practice immunization rate of those indicating that 3 or less of the conditions described were contraindications was 89.7% vs. 74.4% for those endorsing 4 or more contraindications (p = 0.037).

Zimmerman and colleagues found that children treated by of providers who indicated that they would administer an MMR to a well-hydrated 18 month old child who came to their office with watery diarrhea were more likely to receive their MMR vaccine in a timely fashion than patients of providers who indicated that this hypothetical clinical situation was a contraindication to immunization (76% and 62%, respectively, p = 0.007) (Zimmerman et al., 1999). Children seen by providers who were willing to administer the MMR to a child with diarrhea were also significantly more likely to receive DTP #3 and DTP #4 on time. However, these investigators found that there was no difference in rate of timely receipt of DTP #3, DTP #4, or MMR #1 among children whose providers would, or would not, administer a DTP vaccine to a 7 month-old in the office for a mild URI.

To assess the effect of practitioner policy regarding contraindications, Koepke et al. (2001) asked study physicians 3 questions about possibly deferring a DPT in a patient with mild soreness from a previous DTP, in a patient with mild vomiting, or in a children with moderate gastroenteritis. The immunization rate in practices that indicated that they would always, or usually, administer the DTP to children with each of these conditions was higher than that of practices that were more likely to defer the needed DTP when confronted with one or more of these conditions (73% vs. 66%, p < 0.05). In this study, the immunization rate of pediatric practices was significantly higher than in family medicine practices (p < 0.001). After adjusting for type of practice (pediatric or family medicine), there was no statistical association between measured policies regarding contraindications and immunization rate.

Although the results are somewhat mixed, overall the data from these studies suggest that limiting contraindications to vaccination may be an effective practice-based intervention to increase immunization rates. However, the results of observational study must be interpreted cautiously. It is likely that practices that limit contraindications have other, unmeasured, characteristics that are associated with having high levels of fully immunized patients making it difficult to assess the independent effect of evaluated policies. Regardless, even if the effect size of limiting contraindications is modest, this intervention can be implemented with little effort and at no cost.

Reminder/recall systems

Reminder/recall systems are, by far, the best studied practice-based intervention to increase immunization rates. Much of the research has been focused on vaccination programs for adults or for immunizations recommended for special populations of children. For many reasons the results of studies on these populations may not be applicable to routine childhood immunizations. Fortunately, there have been numerous projects designed to specifically assess the efficacy of reminder/recall systems in improving immunization rates in preschool children.

A "reminder" system for immunization describes a process by which parents of young children are contacted about an upcoming immunization that is due. The reminders are either generated by a child's primary care provider or by an agency that has access to a patient's date of birth and dates of immunizations. The process of "recall" usually relates to contacting patients of children who have missed a needed vaccination. In some studies both reminders and recall have been utilized. Multiple methodologies for contacting parents have been assessed in trials including sending parents postcards or letters, personal telephone calls, use of computer generated telephone calls, or combination of multiple techniques. Significant enhancements, such as community outreach and prompts for providers, have been included in some trials in which reminder/recall systems were evaluated.

There are at least 2 published meta-analyses of the efficacy of reminder/recall systems in increasing immunization rates of preschool children (Szilagyi et al., 2000; Jacobson, 2005). Since there was considerable overlap of authorship and included studies it is not surprising that the results of the meta-analyses were similar. In both, reminder/recall systems were found to be effective with odds ratios of 1.45 (95% CI: 1.28 - 1.66) and 2.02 (95% CI: 1.49 - 2.79), respectively. Perhaps more importantly, the measured increase in immunization rates from the various studies included ranged from -2 percent to 34 percent, with a median increase of 15 percent. Most specific reminder/recall interventions, including a letter reminder, computer generated telephone call, personal telephone call, and a combination of a postcard and telephone call, were also found to be effective, although for some interventions there are only data from a very limited number of studies.

There is no doubt that a recall/reminder system, if properly implemented, can increase immunization rates. However, virtually all of the studies in which efficacy was demonstrated were conducted in public health departments, large HMOs, or other agencies with access to sophisticated computerized databases. The applicability of these studies for smaller practices, where the majority of US children are immunized and where resources are more limited, is unclear. Page and colleagues (2002) reported that use of a system to track the vaccination status of practice patients was associated with increased immunization rates (OR 1.48, 95% CI: 1.18 - 1.70). However, in the study by Taylor and colleagues neither the use of a specific tracking system to identify children who were due, or behind in, vaccinations, nor a system to remind parents of an upcoming health supervision appointment was associated with increased immunization rates

among the 112 participating practices (Taylor et al., 2002a). Similarly, Zimmerman and colleagues (1999) could not demonstrate any efficacy of a reminder system in improving immunization coverage; however, only 3 of the 29 study physicians reported using a reminder system. It is possible that the utility of reminder/recall systems in a practice setting might be improved through more extensive use of computerized immunization registries and software to generate practice-level letters or telephone calls to patients due for vaccinations. Alternatively, it is conceivable that local health departments could generate reminder or recall notices using computerized databases.

Immunization audits

Providers who have not formally assessed the vaccine status of the children in their practices tend to overestimate their practices' immunization rates, frequently by a substantial degree (Bordley et al., 1996; Darden and Taylor, 1998). Thus, one might assume that that an audit revealing a lower than anticipated immunization rate would cause practitioners to implement vaccination policy changes designed to increase coverage. However, findings on the efficacy of practice immunization audits are mixed. In a study conducted in public health clinics in Georgia, the use of annual immunization audits with feedback lead to a 46 percent increase in rates over a 6 year period (LeBaron et al., 1997). This increase was much greater than the secular trend in vaccination rates during this period and could not be explained by other changes at the clinic sites. Page and colleagues (2002) also found that use of semi-annual audits to assess coverage was associated higher practice immunization rates (OR 2.00, 95% CI: 1.65 - 2.42). Using a simple chi-square test, in the study by Zimmerman and colleagues, children seen by practitioners who conducted immunization audits were more likely to receive MMR# 1 and DTP#3 than those who were followed by providers who reported that they did not conduct audits; however, after adjusting for confounding variables there were no significant differences in the timeliness of any measured vaccination (Zimmerman et al., 1999). Both Taylor and colleagues (2002a) and Koepke and colleagues (2001) found no significant association between practice immunization audits and rates. Thus, the evidence supporting the use of practice audits to increase vaccination rates is equivocal.

Maximizing the number of vaccines given at one visit

With the licensure of new vaccines for use in infants and the switch from oral to injectable poliovirus vaccine, the number of injections needed to fully vaccinate a preschool child in the US rose dramatically during the 1990's. The obvious consequence of this was that young children either needed up to 5 injections at one visit or needed more visits in order to receive all vaccines recommended during the first two years of life. However, the results of surveys conducted during the decade of the 90's indicated that both parents and providers preferred fewer injections per visit. In a national survey of parents, the median preference for maximal number of injections at one visit was 2 (Taylor et al., 2002b). In another study, 60% of practitioners and 41% of parents had "strong concerns" about a hypotheticcal 7 month old receiving 3 vaccines at one visit. A majority of parents surveyed indicated a preference for returning for a second visit rather than receiving 4 vaccine injections (Woodin et al., 1995). These parental and provider preferences were clearly at odds with the recommended standard of simultaneous administration of all vaccine doses for which a child is eligible at the time of each visit (1993).

In a study conducted during the period 1998 to 2000, pediatricians from 112 practices in 40 states were asked their preferences for the maximum number of vaccine injections administered to a young child at a single visit; the median value was 4.17, with a range of 2-6 injections. After adjusting for the demographic characteristics of the practice and patient population, a practitioner preference for giving more injections at one visit was statistically associated with higher practice immunization rates at 8 months ($p = 0.03$). However, after controlling for other practice policies found to be associated with increased rates, no association between increasing number of injections at one visit and practice immunization rate at 8 months, or 19 months, was found (Taylor et al., 2002a). Other studies of different groups of providers had similar results. Koepke et al. (2001) reported that practices that indicated a willingness to simultaneously administer 4 or more injections at a single visit had higher immunization rates than those administering fewer injections (74% and 65%, respectively, $p < 0.01$). This effect was independent of other practice policies and characteristics; however, after including practice specialty (family medicine or pediatrics) into the regression models the difference in rates was not significantly different. Zimmerman and colleagues (1999) found that children vaccinated by practitioners who indicated that they were "likely" to simultaneously administer 3 injections were more likely to receive MMR#1 and DTP#4 on time than children whose providers were unlikely to administer 3 vaccines at one visit, but the differences were not statistically significant after adjusting for the hierarchal nature of the data.

Overall, the results of these studies suggest that maximizing the number of injections given at one visit may have a modest effect in increasing immunization rates.

CONCLUSIONS

Given the central role immunization plays

in promoting the health of children it is surprising that so few studies have been conducted assessing how to maximize the delivery of vaccines. This is particularly true of trials of specific interventions designed to increase immunization rates. The available evidence strongly support the following findings:

1. School and/or daycare vaccine requirements have played a significant role in maintaining and increasing immunization rates.

2. Removal of financial barriers to vaccination, both through the provision of free vaccine and by providing coverage for care by a primary care provider, has also been shown to be an efficacious intervention.

3. Although research projects on reminder/recall systems have had positive results, the usefulness and sustainability of these systems in the "real world" is less well documented.

The evidence for most other practice-based interventions is weak, however, it is likely that efforts to limit contraindications to vaccination, monitor immunization coverage through periodic audits, and maximize the number of vaccines given at a single visit by a young child can all be used to increase practice immunization rates. Each of the interventions can be implemented with little additional effort and at low cost.

Of all the factors that will influence immunization rates in preschool children in the future, parental health beliefs are the most unpredictable. Attitudes about immunizations have continued to be generally quite positive, however, there is evidence that parental refusal of vaccines for their children is rising (Omer et al., 2006). Several factors might conceivably increase parental wariness about immunizations in the future. First, the effects of new vaccines on improving the individual, or public health, of children are likely to be less dramatic than current immunizations.

For example, even though rotavirus vaccine might be highly efficacious in preventing that infection, young infants who are immunized against rotavirus will still have diarrheal illnesses. This lack of dramatic effect might undermine confidence in new and/or established immunizations. It is also under-appreciated that administering more vaccines increases the chances that a child will experience an adverse event. If a patient receives 5 immunizations, each with a 1% risk of a side effect, the overall chance that the patient will experience a side effect is 5%. In addition, with the administration of vaccines at more times during the first two years of life, the chances of a temporal (but not causal) relationship between a vaccine administration and the onset or diagnosis of a serious condition are increased. Both of these consequences of recommending more immunizations to young children are likely to increase parental concerns about vaccine safety. Finally, with the ever increasing availability and importance of mediums such as the internet, more parents will likely receive the bulk of their information about vaccines from nontraditional sources that are largely negative about this preventive health measure.

REFERENCES

(1993) Standards for pediatric immunization practices. Ad Hoc Working Group for the Development of Standards for Pediatric Immunization Practices. JAMA 269:1817-1822.

(2000) Vaccination coverage among adolescents 1 year before the institution of a seventh grade school entry vaccination requirement--San Diego, California, 1998. MMWR Morb Mortal Wkly Rep 49:101-102, 111.

(2001) Effectiveness of a middle school vaccination law--California, 1999-2001. MMWR Morb Mortal Wkly Rep 50:660-663.

Atkinson WL, Orenstein WA, Krugman S. (1992) The resurgence of measles in the United States, 1989-1990. Annu Rev Med 43:451-463.

Bordley WC, Margolis PA, Lannon CM. (1996) The delivery of immunizations and other preventive services in private practices. Pediatrics 97:467-473.

Briss PA, Rodewald LE, Hinman AR, Shefer AM, Strikas RA, Bernier RR, Carande-Kulis VG, Yusuf HR, Ndiaye SM, Williams SM. (2000) Reviews of evidence regarding interventions to improve vaccination coverage in children, adolescents, and adults. The Task Force on Community Preventive Services. Am J Prev Med 18:97-140.

Clements DA, Zaref JI, Bland CL, Walter EB, Coplan PM. (2001) Partial uptake of varicella vaccine and the epidemiological effect on varicella disease in 11 day-care centers in North Carolina. Arch Pediatr Adolesc Med 155:455-461.

Cutts FT, Orenstein WA, Bernier RH. (1992) Causes of low preschool immunization coverage in the United States. Annu Rev Public Health 13:385-398.

Darden PM, Taylor JA. (1998) Assessing immunization rates in office practice. Pediatr Ann 27:411-416.

Davis MM, Gaglia MA. (2005) Associations of daycare and school entry vaccination requirements with varicella immunization rates. Vaccine 23:3053-3060.

Fairbrother G, Friedman S, Hanson KL, Butts GC. (1997) Effect of the vaccines for children program on inner-city neighborhood physicians. Arch Pediatr Adolesc Med 151:1229-1235.

Feikin DR, Lezotte DC, Hamman RF, Salmon DA, Chen RT, Hoffman RE. (2000) Individual and community risks of measles and pertussis associated with personal exemptions to immunization. Jama 284:3145-3150.

Hinman AR, Orenstein WA, Williamson DE,

Darrington D. (2002) Childhood immunization: laws that work. J Law Med Ethics 30:122-127.

Hutchins SS, Baughman AL, Orr M, Haley C, Hadler S. (2004) Vaccination levels associated with lack of measles transmission among preschool-aged populations in the United States, 1989-1991. J Infect Dis 189 Suppl 1:S108-115.

Jacobson VJ. (2005) Patient reminder and patient recall systems to improve immunization rates. Cochrane Database Syst Rev.

Koepke CP, Vogel CA, Kohrt AE. (2001) Provider characteristics and behaviors as predictors of immunization coverage. Am J Prev Med 21:250-255.

LeBaron CW, Chaney M, Baughman AL, Dini EF, Maes E, Dietz V, Bernier R. (1997) Impact of measurement and feedback on vaccination coverage in public clinics, 1988-1994. JAMA 277:631-635.

Omer SB, Pan WK, Halsey NA, Stokley S, Moulton LH, Navar AM, Pierce M, Salmon DA. (2006) Nonmedical exemptions to school immunization requirements: secular trends and association of state policies with pertussis incidence. JAMA 296:1757-1763.

Orenstein WA, Hinman AR. (1999) The immunization system in the United States - the role of school immunization laws. Vaccine 17 Suppl 3:S19-24.

Orenstein WA, Atkinson W, Mason D, Bernier RH. (1990) Barriers to vaccinating preschool children. J Health Care Poor Underserved 1:315-330.

Page D, Meires J, Dailey A. (2002) Factors influencing immunization status in primary care clinics. Fam Med 34:29-33.

Pediatrics AAo. (2006a) Red Book: 2006 Report of the Committee on Infectious Diseases. In, 27 Edition (Pickering LK BC, Long SS, McMillan JA, ed), pp 1-104. Elk Grove Village, IL: American Academy of Pediatrics.

Pediatrics AAo. (2006b) Red Book: 2006 Report of the Committee on Infectious Diseases. In, 27th Edition (Pickering LK BC, Long SS, McMillan JA, ed), p 847, Elk Grove Village, IL: American Academy of Pediatrics.

Pierce C, Goldstein M, Suozzi K, Gallaher M, Dietz V, Stevenson J. (1996) The impact of the standards for pediatric immunization practices on vaccination coverage levels. JAMA 276:626-630.

Plotkin SL, Plotkin SA. (1994) A short history of vaccinations. In: Vaccines, 2 Edition (Plotkin SA, Mortimer EA, eds), pp 1-11. Philadelphia: WB Saunders Co.

Rodewald LE, Szilagyi PG, Holl J, Shone LR, Zwanziger J, Raubertas RF. (1997) Health insurance for low-income working families. Effect on the provision of immunizations to preschool-age children. Arch Pediatr Adolesc Med 151:798-803.

Salmon DA, Haber M, Gangarosa EJ, Phillips L, Smith NJ, Chen RT. (1999) Health consequences of religious and philosophical exemptions from immunization laws: individual and societal risk of measles. JAMA 282:47-53.

Salmon DA, Moulton LH, Omer SB, DeHart MP, Stokley S, Halsey NA. (2005) Factors associated with refusal of childhood vaccines among parents of school-aged children: a case-control study. Arch Pediatr Adolesc Med 159: 470-476.

Santoli JM, Rodewald LE, Maes EF, Battaglia MP, Coronado VG. (1999) Vaccines for Children program, United States, 1997. Pediatrics 104:e15.

Smith PJ, Stevenson J, Chu SY. (2006) Associations between childhood vaccination coverage, insurance type, and breaks in health insurance coverage. Pediatrics 117:1972-1978.

Strebel PM, Sutter RW, Cochi SL, Biellik RJ, Brink EW, Kew OM, Pallansch MA, Orenstein WA, Hinman AR. (1992) Epidemiology of poliomyelitis in the United States one decade after the last reported case of indigenous wild virus-associated disease. Clin Infect Dis 14:568-579.

Szilagyi PG, Roghmann KJ, Campbell JR, Humiston SG, Winter NL, Raubertas RF, Rodewald LE. (1994) Immunization practices of primary care practitioners and their relation to immunization levels. Arch Pediatr Adolesc Med 148:158-166.

Szilagyi PG, Bordley C, Vann JC, Chelminski A, Kraus RM, Margolis PA, Rodewald LE. (2000) Effect of patient reminder/ recall interventions on immunization rates: A review. JAMA 284:1820-1827.

Szilagyi PG, Rodewald LE, Humiston SG, Pollard L, Klossner K, Jones AM, Barth R, Woodin KA. (1996) Reducing missed opportunities for immunizations. Easier said than done. Arch Pediatr Adolesc Med 150:1193-1200.

Taylor JA, Cufley D. (1996) The association between parental health beliefs and immunization status among children followed by private pediatricians. Clin Pediatr (Phila) 35:18-22.

Taylor JA, Darden PM, Slora E, Hasemeier CM, Asmussen L, Wasserman R. (1997) The influence of provider behavior, parental characteristics, and a public policy initiative on the immunization status of children followed by private pediatricians: a study from Pediatric Research in Office Settings. Pediatrics 99: 209-215.

Taylor JA, Darden PM, Brooks DA, Hendricks JW, Baker AE, Wasserman RC. (2002a) Practitioner policies and beliefs and practice immunization rates: a study from Pediatric Research in Office Settings and the National Medical Association. Pediatrics 109:294-300.

Taylor JA, Darden PM, Brooks DA, Hendricks JW, Wasserman RC, Bocian AB. (2002b) Association between parents' preferences and perceptions of barriers to vaccination and the immunization status of their children: a study from Pediatric Research in Office Settings and the National Medical Association. Pediatrics 110: 1110-1116.

Taylor JA, Darden PM, Brooks DA, Hendricks JW, Baker AE, Bocian AB, Rohder K, Wasserman RC. (2001) Impact of the change to inactivated poliovirus vaccine on the immunization status of young children in the United States: a study from pediatric research in office settings and the National Medical Association. Pediatrics 107: E90.

Waterman SH, Hill LL, Robyn B, Yeager KK, Maes EF, Stevenson JM, Anderson KN. (1996) A model immunization demonstration for preschoolers in an inner-city barrio, San Diego, California, 1992-1994. Am J Prev Med 12: 8-13.

Woodin KA, Rodewald LE, Humiston SG, Carges MS, Schaffer SJ, Szilagyi PG. (1995) Physician and parent opinions. Are children becoming pincushions from immunizations? Arch Pediatr Adolesc Med 149: 845-849.

Zimmerman RK, Mieczkowski TA, Michel M. (1999) Are vaccination rates higher if providers receive free vaccines and follow contraindication guidelines? Fam Med 31: 317-323.

Zimmerman RK, Medsger AR, Ricci EM, Raymund M, Mieczkowski TA, Grufferman S. (1997) Impact of free vaccine and insurance status on physician referral of children to public vaccine clinics. JAMA 278: 996-1000.

BEHAVIORAL INTERVENTIONS FOR PEDIATRIC ASTHMA

Ellen F. Crain and William Crain

INTRODUCTION

Pediatric asthma is a public health epidemic. It is the most common chronic disease of childhood, currently affecting 6.7 million children less than 18 years of age in the United States. In 2003, asthma accounted for 5 million doctor visits and 641,000 visits to emergency departments. Children 5-17 years of age with asthma missed 12.8 million school days (American Lung Association, 2006). Morbidity is disproportionately high among African-American and Puerto Rican children compared with non-Hispanic Caucasians. Asthma also affects poor residents of the inner cities much more than their more affluent suburban counterparts (Weiss et al., 1992).

Until the 1980s, the emphasis in treatment was on compliance with the medical regimen (Mellins et al., 1992). The assumption was fairly widespread that morbidity was due to poor compliance, and, when parents or children failed to comply, they were at fault. Since then, there has been growing awareness that the problem of compliance is considerably more complex. For one thing, several studies (Finkelstein et al., 1995; Weitzman et al., 1990; Crain et al., 1998; Weil et al., 1999) have revealed that many children, especially in poor families, lack access to good medical care and insurance for medications and live in families burdened by mental health problems and poor social support. These conditions can interfere with or overwhelm good compliance and result in poor health outcomes. Moreover, in these same populations, exposure to indoor and outdoor pollutants and allergens has been found to be disproportionately high, also exacerbating asthma despite good compliance.

Attention has shifted to ensuring that parents understand medication use as well as ways to reduce allergen and irritant exposures in the home (Ehnert et al., 1992; Warner et al., 2000). New emphasis has been placed on the application of specific knowledge of asthma management strategies that can be implemented by parents in their particular home environment. Parents are increasingly assigned the role of "knowledgeable experts," who need to know how to manage the home environment and the child's medication schedule (Leickly et al., 1998).

The tremendous increase in the prevalence of a number of chronic diseases in the United States has also revealed limitations in the role of the physician in health maintenance and modified the traditional view of patient compliance. It has become clear that physicians do not have the time or resources to monitor every circumstance or complication of a patient's disease. Patients must learn how to manage their own care. The notion of patients as *compliant* has given way to the concept of the patient as a *partner* with the physician in controlling their disease.

Educational versus Behavioral Interventions

In the 1980's, a series of articles on pediatric asthma deaths suggested that better patient or caregiver knowledge about asthma symptoms and medication use might have significantly reduced the mortality rate (Birkhead et al., 1989; Sears & Beagleole, 1987; Kravis, 1987). The asthma management behavior of caregivers and patients began to be studied, and the following question began to emerge: Are educational programs, which target *knowledge*, effective in reducing asthma morbidity, or do patients need to learn and rehearse *new behaviors* as well? That is, do patients need to know more about asthma, or do they need to practice actual behaviors to successfully manage the disease? This question has become even more relevant as reduction in environmental allergen and irritant exposure has become a major focus of self-management programs.

Wilson-Pessano and McNabb (1985) acknowledged that physician instruction, the transmission of knowledge, is likely to be effective only for children with mild intermittent or easily controlled asthma. Handleman et al. (2004), in a study of explanatory mechanisms for asthma reported by children and their caretakers, expanded on the concept of the effect of knowledge. They found that lack of understanding about the role of asthma medications was only one of several reasons for not giving medications. Moreover, parents' understanding and con-ceptualization was very different from the traditional biomedical model of persistent asthma, suggesting that transmission of know-ledge itself must begin with an understanding of parent concepts and attitudes.

Knowledge-transmission interventions are basically of two kinds. One kind (A) seeks to impart general knowledge about asthma. Examples include a lecture to parents on asthma, its pathophysiology, and treatment, or a videogame for children about asthma, allergens, airway inflammation, and medi-cations. Another version (B) is more specific. It instructs parents or patients on self-management techniques, but does so primarily through teaching through words, diagrams, charts, handouts, homework assignments, and models. Neither type of knowledge-transmission (A nor B) focuses on changing actual behavior during the intervention. Interventions that try to teach new skills, which we will call C, usually involve some form of behavioral rehearsal in addition to providing self-management knowledge during the training. For example, parents might be taught by the health professional about what allergens are and why their reduction is important for controlling

their child's asthma, but then they would observe the health professional using different methods to reduce allergens and then practice the behaviors themselves, while the health professional provides appropriate positive feedback.

Unfortunately, researchers have not focused clearly on the relative usefulness of these three types of intervention. Furthermore, descriptions of the specific methods used in intervention programs are often too brief to indicate which approach has been used. It is likely that some studies included a mixture of the intervention types labeled A, B, and C (most often mixing B, self-management knowledge, with a small amount of C, behavioral rehearsal), but often studies are vague on the matter. Journal editors and publishers contribute to the ambiguity by limiting journal space for methodological descriptions.

The impact of information-transmission interventions (A and B) may be substantial, but there is considerable variation among studies. Some have a substantial effect on important asthma outcomes, including health service utilization and functional morbidity. Others have had effects on knowledge but not on intermediate outcomes such as self-management skills or more distal asthma outcomes such as morbidity, school absences, and quality of life. Rubin et al. (1989) suggested a likely reason for this wide range in effects. In a study of the impact of playing an educational asthma computer game on children's reported asthma management behaviors, the authors noted that the relationship between asthma knowledge and behavior appeared to be nonlinear. That is, knowledge was related to engaging in more of the recommended behaviors only up to a moderate level of knowledge. Above that level, there was no impact on behavior. Moreover, the relationship between know-ledge and asthma management behavior was strongest among children who scored lower on behavioral adjustment, suggesting that knowledge can influence behavior but only when ignorance is the cause of unhealthful behavior. The authors concluded that, "educational interventions for children whose knowledge is already adequate may not increase adherence to recommended practices." This study by Rubin et al. (1989) revealed the limitations of an intervention whose goal was to change self-management through a pure transmission of knowledge, even when the transmission occurred via a fun activity. Information transmission interventions will only improve self-management when lack of knowledge is a barrier to asthma care.

Several reviews of educational programs for pediatric asthma have been published (Wilson-Pessano and McNabb, 1985; Evans and Mellins, 1991; Bauman et al., 1997; Guevera et al., 2005; Bernard-Bonnin et al., 1995). These reviews support the notion that general knowledge transmission alone (A) is the weakest type of intervention, especially when the target outcomes are improved health status and quality of life. Knowledge transmission that focuses on self-management learning (B) and behavioral rehearsal (C) generally lead to more positive outcomes, although the early studies rarely examined the last type (C).

In the table below, we provide an updated review. The table lists behavioral interventions for pediatric asthma culled from the literature since 1985. The last column deserves special comment. In it, we indicate whether the intervention produced clinically meaningful outcomes, such as symptom reduction or a decline in missed school days. It might seem that such as assessment should be objective, but in fact the judgment was not always easy to make. For one thing, outcomes were sometimes reported only as statistically significant or not, with no data provided. When the actual data were presented, only one intervention study reported effect sizes,

and many did not provide means and standard deviations to allow calculation of effect sizes. Determination of meaningful clinical outcomes was therefore subjective. Overall, although there is considerable variability in results, some interventions show substantial positive effects, demonstrating their potential impact and promise.

This updated review of behavioral interventions supports the pattern noted in previous reviews. In terms of clinically significant outcomes, B-type interventions worked better than A, and C-type interventions, behavioral rehearsal, were the most consistently effective of all. However, caution must be exercised in accepting these interpretations of intervention type. The studies varied in terms of patient age, asthma severity, site and intensity of the intervention, and who was targeted for instruction. Most importantly, the interventions were often not well described, so it was not always clear how much behavioral rehearsal, if any, was included. Finally, power analyses were frequently absent, so that interpretation of statistical insignificance was not possible. Nevertheless, the importance of behavioral rehearsal is seen, especially when one is interested in clinically meaningful results. In the next section, we will describe examples of the three types of interventions. After that, we will describe some of the theoretical models that can inform future research.

Example of a Type A Study

An example of the type of intervention we have labeled asthma education only (A) is the report by Dolinar et al. (2000) of a home-based asthma health education program. The investigators enrolled families of children younger than 11 years of age with chronic stable asthma who were receiving care from a pediatrician but had not had an exacerbation. Families were randomized to receive either a single two-hour home-based asthma health education session or, for the control group, a

Table 1: Behavioral interventions for pediatric asthma

Study	Learn-ing Type	Intervention type	RCT (y/n)	Control group	# of subjects Intervention/ Control	Outcomes	Statistical signif-icance	Cinical signif-icance
Rakos et al., 1985	B	Self-administered written self-help program for parents/children	Y	Questionnaire assessments at 0, 2, 6, 12 months	20/23 7-12 year old children with asthma	Self-control skills	Y	
						Self-esteem	N	
						Locus of control	N	
						Parent interruption due to asthma	Y	X
						ER visits	N	
						School absenteeism	N	N
Creer et al., 1988	C	Self-management, modeling, role-playing, skill practice plus medical care	N		123 5-17 year old children with asthma	Parent asthma knowledge	Y	
						Child asthma knowledge	Y	
						# of attacks	Y	Y
						Peak Expiratory Flow Rate	Y	N
						School absences	Y	Y
						Health care costs	Y	X
Shields, 1990	A	Up to 4 group classes for parents and children and telephone instruction by nurses	Y	Usual medical care including basic instruction	127/126 <18 year old children with asthma	ER visits	N	

Column 2, Learning Type: A = knowledge transmission only; B = self-management knowledge transmission which may include very limited skill practice such as use of peak flow meter or inhaler; C = self-management education that emphasizes behavioral rehearsal.
Column 8, Statistical Significance: Y = groups differ with 95% confidence, N = less than 95% confidence that groups differ
Column 9, Clinical Significance: Y=significant, N=not significant, X = cannot judge clinical importance of the outcome

Study	Learning Type	Intervention type	RCT (y/n)	Control group	# of subjects Intervention/Control	Outcomes	Statistical significance	Cinical significance
Dahl et al., 1990	B	4 week behavioral intervention (symptom discrimination., self-management techniques) plus usual medical care with 4-week follow-up	Y	Usual medical care	9/10 children with asthma	B-agonist use	Y	Y
						Days of asthma	Y	Y
						Peak Expiratory Flow Rate	N	
						School days missed	Y	X
Brook et al., 1993	A	Weekly 1 hour lectures for 4 mos. plus written info and routine medical care	Y	Routine medical care	26/28 children with asthma	Asthma knowledge	Y	
Chris-tiansen et al., 1997	B	School based education (5 20-min sessions led by school Nurse Practitioner and written materials)	Y	Baseline and follow-up evaluations	27/15 inner-city 4th graders with asthma	Knowledge	Y	
						Peak Expiratory Flow	Y	
						Monitor technique		
						Inhaler technique	Y	
						Asthma severity	Y	
						Unscheduled Visits	N	
Evans et al., 1999	C	Self-management education (family-focused, clinic-based social work coach) 2 adult group sessions and 1 individual sessions every 2 months; child groups + mattress covers	Y	Morbidity calls every 2 months for 2 years	515/518 inner-city 5-11 year old children with asthma and their parents	Symptom days, year 1	Y	Y
						Symptom days, year 2	Y	Y
						Unscheduled visits	N	

Study	Learning Type	Intervention type	RCT (y/n)	Control group	# of subjects Intervention/Control	Outcomes	Statistical significance	Cinical significance
Tieffenberg et al., 2000	C	Child-centered self-management (5 weekly 2-hour group meetings for parents and children outside hospital; children trained to take lead role in management)	Y	6,12 month interview	355 6-15 year old children with asthma and epilepsy and their parents	Knowledge	Y	
						Family disruption	Y	
						Fewer episodes	Y	Y
						Health service use	Y	X
						ER visits	N	
						Internality	Y	
						School absences	Y	Y
Homer et al., 2000	B	Computer game to teach asthma self-management skills plus printed materials	Y	Reviewed printed educational materials with research assistant	76/61 3-12 year olds with asthma	Asthma knowledge	Y	
						Emergency department visits	N	
						Use of Peak Expiratory Flow Monitor	N	
						Asthma symptoms	N	
Dolenar et al., 2000	A	Home education (single 2-hour home based asthma health education session and booklet)	Y	booklet	20/20 2-10 year olds with asthma	Coping	Y (2/5 subscales)	
						Perception of change in severity	Y	X
						Quality of Life	N	
						Asthma attacks	N	
						Health service use	N	
Liu et al., 2001	A	Education: face-to-face versus group or home video	Y	Usual medical care; no education	31/29/30 1-14 year olds with asthma	Asthma knowledge	Y	

Study	Learning Type	Intervention type	RCT (y/n)	Control group	# of subjects Intervention/ Control	Outcomes	Statistical significance	Cinical significance
Wilson et al., 2001	B	3 nurse-led behavioral/education (+role-play) sessions with cotinine result feedback over 5 weeks	Y	Specialist medical care	44/43 3-12 year olds with asthma	Child anxiety	N	
						Morbidity	Face-to-face only	X
						Acute care visits	Y	Y
Guen-delman et al., 2002	B	Interactive computerized self-management education	Y	Asthma diary for symptom report	66/68 8-16 year olds with asthma	Hospitalizations	N	
						Cotinine/Creatine ratio	N	
						Environmental tobacco smoke exposure	N	
						Activity limitation	Y	Y
Hovell et al., 2002	B	1.5 hours of in-home management education and coaching	Y	Standard asthma management education	97/96 3-17 year olds with asthma	Perceived symptoms	N	
						School absences	N	
						Abnormal Peak Expiratory Flow Rate	Y	Y
						Emergency Department visits	N	
						Hospitalizations	N	
						Urgent calls	Y	
						Parent-reported environmental tobacco smoke exposure	Y	N
						Follow-up parent-reported environmental tobacco smoke exposure	Y	Y
						Urinary cotinine	Y	X
						Mother's cotinine	N	

Study	Learning Type	Intervention type	RCT (y/n)	Control group	# of subjects Intervention/ Control	Outcomes	Statistical significance	Cinical significance
Tsitoura, 2002	A	Education + passive prevention (booklet plus verbal explanation if needed and info on mattress covers, washing toys, and carpet removal + mattress encasement)	Y	booklet	330/306 1.5-3 year olds with asthma	Sensitization to mite allergen	Y	Y
						Eczema, asthma symptoms	Y	Y
Brown et al., 2002	B	Wee wheezers (8 90-minute self-management home-based education sessions by nurse)	Y	Data collection at 0, 3,12 months.	46/49 1-6 year olds with asthma	Less bother 1-3 year olds	Y	X
Bonner, 2002	B	3 monthly workshops plus home visits, and facilitation of MD visits, and improved MD care (Education, modeling, coaching, and physician intervention)	Y	Usual medical care plus data collection	56/63 4-19 year olds with asthma (28% participation rate)	Less bother 4-6 year/olds	N	
						Symptom free days 1-3 year/olds	Y	X
						Symptom free days 4-6 year/olds	N	
						Caregiver Quality of Life 1-3year/olds	Y	
						Asthma management	N	
						Health service use	N	
						Knowledge	Y	

Study	Learning Type	Intervention type	RCT (y/n)	Control group	# of subjects Intervention/ Control	Outcomes	Statistical significance	Cinical signif-icance
Stevens, 2002	A	2 20-minute nurse led education sessions with parent and child plus self-management plan and written booklet	Y	Usual medical care	99/101 18 month-5 year olds with asthma	Health beliefs	Y	
						Self-efficacy	Y	
						Self regulatory skills	Y	
						Symptom persistence	Y	Y
						Activity restriction	Y	Y
						Anti-inflammatory prescriptions	Y	Y
						Health service use	N	
Huss et al. 2003	A	Computer assisted instruction using asthma management game	Y	Written asthma materials and non-asthma health computer game	78/70 7-12 year olds with asthma	Hospitalizations	N	
						Emergency Department visits	N	
						Disability score	N	
						Quality of Life	N	
						Parents asthma knowledge	N	
						Symptoms	N	
						Asthma category	N	
Georgiou et al., 2003	B	Graded asthma management including booklet, phone care and MD detailing	N		404 5-13 year olds with asthma 28% response rate	Asthma knowledge	N	
						Asthma management	N	
						Asthma symptoms	N	
						Quality of Life	N	
						Lost school/work days	Y	Y

Study	Learning Type	Intervention type	RCT (y/n)	Control group	# of subjects Intervention/Control	Outcomes	Statistical significance	Cinical significance
McGhan et al., 2003	C	6 self-management education sessions + behavioral rehearsal	Y	Usual medical care	76/86 7-12 year olds with asthma randomized by school	Day/nighttime symptoms	Y	
						Functional limitations	Y	N
						Impact on family	Y	
						Knowledge	Y	
						Confidence	Y	
						Preventive behaviors	Y	
						Self-efficacy	Y	
						Emergency Department use	Y	N
						Peak Expiratory Flow Rate monitor use	Y	Y
						Unscheduled visits	Y	Y
Krishna, 2003	B	Internet enabled interactive self-management education + traditional education materials	Y	Traditional education materials	119/127 children < 18 years	Missed school	Y	Y
						Parent-rated severity	Y	Y
						Severity of Shortness Of Breath	Y	Y
						Play limitations	Y	Y
						Medication use	Y	Y
						Knowledge	Y	
Clark et al., 2004	B	6 component school-based disease management education program	Y	Phone interview at 0,12,24 months	416/419 2-5th grade randomized by school	Symptom days	Y	Y
						Emergency Department use	Y	Y
						Inhaled corticosteriod use	Y	Y
						Quality of Life	N	
						Daytime symptoms	Y	Y

Study	Learn-ing Type	Intervention type	RCT (y/n)	Control group	# of subjects Intervention/ Control	Outcomes	Statistic al signi-ficance	Cinical signif-icance
Shames et al., 2004	B	Asthma education and self-management video (3 sessions by case manager who also coordinates MD appointments and coaches) plus allergist visit and skin tests)	Y	Usual care	59/60 5-12 year olds with asthma	Nighttime symptoms	N	
						Management by parents	Y	
						School absences	Y (from parent data)	Y
						Science grades	Y	
						Quality of Life physical activity domain	Y	
Morgan et al., 2004	C	Home environment education + modeling & behavioral rehearsal (5 required home visits by educator) + equipment	Y	Evaluation visits and phone evaluation calls	469/468 5-11 year olds with asthma	Quality of Life social activity domain	Y	
						Child asthma knowledge	N	
						Parent asthma knowledge	Y	
						Parent asthma self-management	Y	
						Health service use	N	
						Symptom days	N	
						Days of rescue meds	N	
						Symptoms	Y	Y

Study	Learning Type	Intervention type	RCT (y/n)	Control group	# of subjects Intervention/ Control	Outcomes	Statistical significance	Cinical significance
Henry et al., 2004	A	3 health class lessons for 8th graders	Y	No classes	1787/1656 13-14 year olds with and without asthma randomized by school	Peak Expiratory Flow Rate	N	
						Allergen levels	Y	
						School days missed	Y	Y
						Caretaker plans	Y	
						Unscheduled visits	Y (year 1 only)	Y
						Smokers in home	N	
						Water damage	N	
						Pets in home	N	
						Signs of cockroaches	N	
						Asthma knowledge	Y	
Chiang et al., 2004	B	1-day self-management program (asthma education + modeling)	Y	Regular OPD asthma education from nurse 0/2 weeks, 3,6 months. data collection	33/35 3-14 year olds with asthma	Tolerance	Y	
						Internal control	Y	
						Quality of Life	N	
						Teacher knowledge	Y	
						School policy	Y	
						Asthma knowledge	Y	

Study	Learning Type	Intervention type	RCT (y/n)	Control group	# of subjects Intervention/Control	Outcomes	Statistical significance	Clinical significance
Patterson et al., 2005	B	8 weekly asthma clubs (inhaler practice)	Y	Evaluation only	81/92 7-11 year olds with asthma randomized by school	Self-efficacy	Y	
						Doctor-Patient communication	N	
						Perceived effectiveness of behaviors	N	
						Children's cooperation	N	
						Self-management behavior	Y	
						Activity limitation	N	
						Health service use	N	
						Symptoms	N	
						Quality of Life	N	
Butz AM et al., 2005	B	3 home-based symptom identification/ nebulizer use educations (demonstrate cleaning nebulizer/ describe symptoms)	Y	Standard asthma education	105/105 2-8 year olds with asthma	Spirometry	N	
						Inhaler technique	Y	Y
						Give medications with cough, wheeze, poor speech	Y	X
Velson-Friedrich et al., 2005	B	Open Airways + 5 monthly Primary Nurse Practitioner visits at school clinic	Y	Data collection at 0, 2 wks, 5, 12 mos.	28/24 8-13 year olds with asthma randomized by school	Nebulizer use	N	
						Asthma knowledge	Y	

Study	Learning Type	Intervention type	RCT (y/n)	Control group	# of subjects Intervention/Control	Outcomes	Statistical significance	Cinical significance
McConnell et al., 2005	B	1 peer education session (with modeling) plus mattress cover	Y	Evalation at 0, 4 months	77/73 6-14 year olds with asthma	Asthma self-efficacy	Y	
						Self-esteem	N	
						General self-care	Y	
						Asthma self-care	Y	
						Peak Expiratory Flow Rate	N	
						Acute visits	N	
						Asthma symptoms	N	
						School absences	N	
						Asthma knowledge	Y	
Butz et al., (2005)	B	2 child educational workshops, asthma coloring book, 1-hour parent educational workshop	Y	Quarterly asthma newsletter	122/89 rural 6-12 year olds with persistent asthma	Days of cough/wheeze	Y	X
						Nights of cough/wheeze	Y	X
						Child asthma knowledge grades 1-2	Y	X
						Child asthma knowledge grades 3-5	N	
						Change in child self-efficacy score	Y	X
						Parent knowledge	Y	N
						Parent environmental control knowledge	N	
						Parent self-efficacy	N	
						Child Quality of Life	N	
						Parent Quality of Life	N	
						Emergency Dept. Visits	N	
						Hospitalizations	N	
						Scheduled visits	N	
						Have action plan	N	

Study	Learning Type	Intervention type	RCT (y/n)	Control group	# of subjects Intervention/ Control	Outcomes	Statistical significance	Cinical significance
Krieger et al., 2005	B	Healthy Homes (3-visit, high intensity in-home education (advice, tools, advocacy) plus allergy testing	Y	Low intensity single visit, mattress covers, action plan, limited education, environment assessments	138/136 4-12 year olds with asthma	Behavior for cockroach control	Y	X
						Cockroach count	Y	
						Bed allergen level	Y	
						Quality of Life	Y	
						Health service use	Y	N
						Symptom days	N	
						Activity limits	Y	Y
						Missed school/work	N	
						Controller/reliever use	N	
Eggleston et al., 2005	B	3-visit home-based physical and behavioral education + modeling) HEPA air cleaner, exterminator, skin tests	Y	Phone symptom evaluations	50/50 6-12 year olds with asthma	Particulate matter	Y	
						Cockroach allergen	Y	
						Mouse allergen	N	
						Daytime symptoms	Y	Y
						Nighttime symptoms	N	
						Emergency Room use	N	
						Spirometry	N	
McPherson et al., 2006	A	Asthma information booklet plus interactive CD-Rom, Asthma Files	Y	Asthma information booklet	50/51 7-14 year olds with asthma	Asthma knowledge	Y	
						Asthma locus of control	Y	
						Lung function Forced Expiratory Volume in 1 second	N	
						Peak Expiratory Flow Rate		
						School absences	N	
						General Practice visits	N	
						Hospitalizations	N	

Study	Learn-ing Type	Intervention type	RCT (y/n)	Control group	# of subjects Intervention/ Control	Outcomes	Statistical signif-icance	Cinical signif-icance
Walders et al., 2006	B	Written action plan, peak flow monitor and spacer, education, risk profile, problem solving session, access to 24-hour nurse advice line	Y	Written action plan, metered dose inhaler training, peak flow monitor and spacer	89/86 4-12 year olds with MD-diagnosed asthma and frequent emergency department visits or hospitalization in prior year	Asthma symptom days	N	
						Symptom score	N	
						Asthma related quality of life	N	
						Emergency department visits	Y	Y
Smith et al., 2006	A	Asthma coaching during ED visit and monetary incentive to attend primary care doctor follow-up	Y	Usual discharge instructions to see primary care physician in 3 days	50/42 2-12 year olds	primary care physician visit within 2 weeks	N	
LaRoche et al., 2006	C	3 1-hour modules on symptoms. monitoring, trigger recognition and prevention, and prevention of/ coping with attack, emphasizing collaborative management	Y	Standard psychosocial asthma intervention and no intervention (control group)	12/12/11 Hispanic and black 7-13 year olds with asthma	Emergency Department visits	Y	Y
						Asthma Behavioral Assessment Questionnaire	N	

Study	Learning Type	Intervention type	RCT (y/n)	Control group	# of subjects Intervention/ Control	Outcomes	Statistical significance	Clinical significance
Kercsmar et al., 2006	B	Asthma action plan, individualized problem solving, education, household repairs	Y	Information on how to improve indoor air quality	29/33 2-17 year olds with asthma living in a home with indoor mold	Allergen levels in dust		
						Cockroach	N	
						Dustmite	N	
						Endotoxin	Y: time 1 N: time 2	
						Mouse	N	
						Rat	N	
						Mold	Y	Y
						Maximum symptom days	Y	N
						Exacerbations	N	
						Acute care visits	N	
						Emergency department visits or hospitalizations	Y	Y
						Spirometry	N	
						Functional status	N	
						School absences	N	
						Grade point average	N	
						Asthma knowledge		
Gerald et al., 2006	A	3 educational programs and medical management	Y	Referral to medical doctor or health dept. clinic	736/? In 54 elementary schools, 1st-4th grades	School absences	N	
						Grade point average	N	
						Emergency department visits	N	
						Hospitalizations	N	
						Asthma knowledge	Y	

Study	Learn-ing Type	Intervention type	RCT (y/n)	Control group	# of subjects Intervention/ Control	Outcomes	Statistical signif-icance	Clinical signif-icance
Levy et al., 2006	B	School based nurse case manager (CM), weekly teaching and coaching sessions, follow-up on school absences, care coordination	Y	Usual care	115/128 in 14 elementary schools, ages 6-10 years with parent reported asthma	School absences	Y	Y
						Acute or emergency department visits	Y	N
						Hospital days	Y	N
						Student knowledge	Y (within CM group	
Teach et al., 2006	B	Single emergency department follow-up clinic visit and hypoallergenic bed encasings, metered dose inhaler and spacer	Y	Asthma educational booklet	244/244 12 month-17 year old children with known asthma and high emergency department use or hospitaiza-tion in prior year	Unscheduled asthma visits	Y	Y
						Emergency department visits for asthma	Y	Y
						Use of inhaled corticosteroids at 1 month	Y	Y
						Quality of life	Y	
						Written asthma plan	Y	
						Spacer use	Y	
						Peak Flow Monitor use	N	
						Encasement on bed	Y	
						Smoking in home	Y	
						Linkages/referrals to primary care	N	
Karnick et al., 2007	B	Reinforced asthma education with or without case management	Y	One individualized asthma education session	68/70/74 1 to 16 years	Emergency department visits	N	
						Hospitalizations	N	
						Clinic visits	Y	

Study	Learn-ing Type	Intervention type	RCT (y/n)	Control group	# of subjects Intervention/ Control	Outcomes	Statistical signif-icance	Cinical signif-icance
Joseph et al., 2007	B	Tailored web-based asthma education program, Puff City, with 4 sessions	Y	6 months access to generic asthma website	Urban black youth 15-19 years old (9th-11th graders)	No controller medications	Y	Y
						Controller medications adherent	N	
						Controller medications not adherent	Y	
						Rescue medication available	Y	Y
						Smoking	N	
						Symptom days in the last 2 weeks	Y	Y
						Symptom nights	Y	Y
						School days missed in last 30 days	Y	Y
						Emergency department visits/12 months	N	
						Hospitalizations/12 months	Y	N
						Quality of life	N	

booklet with the same educational content. Families were followed for three months after the intervention, and evaluated at one and three months on parental need for information, coping, and quality of life. The investigators used the Hymovich's Parent Perception Inventory (1998), a self-administered questionnaire that measures coping in families of children with chronic conditions, the Global Rating of Change Questionnaire to evaluate the parent's rating of the change in the child's asthma since the intervention (Juniper et al., 1994), and the Quality of Life Scale (Juniper et al., 1996) to measure caregiver quality of life. They also measured health service utilization and number of asthma exacerbations over the study period. The authors noted that the intervention produced significant improvements in parental need for asthma information, concerns, use of coping strategies, and perception of the child's asthma. Quality of life remained unchanged. Health service use and exacerbation frequency were not reported.

Dolinar et al. (2000) concluded that asthma health education is an important intervention to help parents better manage their child's asthma. They acknowledged that knowledge tests, a frequent measure of the impact of educational interventions, do not provide any information about how families manage their child's asthma. They proposed that, along with measures of coping, quality of life measures would be better for assessing the impact of knowledge interventions, since, "one way parents cope with their child's asthma is by accessing educational information" (p.94). The intervention did produce some positive outcomes, but the study was limited by its failure to report on clinical measures such as health service use. Also, the definition of chronic stable asthma was not described and does not fit into the NAEPP Guideline definitions (National Asthma Education and Prevention Program, 1997). Moreover, the family could not be

enrolled if the child presented with an acute exacerbation. Excluding children with an exacerbation may have selected families who may not have required an intensive program to improve their asthma management skills.

Example of a Type B Study

Type B interventions are also knowledge-based but specifically focus on self-management. This approach is exemplified by the home-based educational intervention described by Brown et al. (2002). The families targeted for this study were from a high-risk population of low-income, urban patients from three pediatric asthma subspecialty clinics and some pediatricians' offices. The child had to be on daily medication for asthma and younger than 7 years of age. Having an asthma exacerbation did not exclude the child or family from participation. The intervention group received eight 90-minute home-based educational sessions delivered by a registered nurse. The intervention was based on the Wee Wheezers program (Stevens et al., 2002) and included educational sessions on symptom recognition and management strategies along with homework. A social worker collected outcome data at 3- and 12-month home visits including symptom-free days, a Paediatric Asthma Quality of Life Questionnaire subscale, asthma management practices, and the number of medical visits. The intervention was associated with significant improvements in symptom-free days and caregiver quality of life for children 1 to 3 years of age but not for children 4 through 6 years of age. There were no differences in caregiver asthma management behaviors or acute care utilization. As the authors noted, this study only demonstrated effects on asthma morbidity and caregiver quality of life in the *younger* subpopulation of patients. There are several interpretations for this finding. One might be that the younger children improved without changes in the family's asthma management behavior, due to the possibility that their wheezing was caused by something other than asthma and resolved over time (misclassification). Alternatively, parents of younger children may have benefited more, in ways that weren't measured, by an educational intervention, since they had less experience with asthma than did parents of older children. However, it is also possible that the older children had more persistent asthma and that an intervention that included only education, without opportunities for behavioral rehearsal, was not intense enough to lead to measurable changes.

Example of a Type C study

An example of an intervention that includes behavioral rehearsal in addition to asthma self-management education is the Environmental Counselor intervention report-ed by Morgan, et al. (2004). Poor, inner-city children 5 to 11 years of age with moderate to severe asthma were randomly assigned to an environmental intervention, "to provide the child's caretaker with the knowledge, skills, motivation, equipment, and supplies necess-ary to perform comprehensive environmental remediation."(p.1070). Environmental reme-diation behaviors were modeled, and feed-back and motivation were provided during behavioral rehearsal. This intervention was one of the first to reduce multiple allergen levels in the home and link those reductions to reduced asthma symptoms and unscheduled asthma visits.

Theoretical Models

Prochaska and Prochaska (2006) noted that "interventions that are theory-driven are likely to produce greatest efficacy, participation, and impacts." An extensive review of behavior change theories may be found in The *Handbook of Behavior Change* (Shumaker et al., 1998). However, most interventions continue to exhibit the weaknesses noted by Bauman et al. (1997) in their review of

psychosocial interventions for children with chronic illness. With a few exceptions, such as the work of Creer et al. (1998) and Clark et al. (2004), most interventions are not clearly tied to behavior change theory, so it is difficult to provide an explanation for their findings. Future research would profit from much tighter links between theory and interventions.

The Health Belief Model

The most widely applied model is The Health Belief Model. It was developed in the 1950's to explain people's poor adherence to preventive medical recommendations (Rosenstock, 1974). It was later used by Becker (1974) to help understand patients' adherence to medical recommendations. It is in this context that the Health Belief Model has gained fairly widespread, if uneven, application in asthma interventions. According to The Health Belief Model, the likelihood of taking preventive health actions depends on the perception that one is at risk for a disease, the perception that the consequences of not taking action against the condition would be serious, and the perception that taking action will have, on balance, more benefits than negative consequences. In this model, cues to action, such as advice from relatives or important others, news articles, or knowing someone with the disease, may trigger taking action.

In a review of models for improving adherence and disease management, Clark and Becker (1998) noted that the Health Belief Model related only to people's attitudes and beliefs, while much of health-related behavior is habitual or depends on skills and is not affected much by attitudes. Also, willingness to adapt new behaviors based on attitudes or beliefs about a disease may be constrained by factors such as income or residence, which are frequently immutable. These factors may be particularly important in pediatric asthma in which the role of environmental tobacco smoke (ETS), for example, is well known. Successful efforts to reduce exposure to ETS have required new models that address change of habitual behaviors that don't respond to knowledge, attitudes, or perceptions (Morgan et al., 2004). Additionally many inner-city residents with asthma face tremendous barriers to taking recommended actions simply by virtue of living in areas with poor housing stock, little green space, and high levels of indoor allergens and diesel particulate matter. Despite these shortcomings, the Health Belief Model remains the most widely referenced theoretical model for health behavior interventions.

Social Cognitive Theory

Perhaps the most promising model is that which Albert Bandura (1986) calls Social Cognitive Theory or the Theory of Self-Efficacy (see Volume 1, Chapter 2). *Self-efficacy* is the belief that one is capable of performing a particular behavior, such as giving an asthma treatment with a spacer and metered dose inhaler or cleaning in ways that reduce allergen levels. Self-efficacy is not a global concept of self-confidence or self-esteem but an assessment of the ability to perform a specific behavior. A related variable in this model is *outcome expectancy*, the belief that a particular outcome will occur if the specific behavior is performed.

Bandura noted that self-efficacy is learned in several ways. The most powerful is through "performance accomplishments," learning through personal experience or practice that enables the individual to gain mastery over a task that had been feared or thought too difficult to perform. The second source of efficacy expectation is vicarious experience, or observation of others who model the behavior. For modeling to be effective in increasing an individual's sense of self-efficacy the model must be similar to the individual whose self-efficacy is to be

affected and the model must be viewed as "overcoming difficulties thorough determined effort rather than with ease." (Wilson et al. 1996). The third method is verbal persuasion, as with a health coach or physician who attempts to convince the child's caretaker to initiate and maintain some useful asthma management behavior. Finally, physiologic state affects efficacy expectations. People who are very tense or agitated are likely to expect failure. This factor may be particularly important in influencing caretaker's efficacy expectations for managing an asthma exacerbation in their child.

The concept of outcome expectations in Bandura's theory is similar to that of perceived benefits in the Health Belief Model, according to Rosenstock et al. (1974). The one construct that is not part of the Health Belief Model is self-efficacy. Rosenstock, et al. (1974) note that making self-efficacy explicit delimits the catch-all category of barriers to action in the Health Belief Model, and enables investigators to better tease apart the factors that contribute to behavior change.

Both outcome expectations (or perceived benefits) and self-efficacy are important for behavior change. Parents and children, especially as they grow older and become more responsible for their self-management, must understand that asthma is a serious problem, and that if they don't act they, or their child, can suffer serious consequences from the condition. They must feel, moreover, that their actions can make a difference, that the possible gains from taking self-manage-ment actions outweigh the required effort. Patients and parents must not face major barriers to action, and they must value their child's health enough to take action.

However, asthma is a chronic, episodic condition that requires planning and complex actions in multiple arenas, including medication adherence and appointment keeping, home allergen and irritant reduction, and trigger avoidance inside and outside the home. In school, control of asthma may require the parent to interact with school officials, obtain medical forms, and establish communication methods with school personnel. Although most parents want their child to be free of asthma symptoms and so have a strong incentive to take action, to be successful, parents must feel competent to implement these specific behaviors.

Despite the urging by Rosenstock et al. (1974) to add self-efficacy as an explanatory variable to the Health Belief Model, even by the mid-1990's, investigators in the National Cooperative Inner-City Asthma Study (NCICAS) were unable to identify a published scale to measure caretaker self-efficacy expectations for important asthma self-management behaviors. Holden et al. (1998) describe a substudy of the NCICAS in which they developed a brief scale to assess self-efficacy, outcome expectations, and response difficulty (barriers). However, neither self-efficacy nor elements of the Health Belief Model were included in an overall model to describe the impact of the NCICAS Asthma Counselor intervention. Use of this scale in other research might help to better characterize the process of successful (or unsuccessful) behavior change by providing a method of determining the amount of change attributable to the elements of the Health Belief-Self Efficacy model.

Theory of Self-Regulation

Noreen Clark and her colleagues have refocused the Health Belief Model plus self-efficacy or Social Cognitive Theory into a theory of self-regulation in which individuals or, in the case of children, their parents, observe and evaluate factors in the social and physical environments, try out solutions to a specific health problem, develop self-confidence when they believe their solution has been effective, and become motivated to repeat that behavior (Clark et al., 2001). Over time, through the process of self-regulation, the individual develops a repertoire of self-management behaviors that work for them. High rates of school absences, days of wheeze and poor functioning, and inappropriate medication use suggest that, most parents are poor self-observers and have difficulty evaluating their situation and taking appropriate action. Self-management education increases what Clark et al. (2001) call the patient's self-regulation skills, which are like the critical thinking skills educators work to instill in children. "Being self-regulating means being observant and making judgments based on observation (versus habit, fear, tradition, etc.)" (p.770). Management strategies are the individual's efforts to control the chronic problem. They may be effective or ineffective; physicians or community health workers can influence the strategy chosen, but in the end, the parent or older child determines what management strategy is used, based on their own observations and evaluations. Self-regulation, like self-efficacy, is very specific to a particular behavior and doesn't generalize to other behaviors. Thus, Clark et al. (2001) noted, an individual does not have a personality trait for self-regulation. However, the ability to self-regulate in one situation, such as making sure to take the child's asthma medicines on vacation, may help a parent to be or become more self-regulating in another situation.

Clark at al. (2001) note that the motivating factor for parents taking self-regulating action is their personal goal for the child, which may be very different from the physician's goal. They also note that, "when an educator or clinician … has a different goal than the individual, the opportunity for successful goal attainment is attenuated. When the clinician and educator focus on achieving the patient's personal goal, the chances are greater that the therapeutic regimen will appeal to the interests of the patient (or parent) and be implemented by him or her." (p.772)

The effect of the lack of theory on program evaluation

Most pediatric asthma interventions have not made explicit their theoretical underpinnings, so it is difficult to evaluate how well any particular model predicts success. A few have stated that they are founded on principles of the Health Belief Model and Social Cognitive Theory, for example, but almost no studies have provided information relating components of the intervention specifically to elements of the theories on which they are said to be based. One recent successful intervention, the Inner-City Asthma study, was reported to be based on both of the above theories (Crain et al., 2002). As noted above, this study was one of the first to show that a home-based educational intervention could lead to reduced levels of several allergens in the home of children with moderate to severe asthma and that the reduction persisted in the intervention group for up to a year after the home-based Environmental Counselor program had ended. Moreover, reductions in allergen levels in the intervention group were associated with significantly fewer asthma symptom days during both the intervention and follow-up years. This effect translated into 34 fewer days with reported wheeze during the two years of the study among children in the intervention group compared with the control group, similar to the effect of inhaled corticosteroids in a randomized controlled trial of asthma medications (The Childhood Asthma Management Program Research Group, 2000). In addition, the intervention group had significantly fewer unscheduled asthma visits to the emergency department or clinic during the intervention year. At the first home visit, the Environmental Counselor asked the caretaker what her goals were with regard to her child's asthma or what she most wanted her child to be able to do. The counselor then organized the program activities around the caretaker's goals; successful performance of the activities would help the caretaker achieve her personal goal for her child's asthma. The caretaker was taught strategies to reduce exposures to all indoor allergens to which the child was sensitized and to environmental tobacco smoke. Although caretaker self-efficacy was not measured at baseline or at the end of the intervention period, the intervention focused on the caretaker's feelings that he or she was performing behaviors competently; counselor feedback was as consistently positive as realistically possible.

The Environmental Counselor also provided a brief knowledge-transmission component, and modeled the skills that the caretaker was to perform for each specific allergen and irritant reduction behavior. Barriers to the caretaker performing the behaviors were discussed at each visit and plans made to help the caretaker overcome those barriers. Finally, certain important pieces of equipment such as a HEPA air cleaner and vacuum cleaner, mattress and pillow encasements, and cleaning supplies were provided to overcome the barriers of cost, lack of knowledge of what and where to purchase the equipment, and time.

A brief look at another home environmental intervention that addressed airborne pollutants and indoor allergens among inner-city Baltimore children with asthma highlights the difficulty we have in comparing even similar interventions in terms of their effectiveness (Eggleston et al., 2005). This intervention, reported by Eggleston, et al. (2005), consisted of a combination of physical and behavioral educational interventions. It reduced cockroach, but not mouse, allergen levels as well as daytime symptoms over the first nine months but did not have an impact on spirometry findings, nighttime symptoms, emergency department visits, or quality of life. Though the investigators did not specifically tie any components of the intervention to a theoretical model, they did note that the "content and sequence of the interventions were tailored to increase awareness, establish goals, and increase self-efficacy" (Eggleston et al., 2005). The home educator provided the caretaker with information about the child's allergy testing, emphasizing that the child has a health problem. The educator also showed the caretaker the results of a home environmental survey as well as home levels of allergens and pollutants and provided information about how to reduce the child's exposure to environmental tobacco smoke and indoor allergens. Behaviors to reduce exposure were modeled, but it is not clear if the caretaker was able to rehearse them and receive feedback. Were the differences in the findings of these two interventions due to greater or lesser fidelity to a model of behavior change or to factors associated with the populations in which they were implemented? We do know that the Inner-City Asthma Study addressed a broader array of allergens and irritants than the Baltimore project, but the role of this difference is not clear. Because the details of program implementation and the degree to which elements of the intervention were tied to theory were not elaborated, it is not possible to know whether the limited impact of the Baltimore intervention was due to program deficiencies or characteristics of the population and the environment in which it was tested.

In the absence of a description of the pathway through which an intervention impacts morbidity, intermediate pathway variables are rarely measured. Thus, investigators rarely provided a description of how the intervention improved or failed to improve the selected asthma outcomes. Because so many factors affect the morbidity, school absences, and health service utilization of children with asthma, the absence of a model of how an intervention affects outcomes means that confounding variables are frequently unaccounted for in the model and therefore not measured. Thus, program failure cannot be explained nor can the program be strengthened or refocused. The table below summarizes the most important elements that behavioral interventions for pediatric asthma should include (Table 2).

Table 2: Elements of successful pediatric asthma interventions

1.	Provide clear description of the pathway from intervention to expected outcome
2.	Ensure measurement of pathway variables and confounders based on the descriptive model
3.	Ensure that the intervention addresses parents perceptions and health beliefs in addition to their level of knowledge about asthma
4.	Identify barriers to improved self-management
5.	Focus the intervention around the parents' goals for their child
6.	Include opportunities for behavioral rehearsal
7.	Provide problem solving strategies for parents to enable them to successfully deal with new barriers to self-management after the intervention is withdrawn
8.	Address important content areas including: home allergen and irritant reduction, understanding, avoiding and managing asthma triggers, increasing medication and appointment-keeping adherence, proper use of asthma medications, spacers, and metered dose inhalers, and learning strategies to function as a partner with the child's provider
9.	Report morbidity outcomes in terms of days or visits per year and pulmonary function data in terms of change in percent predicted value so that clinical importance of the findings can be determined and compared across studies that enroll children with similar asthma severity

SUMMARY AND CONCLUSION

Despite huge advances in our understanding of the pathophysiology and medical therapy of pediatric asthma, patients and families have had to assume growing responsibility for the management of the disease. Initially, study of caretakers' asthma management behaviors led physicians to focus their efforts on increasing parents' knowledge about asthma. Gradually, it became clear that the transmission of knowledge had limited effect on proximal outcomes like asthma management behaviors or on more distal outcomes such as days of wheeze, disruption of play, or health service utilization. Researchers began to shift their focus to self-management knowledge and behavioral rehearsal. To date, interventions that include behavior rehearsal seem to be the most effective, especially when it comes to clinically significant distal outcomes.

Although many studies mentioned theoretical models, such as the Health Belief Model or the Self-Efficacy Model, most interventions have not closely tied their intervention components to specific theories of behavior change. Few, if any, studies have included measures of key variables in these theories such as self-efficacy or outcome expectancy.

In future research, progress can be made in three ways. First, investigators need to more clearly describe their interventions. It would help if journal editors recognized this need and gave more space for more detailed descriptions of study methods. The description of one's methods is central to scientific progress; if others know what was done, they can test whether replication of the procedure leads to similar results. Secondly, investigators should use standard definitions and standard measures. They should try, where possible, to use the same process and outcome measures and to include clinical outcomes. They should also clearly describe

their enrollment criteria and use standard definitions of severity, so that the effectiveness of interventions can begin to be compared. A third goal of future research is to tie interventions to theory. Theory enables researchers to organize concepts. Without this organization, research may omit measurement of key process variables and fail to learn from previous intervention trials. Greater attention to the methodological strengths of successful interventions should increase the chance that interventions will consistently help children with asthma and their families live normal lives and have improved quality of life.

REFERENCES

Bandura A. (1986) Social foundations of thought and action: A social cognitive theory. Englewood Cliffs, NJ: Prentice-Hall.

Bauman LJ, Drotar D, Leventhal JM, Perrin EC, Pless IB. (1997) A review of psychosocial interventions for children with chronic health conditions. Pediatrics 100: 244-251.

Becker MH. (1974) The health belief model and sick role behavior. Health Education Monographs 2:409-419.

Bernard-Bonnin A, Stachenko S, Bonin D, Charette E, Rousseau E. (1995) Self management teaching programs and morbidity of pediatric asthma: A meta-analysis. J Allergy Clin Immunol 95:34-41.

Birkhead GB, Attaway NJ, Strunk RC, et al. (1989) Investigation of a cluster of deaths of adolescents from asthma: evidence implicating inadequate treatment and poor patient adherence with medications. J Allergy Clin Immunol 84:484-491.

Bonner S, Zimmerman BJ, Evans D, Irigoyen M, et al. (2002) An individual-ized intervention to improve asthma management among urban Latino and African-American families. J Asthma 39: 167-179.

Brook U, Mendelberg A, Heim M. (1993) Increasing parental knowledge of asthma decreases the hospitalization of the child: A pilot study. J Asthma 30:45-49.

Brown JV, Bakeman R, Celano MP, Demi AS, et al. (2002) Home-based asthma education of young low-income children and their families. J Pediatric Psychology 27:677-688.

Butz AM, Syron L, Johnson B, Spaulding J, et al. (2005) Home-based asthma self-management education for inner-city children. Public Health Nursing 3:189-199.

Butz A, Pham L, Lewis L, Lewis C, et al. (2005) Rural children with asthma: Impact of a parent and child asthma education program. J Asthma 42:813-821.

Chiang LC, Huang JL, Yeh KW, Lu CM. (2004) Effects of a self-management asthma educational program in Taiwan based on PRECEDE-PROCEED model for parents with asthmatic children. J Asthma 41:205-215.

Christiansen SC, Martin SB, Schleicher NC, Koziol JA, et al. (1997) Evaluation of a school-based asthma education program for inner-city children. J Allergy Clin Immunol 100: 613-617.

Clark NM, Brown R, Joseph CLM, Anderson EW, et al. (2004) Effects of a comprehensive school-based asthma program on symptoms, parent management, grades, and absenteeism. Chest 125: 1674-1679.

Clark NM, Beker MH. (1998) Theoretical models and strategies for improving adherence and disease management, in Shumaker SA, et al (eds) The Handbook of Health Behavior Change, 2nd ed, op.cit., pp.5-32.

Clark NM, Gong M, Kaciroti N. (2001) A model of self-regulation for control of chronic disease. Health Educ and Behavior 28:769-782.

Crain EF, Walter M, O'Connor GT, et al. (2002) Home and allergic characteristics of children with asthma in seven U.S. urban communities and design of an environmental intervention: the Inner-City Asthma Study. Environ Health Perspect 110:939-945.

Crain EF, Kercsmar C, Weiss KB, Mitchell H, Lynn H. (1998) Reported difficulties in access to quality care for children with asthma in the inner city. Arch Pediatr Adolesc Med 152:333-339.

Crain W. (2000) Theories of Development: Concepts and Applications, 5th ed., Ch.9: Bandura's social learning theory, Upper Saddle River, NJ: Prentice-Hall, pp.197-216.

Creer TL, Backial M, Burns KL, Leung P, et al. (1988) Living with asthma: Genesis and development of a self-management program for childhood asthma. J Asthma 25:335-362.

Dahl J, Gustafsson D, Melin J. (1990) Effects of a behavioral treatment program on children with asthma. J Asthma 27:41-46.

Data from The American Lung Association, http://www.lungusa.org, Asthma and Child Fact Sheet.

Dolinar R-M, Kumar J, Coutu-Wakulczyk G, Rowe BH. (2000) Pilot study of a home-based asthma health education program. Patient Education and Counseling 40:93-102.

Eggleston PA, Butz A, Rand C, Curtin-Brosnan JC, et al. (2005) Home environmental intervention in inner-city asthma: A randomized controlled clinical trial. Ann Allergy Asthma Immunol 95: 518-524.

Ehnert B, Lau-Schadendorf S, Weber A, Buettner P, et al. (1992) Reducing domestic exposure to dust mite allergen reduces bronchial hyperreactivity in sensitive children with asthma. J Allergy Clin Immunol 90:135-138.

Evans D, Mellins RB. (1991) Educational programs for children with asthma.

Pediatrician 18:317-323.

Evans R, Gergen PJ, Mitchell H, Kattan M, et al. (1999) A randomized clinical trial to reduce asthma morbidity among inner-city children: Results of the National Cooperative Inner-City Asthma study. J Pediatr 135: 332-338.

Finkelstein JA, Brown RW, Scheider LC, Weiss ST, et al. (1995) Quality of care for preschool children with asthma: the role of social factors and practice setting. Pediatrics 97:389-394.

Georgiou A, Buchner DA, Ershoff DH, Blasko KM, et al. (2003) The impact of a large-scale population-based asthma management program on pediatric asthma patients and their caregivers. Ann Allergy Asthma Immunol 90:308-315.

Gerald I, Redden D, Witich AR, Hains C, et al. (2006) Outcomes for a comprehensive school-based asthma management program. J School Health 76:291-296.

Guendelman S, Meade K, Benson M, Chen YQ, Samuels S. (2002) Improving asthma outcomes and self-management behaviors of inner-city children. Arch Pediatr Adolesc Med 156:114-120.

Guevera JP, Wolf FM, Grum CM, Clark NM. (2005) Effects of educational interventions for self-management of asthma inchildren and adolescents: Systematic review and meta-analysis. BMJ 326:1-6.

Handelman L, Rich M, Bridgemohan CF, Schneider L. (2004) Understanding pediatric inner-city asthma: An explanatory model approach. J Asthma 41:167-177.

Henry RL, Gibson PG, Vimpani GV, Francis JL, Hazell J. (2004) Randomized controlled trial of a teacher-led asthma education program. Pediatric Pulmonol 38:434-442.

Holden G, Wade SL, Mitchell H, Ewart C, Islam S. (1998) Caretaker expectations and the management of pediatric asthma in the inner-city: A scale development study. Social Work Research 22:51-59.

Homer C, Susskind O, Alpert HR, Owusu C, et al. (2000) An evaluation of an innovative multimedia educational software program for asthma management: Report of a randomized controlled trial. Pediatrics 106:210-215.

Hovel MF, Meltzer SB, Wahlgren DR, Matt GE, et al. (2002) Asthma management and environmental tobacco smoke exposure reduction in Latino children: A controlled trial. Pediatrics 110: 946-956.

Huss K, Winkelstein M, Nanda J, Naumann PL, et al. (2003) Computer game for inner-city children does not improve asthma outcomes. J Pediatr Health Care 17:72-78.

Janz NK, Becker MH. (1984) The health belief model: A decade later. Health Ed Quarterly, 11:1-47.

Joseph CLM, Peterson E, Havstad S, Johnson CC, et al. (2007) A web-based tailored asthma management program for urban african-american high school students. Am J Respir Crit Care Med 175: 888-895.

Karnick P, Margellos-Anast H, Seals G, Whitman S, et al. (2007) The pediatric asthma iintervention: A comprehensive cost-effective approach to asthma management in a disadvantaged inner-city community. J Asthma 44:39-44.

Kercsmar CM, Dearborn DG, Schluchter M, Xue L, et al. (2006) Reduction in asthma morbidity in children as a result of home remediation aimed at moisture sources. Environ Health Perspect 114:1574-1580.

Kravis LP. (1987) An analysis of fifteen childhood asthma fatalities. J Allergy Clin Immunol 80:467-472.

Krieger JW. Talarp TK, Song L, Weaver M. (2005) The Seattle-King County Healthy Homes Project: a randomized, controlled trial of a community health worker intervention to decrease exposure to indoor asthma triggers. Am J Public Health 95:652-659.

Krishna S, Francisco BD, Balas A, Konig P,

et al (2003) Internet-enabled interactive multimedia asthma education program: A randomized trial. Pediatrics 111:503-510.

LaRoche MJ, Koinis-Mitchell D, Gualdron L. (2006) A culturally competent asthma management intervention: a randomized controlled pilot study. Ann Allergy Asthma Immunol 96: 80-85.

Leickly FE, Wade SL, Crain E, Kruszon-Moran D, et al. (1998) Self-reported adherence, management behavior, and barriers to care after an emergency department visit by inner city children with asthma. Pediatrics 101, URL:http://www.pediatrics.org/cgi/content/full/101/5/e8.

Levy M, Heffner B, Stewart T, Beeman G. (2006) The efficacy of asthma case management in an urban school district in reducing school absences and hospitalizations for asthma J Sch Health 76:320-324.

Liu C, Feekery C. (2001) Can asthma education improve clinical outcomes? An evaluation of a pediatric asthma education program. J Asthma 38:269-278.

McConnell R, Milam J, Richardson J, Galvan J, et al. (2005) Educational intervention to control cockroach allergen exposure in the homes of Hispanic children in Los Angeles: Results of the La Casa study. Clin Exp Allergy 35:426-433.

McGhan SL, Wong E, Jhangri GS, Wells HM, et al. (2003) Evaluation of an education program for elementary school children with asthma. J Asthma 40:523-533.

McPherson AC, Glazebrook C, Forster D, James C, Smyth A. (2006) A randomized, controlled trial of an interactive educational computer package for children with asthma. Pediatrics 117: www.pediatrics.org/cgi/doi/10.1542/peds2005-0666.

Mellins RB, Evans D, Zimmerman B, Clark NM. (1992) Patient compliance. Are we wasting our time and don't know it? Am

Rev Resp Dis 146:1376-1377.

Morgan WJ, Crain EF, Gruchalla RS, O'Connor GT, et al. (2004) Results of a home-based environmental intervention among urban children with asthma. N Engl J Med 351:1068-1080.

Patterson EE, Brennan MP, Linskey KM, Webb DC, et al. (2005) A cluster randomized intervention trial of asthma clubs to improve quality of life in primary school children: the School Care and Asthma management Project (SCAMP). Arch Dis Child 90:786-791.

Prochaska JO, Prochaska JM. (2006) An update on maximum impact practices from a transtheoretical approach, in Best Practices in the Behavioral Management of Chronic Disease, v.1, Ch.1, Institute for Brain Potential, California: Los Altos, p.1.

Rakos RF, Grodek MV, Mack KK. (1985) The impact of a self-administered behavioral intervention program on pediatric asthma. J Psychosomatic Research 29: 101-108.

Rosenstock IM. (1974) Historical origins of the Health Belief Model. Health Education Monographs 2:328-335.

Rosenstock IM, Strecher VJ, Becker MH. (1988) Social learning theory and the health belief model. Health Educa Quarterly 15:175-183.

Rubin DH, Bauman LJ, Lauby JL. (1989) The relationship between knowledge and reported behavior in childhood asthma. J Dev Behav Pediatr 10:307-312.

Sears MB, Beagleole R. (1987) Asthma morbidity and mortality: New Zealand. J Allergy Clin Immonol 80:383-388.

Shames RS, Sharek P, Mayer M, Robinson TN, et al. (2004) Effectiveness of a multicomponent self-management program in at-risk, school-aged children with asthma. Ann Allergy Asthma Immunol 92:611-618.

Shields MC, Griffin KW, McNabb WL.

(1990) The effect of a patient education program on emergency room use for inner-city children with asthma. Am J Public Health 80:36-38.

Shumaker sA, Schron EB, Ockene JK, McBee WL (eds). (1998) The Handbook of Health Behavior Change, 2nd ed. New York: Springer Publishing Company.

Smith SR, Jaffe DM, Highstein G, Fisher EB, et al. (2006) Asthma coaching in the pediatric emergency department. Acad Emerg Med 13:835-839.

Stevens CA, Wesseldine LJ, Couriel JM, Dyer AJ, et al. (2002) Parental education and guided self-management of asthma and wheezing in the pre-school child: a randomised controlled trial. Thorax 57:39-44.

Teach SJ, Crain EF, Quint DM, Hylan ML, et al. (2006) Improved asthma outcomes in a high-morbidity pediatric population: Results of an emergency department-based randomized clinical trial. Arch Pediatr Adolesc Med 160:535-541.

Tieffenberg JA, Wood EI, Alonso A, Tossutti MS, Vicente MF. (2000) A randomized field trial of ACINDES: A child-centered training model for children with chronic illnesses (asthma and epilepsy). J Urban Health 77: 280-297.

Tsioura S, Mestoridou K, Botis P, Karmaus W, et al. (2002) Randomized trial to prevent sensitization to mite allergens in toddlers and preschoolers by allergen reduction and education. Arch Pediatr Adolesc Med 156: 1021-1027.

Velsor-Friedrich B, Pigott T, Srof B. (2005) A practitioner-based asthma intervention program with African-American inner-city school children. J Pediatric Health Care 19:163-171.

Walders N, Kercsmar C, Schluchter M, Redline S, et al. (2006) An interdisciplinary intervention for undertreated pediatric asthma. Chest 129: 292-299.

Warner JA, Frederick JM, Bryant TN, et al. (2000) Mechanical ventilation and high efficiency vacuum cleaning: a combined strategy of mite and mite allergen reduction in the control of mite-sensitive asthma. J Allergy Clin Immunol 105:75-82.

Weil CM, Wade SL, Bauman LJ, Lynn H, Mitchell H, Lavigne J. (1999) The relationship between psychosocial factors and asthma morbidity in inner-city children with asthma. Pediatrics 104: 1274-1280.

Weiss KB, Gergen PJ, Crain EF. (1992) Inner city asthma: The epidemiology of an emerging US public health concern. Chest 101:363S-367S.

Weitzman M, Gortmaker S, Sobol A. (1990) Racial, social, and environmental risk factors for childhood asthma. Am J Dis Child 144: 1189-1194.

Wilson SR, Yamada EG, Sudhakar R, Roberto L, et al. (2001) A controlled trial of an environmental tobacco smoke reduction intervention in low-income children with asthma. Chest 120: 1709-1722.

Wilson-Pessano SR, McNabb WL. (1985) The role of patient education in the management of childhood asthma. Prev Med 14:670-687.

BEHAVIORAL INTERVENTIONS FOR AUTISM SPECTRUM CONDITIONS

Gina Owens, Kate Gordon, and Simon Baron-Cohen

INTRODUCTION

Autism spectrum conditions (ASC) (also referred to as autism spectrum disorders (ASD)) including the diagnostic categories of classic autism and Asperger syndrome, are a group of pervasive developmental outcomes characterized by atypical development in three domains:

- Reciprocal social interaction
- Verbal and nonverbal communication
- Behavior (restricted, repetitive interests and stereotyped behaviors)

As the name suggests there is a spectrum of ability in each of the three areas described above. Autism may also be accompanied by learning disability. The exact nature of the problems experienced by an individual child will vary considerably depending on language ability, cognitive ability and chronological age.

A low functioning child may have little or no speech, will show little or no interest in people (preferring objects) and might engage in significant nonfunctional or repetitive behavior. At the other end of the spectrum, individuals with high functioning autism may have fluent speech but difficulties with the pragmatic aspects of language; they may engage in social inter-actions but in a one-sided or odd way and they may have narrow interests pursued to an obsessive level.

Individuals with ASC often show reduced interest in social interactions and often try to avoid them. Often there is a lower frequency of *initiating* social contact (Carter et al., 2005). Where children do participate in social exchanges, they are often characterized by a lack of awareness of social rules or of how they might appear to others. Interactions may

also be difficult for the communication partner to sustain.

Early problems with joint attention are recognized as pivotal to the development of social problems for individuals with ASC (Charman, 2003). Joint attention involves the coordination of attention between people and objects in order to share an experience. It includes sharing affect with another person, following another's gaze or point and directing another's attention to objects or events in order to share an experience (Bakeman and Adamson, 1984). Impaired joint attention is thought to reflect a lack of basic awareness of other people's interests and intentions (Tomasello, 1999) leading to a deficit in social reciprocity and reflecting a disability in understanding other people's mental states (Baron-Cohen and Howlin, 1993).

Communication problems are usually the first signs to be recognized in children with ASC (Paul and Sutherland, 2005). A proportion of individuals with autism fail to develop any functional speech (Lord and Bailey, 2002) and these individuals also have impairments in non-verbal communica-tion such as gestures and facial expression. When speech develops, most children show slow or unusual development and some have a regression of spoken language skills. Those who speak fluently have problems with the pragmatic use of language (Baron-Cohen, 1988) and may have unusual speech quality in terms of tone, pitch or volume. Similar to its role in social development, joint attention has also been identified as important for later language development (Charman, 2003).

The third area of atypical behavior lies in

the presence of repetitive stereotyped behavior, ritualistic behavior and obsessive interests. Repetitive behaviors include mannerisms such as hand-flapping or spinning. Individuals may also adhere to a strict routine in their daily lives. It is also common for individuals with ASC to have intense and unusual interests that they pursue to an obsessive degree. Individuals can become very rigid in their routines, and their obsessions can be very disruptive to the lives of the individuals and their families (Schulman, 2002).

BEST PRACTICE IN BEHAVIORAL INTERVENTION FOR CHILDREN WITH ASC

Many interventions have been developed to help children with ASC improve in one or more of the areas described above (see Simpson et al., 2005 for a recent comprehensive review). However, there is no cure for ASC and few interventions have been found to have long lasting benefits. This chapter focuses on interventions that include a behavioral component (non-medical interventions) and are discussed with regard to the quality of evidence in support of their effectiveness.

Despite the wide variety of interventions that have been developed, there are relative-ly few randomized controlled trials (RCTs) in the literature (Table 1). Randomized controlled trials provide the only means for eliminating systematic bias between treatment groups, enabling causal inferences about the effects of a treatment to be drawn (Harrington et al., 2002). Given their capacity to address issues of internal and external validity, RCTs are considered the 'gold standard' in treatment studies and their use within ASC intervention research has been widely encouraged (Charman and Howlin, 2003; Lord et al., 2006). A further problem with evaluating the relative effectiveness of different interventions is the lack of standardized outcome measures. Outcome measures vary widely, making it difficult for parents and professionals to compare the effectiveness of one intervention to another. A charity has recently been set up to fund research into the effectiveness of different interventions and has a useful website that provides up to date information about a wide range of interventions and their supporting scientific evidence (www.researchautism.net). This is a useful starting point for parents and professionals.

As mentioned previously, there are considerable individual differences in the features of ASC. Children may also show associated problems such as anxiety (Muris et al., 1998; Gilliott et al., 2001), hyper-activity (Frazier et al., 2001; Goldstein and Schwebach, 2004) self-injury, epilepsy, gut problems, and sensory problems (Keintz and Dunn, 1997), to name just a few. At present, little is known about which interventions are effective for children with different features and personality characteristics. Until there is a wide base of well-conducted RCTs that use standardized outcome measures, it will be difficult to make recommendations in terms of best practice, and the findings from studies should be interpreted with caution. What is clear, at present, is that there is no single approach that works for every child.

Below is a summary of behavioral interventions that have had some empirical evaluation, a few through RCTs, most through control-group comparisons or multiple baseline and reversal designs. This review is not comprehensive, but will attempt to evaluate interventions that seem promising in the following areas: comprehensive approaches, language and communication training, alternative communication strategies, social skills training, stereotyped/repetitive behavior, and other problems associated with ASC (Table 2).

Table 1. Randomized controlled trials of psychosocial interventions for ASC

Study	Intervention	Participants	Outcomes	Limitations/future directions
Smith, Groen & Wynn (2000)	ABA (24 hours/week from therapist and 5 hours/week from parents for 1-2 years), compared to parent training control group	N=28 (14 with ASC); Age = 3yrs; IQ = 35-75	Greater gains for ABA group in educational placement, IQ, visual-spatial skills and language but not adaptive behavior. Significantly more children in the behavioral treatment group were in less restrictive educational placements compared to controls at follow-up (age 7-8yrs)	Small sample size, limited validity of outcome measures and need follow-up.
Drew et al. (2002)	Home-based parent training program in speech and language therapy (6 weeks) focuses on joint attention, joint action routines and behavior regulation. Comparison to standard local provision.	N = 25 (13 in intervention; 12 in control group)	Modest improvement in receptive and expressive language at 12 month follow-up for intervention group.	Contamination of treatment conditions by parents in control group seeking other intervention. Reliance on parent report.
Aldred et al. (2004)	Parent training program. Monthly therapist for 6 months; further 6 months of twice-monthly consolidation sessions focused on parents promoting intentional communication in their children. Comparison to routine care.	N = 28 (14 in treatment; 14 in control group); Age = 51 months.	Improvement in standardized measures and observational measures of social interaction and expressive language in treatment group. Language improvement most significant in older, lower functioning children.	Need replication on larger independent samples, longer follow-up period and comparison to other interventions.
Kasari, Freeman & Paparella (2005)	Comparison of two interventions and a control. Interventions taught either joint attention or symbolic play using behavioral techniques (prompting and reinforcement) for 30mins/day for 5-6 weeks. Comparison with no intervention control group.	N = 58 (20 in Joint attention group, 21 in symbolic play group, 17 in control group) Age = 3-4yrs	Measured joint attention, play skills and mother/child interactions before and after intervention. Both interventions were successful at teaching the behaviors targeted (joint attention or symbolic play) in comparison to controls. Skills generalized to parent-child interactions.	Need to evaluate long-term effects of this intervention.
Yoder & Stone (2005)	Response Education and Prelinguistic Milieu Therapy (RPMT) compared to the Picture Exchange Communication System (PECS) (1hour/week for 6 months)	N = 36; Age = 18-60 months;	RPMT increased the frequency of turn-taking and initiation of joint attention more than PECS, only for children who started treatment with some initiating of joint attention. PECS facilitated generalized requests more than RPMT in children with very little initiation of joint attention prior to intervention.	Data coders not blind to treatment allocation. Need to look at long term outcomes.

		N=84; Age = 4-11 yrs	Significant increases in observed rates of children's use of pictures for communication and rates of children's spontaneous communication immediately following the training period. These effects did not persist in a subset of the children who were followed-up approximately 9 months later. There was no significant increases in speech	Observations restricted to class snack times. No measure of treatment fidelity. Data coders not blind to treatment groups.
Howlin et al (2007)	Picture Exchange Communication System training for teachers (PECS training workshop and 6 half-day follow-up visits to the classrooms by PECS consultants over 5 months) compared to children in similar classes whose teachers received no PECS training			

Table 2. Commonly used behavioral interventions for autism spectrum conditions

Comprehensive Approaches	Language and Communication	Alternative communication	Social skills	Repetitive behaviors	Associated Difficulties
Intensive behavioral treatments: Applied Behavior Analysis (ABA)	Discrete trial training	Signing	Peer-mediated interventions	Behavior Modification Procedures	Cognitive Behavioral Therapy
Relationship Development Intervention (RDI)	Pivotal Response Training (PRT)	Functional communication training	Cognitive behavioral approaches	Teaching Alternative Activities	
	Joint attention and play skills training	Voice output communication aids (VOCAs)	Social skills groups		
Son Rise	*Parent training programs:* More Than Words;	Picture systems	Assistive Technology		
Psycho-educational: TEACCH	Responsive Education and Prelinguistic Milieu Therapy (RPMT)				

Comprehensive intervention programs

Applied behavior analysis (ABA) approaches are commonly used in ASC intervention either as techniques for teaching specific skills (e.g. discrete language training as described in the 'Language and Communication' section) or to form the basis of comprehensive intervention programs (Romanczyk and Gillis, 2005) that target all three types of behavioral problem. In comprehensive ABA, the skills and behavior of each child are assessed, and appropriate functional skills to be taught are chosen with respect to the child's ability. The teaching environment is continually analyzed to optimize class-room structure, adapt instructional activities, and to develop meaningful curricula. Principles of operant conditioning (see Glossary) are used to teach the behaviors identified during assessment. Discrete trial teaching (DTT) is used where a stimulus is presented to the child and the child is rewarded for correct responses (see Glossary).

ABA therapists give short and clear instructions with carefully planned prompts and reinforce closer and closer approximations to correct responses. Complex behaviors are taught by breaking them down into smaller components. These are taught separately before being 'chained' together into a whole. The antecedents and consequences of problematic behaviors are monitored using functional analysis (see Glossary) and are altered in order to improve the child's skills. ABA treatment programs can be very intensive (up to 40 hours per week has been recommended by some interventionists) and progress from 1:1 interactions to small groups then larger groups, and from very structured settings to less structured, 'naturalistic' settings.

ABA became popular following the work of Ivar Lovaas (1987), who evaluated the effectiveness of an intensive early behavioral intervention. This study claimed that following 40 hours a week of 1:1 ABA, 47% of children with ASC achieved 'normal educational and intellectual functioning', i.e. they obtained average or above average IQ scores, and successfully completed first grade at a regular school. Out of the remaining children in this group, 42% improved marginally and two children did not improve at all. Only one child in the comparison groups (who received 10 hours per week intervention, or no intervention) successfully completed first grade at school and achieved an average IQ score. At 3- to 6-year follow-up, gains had persisted for the children who had improved to the 'normal' educational and intellectual level (children in the other groups were not followed-up; McEachin et al., 1993). Since this early evaluation, ABA has become the most widely studied of all psychosocial interventions (Volkmar et al., 2004). However, the early work conducted by Lovaas and his colleagues (1987) has proved to be somewhat controversial and the validity of the findings has come under considerable scrutiny (Smith, 1999).

In reaction to the widespread criticism of the early ABA studies, attempts have been made to study the effectiveness of intensive behavioral treatment (IBT) more systematically. Smith, Groen and Wynn (2000) carried out a randomized controlled trial of IBT and found children made greater gains than controls on educational placement, tests of IQ, visual-spatial skills and language but not on adaptive behavior (Table 1). This program was effective despite being less intensive (though arguably more feasible) than other ABA interventions.

Eiskeith, Smith and colleagues (2002) studied 13 children (aged 4 to 7 years) who received school-based IBT for 29 hours per week plus consultation for 1 year compared to 12 children who received eclectic 1:1 therapy in school at the same level of

GLOSSARY

Backward-chaining is a format used for teaching a sequence of actions necessary to complete a task. A sequence of physical prompts is faded one by one over a number of trials. The prompt for the last step in the sequence is faded first. In the example of PECS training, physical prompts to pick up, extend and exchange the picture are taught. The spontaneous exchange is taught first and the prompt to pick up the picture is the last to be faded.

Discrete trial training is a way of teaching behavior through prompting and reinforcing correct responses. For example, an instruction is given to a child by a teacher and the goal is for the child to respond correctly. The teacher can give a prompt to help the child respond correctly. When the child produces a correct response they are given a reward (reinforcement). The same response can be practiced in several different discrete trials with pauses between each one until the child masters the response.

Establishing operations are environmental events that influence the reinforcement value of other events, and therefore change the likelihood of certain types of communication such as requesting for the reinforcing event or item. Manipulation of establishing operations is an approach used with children with autism to increase their initiation of requests.

Functional Analysis is a systematic method for studying inappropriate, inadequate or maladaptive behavior. The goal of functional analysis is to ascertain the motivation for a target behavior so that it can be modified or replaced with a more appropriate behavior. First, a specified behavior is described in detail in terms of its context, what causes it (its antecedents) and what its consequences are. The antecedents and consequences are then systematically altered to observe behavioral differences and to determine the function of the behavior more precisely.

Incidental Teaching is an approach to teaching that is based on a child's interests and motivation. Rather than taking place in a classroom or clinical setting, learning opportunities are found in everyday activities. For example, a teacher might place a desired toy or activity in sight but out of reach of a child. Once the child shows an interest in the toy, the teacher can prompt the child to make an appropriate request or elaboration on their initial expression of interest. For example, a child may say 'teddy' to request a teddy, and the teacher might ask 'what color teddy?'. If the child says 'brown', then they are allowed to play with the teddy for a while.

Operant conditioning is the use of consequences to modify the occurrence and form of behavior.

Time-Delay Procedures can be used to increase spontaneity of a trained response. In the context of speech training, the time delay before a response is modeled is gradually extended over a number of trials in order to increase the likelihood that the child will spontaneously produce the spoken request.

intensity. Children were assigned to the two groups according to the availability of personnel at the time that each child was referred to the specialist school service. The IBT group demonstrated greater improvement than the control group on several measures such as IQ, language and adaptive behavior. In this study, children were not randomly assigned to groups. The children were also relatively able (all were selected to have IQ over 50), so findings may not generalize to children with lower functioning.

Overall, the effectiveness of intensive ABA intervention programs requires further research. Concerns remain over the outcome measures used in these studies. For example, difficulties arise with regard to school placement as a measure as this is likely to be influenced by a number of factors other than intervention (e.g. parental preference and variation in local regulations). Also, improvements in IQ scores or placement in mainstream school cannot necessarily be equated to a reduction in pervasive social communication impairments. Further, the extent to which the improvements can be generalized to everyday life and their impact later on in childhood is yet to be fully understood.

Aside from ABA, other intensive intervention programs have been developed and reported in the literature. The 'Son Rise' program (Kaufman, 1994) is a home-based program where parents are regarded as the key 'therapists'. Families attend workshops mostly run in the USA, often lasting many weeks, where they are trained to engage with their children through energetic and exciting interactive play sessions and to get involved with their child's repetitive behaviors. The program undoubtedly provides an optimistic and empowering approach for parents, however there are considerable financial and emotional commitments required. While the program makes strong claims about improving social communication, and even 'curing' ASC, this is based on anecdotal reports rather than controlled research.

The Relationship Development Intervention Program (RDI) specifically targets deficits in children's experience-sharing abilities, such as gaze direction (Baron-Cohen, 1995a) and facial expression (Hobson, 1986; Golan and Baron-Cohen, 2006), by identifying their individual strengths and needs (Gutstein and Sheeley, 2002). Activities follow a sequence starting with those targeting prelinguistic skills. The primary focus is to engage children in a social relationship that is fun and motivating, using indirect prompts such as invitations to interact, thus fostering the development of communication skills. Parents are trained to build motivation, modify communicative style and communication environments and to generalize skills into everyday life. Following this, parents receive visits and evaluation from consultants and use video footage to get feedback on their practice.

The TEACCH program (Treatment and Education of Autistic and Related Communication Handicapped Children) focuses on the role of structure in the learning environment of children with ASC (Schopler et al., 1995) and is widely used in special education classrooms. By using supports such as timetables and work schedules, tasks are given a visual structure and are therefore made more predictable and meaningful for the child. TEACCH appears to be a useful tool for teachers. It provides a system for organizing work tasks and is widely used in conjunction with other methods such as alternative communication (discussed later in this chapter). Ozonoff and Cathcart (1998) conducted a controlled study of the effectiveness of TEACCH for young children with ASC. The first 11 children whose parents volunteered to participate in the study were allocated to the active treatment group and the next 11 to the control group. The program was implemented in the children's homes over a period of 4 months. By the end of the training, children in TEACCH were performing significantly better on tests of non-verbal skills and cognitive abilities compared to the control group, though outcome in terms of social communication skills was not measured.

Conclusion

Intensive behavioral treatment programs often require very high levels of commit-ment in terms of time, energy and emotion. There are also substantial financial costs for therapists and resources. For many parents or families these costs are very difficult to meet. While beneficial interventions should be available to all children who need them, in the absence of good evidence of effectiveness, such commitments should be made with caution. Psychoeducational approaches are probably the most common route of access to intervention for children with autism but require further empirical evaluation to establish the extent of their effectiveness. In general, comprehensive interventions require more systematic investigation focusing on what specific aspects of the program are effective, which symptoms they effectively address and which children are likely to respond best.

Language and communication interventions

Spoken language training

During the 1970s and 1980s, discrete-trial teaching of speech (see Glossary) was predominant within behavioral programs for individuals with ASC (Lovaas, 1977). However, more detailed examination of effectiveness suggested that children with significant impairment in language skills and social development were unlikely to develop any communicative speech through the use of such techniques. Where children did learn speech, outcomes in terms of spontaneity and flexibility were disappointing (Howlin, 1981).

One method that attempts to increase spontaneity of speech is the use of time-delay procedures (see Glossary). Within a requesting routine, for example, appropriate vocalizations are modeled and the time delay prior to the model is gradually extend-ed, increasing the likelihood that the child themselves will spontaneously produce the spoken request (Charlop et al., 1986). Overall, the weakness of this type of approach is that even where speech is taught, the style of communication is often passive and prompt-dependent and not necessarily used outside of the training situation (Paul and Sutherland, 2005).

Incidental language teaching adopts a more naturalistic approach (see Glossary). Speech training takes place during normal activities and children's own initiated behavior is the focus of the teaching paradigm. In a review of studies of language training, Delprato (2001) found that compared to discrete-trial training, such naturalistic approaches were more effective and also that outcomes were better in terms of generalization. An example of an incidental approach to teaching language is Pivotal Response Training (PRT; Koegel et al., 1987). PRT teaches cue responsiveness during everyday activities, capitalizing on children's preferred items or activities and motivation to communicate (Koegel, 1995). Studies have reported that, in the short term at least, children have made gains in language use and social skills following PRT and were able to use these with some flexibility, spontaneity and generalization (Koegel and Koegel, 1996).

Taylor et al. (2005b) report another example of a naturalistic behavioral approach to teaching spontaneous use of language in a natural setting by 'systematic manipulation of establishing (see Glossary). Its effectiveness for eliciting spontaneous initiations towards peers was studied in three children with ASC. After training, all three children were able to make spontaneous requests for desired snack items or toys from a peer, where none had readily displayed this behavior prior to training. Evidence of true generalization was limited however, and as the items of interest were always visibly present, it is difficult to demonstrate that the communication was spontaneous. Addition-ally, one child experienced difficulty when he found himself in a situation where a peer refused a request. This example illustrates a potential problem with training children to use speech in the absence of the pragmatic knowledge gained through prior development of communicative intent and function (Wetherby and Prizant, 2005).

'Minimal speech' (Potter and Whittaker, 2001) can also be considered as a naturalistic approach to speech training. Unlike discrete trials or incidental teaching, 'minimal speech' focuses primarily on changing the communication behavior of the teacher or parent (rather than the child) in order to encourage the child to initiate communication. Adults are encouraged to speak less, introduce pauses and remove prompts to induce children to communicate spontaneously. Where necessary, nonverbal prompts are used and single words are modeled. This approach is similar to the communicative style used by many people who work with individuals with ASC and Potter and Whittaker (2001) describe anecdotal evidence of the efficacy of this intuitive approach. To date, this approach has not been evaluated in an RCT (Paul and Sutherland, 2005).

It is possible that core deficits in reciprocal social interaction may limit the practical use of language skills learned in these interventions. Additionally, non-verbal communication abilities may exceed verbal abilities in many individuals with ASC and thus other programs have aimed to improve more basic communication skills. (Camaioni et al., 1997; Camaioni et al., 2003). These are described in the next section.

Communication training

Developmental approaches to communi- cation intervention aim to provide opportunities for meaningful communication to occur. Children's intentional actions and/or communicative acts are responded to or expanded upon by a trainer or parent and further communication behaviors are taught through modeling. To some extent, such approaches aim to replicate what would typic- ally happen in very early social communi- cative interactions. Interventions focus on development of prelinguistic nonverbal skills, such as joint attention, as a prerequisite to developing language. It is of interest that many interventions consider the establishment of joint attention as critical for later social development, an idea that is now well- established (Baron-Cohen, 1989; Charman, 2003).

Kasari, Freeman and Paparella (2005) have recently conducted an RCT to evaluate the efficacy of joint attention and symbolic play interventions (Table 1). Applied behavior analysis and developmental procedures of responsive and facilitative interactive methods were applied by trainers during discrete trials to teach particular treatment goals. The main difference between the two interventions was the goals focused upon during the sessions. Examples of joint attention treatment goals include teaching coordinated joint looking and following a distal point. Examples of play treatment goals include teaching how to combine objects during play, making object substitutions and using a doll as an agent. Joint attention treatment sessions incorporated imitation and engineered play routines, whilst the play treatment session focused on object combinations that were increasingly symbolic but not contingent on joint attention. In terms of measuring outcome, joint attention skills were measured using a semi-structured assessment of early social communication skills. Functional and symbolic play skills were assessed from a 15-20 minute observation of the child playing with a standard array of toys. In addition, a 15- minute videotape of a caregiver-child interaction was also coded for joint attention skills and child's play. Results indicated that the interventions were successful and that skills were generalized to interactions between children and their caregivers. This approach warrants follow-up to assess the longer term impact of this training.

Enhancing early nonverbal social communication skills by targeting parental communication has become recognized as an important and useful approach (Reddy et al., 1997; Siller and Sigman, 2002). Responsive Education and Prelinguistic Milieu Therapy (RPMT; Yoder and Warren, 2002) incorporates a parent training component with an incidental teaching approach in one-to-one sessions between a child and trainer. The therapy sessions teach children to initiate joint attention and increase their prelinguistic intentional communication behaviors. Prompts, gradually faded, are used to elicit behaviors such as pointing to request (i.e. imperative communication). Modeling is used to teach children to initiate shared attention with another person such as directing another's attention to a different item using gaze switching or pointing (i.e. joint attention). This intervention was developed for use with children with developmental disabilities, though a recent RCT (Table 1) showed RPMT was successful at increasing the frequency of initiated joint attention amongst young children with ASC who had some joint attention initiation behavior to start with (Yoder and Stone, 2005).

The 'More Than Words' program (Sussman, 1999) focuses on enhancing parents' ability to observe their child, to engage in structured routines of joint attention, and to make use of everyday opportunities to teach communication and social skills. McConachie, Randle, Hammal and Le Couteur (2005) recently completed a controlled trial of this training course for parents of children with suspected ASC in the UK. According to parental report, by follow-up, children in the intervention group had a significantly larger vocabulary than the children in the control group. A significant effect of the intervention on facilitative communication behavior during parent-child interactions was also observed but this was only seen amongst the parents whose children had confirmed diagnoses of ASC from the outset.

Two further RCTs have been conducted to test the effectiveness of parent training programs (Table 1). Drew et al. (2002) conducted a RCT of a home-based program where parents received training from a speech and language therapist in how to develop joint attention and joint action routines with their children. They were also advised on behavior regulation. At 12 month follow-up modest but statistically significant improvements in receptive and expressive language were seen in the training group compared to a 'local provision only' group, although the authors did acknowledge the limitations of using parent report as their outcome measure.

Aldred and colleagues (2004) conducted a similarly sized RCT to test the effectiveness of a parent training program that focused on teaching parents about the developmental 'building blocks' of social interaction and communication. Parents were encouraged to be sensitive to their child's actions, leading to an increase in joint attention and reciprocity and action routines. Repeated scripts and introduction of pauses and teasing were taught to promote children's intentional communication. Compared to routine care, the intervention led to significant improvement on standardized measures of social interaction and expressive language, and in observational measures of parent-child interactions. Reduction in autistic 'symptoms' was most substantial in the younger children who received the intervention. Improvement in expressive language was most significant for children who were lower functioning and older.

Conclusion

It is encouraging to see RCTs in this area.

Studies have shown that children with ASC have the potential to improve their communicative abilities and some have attempted to examine which particular children benefited most from particular interventions. Further studies are now needed to examine the broader and longer term impacts of these programs. Until more systematic research is done, few conclusive recommendations can be made about best practice for particular children.

Alternative and augmentative communication systems

Alternative and Augmentative Communication (AAC) systems (e.g. sign language, pictures/symbols, or computerized devices that emit speech) provide non-verbal means for conventional communication within the context of daily activities. They also have the potential to increase an individual's capacity to spontaneously initiate functional communication (Romski and Sevcik, 2005). Duchan (1987) emphasized the importance of teaching the pragmatic aspects of communication, irrespective of the form used: by enabling independent communication (e.g. by using an AAC system), the 'power' of one's own behavior to direct the behavior of another in order to reach a goal is explicitly demonstrated. In addition to enabling functional communication, AAC has also been associated with a decrease in unwanted behavior and has been used successfully to replace challenging behavior in individuals with ASC (Mirenda, 1997; Charlop-Christy et al., 2002). Despite their potential as alternative communication modes for children with ASC, there is little evidence that AACs can stimulate or accelerate the development of speech itself (Paul and Sutherland, 2005; Rogers, 2006). Nevertheless, AACs are widely used with children with ASC. Some of the most commonly used approaches are discussed below.

Sign language

Studies have demonstrated that children with ASC can and do acquire signs, and it has been argued that the opportunities for social interaction provided by signing can have a significant impact on an individual's social and practical skills (Von Tetzchner and Martinsen, 2000). An advantage of using sign language with children with ASC is the less transient nature of the visual symbols, compared to spoken language. Signing and the use of signing alongside speech training have been consistently demonstrated to be more effective than speech training alone (Goldstein, 2002).

Studies have reported that children with ASC can have difficulties in learning to use sign language (Yoder and Layton, 1988). The limited success of signing with children with ASC is not surprising given that it requires imitation skills, symbolic processing, and social and receptive language skills, all well-documented impairments in children with ASC (Howlin, 2006). Additionally, there is no evidence to suggest that acquisition of a sign vocabulary has any impact on wider communication skills such as spontaneity in initiating communicative interactions (Goldstein, 2002). With regard to enhancing spoken language, a study of children with ASC who had minimal speech suggested that while teaching signing did not necessarily prevent speech development, it did not accelerate spoken language development either (Yoder and Layton, 1988). For those who are able to acquire sign language, this may well offer a very practical alternative to spoken words, however, the acquisition of flexible communication using signing in a child with ASC is rare (National Research Council, 2001).

Functional Communication Training

Functional Communication Training (FCT) identifies behaviors that are potentially communicative and seeks to replace them with functional, socially acceptable forms of communication (Durand and Merges, 2001). Acts that are sometimes identified as having communicative potential include challenging behavior, aggression and self-injury as well as idiosyncratic behaviors such as hand flapping. FCT begins with the assessment of these behaviors in order to understand their function and seeks to replace them with forms that are more adaptive and easier to interpret, thus enabling children to become more effective communicators. Keen et al. (2001) studied the implementation of FCT in a classroom environment, reporting how behaviors in four young children with ASC were successfully replaced with alternative forms of communication. In some cases, children were taught to replace behaviors with gestures or pictures/symbols. Above all, the success of this approach appears to depend on careful and thorough training of implementers: Keen et al. (2001) highlight the importance of the consistency of teacher-provided opportunities, acknowledgements and reactions in the children's acquisition of the alternative skills. The authors emphasized the need for further study of the generalization and maintenance of communication skills taught in this way.

Voice output communication aids

Voice output communication aids (VOCAs) are portable communication devices that can produce synthesized or recorded speech output. Such devices vary in complexity: they can be simple single-switch units or may hold thousands of communication messages. The strength of these systems is their capacity to provide verbal models for speech, however, there is only preliminary evidence of the efficacy of such devices for individuals with ASC (National Research Council, 2001). Despite their sophistication, VOCAs have been criticized for their failure to tackle the central issue of the deficit in initiation of communication (Paul and Sutherland, 2005) although there are reports of children successfully using VOCAs to repair communicative break-downs and to make spontaneous requests (Sigafoos et al., 2004a; Sigafoos et al., 2004b). Currently, little is known about which children might respond to VOCA training overall. Considering the financial commitment involved, a greater understanding is necessary of how and for whom VOCAs are effective.

Pictures/symbols

Like signing, visual pictures or symbols provide a non-transient form for communication that capitalizes on the visual strengths of many children with ASC (Schuler et al., 1997). Unlike signing, picture communication symbols seem to make fewer cognitive and motor demands on the user (Chambers and Rehfeldt, 2003) and the symbols themselves may be easier to interpret for the receiver. Pictures and photographs are widely used with individuals with ASC to communicate needs or to introduce new activities. Various picture-symbol systems have been used over the last 20 years. Reichle and Brown (1986) reported individ-uals with ASC communicating using Rebus symbols (cartoon-style symbol cards with the written label placed beneath the picture). The TEACCH system (see 'Comprehensive Programs' section) uses picture-symbols on visual timetables and work stations to enable individuals with ASC to be independent in completing tasks. As with signing, there is limited scientific evidence to support the benefits of picture and symbol communication systems (Howlin, 2006).

The Picture Exchange Communication System (PECS; Bondy and Frost, 1994) was developed specifically for children with ASC and is widely used in educational settings. Its primary aim is to teach spontaneous and functional communication in a social context and highlights the importance of teaching social approach (Bondy and Frost, 1998). PECS takes a 'functional-developmental' approach to teaching communication, incorporating principles of early intentional communication development into a training program that enables children to make meaningful communication that is appropriate to their needs (Prizant and Wetherby, 2005). In contrast to many other alternative communication systems, PECS requires no skills in pointing or eye contact. Unlike signing, no imitative ability is needed and PECS training has been specifically designed to eliminate physical modeling or prompting, thus maximizing truly spontaneous communication.

The PECS training protocol is detailed in a comprehensive manual (Bondy and Frost, 2002) and is based on behaviorist principles (Skinner, 1957). Physical prompts, faded by 'backward-chaining' (see Glossary) are used to shape a non-communicative reach for an item into a functional communicative exchange. The child is taught to pick up and exchange a symbol for a desired item. This request is reinforced by receipt of the item. In addition to giving the item, the adult might respond using verbal reinforcement, but prompts are not used (e.g. 'Biscuit! You want a biscuit!'). Once a child can use symbols with some flexibility and has learned to seek out a communication partner in several settings, training moves on to picture discrimination, 'vocabulary' extension and making sentences.

Studies have demonstrated that children with ASC with little or no functional communication can be successfully taught to use PECS to make requests. Increases in spontaneously initiated communication have been observed when children use PECS (Charlop-Christy et al., 2002; Kravits et al., 2002; Magiati and Howlin, 2003) and some children have been reported to have developed spoken language during or after learning PECS (Bondy and Frost, 1994;

Schwartz et al., 1998). Decreases in disruptive behavior have also been associated with increases in PECS communication (Charlop-Christy et al., 2002; Magiati and Howlin, 2003). The vast majority of studies of PECS have been small scale, without controls and with findings that are difficult to generalize to a wider population. Further research is needed need to properly understand the broader impact of PECS and its long-term effectiveness for children with ASC. One RCT found that children with less joint-attention behavior benefited more from PECS than another communication intervention (RMPT, described earlier) in terms of increases in requesting behavior (Yoder and Stone, 2005; see Table 1). The effectiveness of school-based PECS training has recently been investigated in a large scale RCT (Howlin et al., 2007, see Table 1). This study showed significant effects of training teachers to implement PECS on overall rates of children's use of pictures to communicate and overall rates of spontaneous communication, although these effects did not persist when the children were observed again approximately 9 months later. No effect of PECS on children's rate of speech was seen.

Conclusion

Overall, research suggests that alternative communication systems are promising in terms of increasing functional communica-tion. Further RCTs are needed to evaluate whether they are effective in the long-term for improving spontaneous, flexible language that can be generalized across settings, and to investigate which approaches are most suitable for which individuals.

Social Skills Interventions

There are many different approaches that address social difficulties for children with ASC. At present, there are no randomized controlled trials in this area evaluating their effectiveness. Below is a summary of the small-scale studies carried out in this area.

Peer Mediated Interventions

Peer-mediated approaches are promising social skills interventions for preschool and school-age children with ASC and can be used to encourage both specific social skills and broader interactions and relationships (Rogers, 2000; McConnell, 2002). In peer-mediated interventions typically-developing peers are trained by an adult to initiate, elicit, prompt and reinforce social behaviors for children with ASC. The adult then prompts the peers to interact with the child during specific activities or play sessions. For example, they may be taught to initiate sharing, helping, giving affection or giving praise. The peers themselves are reinforced for their participation, but reinforcements are slowly reduced so adult prompting is no longer required (Odom et al., 1992).

The cumulative results from small scale multiple-baseline and reversal studies indicate that peer-mediated strategies are helpful to increase the social behavior of young children with ASC (Strain et al., 1979; Goldstein et al., 1992; McGee et al., 1992; Kamps et al., 1994; Kamps et al., 1997; Odom et al., 1999; Whitaker, 2004). Results suggest that using multiple peer trainers improves generalization of skills (Kamps et al., 1994; Mudschenk and Sasso, 1995) and that if the trained peers evaluate themselves and monitor their own progress, generalization and maintenance of the skills across settings is improved (Sainato et al., 1992). Superior outcomes seem to occur when multiple same-age peers with high social status are used as 'interventionists' (Sasso et al., 1998). Parents can also be taught to train siblings to use peer-mediated approaches at home to improve child-sibling interactions (Strain et al., 1994b).

Pivotal Response Training (PRT) has also been implemented by peers to help improve social and communication skills of children with ASC. PRT is used to teach pivotal behaviors that are expected to have an impact on other associated behaviors. One important 'pivotal' behavior is motivation. A child can be motivated to learn a new skill (such as social responses) through using the child's own interests. Motivation is maintained by varying the learning activities and combining new learning tasks with those the child has already mastered. The child or adult conducting the PRT will also make sure the child is paying attention before using very clear, simple directions. The target child is given plenty of time to respond. For example, if a child particularly enjoys playing on the swing but fails to take turns with other children, their enjoyment of swinging can be used to help them practice taking turns. The child can be asked whether they want to swing first or second, and after an appropriate time can be prompted to let another child have a turn. Multiple-baseline studies have shown improvements in social interaction, socio-dramatic play and communicative interactions for school-age children following peer-implemented PRT (Koegel and Frea, 1993; Pierce and Schreibman, 1995; Thorp et al., 1995; Pierce and Schreibman, 1997).

Another variation of peer mediation is the 'circle of friends' approach (Taylor, 1997). This is an educational approach that facilitates the inclusion of children with disabilities into the mainstream classroom through the encouragement of peer inter-actions. Few studies have been carried out to evaluate its effectiveness, but preliminary baseline studies suggest it can be effective at increasing successful social initiations and responses (Whitaker et al., 1998; Kalyva and Avramidis, 2005).

LEAP (Learning Experiences: An Alternative Program for Preschoolers and Parents; Strain and Cordisco, 1993) is an early preschool program that focuses on the social development of young children with ASC through a combination of peer mediation, developing educational programs, and behavioral training for parents. In LEAP, peer mediation is prompted throughout the whole school day, rather than only during specific time-periods (Kohler and Strain, 1999; Strain and Hoyson, 2000). Results from longitudinal baseline studies found significant gains for 6 children with ASC in positive social interactions, behavior and developmental progress.

On the whole, peer-mediated interventions seem promising, but large-scale, RCT studies are needed to make positive conclusions about their efficacy. Peer-mediated interventions mean child-child interactions are learned directly so, in theory, generalization of skills to new peer partners and new contexts is easier. However, studies to date suggest generalization is still difficult to achieve and new peers must be continually trained to ensure children with ASC reap the most benefits. A further consideration based on studies of peer-mediated approaches is that the ability to initiate social contact following inter-vention does not improve as much as the ability to respond to others' social inter-actions (Goldstein et al., 1992; Sainato et al., 1992; Rogers, 2000). This may be due to the slightly intrusive and 'adult-like' interactive style that is fostered by peer mediation (Roeyers, 1995). Learning to initiate social contact is a critical skill to master: unless children with ASC learn to initiate social interactions, typically developing children with whom they interact may give up their efforts, and the opportunity for participating in social interaction is reduced. It is important that interventions can demonstrate these effects and that they generalize skills to untrained peers and new situations.

Cognitive Behavioral Approaches

Cognitive behavioral interventions are used to teach children with ASC to monitor and manage their own behavior through changing their perceptions, self-understand-ing and beliefs, based on the assumption that change is most likely to occur when a child is actively involved in their own behavior management. For this reason, cognitive behavioral methods are most appropriate for ASC children with a greater than average level of self-understanding and self-aware-ness and are thus mostly used with school-age children and adolescents with high-functioning autism or Asperger Syndrome.

Self-monitoring and self-management techniques are two cognitive behavioral approaches used. Children are taught to be aware of certain target behaviors and their impact on learning. They are then trained to monitor their behavior with the goal of reducing maladaptive behavior or increasing the frequency of appropriate behavior and alternative strategies. The need for external reinforcement from adults or peers is reduced as the child becomes more independent in their behavior management (Quinn et al., 1994). For example, children can be trained to use a wrist counter to tally the frequency of their appropriate verbal responses to other people's social initiation. Frequencies are converted to points and exchanged for rewards though, these rewards should be quickly faded (Koegel et al., 1992). Several multiple-baseline studies across settings have shown that such strategies do improve social interactions of higher-functioning children with ASC (Strain et al., 1994a; Shearer et al., 1996), though evidence that the skills are maintained once the procedure is stopped is variable.

Cognitive-behavioral techniques have also been used to teach social-emotional functioning in classroom settings. One study evaluating a 7 month cognitive behavioral intervention found an increase in interper-sonal problem-solving, affective knowledge and social interactions following intervention for 15 children (8-17 yr olds) with high functioning ASC (Bauminger, 2002), though there was no comparison group in this study.

Cognitive scripts are another method used to teach appropriate interaction in a wide variety of contexts to verbal school-age children. These might be more appropriate for children with lower levels of self-understanding and self-awareness. A cognitive script is a repeated script of a familiar event that children with ASC can use in a particular set of circumstances, for example, to initiate a social interaction. Scripts are first written by an adult and their correct use is modeled by adults or through videotapes. The child rehearses the script before using it in appropriate contexts. The child's reliance on the script is gradually faded until it is not used at all (Odom et al., 1992). Results from small scale, multiple-baseline and reversal studies suggest that the use of scripts has a positive impact on children's pro-social behavior (Sasso et al., 1990), interaction skills (Goldstein and Cisar, 1992) and the frequency and duration of social interactions (Kamps et al., 1992b; Gonzalez-Lopez and Kamps, 1997). One commonly used variation of cognitive scripts is Gray's social stories (Gray and Garand, 1993; Gray, 1994; Gray, 1998). These are individually written stories that describe social cues, address the feelings and reactions of others and provide appropriate responses to specific social situations. Social stories are widely used for children with ASC, yet there is limited research evaluating their effectiveness. Case studies that have been published report variable outcomes in terms of social behavior (Swaggart et al., 1995; Lorimer et al., 2002; Bledsoe et al., 2003; Delano and Snell, 2006; Reynhout and Carter, 2006) suggesting that the technique may be more effective with some children than others.

Cognitive scripts are low-cost and easy to implement and can be taught by teachers, parents, and other professionals without complex training. They can be also be used in multiple settings, increasing the likelihood of skill generalization. However, at present the research supporting their effectiveness is limited and their comparative effectiveness to other approaches is not known.

Social Skills groups

Social skills groups are suitable for children and adolescents with high functioning autism and Asperger Syndrome, and allow members to practice skills in reasonably naturalistic environments. They are used as part of the TEACCH program and may be used in clinic-based or school-based settings. Several authors have outlined suggestions about how to run social skills groups, and for whom they are most suitable (Mesibov, 1986; Krasny et al., 2003). However, as yet there is little empirical evidence to guide how often, with whom, in which contexts and with which curricula the groups are most successfully implemented.

School-based social skills interventions have focused on increasing a broad range of skills in short and frequent classroom sessions (Matson et al., 1991; Kamps et al., 1992a), or have focused on teaching specific skills such as eye-contact and play with preferred toys (Koegel and Frea, 1993; Baker et al., 1998). Both approaches have shown improvements in skills taught in small-scale, multiple baseline studies. Some group studies have focused on teaching theory of mind skills to children with ASC. Theory of mind is the ability to understand other people's mental states, and is thought to be a core deficit in ASC (Baron-Cohen, 1995b). It is also thought of as the cognitive component of empathy (Baron-Cohen and Wheelwright, 2004). Teaching individuals this skill has resulted in improvement on experimental tasks compared to controls, but not in natural settings (Hadwin et al., 1997) or on ratings of social behaviors (Ozonoff and Miller, 1995).

Social skills groups carried out in clinic settings are generally delivered less frequently (e.g. weekly) for a longer amount of time (usually 1 hour) than in school settings and usually without the presence of typically developing peers. Barry et al. (2003) evaluated the effectiveness of an outpatient social skills group for 4 children with high functioning ASC. The groups were run for 8 weeks for 2 hours per week and focused on teaching initiations and responses in greetings, conversations and play interactions through social scripts and group activities. Improvements were found with peers in greeting and play skills but not conversational skills. The children involved also reported greater feelings of social support from classmates after the group. Parent reports of progress showed improve-ments only in greeting skills, suggesting that although skills were learned in the clinic setting, they did not completely generalize to other contexts.

Solomon et al. (2004) evaluated the effectiveness of a 20 week group intervention for 8-12 year olds with high functioning autism or Asperger Syndrome. They used a 'social adjustment enhancement curriculum' which focused on emotion recognition, theory of mind skills, executive function skills, group problem-solving and basic conversation skills and included psycho-educational training for parents. Following twenty 1½ hour sessions in groups of four or five, the nine boys in the intervention group improved significantly in their ability to recognize facial expressions and solve problems compared to a waiting list control.

A larger scale study was carried out to investigate the effectiveness of a social skills group based around LEGO® play for 6 – 16 year olds with ASC (LeGoff, 2004). In LEGO Therapy, children built LEGO® sets collaboratively in groups of 5 or 6 (children with ASC and some typically-developing peers) which required verbal and non-verbal communication, collaboration, joint problem-solving, joint creativity and joint attention to the task. Groups lasted 90 minutes and were accompanied by 1 hour individual sessions

once a week in a clinic setting over an average period of 24 weeks. A waiting-list control design was used, and 47 children were included in the study. Following intervention, children in the LEGO® therapy group improved significantly more than the control group in the number of social initiations they made to peers, and in the duration of their social interactions in the school playground.

Overall, school-based and clinic-based social skills groups could be effective interventions, especially for higher functioning individuals. However, at this stage research findings are limited. Detailed manuals of the different curricula and intervention procedures need to be published and large scale comparative RCT studies need to be carried out.

Assistive Technology for Social Skills

Assistive technology (AT) can be used for a wide range of skills, including social interaction, communication, daily living skills, and independence (see Golan et al., 2006 for a comprehensive review). AT can be as simple as a visual schedule or as complex as a virtual reality system and can vary from low to high tech levels. It can be used to teach social rules, emotion under-standing and pro-social behaviors. AT may be particularly useful for children with ASC due to the systematic nature of the technology. Individuals with ASC show good and sometimes superior skills in 'systemizing' (Baron-Cohen, 2006). Systemizing is the drive to analyze and build systems in the world in order to predict events. AT might be able to harness this affinity to help children cope with areas of difficulty such as social functioning.

Low-tech AT includes social scripts, social stories and visual schedules that have been discussed earlier. Mid-tech AT includes battery-operated or electricity-based products. One example of teaching social skills using mid-tech AT is using videotapes of TV programs (e.g. 'Saved by the Bell' and 'Third Rock from the Sun') to model appropriate and inappropriate social interactions (Myles and Southwick, 2005). Research is needed to evaluate whether these approaches are effective.

High-tech AT usually involves specifically designed computer software. This has several advantages for children with ASC. Computer environments are predictable and free from social demands, children can work at their own pace and level, and lessons can be repeated until they are understood. Computerized rewards can also be used to maintain motivation. Software is commercially available to teach various social skills. A few examples include *Social Skills Builder* (www.socialskillsbuilder.com), *Mind Read-ing* (Baron-Cohen et al., 2004), *Gaining Face* (http://ccoder.com/GainingFace/), *The Emotion Trainer* (Silver and Oakes, 2001) and *Fun with Feelings* (www.ultimate learning.net). The *Mind Reading* DVD has been recently evaluated. It is an interactive DVD suitable for 4 years to adulthood that is designed to teach emotions and mental state understanding (Baron-Cohen et al., 2004). It is organized in a systematic taxonomy of 412 emotions and mental states that can be learned through an emotions library, a learning center or a games zone. Facial expressions, tone of voice and contexts are addressed. Its effectiveness was evaluated for adults (Golan and Baron-Cohen, 2006) and for 8-11 year olds with high functioning autism and Asperger Syndrome (Golan and Baron-Cohen, in preparation). Children used *Mind Reading* for 20 hours over a 10 week period. In comparison to matched controls who received no intervention, children significant-ly improved in their ability to recognize emotions. However, the skills did not generalize beyond the material included in the software or stimuli closely related to those which appeared in the program.

The reason for a lack of generalization of skills could be due to the unnatural nature of computerized interventions (Parsons and Mitchell, 2002). The best way forward could be to use AT in conjunction with real-world human interaction, and more research is needed to focus on the outcomes of such collaborations. One such way of combining AT with real life situations is the Portable Affect Reference Learning Environment (PARLE; Bishop, 2003). This system is a database that can be accessed via internet-based mobile phones in real-time social situations to translate idioms and common phrases into more meaningful expressions. It also includes explanations and possible responses to such phrases. For example, if during a social interaction a person with ASC is asked, 'Cat got your tongue?' they could interpret this literally and the situation may become confusing. With PARLE, the individual can type the confusing phrase into the database and it is translated into an open-ended question such as, 'You appear quiet, how come?' Individuals with ASC have reported that PARLE was easy to use, efficient and useful both at home and in public. This system could be a valuable support for higher functioning adolescents with ASC, enabling them to learn through real-life interactions. However, there are concerns that this might not be an approach for everyone. For example, individuals with social phobia who tried PARLE found it embarrassing to use in public.

Conclusion

Overall, research evaluating methods to help improve the social skills of children with ASC is limited due to the lack of large scale RCTs. There are several promising approaches which deserve further evaluation, but no recommendations of which approach to use with which children can be made until the evidence base is greater.

Repetitive and Stereotyped Behaviors

The term repetitive behavior refers to a large variety of behaviors, interests and activities, all of which could be the result of different underlying brain functions (Militerni et al., 2002). These occur in many conditions, but are particularly common in ASC (Schreibman, 1988; Carcani-Rathwell et al., 2006). All are characterized by a high degree of repetition, rigidity, invariance and inappropriateness (Turner, 1999). Some researchers have loosely classified repetitive behaviors into lower level and higher level categories. Lower level repetitive behaviors include repetitive motor behaviors (e.g. hand flapping or body rocking), whereas higher level repetitive behaviors include circumscribed interests (such as fans or serial numbers), resistance to change and rigid routines and rituals (Turner, 1999). Though both types of repetitive behavior are present in individuals with ASC, stereotyped movements and vocalizations have been the focus of most intervention as these tend to cause the most significant problems with daily life, learning and adaptive functioning (Risley, 1968; Koegel and Covert, 1972). Some repetitive behaviors may not have a function (e.g. involuntary movement associated with seizure disorders), and behavior modification procedures are not likely to reduce such behaviors. Most repetitive behaviors are not related to seizures and the recently proposed hyper-systemizing theory sees repetitive behavior as the behavioral expression of the autistic brain drawn to systemize all data (Baron-Cohen, 2006). According to this theory, repetitive behavior is not 'purposeless' but is a sign that the mind of someone with an ASC cannot help but systemize. Seen in this more 'intelligent' light, it may be a sign of the individual's learning style rather than a 'symptom' to be reduced or eradicated. Harnessed appropriately, systemizing can lead to remarkable achievements in fields like calculation and intuitive physics (Baron-Cohen et al., 1999). However, in what

follows, we summarize studies that have aimed to reduce problematic repetitive behavior. To date no randomized controlled trials of these approaches have been carried out, rather, research mostly consists of case studies with varied results. These are summarized below.

Behavior modification procedures

Some repetitive behaviors might be learned and maintained because of the perceptual, tactual or auditory stimulation they provide (Lovaas et al., 1987). They can be thought of as having 'self-reinforcing' properties, i.e. the performance of the behavior itself provides sensory stimulation that is inherently rewarding (e.g. repetitive vocalizations provide auditory stimulation). Behavior such as this is very resistant to change, and interventions have tried punishments such as time out (Harris and Wolchik, 1979), overcorrection (Azrin et al., 1973; Wells et al., 1977; Maag et al., 1986) or even a slap (Koegel and Covert, 1972; Koegel et al., 1974) and electric shock (Risley, 1968) to try and reduce the frequency of these behaviors, although some of these are generally regarded as unethical. More recent case studies have looked at the effects of blocking repetitive behaviors (e.g. by physical restraint), however, results are not simple to interpret. Although some case studies have shown response blocking to lead to a decrease in repetitive behavior blocking has also been associated with lowered adaptive behavior, increases in different stereotyped behavior, and sometimes aggression (Lerman et al., 2003).

An alternative approach has been to reward individuals for not engaging in a repetitive behavior. This can be done by reinforcing (rewarding) other more appropriate behaviors, or by reinforcing behaviors that are incompatible with the target behavior (Harris and Wolchik, 1979; Fellner et al., 1984; Handen et al., 1984;

Haring et al., 1986; Nuzzolo-Gomez et al., 2002). Children have also successfully been taught an effective self-management procedure (see social skills section) to reinforce the absence of their own repetitive behavior (Koegel and Koegel, 1990). Other approaches have used visual cues to prompt times when it is or is not appropriate to engage in repetitive behavior (Conroy et al., 2005). Though results from these procedures seem fairly promising, recent studies have shown that while being successful in decreasing the rate of repetitive behaviors, they can also increase the persistence of the behavior (Mace, 2000; Nevin and Grace, 2000; Ahearn et al., 2003).

A meta-analysis looking at several studies of behavior modification procedures found overcorrection and punishments to be most effective in reducing repetitive behavior, followed by rewarding alternative adaptive behaviors (Didden et al., 1997). This is a complex area, and factors controlling the effectiveness of behavior modification procedures require further systematic investigation.

Not all repetitive behaviors are self-reinforcing, but may serve functions other than sensory stimulation. Functional assessment is often used for those with severe learning disability to ascertain what function a repetitive behavior serves. This knowledge is then used to develop intervention strategies (e.g. by gradually removing the reinforcement of the target behavior). For example, as previously discussed, certain behaviors may serve a communicative purpose. Functional Communication Training is used to replace these behaviors with more conventional functional means of communication. Specific reinforcers of target repetitive behaviors can be identified through the use of rating scales, through observation or through structured assessments. These analyses have shown that there is a wide variety of functions associated with repetitive and stereotyped behavior

across individuals with ASC (Kennedy et al., 2000). This should be taken into account when developing behavioral interventions.

The approaches described above may be useful in reducing repetitive behavior and self-injurious behavior, but there is not sufficient evidence to make general recommendations for intervention of individuals with ASC. There have been no RCTs in this area, and there is little evidence that improvements generalize across settings or are maintained once the intervention is discontinued. There are also concerns with these procedures, as the methods found to be most effective (overcorrection and punishments) have ethical and moral considerations.

Teaching Alternative Activities

Rather than seeking to reduce unwanted behaviors it is also possible to teach and prompt other appropriate activities as alternatives to undesirable behavior. Early studies found that teaching appropriate play behaviors did lead to a reduction in the number of repetitive movements in children with ASC (Eason et al., 1982). Later studies demonstrated that prompting interaction with an alternative activity was necessary to decrease rates of repetitive behavior (Britton et al., 2002). Prompting correct responses using verbal and visual cues has also been found to help reduce repetitive behavior and increase appropriate behavior (MacDuff et al., 1993; Pierce and Schreibman, 1994; Symons and Davis, 1994). In some cases these gains generalized to other tasks and settings.

Piazza et al. (2000) found that the provision of alternative behaviors is most effective when the alternative item produces the same type of sensory stimulation as would be produced by the repetitive behavior. For example, the repetitive vocalizations of children and adolescents with ASC have been significantly reduced when more appropriate forms of auditory stimulation (i.e. music) were provided (Falcomata et al., 2004).

However, care must be taken with these particular interventions. The constant playing of music may also interfere with necessary auditory input (e.g. instructions) and may inhibit appropriate verbalizations. One way around this may be to combine this approach with a reinforcement procedure. For example, a four year old with ASC showed a reduction in vocal stereotypies when given access to toys that made noises. Because it was not appropriate to provide these toys all the time, they were used as reinforcement for the absence of vocalizations. This method showed significant reductions in vocalizations in a multiple base-line design and was maintained for 1 year in a classroom setting (Taylor et al., 2005a). Although results from this study cannot be generalized to the wider population, its findings suggest that important gains can be made by combining different approaches for the treatment of repetitive behavior.

Conclusion

Overall our knowledge about the most effective forms of intervention to address repetitive behaviors remains limited. The findings from case reports and small studies can be drawn upon, however, there is no single best solution. More investigation is needed into which specific approaches might work for specific children and for specific behaviors.

Associated difficulties

In addition to the triad of impairments, children with ASC may also show associated difficulties such as co-morbid anxiety (Muris et al., 1998; Gilliott et al., 2001), hyperactivity (Frazier et al., 2001; Goldstein and Schwebach, 2004) and sensory problems (Keintz and Dunn, 1997), to name a few. This is an important area upon which to focus in order to treat the full range of symptoms seen in individuals with ASC. Findings from a randomized controlled trial have shown that cognitive behavior therapy can be effective at treating anxiety in children with Asperger syndrome (Sofronoff et al., 2005). Future studies should evaluate effective interventions for all symptoms associated with ASC.

DISCUSSION: THE NEED FOR FURTHER RESEARCH

Though a wide variety of behavioral and psychosocial interventions for ASC exists, at present the research evaluating the effectiveness of different approaches is limited. There is also little evidence of the extent to which improvements seen in research studies are truly generalized to other situations with new people or contexts. Further, where improvements are seen, few studies have reported what, if any, lasting impacts the intervention had. Recently there has been a promising increase in the number of randomized controlled trials in this area. Such studies are crucial to test the causal link between any intervention and the changes seen following an intervention period. In particular, randomized comparison trials comparing two or more different approaches are useful for drawing conclusions about specific aspects of programs that are effective.

The wide variety of approaches that have been used to measure change demonstrates the divergence in what constitutes functional improvement following intervention. Many studies have tended to test outcomes only for the specific problems they have targeted rather than a broader spectrum of autism symptoms. For these reasons it is not easy to compare the overall effectiveness of interventions for autism against one another. Additionally, if a procedure for reducing one symptom produces worsening of another, this will not be detected. Adoption of a research convention using a standard set of instruments for confirming diagnosis and IQ, as well as for changes in social, language and communication skills has been suggested, (Jordan et al., 1998; Goldstein, 2002;

Charman and Howlin, 2003; Lord et al., 2005). A similar format for the reporting of such information would also be useful to allow study findings to be more easily compared and/or combined.

Where interventions are shown to be effective in some way, it is unlikely that any one intervention will be equally beneficial for all children. Currently, however, virtually nothing is known about which children would benefit most from which interventions. There are vast differences between children with ASC in terms of cognitive and symbolic understanding, language level, and symptom severity, as well as factors influenced by their families and their environment. The way in which individuals respond to intervention is likely to be moderated by some, if not all of these factors. It is therefore extremely important that future intervention research focuses not just on the question of whether an approach works, but for whom.

REFERENCES

Ahearn WH, Clark KM, Gardenier NC. (2003) Persistence of stereotypic behavior: examining the effects of external reinforcers. J Applied Behavior Analysis 36:439- 448.

Aldred C, Green J, Adams C. (2004) A new social communication intervention for children with autism: pilot randomised controlled treatment study suggesting effectiveness. J Child Psychol Psychiatr 45:1420-1430.

Azrin NH, Kaplan SJ, Foxx RM. (1973) Autism reversal: Eliminating stereo-typed self-stimulation of retarded individuals. Am J Mental Deficiency 78: 241-248.

Bakeman R, Adamson L. (1984) Coordinat-ing attention to people and objects in mother-infant and peer-infant inter-action. Child Dev 55:1278-1289.

Baker MJ, Koegel RL, Koegel LK. (1998) Increasing the social behavior of young children with autism using their obsessive behaviors. J Assoc Pers Sev Handicaps 23:300-308.

Baron-Cohen S. (1988) Social and pragmatic deficits in autism: cognitive or affective? J Autism Development Disorders 18:379-402.

Baron-Cohen S. (1989) Joint attention deficits in autism: towards a cognitive analysis. Dev Psychopathol 1:185-189.

Baron-Cohen S. (1995a) The Eye-Director Detector (EDD) and the Shared Attention Mechanism (SAM): two cases for evolutionary psychology. In: Joint attention: its role in development (Moore C, & Dunham, P, ed): Laurence Erlbaum.

Baron-Cohen S. (1995b) Mindblindness: an essay on autism and theory of mind. Boston: MIT Press/Bradford Books.

Baron-Cohen S. (2006) Two new theories of autism: hyper-systemising and assorta-tive mating. Arch Dis Childhood 91:2-5.

Baron-Cohen S, Howlin P. (1993) The theory of mind deficit in autism: some questions for teaching and diagnosis. In: Understanding other minds: perspectives from autism (Baron-Cohen S, Tager-Flusberg H, Cohen DJ, eds): Oxford University Press.

Baron-Cohen S, Wheelwright S. (2004) The empathy quotient: an investigation of adults with Asperger syndrome or high functioning autism, and normal sex differences. J Autism Development Disorders 34:163-175.

Baron-Cohen S, Golan O, Wheelwright S, Hill JJ. (2004) Mind Reading: the interactive guide to emotions. In. London: Jessica Kingsley Ltd (www.jkp.com).

Barry TD, Klinger L, Lee JM, Palardy N, Gilmore T, Bodin SD. (2003) Examining the effectiveness of an outpatient clinic-based social skills group for high-functioning children with autism. J Autism Development Disorders 33:685-701.

Bauminger N. (2002) The facilitation of

social-emotional understanding and social interaction in high-functioning children with autism: intervention outcomes. J Autism Development Disorders 32:283-298.

Bishop J. (2003) The internet for educating individuals with social impairments. Journal of Computer Assisted Learning 19:546-556.

Bledsoe R, Myles BS, Simpson RL. (2003) Use of social story intervention to improve mealtime skills of an adolescent with Asperger Syndrome. Autism 7:289-295.

Bondy AS, Frost LA. (1994) The Picture Exchange Communication System. Focus on Autistic Behavior 9:1-19.

Bondy AS, Frost LA. (1998) The Picture Exchange Communication System. Sem Speech Language 19:373-389.

Bondy AS, Frost LA. (2002) PECS: Picture Exchange Communication System Training Manual (2nd ed.). Cherry Hill, NJ: Pyramid Educational Consultants Inc.

Britton LN, Carr J, Landaburu H, Romick K. (2002) The efficacy of non-contingent reinforcement as a treatment for automatically reinforced stereotypy. Behavioral Interventions 17:93-103.

Camaioni L, Perucchini P, Muratori F, Milone A. (1997) Brief report: A lon-gitudinal examination of the commun-icative gestures deficit in young children with autism. J Autism Dev Disord 27:715-725.

Camaioni L, Perucchini P, Muratori F, Parrini B, Cesari A. (2003) The communicative use of pointing in autism: developmental profile and factors related to change. European Psychiatry 18:6-12.

Carcani-Rathwell I, Rabe-Hasketh S, Santosh P. (2006) Repetitive and stereo-typed behaviours in pervasive develop-mental disorders. J Child Psychol Psychiatr 47:573-581.

Carter AS, Ornstein Davies N, Klin A, Volkmar FR. (2005) Social development

in autism. In: Handbook of autism and pervasive developmental disorders (3rd ed.) (Volkmar FR, Paul R, Klin A, Cohen D, eds), pp 312-334. Hoboken, NJ.: John Wiley & Sons, Inc.

Chambers M, Rehfeldt RA. (2003) Assess-ing the acquisition and generalization of two mand forms with adults with severe developmental disabilities. Res Dev Disabil 24:265-280.

Charlop-Christy M, Carpenter M, LeBlanc L, Kellet K. (2002) Using the picture exchange communication system (PECS) with children with autism: assessment of PECS acquisition, speech, social-communicative behavior, and problem behavior. J Appl Behav Anal 35:213-231.

Charlop MH, Schreibman L, Thibodeau MG. (1986) Increasing spontaneous verbal responding in autistic children using a time delay procedure. J Appl Behav Anal 18:155-166.

Charman T. (2003) Why is joint attention a pivotal skill in autism? Philosophical Transactions of the Royal Society, Series B Biological Sciences 358:315-324.

Charman T, Howlin P. (2003) Research into early intervention for children with autism and related disorders: Methodo-logical and design issues. Autism 7:217-225.

Conroy M, Asmus J, Sellers J, Ladwig C. (2005) The use of an antecedent-based intervention to decrease stereotypic behavior in a general education classroom: a case study. Focus on Autism and Other Developmental Disabilities 20:223-230.

Delano M, Snell ME. (2006) The effects of social stories on the social engagement of children with autism. Journal of Positive Behavior Interventions 8:29-42.

Delprato DJ. (2001) Comparisons of discrete-trial and normalized behavioral language intervention for young children with autism. J Autism Dev Disord 31:315-325.

Didden R, Duker PC, Korzilius H. (1997)

Meta-analytic study on treatment effectiveness for problem behaviors with individuals who have mental retardation. Am J Ment Retard 101:387-399.

Drew A, Baird G, Baron-Cohen S, Cox A, Slonims VW, S., Swettenham J, Berry B, Charman T. (2002) A pilot randomised control trial of a parent training intervention for preschool children with autism- Preliminary findings and methodological issues. European Child and Adolescent Psychiatry 11:266-272.

Duchan JF. (1987) Perspectives for understanding children with communication disorders. In: Understanding exceptional children and youths (Knoblock P, ed). Boston: Little, Brown and Co.

Durand VM, Merges E. (2001) Functional communication training: a contemporary behavior analytic intervention for problem behavior. Focus on Autism and Other Developmental Disabilities 16: 110-119.

Eason LJ, White MJ, Newsom C. (1982) Generalized reduction of self-stimulatory behavior: An effect of teaching appropriate toy play to autistic children. Analysis and Intervention in Developmental Disabilities 2.

Eikeseth S, Smith T, Jahr E, Eldevik S. (2002) Intensive behavioural treatment at school for 4- to 7-year old children with autism. Behavior Modification 26:49-68.

Falcomata TS, Raone HS, Hovanetz AN, Kettering TL, Keeney KM. (2004) An evaluation of response cost in the treatment of inappropriate vocalizations maintained by automatic reinforcement. J Appl Behav Anal 37:83-87.

Fellner DJ, Laroche M, Sulzer-Azaroff B. (1984) The effects of adding interruption to differential reinforcement on targeted and novel self-stimulatory behaviors. J Behav Ther Exp Psychiatry 415:315-321.

Frazier JA, Biederman J, Bellordre CA, Garfield SB, Geller DA, Coffey BJ, Faraone SV. (2001) Should the diagnosis of attention deficit/ hyperactivity disorder be considered in children with pervasive developmental disorder? Journal of Attention Disorders 4:203-211.

Gilliott A, Furnis F, Walter A. (2001) Anxiety in high-functioning children with autism. Autism 5:277-286.

Golan O, Baron-Cohen S. (2006) Systemizing empathy: Teaching adults with Asperger Syndrome and High Functioning Autism to recognize complex emotions using interactive multimedia. Dev Psychopathol 18:591-617.

Golan O, Baron-Cohen S. (in preparation) Teaching children with Asperger Syndrome and High Functioning Autism to recognize emotions using interactive multimedia.

Golan O, LaCava P, Baron-Cohen S. (2006) Assistive technology as an aid in reducing social impairments in autism spectrum conditions. In: Autism: Beyond Early Interventions: Profession-al guide to options for school-age children and their caregivers (Gabriels RL, Hill DE, eds). London: Guilford Press.

Goldstein H. (2002) Communication intervention for children with autism: A review of treatment efficacy. J Autism Dev Disord 32:373-396.

Goldstein H, Cisar CL. (1992) Promoting interaction during sociodramatic play: Teaching scripts to typical preschoolers and classmates with disabilities. J Appl Behav Anal 25:265-280.

Goldstein H, Kaczmarek L, Pennington R, Shafer K. (1992) Peer mediated intervention: Attending to, commenting on, and acknowledging the behavior of preschoolers with autism. J Appl Behav Anal 25:289-305.

Goldstein S, Schwebach AJ. (2004) The comorbidity of pervasive developmental disorder and attention deficit hyperactivity disorder: Results of a retrospective chart review. J Autism Dev

Disord 34:329-339.

Gonzalez-Lopez A, Kamps DM. (1997) Social skills training to increase social interactions between children with autism and their typical peers. Focus on Autism and Other Developmental Disabilities 12:12-14.

Gray CA. (1994) Comic strip conversations: Colorful, illustrated interactions with students with autism and related disorders. Jenison, MI: Jenison Public Schools.

Gray CA. (1998) Social stories and comic strip conversations with students with Asperger syndrome and high-function-ing autism. In: Asperger syndrome or high-functioning autism? Current issues in autism (Schopler E, Mesibov GB, eds), pp 167-198. New York, NY: Plenum Press.

Gray CA, Garand JD. (1993) Social stories: improving responses of students with autism with accurate social information. Focus on Autistic Behavior 8:1-10.

Gutstein S. (2006) Preliminary evaluation of the Relationship Intervention Program. J Autism Dev Disord

Gutstein S, Sheeley R. (2002) Relationship Development Intervention with young children. Social and Emotional Develop-ment Activities for Asperger Syndrome, Autism, PDD and NLD. London: Jessica Kingsley Publishers.

Hadwin J, Baron-Cohen S, Howlin P, Hill K. (1997) Does teaching a theory of mind have an effect on social communication in children with autism? J Autism Dev Disord 27:519-538.

Handen BL, Apolito PM, Seltzer GB. (1984) Use of differential reinforcement of low rates of behavior to decrease repetitive speech in an autistic adolescent. J Behav Ther Exp Psychiatry 15:359-364.

Haring TG, Breen CG, Pitts-Conway V, Gaylord-Ross R. (1986) Use of differential reinforcement of other behavior during dyadic instruction to reduce stereotyped behavior of autistic students. Am J Mental Deficiency 90:694-702.

Harrington RC, Cartwright-Hatton S, Stein A. (2002) Annotation: Randomised Trials. J Child Psychol Psychiatry & Allied Disciplines 43:695-704.

Harris SL, Wolchik S. (1979) Suppression of self-stimulation: Three alternative strategies. J Appl Behav Anal 12:185-198.

Hobson RP. (1986) The autistic child's appraisal of expressions of emotion. J Child Psychol Psychiatry 27:321-342.

Howlin P. (1981) The effectiveness of operant language training with autistic children. J Autism Dev Disord 11:89-106.

Howlin P. (2006) Augmentative and alternative communication systems for children with autism. In: Social and communication development in autism spectrum disorders: Early identification, diagnosis, and intervention (Charman T, Stone W, eds). London: Guilford Press.

Howlin P, Gordon RK, Pasco G, Wade A, Charman T. (2007) The effectiveness of Picture Exchange Communication System (PECS) training for teachers of children with autism: a pragmatic, group randomised controlled trial. J Child Psychol Psychiatr 48(5): 473-481.

Jordan R, Jones G, Murray D. (1998) Educational interventions for children with autism: a literature review of recent and current research. Birmingham: School of Education, University of Birmingham.

Kalyva E, Avramidis E. (2005) Improving communication between children with autism and their peers through the 'Circle of Friends': A small-scale intervention study. Journal of Applied Research in Intellectual Disabilities 18:253-261.

Kamps DM, Potucek J, Lopez AG, Kravits T, Kemmerer K. (1997) The use of peer networks across multiple settings to improve social interaction for students with autism. Journal of Behavioral

Education 7:335-357.

Kamps DM, Barbetta PM, Leonard BR, Vernon S, Dugan EP, Delquadri JC. (1994) Classwide peer tutoring: An integration strategy to improve reading skills and promote peer interactions among students with autism and general education peers. J Appl Behav Anal 27:49-61.

Kamps DM, Leonard BR, Vernon S, Dugan EP, Delquadri JC, Gershon B, Wade L, Folk L. (1992a) Teaching social skills to students with autism to increase peer interactions in an integrated first-grade classroom. J Appl Behav Anal 25:281-288.

Kamps DM, Leonard BR, Vernon S, Dugan EP, Delquadri JC, Gerson B, Wade L, Folk L. (1992b) Teaching social skills to students with autism to increase peer interactions in an integrated first grade classroom. J Appl Behav Anal 25:281-288.

Kasari C, Freeman S, Paparella T. (2005) Joint attention and symbolic play in young children with autism: a randomized controlled intervention study. J Child Psychol Psychiatry 47 611-620.

Kaufman B. (1994) Son-Rise: The miracle continues. Tiburon, CA: H.J. Kramer.

Keen D, Sigafoos J, Woodyatt G. (2001) Replacing prelinguistic behaviors with functional communication. J Autism Dev Disord 31:385-398.

Keintz MA, Dunn W. (1997) A comparison of the performance of children with and without autism on the Sensory Profile. Am J Occup Ther 51:530-537.

Kennedy C, Meyer K, Knowles T, Shukla S. (2000) Analyzing the multiple functions of stereotypical behavior for students with autism: Implications for assessment and treatment. J Appl Behav Anal 33:559-571.

Koegel LK. (1995) Communication and language intervention. In: Teaching children with autism: Strategies for initiating positive interactions and improving learning opportunities (Koegel RL, Koegel LK, eds), pp 17–32. Baltimore, MD: Brookes Publishing.

Koegel LK, Koegel RL. (1996) The child with autism as an active communicative partner: Child-initiated strategies for improving communication and reducing behavior problems. In: Psychosocial treatments for child and adolescent disorders: Empirically based strategies for clinical practice (Hibbs ED, Jensen PS, eds), pp 553-572. Washington, D.C.: American Psychological Association.

Koegel LK, Koegel RL, Hurley C, Frea WD. (1992) Improving social skills and disruptive behavior in children with autism through self-management. J Appl Behav Anal 23:119-127.

Koegel RL, Covert A. (1972) The relationship of self-stimulation to learning in autistic children J Appl Behav Anal 5:381-387.

Koegel RL, Koegel LK. (1990) Extended reductions in stereotypic behavior of students with autism through a self-management treatment package. J Appl Behav Anal 23:119-127.

Koegel RL, Frea WD. (1993) Treatment of social behavior in autism through the modification of pivotal social skills. J Appl Behav Anal 26:369-377.

Koegel RL, O'Dell MC, Koegel LK. (1987) A natural language paradigm for teaching nonverbal autistic children. J Autism Dev Disord 17:187-199.

Koegel RL, Firestone P, Kramme KW, Dunlap G. (1974) Increasing spontan-eous play by suppressing self-stimula-tion in autistic children. J Appl Behav Anal 7:521-528.

Kohler FW, Strain PS. (1999) Maximizing peer-mediated resources in integrated preschool classrooms. Topics in Early Childhood Special Education 19:92-102.

Krasny L, Williams BJ, Provencal S, Ozonoff S. (2003) Social skills interventions for the autism spectrum: Essential ingredients and a model curriculum. Child Adolesc Psychiatr Clin N Am 12:107-122.

Kravits T, Kamps DM, Kemmerer K, Potucek J. (2002) Brief report: Increasing communication skills for an elementary-aged student with autism using the picture exchange communica-tion system. J Autism Dev Disord 32.

LeGoff DB. (2004) Use of LEGO as a Therapeutic Medium for Improving Social Competence. J Autism Dev Disord 34 557-571.

Lerman D, Kelley M, Vorndran C, Van Camp C. (2003) Collateral effects of response blocking during the treatment of stereotypic behavior. J Appl Behav Anal 36:119-123.

Lord C, Bailey A. (2002) Autism Spectrum Disorders. In: Child and Adolescent Psychiatry (4th ed) (Rutter M, Taylor E, eds). Oxford: Blackwell.

Lord C, Wagner A, Rogers SJ, Szatmari P, Aman M, Charman T, et al. (2006) Challenges in evaluating psychosocial interventions for autistic spectrum disorders. J Autism Dev Disord 35(6): 695-708.

Lord C, Wagner A, Rogers SJ, Szatmari P, Aman M, Charman T, Dawson G, Durand VM, Grossman L, Guthrie D, Harris SL, Kasari C, Marcus L, Murphy S, Odom SL, Pickles A, Scahill L, Shaw E, Siegel B, Sigman M, Stone W, Smith T, Yoder PJ. (2005) Challenges in evaluating psychosocial interventions for autistic spectrum disorders. J Autism Dev Disord 35:695-708.

Lorimer PA, Simpson RL, Myles BS, Ganz J. (2002) The use of social stories as a preventative behavioral intervention in a home setting with a child with autism. Journal of Positive Behavioral Interventions 4:53-60.

Lovaas O. (1987) Behavioural treatment and normal educational and intellectual functioning in young autistic children. J Consult Clin Psychol 55:3-9.

Lovaas OI. (1977) The autistic child: Language development through behavior modification. New York, N.Y.: Irvington Press.

Lovaas OI, Newsom C, Hickman C. (1987) Self-stimulatory behavior and perceptual development. J Appl Behav Anal 20:45-68.

Maag J, Rutherford R, Wolchik S, Parks B. (1986) Comparison of two short overcorrection procedures on the stereotypic behavior of autistic children. J Autism Dev Disord 16:83-87.

MacDuff GS, Krantz PJ, McClannahan LE. (1993) Teaching children with autism to use photographic activity schedules: Maintenance and generalization of complex response chains. J Appl Behav Anal 26:89-97.

Mace FC. (2000) Clinical applications of behavioral momentum [commentary]. Behav Brain Sci 23:105-106.

Magiati I, Howlin P. (2003) A pilot evaluation study of the Picture Exchange Communication System (PECS) for children with autistic spectrum disorders. Autism 7:297-320.

Matson JL, Fee VE, Coe DA, Smith D. (1991) A social skills program for developmentally delayed preschoolers. J Clin Child Psychol 20:428-433.

McConachie H, Randle V, Hammal D, LeCouter A. (2005) A controlled trial of a training course for parents of children with suspected autism spectrum disorder. J Paediatr 147:335-340.

McConnell SR. (2002) Interventions to facilitate social interaction for young children with autism: Review of available research and recommendations for educational intervention and future research. J Autism Dev Disord 32:351-372.

McEachin J, Smith T, Lovass O. (1993) Long

term outcome for children with autism who received early intensive behavioural treatment. Am J Ment Retard 97:359-372.

McGee GG, Almeida MC, Sulzer-Azaroff B, Feldman RS. (1992) Promoting reciprocal interactions via peer incidental teaching. J Appl Behav Anal 25:117-126.

Mesibov GB. (1986) A cognitive program for teaching social behaviors to verbal autistic adolescents and adults. In: Social behavior in autism (Schopler E, Mesibov GB, Kunce LJ, eds), pp 265-283. New York, : Plenum Press.

Militerni R, Bravaccio C, Falco C, Fico, Palermo MT. (2002) Repetitive behaviors in autistic disorder. Eur Child Adolescent Psychiatry 11:210-218.

Mirenda P. (1997) Functional communication training and augmentative communication: A research review. Augmenta-tive and alternative communication 13.

Mudschenk NA, Sasso GM. (1995) Assessing sufficient social exemplars for students with autism. Behav Disord 21:62-78.

Muris P, Steerneman P, Merckelbach H, Holdrinet I, Meesters C. (1998) Comorbid anxiety symptoms in children with pervasive developmental disorders. J Anxiety Dis 12:387-393.

Myles BS, Southwick J. (2005) Asperger Syndrome and difficult moments: Practical solutions for tantrums, rage and meltdowns. Shawnee Mission, KS: Autism Asperger Publishing Company.

National-Research-Council. (2001) Educating children with autism: Committee on educational interventions for children with autism. Division of behavioural and social sciences and education. In. Washington DC: National Academy Press.

Nevin JA, Grace RC. (2000) Behavioral momentum and the law of effect. Behav Brain Sci 23:73-130.

Nuzzolo-Gomez R, Leonard M, Ortiz E, Rivera C, Greer RD. (2002) Teaching children with autism to prefer books or toys over stereotypy or passivity. Journal of Positive Behavior Interventions 4:80-87.

Odom SL, Chandler LK, Ostrosky M, McConnell SR, Reaney SR. (1992) Fading teacher prompts from peer-initiation interventions for young children with disabilities. J Appl Behav Anal 25:307-317.

Odom SL, McConnell SR, McEnvoy MA, Peterson C, Ostrosky M, Chandler LK, Spicuzza RJ, Skellenger A, Creighton M, Favazza PC. (1999) Relative effects of interventions for supporting the social competence of young children with disabilities. Topics in Early Childhood Special Education 19.

Ozonoff S, Miller JN. (1995) Teaching theory of mind: A new approach to social skills training for individuals with autism. J Autism Dev Disord 25:415-434.

Ozonoff S, Cathcart K. (1998) Effectiveness of a home program intervention for young children with autism. J Autism Dev Disord 28:25-32.

Parsons S, Mitchell P. (2002) The potential of virtual reality in social skills training for people with autistic spectrum disorders. J Intellect Disabil Res 46:430-443.

Paul R, Sutherland D. (2005) Enhancing early language in children with autism spectrum disorders. In: Handbook of autism and pervasive developmental disorders (3rd ed) (Volkmar FR, Paul R, Klin A, Cohen D, eds), pp 946-976. Hoboker, N.J.: John Wiley and Sons, Inc.

Piazza CC, Hanley GP, Fisher WW. (2000) Functional analysis and treatment of cigarette pica. J Appl Behav Anal 29:437-449.

Pierce K, Schreibman L. (1994) Teaching daily living skills to children with autism in unsupervised settings through pictorial self-management. J Appl Behav Anal 27:471-481.

Pierce K, Schreibman L. (1995) Increasing complex social behaviors in children with autism: Effects of peer-implemented pivotal response training. J Appl Behav Anal 28:285-295.

Pierce K, Schreibman L. (1997) Multiple peer use of pivotal response training social behaviors of classmates with autism: Results from trained and untrained peers. J Appl Behav Anal 30:157-160.

Potter C, Whittaker C. (2001) Enabling communication in children with autism. London: Jessica Kingsley.

Prizant B, Wetherby AM. (2005) Critical issues in enhancing communication abilities for persons with autism spectrum disorders. In: Handbook of autism and pervasive developmental disorders (3rd ed.) (Volkmar FR, Paul R, Klin A, Cohen D, eds), pp 925-945. Hoboken, N.J.: John Wiley & Sons.

Quinn C, Swaggart BL, Myles BS. (1994) Implementing cognitive behavior management programs for persons with autism: Guidelines for practitioners. Focus on Autistic Behavior 9:1-13.

Reddy V, Hay D, Murry L, Trevarthen C. (1997) Communication in infancy: Mutual regulation of affect and attention. In: Infant development: Recent advances (Bremner G, Slater A, Butterworth G, eds), pp 247-274. Hove, UK.: Psychological Press.

Reichle J, Brown L. (1986) Teaching the use of a multipage direct selection communication board to an adult with autism. J Assoc Pers Sev Handicaps 11:68-73.

Reynhout G, Carter M. (2006) Social stories for children with disabilities. J Autism Dev Disord 36:445-469.

Risley TR. (1968) The effects and side effects of punishing the autistic behaviours of a deviant child. J Appl Behav Anal 1:21-34.

Roeyers H. (1995) Peer mediated proximity intervention to facilitate the social interactions of children with a pervasive developmental disorder. British Journal of Special Education 22:161-163.

Rogers SJ. (2000) Interventions that facilitate socialization in children with autism. J Autism Dev Disord 30:399-409.

Rogers SJ. (2006) Evidence based interventions for language development in young children with autism. In: Social communication development in autism spectrum disorders: Early identification, diagnosis and intervention (Charman T, Stone W, eds). London: Guilford Press.

Romanczyk RG, Gillis JM. (2005) Treatment approaches for autism: Evaluating options and making informed choices. In: Autism spectrum disorders: identification, education, and treatment (3rd ed.) (Zager D, ed), pp 515-535. Mahwah, N.J.: Lawrence Erlbaum Associates.

Romski M, Sevcik RA. (2005) Augmenta-tive communication and early interven-tion: myths and realities. Infants and Young Children 18:174-185.

Sainato DM, Goldstein H, Strain PS. (1992) Effects of self-evaluation on preschool children's use of social interaction strategies with their classmates with autism. J Appl Behav Anal 25:127-141.

Sasso GM, Melloy KJ, Kavale K. (1990) Generalization, maintenance, and behavioral co-variation associated with social skills training through structured learning. Behavioral Disorders 16:9-22.

Sasso GM, Mundschenk, Melloy KJ, Casey SD. (1998) A comparison of the effects of organismic and setting variables on the social interaction behavior of children with developmental disabilities and autism. Focus on Autism and Other Developmental Disabilities 13:2-16.

Schopler E, Mesibov GB, Hearsey K. (1995) Structured teaching in the TEACCH system. In: Learning and cognition in autism (Schopler E, Mesibov GB, eds), pp 243-268. New York: Plenum Press.

Schreibman L. (1988) Autism. Newbury Park, C.A.: Sage Publications.

Schuler AL, Prizant B, Wetherby AM. (1997) Enhancing language and communication development: Prelin-guistic approaches. In: Handbook of autism and pervasive developmental disorders (2nd ed.) (Cohen DJ, Volkmar FR, eds), pp 539-571. New York: Wiley.

Schulman C. (2002) Bridging the process between diagnosis and treatment. In: Autism- From research to individual practice (Gabriels RL, Hill DE, eds), pp 25-46. London: Jessica Kingsley.

Schwartz IS, Garfinkle AN, Bauer J. (1998) The picture exchange communication system: Communicative outcomes for young children with disabilities. Topics in Early Childhood Special Education 18:144-159.

Shearer DD, Kohler FW, Buchan KA, McCullough KM. (1996) Promoting independent interactions between preschoolers with autism and their nondisabled peers: An analysis of self-monitoring. Early Educ Dev 7:205-220.

Sigafoos J, Drasgow E, Halle JW, O'Reilly M, Seely-York S, Edrisinha C, et al. (2004a) Teaching VOCA use as a communicative repair strategy. J Autism Dev Disord 34:411-422.

Sigafoos J, O'Reilly M, Seely-York S, Weru J, Son SH, Green VA, et al. (2004b) Transferring AAC intervention to the home. Disabil Rehabil 26:1330-1334.

Siller M, Sigman M. (2002) The behaviours of parents of children with autism predict the subsequent development of their children's communication. J Autism Dev Disord 32:77-89.

Silver M, Oakes P. (2001) Evaluation of a new computer intervention to teach people with autism or Asperger syndrome to recognize and predict emotions in others. Autism 5:299-316.

Simpson RL, de Boer-Ott S, Griswold DE,

Smith Myles B, Byrd J, Ganz J, Tapscott Cook K, Otten K, Ben-Arieh J, Kline SA, Garriott Adams L. (2005) Autism Spectrum Disorders: Interventions and treatments for children and youth. Thousand Oaks, CA.: Corwin Press.

Skinner BF. (1957) Verbal Behaviour. Englewood Cliffs, N.J.: Prentice Hall.

Smith T. (1999) Outcome of Early Intervention for Children with Autism. Clinical Psychology: Science and Practice 6:33-49.

Smith T, Groen AD, Wynn JW. (2000) Randomized trial of intensive early intervention for children with pervasive developmental disorder. Am J Ment Retard 105:269-285.

Sofronoff K, Attwood AJ, Hinton S. (2005) A randomised controlled trial of a CBT intervention for anxiety in children with Asperger's Syndrome. J Child Psychol Psychiatry 46:1152-1160.

Solomon M, Goodlin-Jones BL, Anders TF. (2004) A social adjustment enhancement intervention for high functioning autism, Asperger Syndrome and pervasive developmental disorder. J Autism Dev Disord 34:649-668.

Strain PS, Cordisco L. (1993) The LEAP preschool model: Description and outcomes. In: Preschool education programs for children with autism (Harris SL, Handleman J, S., eds). Austin, TX: Pro-Ed.

Strain PS, Hoyson M. (2000) The need for longitudinal, intensive social skill intervention: LEAP follow-up outcomes for children with autism. Topics in Early Childhood Special Education 20:116-122.

Strain PS, Kerr MM, Ragland EU. (1979) Effects of peer-mediated social initiations and prompting/reinforcement procedures on the social behavior of autistic children. J Autism Dev Disord 9:41-54.

Strain PS, Kohler FW, Storey K, Danko CD. (1994a) Teaching preschoolers with autism to self-monitor their social interactions: An analysis of results in home and school settings. J Emotion Behav Disord 2:78-88.

Strain PS, Kohler FW, Storey K, Danko CD. (1994b) Teaching preschoolers with autism to self-monitor their social interactions: An analysis of results in home and school settings. J Emotionand Behav Disord 2:78-88.

Sussman F. (1999) More Than Words: Helping parents promote communication and social skills in children with autism spectrum disorder. Toronto.

Swaggart BL, Gagnon E, Bock SJ, Earles TL, Quinn C, Myles BS, Simpson RL. (1995) Using social stories to teach social and behavioral skills to children with autism. Focus on Autistic Behavior 10:1-16.

Symons FJ, Davis MH. (1994) Instructional conditions and stereotyped behavior: The function of prompts. J Behav Ther Exp Psychiatry 25:317-324.

Taylor B, Hoch H, Weissman M. (2005a) The analysis and treatment of vocal stereotypy in a child with autism. Behavioral Interventions 20:239-253.

Taylor B, Hoch H, Potter B, Rodriguez A, Spinnato D, Kalaigian M. (2005b) Manipulating establishing operations to promote initiations towards peers in children with autism. Res Dev Disabil 26:385-392.

Taylor G. (1997) Community building in schools: developing a 'circle of friends'. Education Child Psychol 14:3.

Thorp DM, Stahmer AC, Schreibman L. (1995) Effects of sociodramatic play training on children with autism. J Autism Dev Disord 25:265-282.

Tomasello M. (1999) Having intentions, understanding intentions and under-standing communicative intentions. In: Developing theories of intention: social understanding and self-control (Zelazo PD, Astington JW, Olson DR, eds), pp

63-75. Mahwah, NJ: Lawrence Erlbaum Associates.

Turner M. (1999) Repetitive behaviour in autism: A review of psychological research. J Child Psychol Psychiatry 40:839-849.

Volkmar FR, Lord C, Bailey A, Schultz RT, Klin A. (2004) Autism and pervasive developmental disorders. J Child Psychol Psychiatry 45:135-170.

Von Tetzchner S, Martinsen H. (2000) Introduction to augmentative and alternative communication. London: Whurr.

Wells KC, Forehand R, Hickey K. (1977) Effects of a verbal warning and overcorrection on stereotyped and appropriate behaviors. Journal of Abnormal Child Psychology 5:387-403.

Wetherby AM, Prizant B. (2005) Enhancing language and communication develop-ment in autism spectrum disorders: Assessment and intervention guidelines. In: Autistic Spectrum Disorders: Ident-ification, education, and treatment (3rd ed.) (Zager D, ed). Mahwah, N.J.: LEA.

Whitaker P. (2004) Fostering communica-tion and shared play between mains-tream peers and children with autism: approaches, outcomes and experiences. British Journal of Special Education 31:215-222.

Whitaker P, Barratt P, Joy H, Potter M, Thomas G. (1998) Children with autism and peer group support: using 'circle of friends'. British Journal of Special Education 25:60-64.

Yoder PJ, Layton TL. (1988) Speech following sign language training in autistic children with minimal verbal language. J Autism Dev Disord 18:217-230.

Yoder PJ, Warren SF. (2002) Effects of prelinguistic milieu teaching and parent responsivity education on dyads involving children with intellectual disabilities. J

Speech Lang Hear Res 45:1158-1174.

Yoder PJ, Stone WL. (2005) Randomized comparison of two communication interventions for preschoolers with autism spectrum disorders. J Consult Clin Psychol 74(3): 426-35.

BEHAVIORAL INTERVENTIONS FOR EATING DISORDERS

Phillipa J. Hay

INTRODUCTION

Current diagnostic schemes define three groups of Eating Disorders: anorexia nervosa, bulimia nervosa (APA, 1994, WHO, 1992) and Eating Disorders not Otherwise Specified (EDNOS) (APA, 1994) or atypical anorexia nervosa and atypical bulimia nervosa (WHO, 1992). The former are well-defined Eating Disorders, but are less common than EDNOS in both clinic samples (excepting tertiary centers) and community surveys (Fairburn and Bohn, 2005). Anorexia nervosa is a disorder of self-maintained starvation and severe weight loss with extreme fear of weight gain. Bulimia nervosa is characterized by recurrent episodes of binge eating, extreme weight and shape concerns, and compensatory behaviors, such as self-induced vomiting or laxative misuse (purging form) or fasting or excessive exercise (non-purging form). People with bulimia nervosa are of normal or above normal weight by definition. EDNOS includes binge eating disorder (BED), which is characterized by recurrent binge eating in the absence of regular extreme weight control behaviors. The remainder of EDNOS mostly comprises people whose (i) symptom severity excludes them from a diagnosis of bulimia nervosa or anorexia nervosa, for example they fail to meet the frequency requirement for binge eating episodes, or their 'binge' eating episodes are not 'objectively' large or (ii) a range of disorders characterized by extreme weight control methods (APA, 1994; WHO, 1992).

Anorexia nervosa is found in less than 0.5%, bulimia nervosa in about 1%, and EDNOS, including BED, in 3-5% of young women (Ghaderi and Scott, 2001). The peak age of onset of common eating disorders, i.e., bulimia nervosa and EDNOS, is in late adolescence and young adulthood (Stice, 1998; Hay, 2003).

Risks related to Eating Disorders

A meta-analytic review (Stice, 2002) of prospective and randomized controlled experimental studies evaluated the effect size of a number of risk factors and found support for increased body weight as a risk factor for body dissatisfaction and dieting, and body dissatisfaction as a risk factor for dieting, negative affect and eating pathology. Negative affect, perfectionism, impulsivity and substance use were also notable risk factors for eating pathology. However, not all the studies in this review were of participants who had developed clinical eating disorders. Eating disorders have frequent medical complications, increased risk of obesity and high levels of co-morbidity with both depression and anxiety (APA, 2000). Community and clinic-based surveys, across "Western" countries (Crow and Peterson, 2003; Mond et al., 2004; Doll et al., 2005) have found impaired quality of life and moderate to high disability in people with BN and EDNOS.

Predictors of Treatment Outcome

Consistent predictors of outcome in eating disorders have often been elusive. The National Institute for Clinical Excellence systematic search (NICE, 2004) found only four consistent pre-treatment predictors of poorer outcome for treatment of bulimia nervosa: features of borderline personality disorder, concurrent substance misuse, low motivation for change and a history of obesity. In addition, early progress in therapy has predicted a better outcome at one (Agras et al., 2000a) and three years (Carter et al., 2002) and a recent study has found higher 'weight suppression' i.e., the discrepancy between and individual's highest weight ever and his or her present weight, to be associated with a higher dropout rate and poorer symptomatic outcome in people treated for bulimia nervosa with cognitive behavior therapy (Butryn et al., 2006).

OVERVIEW OF PSYCHOTHERAPIES IN EATING DISORDERS
General principles

It is not known which, if any, treatment approaches are most commonly used worldwide in anorexia nervosa, and while cognitive-behavioral therapy for bulimia nervosa is now endorsed by leading authorities (e.g. NICE, 2004; APA, 2000) a range of other individual therapies have been described and are used for people with bulimia nervosa. It is likely that use is influenced by factors such as availability of training and ongoing supervision for therapists, and health resource issues for consumers and providers that are outside the scope of this review. Here, we will focus on those therapies that are in current use (e.g. as reflected in clinical practice guidelines) and have evidence of efficacy from at least one randomized controlled trial (RCT; see Part 3 below).

Most individual therapy for bulimia nervosa and EDNOS sufferers is conducted on an outpatient basis. While evidence is currently insufficient to support outpatient as opposed to inpatient programs (Meads et al., 1999) the focus of treatment of anorexia nervosa has also moved from long-term inpatient programs with outpatient follow up, to more commonly outpatient care, with hospital backup (Garner and Needleman, 1997). Care is usually offered in individual or group sessions, and family therapy is more usual in child or adolescent settings. Detailed accounts are found in Garner and Garfinkel (1997). It is thought that severely ill patients are usually best treated in a specialised unit, at least until nutritional state is restored. Inpatient regimes have moved away from strict programs emphasising weight gain towards more 'humane' approaches that place less emphasis on weight gain and more on psychological, family, and interpersonal issues, and shorter inpatient treatments followed by partial or day hospitalization or outpatient programs (e.g. Touyz et al., 1984). These approaches are popular in that they can incorporate individual, group and family therapies, as well as refeeding, are cost-efficient and allow patients to continue with education and maintain contact with family and friends. The frequency and duration of therapy is diverse and there does not appear to be a 'standard' (see also 'Karolinska and other programs' below).

Individual and group psychotherapies
Psychodynamic therapy

Psychodynamic therapies have the longest history of therapies for eating disorders. They have developed from open-ended to more time-limited structured approaches (Dare and Crowther, 1995). A key figure in the application of such therapies in anorexia nervosa was Bruch (1973). She described the core therapeutic elements to change in anorexia nervosa as developing an understanding of the meaning of food for the patient, and helping the patient find alternatives to anorexic self-experience and self-expression.

These therapies are long-term and therapist time intensive by their nature. They also require specific training that may often be not readily accessible or available. Dare and colleagues (Dare and Crowther, 1995) have developed focal psychoanalytic therapy (FPT) for anorexia nervosa, as a standardized form of time-limited psychoanalytic therapy that may be both more readily accessible and disseminated, and subject to empirical evaluation. The therapist takes a non-directive stance, gives no advice about the eating behaviors or other problems of symptom management, but addresses: 1) the unconscious and conscious meanings of the symptom in terms of the patient's history and family experiences, 2) the effects of the symptom and its influence on current interpersonal relationships, and 3) the manifestation of those influences in the patient's relationship with the therapist. A non-directive stance can, however, present challenges in child and adolescent treatment settings, given parental pressure for a 'cure', and the expectation of active interventions by pediatricians rather than rehabilitative approaches.

Self-psychology for eating disorders such as bulimia nervosa (Goodsitt, 1997) has developed out of the older psychodynamic traditions. This approaches bulimia nervosa as a specific case of the pathology of the self. The patient does not rely on people to fulfill their personal needs (e.g. self-esteem). They rely instead on a substance, food, to fulfill personal needs. Therapy progresses when the patient moves to rely on humans, starting with the therapist.

Cognitive-behavior, cognitive and behavior therapies

Cognitive-behavior therapy (CBT), cognitive therapy (CT) and behavior therapy (BT) are time-limited manual-based therapies that address abnormal cognitions (beliefs) and behaviors thought to promote and maintain the disorder. Garner and colleagues (1997) describe CBT for anorexia nervosa as a therapy that addresses the patient's set of beliefs, attitudes and assumptions about the meaning of body weight. The therapy challenges the belief that thinness is the principal construct for self-worth and weight gain should be feared. The treatment identifies the combination of positive and negative reinforcers that maintain the patient's behavior and that help explain the ego-syntonic nature of the illness, namely those behaviors, values, or feelings, which are in harmony with or acceptable to the needs and

goals of the person. Strategies are proposed that challenge these beliefs and behaviors to normalize eating patterns. Fairburn and colleagues (2003) have subsequently developed an alternate CBT approach, modelled on CBT for bulimia nervosa (see below), that also addresses four key illness-maintaining factors, namely clinical perfectionism, low self-esteem, mood intolerance and interpersonal difficulties. They note this approach is not inconsistent with the involvement of the family "in the treatment of young cases". Forms of CBT have also been evaluated in a post-hospitalization trial in anorexia nervosa (e.g. Pike et al., (2003)).

A more recent non-specific therapy for anorexia nervosa, that is less directive than earlier forms of CBT, but includes many behavioral elements, has been developed in New Zealand (McIntosh et al., 2005). It is called non-specific clinical management (NSCM). NSCM includes psychoeducation, "care" and supportive psychotherapy, with a focus on resumption of normal eating and weight gain, strategies for weight maintenance, information about energy requirements and re-learning to eat normally. It thus incorporates elements of nutritional counselling and some behavioral weight restoration strategies. Treatment is relatively short, comprising 20 one-hour manual-based sessions over a minimum of 20 weeks.

A specific form of CBT has been developed for bulimia nervosa, termed CBT-BN (Fairburn et al., 1993; NICE, 2004). This uses three overlapping phases. Phase one aims to educate the person about bulimia nervosa. People are helped to increase regularity of eating, and resist urges to binge or purge. Phase two introduces procedures to reduce dietary restraint (e.g. broadening food choices). In addition, cognitive procedures supplemented by behavioral experiments are used to identify and correct dysfunctional attitudes, beliefs, and avoidance behaviors, and problem solving is introduced. Phase three is the maintenance phase. Relapse prevention strategies are used to prepare for possible future set backs. The standard CBT-BN regime for adults is 19 sessions over 20 weeks (Fairburn et al., 1993). A further variation, sometimes used as a comparison therapy, is behavior therapy (BT), which applies behavioral strategies only, such as keeping a diary of eating patterns, exposure to "normal" eating, and techniques to help distract from extreme weight control behaviors such as vomiting. The highly structured, and manualized nature of CBT and BT has rendered them amenable to empirical evaluation and widespread dissemination, and CBT-BN has been endorsed as a first line evidenced based therapy in leading guidelines (e.g. APA, 2000; NICE, 2004) and systematic reviews (e.g. Hay and Bacaltchuk, 2005). CBT is most commonly provided as an individual therapy although it has been found to be as effective in group format in EDNOS (see Nevonen and Broberg, 2006 below).

In the 1980s, a modification of the exposure and response prevention therapy developed for obsessive compulsive disorder was developed for adults with bulimia nervosa. It involved exposure to food and then psychological prevention strategies to reduce weight-control behavior, such as vomiting after eating, until the urge or compulsion to vomit receded (Leitenberg et al., 1988; Carter et al., 2002). In RCTs evaluating its efficacy with CBT-BN compared to a wait-list control, and in enhancing the effectiveness of CBT-BN alone, it was found to add little to the parent treatment (e.g. Agras et al., 1989; also see Hay et al., 2004 for a meta-analysis of this form of therapy). It does not appear to have gained widespread support for its use.

Griffiths and colleagues (1996) have developed hypnobehavioral psychotherapy for BN. It uses a combination of behavioral techniques, such as self-monitoring to change maladaptive eating, and hypnotic techniques to reinforce and encourage behavior change. However, only a single short term RCT (Griffiths et al., 1996; 1994) has been conducted.

There have been a number of other attempts to enhance CBT for bulimia nervosa but as yet none is known to have widespread support. For example, ecological momentary assessment (EMA), which enforces an intensive real-time monitoring schedule, did not significantly enhance the effects of self-monitoring in a small RCT (le Grange et al., 2002). A more promising but yet unproven approach is that of Fairburn and colleagues' (2003) 'transdiagnostic therapy' described above. Finally, many with BED are also overweight or obese and adding strategies that help address the weight disorder, such as exercise (see Pendleton et al., 2002, below) may be important to longer term outcome.

Other 'behavioral' therapies

Cognitive-analytic therapy (CAT) is a treatment that combines elements of CT and brief-focused psychodynamic therapy. CAT integrates active symptom management, and has been recommended as a viable alternative to CBT for anorexia nervosa (Garner and Needleman, 1997). People are helped to evolve a formal, mapped-out structure of the place of anorexia nervosa in their experience of themselves and their early and current relationships. This is drawn in diagrammatic form, and the figure may be modified over the course of the treatment (Treasure et al., 1995). Treatment is conducted in 20 weekly sessions, with monthly "booster" sessions over three months. Therapists require specific training and supervision.

Cognitive orientation theory aims to generate a systematic procedure for exploring the meaning of a behavior around themes, such as avoidance of certain emotions. Therapy for modifying behavior focuses on systematically changing beliefs related to themes, not beliefs referring directly to eating behavior. No attempt is made to persuade the patient that their beliefs are incorrect or maladapative (Bachar et al., 1999). This is however a little used therapy with only one very small and inconclusive trial.

Finally, dialectical behavior therapy is a type of behavioral therapy that views emotional dysregulation as the core problem in bulimia nervosa, with binge eating and purging understood as attempts to influence, change, or control painful emotional states. Patients are taught a repertoire of skills to replace dysfunctional behaviors (Safer et al., 2001). While this is a promising approach there has only been one short term (20 week) RCT of its use in 31 women. This trial found that dialectical behavior therapy significantly increased cessation of binge eating or purging (28.6% abstinence) compared with people on a wait list control (0% abstinence; relative risk (RR) 0.75) and significantly reduced bulimic symptom scores and dietary restraint scores compared with wait list control over 20 weeks (bulimic symptom scores: standardized mean difference (SMD) -1.35, 95% confidence interval (CI): -2.17 - -0.53; dietary restraint scores: SMD -0.80, 95% CI: -1.56 - -0.04). However, it found no significant difference in depression scores between dialectical behavioral therapy and wait list control (SMD -0.33, 95% CI: -1.07 - $+0.40$). (These results are drawn from data supplied to authors of a systematic review and calculated using the REVMAN program (Hay et al., 2004)).

Interpersonal psychotherapy

Interpersonal psychotherapy (IPT) was first developed for treatment of depression and was later modified for treatment of BN (Fairburn et al., 1991). Like CBT, it is a manual-based therapy and thus readily amenable to empirical evaluation. In bulimia nervosa it uses three overlapping phases. The first phase analyses the interpersonal context of the eating disorder leading to a formulation of the patient's problem area(s) that then form the focus of the second phase. The third phase aims at monitoring progress in making interpersonal changes and exploring ways to cope with further interpersonal difficulties. In bulimia nervosa, but not necessarily in anorexia nervosa, the patient is not encouraged to pay attention to eating patterns or body attitudes.

Specific training for this treatment is required, and it is unclear how common its use by therapists has become. It has been evaluated in longitudinal studies in comparison with CBT-BN with some support (see below) but with little support in one short-term trial of anorexia nervosa in adults (McIntosh et al., 2005).

Feminist therapy

Feminist therapy rests on the proposition that cultural constructions of gender are central to understanding and treating eating disorders. Katzman and Lee (1997), Striegel-Moore (1995) and Wooley (1995) are key figures in the integration of feminist and transcultural approaches to eating disorders. Other descriptions are found in Dolan (1994). Although addressing feminist issues has 'face validity' for a disorder in which 90% of sufferers are women with body image concerns, there are no RCTs evaluating its approach and it is uncertain how commonly it is used.

Motivational enhancement therapy

Vitousek et al. (1998) and Ward et al. (1996) have developed motivational enhancement therapies (METs) in eating disorders. This treatment is based on a model of change with focus on stages of change and it targets the ego-syntonic aspects of the illness that are in harmony with the person's own needs and goals. Stages of change represent constellations of intentions and behaviors through which individuals pass as they move from having a problem to doing something to resolve it. People in 'pre-contemplation' show no intention to change. People in 'contemplation' acknowledge they have a problem and are thinking about change, but have not yet made a commitment to change. People in the third 'action' stage are actively engaged in overcoming their problem while people in 'maintenance' work to prevent relapse. The aim of MET is to help patients move from earlier stages into 'action', utilizing cognitive and emotional strategies. For example with pre-contemplators, the therapist explores perceived positive and negative aspects of abnormal eating behaviors. Open-ended questions are used to elicit client expression, and reflective paraphrase is used to reinforce key points of motivation. During a session following structured assessment, most of the time is devoted to providing feedback to the client. Therapy then progresses to helping the patient develop and consolidate a change plan (Prochaska, 1992).

This is a widely used approach in psychiatry and psychology, and has applicability in anorexia nervosa where there is often strong resistance to change. As an approach, it would arguably be a useful adjunct to other specific therapies, but is as yet unsupported by evidence. We found one RCT, which compared four sessions of motivational enhancement therapy versus CBT (Treasure et al., 1999). It found no significant difference between motivational enhancement therapy and CBT in achieving a clinically significant reduction in binge frequency in participants with bulimia nervosa after 4 weeks (17/25 [68%] with CBT versus 23/43 [53%] with motivational enhancement therapy; RR 1.3, 95% CI: 0.9 - 1.9). (These results are drawn from data supplied to authors of a systematic review and calculated using the REVMAN program (Hay et al., 2004)).

Self-help therapy

Self-help therapy in eating disorders is a modified form of cognitive behavioral therapy, in which a treatment manual is provided for people to proceed with treatment on their own, or with support from a non-professional. Guided self-help usually implies that the support person may have some professional training, but is usually not a specialist in eating disorders. A good discussion of the development and types of self-help can be found in Williams (2003).

These approaches have received considerable interest and support for their relative efficacy. A recent systematic review of RCTs of any form of self-help for bulimia nervosa or BED was conducted by Stefano et al. (2006). In this review, the search date was June 2004, 7 databases and one hand search were done, Cochrane quality criterion were used to appraise RCTs, and two unblinded reviewers checked data extraction. Nine RCTs were included, 5 which used the published manual "Overcoming binge eating" (Fairburn, 1995), one "Bulimia Nervosa: A guide to recovery" (Cooper, 1995) and one "Getting better Bit(e) by Bit(e)" (Schmidt and Treasure, 1993). The primary outcome was 100% remission from binge eating. Two trials were of participants with BED, four with bulimia nervosa and three with mixed diagnoses. Five meta-analyses were conducted. The first was the only one that reached significance, namely any form of self-help (SH) versus wait-list (WL) achieved 26.5% versus 6.5% remission rates (n=5 trials, RR 0.76, 95% CI: 0.59-0.98). Significant heterogeneity was found however. There were no significant differences in non-completion rates or in remission rates for the four meta-analyses of pure SH versus WL (n=4 trials), guided SH versus WL (n=3 trials), guided SH versus pure SH (n=4 trials) or any SH versus CBT (pure or plus IPT) (n=2 trials).

Family therapies

Family therapy has been largely developed for use in treatment of adolescents and children with anorexia nervosa, and is likely the most common approach for treating these patients world-wide. It has also received the most research attention and like CBT-BN been endorsed in evidence based treatment guidelines (e.g. NICE, 2004; APA, 2000; and Beumont et al., 2004). A variety of family therapies have been evaluated based on family systems theory, that include strategic, structural and the Milan approaches (Lock and le Grange, 2005). The Maudsley approach builds on these and has three phases; the first focuses on re-feeding the patient and includes a family meal, the second on negotiations for a new pattern of relationships and the third on the establishment of a healthy adolescent or young adult relation-ship with the parents in which the distorted eating does not constitute the basis of inter-action. This includes working towards increas-ed personal autonomy for the adolescent.

Other approaches include: 1) "family group psycho-education" where families are seen together in a class format, 2) conjoint family therapy and "separated" family therapy (patients and parents are seen separately) 3) behavioral family systems therapy where parents, as in the Maudsley approach, are encouraged to take responsibility for re-feeding their child and additionally are trained in specific communication and problem-solving skills after the re-feeding period, and 4) a form of structural family therapy, with and without individual body awareness therapy (focusing on correcting the distorted body image).

Karolinska and other programs

Many services for anorexia nervosa have developed particular approaches. Bergh et al. (2002) of the Karolinska Institute in Sweden have developed a novel variant of a predominantly nutritional and behavioral regime, and they have uniquely compared this to a 'no treatment' arm in a RCT. Their approach incorporates computer-supported feedback to participants on satiety ratings.

Short-term weight gain goals of at least 2 kg are negotiated, and then re-negotiated as weight increases. Patients are then trained to eat in front of a computer monitor, the "mandometer". Once a day they eat from a plate resting on a scale. They record their level of satiety at 1 minute intervals while eating, and are asked to follow a linear curve for eating rate. The latter is modified until they are trained to eat progressively more, ingesting 350 grams each 10-15 minutes. After eating they rest in a warm room. (The latter is based on findings from animal studies where activity levels decrease with warming). There is a graded reduction in restriction of physical activity until remission. In addition participants have two other daily meals (with supplements) and between-meal snacks. Short-term social and occupational goals are set and modified each second week. Treat-ment continues for as long as necessary, typically from 6 months to more than 2 years. In an RCT with a wait-list as control, all but one of 11 patients in the treatment group were in remission after a median of 14.4 months of treatment and none of eight patients in the control group went into remission during a 21.6 month observation period. Whether it is the intensity of the regime or the computer aided satiety monitoring that is the efficacious part of the program remains to be tested, but similar outcomes are reported from other open trials of intensive programs (Meads, 1999).

SYSTEMATIC REVIEW OF LONGITUDINAL TRIALS OF THERAPIES

Methods of systematic review

A search was conducted for RCTs with at least one year follow-up (or otherwise of interest or high quality), that have evaluated psychotherapies in common current use (see below) for anorexia nervosa, bulimia nervosa, BED and EDNOS according to DSM-IV (APA, 1994) criteria or its equivalent.

The search strategy first sourced RCTs via peer-reviewed meta-analyses and other systematic reviews of treatments, including psychotherapy, for eating disorders that were published in 2004 and 2005, namely NICE (2004), Hay et al., (2004), Claudino et al., (2005), Hay and Bacaltchuk (2005), Bacaltchuk and Hay (2005a; 2005b), Treasure and Schmidt (2005). A systematic database search of MEDLINE and PSYCHLIT using the terms "therapy and ('binge eating disorder' or 'bulimia' or 'anorexia nervosa')" was then done for the year 2005 to January 2006 to search for more recent RCTs. Trials were evaluated according to published quality criterion guidelines (namely CONSORT, www.consort-statement.org, Cochrane Collaboration CCDAN group, www.cochrane.org, and Clinical Evidence, www.clinicalevidence.com) and were included if they were: (i) randomized, (ii) had at least 12 months follow-up and (iii) had drop-out rate <50%.

"Behavioral" approaches in common and/or current use and that had an evidence base of at least one longitudinal RCT, included the following: cognitive behavioral treatment (CBT) and other psychological approaches with a behavioral component, interpersonal psychotherapy (IPT), family therapy, self-help approaches, and these therapies in combination with antidepressant therapy. Trials of therapies not in common current use for eating disorders were excluded (a list of excluded studies is available from the author upon request). These included a range of therapies that were obscure (such as cognitive orientation therapy) and also that had been found to be ineffective (such as exposure response prevention enhancement of CBT). Also not included were studies evaluating behavioral therapies designed to address weight loss in people with obesity as well as an eating disorder, unless the aim of treatment was also to attenuate eating disorder symptoms.

Outcomes of longitudinal (at least 1-year) randomized controlled studies were evaluated, where reported, across medical (weight/body mass index), psychiatric outcome status (e.g. abstinence from bulimic behaviors/frequency of eating disorder symptoms) and quality of life and/or social function domains. Where both significant and able to be calculated, the magnitude of effect is reported in terms of relative risk reduction random effects (RR) model (e.g. percent 'recovery' in anorexia nervosa or abstinence from binge eating and/or purging behaviors in bulimia nervosa and binge eating disorder) and/or standardized mean difference (SMD) in bulimic or other eating disorder symptom severity, with 95% confidence intervals, according to intention to treat principles where data were available. These were calculated using the REVMAN statistical program as available from the Cochrane Collaboration (www.cochrane.org). The RR is the ratio of the proportion of cases having a positive outcome in the two groups. A ratio of 1 infers equal risk in both groups, and if 1 is within the 95% confidence interval the result is not statistically significant. In the analyses in this review a convention is taken that if RR is < 1 the active or experimental treatment is favored over the control for a binary outcome e.g. numbers not achieving abstinence from binge eating abstinence. The SMD reports the difference between the means or averages of a continuous outcome measure (e.g. frequency of binge eating) and by convention 0 infers no difference between the mean outcomes of two groups and <0 favors the active or experimental group over the control group (namely e.g. the former has a lower mean frequency of binge eating). If 0 is within the 95% confidence interval of the SMD then the result is not significant.

Results of review

Twenty-five RCTs were identified for inclusion from a total pool of 79 trials. The most common reason for exclusion of an RCT was failure to have at least one year follow-up (n=46 trials). Two anorexia nervosa trials in particular were included with less than one year follow-up: Dare et al. (2001) was included because it is of interest in that it attempted to evaluate and compare some of the more commonly known approaches in AN, and McIntosh et al. (2005) was included as longitudinal follow-up is reported as being in progress and it has attracted considerable interest with unexpected findings. The 25 RCTs are summarized in Tables 1, 2 and 3.

Bulimia Nervosa Trials

There were eight trials in bulimia nervosa, the majority of CBT-BN, other CBT, and combinations. There was only one comparing CBT-BN with a no treatment or wait-list control group. Where compared with another therapy, in one trial CBT-BN was found superior to interpersonal psychotherapy at the end of treatment, but not at follow-up. CBT has been found to be at least as effective as an anti-depressant, but it is likely more acceptable as higher dropouts have been found in participants randomized to the drug arm of trials (see also Bacaltchuk and Hay, 2005a; 2005b). Guided self-help CBT was supported in one trial, and a second found CBT may be effectively provided in a group setting. CBT appears more effective than BT alone. The quality of trials in the present review was variable; only one had adequate allocation concealment, five had blind outcome asses-sors, and four used intention-to-treat analyses.

Anorexia nervosa trials

There were eleven trials in anorexia nervosa, and two of these were post-hospitalization trials after relative weight restoration. Most trials were inconclusive, although cognitive orientation and 'routine care' therapy performed poorly. Trials were also very small with only four having more than 50 participants, only three utilizing blind

outcome assessors and only three using adequate allocation concealment, however, most (n=7) used intention-to-treat analyses. The new NSCM approach showed some promise, but most participants did poorly in this and other trials. Only four trials applied manualized therapies.

BED and EDNOS trials

There are six trials of BED, EDNOS or mixed diagnostic groups. Outcomes in these trials are relatively better although not consistently so. CBT is the most evaluated treatment, although it has proven difficult to demonstrate that it is more effective than an alternative therapy, namely IPT. In one trial, exercise was found to enhance psychological approaches in those with co-morbid obesity. Four trials used intention-to-treat analyses, one had adequate allocation concealment, and none had blinded outcome assessment.

CONCLUSIONS AND FUTURE DIRECTIONS

This review points to an important issue, namely that all systematic reviews are not the same even when drawing on the same sources of evidence. However, although the present review reports many fewer RCTs (as most previous reviews had not set a follow-up of a year as a criterion for inclusion of RCTs) the results are consistent with other identified systematic reviews and guidelines. There is a limited body of evidence to support CBT-BN for treatment of bulimia nervosa in adults, and a even more limited body of evidence for family therapy as treatment of anorexia nervosa in adolescents and children. CBT combined with weight management strategies, particularly exercise in adults with BED and a weight disorder, and self-help (especially guided CBT self-help) in bulimia nervosa, BED and EDNOS adults show promise. In most trials treatment effects in bulimia nervosa, EDNOS and BED appear to be sustained or increase over time. An overview

Table 1. Randomized Controlled Trials of Therapies for Bulimia Nervosa: Between group differences in binge eating frequency and percent abstinence at end of therapy and at one year follow-up.

Study	Trial Quality	Participants per group and setting	Intervention	Outcome at End of treatment	Outcome at 1-year
Sundgot-Borgen, 2002	Unclear allocation concealment, No ITT analysis, Assessors not blind, Follow-up 18 months	n=64, 5(8%) dropouts gender not specified adults Recruitment:outpatients Setting: specialist Country: Norway	1) Cognitive behavioral therapy (CBT) group 2) Nutritional counseling 3) exercise (EX) 4) waitlist (WL)	Mean bingeing: 1) 7.9 (2.95) 2) not provided 3) 7.3 (2.72) 4) not provided. Data from authors found CBT significantly fewer bulimic symptoms than WL: SMD -1.35 (-2.17, -0.53)[1]	Recovery greatest in EX group 1) 31%, 2) 24%, 3) 53%, 4) not provided
Agras, 2000b	Multi-site, Adequate allocation, Concealment, Assessors blinded, ITT analysis done	n=220, 61 (28%) dropouts Gender: not specified Adults Diagnosis: BN purging type Recruitment: media advertising and referrals Country: USA	1) CBT-Bulimia Nervosa (BN) 2) Interpersonal therapy (IPT)	SMD -0.34 (-0.61, -0.08) RR 0.76 (0.67, 0.86) 29% vs 6 % abstinence Other: no significant effects on psychosocial function or dropouts	Abstinence: 1) 31% 2) 19% NS
Fairburn, 1991	Unclear allocation, Concealment, ITT not done, Assessors blinded, Follow-up 5 years	n=73, 13 (18%) dropouts, all female, Adults BN (DSM-IIIR) Recruitment: primary and secondary care Setting: tertiary	1) CBT-BN 2) IPT 3) Behavioral Therapy (BT)	Abstinence: SMD -0.34 NS, RR 0.87 NS, 1) 60%, 2) 54%, 3) 54%, NS No significant differential effects on dropouts, depression, psychosocial function or weight	Outcome poor in BT group and attrition high (48%) Abstinence: 1) 36%, 2) 44%, 3) 20% CBT superior to BT Treatment effects maintained at 5 years
Fairburn, 1986	Unclear allocation, Concealment, ITT not done but supplied by authors[1], Assessors blinded	N=24, 2 (8%) dropouts All female, adults BN-P (Russell, 1979) Recruitment primary care Setting: Tertiary Country: UK	1) CBT-BN 2) Focal psychotherapy	Abstinence: SMD 0.19 NS No significant effects on dropouts, depression, psychosocial function, general psychiatric symptoms or weight	Abstinence: SMD 0.42 NS Effects maintained over time

SMD: Standardized mean difference in bulimic symptoms or binge eating symptom severity frequency, 95% CI <0 indicates significantly better outcomes
RR: Relative Risk of abstinence from binge eating or binge eating and vomiting, 95% CI <1 indicates significantly better outcomes
NS: not significant, [1]Data reported in Hay et al. (2004).

Table 1. continued

Study	Trial Quality	Participants per group and setting	Intervention	Outcome at End of treatment	Outcome at 1-year
Bailer, 2003	Unclear allocation, Concealment ITT analysis done Assessor blind	N=81, 25 (31%) dropouts, Gender: not specified, Age: all > 17 years DSM-III Bulimia Community recruitment Setting: specialist Country: Germany	3) Guided self-help (GSH) (Schmidt and Treasure) 4) Group CBT-BN	Abstinent: SMD -0.48 (-0.92, -0.03); RR 1.05 NS 1) 8%, 2) 12% No significant differences in dropouts, improved depression: SMD -0.55 (-1.09, -0.02)	Abstinent: 1) 23%, 2) 15%, NS
Mitchell, 1990	Unclear allocation, Concealment, No ITT analysis, Unclear if assessors blind, 10-year follow-up (Keel et al., 2002)	N=171, 27% dropouts All female Adults Recruitment specialist Clinic and community Setting: specialist Country: USA	1) CBT and imipramine 2) CBT and placebo 3) Imipramine 4) Placebo 5) CBT in group	CBT superior to drug therapy and placebo on all measures including bulimic symptoms and depression, 51% symptom free versus 16% in drug arm	10 year: NS effects of active treatment group on bulimic symptoms & depression, but those in placebo group had worse social adjustment (p<0.05)
Agras, 1992	Unclear allocation Concealment ITT analysis done Assessor blind	N=71, 14% dropouts Gender not specified Adults Recruitment specialist Clinic and community Country: USA	1) Desipramine 16 weeks 2) Desipramine 24 weeks 3) CBT 4) CBT + Desipramine 16 weeks 5) CBT + Desipramine 24 weeks	24 week desipramine and CBT and combined superior (p<0.01) to 16 weeks desipramine; NS differences between the first 3	Abstinence 1) 17% 2) 50% 3) 52% 4) 33% 5) 50% Poorer outcome in groups with 16 week desipramine: RR 0.47 (0.22-0.99)
Nevonen, 2006	Unclear allocation Concealment ITT analysis done Assessor blinding unclear	N=82, 27% dropouts All female Adults Specialist referrals Country: Sweden	1) Individual CBT and IPT 2) Group CBT and IPT	NS differences in eating disorder symptoms and interpersonal problems. Psychiatric symptoms, depression or dropouts Abstinence rate: 1) 31%, 2) 45%	Abstinent rate: 1) 33%, 2) 33% At 2.5 years 1) 38%, 2) 30%

SMD: Standardized mean difference in bulimic symptoms or binge eating symptom severity frequency, 95% CI <0 indicates significantly better outcomes
RR: Relative Risk of abstinence from binge eating or binge eating and vomiting, 95% CI <1 indicates significantly better outcomes
NS: not significant, [1]Data reported in Hay et al. (2004).

Table 2. Randomized Controlled Trials of Therapies for Anorexia Nervosa: Between group differences in weight and 'recovery' at end of therapy and at one year follow-up.

Study	Trial Quality	Participants per group and settings	Intervention(s)	Outcome at end of treatment	Outcome at 1-year
Dare, 2001	Adequate allocation concealment, Assessors not blind, ITT analysis done	N=84, 36% dropouts Adults, 2 males Specialist treatment referrals Country: UK	1) Focal psychoanalytic (FAT) 2) Cognitive-analytic manual 3) Family therapy 4) Routine care	1) 33%, 2) 27%, 3) 36%, 4) 5%, FAT had a higher recovery rate than routine care: RR 0.7 (0.51, 0.97) but not 2 or 3; no differences in dropouts, in routine care one died and more were hospitalized (p<0.05).	One year was end of treatment
Treasure, 1995	Unclear allocation concealment, Assessors not blind, ITT analysis done	N=30, 33% dropouts, Adults, 1 male, Country: UK	1) Educational BT 2) Cognitive-analytic therapy manual	NS differences between groups in numbers recovered or weight	37% poor outcome, NS difference in numbers recovered or weight between groups
Bachar, 1999[1]	Unclear allocation concealment, No ITT analysis, Assessors part blinded	N=13, 5 dropouts All female, Adults and adolescents Specialist recruitment Setting: specialist Country: Isreal	1) Self-psychology and Nutritional Counseling 2) Cognitive orientation and Nutritional Counseling 12 months	BMI>17.5 and menstruating: RR 0.29 (0.09, 0.92) 1: 5/7, 2: 0/6 No differences in dropout	<50% followed and data not reported
Bergh, 2002	Adequate allocation concealment, Assessors not blind, Not clear ITT, but only 1 dropout	N=19 Adolescents Specialist treatment Referrals Country: Sweden	1) Karolinska approach 2) Waitlist Four were inpatients at some points	1) 10/11 in remission after 14.4 months versus none in 2) RR 15.8 (1.06, 234.9) Information supplied to author	Not specified
Channon, 1989	Unclear allocation concealment, ITT analysis done, Assessors not blind	N=24, 3 dropouts Russell criterion (1983) All female Specialist treatment Referrals Country: UK	Six months therapy 1) CBT 2) BT 3) 'eclectic'	All participants improved, data could not be extracted for further statistical testing of outcomes, NS difference in dropouts	All improved, NS group differences in weight, nutritional function, menses, Eating Disorder Inventory drive for thinness, psychosexual function and mood

SMD: Standardised mean difference in eating disorder symptoms or weight (BMI), 95%CI <0 indicates significantly better outcomes
RR: Relative Risk of reaching a 'recovered' intermediate or good outcome (i.e., Morgan and Russell: weight >85% mean for age, gender, height, with menstruation), 95% CI <1 indicates significantly better outcomes, NS: not significant,
1. There were also 13 patients with bulimia nervosa on this trial, but as this is not a common therapy for bulimia nervosa and the numbers were very small this aspect of the study has not been included here.
2. There were also 23 patients with bulimia nervosa in this trial, but as this is not a common therapy for bulimia nervosa and the numbers were very small this aspect of the study has not been included here.

Table 2 continued

Study	Trial Quality	Participants per group and settings	Intervention(s)	Outcome at end of treatment	Outcome at 1-year
Crisp, 1991	Unclear allocation concealment, ITT analysis done, Assessors blind	N=90, 19% dropouts All female, young adults Specialist referrals over 5 years, Country: UK	1) Inpatient and 12 outpatient sessions 2) Individual/family therapy, 12 sessions 3) 10 outpatient groups All had a behavioral approach to diet and weight gain plus individual and family psychotherapy 4) No treatment	Variable end of treatment, data not published, one in group therapy (3) died	Individual/family therapy(2), better socioeconomic adjustment $p<0.05$, weight gain greater in active treatment groups (1-3) vs. inactive (4) $p<0.01$, no other between group differences and all groups had significant improvement $p<0.05$
Hall, 1987	Unclear allocation concealment, ITT analysis done, Assessors blind	N=30, 17% dropout All female, adults and adolescents, Specialist referrals Country: UK	1) 12 sessions mixed individual and family psychotherapy 2) 12 dietician sessions individual and family	Significant overall weight gain but NS difference between groups	NS difference between group except 1) better social and sexual adjustment ($p<0.01$) and numbers 'recovered': 4/15 versus 0/15, RR 0.73 (0.54, 1.00)
Robin, 1999	Unclear allocation concealment, Assessors not blind, No ITT analysis	n=37, no dropouts 7 did not have follow-up All female, Adolescents Country: USA	1) Behavioral family systems (BFST) 2) Individual ego-oriented (EGIT) therapies Over 12-18 months	BFST > weight gain ($p<0.001$) and more menstruating ($p<0.03$), NS differences eating attitudes, depression, maturity, family conflict	BFST > weight gain ($p<0.02$), No other differences, Significant time effects for most measures except general family conflict
McIntosh, 2005	Adequate allocation concealment, Blind outcome assessors, ITT analysis done	n=56, AN and EDNOS-AN BMI: 15.5-19 Country: New Zealand	1) CBT 2) IPT 3) Non-specific clinical management (NSCM) 20 weekly sessions manualized	Good outcome: 1) 32%, 2) 10%, 3) 56% 1 vs 2: RR 0.76 (0.54, 1.06) and lower restraint: (SMD -0.74, -1.38 – 0.09) but NS differences in weight, GAF or depression 1 vs 3: 3>1 global improvement, restraint and GAF, but not depression or weight 2 vs 3: NS differences	In progress

SMD: Standardised mean difference in eating disorder symptoms or weight (BMI), 95%CI <0 indicates significantly better outcomes
RR: Relative Risk of reaching a 'recovered' intermediate or good outcome (i.e., Morgan and Russell: weight >85% mean for age, gender, height, with menstruation), 95% CI <1 indicates significantly better outcomes, NS: not significant

Table 2 continued

Study	Trial Quality	Participants per group and settings	Intervention(s)	Outcome at end of treatment	Outcome at 1-year
Post-hospitalization trials					
Russell, 1987	Unclear allocation concealment, Assessors not blind, ITT analysis done	N=57², 9% dropout Mixed adults and adolescents, 7 male 5 year follow-up Country: UK	1) Maudsley family therapy 2) Individual supportive therapy	Same as one year, effects maintained at 5 years Eisler et al., 1997	22 (39%) good or Between group data presented by subgroups. Significant difference only in subgroup 1 (onset≤18, duration<3 years): 9/10 family versus 2/11 individual had good or intermediate outcomes
Pike, 2003	Unclear allocation concealment, Assessor blinding not specified	N=33, 15 early dropout Adults, all within 95% ideal body weight, all women Clinic recruitment Country: USA	1) Manualized CBT 2) Nutritional counseling 50 sessions over 1-year	Same as one year	8/18 (39%) good outcome, χ^2=5.89, p<0.02, Survival analysis, longer mean time to relapse in CBT group: 1) 43.79, 2) 27.21, long rank statistic 8.39, p<0.004

SMD: Standardised mean difference in eating disorder symptoms or weight (BMI), 95%CI <0 indicates significantly better outcomes
RR: Relative Risk of reaching a 'recovered' intermediate or good outcome (i.e., Morgan and Russell: weight >85% mean for age, gender, height, with menstruation), 95% CI <1 indicates significantly better outcomes
NS: not significant,
1. There were also 13 patients with bulimia nervosa on this trial, but as this is not a common therapy for bulimia nervosa and the numbers were very small this aspect of the study has not been included here.
2. There were also 23 patients with bulimia nervosa in this trial, but as this is not a common therapy for bulimia nervosa and the numbers were very small this aspect of the study has not been included here.

Table 3. Randomized Controlled Trials of Therapies for BED, EDNOS and mixed diagnostic groups: Between group differences in binge eating frequency and percent abstinence at end of therapy and at one year follow-up.

Study	Trial quality	Participants per group and settings	Intervention(s)	Outcome at End active Rx	Outcome at 1-year
Wifley, 1993	Allocation concealment unclear, ITT analysis done, Assessor not blind	N=56, 9 (16%) dropouts All female, adults BN nonpurging, DSM-IIIR Recruitment: community Setting: tertiary Country: USA	1) CBT 2) IPT Conducted in groups	Abstinence: 1) 27%, 2) 44%, SMD: NS, RR: NS NS differences in dropouts, depression, or psychosocial function	NS differences, effects maintained
Wifley, 2002	Allocation concealment unclear, ITT analysis done, Assessor not consistently blind	N=162, 16 (10%) dropouts 83% female, older adults, all BMI>27 BED DSM-IIIR Recruitment: community Setting: tertiary Country: USA	1) CBT 2) IPT Conducted in groups	Abstinence: 1) 79%, 2) 73%, SMD: NS, RR: NS IPT less dietary restraint	1) 72%, 2) 70% maintained abstinence BMI remained stable Dietary restraint reduced in both groups
Pendleton, 2002	Unclear allocation concealment, ITT not done, Assessor not blind	N=114, 26% dropouts All female, adults Community recruitment BED Country: USA	1) CBT, exercise (EX) consisting of 3 times per week, 45 minute sessions of aerobics, and maintenance (M) 2) CBT and EX 3) CBT and M 4) CBT	Abstinence: 1) 16/29, 55% 2) 10/28, 36% 3) 5/28, 18% 4) 7/29, 24% With EX: 46%, without EX: 22%, RR 2.17 (1.22, 3.86) and with EX had significantly greater reductions in weight and depression	Abstinence at 16 months: 1) 14/29, 48% 2) 13/28, 46% 3) 9/28, 32% 4) 3/29, 10% with EX: 47%, without EX: 19%, RR 2.45 (1.35, 4.46) and with EX had significantly greater reductions in weight and depression

SMD: Standardised mean difference in bulimic symptoms or binge eating symptom severity frequency, 95% CI <0 indicates significantly better outcomes
RR: Relative risk of abstinence from binge eating or binge eating and vomiting, 95% CI <1 indicates significantly better outcomes
NS: not significant NC: nutritional counseling
1. All of the criteria for bulimia nervosa are met except that the binge eating and inappropriate compensatory mechanisms occur at a frequency of less than twice a week or for duration of less than 3 months.

Table 3 continued

Study	Trial quality	Participants per group and settings	Intervention(s)	Outcome at End active Rx	Outcome at 1-year
Molinary, 2005	Unclear allocation concealment, ITT not done, Assessor not blind	N=65, 8% dropouts All female and obese, adults Obese hospital patients with BED Country: Italy	One year, all participants received diet and NC 1) CBT for BED 2) Fluoxetine 20-60 mg 3) Combined CBT and fluoxetine	Lower binge eating frequency and greater weight loss with CBT versus combined versus fluoxetine, p<0.001	One year same as end of treatment
Palmer, 2002	Adequate allocation concealment, ITT done, Assessor not blinded	N=121, 30 (25%) dropouts Only 4 male, adults Mixed diagnoses: BN, BED, EDNOS Recruitment: outpatient Setting: tertiary Country: UK	1) 1 session guided self-help (GSH) 2) phone GSH 3) face-to-face GSH 4) WL	Abstinence: 1) 6% 2) 14% 3) 10% 4) 0% NS differences	Abstinence: 1) 22% 2) 21% 3) 23% 4) 23%
Nevonen, 2005	Unclear allocation concealment, ITT analysis done Assessor blinding unclear	N=35, 14% dropouts All female, adults EDNOS Types 3[1] Specialist referrals Country: Sweden	1) Individual CBT and IPT 2) Group CBT and IPT	Abstinent: 1) 10%, 2) 10% NS differences in eating disorder symptoms, interpersonal problems, psychiatric symptoms, depression or dropouts	Abstinent at 1 year: 1) 53%, 2) 83% Abstinent at 2.5 years: 1) 59%, 2) 67% Only significant difference was lower psychiatric symptoms at 2.5 years for group therapy

SMD: Standardised mean difference in bulimic symptoms or binge eating symptom severity frequency, 95% CI <0 indicates significantly better outcomes

RR: Relative risk of abstinence from binge eating or binge eating and vomiting, 95% CI <1 indicates significantly better outcomes

NS: not significant NC: nutritional counseling

1. All of the criteria for bulimia nervosa are met except that the binge eating and inappropriate compensatory mechanisms occur at a frequency of less than twice a week or for duration of less than 3 months.

of the evidence base for these approaches is summarized on Table 4.

Nevertheless, there are many unanswered questions and overall the numbers of longitudinal trials are very low and of variable quality. Frequently, studies of anorexia nervosa were underpowered. Many trials had unclear allocation concealment, and potential for bias in outcome assessments. There is insufficient research comparing active treatments with no treatment or wait-list groups.

Table 4. Comparative levels of evidence supporting behavioral therapies in anorexia nervosa, bulimia nervosa and eating disorder not otherwise specified (EDNOS).

Therapy	Level of Evidence support*		
	Anorexia Nervosa	Bulimia Nervosa	EDNOS
Cognitive behavior therapy	B	A	B
Family Therapy	B	D	n.a.
Interpersonal Psychotherapy	D	B	C
Self-help – structured manuals	n.a.	B	B
Non-specific clinical management	B	n.a.	n.a.
Psychodynamic therapies (e.g. focal analytic therapy)	C	C	n.a.
Cognitive analytic therapy	B	n.a	n.a.
Structured inpatient programs	B	n.a	n.a.
Dialetical Behavior Therapy	n.a.	B	B
Motivational Enhancement Therapy	C	D	n.a.
Feminist therapies	C	C	C

*Levels of Evidence
   A. Systematic review and meta-analysis of one or more randomized controlled trials
   B. At least one well conducted RCT
   C. Other controlled (e.g. case-control, historical controls), case series or consensus opinion from experts
   D. RCT not supportive
   n.a. not applicable to this eating disorder diagnostic group – either not well studied or not an indicated therapy

There is room for improvement in all approaches, and particularly many people with anorexia nervosa have a poor outcome even with the 'best' of treatments. Attempts to enhance CBT-BN, particularly with IPT (although this appears promising), have yet to be proven. It is not know which of a range of approaches in either individual or family therapy for anorexia nervosa is most efficacious. This is highlighted by the unexpected results of the McIntosh et al. (2005) trial, where participants receiving non-specific clinical management, the control condition, had better outcomes than participants receiving either cognitive behavioral therapy or interpersonal therapy.

A question of concern is why is there is so little evidence base in particular for the treatment of anorexia nervosa, the 'oldest' of the Eating Disorders and the one with most disability? It is possible that participants and health care providers are reluctant to take the chance of randomization to a potentially less effective therapy where the illness is severe and risk may be high. It is also more common in children and adolescents, and often RCTs are less common where dual consent issues are present. It is also relatively less common than other eating disorders. A leading authority (Fairburn, 2005) has suggested that, given the poor outcome of RCTs in anorexia nervosa to date, further RCTs should not be conducted without preliminary data (from e.g. open trials) to support them.

Finally, in this review CBT-BN was found to lead to symptomatic change earlier than IPT for people with bulimia nervosa (e.g. Fairburn et al., 1991; Agras et al., 2000a). Further studies should emulate these, namely they should attempt to assess outcome during treatment and at follow-up, in addition to the beginning and end of treatment. This enables the mechanism and the rate of change to be studied.

USEFUL RESOURCES FOR HEALTH PROFESSIONALS
Self-help CBT books:
GC Fairburn. (1995) *Overcoming Binge Eating.* New York: The Guilford Press.

Peter Cooper. (1995) *Bulimia Nervosa and Binge Eating. A guide to recovery.* London: Robinson Press and New York: New York University Press, Reprint edition.

Schmidt U, Treasure T. (1993) *Getting Better BitE BitE: A Survival Kit for Sufferers of Bulimia Nervosa and Binge Eating Disorders.* Psychology Press.

Contemporary consensus guidelines have recently been published by the American Psychiatric Association: Practice Guideline for the Treatment of Patients with Eating Disorders Third edition online at http://www.psych.org and in the June 2006 issue of the American Journal of Psychiatry.

A good account of *medical issues* is found in: Birmingham L, Beumont P. (2004) *Medical management of eating disorders.* Cambridge: Cambridge University Press.

A good account of the *details of therapies* is found in: Garner DM, Garfinkel PE (eds). (1997) *Handbook of Treatments for Eating Disorders.* 2nd edition. New York: The Guilford Press: 67-93

A good overview *for consumers and their families, of bulimia nervosa* is found in: Lilly RZ, Hay PJ, Tonks A. (2003) Bulimia nervosa. British Medical Journal 327: 380-383.

A good overview *for consumers and their families, of anorexia nervosa* is found in: Treasure J. (1997) *Anorexia Nervosa A survival guide for families friends and sufferers.* Psychology Press.

A good account of the eating disorders and their treatments *in the context of adolescence* is found in: Jaffa T, McDermott, B. (eds) (2006) *Eating Disorders in Children and Adolescents.* Cambridge: Cambridge University Press.

An in-depth discussion of *ethical and legal aspects of treatment* is found in: Vandereycken W, Beumont P (eds). (1999) *Treating Eating Disorders: Ethical, Legal and Personal Issues.* London: Athlone.

REFERENCES
American Psychiatric Association (APA). (1994) Diagnostic and Statistical Manual of Mental Disorders (Fourth Edition), Washington, DC:APA.

American Psychiatric Association. (2000) Practice Guidelines for the treatment of patients with eating disorders (Revision) Am J Psychiatry 157 Jan Suppl.:1-39.

Agras WS, Schneider JA, Arnow B, Raeburn SD, Telch CF. (1989) Cognitive-behavioral and response-prevention treatments for bulimia nervosa. J Consult Clin Psychol 57:215–221.

Agras WS, Rossiter EM, Arnow B, Telch CF, Raeburn SD, Bruce B, Koran LM. (1992) Pharmacologic and cognitive-behavioural treatment for bulimia nervosa: a controlled comparison. Am J Psychiatry 149: 82-87.

Agras WS, Rossiter EM, Arnow B, Telch CF, Raeburn SD, Bruce B, Koran LM. (1994) One-year follow-up of psychosocial and pharmacologic treatments for bulimia nervosa. J Clin Psychiatry 55:179-213.

Agras WS, Crow S, Halmi K, Mitchell JE, Wilson GT, Kraemer HC. (2000a) Outcome predictors for the cognitive-behaviour treatment of bulimia nervosa: Data from a multisite study. Am J Psychiatry 157: 1302-08.

Agras WS, Walsh BT, Fairburn CG, Wilson GT, Kraemer HC. (2000b) A multicenter comparison of cognitive-behavioral therapy and interpersonal psychotherapy for bulimia nervosa. Arch Gen Psychiatry 54: 459-65.

Bachar E, Eytan B, Yael L, Shulamit K, Berry EM. (1999) Empirical comparison of two psychological therapies. Self Psychology and Cognitive Orientation in the Treatment of Anorexia and Bulimia. J Psychother Pract Res 2:115-28.

Bacaltchuk J, Hay P. (2005a) Antidepressants versus placebo for people with bulimia nervosa (Cochrane Review). In: The Cochrane Library Issue 2. Chichester, UK: John Wiley and Sons, Ltd.

Bacaltchuk J, Hay P. (2005b) Antidepressants versus psychological treatments and their combination for people with bulimia nervosa (Cochrane Review). In: The Cochrane Library Issue. Chichester, UK: John Wiley and Sons, Ltd.

Bailer U, de Zwaan M, Leisch F, Strnad A, Lennkh-Wolfsberg C, El-Giamal N, Hornik K, Kasper S. (2003) Guided self-help versus cognitive behavioural group therapy in the treatment of bulimia nervosa. Int J Eat Disord 35:522-37.

Bergh C, Brodin U, Lindberg G, Sodersten P. (2002) Randomized controlled trial of a treatment for anorexia and bulimia

nervosa. Proc National Acad Sciences 99:9486-91.

Beumont P, Hay P, Beumont D, Birmingham L, Derham H, Jordan A, Kohn M, McDermott B, Marks P, Mitchell J, Paxton S, Surgenor L, Thornton C, Wakefield A, Weigall S; Royal Australian and New Zealand College of Psychiatrists Clinical Practice Guidelines Team for Anorexia Nervosa. (2004) Australian and New Zealand clinical practice guidelines for the treatment of anorexia nervosa. Australian N Z J Psychiatry 38:659-70.

Bruch H. (1973) Eating disorders: Obesity, anorexia nervosa and the person within. New York: Basic Books.

Butryn ML, Lowe MR, Safer DL, Agras WS. (2006) Weight suppression is a robust predictor of outcome in the cognitive-behavioral treatment of bulimia nervosa J Abnorm Psychol 115:62-7.

Carter FA, Bulik CM, McIntosh VV, Joyce P. (2002) Cue reactivity as a predictor of outcome with bulimia nervosa. Int J Eat Disorders 31:240-50.

Carter FA, McIntosh VVW, Joyce PR, Sullivan PF, Bulik CM. (2003) Role of exposure with response prevention in cognitive-behavioral therapy for bulimia nervosa: Three-year follow-up results. Int J Eat Disorders 33;127-35.

Channon S, de Silva P, Hemsley D, Perkins R. (1989) A contolled trial of cognitive-behavioural and behavioural treatment of anorexia nervosa. Behav Res Ther 27:529-35.

Claudino AM, Hay P, Lima MS, Bacaltchuk J, Schmidt U, Treasure J. (2006) Antidepressants for anorexia nervosa. Cochrane Database Syst Rev. 25(1):CD004365.

Cooper P. (1995) Bulimia nervosa and Binge Eating: A guide to recovery London: Robinson Press.

Crisp AH, Norton K, Gowers S, Bowyer C, Yeldham D, Levett G, Bhat A. (1991) A controlled study of the effect of therapies aimed at adolescent and family psychopathology in anorexia nervosa. Br J Psychiatry 159:325-33.

Crow SJ, Peterson CB. (2003) The economic and social burden of eating disorders: A review. In Eating Disordes. ED Maj M, Halmi K, Lopez-Ibor JJ, Sartorius N. John Wiley and Sons , pp 384-423.

Dare C, Crowther C. (1995) Living dangerously: psychoanalytic psycho-therapy of anorexia nervosa. In: Szmulker G, Dare C, Treasure J, editor(s). Handbook of Eating Disorders: Theory, treatment and research. Chichester: John Wiley and Sons, 125-139.

Dare C, Eisler I, Russell G, Treaure J, Dodge L. (2001) Psychological therapies for adults with anorexia nervosa. Br J Psychiatry 178: 216-21.

Dolan B. Gitzinger I. (1994) Why women? Gender issues and eating disorders. London: The Athlone Press.

Doll HA, Petersen SE, Stewart-Brown SL. (2005) Eating disorders and emotional and physical well-being: Associations between student self-reports of eating disorders and quality of life as measured by the SF-36. Qual Life Res 14:705-17.

Eisler I, Dare C, Russell GF, Szmukler G, le-Grange D, Dodge E. (1997) Family and individual therapy in anorexia nervosa. A 5-year follow-up. Arch Gen Psychiatry 54: 1025-30.

Fairburn CG. (1995) Overcoming binge eating. New York, NY: Guilford Press.

Fairburn CG. (2005) Evidenced based treatment of anorexia nervosa. Int J Eat Disorders 37: S26-S30.

Fairburn C, Bohn K. (2005) Eating Disorder NOS (EDNOS): An example of the troublesome "Not otherwise Specified" (NOS) category in DSM-IV. Behav Res Ther 43:691-701.

Fairburn CG, Kirk J, O'Connor M, Cooper PJ. (1986) A comparison of two psycho-logical treatments for bulimia nervosa. Behav Res Ther 24:629-43.

Fairburn CG, Jones R, Peveler R, Carr SJ, Solomon RA, O'Connor ME et al. (1991) Three psychological treatments for bulimia nervosa: A comparative trial. Arch Gen Psychiatry 48: 463-9.

Fairburn CG, Marcus MD, Wilson GT. (1993) Cognitive behaviour therapy for binge eating and bulimia nervosa: A comprehensive treatment manual. In: Fairburn CG, Wilson GT, eds. Binge Eating: Nature, Assessment and Treatment. New York: Guildford Press, 361-404.

Fairburn CG, Cooper Z, Shafran R. (2003) Cognitive behaviour therapy for eating disorders: a "transdiagnostic" theory and treatment. Behav Res Ther. 41:509-28.

Fairburn CG, Shafran R, Cooper Z. (1999) A cognitive behavioural theory of anorexia nervosa. Behav Res Ther. 37:1-13.

Garner DM Garfinkel PE. (1997) Handbook of treatment for eating disorders. 2nd edition. New York: The Guilford Press.

Garner DM, Needleman LD. (1997) Sequencing and integration of treatments. In: Garner DM, Garfinkel PE, editor(s). Handbook of treatment for eating disorders. 2nd edition. New York: The Guilford Press, 50-66.

Garner DM, Vitousek KM, Pike KM. (1997) Cognitive-behavioural therapy for anorexia nervosa. In: Garner DM, Garfinkel PE, editor(s). Handbook of Treatments for Eating Disorders. 2nd edition. New York: The Guilford Press, 67-93.

Ghaderi A, Scott B. (2001) Prevalence, incidence and prospective risk factors for eating disorders. Acta Psych Scand 104: 122-130.

Goodsitt A. (1997) Eating Disorders: A self-psychological perspective. In: Garner DM, Garfinkel PE, editor(s). Handbook of Treatments for Eating Disorders. 2nd edition. New York: The Guilford Press,

205-228.

Gowers S, Bryant-Waugh R. (2004) Management of child and adolescent eating disorders: the current evidence base and future directions. J Child Psychol Psychiatry 45:63-83.

Gowers S, Norton K, Halek C, Crisp AH. (1994) Outcome of outpatient psychotherapy in a random allocation treatment study of anorexia nervosa. Int J Eat Disord 15:165-77.

Griffiths RA, Hadzi-Pavlovic D, Channon-Little L. (1994) A controlled evaluation of hypnobehavioural treatment for bulimia nervosa: Immediate Pre-Post Treatment effects. Europ Eating Disorders Rev 2: 202-20.

Griffiths RA, Hadzi-Pavlovic D, Channon-Little L. (1996) The short-term follow-up effect of hypnobehavioural and cognitive behavioural treatment for bulimia nervosa. Europ Eating Disorders Rev 4:12-31.

Grilo CM, Masheb RM. (2005) A randomized controlled comparison of guided self-help cognitive behavioural therapy and behavioural weight loss therapy for binge eating disorder. Beh Res Therapy 43:1509-25.

Grilo CM, Masheb RM, Wilson GT. (2005) Efficacy of cognitive behavioral therapy and fluoxetine for the treatment of binge eating disorder: a randomized double-blind placebo-controlled comparison. Biol Psychiatry 57:301-9.

Hall A, Crisp AH. (1987) Brief psychotherapy in the treatment of anorexia nervosa: outcome at one year. Br J Psychiatry 151:185-91.

Hay PJ. (2003) Quality of life and bulimic eating disorder behaviors. Int J Eat Disord 33: 434-42.

Hay PJ, Bacaltchuk J. (2005) Bulimia nervosa. Clin Evid 14: 834-845.

Hay PJ, Bacaltchuk J, Stefano, S. (2004) Psychotherapy for bulimia nervosa and binge eating. Cochrane Database Syst

Rev. 3:CD000562.

Hay P, Bacaltchuk J, Claudino A, Ben-Tovim D, Yong PY. (2003) Individual psychotherapy in the outpatient treatment of adults with anorexia nervosa. Cochrane Database Syst Rev. 4: CD003909.

Katzman MA, Lee S. (1997) Beyond body image: The integration of feminist and transcultural theories in the understanding of self-starvation. Int J Eat Disord. 22: 385-94.

Keel PK, Mitchell JE, Davis TL, Crow SJ. (2002) Long-term impact of treatment in women diagnosed with bulimia nervosa. Int J Eat Disord 31:151-8.

Le Grange D, Gorin A, Dymek M, Stone A. (2002) Does ecological momentary assessment improve cognitive behavioral therapy for Binge eating Disorder? A pilot study. Europ Eat Dis Rev 10:316-28.

Leitenberg H, Rosen J, Gross J, Nudelman S, Vara LS. (1998) Exposure plus response-prevention treatment of bulimia nervosa. J Consult Clin Psychol 56:535-41.

Lock J, le Grange D. (2005) Family based treatment of eating disorders Int J Eat Disord 37:S64-S67.

McIntosh VVW, Jordan J, Carter F, Luty SE, McKenzie JM, Bulik CM, Frampton CMA, Joyce PR. (2005) Three psychotherapies for anorexia nervosa: a randomized controlled trial. Am J Psychiatry 162: 741-7.

Meads C, Gold L, Burls A, Jobanputra P. (1999) In-patient versus out-patient care for eating disorders. DPHE Report no 17 University of Birmingham.

Molinari E, Baruffi M, Croci M, Marchi S, Petroni ML. (2005) Binge eating disorder in obesity: Comparison of different therapeutic strategies. Eat Weight Dis 10: 154-61.

Mond JM, Rodgers B, Hay PJ, Korten A, Owen C, Beumont PJV. (2004) Disability associated with community cases of commonly occurring eating disorders ANZ J Pub Health 28: 246-51.

Mitchell JE, Pyle RL,Eckert ED, Hatsukami D, Pomeroy C, Zimmerman R. (1990) A comparison study of antidepressants and structured intensive group psychotherapy in the treatment of bulimia nervosa. Arch Gen Psychiatry 47: 149-57.

National Institute for Clinical Excellence (NICE). (2004) Eating Disorders: Core interventions in the treatment and management of anorexia nervosa, bulimia nervosa and related disorders. Clinical Guideline number 9. London: NICE.

Nevonen L, Broberg AG (2005) A comparison of sequenced individual and group psychotherapy for eating disorder not otherwise specified Europ Eat Disord Rev 13:29-37.

Nevonen L, Broberg AG. (2006) A comparison of sequenced individual and group psychotherapy for patients with bulimia nervosa. Int J Eat Disord 39:117-27.

Palmer RL, Birchall H, McGrain L, Sullivan V. (2002) Self-help for bulimic disorders: a randomised controlled trial comparing minimal guidance with face-to-face or telephone guidance. Br J Psychiatry 181: 230-5.

Pendleton VR, Goodrick GK, Poston WSC, Reeves RS, Foreyt JP. (2002) Exercise augments the effects of cognitive-behavioural therapy in the treatment of bulimia nervosa. Int J Eat Disord 31:172-84.

Pike KM, Walsh BT, Vitousek K, Wilson GT, Bauer J. (2003) Cognitive behavior therapy in the posthospitalization treatment of anorexia nervosa. Am J Psychiatry 160:2046-9.

Prochaska, JO, DiClemente, CC, Norcross, JC. (1992) In search of how people change: Applications to addictive behaviors. Am Psychol 47:1102-14.

Robin AL, Gilroy M and Deniis AB. (1998) Treatment of eating disorders in children and adolescents. Clin Psychol Rev 18: 421-46.

Robin AL, Siegel PT, Moye AW, Gilroy M, Dennis AB, Sikand A. (1999) A controlled comparison of family versus individual therapy for adolescents with anorexia nervosa. J Am Acad Child Adolesc Psychiatry 38:1482-9.

Russell GF, Szmukler GI, Dare C, Eisler I. (1987) An evaluation of family therapy in anorexia nervosa and bulimia nervosa. Arch Gen Psychiatry 44:1047-56.

Safer DL, Telch CF, Agras WS. (2001) Dialectical behavior therapy for bulimia nervosa. Am J Psychiatry 158:632-4.

Schmidt U, Treasure T (1993) Getting Better BitE BitE: A Survival Kit for Sufferers of Bulimia Nervosa and Binge Eating Disorders. Psychology Press.

Stefano S, Bacaltchuk J, Blay S, Hay P. (2006, in press) Self-help treatments for disorders of recurrent binge eating: a systematic review. Acta Psychiatr Scand.

Stice E. (2002) Risk and maintenance factors for eating pathology: A meta-analytic review. Psychol Bull128:825-48.

Stice E, Killen JD, Hayward C, Taylor CB. (1998) Age of onset for binge eating and purging during late adolescence A 4-year survival analysis. J Abnorm Psychol 107:671-5.

Striegel-Moore RH. (1995) A feminist perspective on the etiology of eating disorders. In: Brownell KD, Fairburn CG, editor(s). Eating Disorder and Obesity. A comprehensive handbook. New York: The Guilford Press, 224-9.

Sundgot-Borgen J, Rosenvinge JH, Bahr R, Schneider L Sundgot. (2002) The effect of exercise, cognitive therapy, and nutritional counselling in treating bulimia nervosa. Med Sci Sports Exercise 34:190-5.

Touyz SW, Beumont, PJV, Glauin D, Phillipa T, Cowie I. (1984) A comparison of lenient and strict operant conditioning progarammes in refeeding patients with anorexia nervosa. Br J Psychiatry 144: 517-20.

Treasure J, Schmidt U. (2005) Anorexia nervosa. Clin Evid 13: 1148-57.

Treasure J, Todd G, Brolly M, Tiller J, Nehmed A, Denman F. (1995) A pilot study of a randomized trial of cognitive analytical therapy vs educational behavioural therapy for adult anorexia nervosa. Behav Res Ther 33:363-7

Treasure JL, Katzman M, Schmidt U. (1999) Engagement and outcome in the treatment of bulimia nervosa: first phase of a sequential design comparing motivation enhancement therapy and cognitive behavioural therapy. Behav Res Ther 37: 405-18.

Vitousek KM, Watson S, Wilson GT. (1998) Enhancing motivation for change in treatment resistant eating disorders. Clin Psychol Rev 18:391-420.

Ward A, Troop N, Todd G, Treasure J. (1996) To change or not to change - 'How' is the question? Br J Med Psychol 69:139-46.

Wilfley DE, Agras WS, Telch CF, Rossiter EM, Schneider JA, Cole AG, Sifford LA, Raeburn SD. (1993) Group cognitive behavioural and group interpersonal psychotherapy for the nonpurging bulimic individual: a controlled comparison. J Consult Clin Psychol 61:296-305.

Wilfley DE, Welch RR, Stein RI, Spurrell EB, Cohen LR, Saelens BE, Dounchis JZ, Frank MA, Wiseman CV, Matt GE. (2002) A randomized comparison of group cognitive-behavioral therapy and group interpersonal psychotherapy for the treatment of overwieght individuals with binge-eating disorder. Arch Gen Psychiatry 59:713-21.

Williams C. (2003) New technologies in self-help: another effective way to get better? Eur Eat Disord Rev 11:170–82.

Wooley SC. (1995) Feminist influences on the treatment of eating disorders. In: Brownell KD, Fairburn CG, editor(s).

Eating Disorders and Obesity A comprehensive handbook. New York: The Guilford Press, 294-298.

World Health Organization (WHO). (1992) The ICD-10 Classification of Mental and Behavioural Disorders. Clinical descriptions and diagnostic guidelines. Geneva: WHO.

PRIMARY PREVENTION OF OBESITY

Nancy E. Sherwood and Robert W. Jeffery

INTRODUCTION

Obesity is a major public health problem in the United States. Increases in the prevalence of obesity over the last few decades have been dramatic in all age and social groups, heightening concern about health risks for children, adolescents, and adults (Center for Disease Control and Prevention, 2002a, 2002b; Kuczmarski et al., 1994; Mokdad et al., 1999; Must et al., 1999). Currently, over half of US adults and 15% of US children and adolescents are overweight and upward trends in prevalence show no sign of slowing (Center for Disease Control and Prevention, 2002a, 2002b). A continuation of current trends seems quite likely to lead to substantial increases in the number of people affected by obesity-related health conditions and in premature mortality (National Heart, Lung and Blood Institute, 1999; World Health Organization, 1997). Increased obesity is also likely to promote increases in psychosocial comorbidities, including binge eating disorder, depression, social bias, and discrimination (Falkner et al., 1999; Gortmaker et al., 1993; Marcus, 1993; Wadden and Stunkard, 1985). The economic burden of obesity is also sizeable. It adversely affects the costs of individual health care including obesity treatment and premature disability and death contribute to lost productivity (Oster et al., 1999; Thompson et al., 1998; Wolf and Colditz, 1996). Estimates of the total economic burden of obesity are as high as $100 billion per year (Wolf, 1998).

Given the alarming increase in obesity and the difficulty and cost of treating it, more and more attention is being paid to how it can be prevented. Although the field of obesity treatment has been making advances for over 30 years, research on obesity prevention is just emerging. The primary prevention of obesity is rapidly becoming a public health priority. It has been argued that prevention of weight gain may be easier, less costly and more effective than treating obesity after it has fully developed (World Health Organization, 1997). The goal of the chapter is to review the literature on primary prevention strategies for obesity and to discuss implications for future research in this area.

Although individuals are at risk for unhealthy weight gain at any point in their lives, several risk periods for excessive weight gain have specifically been identified and discussed: early adolescence, young adulthood (25 to 34 years of age), and for women, pregnancy and menopause (Obarzanek and Pratt, 2003; Wing, 1998). Additionally, certain population sub-groups have been identified as at particularly high risk for obesity and thus in need of preventive services (e.g., American Indians, African American females) (Cabellaro et al., 1998; Obarzanek and Pratt, 2003). This review focuses on intervention studies that have sought to prevent obesity by improving eating behavior and/or activity patterns. It includes prevention programs that have been conducted across different age and cultural groups. To identify obesity prevention studies, we conducted a computerized search of English-language peer-reviewed literature (in MEDLINE), searched our own files, consulted with colleagues, and searched the references of identified papers. Four studies with adults and ten studies with children or adolescents were identified. The review is restricted to studies in which prevention of obesity or weight gain was the specific goal and that utilized randomization to treatment and comparison groups. Studies are overviewed in Table 1.

Children and Adolescents

Primary prevention of obesity in childhood and adolescence is a critical need. Childhood-onset obesity is related to an increased likelihood of obesity later in life. The likelihood of persistence of obesity from childhood to adulthood is related to the degree and duration of obesity, family adiposity and age of the child. A recent study that tracked 854 infants over 21-29 years found that among obese 6 year olds about 50% remained obese. However, by the age of 10-14 years, 80% of obese children with at least one obese parent remained obese (Whitaker et al., 1997). Although obesity-associated morbidities occur most frequently in adults, consequences of excess weight, such as type 2 diabetes, are now occurring with greater frequency among obese adolescents (Fagot-Campagna et al., 2000). Obesity prevention programs for youth that have been conducted in both school and community-based settings are reviewed.

School-based Obesity Prevention Programs

Schools have the potential to make valuable contributions to the prevention of childhood obesity. More than 95% of youth, ages 5-17 are enrolled in school, and no other institution has as much continuous and intensive contact with children during their first two decades of life. The availability of classroom health education, physical education programs, food service, health services, and family contact make schools an attractive target for providing obesity interventions in a comprehensive manner. Although a number of school-based health promotion interventions have been conducted that focus on reduction of risk for cardiovascular disease (Nader et al., 1999), or on promoting healthy eating (Baranowski et al., 2000) and physical activity (Sallis et al., 1997), the small number of school-based studies that have focused specifically on obesity prevention are reviewed here.

Pathways

Across both genders and the age span, American Indians have a high prevalence of obesity and obesity-related health problems (Story et al., 2001). Pathways was a multisite school-based study designed to reduce the prevalence of obesity in American Indian school children (Cabellaro et al., 1998). Pathways was based on a partnership between five universities and seven American Indian communities: Gila River Indian Community, Tohono O'odham (University of Arizona); White Mountain Apache, San Carlos Apache (Johns Hopkins University); Oglala Lakota, Sicangu Lakota (University of Minnesota); and Navajo (University of New Mexico). Forty-one schools were randomized to either intervention (n = 21) or control (n = 20) conditions. Four integrated intervention components delivered in grades 3 through 5 included a classroom curriculum, school food service, physical activity, and family component. The classroom curriculum consisted of culturally appropriate lessons that focused on promoting healthful, low-fat eating behaviors, and increasing physical activity. The lessons were presented to each intervention school via two 45-minute sessions per week for a 12-week period during each school year. The school food service component involved working with food service staff to lower the amount of fat in breakfast and lunch meals to no more than 30% of total. The physical activity component included modifications in the frequency and quality of physical education classes (e.g., a minimum of three 30-minute sessions per week), the introduction of classroom activity breaks, and encouragement of active play during recess periods. The family intervention component included take-home materials for families and family gatherings at a school. After 3 years, no significant differences in the primary outcome variable (percent body fat) were observed (Lohman et al., 2001).

Table 1. Description of obesity prevention studies and major outcomes

Study Name	Study Type and Population	Intervention Description	Major Outcomes
Pathways Lohman et al., 2001; Himes et al., 2001; Going et al., 2001	Multi-site, group randomized trial 1: 21 schools 2: 20 schools from seven American Indian Communities	1: 3-year, multi-component intervention (e.g., classroom curriculum, school food service, physical activity, and family components) delivered in grades 3-5. 2: Control	No significant effect for BMI or PBF at 3 years. There were reductions in school service fat calories and child-reported fat intake.
Planet Health Gortmaker et al., 1999	Group randomized trial 1: 5 schools 2: 5 schools	1: 2-year, multidisciplinary (e.g., language arts, math, science and social studies), multi-component (e.g., classroom curriculum, physical activity, fitness funds) intervention 2: Control	**Obesity prevalence among girls at 2 years:** 1: 20.3%, 2: 23.7%, p< .03 **Greater remission of obesity among girls at 2 years:** 1: 31.5%, 2: 19.1%, p < .04
Robinson et al., 1999	Randomized trial 1: 1 school 2: 1 school	1: 6-month, 18-lesson classroom curriculum to reduce TV, videotape, and videogame use. 2: Control	At 6 months, **Decreased BMI:** 1. 18.7 (3.8), 2: 18.8 (3.8), p <.002 **Decreased Triceps skinfold thickness:** 1. 15.5 (6.0), 2: 16.5 (5.3), p < .002 **Decreased Waist circumference:** 1: 63.6 (9.0), 2: 64.7 (8.9) , p < .001 **Decreased Waist to hip ratio:** 1:0.83 (0.06), 2:0.84 (0.05), p <.001 There were also significant decreases in TV watching.
Dance for Health Flores et al., 1995	Randomized trial 1: 43 students 2: 38 students	1: 12-week "Dance for Health" physical activity curriculum (3 times per week) and health education curriculum (2 times per week) 2: Control	Decrease in BMI among girls at 12 weeks: 1: 22.1 (6.0), 2: 22.5 (4.4) , p < .05
Stolley and Fitzgibbon 1997	Randomized trial of African American girls and their mothers 1: 32 2: 33	1: 11-week culturally-tailored intervention based on the "Know Your Body" Program 2: Control	No significant differences in BMI were found. Intervention girls reported lower percent of calories from fat compared to control girls
GO GIRLS! Resnicow et al. 2000	Uncontrolled trial 1: 57 overweight, adolescent African American girls	1: 6-month culturally tailored program with three components: 1) interactive educational/behavioral sessions; 2) physical activity (e.g., dance); 3) Food preparation	No significant BMI, PBF, physical activity, or dietary intake differences between "high" and "low" attenders.

Study Name	Study Type and Population	Intervention Description	Major Outcomes
GEMS: Baylor Baranowski et al. (2003)	Randomized trial of 8 year old African American girls 1: 19 2: 16	1: 12-week program including a 4-week summer day camp followed by an 8-week Internet component for girls and their parents 2: 4-week Control summer day camp and 8-week general health Internet component for girls and their parents	No significant BMI, dietary intake or physical activity differences
GEMS: Stanford Robinson et al. (2003)	Randomized trial of 8-10 year old African American girls 1: 28 2: 33	1: 12-week program including dance classes offered five days per week and a home-based media use reduction program 2: Health Education program to promote healthful diet and physical activity including monthly community health lectures and newsletters	No significant BMI, dietary intake or physical activity differences
GEMS: Minnesota Story et al. (2003)	Randomized trial of 8-10 year old African American girls 1: 26 2: 28	1: 12-week program including a two day per week after school program with physical activity and nutrition components and a family-based component 2: Monthly Saturday morning program focused on self-esteem and cultural enrichment	No significant BMI, dietary intake or physical activity differences
GEMS: Memphis Beech et al. (2003)	Randomized trial of 8-10 year old African American girls 1: 21 child-targeted 2: 21 parent-targeted 3: 18	1: 12-week program targeting children, weekly 90 minute sessions focused on physical activity and nutrition. 2: 12-week program targeting parents, weekly 90 minute sessions focused on physical activity and nutrition. 3: : Monthly program meetings designed to enhance and prevent declines in self-esteem	No significant BMI. or physical activity differences. Girls in the parent-targeted intervention reported consuming fewer sweetened beverages compared to control girls.

Study Name	Study Type and Population	Intervention Description	Major Outcomes
Pound of Prevention-Pilot Forster et al. (1988)	Randomized trial 1: 110 2: 109	1: 12-month intervention including monthly newsletters, financial incentives and an optional 4-session education course 2: Control	**Decrease in weight at 1 year:** 1: -2.1 lbs (0.6), 2: -0.3 lbs (0.6), p < .03
Pound of Prevention Jeffery and French (200)	Randomized trial 1: 197 Education Only 2: 198 Education Plus Lottery 3: 414	1: 3-year intervention including monthly newsletters, optional in-person and home-based activities 2: 3-year intervention including monthly newsletters, optional in-person and home-based activities, and financial incentives 3: Control	No significant weight, dietary intake or physical activity differences.
Klem et al. (2000)	Randomized trial 1: 33 Group 2: 32 Correspondence 3: 37	1: 10-week intervention with weekly group meetings 2: 10-week intervention with weekly mailed lessons 3: Control	**Decrease in weight at 10-weeks between Group and Control:** 1: -1.9[a] kg. (1.8), 2: -1.1 [a,b] (2.1), 3: -0.2[a] (1.3). p < .03. No significant weight differences were observed at 6-month follow-up.
Women's Healthy Lifestyle Project Kuller et al. (2001)	Randomized trial 1: 260 2: 275	1: 5-year cognitive-behavioral program including 10 weekly sessions, 5 biweekly sessions, 3 bimonthly group meetings and group, mail or phone contact every 2-3 months 2: Control	**Decrease in weight at 6, 18, 30, 42, and 54 month follow-up:** 6 months, 1: -10.7 lbs, 2: -0.5 lbs, p < .05 18 months, 1: -6.7 lbs, 2: -0.6 lbs, p < .05 30 months, 1: -4.7 lbs, 2: +2.1 lbs, p < .05 42 months, 1: -2.2 lbs, 2: +3.6 lbs, p < .05 54 months, 1: -0.2 lbs, 2: +5.2 lbs, p < .05

Abbreviations: BMI=body mass index, PBF=percent body fat,

However, the Pathways intervention was effective at reducing fat calories in the school food service, and the reported fat intake among participants (Himes et al., 2001). Promising trends for physical activity increases in the intervention schools were observed (Going et al., 2001).

Planet Health

Planet Health was a school-based health behavior intervention program designed to reduce the prevalence of obesity among youth in grades 6-8 (Gortmaker et al., 1999). Ten schools were randomized to either intervention (n = 5) or control (n = 5) conditions. The interdisciplinary intervention took place over a 2-year period. Planet Health sessions focused on four behavioral changes: reducing television viewing to less than 2 hours a day, increasing moderate and vigorous physical activity, decreasing consumption of high fat foods, and increasing consumption of fruits and vegetables to five a day or more. A unique aspect of Planet Health was its interdisciplinary curriculum approach. The intervention material was integrated into instruction for traditional subject areas (i.e., language arts, math, science and social studies) and physical education classes. Each intervention school received the Planet Health program of teacher training workshops, classroom lessons, physical education materials, wellness sessions and fitness funds. Each year, the four behavioral goals were addressed in one lesson per major subject area, so that a total of 16 core lessons were taught per year. An additional lesson developed a 2-week school-wide "Power Down" campaign to reduce television viewing at home. The physical education component of the curriculum included thirty 5-minute microunits during each school year. Physical education materials included student self-assessment and goal setting related to both inactivity and activity. Students were encouraged to replace inactive time with moderate and vigorous activity. Monetary incentives of $400 to $600 were made available to teachers in intervention schools who submitted proposals for student activities consistent with Planet Health themes. Two-year outcome evaluation of the Planet Health program was promising. A gender difference in the effectiveness of the intervention was noted, with girls responding more positively than boys. Obesity prevalence among girls in the control schools increased from 21.5% to 23.7% over the 2-year intervention period, while obesity prevalence among girls in the intervention schools decreased from 23.6% to 20.3%. Controlling for baseline levels of obesity, the prevalence of obesity among girls

in the intervention schools was reduced compared to girls in the control schools (OR = 0.47, 95% CI = 0.24-0.93, p < .03). Additionally, greater remission of obesity among girls in the intervention schools compared to the control schools was observed (OR = 2.16, 95% CI = 1.07-4.35, p < .04). Examination of changes in the behavioral targets revealed that reductions in television viewing were associated with decreases in obesity among the girls; a similar effect was not reported for boys.

School-based Media Use Reduction

Robinson (1999) conducted a randomized controlled trial to examine the effects of a school-based intervention focused on reducing television, videotape and video game use on changes in adiposity, physical activity and dietary intake in third and fourth grade children. One school received the intervention and one school served as the control group. The intervention consisted of an 18 lesson, 6-month classroom curriculum to reduce media use.

Key intervention components included: self-monitoring of media use, a 10-day "TV Turn-Off" period, encouragement of limiting media use to 1 hour per day, parent newsletters, and "TV allowance" gadgets in each home that allowed parents to control the total amount of television access time per week. Children were also encouraged to become selective viewers of the media and advocates for reduced media use. Six-month outcome data showed that children in the intervention school showed significant relative decreases in body mass index (BMI; Adjusted change=-0.45, CI=-0.73 to -0.17, p < .002), tricep skin-fold thickness (Adjusted change=-1.47, CI=-2.41 to -0.54, p < .002), waist circumference (Adjusted change=-2.30, CI=-3.27 to -1.33, p < .001), and waist-to-hip ratios (Adjusted change=-0.02 (-0.03 to -0.01) compared to children in the control school. Statistically significant decreases in children's reported TV watching and meals eaten in front of the TV were observed in the intervention group relative to the controls. No significant differences between the two schools, however, were observed for changes in high fat food intake, moderate-to-vigorous physical activity, or fitness.

Dance for Health

Dance for Health (Flores, 1995) was a 12-week school-based intervention program designed to maintain or decrease weight and increase physical activity among low-income African American and Hispanic students. Forty-three students were randomized to Dance for Health and 38 to usual physical activity. Those in the intervention class received a health education curriculum twice a week and a mandatory dance oriented physical education class three times a week. The dance curriculum included 40 minutes for moderate-to-high intensity dance to culturally appealing, student chosen music, and 10 minutes for warm-up and cool down. The 25-session health education component addressed nutrition, exercise, obesity, unhealthy weight practices smoking prevention, substance abuse, stress management, and peer pressure. The 30-minute sessions included 10 minutes of didactics and 20 minutes of more interactive activities. Outcome evaluations were more promising for girls compared to boys. Girls in the intervention group had a significantly greater change in BMI compared to girls in the control group (intervention girls, -0.8 % change; control girls, +0.3% change).

Community-based Obesity Prevention Studies

Although the majority of health promotion programs for children have been provided in school settings, community-based programs represent untapped potential for obesity prevention interventions (Yung and Hammond, 1997). Although the school

environment confers many advantages including the reduction of barriers of cost and transportation and the provision of access to a large, already assembled population, schools may be limited in their ability to focus on culturally unique needs and characteristics because they typically serve children of different ethnic and cultural backgrounds. In contrast, many community-based health and social service organizations primarily serve one ethnic minority group and have positive reputation and connections in the community (Isaacs and Benjamin, 1991). Given the advantage community-based programs have in tailoring interventions for specific cultural groups, to date, community-based obesity prevention programs described in the literature have been targeted towards African American girls who are at particularly high risk for obesity and associated health consequences.

Obesity Prevention for African American Girls

Stolley and Fitzgibbon (1997) conducted the first published community-based obesity prevention study for African American girls. Participants were 65 African American girls and their mothers who lived in the inner city of Chicago and attended a local tutoring program. Interested mothers and daughters were randomized to either the treatment or attention placebo control group. Upon completion of baseline assessments, the groups attended separate one-hour program sessions for an 11-week period. The culturally tailored intervention program, based on the Know Your Body Program, focused on adopting a low-fat, low-calorie diet and increased physical activity. Key culturally-tailored components of the intervention included: 1) incorporating parental participation; 2) holding the program at the tutoring site for easy access and safety; 3) incorporating participants' food preferences and ease of access to specific foods into the dietary change component of the program; 4) using culturally relevant music and dance for intervention activities; and 5) using appropriate materials from magazines geared towards African Americans. Although no treatment effects on BMI were reported, results showed significant differences between the treatment and control mothers for daily saturated fat intake and percentage of calories from fat. Daughters in the treatment group also reported lower percent calories from fat relative to girls in the control group.

GO GIRLS!

GO GIRLS! was a pilot, community-based, nutrition and physical activity program designed for inner city, overweight African American girls (Resnicow et al., 2000). Participants were overweight (BMI $\geq 85^{th}$ percentile for age and sex), 11 to 17 year-old African American girls who were recruited through public housing developments. Given the developmental nature of the program, no control group was included. The 6-month program included biweekly group sessions for the first 4 months and weekly sessions for the last 2 months. Each session included three components: 1) an interactive educational or behavioral session focused on program goals; 2) 30 to 60 minutes of physical activity (e.g., Hip Hop, Funk and "Afrobics" aerobic dance); and 3) preparation and tasting of low-fat, portion-controlled recipes (e.g., low-fat macaroni and cheese, oven "fried" chicken). Results showed that girls who were classified as "high attenders" (e.g., girls who attended at least half of the sessions) reported lower total energy and percentage of energy intake from fat at follow-up compared to "low attenders" although these differences were not statistically significant. No statistically significant differences between "high" and "low" attenders were observed for measures of physical activity, BMI, and percent body fat.

Girls health Enrichment Multi-site Studies (GEMS)

Phase I of GEMS was a National Heart, Lung, and Blood Institute-sponsored multicenter research program to develop and test 12-week pilot interventions to prevent excessive weight gain in 8 to 10 year old African-American girls (Obarzanek and Pratt, 2003). The GEMS initiative was funded given the lack of available information regarding what types of interventions, delivery channels and settings, and intervention messages would be most effective for preventing obesity in African American girls. Four field centers participating in GEMS (University of Memphis, University of Minnesota, Baylor College of Medicine, and Stanford University) independently developed and tested their own interventions but shared common eligibility criteria and key measurements. Since the pilot studies had a relatively short intervention period of 12 weeks and include small numbers of girls, they were not powered to detect statistically significant differences in weight, diet and activity outcomes. However, the descriptions of the programs and results provide valuable information in this developing area of research.

The Baylor GEMS Pilot Study: The Fun, Food and Fitness Project (Baranowski et al., 2003).

Thirty-five 8-year-old African American girls and their parents or caregivers were randomly assigned to the treatment (n = 19) or control (n = 16) condition. Intervention goals were as follows: 1) increase girls' fruit and vegetable consumption; 2) increase girls' intake of water; and 3) increase girls' participation in moderate to vigorous physical activity to 60 minutes per day. The intervention condition included a four-week summer day camp followed by an 8-week Internet intervention component for girls and their parents. The intervention day camp included training in dance, educational games to increase physical activity and fruit and vegetable intake, snack recipe preparation, goal setting, buddy groups, and the use of camp cheers as mnemonics for decision making, problem-solving and asking behaviors. The intervention websites for girls and parents featured a different message each week (e.g., fun physical activity at home, choosing fruits and vegetables for snacks). The girls intervention website featured a comic book with characters who attended the GEMS summer camp and were trying to obtain the diet and activity goals, problem solving activities, review of goal attainment for the previous week's goal, opportunities to set new goals, a photo album of girls from camp, an "ask the expert" feature, and linkages to websites that might be of interest to girls. The intervention parent web-site mirrored the girl website and included a comic book featuring parent/child interactions that modeled desired parenting behaviors, a parent poll of how best to encourage lifestyle changes, goal-setting activities, recipes, an "ask the expert" feature, and links to other websites, including the girls' website. The control condition included a "usual" 4-week summer day camp followed by an 8-week Internet program that asked girls to log-on once a month and provided links to general health and homework websites. The control parent website offered links to the girls' website as well as other websites with information on general health issues. Results showed no significant differences in BMI either at the end of the summer camp or at the end of the 12-week intervention period. However, at the end of the summer camp, there was a trend for lower BMI among the heavier girls in the intervention group compared to the heavier girls in the control group. Although trends were in the hypothesized direction, no significant treatment group differences were observed for physical activity or dietary intake behaviors.

The Stanford GEMS Pilot Study (Robinson et al., 2003)

Sixty-one 8 to 10 year old African American girls and their parents or caregivers were randomly assigned to the treatment (n = 28) or control (n = 33) condition. Intervention goals were to increase time spent in moderate-to-vigorous physical activity and to decrease time spent engaging in sedentary activity. GEMS Jewels dance classes were offered 5 days per week at three neighborhood community centers. Girls were encouraged to attend the dance classes as often as possible during the 12-week intervention period. Each daily session lasted for up to 2.5 hours (3:30 to 6:00 p.m.), beginning with a one-hour homework period and a healthful snack followed by 45 to 60 minutes of moderate-to-vigorous dance. Classes included traditional African dance, Hip-Hop, and Step. Each session ended with a 30-minute GEMS talk that focused on the meaning and importance of dance in the girls' lives and the African-American community and culture. Additional activities included costume creation, videotaping, and performances for families and friends. Female African American college students and recent college graduates with dance expertise led the sessions. The START (Sisters Taking Action to Reduce Television) intervention included five lessons delivered during home visits over the 12-week intervention period. A female African-American intervention specialist scheduled lesson times with each family and delivered the intervention to the participating girl and other family members who were available. The strategies promoted for reducing television viewing included nonselective reductions in total hours and/or access to television; selective reductions by day, time, context, or content; and displacement of viewing time with other activities (e.g., dance). Specific behaviors included self-monitoring, a 2-week TV-turnoff, and budgeting viewing hours. The lessons incorporated African and African-American history and cultural themes. Families were also given electronic TV time managers to help with budgeting TV time (TV Allowance, Miami, FL). Additionally, five newsletters were mailed to parents/guardians to reinforce the lessons and communicate updates on dance class activities. Girls and families randomized to the control group received a state-of-the-art information-based health education program that focused on promoting healthful diet and activity patterns. The control intervention included monthly community health lectures delivered by volunteers from the African-American task forces of the local chapters of the American Heart Association and the American Diabetes Association and 11 "Felicia's Healthy News Flash" newsletters mailed to girls and 5 "Stanford GEMS Health Report" newsletters mailed to parents. Newsletter content focused on reducing risks for obesity, heart disease, stroke, hypertension, and diabetes and included age-appropriate and culturally targeted educational materials from federal health agencies. Results showed that, although not statistically significant, there was a trend for girls in the intervention group to have a lower BMI at follow-up compared to girls in the control group. Nonsignificant trends for lower waist circumference; increased after-school physical activity; and reduced television, videotape, and video game were also observed. The treatment group significantly reduced reported household television viewing and dinners eaten while watching television.

The Minnesota GEMS Pilot Study: An After-School Obesity Prevention Program
(Story et al., 2003)

Fifty-four 8 to 10 year old African American girls and their parents or caregivers were randomly assigned to the treatment (n = 26) or control (n = 28) condition. Girls in the intervention group participated in a 12-week after-school program called "Girlfriends for KEEPS," where KEEPS stood for Keys to Eating, Exercising, Playing, and Sharing. Intervention goals included: 1) increasing frequency of participation in sustained, moderate-to-vigorous intensity activities; 2) decreasing time spent in sedentary activities; 3) promoting enjoyment, physical competence, and self confidence in a range of physical activities; 4) decreasing consumption of high-fat foods; 5) increasing consumption of fruits and vegetables; 6) decreasing consumption of sweetened beverages; and 7) adopting healthy weight-related eating practices (e.g., portion size awareness, eating when hungry). Intervention meetings, designed in a "club meeting" format, were held twice a week for one hour after school at each of the three elementary schools. The intervention was taught by trained African-American GEMS staff. Club activities were comprised of fun, culturally appropriate, interactive, hands-on activities that emphasized skill building and practice of the particular health behavior message for that week. Weekly messages included drinking water more often than soda pop, increasing the consumption of fruits and vegetables, drinking low-fat milk, selecting low-fat foods for snacks, eating smaller portions of snacks, choosing smaller-sized and lower-fat entrees in fast food restaurants, increasing physical activity, watching less television, and enhancing self-esteem. A healthful snack, sometimes prepared by the girls, was offered at each club meeting. Girls participated in physical activity for a minimum of 20 minutes during each session. A variety and choice of activities were included such as dancing (ethnic, hip hop, aerobic), double-dutch jump rope, relay races, tag, and step aerobics. To keep girls' interest and participation, incentives were built into the program for attendance, setting short-term goals, and completing activities. These included attendance beads that together made a bracelet by the end of the intervention, water bottles, pedometers, jump ropes, and t-shirts. The intervention also included a family component designed to reinforce and support the healthy eating and physical activity messages delivered in the after-school program. The family component included weekly family packets sent home to the parents, family night events, encouragement telephone calls to parents to reinforce and support diet and activity goals they set for their family, and organized neighborhood walks. Girls randomized to the control condition participated in the "GEMS Club", a non-nutrition/physical activity low-intensity program that focused on promoting positive self-esteem and cultural enrichment. Participants attended monthly Saturday morning meetings (three meetings during the 12-week period), which included arts and crafts, self-esteem activities, creating memory books, and a workshop on African percussion instruments. Result showed no significant treatment group differences in BMI upon completion of the 12-week intervention period. However, promising trends were noted with girls in the intervention group showing higher levels of physical activity relative to girls in the control group at the follow-up measurement.

The Memphis GEMS Pilot Study: Child- and Parent-Targeted Interventions (Beech et al., 2003)

Sixty 8 to 10 year old African American girls were randomized to one of three groups: 1) a child-targeted intervention program; 2) a parent/caregiver-targeted program; or 3) a control condition. The child- and parent-targeted interventions were similar, allowing for evaluation of two different approaches to obtain the same objectives. Intervention goals included: 1) choosing a nutritionally balanced eating plan, including the reduction of high-fat food intake (particularly fast foods); 2) increasing water consumption and reducing

sweetened beverage intake; 3) increasing fruit and vegetable intake; and 4) promoting nutrition-related healthy behaviors and the recognition of health-compromising behaviors such as eating while watching television, meal skipping, and snacking when not hungry; 5) increasing the frequency of moderate to vigorous physical activity; 6) decreasing the frequency of sedentary behaviors; and 7) promoting enjoyment and self-efficacy in physical activity. The child-targeted intervention entitled "GEMS Jamboree" included weekly 90-minute intervention sessions for 12 weeks. Program structure included the following: 1) an introduction consisting of a welcome and a discussion of the basic concepts for the day (15 minutes); 2) a "Movin' It" physical activity component (30 minutes); 3) a "Munchin' It" nutrition component (30 minutes); and 4) a "Taking it Home" segment (15 minutes) in which the concepts of the day were reviewed, incentives (small gifts) were given, and motivation for healthy eating and the maintenance of physical activity were provided. The primary activity for the physical activity component was hip-hop aerobics. The nutrition component included interactive strategies designed to promote the dietary intake goals (e.g., taste testing, food preparation, food art). The parent-targeted intervention entitled "Eating and Activity Skills for Youth" (EASY) also included weekly 90-minute intervention sessions during the 12-week period. Program structure included: 1) "EASY Moves", a dance-based physical activity component; 2) "EASY Tips", a didactic nutrition segment; and 3) "EASY Fun", a segment alternating food preparation and nutrition-related games. The weekly intervention concluded with a session used to reinforce key points and to provide take-home materials (i.e., healthy recipes and small thematic incentives related to the weekly concepts). Childcare was provided, with non-nutrition or physical activity-related activities designed for the 8 to 10 year old daughters. Girls randomized to the control group attended three monthly 90-minute sessions over the 12-week pilot study that focused on improving self-esteem. Control group activities included arts and crafts, "friendship-building"/social support-type activities (e.g., "trust" games), and enjoyable games. Personalized greeting cards and general health information were mailed to participants bimonthly to maintain contact and build rapport. Results showed that compared to girls in the comparison condition, girls in the active conditions combined showed a nonsignificant trend for reduced BMI and waist circumference. Statistically significant intervention effects were observed for sweetened beverages, with girls in the parent-targeted intervention consuming fewer sweetened beverages compared to girls in the control group. No significant treatment group effects were observed for the physical activity or other dietary intake variables.

Two field centers from GEMS Phase I, the University of Memphis and Stanford University, are currently evaluating 2-year obesity prevention interventions for pre-adolescent African American girls in full-scale randomized trials

Adulthood

Both normal weight and overweight individuals are at risk for weight gain during adulthood. Between the ages of 30 and 55 years, average weight gain per year among adults in the US is .5 to 1 kg (Williamson et al., 1991). Slowing this rate of weight gain may help reduce the population impact of obesity. Behavior changes required to achieve and maintain large weight losses are difficult for most people. However, the premise behind weight-gain prevention programs is that behavior changes needed to prevent or reverse small weight gains with age may be easier to sustain.

Pound of Prevention (POP)

The POP studies (Forster et al., 1988; Jeffery and French, 1997, 1999) were the first completed obesity prevention studies in adults. The POP program was based on the hypothesis that gradual weight gain in adults is due in large part to the fact that people are not very attentive or motivated to correct the small changes in weight that lead to obesity or the small changes in eating and exercise habits that could prevent these weight gains. The goal of the POP interventions were to encourage participants to make small changes in their eating and activity habits to prevent weight gain with age. In the initial POP study, 219 participants were randomized to either weight-gain prevention treatment or no treatment for a 1-year period. Participants in the treatment group received monthly newsletters relating to weight management, participated in a financial incentive system, and were offered an optional four-session education course in the sixth month of the program. Significant treatment effects for weight change were found. At 1-year follow-up, participants in the intervention group showed a new weight loss of 1.8 lb compared to participants in the control group. Moreover, 82% of the intervention participants maintained or lost weight compared to 56% of control group participants.

In the full-scale POP study, participants were randomized to one of three conditions: Control (n = 414), Education (n = 197) , or Education Plus Lottery (n = 198) (Jeffery and French, 1999). Participants in the two education groups received monthly newsletters for 3 years that focused on five program messages. Education messages included: 1) paying attention to weight by self-weighing ≥ 1 time per week; 2) eating two servings of fruit per day; 3) eating three servings of vegetables each day; 4) reducing intake of high-fat foods; and 5) walking three times a week for ≥ 20 minutes. Participants returned a prestamped postcard each month on which they recorded adherence to program messages and their current weight. Participants in the Education Plus Lottery condition were offered a $100 lottery drawing each month for members who returned their postcards. Once every 6 months, participants were invited to participate in additional intervention in-person and home-based activities. Activities included four-session weight control classes, aerobics classes, a correspondence weight-loss course, and a home-based walking "marathon" competition. Participants in the POP study were on average 38 years old and were primarily female. About half of the participants were married. The average BMI was about 26 in the control and education + incentive groups, but was 27.5 in the education only group. Of note, study population included 400 low-income participants recruited from low-income neighborhoods and WIC clinics.

Participants returned an average of 68% of the newsletter postcards across the 3-year intervention period. Upon completion of the study, 80% reported having read most or all of the newsletters. Twenty-five percent of the participants participated in ≥ 1 supplementary activity (e.g., POP marathon, weight-loss correspondence course). Of note, the supplementary correspondence options were considerably more popular than the in-person opportunities (Sherwood et al., 1998). The overall mean weight change observed in the study population over 3 years was a gain of 1.7 kg, approximately .5 kg per year. Sixty-three percent of participants gained weight whereas only 37% maintained or lost weight. Point estimates for weight gain were slightly lower in both intervention groups than in the control group at each year. However, these differences fell far short of statistical significance. No significant intervention group differences were observed for energy intake, fat intake, or exercise. Significant group differences were observed for self-weighing frequency and a healthy weight-loss

practice index that included behaviors such as increasing fruit and vegetable intake and increasing exercise that were promoted by the POP program. Although POP was not successful in achieving its primary objective, several aspects of the results were informative. Newsletter mailings were shown to be a cost-effective way of communicating with large numbers of people over an extended period of time. Favorable behavioral, knowledge, and weight trends in the intervention groups were encouraging.

Obesity Prevention for Women

Klem et al. (2000) evaluated the acceptability of three different formats for prevention of weight gain among 25 to 34 year old women. One hundred two recruited participants were randomly assigned to one of three treatment formats: a weekly group meeting focused on modest dietary and physical activity changes, a weekly correspondence course with similar content, and a no-treatment control group who received a lifestyle brochure. After participants were assigned to a treatment group, they were asked whether they were willing to participate in that treatment format. Participants who refused were omitted from the study. Although similar numbers of randomized women verbally agreed to participate in their assigned treatment, a greater percentage of women actively participated in the correspondence option. Program efficacy was assessed by examining weight change at posttreatment (10 weeks) and 6-month follow-up. Of the 55 women who participated in the measurement session at the end of the 10-week intervention, participants in the group format showed the largest short-term changes in weight (group format: mean = -1.9 kg, sd = 1.8; correspondence format: mean = -1.1 kg, sd = 2.1; and control group: mean = -0.2 kg, sd = 1.3; p < .03). At 6-month follow-up, however, no significant treatment group differences in weight loss were observed.

Women's Healthy Lifestyle Project

The Women's Healthy Lifestyle Project tested the hypothesis that reducing consumption of saturated fat and cholesterol by decreasing total and fat calories and moderately increasing physical activity among "healthy" women would prevent the rise in LDL cholesterol and weight gain during menopause (Kuller et al., 2001; Simkin-Silverman et al., 1998 ; Simkin-Silverman et al., 1995). The intensive phase of the intervention consisted of 10 weekly sessions and then biweekly sessions for an additional 10 weeks. The maintenance phase included 3 monthly group meetings; 3 bimonthly group meetings; and group, mail, or telephone contact every 2 to 3 months thereafter. Additionally, participants were invited to attend a 6-week refresher program and received quarterly newsletters. Social and educational gatherings were held two to three times per year. Intervention goals were as follows: 1) lower fat intake to 25% of daily calories; 2) lower saturated fat intake to 7%; 3) lower cholesterol to 100 mg/day; 4) increase level of moderate intensity physical activity; and 5) prevent future weight gain by achieving a modest weight loss in all participants. Normal weight participants with a BMI < 24.4 were given a 5-lb weight-loss goal, mildly overweight participants with a BMI 24.5 to 26.4 were given a 10-lb weight-loss goal, and moderately overweight participants with a BMI ≥ 26.5 were given a 15-lb weight-loss goal. Both groups attended follow-up visits at 6, 18, 30, 42, and 54 months. Attendance at the follow-up visits averaged 93%, with 95% returning for the 54-month assessment. Across all the time periods, there was a significant weight change difference between the intervention and comparison group. Among women in the comparison group who participated in the assessments only and received no intervention, weight remained stable initially and then the typical increases in weight over time were observed so that at the end of the study participants were on average 5 lb heavier. Women in the intervention group initially lost weight and then gradually gained weight over time. Due to the initial weight loss, however, at the end of the 54-month period, women in the intervention group were at about their baseline weight as opposed to 5 lb heavier.

SUMMARY AND RECOMMENDATIONS

The field of obesity prevention has emerged in response to the worsening obesity epidemic and the lack of long-term success of obesity treatment programs. It has been suggested that obesity prevention may be more effective than obesity treatment, however, work in this area is in the early stages and empirical data supporting this view are lacking. This chapter has reviewed several weight-gain prevention programs targeted towards youth, adults, and specific ethnic groups. Programs have been conducted in both school and community settings, have been generally well received by participants, and have shown positive behavior change trends. To date, outcome evaluations have not yielded consistent effects on BMI and obesity prevalence. Considerably more work needs to be done in the area of obesity prevention before conclusions can be made about its efficacy and definitive recommendations can be made about best practices. Given the current state of obesity prevention, we suggest preliminary recommendations, areas for further investigation, and challenges for the primary prevention of obesity.

Recruitment and Retention

Recruitment and retention of participants in obesity prevention trials is a critical first step toward reducing the prevalence of obesity. Obesity prevention programs must be tailored to the audience of interest and packaged in such a way as to be attractive and accessible to participants. The majority of obesity prevention programs published in the literature have been successful in recruiting and retaining participants. The most impressive long-term follow-up rate was observed in the Women's Healthy Lifestyle trial with 95% of participants completing a 54-month follow-up assessment (Kuller et al., 2001). Community-based programs targeting youth have also shown high retention rates, however, such programs have been short-term, ranging from 10 weeks to 6 months. Maintaining high levels of interest and participation among youth and families over longer periods of time may be challenging.

Recruitment messages for obesity prevention programs have ranged from emphasizing preventing weight gain specifically (Jeffery and French, 1999) to focusing on more general messages of promoting healthy eating and physical activity (Baranowski et al., 2003; Beech et al., 2003; Robinson et al., 2003; Story et al., 2003). Recruitment messages need to capture the attention of the audience of interest. Obesity prevention programs targeting youth must focus not only on the health benefits of participation, but also on the social benefits of taking part. Another key issue for obesity prevention programs is attracting a target audience of normal weight adult participants. Participants in weight-gain prevention programs to date have tended to be heavier, with normal weight individuals less likely to participate. Since even normal weight adults are at risk for weight gain with age, strategies for attracting such participants to obesity programs are needed.

The optimal treatment modality for different audiences also needs further attention. Research with adults suggests a stronger preference for correspondence versus in-person programs (Klem et al., 2000;

Sherwood et al., 1998). Participants in the POP program were significantly more likely to take part in correspondence options compared to face-to-face program options. Klem et al. also reported that participants were more likely to take part in a correspondence program versus an in-person group program. However, short-term results suggested that participants in the in-person program lost more weight compared to those in the correspondence program. The efficacy of face-to-face programs may be enhanced by the greater accountability, structure, and support that is provided by this modality. Strategies for enhancing the intensity and effectiveness of correspondence programs are needed given their popularity and potential to reach a larger audience. A combination of initial face-to-face sessions and subsequent correspondence options as used in the Women's Healthy Lifestyle trial may be a viable option. Future weight-gain prevention efforts should focus on ways of increasing impact of correspondence contacts (e.g., tailoring of messages, increased frequency) and modalities for correspondence options (e.g., mail- or phone-based strategies, internet programs).

Intervention Goals

Refining intervention goals for obesity prevention is another key area for future investigation. Weight-gain prevention programs have tended to use strategies "inherited" from obesity treatment research. Diet-related intervention recommendations have included reductions in energy intake, fat intake and sweetened beverages, and increases in fruit and vegetable intake. Activity-related messages have included a focus on increasing time spent in moderate-to-vigorous physical activity and decreasing time spent in sedentary pursuits, primarily television viewing. An open question is whether weight-gain prevention strategies should be different from obesity treatment strategies, and, if so, in what ways should they be different?

The optimal specificity and intensity of obesity prevention messages deserves further investigation. The Pound of Prevention program included five messages: 1) paying attention to weight by self-weighing ≥ 1 time per week; 2) eating two servings of fruit per day; 3) eating three servings of vegetables each day; 4) reducing intake of high-fat foods; and 5) walking three times a week for ≥ 20 minutes (Jeffery and French, 1999). Although four of the five messages were quite specific, the message regarding reducing intake of high-fat foods was fairly general. Increasing the specificity of this message may have helped participants to better understand and adhere to program goals. For example, the Women's Healthy Lifestyle trial included specific recommendations about percent of calories from fat and saturated fat (Kuller et al., 2001).

In addition to greater specificity, obesity prevention messages may need to be more intense. An example of a more intense program goal could be the recommendation to lose weight as a weight-gain prevention strategy. Participants in the Women's Healthy Lifestyle trial were given a weight-loss goal depending upon their starting weight (Kuller et al., 2001). Evaluation data showed that women in the intervention group initially lost weight although they gradually gained weight over time. Due to the initial weight loss, however, at the end of the 54-month follow-up period, women in the intervention group were at about their baseline weight compared to women in the control group, who were approximately 5 lb heavier on average. These data suggest that modest weight-loss goals may be effective in preventing weight gain for as long as 5 years and are consistent with the results of two recent observational studies that have shown that weight losses of unknown cause over periods of 1 or 2 years are typically followed by weight regain, but that

there are net benefits relative to no weight loss lasting as long as 4 years (Field et al., 2001; Jeffery et al., 2002).

In addition to determining the optimal intensity and specificity of obesity prevention messages, more information is needed about what goals to include for which subgroups of individuals. Dietary intake goals in prevention programs have included recommendations about specific food groups (e.g., increases in fruit and vegetable intake, reductions in sweetened beverages, increases in water consumption) and macronutrient intake (e.g., reductions in fat intake). Obesity prevention programs may also need to include messages about total energy intake. Activity-related goals have included both increases in physical activity and decreases in sedentary behavior. Media use reduction appears to be a promising obesity prevention strategy among youth and should be explored as a strategy for adult populations. Weight-gain prevention programs also focus on behavioral strategies such as self-monitoring weight and teaching individuals to respond to small weight gains by making moderate behavioral changes such as increasing physical activity and/or decreasing caloric intake. Little information in known, however, about which of the above noted factors is most strongly associated with success in preventing excessive weight gain.

To summarize, challenges for obesity prevention programs include: 1) optimal recruitment and retention strategies and treatment modalities for different audiences; 2) increasing the intensity and specificity of program messages; 3) increasing the intensity and duration of programs; and 3) strategies for sustaining motivation for behavioral changes.

REFERENCES

Baranowski T, Baranowski J, Cullen KW, Thompson DI, Nicklas T, Zakeri IF, Rochon J. (2003) The Fun, Food and Fitness Project (FFFP): The Baylor

GEMS pilot study. Ethn Dis 13 (Suppl 1): S1-30-S1-39.

Baranowski T, Davis M, Resnicow K, Baranowski J, Doyle C, Lin LS, Smith M, Wang DT. (2000) Gimme 5 fruit and vegetables for fun and health: Outcome evaluation. Health Educ Behav 27:96-111.

Beech BM, Klesges RC, Kumanyika SK, Murray DM, Klesges L, McClanahan B, Slawson D, Nunnally C, Rochon J, McLain-Allen B, Pree-Cary J. (2003) Child- and parent-targeted interventions: The Memphis GEMS pilot study. Ethn Dis 13(Suppl 1): S1-40-S1-53..

Cabellaro B, Davis S, Davis CE, Ethelbah B, Evans M, Lohman T, Stephenson L, Story M, White J. (1998) Pathways: A school-based program for the primary prevention of obesity in American Indian children. J Nutr Biochem 9: 535-543.

Centers for Disease Control and Prevention (2002a). Prevalence of overweight among children and adolescents: United States, 1999-2000. Accessed on 1/15/03: http://www.cdc.gov/nchs/products/pubs/pubd/hestats/overwght99.htm

Centers for Disease Control and Prevention (2002b) Prevalence of overweight and obesity among adults: United States, 1999-2000. Accessed on 1/15/03: http://www.cdc.gov/nchs/products/pubs/pubd/hestats/obese/obse99.htm

Fagot-Campagna A, Pettitt DJ, Engelgau MM, Burrows NR, Geiss LS, Valdez R, Beckles GL, Saaddine J, Gregg EW, Williamson DF, Venkat Narayan KM. (2000) Type 2 diabetes among North American children and adolescents: An epidemiologic review and a public health perspective. J Pediatr 136:664-672.

Falkner NH, French SA, Jeffery RW, Neumark-Sztainer D, Sherwood NE, Morton N. (1999) Mistreatment due to weight: Prevalence and sources of perceived mistreatment in women and men. Obes Res 7:572-576.

Field AE, Wing RR, Manson JE, Spiegelman DL, Willett WC. (2001) Relationship of a large weight loss to long-term weight change among young and middle-aged US women. Int J Obes Relat Metab Disord 25:1113-1121.

Flores R. (1995) Dance for health: Improving fitness in African American and Hispanic adolescents. Public Health Rep 110:189-193.

Forster JL, Jeffery RW, Schmid TL, Kramer FM. (1988) Preventing weight gain in adults: A Pound of Prevention. Health Psychol 7:515-525.

Going SB, Stone E, Harnack L, Thompson J, Norman J, Stewart D, Corbin C, Hastings C, Eklund J; The Pathways Collaborative Research Group. (2001) The effects of the Pathways Obesity Prevention Program on physical activity in American Indian school children. Fed Am Soc Experi Biol 15:abstract 836.4.

Gortmaker SL, Must A, Perrin JM, Sobol AM, Dietz WH. (1993) Social and economic consequences of overweight in adolescence and young adulthood [see comments]. N Engl J Med 329:1008-1012.

Gortmaker SL, Peterson K, Wiecha J, Sobol AM, Dixit S, Fox MK, Laird N. (1999) Reducing obesity via a school-based interdisciplinary intervention among youth: Planet Health. Arch Pediatr Adolesc Med 153:409-418.

Himes JH, Cunningham-Sabo L, Gittelsohn J, Harnack L, Ring K, Suchindran C, Thompson J, Weber J; The Pathways Collaborative Research Group. (2001) Impact of the Pathways intervention on dietary intake of American Indian school children. Fed Am Soc Experi Biol 15:abstract 836.3.

Isaacs M, Benjamin M. (1991) Toward a Culturally Competent System of Care: Programs which Utilize Culturally Competent Principles, II. Washington,

DC: CASSP Technical Assistance Center, Center for Child Health and Mental Health Policy, Georgetown University Child Development Center.

Jeffery RW, French SA. (1997) Preventing weight gain in adults: Design, methods and one year results from the Pound of Prevention study. Int J Obes Relat Metab Disord 21:457-464.

Jeffery RW, French SA. (1999) Preventing weight gain in adults: The Pound of Prevention study. Am J Public Health 89:747-751.

Jeffery RW, McGuire MT, French SA. (2002) Prevalence and correlates of large weight gains and losses. Int J Obes Relat Metab Disord 26:969-972.

Klem ML, Viteri JE, Wing RR. (2000) Primary prevention of weight gain for women aged 25-34: The acceptability of treatment formats. Int J Obes Relat Metab Disord 24:219-225.

Kuczmarski RJ, Flegal KM, Campbell SM, Johnson CL. (1994) Increasing prevalence of overweight among US adults: The National Health and Nutrition Examination Surveys, 1960-1991. JAMA 272:205-211.

Kuller LH, Simkin-Silverman LR, Wing RR, Meilahn EN, Ives DG. (2001) Women's Healthy Lifestyle Project: A randomized clinical trial: Results at 54 months. Circulation 103:32-37.

Lohman TG, Going S, Stewart D, Cabellaro B, Stevens J, Himes J, Weber J, Thompson J, Davis E, Norman J; The Pathways Collaborative Research Group. (2001) The effect of Pathways Obesity Prevention Study on body composition in American Indian children. Fed Am Soc Experi Biol 15:abstract 836.9.

Marcus M. (1993) Binge eating in obesity. In: Binge Eating, Nature, Assessment, and Treatment (Fairburn CG, Wilson GT, eds), pp 77-96. New York, NY: Guilford Press.

Mokdad AH, Serdula MK, Dietz WH, Bowman BA, Marks JS, Koplan JP. (1999) The spread of the obesity epidemic in the United States, 1991-1998. JAMA 282:1519-1522.

Must A, Spadano J, Coakley EH, Field AE, Colditz G, Dietz WH. (1999) The disease burden associated with overweight and obesity. JAMA 282: 1523-1529.

Nader PR, Stone EJ, Lytle LA, Perry CL, Osganian SK, Kelder S, Webber LS, Elder JP, Montgomery D, Feldman HA, Wu M, Johnson C, Parcel GS, Luepker RV. (1999) Three-year maintenance of improved diet and physical activity: The CATCH cohort. Arch Pediatr Adolesc Med 153:695-704.

National Heart, Lung and Blood Institute. (1999) Clinical guidelines on the identification, evaluation, and treatment of overweight and obesity in adults. Bethesda, MD: NIH, NHLBI.

Obarzanek E, Pratt CA. (2003) Girls health Enrichment Multi-site Studies (GEMS): New approaches to obesity prevention among young African-American girls. Ethn Dis 13(Suppl 1): S1-1-S1-5.

Oster G, Thompson D, Edelsberg J, Bird AP, Colditz GA. (1999) Lifetime health and economic benefits of weight loss among obese persons. Am J Public Health 89:1536-1542.

Resnicow K, Yaroch AL, Davis A, Wang DT, Carter S, Slaughter L, Coleman D, Baranowski T. (2000) GO GIRLS!: Results from a nutrition and physical activity program for low-income, overweight African American adolescent females. Health Educ Behav 27:616-631.

Robinson TN. (1999) Reducing children's television viewing to prevent obesity: A randomized controlled trial. JAMA. 282:1561-1567.

Robinson TN, Killen JD, Kraemer HC, Wilson DM, Matheson DM, Haskell WL, Pruitt LA, Powell TM, Owens AS,

Thompson NS, Flint-Moore NM, Davis GJ, Emig KA, Brown RT, Rochon J, Green S, Varady A. (2003) Dance and reducing television viewing to prevent weight gain in African-American girls: The Stanford GEMS pilot study. Ethn Dis 13(Suppl 1):S1-65-S1-77.

Sallis JF, McKenzie TL, Alcaraz JE, Kolody B, Faucette N, Hovell MF. (1997) The effects of a 2-year physical education program (SPARK) on physical activity and fitness in elementary school students. Sports, Play and Active Recreation for Kids. Am J Public Health 87:1328-1334

Sherwood NE, Morton N, Jeffery RW, French SA, Neumark-Sztainer D, Falkner NH. (1998) Consumer preferences in format and type of community-based weight control programs. Am J Health Promo 13:12-18.

Simkin-Silverman LR, Wing RR, Boraz MA, Meilahn EN, Kuller LH. (1998) Maintenance of cardiovascular risk factor changes among middle-aged women in a lifestyle intervention trial. Womens Health 4:255-271.

Simkin-Silverman L, Wing RR, Hansen DH, Klem ML, Pasagian-Macaulay AP. Meilahn EN, Kuller LH. (1995) Prevention of cardiovascular risk factor elevations in healthy premenopausal women. Prev Med 24:509-517.

Stolley MR, Fitzgibbon ML. (1997) Effects of an obesity prevention program on the eating behavior of African American mothers and daughters. Health Educ Behav 24:152-164.

Story M, Davis S, Ethelbah B, Himes J, Holy Rock B, Stephenson L, Stevens J, Stone E; The Pathways Collaborative Research Group. (2001) Childhood obesity: A priority for prevention in American Indian school children. Fed Am Soc Experi Biol 15:abstract 836.10.

Story M, Sherwood NE, Himes JH, Davis M, Jacobs DR, Cartwright Y, Smyth M,

Rochon J. (2003) An after-school obesity prevention program for African-American girls: The Minnesota GEMS pilot study. Ethn Dis 13(Suppl 1):S1-54-S1-64.

Thompson D, Edelsberg J, Kinsey KL, Oster G. (1998) Estimated economic costs of obesity to US business. Am J Health Promot 13:120-127.

Wadden TA, Stunkard AJ. (1985) Social and psychological consequences of obesity. Ann Intern Med 103:1062-1067.

Whitaker RC, Wright JA, Pepe MS, Seidel KD, Dietz WH. (1997) Predicting obesity in young adulthood from childhood and parental obesity. N Engl J Med 337:869-73.

Williamson DF, Kahn HS, Byers T. (1991) The 10-year incidence of obesity and major weight gain in black and white US women aged 30-55 years. Am J Clin Nutr 53:1515S-1518S.

Wing RR. (1998) Obesity. In: Behavioral Medicine and Women: A Comprehensive Handbook (Blechman EA, KD Brownell KD, eds), pp 397-401. New York, NY: Guilford Press.

Wolf AM. (1998) What is the economic case for treating obesity. Obes Res 6(suppl):2S-7S.

Wolf AM, Colditz GA. (1996) Social and economic effects of body weight in the United States. Am J Clin Nutr 63:466S-469S.

World Health Organization. (1997, June) Obesity: Preventing and managing the global epidemic. Report of a WHO Consultation on Obesity, Geneva, Switzerland.

Yung B, Hammond W. (1997) Community-based interventions. In: Health-Promoting and Health-Compromising Behaviors Among Minority Adolescents (Wilson D, Rodriguez J, Taylor W, eds), pp. 269-297. Washington, DC: American Psychological Association.

LONG-TERM OUTCOMES OF TREATMENT FOR ATTENTION-DEFICIT/HYPERACTIVITY DISORDER

Jonathan D. Schmidt and Bradley H. Smith

INTRODUCTION

Attention-Deficit/Hyperactivity Disorder (ADHD) is one of the most commonly diagnosed and treated disorders among school-aged children (Barkley, 2006). Recent estimates are that 3-7% of school children in the US meet diagnostic criteria for ADHD (American Psychiatric Association, 2000). Enormous resources are spent on treating ADHD with annual costs estimated to be between $36 billion and $42.5 billion annually (Pelham et al., 2007). The number of children treated for ADHD in 1997 was estimated at 2,158,000, up from an estimated 493,000 in 1987 (Olfson et al., 2003). Furthermore, ADHD is one of the most common reasons for referral to special education, which costs an average of about $16921 per pupil per year compared to about $7552 for students in regular education settings (National Education Association, 2004)). Thus, it seems reasonable to ask if the tremendous investment in the treatment of ADHD is justified by the outcomes.

A critical consideration when evaluating the value of treatment for ADHD is the long-term outcomes of treatment. We are not aware of any comprehensive reviews of the long-term studies of treatment for ADHD that have been conducted in the past eight years (see Kupfer et al., 2000). This review makes an important contribution to the literature by presenting an update on the studies that provide information on the long-term results of treatment of ADHD. Moreover, we provide a methodological review designed to guide needed advances in research on the treatment of ADHD. Foremost among these recommendations is the need to switch from an acute care to chronic care model of managing ADHD, which is a chronic disorder.

Prior to reviewing the studies, we provide a brief background on the diagnosis and nature of ADHD. Then we present our review criteria, which focus on the efficacy, safety, and practicality of the various treatments for ADHD. These criteria are intended to emphasize not only the importance of scientific rigor and clinical safety, but also the importance of considering the availability, acceptability, generalizability, and feasibility of treatments for ADHD. After reviewing the efficacy, safety, and practicality considerations, we use these criteria to evaluate the various treatments for ADHD that have been studied with at least a four-month follow-up. At the conclusion of the review, we provide an overview of the treatment literature with an emphasis on clinical implications and future directions for research.

Diagnosis and Description of ADHD

ADHD is defined by two clusters of symptoms: inattention and hyperactivity/ impulsivity. These core symptoms of ADHD are correlated with each other, but there is growing information that they are distinct from each other even though they often co-occur (Barkley, 2006). Thus, a person diagnosed with ADHD can have problems related to inattention, hyperactivity/impulsivity, or both. Some have argued, that other dimensions of ADHD exist (e.g. sluggish cognitive tempo). These dimensions have not yet been incorporated into the definition of ADHD and the eventual status of these potential dimensions of ADHD is uncertain.

The first documentation of ADHD in professional literature was by Still (1902), when he described a group of children who were excessively active, distractible, and poor at sustaining their attention to tasks. Initially many thought that ADHD was due to brain damage, but that hypothesis has been completely discredited by several decades of research (Barkley, 2006). Formal definitions of the disorder have shifted from a focus on hyperactivity as the core problem (i.e., Hyper-kinetic Reaction of Childhood), to attention as the core problem (Attention Deficit Disorder with or without hyperactivity), to a unitary disorder (Attention-Deficit Hyperactivity Disorder), to the current definition that has three subtypes of ADHD: Predominately Inattentive, Predominantly Hyperactive/ Impulsive, and Combined (American Psychiatric Association, 2000).

It is evident from the various subtypes that ADHD is a heterogeneous disorder than can be complicated to assess. A detailed discussion of assessment for ADHD is beyond the scope of this chapter (see Smith, et al., 2006 for more information on assessing ADHD). For present purposes it suffices to say that the DSM-IV presents the most widely accepted criteria for assessing ADHD. Exact DSM-IV diagnostic criteria are listed in Table 1. The key elements of the DSM-IV ADHD diagnosis can be summarized by the following seven concepts.

(1) Individuals with ADHD can have problems related to inattention, hyperactivity/ impulsivity, or both.

(2) ADHD is a developmental disorder of attention span and/or hyperactivity/impul-sivity in which these deficits are significantly inappropriate for the person's age.

(3) The disorder should have an onset in early childhood.

(4) The condition is generally chronic or persistent over time.

(5) The core symptoms are significantly pervasive or cross-situational in nature.

(6) The deficits are not the direct result of severe language delay, deafness, blindness, or another psychiatric condition.

(7) The core symptoms of ADHD must be causally associated with significant impairment in educational, social, vocational, physical, or other significant areas of life functioning.

Thirty years ago there was a widespread belief that ADHD was a self-limiting disorder that typically remitted shortly after puberty (Brown and Borden, 1986). However, in the past three decades, several well-conducted longitudinal studies have shown that 43-80 percent continue to have the disorder into adolescence (Barkley et al., 1990; Biederman et al., 1996; Mannuzza et al., 1998; Weiss and Hechtman, 1993). Many of the children with ADHD who putatively "outgrow" their symptoms during adolescence are often borderline cases that switch back and forth between diagnosed and non-diagnoses status (Barkley, 2006). Moreover, those who have subclinical levels of ADHD as adolescents are often significantly impaired relative to their peers (Molina and Pelham, 2003).

Many of these borderline cases might maintain a diagnosis of ADHD if more developmentally appropriate diagnostic criteria were employed. Unfortunately, the DSM-IV criteria were written for and field-tested primarily with children in mind. As a consequence, some of the DSM-IV symptoms for ADHD are irrelevant to adolescents, who generally show a decline in hyperactive behavior. For example, statements like "runs or climbs excessively" or "fails to remain in seat" no longer apply to post-pubescent individuals with ADHD. On the other hand, the DSM-IV symptoms of inattention seem to be relatively stable for teens and young adults (Smith et al., in press). A key clinical and research implication of the chronic nature of ADHD is that the treatments that have been tested are not expected to cure ADHD. Numerous reversal studies have shown that if treatments are effective in treating ADHD, when participants who are positive responders to intervention have the intervention removed the effects are short lived. This is true for both

TABLE 1. DSM-IV Criteria for ADHD

A. Either (1) or (2):

(1) six (or more) of the following symptoms of **inattention** have persisted for at least 6 months to a degree that is maladaptive and inconsistent with developmental level:

Inattention

(a) often fails to give close attention to details or makes careless mistakes in schoolwork, work, or other activities

(b) often has difficulty sustaining attention in tasks or play activities

(c) often does not seem to listen when spoken to directly

(d) often does not follow through on instructions and fails to finish schoolwork, chores, or duties in the workplace (not due to oppositional behavior or failure to understand instructions)

(e) often has difficulty organizing tasks and activities

(f) often avoids, dislikes, or is reluctant to engage in tasks that require sustained mental effort (such as school work or homework)

(g) often loses things necessary for tasks or activities (e.g., toys, school assignments, pencils, books, or tools)

(h) is often easily distracted by extraneous stimuli

(i) is often forgetful in daily activities

(2) six (or more) of the following symptoms of **hyperactivity–impulsivity** have persisted for at least 6 months to a degree that is maladaptive and inconsistent with developmental level:

Hyperactivity

(a) often fidgets with hands or feet or squirms in seat

(b) often leaves seat in classroom or in other situations in which remaining seated is expected

(c) often runs about or climbs excessively in situations in which it is inappropriate (in adolescents or adults, may be limited to subjective feelings of restlessness)

(d) often has difficulty playing or engaging in leisure activities quietly

(e) is often "on the go" or often acts as if "driven by a motor"

(f) often talks excessively

Impulsivity

(g) often blurts out answers before the questions have been completed

(h) often has difficulty awaiting turn

(i) often interrupts or intrudes on others (e.g., butts into conversations or games)

B. Some hyperactive–impulsive or inattentive symptoms that caused impairment were present before age 7 years.

C. Some impairment from the symptoms is present in two or more settings (e.g., at school [or work] and at home).

D. There must be clear evidence of clinically significant impairment in social, academic, or occupational functioning.

E. The symptoms do not occur exclusively during the course of a Pervasive Developmental Disorder, Schizophrenia, or other Psychotic Disorder, and are not better accounted for by another mental disorder (e.g., Mood Disorder, Anxiety Disorder, Dissociative Disorder, or a Personality Disorder).

Code based on type:

314.01 Attention-Deficit/Hyperactivity Disorder, Combined Type: if both Criteria A1 and A2 are   met for the past 6 months.

314.00 Attention-Deficit/Hyperactivity Disorder, Predominantly Inattentive Type: if Criterion A1 is   met but Criterion A2 is not met for the past 6 months pharmacological and behavioral treatments (Smith et al., 2006). Thus, treatment for ADHD needs to be approached from the standpoint of chronic care.

Similar to a disease like diabetes, failures in day-to-day compliance with treatment for ADHD have immediate implications for current functioning and the accumulation of impairing consequences. For instance, forgetting to give a child with ADHD their morning dose of stimulant medication can result in a problem at school that day (e.g., disrupting the classroom) which can create other problems (e.g., missing instructional time due to an in-school suspension). The consequences of these impairments accumulate over time (e.g., experiencing academic failure and frustration from doing poorly on a test because a review of the material was conducted while the child was excluded from the classroom). Eventually, the impairing consequence may evolve into the serious academic, social, and vocational impairments that characterize ADHD (DuPaul and Stoner, 1994; Barkley, 2006).

The implications of the fleeting nature of treatment for ADHD is that even though treatments for ADHD may not cure the disorder, compliance with effective treatments should lead to better outcomes by preventing the accumulation of ADHD-related impairments. Thus, studies that evaluate the effectiveness of treatment for ADHD need to be longitudinal and determine if symptoms and related impairment are effectively controlled over time. Thus, a critical consideration for long-term studies of ADHD also is to measure impairment and compliance with treatment. Contrary to this ideal, however, a major review of the literature on ADHD conducted by the National Institutes on Health Consensus Forming Conference concluded that there was a dearth of longitudinal research on ADHD, and the panel of reviewers strongly endorsed the need to conduct longitudinal studies (Kupfer et al., 2000).

The purpose of this review is to examine the current state of longitudinal treatment literature on ADHD. This review provides shows the number of longitudinal studies published in the peer reviewed literature has increased since the NIH Consensus Forming Conference. However, this review also shows that the literature is still very limited in terms of the number and nature of studies. Taken together, we believe this is the most comprehensive review of long-term outcomes of treatment for ADHD that has been completed to date. This is a disparate literature spanning a broad range of research designs, measures, and populations. Due to the heterogeneity of studies and limited number of similar studies, this literature cannot yet be subjected to quantitative review (e.g., meta-analysis). Nevertheless, we thought it was necessary to provide a broad synthetic framework for examining and comparing the available treatments. Therefore, we rated each treatment on the parameters of efficacy, safety, and practicality (see Table 2). These parameters are explained in detail in the next three sections and were used previously in Smith et al., (2000).

Efficacy, Safety, and Practicality Criteria

The criteria used for evaluating efficacy were similar to those adapted by a recent task force on child psychopathology treatment that was commissioned by the American Psychological Association (Lonigan et al., 1998).

These criteria have two levels of empirical support: well-established and probably efficacious. We added two additional levels: promising but not validated and probably ineffective.

The criteria for *well-established interventions* for childhood disorders require that either (a) there are two or more well-conducted group-design studies completed by different research teams or (b) there are several well-conducted single-case study designs completed by independent investigators showing the treatment is either superior to placebo or is at least as good as an existing well-established treatment in a study with sufficient statistical power. The criteria for *probably efficacious interventions* require either (a) two studies demonstrate the intervention is more effective than a no-treatment control group or (b) there are two well-conducted group-design studies, but they are by the same investigators or group of investigators. For well-established and probably efficacious interventions, it is important to have clearly specified sample characteristics. Furthermore, the use of sufficiently detailed treatment manuals that allow for rapid treatment dissemination, and procedures to measure the effects of adherence to the manuals are highly desirable.

Our criteria for *promising, but not validated* treatments were that there was at least one well-controlled study or a limited number of high-quality case studies that suggested the treatment is effective. Our criteria for *probably ineffective* treatments was that there was at least one study showing null or negative results and no studies showing positive results.

To help summarize our results and compile an overall treatment quality score that included efficacy, safety, and practicality, we created a quantitative score for each of these three dimensions. With regard to efficacy, well-established treatments were given a 3. Probably efficacious treatments were given a

2. Promising but not validated treatments were given a 1. Probably ineffective received a zero.

Safety

There are debates in the public and professional literature regarding the safety of medications for treating children and adolescents with ADHD (Barkley, 1998). Although all of these drugs meet the minimum safety standards of the Food and Drug Administration, not all of the drugs are equally safe and many have been tested on adults only. Furthermore, once a drug has been approved for any purpose, it can be used at the physician's discretion. Consequently, drugs that are FDA approved to treat one problem (e.g., depression in adults) might be used to treat another problem (e.g., ADHD in adolescents) even though there is no extant data on (a) the safety of the drug to treat that problem, and (b) the efficacy of the drug for that problem. This practice, sometimes called "off-label prescribing," is very common in child and adolescent psychiatry.

Given the lack of consistency in safety data, it is not surprising that opinions regarding the safety of drugs vary depending on which criteria are selected. In this review, we focused on reports of sudden or premature death associated with doses in the therapeutic range, the risk of a fatal overdose, and the risk of acute and long-term impairment from doses given in the normal therapeutic range. Although debatable, we considered phenomena such as potential growth suppression from treatment with stimulant medication to be a possible long-term negative outcome (Jensen et al., 2004). Similarly controversial, is the assumption that grouping antisocial children in settings that are not highly structured can promote the development of anti-social behavior and substance abuse (Dishion et al., 1999).

All treatments started with a safety score of three. One point was subtracted if the drug had a relatively high risk for fatal overdose, defined in this review as likely to be fatal if one week's supply of medication was consumed at once. One point was subtracted if there were occasionally life-threatening or health impairing side effects at therapeutic doses (e.g., cardiac arrythmias or seizures). A point could also be deducted if there was the possibility of long-term negative consequences from the treatment (e.g., growth suppression or elevated rates of delinquent behavior).

It is important to note that safety considerations are not limited to pharmacological treatments. A commonly endorsed ethical principle is that the benefits of treatment should far outweigh the costs incurred in the treatment process (e.g., (McFall, 2000). The current APA criteria for evaluating the empirical support of treatments do not include cost-benefit considerations. More specifically, the APA task force criteria for evaluating psychosocial treatments are purely inclusive because they are based only on data that evaluates whether or not the treatment is associated with positive outcomes (Chambless et al., 1996). These standards for evaluating empirical support do not have any systematic means of including evidence of harmful effects. This limited perspective would clearly be inappropriate for medication treatment, and seems inappropriate for psychosocial treatment. Presumably, these less than perfect first generation of evolving standards for evaluating treatment (Weisz and Hawley, 1998) will continue to be refined and will soon include criteria for identifying likely negative side effects that detrimentally affect the safety and practicality of the intervention.

Practicality

The issues of practicality are germane to controlled clinical studies (i.e., studies of treatment efficacy), but have their most profound impact on utility of treatments in natural settings (i.e., the treatment effectiveness). Key issues defining treatment practicality are (a) tolerability, which includes acceptability, acute side effects, and factors affecting compliance, (b) dissemination of treatments from research to applied settings, and (c) cost-effectiveness (Lonigan et al., 1998; McKay et al., 1996).

No matter how effective a treatment may be, if families are unwilling to try it (e.g., electroconvulsive therapy for depression) the intervention will be useless. Parents seem to prefer treatments for ADHD that include a strong psychosocial component (Jensen et al., 1998). It is not known, however, if this initial preference translates into better compliance and outcomes for their children with ADHD.

Another factor affecting practicality is tolerability defined as whether or not there are annoying side effects. Literature from child samples suggests side effects of stimulant medications for ADHD are usually reversible and often dose-dependent (Barkley et al., 1990; Pelham, Jr., 1999; Pelham, Jr. and Gnagy, 1999). Similar results have been found with adolescents with ADHD (Smith et al., 1998). Furthermore, many side effects diminish with daily use of stimulant medication (Barkley, 2006). Nevertheless side effects may make the treatment unpleasant in the short run and lead to premature termination of medication. Moreover, even among those who have well-documented positive responses to pharmacological treatment, there is a steady decline in use of stimulant medication after peak use at around age 8 (Zuvekas et al., 2006). This decline appears to be more of a matter of adherence rather than a lessening in effectiveness of stimulants in treating ADHD (Smith et al., 1998).

Another practicality issue is the complexity of demands made upon children and families for administering the treatment. For example, a once-a-day dose is more feasible than complicated multiple dose regimens. Practicality is also influenced by access factors such as cost and service delivery models. Thus, the benefits of once-a-day dosing may be overshadowed by the high cost of some of these medicines.

Different service delivery models, such as in-office versus in-home treatments, are likely to be associated with compliance with treatment. Paradoxically, treatments that have a higher cost may diminish the effectiveness of treatment if the stakeholder paying for the treatment (e.g., a parent or HMO) refuses to pay because they have not been persuaded that the treatment has a favorable cost-benefit ratio (Henggeler et al., 1998).

Once the practical issues of tolerability and cost have been addressed, one needs to consider the extent to which treatments generalize from controlled efficacy studies. A meta-analysis by Weisz and colleagues (Weisz et al., 1987) indicates that treatment provided in controlled clinical studies is far more effective than treatment delivered in the community. Some recent studies echo the results of Weisz and colleagues. For example, pharmacological treatment for ADHD was more effective in the context of research protocol than when received as part of treatment as usual in the community (MTA Collaborative Group, 1999). Similarly, multi-systemic family treatment was far more effective when provided by academic versus non-academic service organizations (Huey et al., 2000).

More dramatically, a meta-analysis found that the mean effect size for treatment in research settings was large (e.g., an effect size of 0.6 standard deviation change), whereas the mean effect size in community settings was zero (Weisz et al., 2004). This suggests that either there is no effect of treatment or that half of the children receiving treatment in the community get worse, thus counter-balancing the children who get better. In this later scenario, community-based child therapy is often harmful. In the former scenario, it is merely ineffective. Understanding the reasons for this discrepancy in efficacy between academic and non-academic service delivery models should be a high research priority and should be a cautionary note for the interpretation of the studies in this review.

To summarize, our criteria regarding practicality of treatments are preliminary and reflect our judgment rather than a systematic summary such as would be done in a meta-analysis. Nevertheless, rankings of this sort are common in the psychotherapy literature and the efficacy criteria are similar to those used by the APA Task Force on evidence-based treatments (e.g., Chambless et al., 1996). The proposed practicality scores are designed to call attention to important issues affecting the impact of treatment, which has been incorporated into some more recent rating systems (Biglan et al., 2003). All treatments started with a practicality score of 3, thus giving efficacy, safety, and practicality equal weight. One point was deducted for practicality if the treatment was unlikely to be disseminated with sufficient fidelity. One point was deducted if the treatment regimen was inconvenient, such as requiring multiple daily dosing, or expensive, such as requiring an hour or more of therapist contact each week for several weeks. One point was deducted if there were known problems with compliance.

REVIEW OF STUDIES

We selected studies for this review based on the following criteria. First, in order to achieve a minimum level of quality, we only considered studies that were doctoral dissertations or published in peer-reviewed journals. Second, the study needed to have a comparison group that allowed for inference regarding treatment efficacy and calculation of effect size. Third, the study needed to measure treatment outcomes in terms of ADHD symptoms. Fourth, we sought studies that represented a long-term follow-up, which we originally thought would be a follow-up of at least a year. There were only six studies

Table 2: Efficacy, Safety, and Practicality Rating System Criteria

Efficacy	Safety	Practicality
3- Series of well-controlled studies with independent replication showing superiority to another treatment on ADHD symptoms or problems specific to ADHD.	Start with a safety score of 3 and subtract points for risk factors.	Start with a practicality score of 3 and subtract points for barriers to acceptability, feasibility, and sustainability.
2- Series of well-controlled studies, but independent replication lacking or failed to show superiority.	-1 if there is a reasonable risk of a fatal side effect (e.g., fatal drug overdose).	-1 if the treatment is extremely complex and unlikely to be disseminated with sufficient fidelity.
1- A promising study or some conflicting studies with the preponderance of data favoring efficacy	-1 if there are occasional life threatening or health impairing side effects (e.g., "boxed warnings")	-1 if the treatment is not cost effective compared to equally efficacious alternative treatments
0 – no available research or the available studies found no benefit	-1 Research has demonstrated a significant risk of long term negative consequences (e.g., deviancy training).	-1 if there are problems with acceptability or tolerability (e.g., due to beliefs about the treatment or annoying side effects).
Note- If there are a series of well-conducted, independently replicated studies finding null or negative results, then this is an empirically invalidated treatment that should not be used even if it is safe and people like it.	Note – If a drug is banned by the FDA (e.g., ephedra) or shown to be harmful to a significant subset of patients, then the treatment should not be used.	Note- Some interventions studied in research settings are so intensive that they will never be available to the general public (e.g., MTA psychosocial intervention). Interventions such as these should have a Practicality score of zero.

with a follow-up of one year or more. We relaxed the follow-up period instead to at least 4 months. This minimum length of follow-up is somewhat arbitrary, but appeared to us to be a reasonable cutoff between short-term follow-up (i.e., three months or less) and longer-term follow-up.

Studies meeting these criteria were identified as eligible through a review of the literature by searching Psyc Info, Web of Science, and PubMed. A reverse literature search was done in order to identify other potential articles that had cited the ones already found. Key words used for the search included hyperactivity, ADHD, ADD, stimulants, psychosocial treatments, follow-up, behavioral interventions, multimodal treatment, pharmacological, externalizing behaviors and other combinations of these words. The reference lists of eligible articles found in this search were also scanned to identify additional studies.

The review found five broad areas of intervention that have been studied in the long-term treatment literature: (1) parent training, (2) parent training combined with child-focused groups, (3) child-focused intervention, (4) medication, and (5) comprehensive multimodal treatment. These groupings often contained studies that were very different in content or intensity, such as 10 weekly parenting sessions lasting 90 minutes each or intensive parent training with an average of 48 hours of contact in 12 weeks. Consequently, these treatments are rated separately (see Table 3).

Of note, many studies examined multiple therapies. For example one study compared parent training with (a) parent training plus a child-focused intervention and (b) a control group. This study contributed to both the parent training and the parent training combined with child-focused intervention. Thus, this study and some others, contribute multiple times to the review.

Some studies had no untreated control group, so some interventions are compared with other interventions. These designs make it difficult to interpret effect sizes. However, they do provide some information about relative efficacy. In such cases, the studies are grouped by the intervention for which inference about relative efficacy was possible.

For example, one study compared parent training with parent training plus individual cognitive behavior therapy for the child. This study is grouped with child-focused therapies because this study does not provide information about the efficacy of the parent training, but it does provide information of the relative efficacy of parent training plus child-focused intervention compared to parent training alone.

Behavioral Parent Training

The literature review located only three studies where it was possible to glean information regarding the long-term effects of improving parent's behavioral control of their children. This section provides a description of each study and concludes with an overview of the evidence base for the efficacy, safety, and practicality of behavioral parent training interventions for ADHD. The studies are presented in chronological order.

Table 3: Studies of Parent-Focused Intervention

Study	Type of Treatment	Treatment Duration	Follow-up	Efficacy	Safety	Practicality
Strayhorn and Weidman, 1991	Parent-child Interaction Training	Variable	1 year	Support for the underlying theory, but few significant findings relative to controls	No problems	Limited parent participation probably limited the effect size
Shelton et al., 2000	Parent training	10 weeks	2 years	No effects reported relative to a control group	No problems	Poor attendance at parent training groups
Wilmshurst, 2002	Community-Based Family Preservation Using Multi-systemic Therapy	12 weeks with mean contact of 48 hours	1 year	Compared favorably to 12 weeks of inpatient care	No problems	Requires special training and unique staffing patterns

Parent-Child Interaction Training (Strayhorn and Weidman, 1991)

Strayhorn and Weidman (1991) evaluated the effects of a parent-child interaction training program on attention deficit symptoms of 84 preschool children. Participants were randomly assigned to a minimal treatment control group or a more intensive treatment experimental group. In the experimental group parents were given training in parent-child interaction skills. This involved training parents to model prosocial behavior, engage their children in conversation, read stories with their children, and use dramatic play to teach their children about prosocial behavior (Strayhorn and Weidman, 1991). The control group was given a pamphlet on parenting and watched two videotapes discussing the use of time-out (Patterson, 1982) and positive reinforcement (Research Press, 1983).

Families were recruited through Head Start centers, advertisements and flyers, referrals from health professionals, and word of mouth. Of note, in contrast to many studies, which are primarily with Caucasian males, 64% of the sample was African-American and 57% were female. According to a DSM-III-R checklist, 39% of the children's caretakers endorsed at least 8 or more of the 14 criteria that permitted a diagnosis of ADHD, and 32% of children's parents noted 5 or more of the 9 criteria listed for oppositional defiant disorder (ODD). A total of 77 parents and 84 children completed the study, however, teacher ratings were only obtained for 56 of the children in the study. At one year follow-up, no families had received additional treatment after the interventions concluded.

The primary outcome measures in this study, as stated by the authors, were ADHD symptoms and internalizing symptoms on the teacher and parent Behar Preschool Behavior Questionnaire. Researchers also analyzed the correlation of improvement in parenting behaviors from pre-intervention to post-intervention with the child's hyperactivity ratings from pre-intervention to follow-up.

Parent ratings on the Behar showed there were no significant differences found between groups when testing the reduction of ADHD symptoms in children from the parent-child interaction program. Teacher reports did show a significant reduction in ADHD hyperactivity symptoms. This was not found in the initial post-test and thus may represent a "sleeper" effect (Strayhorn and Weidman, 1991). However, low power and a considerable number of missing teacher ratings suggest these data should be interpreted cautiously.

Of note, parents who improved the most in videotaped interactions with their children had the largest reductions in ADHD hyperactive symptoms in the classroom ($r=0.38$, $p<.01$). This finding supports the underlying intervention theory; specifically that parent behavior mediates change in child functioning. Nevertheless, as mentioned above, parent ratings on the Behar Composite showed no significant difference between the experimental and control groups at the one-year follow-up. This suggests that the intervention did not have a sufficient effect on parenting behaviors.

A key consideration with this study is that only 26 of 40 parents (65%) completed the training exercises, only 17 (42.5%) had at least one monitored play session with their child, and only 14 (35%) met the criterion level for mastery of the procedures. Thus, there are legitimate questions regarding whether or not the full potential of the procedure was tapped in this study.

Parent Groups for High-risk Kindergarten Students (Shelton et al., 2000)

This study was designed to identify high-risk kindergarten students and provide early intervention. A total of 158 children were assigned to one of four groups during their first year in kindergarten: (1) a no-treatment control group, (2) parent training only groups,

(3) special treatment classroom, and (4) a parent training combined with the special classroom treatment group. More details of the study are reported in a subsequent section of this review (i.e., parent training combined with child-focused intervention).

Parents in this study were offered a 10-week parenting program that focused on identifying the causes of behavior problems, rewarding children for non-disruptive behavior, setting up a token system to encourage positive behavior, and methods for handling disruptive behavior in different situations. Evaluation of the data at post-treatment showed that there was no significant effect of the parent training program that was implemented. This should not, however, be attributed to a failure of the efficacy of parent training. Rather, this poor outcome seems to be due to low attendance rates at the parent training sessions. It appears that it may be difficult to engage parents of high-risk kindergarten but not clinically-referred students in parent training groups.

Community-Based Family Preservation (Wilmshurst, 2002)

In this study, children with emotional and behavioral disorders between the ages of 6 and 14 were quasi-randomly assigned (based on bed availability) to receive 3 months of treatment in either a 5-day residential (5DR) program or a community-based family preservation treatment (FP) (Wilmshurst, 2002). The focus of the 5DR was brief solution focused therapy with the child alone, and active involvement from the parent/parents was expected, whereas the FP program focused on teaching and using cognitive-behavioral and behavioral techniques within the family. The FP program was based on Multisystemic Family Therapy (Henggeler et al., 1992) therefore it focused on allowing for intensive home support. Workers were available 24 hours a day, 7 days a week for up to 12 hours a week.

The average family contact time during the 3-month session was 48.33 hours. Furthermore, after the completion of the FP program, continued support was offered in parent support groups by community agencies.

The primary goal of the FP intervention was for the therapist to teach the children and their families to find solutions to problems by focusing on family strengths, and the use of problem solving, cognitive-behavioral, and behavioral strategies. Therapists acted as guides by first observing the problem behaviors, and then conversing with the parents to develop interventions through reframing and contingency management.

The 5DR program was a residential treatment program that operated Monday through Friday, allowing the children to return home for weekends. It consisted of a 3-month residential placement phase for 5 days a week, and a 3-month reintegration phase. Only 9 subjects at a time could participate in this treatment due to housing constraints. The 5DR was reportedly based on brief solution focused therapy (Miller et al., 1996). This approach emphasized the child's responsibility for change, with client-focused training in self-regulation skills related to problem identification, coping, self-monitoring, competence (self-efficacy), and use of available resources. In the residential placement phase clinicians worked with the family at a clinic for 1 hour every 2 weeks doing therapy sessions and focusing on solution time questions. Overall, the mean family contact time was 26.11 hours while in the residential phase, and 18.14 hours for the reintegration phase, for a total of 42.25 hours.

Overall 65 children completed the study, with 38 children in the FP program and 27 children in the 5DR program. All children who participated in the study were assigned to the same mental health agency by the Children's Services Network for being at-risk and needing services. Children were then rated by case mangers using the Children's

Services Network Assessment of Risks and Needs (CSNARN) rating scale. Children whose rating was in the high to very high range (i.e., the most clinically severe) were referred to the program director responsible for intensive service placement before being referred to a case manager. At this point, participants were assigned by alternate draw to either the FP or 5DR program based on the availability of treatment. All participants in the study had one therapist who was responsible for the organization and administration of all services during their 3 months of treatment.

The primary outcome measures in this paper, as stated by the author, were parent report measures, specifically the Social Skills Rating System (SSRS) and the Standardized Client Information System (SCIS). Both measures were administered prior to treatment, after treatment, and 1 year after treatment. Teacher ratings were also collected but interpretability of the teacher ratings is questionable because (a) almost half of the teacher ratings were missing, and (b) pre- to follow-up ratings were done by different teachers. Of note, according to parent report, at baseline this was a very severe population with at least 70% having co-occurring symptoms in the clinical range for both externalizing and internalizing disorders.

At one-year follow-up, comparison of the FP and 5DR treatment groups indicated that FP was superior. For instance, 63% of youth in FP had significant reduction for ADHD as compared to only 11% of the 5DR. Only individuals in the FP program had a significant reduction in internalizing symptoms from pretreatment to 1-year follow-up as evidenced by both parent and teacher ratings. In contrast, as measured by the reliable change index, there was a worsening of symptoms for participants in the 5DR program in terms of generalized anxiety ($X^2=10.51$, $p=.01$), separation anxiety ($X^2=6.66$, $p=.01$), and depression ($X^2=11.64$,

$p=.001$) when compared to FP group participants. Both teachers and parents reported an increase in this area. The reason for the deterioration for the 5DR group in terms of internalizing symptoms is unclear, but raises questions about the safety of inpatient programs for treating high-risk youth.

Overall, the Wilmshurst study suggests that the FP (Family Preservation) model, including combined cognitive behavior therapy and behavior support for effective parenting, is a worthwhile model for treating children with ADHD who also show severe emotional and behavioral problems. On the other hand, as reiterated in the next section, the 5DR model is not recommended due to limited efficacy and concerns about safety and practicality.

Parent Focused Intervention: Overview and ESP Ratings

The literature review located only three studies that provided information on the long-term effects of improving parent's behavioral control of their children (see Table 3). Two studies were with relatively young children with ADHD using a standard dose of group parenting intervention (e.g., about 10 sessions lasting 90 minutes each). The other study was with very high-risk youth using an intensive intervention, namely Multisystemic Therapy (MST) delivered in a community-based family preservation model.

In terms of efficacy, the parent training groups with parents of younger children yielded small effect sizes and mostly non-significant results relative to no treatment controls. On the other hand, MST compared favorably to inpatient therapy. Because these interventions are so different, we rated efficacy separately, giving a 2 for MST and a 1 for parent training groups. To achieve higher efficacy scores, there need to more long-term studies of parenting interventions that replicate or extend these results.

None of the studies reported negative effect sizes that were consistently found across multiple measures. None of the studies reported any harmful side effects of the parent interventions. Therefore, we awarded behavior parent training the highest possible safety score (3) to the parenting interventions. As noted in the next section, there did appear to be some negative effects of the inpatient (5DR) program.

In terms of practicality, there were problems with engaging parents of young children in the parenting groups. It is likely that this poor engagement contributed to the small effect sizes of these interventions. Thus, we deducted one practicality point due to low acceptability, thus giving the parenting groups for young children with ADHD a practicality score of 2.

In terms of practicality of MST, this intensive treatment has been shown to (a) be dependent on fidelity of implementation, (b) requires extensive training, and (c) has not been implemented with sufficient fidelity in many sites when researchers have conducted effectiveness studies (Hengeller et al., 1997). Thus, MST loses at least one practically point for complexity and we gave MST a

practicality score of 2.

Taken together, the ratings parenting interventions for ADHD ranged from 5 to 6 on a 9-point scale, which suggests there is considerable room for improvement. Key areas of improvement are related to efficacy and practicality. Also, considering that parent training in behavioral management is a nearly ubiquitous recommendation for treating ADHD, there are shockingly few controlled studies of this important intervention.

Combining Child-Focused Intervention with Complementary Parenting Training

The section reviews studies that (a) focus on providing self-control, social, and other ADHD relevant coping skills to children, and (b) provide a parent-training component designed to help the parents support and extend the child skills. The literature review located only 4 studies that provided information on these types of studies (see Table 4). This section provides a description of each study and concludes with an overview of the efficacy, safety, and practicality of this approach to treating ADHD. The studies are presented in chronological order.

Table 4: Combining Child-Focused with Parent-Focused Intervention

Study	Type of Treatment	Treatment Duration	Follow-up	Efficacy	Safety	Practicality
Horn et al, 1991	Behavioral Parent Training Plus Child Self-Control Training	12 weekly 90-minute sessions for parents and children	8 months	Combined was superior to parent or child alone	No problems reported but deviant peers were grouped	No major problems reported
Fehlings et al., 1991	Child Cognitive Behavioral Therapy plus Parent CBT generalization training	16 individual 1-hour child sessions plus eight 2-hour family sessions	Five months	The authors report positive effects of CBT plus PT, but design problems cloud causal inference	No problems	An intensive intervention with questionable incremental effects of individual CBT

Study	Type of Treatment	Treatment Duration	Follow-up	Efficacy	Safety	Practicality
Pfiffner and McBurnet, 1997	Social Skills Training (SST) and SST plus Parent Training	Eight 90-minute sessions	4 months	Weak effects on social skills, no effect on ADHD problems	No problems reported	Providing conjoint child sessions with parent sessions may improve acceptability
Springer, 2004	Cognitive Behavioral Therapy for ADHD plus Parent Training	10 ninety-minute sessions for parents and children	4 months	Not interpretable	Some low child self-ratings in the adherence monitoring group	No major problems reported
Hauch, 2005	Child Training based on Social Learning Theory plus Parent Training	10 weeks	16 months	Comprehensive Parent training was superior to Child Therapy alone based on parent reports but not teacher reports	High structure and low staff to child ratio likely preclude problems with grouping deviant peers	No major problems reported

Child Self-Control Training plus Parent Training (Horn et al., 1990)

In this study, 42 elementary school age children diagnosed with ADHD were randomly assigned to receive one of three treatments: (1) behavioral parent training (PT), (2) self-control instruction (SC), or (3) a combination of the two (PTSC). Children were diagnosed as having ADHD from a clinical interview that used DSM-III-R criteria, a completion of the Conner's Parent Rating Scale (CPRS) and the Conner's Teacher Rating Scale (CTRS). To be in the study children had to fall at least 2 standard deviations above the mean on the CPRS and CTRS forms, and have an agreement between an independent reviewer and the interviewer from the interview conducted with the parents. Children also had to be free of medication, intellectual deficits, and have an absence of psychoses in both the parents and the child.

Regardless of placement, each treatment group was broken down into additional groups of 7 families, and received 12 weekly 90-minute group therapy sessions. School consultation was also conducted for each treatment group and instructed the teacher on how to prompt for and promote the usage of the target skill the students were learning in their instructional groups.

In the PT group sessions consisted of

didactic presentations, discussions, and role plays that employed social learning theory principles to managing their children's behavior (Horn et al., 1990). Parents were assigned homework tasks that included informative reading. The readings instructed them on strategies they should use to deal with their children when exhibiting behavior problems, and on how to promote individualized behavior management plans with their children. A daily home report card was used with the teachers of any of the children whose parents were in this group.

The SC therapy was conducted in groups of seven children. Children were taught problem solving plans that focused on self-control strategies that involved thinking through a problem step by step and relaxations skills to use when dealing with academic or interpersonal problems. A token reward system was used for behavioral control of subjects during SC training. Teachers of the child participants were instructed on how to prompt for and reinforce students for the use of the skills they had learned in their weekly therapy groups.

From pre-treatment to 8 month follow-up, the largest changes in parent-report of the Externalizing, Hyperactivity, and Total scores of the CBCL were found for the combined treatment group (p<.001). This indicates that there was a decrease in ADHD behaviors in the home for individuals who were in the combined treatment group. Statistically significant changes from pre-treatment to follow-up were also found for the PT and SC groups on the CBCL Total and Externalizing scales, but effects were not as large as the combined treatment. Also, when researchers combined treatments and looked for responders (individuals who had a positive response to treatment) vs. non-responders (individuals who did not respond to the treatment), the combined treatment group had the most clinically significant responders to treatment (8 out of 11), 5 more than the other

two treatments (3 per treatment). However, results were only generalized to the home setting; when comparing the three treatments against each other, none were found to have a significantly greater effect on school behavior and no significant changes in school behavior were found at follow-up.

Individual CBT Therapy Plus Family Facilitation of CBT (Fehlings et al., 1991)

In this study researchers examined the effects of cognitive behavioral therapy (CBT) training delivered to 7 to 13 year olds diagnosed with ADHD. Research participants were referred to a clinic by pediatricians or school board members. Inclusion criteria required that the children be between the ages of 7 and 13, not be on stimulant medication, not have any major psychiatric disorders, have an IQ of at least 85, and have a diagnosis of ADHD. Children were diagnosed as ADHD by prior history, an interview, and a rating of at least 15 on the Parent Conner's Abbreviated Symptoms Questionnaire (CASQ). No breakdown in demographics from the sample was provided in the paper.

Children in the CBT group received 12 individual sessions with a behavioral therapist at a rate of two sessions per week. Children were taught steps to solve problems through modeling, self-instructional training, and other behavioral techniques. Also, children in this group and their families participated in eight 2-hour sessions at their homes. One session was delivered every 2 weeks. In family sessions parents were informed about ADHD and given instructional steps on how they could promote CBT strategies in their children.

The comparison condition in the study was 6 weeks of supportive therapy. Children in the supportive therapy control group spent the same amount of time with a therapist, however, the therapist provided supportive listening instead of CBT strategy instruction. The CBT and supportive therapy conditions were implemented according to a standard manual, and the individual sessions were videotaped and coded for fidelity to the manual and the therapist's positive manner.

A total of 25 children completed the study, 12 receiving CBT and 13 the supportive control. The primary outcomes were parent-reported measures. At 5 month follow-up researchers found that parent's ratings of their child's hyperactivity decreased in the CBT group, but there was no significant change in either the Self-Control Rating Scale or the Behavior Problems Checklist-Attention Problems subscale. These findings provide no support for the cognitive behavioral treatment and might simply reflect the behavioral training the parents received. It is noteworthy, however, that the self-esteem of the child was found to increase for subjects in the CBT group.

Overall the measures used in this study were sound, but low statistical power due to the small sample is a major concern regarding the stability of the findings. Furthermore, we are concerned that the individual CBT condition was confounded with eight 2-hour sessions of parent training. This confound makes it unclear if the positive effects relative to supportive individual therapy were due to CBT, the behavioral intervention, or some combination of the two. Another confound is that the CBT therapists were rated as more positive than the supportive therapists. Thus, therapeutic alliance, rather then the efficacy of CBT, might account for some group differences.

Social Skills Training Plus Parenting Training *(Pfiffner and McBurnett, 1997)*

The purpose of this study was to assess the effects of a social skills training (SST) and parent training (PT) on the social skills of 27 children ages 8-10 who had a diagnosis of ADHD. The children and their parents were randomly assigned within gender to one of three training groups: (1) a social skills

training group with parent-mediated generalization (SST-PG), (2) a child-only SST group, or (3) a wait-list control group.

The SST with children consisted of eight 90-minute sessions and focused on some of the negative behaviors children with ADHD exhibit when interacting with their peers (aggressiveness, impulsiveness, intrusiveness, and irritability) (Pfiffner and McBurnett, 1997). The program taught social skills in a hierarchical fashion on topics such as how to have good sportsmanship, accept consequences, ignore provocation, be empathetic, and deal with emotions, plus taught a five-step procedure for problem solving. Skills were taught to children using didactic instruction, symbolic modeling with the use of puppets, role-playing, and behavior rehearsal. Children then participated in games where they were rewarded with "good sports bucks" for exhibiting target skills. Parents were informed of the child's target skills and were instructed to give their children good sports bucks as a reward for exhibiting the skills at home. All children were assigned to practice the skill of the week at home and at school as a homework assignment.

In the SST-PT group parents were taught the skills that their children were working on in their groups. Parents observed their child in the group through a one-way mirror so that a psychologist could instruct the parents on when to prompt for and reward the child for use of a target social skill. In the SST-PT group teachers and parents met to discuss the target skill for that week, and the teachers filled out daily report cards indicating how well the child had exhibited the behaviors. Goals were set up at home that would allow the student to earn good sports bucks for using the target skills in school. Parents in the SST group received the same handouts as parents in the SST-PG group, but did not attend group meetings, receive good sports bucks, or have the teachers fill out daily report cards.

Participants were recruited from newspaper advertisements and referrals to a clinic that specialized in dealing with children who have an ADHD diagnosis. Subjects needed to meet several criteria indicating a diagnosis of ADHD before being accepted into the study. First, when rated by parents, subjects needed a mean score at or above 1.5 on a subscale assessing ADHD from the Conners, Loney, and Milich Rating Scale (CLAM) or the Swanson, Nolan, and Pelham Revised Rating Scale (SNAP-R). Second, participants needed a T score of 60 or higher on the Attention Problem subscale of the CBCL. Lastly, children had to be diagnosed as having either ADHD or undifferentiated attention deficit disorder (UADD) according to DSM-III-R criteria after a clinical interview with their mothers.

Nineteen of the subjects met criteria for Oppositional Defiant Disorder, 3 for Conduct Disorder, 4 for separation anxiety disorder, 5 for overanxious disorder, and 2 for dysthymic disorder. Twelve of the subjects were on stimulants during the study. Of note, all participants in this study were Caucasian except for one African-American family. Also, most of the families that were used in this study had two parents, and were of middle to upper socioeconomic class.

The primary outcome measures were parent and teacher reported measures of social skills. Overall, being in a treatment group led to an improvement in parent ratings of their child exhibiting social skills when compared to the control group. Significant differences in ratings of social skills were not found between the SST and SST-PT groups, indicating that the parent generalization component was not useful in increasing the amount of positive social skills exhibited by the child. Also of note, teacher and parent ratings failed to find significant differences between the two groups when compared against the control groups on externalizing behavior and problem behavior from pre

treatment to follow-up. This raises questions about the importance of social skills as an intervention target.

An important methodological consideration is that different teachers filled out the SSRS rating forms at pre-treatment and follow-up, and at neither assessment point did the two treatment groups show significant differences on behavior problems from the control group. Since changes were noticed in parental scores, but not teacher scores, this leaves the validity of the treatment in question. Parents may have had reactivity to the measure since they filled out the form more than once, whereas a different teacher filled the form out at the pre-intervention and follow-up phases for the child participants, allowing for a more accurate depiction of the child's true behavior. Or, it is possible that the parents had expectations of the experimental situations, and their responses to the forms were convoluted due to this bias.

Another methodological consideration was that many participants in the control group also had an increase on their scores on the outcome measures, indicating that studies of children with ADHD are encumbered by time threats to causal inference, such as maturation, regression, instrumentation, and reactivity. Having a wait-list or untreated control group, such as the one in this study, is one of the best ways to reduce uncertainty in causal inference related to these time threats.

CBT for ADHD plus Parent Training (Springer, 2004)

The purpose of this study was to analyze the effects of an early intervention program for 51 children between the ages of 4 and 8.5 that had a diagnosis of ADHD combined type. Children were assigned to one of three groups for 10 weeks of treatment: (1) child group training only (C1), (2) child and parent group training (C2), or (3) a child and parent group training with an adherence measure (C3).

Children's group training (CGT) sessions

used cognitive-behavioral methods to address common problems in children with ADHD such as impulsivity, difficulty with stress and anger management, and deficits in social skills. Children were taught methods to address these problem areas through didactic instruction, modeling, role-playing, behavior rehearsal, coaching, and games. A token economy system was used during the sessions to encourage the children to participate in order achieve more success in mastering target skills. At the end of each session, children self-evaluated whether they were successful in following directions, using their words, and keeping their hands and feet under control. Children were rewarded with a sticker they could place in a book for each goal they achieved. Children also had an "All About Me" workbook were they recorded their progress evaluation with a therapist (e.g. behavior goal charts) as well as personal information about themselves.

Parent training groups (PTG) consisted of 10 weekly 90-minute sessions based on a modified version of Barkely's parent training curriculum (Barkley, 1990) The PTG focused on teaching parents how to use various behavioral techniques, deal with stress, improve communication between themselves and their child diagnosed with ADHD, as well as facts about ADHD. Handouts containing information on various behavioral techniques and strategies were distributed weekly so the parents would have the ability to reinforce the skills being taught to their children. Parents in C3 also filled out a Parental Adherence Measure (PAM) at the beginning of each parent training session beginning with session 3.

Participants for this study were recruited in a variety of ways. Some parents contacted the Center for Psychological Services at Farleigh Dickinson University after receiving a referral from the school, pediatrician, or mental health professional. Other subjects responded to an ad in the paper, or heard about it on the internet or by word of mouth. All children had a primary diagnosis of ADHD Combined Type by a professional, exhibited clinically elevated scores on several child assessment measures, and their parents had a score in the 80th percentile or above on the child domain of the Parent Stress Index-III. Participants were required to pay for treatment, but the cost to the family of each intervention was not specified in the paper.

The author used a large number of outcome measures, including the Child Behavior Checklist, Conner's Parent Rating Scale Revised, Social Skills Rating System Parent Form, Conner's Teacher Rating Scale Revised, and the Social Skills Rating System Teacher From. These measures were administered to parents and teachers prior to treatment, post-treatment, and at the 4-month follow-up. Repeated measures ANOVA found no group by time interactions, indicating that there were no statistically significant treatment effects. However, the ANOVAs were conducted with low power and a myriad of other statistical measures were presented including effect sizes, reliable change, and t-tests for pre to follow-up.

Generally speaking, due to the huge number of measures and statistical analyses, the pattern of results was very confusing. For example, parents in the C3 group reported significant improvements for parental efficacy at the four-month follow up. Furthermore, C3 had the highest percentage of participants who showed reliable change with recovery in terms of parental stress and child internalizing, externalizing, hyperactivity, and social problems across home and school settings. However, their children showed a decrease in cognitive competence, physical competence, peer acceptance, and maternal acceptance. Many other measures showed contradictory patterns.

The most conservative approach to assessing the results of this study is to examine ANOVAs, which generally found non-significant results. Due to the small sample size and no reports of statistical power, however, the ANOVAs are not readily interpreted. Unfortunately, the other measures (e.g., effect sizes and measures of clinically significant change) were often contradictory. Therefore, we deemed the results of this study to be unable to be interpreted with regard to efficacy.

Intensive Parent Training Plus Child Cognitive Behavioral Therapy (Hauch, 2005)

Hauch (2005), like Springer (2004), was a doctoral dissertation. The purpose of the Hauch (2005) study was to evaluate the effects of the Child ADHD Multimodal Program (CAMP) with children ages 5 to 7 years who had a diagnosis of ADHD Combined Type. Despite the use of term "multimodal" in the name of the therapy, as described below, the intensive program was parent focused. In contrast, what we deem to be multimodal treatment involves a combination of truly different modes, such as medication, parent training, intensive child-focused, and school-based intervention.

In Hauch (2005), the CAMP consisted of (1) a child training (CT) group that promoted social skills, impulse control, and anger management, (2) a parent training (PT) group designed to compliment the child training, and (3) an additional home/school-based behavioral component. This study adds to the 4-month Hall and Reddy (2002) report that consisted of 20 children and 19 families who were randomly assigned to participate in the CAMP or a CT only group.

The CT group was based on philosophies from Bandura's social learning theory, Torbert's cooperative games, and Goldstein's Skill Streaming approach (Hauch, 2005). Individuals in the CT group were trained about the purpose of verbal and nonverbal prompts, and the use of self-control strategies. A token economy system was used with the children when in groups to maintain high levels of participation that would theoretically lead to a "mastery" of skills. When a new skill or strategy was introduced, group leaders modeled for the children how to use the skill appropriately. The children then engaged in role plays to practice using the target skill and were given corrective feedback by therapists. At the end of each session, children self-evaluated whether they were successful in following directions, using their words, and keeping their hands and feet under control. The ratio of children to therapists was 2:1 and the average number of treatment hours was 1.5.

The PT portion, which consisted of 10 weekly sessions, was only given to CAMP families and was modified from Barkley's (1990) parent training program. The overall goals of the PT were to teach parents: details about ADHD, how to implement and maintain the use of behavioral techniques, how to recognize their child's strengths' and weaknesses, anger and stress management techniques, and how to interact with their children and school personnel in order to achieve more success with the child's behavior and goals. Handouts containing information on various behavioral techniques and strategies were distributed weekly to reinforce the skills the children were learning. CAMP families were given home- and school-based behavioral consultation. Therapists had an average of 3.3 consultation sessions with teachers and an average of 5.4 consultation sessions with parents. The average number of treatment hours per week for individuals receiving the CAMP was 4.

Initially, parents contacted the ADHD Clinic at Farleigh Dickinson University for treatment after hearing about the program from physicians or word of mouth, seeing advertisements, or seeing internet web pages. Families were then randomly drawn from a pool and offered the option to participate in the study. To participate in this study all children had to have a diagnosis of ADHD

Combined Type by a licensed professional, have elevated scores on several standardized assessment measures, and have their parent score in the 70th percentile or higher on the Child Total Scale of the Parenting Stress Index III. After screenings, 9 children met the criteria for ODD, 2 for CD, and 5 for Anxiety Disorders. Also of note, 12 of the children who participated were taking Ritalin or Adderall during treatment. Children whose parents were separated or in the divorce process, children who had been sexually abused within the past 18 months, and children who had a significant loss in the past year were excluded from the study.

Numerous measures were used in this study for the 4-month follow up, as stated by the researcher, included the SSRS-PF, SSRS-TF, the CPRS-R, and the CBCL. Measures that were also administered at the 16-month follow up for externalizing and ADHD behaviors included the Conner's Parent Short form and the Home Situations Questionnaire Revised (HSQ-R).

"At the 16-month follow-up the CAMP was found to be clinically superior to the CT group on externalizing problems, parental stress, parental efficacy, and family routines. Individuals in the CAMP also showed greater percentages of reliable change with recovery on the oppositional, cognitive problems/inattention, and ADHD scales of the Conner's Parent Short form" (Hauch, 2005). No teacher data were collected at the 16-month follow-up.

Overview of Child-Focused Interventions Combined with Parent Training and ESP Ratings

The content of the parenting sessions was similar across studies and dose of parenting intervention in these studies was similar. Specifically, the interventions were provided in 8 to 12 weeks and the parent interventions were provided in weekly 60 to 90 minute sessions. This content and dose is similar to many standardized and empirically validated parenting protocols (e.g., Sanders, 1999; Webster-Stratton et al., 2001) and, therefore, provides an appropriate backdrop for evaluating the incremental effect of child-focused interventions.

In terms of efficacy, the child-focused interventions had little or no efficacy when compared to the parenting interventions. Indeed, there appeared to be minimal effects of child-focused interventions even when the interventions were compared to no treatment controls. Thus, the efficacy for adding child-focused interventions to parenting interventions appears to be zero. An important caveat is that this rating is based on a limited number of relatively brief child interventions with elementary school aged children. It seems plausible that child-focused interventions may be more powerful with older children (e.g., middle-school age).

Safety concerns with group-based treatments for children with behavior problems were raised several years ago (Dishion et al., 1999). Subsequent reviews have found possible iatrogenic effects of grouping deviant youth together (Dodge et al., 2006; Rhule, 2005). There are some differing results, however, with some reviews finding no negative effects in well-structured psychotherapy groups (Weiss et al., 2005). Nevertheless, we are concerned about possible deviancy training and deducted one point for safety when poorly behaved children are grouped together.

Another safety consideration is the potential for an escalation in parent-child conflict when both are involved in therapy. This has been noted in at least one study (Barkley et al., 2001). No such problems were reported in the studies reviewed. Due to the uncertainly on this issue, and the uncertainty regarding deviancy training, we did not deduct an additional point for safety in these studies. However, we strongly recommend that future studies monitor the peer deviancy and parent-child conflict issues very carefully.

Finally, the issue of practicality did not receive extensive comment in these studies. Parent satisfaction, fidelity, and other issues were minimally examined in these studies which is a serious methodological deficiency in our opinion. We should note that organizing outpatient groups is notoriously difficult and is not always adequately supported by clinics and third party providers. As seen in the section on parent training, there can be major problems with getting parents to attend parent training sessions. Taken together, we deducted one point from practicality for this type of intervention (see Table 7).

Child-Focused Intervention

In this section, we review studies where the focus of the causal inference was the efficacy of child focused-intervention alone. Only two studies contributed to this section (see Table 5). We provide a detailed description of the Shelton et al. (2000) intensive classroom study and a brief summary of the pertinent results from Pfiffner and McBurnett (1997). Then, we rate the long-term efficacy, safety, and practicality of these child-focused interventions.

Table 5: Studies of Child-Focused Intervention

Study	Type of Treatment	Treatment Duration	Follow-up	Efficacy	Safety	Practicality
Shelton et al., 2000	Special Treatment Classroom	1 year	2 years	No effects reported when compared to control group	Possible iatrogenic effects from grouping deviant peers	Not cost effective compared to alternatives
Pfiffner and McBurnett, 1997	Social Skills and Self-control Training	Eight consecutive weekly 90 minute sessions	4 months	Decreases in disruptive behavior should be interpreted cautiously due to lack of adequate control group	Grouping of deviant peers	Not cost effective compared to alternatives

Intensive Classroom Intervention (Shelton et al., 2000)

In this study, which was mentioned briefly in the section on parent training, 158 preschool children were assigned to one of four groups during their first year in kindergarten: (1) a no-treatment control group, (2) parent training only groups, (3) special treatment classroom, and (4) a parent training combined with the special classroom treatment group. Children were identified as having high levels (>+1.5 SD) of disruptive behavior and to be eligible for the experiment needed to meet 2 criteria: (1) significantly elevated scores on either the ADHD or impulsive-hyperactive scale and on the oppositional defiant disorder (ODD) or conduct problems (CP) factors of the Revised Conner's Parent Rating Scale. Children were returned to their community for first grade.

Initially, a 10-week parenting program was implemented that focused on identifying the causes of behavior problems, rewarding children for non-disruptive behavior, setting up a token system to encourage positive behavior, and methods for handling disruptive behavior in different situations. Evaluation of the data at post-treatment showed that there was no significant effect of the parent training program that was implemented, although this may have been due to low attendance rates. For this reason, the 2-year follow-up paper compares the subjects who did receive a treatment classroom intervention (n=74) and those who did not (n=77). Hence, we listed this study as a child-focused intervention.

Teachers were offered advice for behavioral interventions for the children they would be teaching. The special treatment classroom intervention was similar to regular kindergarten classrooms with a teacher and teacher aide. Also, a master teacher who was experienced in behavioral treatment programs worked in each classroom for half a day (Shelton et al., 2000). Behavioral interventions such as token systems, time out, social skills training, response cost, and self-control instruction were implemented in the classes.

When students with disruptive behavior in the study were compared to a community control group the study participants scored significantly higher on CBCL attention, aggression, delinquency, anxiety, social, and thought problems scales indicating this is a representative sample of a group with behavior problems. No significant results were found for being in the treatment group according to DISC-P and CBCL scores in the home. No significant results were found in the school either as indicated by measures of social skills or on behavioral scores from the CBCL.

Social Skills Training (Pfiffner and McBurnett, 1997)

As stated previously, this study found limited changes in social skills as rated by parents compared to parent reports in a wait-list control group. Importantly, social skills training did not result in any detected changes in ADHD-related problems and had no effect on behavior reported by teachers. Thus, this study raises questions about the (a) the efficacy and generalizability of social skills training, and (b) the underlying treatment theory that changes in social skills might mediate changes in ADHD-related problems. In terms of safety, we were concerned with the grouping of deviant peers. In terms of practicality, providing parent groups simultaneously with child groups may be a good way to engage parents in the intervention process (McKay et al., 1996).

Overview of Child-Focused Intervention and Efficacy, Safety, and Practicality Ratings

The two child-focused interventions studied are examples of what might be considered to be reasonable interventions for children with ADHD. One is a very intensive intervention similar to what might be given to a child with ADHD who is classified as emotionally/behaviorally disturbed. This intensive intervention has virtually no beneficial effect. This is consistent with extensive reviews of the literature that have found no benefit of special education classrooms that group deviant youth. Indeed, a well conducted meta-analytic review found a negative effect of such interventions (Lipsey and Wilson, 1993).

Considering that social skills problems are rife among children with ADHD, social skills training seems like a reasonable intervention. Studies, however, have not supported this supposition. Thus, the Pfiffner and McBurnett (1997) study adds to a series of studies finding limited efficacy of social skills training.

Taken together, the studies reviewed found no support for the efficacy of child-focused interventions, so the efficacy was rated as zero. Grouping peers with behavior problems in classrooms for a whole year is very likely to cause harm, for a variety of reasons including deviancy training. Therefore, we rated the classroom intervention as having a safety score of only 1 and the group social skills training as having a safety score of 2.

The intensive classroom intervention has some significant implementation challenges, both procedurally and in terms of funding and sustainability. Therefore, this intervention loses two points for practicality, and has a score of 1. Social skills training in outpatient groups has some problems with implementation, but is a fairly common practice that seems acceptable to parents. Accordingly, we gave the social skills training groups a practicality score of 2.

Pharmacological Intervention

Although the focus of this review is on psychosocial interventions, the sheer popularity and established efficacy of pharmacological interventions necessitates that this topic be covered in this review. This is consistent with other reviews that focused primarily on psychosocial interventions (Pelham, Jr. et al., 1998). Unlike the review of the psychosocial interventions, our review here is not exhaustive. Rather it focuses on the Multimodal Treatment Study of ADHD (MTA), which is widely regarded as the best longitudinal study of treatment for ADHD to be conducted to date. Because there is only one study reviewed, there is no separate table for pharmacological intervention.

The MTA was primarily designed to answer questions about the long-term efficacy of the best-supported treatments for AD/HD and if there was any difference in clinical outcome when the treatments were used separately or in combination. To address this issue children were randomly assigning children to four treatment groups: medication alone (MedMgt), behavior modification alone (Beh), the combination of medication and behavior modification (Comb), and community comparison (CC). In order to be eligible for the study, children had to be between ages 7-9.9, be in grades 1-4, meet DSM-IV diagnostic criteria for ADHD Combined Type via Parent Diagnostic Interview Schedule for Children (supplemented by teacher reported symptoms if the case was near the diagnostic threshold), and be living with the same caretaker for at least the previous six months. Youth with co-morbid internalizing or externalizing psychiatric disorders were included as long as these conditions did not require treatment incompatible with study treatments.

Important characteristics of the MTA sample selected for the study included variables identified a priori as potential moderators of treatment: gender (20% female), prior medication status (31%), ODD or CD diagnoses (40% and 14%), DSM IIIR anxiety disorder (34% with simple phobia alone not included), and numbers of youth whose families were receiving welfare, public assistance, or SSI (19%). Important to note is that the 579 children represented 13% of those initially contacting the project, 25% of those passing an initial rating scale screening, or 62% of those completing the diagnostic interview and evaluation of school cooperation.

The medication treatment (in both MedMgt and Comb conditions) provided in the MTA occurred in a much more rigorous and intensive way than is typical in clinical practice. All medication treatment provided by the MTA included an initial 28-day double-blind, placebo-controlled titration consisting of placebo plus four different doses of methylphenidate (5, 10, 15, and 20mg) randomly given over the titration period. Approximately, 89% of youth assigned to MedMgt or Comb successfully completed titration; of these, 68.5% were assigned to initial doses of methylphenidate averaging

30.5 mg/day given 3 times per day, of the remaining group of youth who completed titration but were not started on methylphenidate, 26 received an unblinded titration of dextroamphetamine because of unsatisfactory methylphenidate response and 32 were given no medication because of a robust placebo response. Of note is that of the 289 subjects assigned to MedMgt or Comb, 17 families refused titration and another 15 subjects did not complete titration (11 due to side effects or problems with titration) and 4 of whom inadequate amounts of titration data were gathered (MTA Cooperative Group, 1999a).

Youth assigned to the CC condition received no intervention by the MTA staff, but sought treatment as usually provided in the community. Referrals to non-MTA providers were made as necessary for these families; all CC youth and families returned for assessments at the same time as youth in the other three conditions of the study. Initially, it was thought that the CC group would provide a minimal or no treatment comparison group. However, about two-thirds of the children in the CC group received medication for AD/HD.

Treatments were delivered over a 14-month period and this review focuses on results at the one-year follow-up. Outcomes in this study were assessed using a large number of measures in multiple domains, including verbal-report information (via interview and paper/pencil measures) by parents, teachers, and children, direct observation in the clinic and school, and computerized assessments of attention. The major outcome domains that have received attention in the literature are: ADHD symptoms, oppositional/aggressive symptoms social skills, internalizing symptoms, parent-child relations parental discipline, and academic achievement.

All four MTA groups showed symptom reduction over time, but this could be due to maturation or other artifacts of time.

Therefore, this review focuses on between group comparisons. In the 24-month MTA outcome, the investigators focused on AD/HD symptoms plus four other areas of outcome deemed to be important and validly measured (MTA Cooperative Group, 2004a). These areas were oppositional symptoms, social skills, negative/ineffective parenting, and reading achievement. In this analysis, which focused on group means, the MTA intensive medication groups experienced a greater reduction in ADHD symptoms and oppositional/aggressive symptoms than the CC group. Furthermore, the long-term effects were apparently mediated by use of medication, thus providing support for this mechanism of intervention.

Overall, the efficacy of the MTA intensive medication management (MedMgt) intervention was high, showing clear advantages of this approach relative to typical community care in which about two-thirds of the participants received medication. Thus, something about the intensive medication management seemed to improve the efficacy of an efficacious intervention. The added efficacy may be due to the higher dose of medication in the MedMgt group relative to CC. Also, non-pharmacological factors, such as rapport and supportive counseling, could account for added efficacy of MegMgt versus CC.

Although stimulant medications, such as methyphenidate, have been given to millions of children with hardly any serious problems, there have been some concerns about using stimulant medication. For children taking stimulants there are concerns with issues such growth suppression, potentially elevated risk for substance abuse, and hypertension. Furthermore, in the MTA, children who did not respond to stimulants were given drugs that have the risk of some serious toxic effects. Therefore, the MTA MedMgt intervention was given a safety score of 2.

In terms of practicality, the MTA showed that compliance was critical for the intervention effects. Unfortunately, compliance with medication for ADHD has been poorly studied and the few studies suggest that compliance is far less than optimal. Furthermore, many parents consider medication for ADHD to be unacceptable. Moreover, the MedMgt intervention is unlikely to be available to most families. As a result, the MedMgt condition in the MTA received a practicality score of zero due to problems with compliance, acceptability, and availability.

Intensive Multimodal Treatment

Intensive multimodal treatment can describe a broad range of therapies. For present purposes, we defined "intensive" as an intervention that exceeded the typical dose of that therapy (e.g., a total of 10 sessions delivered in 90 minute weekly meetings). We defined "multimodal" as treatments using at least two substantially different modalities such as medication management, parent training, or school-based intervention.

According to our definition of intensive therapy, a few studies previously reviewed are intensive treatments. These include the MST and 5DR interventions in Wilmshurst (2002) and the CAMP intervention in Hauch (2005). However, these treatments are not multimodal by our definition because MST and CAMP focused primarily on parenting and the 5DR treatment was primarily child-focused.

According to our literature search only two studies have examined the long-term effects of intensive multimodal treatment. One is the MTA, which had two multimodal arms. One of these is the intensive behavioral intervention (Beh) group that focused on parent training, intensive school-based intervention, and a therapeutic summer program for the children with ADHD. The MTA COMB group combined intensive medication management (MedMgt) with the intensive behavioral interventions (Beh). The MTA was described in the previous section and relevant issues are presented in this section. The other study is called the "New York/Montreal collaborative study" or the NYM for short. This section describes the NYM study, then reviews the efficacy, safety, and practicality of combining intensive pharmacological and multimodal psychosocial treatment.

The New York Montreal Study *(Abikoff et al.,2004.*

The New York/Montreal Study (Klein et al., 2004) was conducted at about the same time as the MTA study but, for reasons we have not been able to determine from the articles, the results were not published until much later. In this study researchers examined the effects of multimodal treatment on 103 children ages 7-9 who had a diagnosis of ADHD. Children were randomly assigned to 1 of 3 treatments for 2 years: (1) methylphenidate only (M); (2) methylphenidate plus multimodal psychosocial treatment (M+ MPT); or (3) methylphenidate plus attention psychosocial control treatment (M+ ACT).

All children in the New York/Montreal Study (NYM) initially entered a 5-week trial of methylphenidate followed by a 4-week placebo trial. Children were administered medication three times a day (t.i.d.) 7 days a week with doses titrated upward until the maximum benefits were found at the lowest dosage possible at which point the dose was maintained. Children were considered methylphenidate responders if they (a) had a positive clinical response while on the medication, (b) relapsed during the placebo period and (c) had an absence of cognitive deterioration due to methylphenidate (Klein et al., 2004). Only individuals who met these three criteria were allowed to participate in the NYM study. Thus, the design of the NYM study tests the incremental effect of providing psychosocial intervention to children who respond positively to methylphenidate.

Regardless of which treatment group children and their families were assigned to, all children were administered methylphenidate for 2 years. This required families to meet with a child psychiatrist once a month to monitor the effects of the medication, and adjust the dosage when needed. A total of 22 did not complete the protocol for a variety of reasons such as immediate dropout because of dissatisfaction with treatment assignment, the parents deciding that the child no longer needs treatment, the parents wanting more treatment for their child, problems with attendance, or inability to meet study demands.

A variety of common ADHD issue areas were addressed in the multimodal psychosocial treatment (MPT) condition. The first year of psychosocial treatments involved twice-weekly visits, whereas the second year only required twice monthly follow-up booster sessions. Children received group social skills training and academic remediation skills, and individual psychotherapy. Parents participated in parent training. A 75% attendance rate was required for all families and make-up sessions were provided. Individuals in the attention control group (ACT) received group training in normal development (for parents) and supportive counseling (for children). After one year, children were switched to single-blind placebo conditions and methylphenidate was reissued when needed

This study was conducted at one medical center located in New York and one in Montreal. Participants were obtained from referrals from school and community resources for children who were exhibiting behavior problems in the school and at home. All participants met the DSM-III-R criteria for ADHD based on a parent interview with the DISC-P2 as well as parent and teacher reports. Also, all children had a mean teacher rating of at least 1.5 on the hyperactivity

factor or Hyperkinesis Index of the CTRS on at least 2 separate occasions. Additional criteria that had to be met in order for families to participate included that the child: was medication-free 2 weeks before the evaluation, had an IQ within the normal range, was living with at least one parent (81.2% lived with both parents), and had telephone access. Also of note, children were excluded if they had a learning disorder, psychosis, or conduct disorder. Approximate-ly 53.4% of the sample met the criteria for ODD. Children were also excluded if they did not have significant behavioral deterioration over the 4 week placebo period when compared to the methylphenidate trial.

The primary measures for assessment, as stated by the authors, included the CPRS, the Home Situations Questionnaire (HSQ), and the CTRS. In addition, observers viewed the students in their academic and gym classes using the Classroom Observation code form. After gym observations observers completed the CTRS Hyperkinesis Index and IOWA CTRS. Parents, teachers, and psychiatrists were aware of the child's group assignment, but raters at school were blind to treatment condition which was easy to accomplish because no treatment was provided at school.

At the 2-year follow-up, there were not significant group or interaction effects on any of the parent or teacher rating. Psychiatrists' ratings of ADHD symptoms in the school and home did not differ in the treatment groups. Classroom observations also failed to yield significant group effects. M+MPT was not found to be more effective than M or M+ACT. It was expected that participants in the combination treatments would have more methylphenidate discontinuation then the methylphenidate group alone, but this hypothesis was not supported by the data.

The results of the NYM study suggest that there was no incremental benefit of providing intensive psychosocial treatment to children who responded positively to methylphenidate.

It is noteworthy, however, that the psycho-social interventions selected for this study (e.g., individual therapy) have questionable efficacy for treating ADHD. Furthermore, fidelity checks in the study found that the parenting interventions produced no changes in parenting behavior. Thus, the NYM did not implement a credible intensive psychosocial intervention.

In terms of safety, because the NYM study used methylphenidate, the medication arm of this study is very safe. Greater risks are incurred with some other drugs used to treat ADHD, with the possible exception of other stimulants and atamoxatine (see Smith et al., 2006). Nevertheless even stimulants raise some concerns, such as potential growth suppression, so we deducted one point for safety.

In terms of practicality, three points were deducted. One was due to the problems with compliance. Another point was lost due to tolerability, with 22 out of 103 subjects withdrawing from the study due to lack of tolerance for the procedures. Also, because this intervention was so complex and intense, it is unlikely that this intervention will be widely available to families outside of research studies. Thus, the overall practicality score for the NYM study was a zero.

Multimodal Treatments in the MTA

The behavioral treatments in the MTA were very intensive with parenting training, two major child-focused interventions, and school-based services based primarily on behavioral modification principles. Briefly, the parenting intervention consisted of 27 group and 8 individual sessions in less than one year. Child-focused behavioral treatment consisted of (a) an intensive summer treatment program that the children attended for 8 weeks, 9 hours a day and (b) 12 weeks of having paraprofessional aides at school working in the child's classroom. Furthermore, there were intensive school

consultation services consisting of 10 to 16 sessions of teacher consultation. Families attended an average of 77.8% of parent training sessions, 36.2 of 40 possible Summer Treatment Program days, 10.7 teacher consultation visits, and 47.6 (of 60) possible days with a classroom aid. Children in the Comb condition received all of the behavioral intervention, plus the complete MedMgt intervention, which was described previously.

At the 24-month follow-up it appears that the trends in the data favor the Comb treatment over the other three conditions, but this conclusion may depend on how those data are analyzed (Smith et al., 2006). For instance, the Comb and MedMgt conditions had significantly different scores on ADHD symptoms and related problems compared to the Beh and CC conditions. However, there were no mean group differences between the Beh and CC groups, suggesting that the MTA behavior management was not better than usual community care, with CC heavily dependent on medication. Also, there were not mean differences between the Comb and MedMgt groups, which some interpreted to mean that the behavioral intervention added nothing to intensive medication management.

A different picture of the MTA emerges, however, if one examines variables other than group differences in ADHD and ODD/CD symptoms. For instance, the normalization rates were 48%, 37%, 32%, and 28%, for Comb, MedMgt, Beh, and CC, respectively (MTA Cooperative Group, 2004a). Further-more, analyses of group differences found that that Comb group was better than the other groups with regard to child social skills, negative/ineffective parenting, and reading achievement. Thus, as the effects of the MTA study had faded since the discontinuation of treatment, the long-term effects of the Comb intervention appear to emerge as the most efficacious treatment for ADHD in the MTA study.

The MTA Cooperative Group conducted

analyses on the relationship between treatment participation and outcomes (MTA Cooperative Group, 2004b). In this analysis mediators were defined as acceptance of treatment and attendance at treatment sessions. Overall, there was an effect of compliance on treatment outcome and the Comb condition was apparently more robust to noncompliance than MedMgt. It is also noteworthy that at the 14-month follow-up, satisfaction scores by parents for Comb and Beh were equal to each other and significantly better than parent satisfaction scores for the MedMgt condition (MTA Cooperative Group, 1999a). Given the emphasis placed on consumer satisfaction, this is not a trivial matter. Indeed, the highest attrition rates were for the MedMgt condition.

The efficacy, safety, and practicality ratings (ESP) are given in Table 6. Because of the strength of the MTA design, consistencies with other studies of combined treatment, and the superiority of the Comb condition to the other three MTA conditions

we gave the MTA Combined treatment condition the highest possible score for efficacy. Although the treatment effect faded somewhat from 14 to 24 months, there was still support for the efficacy of the MedMgt, Beh, and CC conditions; however, CC and Beh were consistently behind MedMgt. Thus, we gave efficacy ratings of 2 to MedMgt and 1 to CC and Beh.

In terms of safety, we gave the MTA Comb and MedMgt conditions scores of 2 due to potential long-term risks from taking medication. For children taking stimulants we were concerned with issues including growth suppression, which was reported at the 24-month follow-up. The risk for safety with the MTA Behavioral intervention was potential deviancy training especially during the summer treatment program portion, so we deducted safety points when children were in the summer treatment program. We should note, however, that the highly controlled environment might preclude deviancy training.

Table 6: Treatments from the MTA

Type of Treatment	Efficacy	Safety	Practicality
Medication Management	Superior to Beh and CC	Growth suppression	Very unlikely to be available to general public, medication was not administered to subjects as prescribed
Behavioral Training	Superior to CC, but results were far less robust when compared to Medication and Combined treatments	Possible deviancy training	Very unlikely to be available to general public
Medication Management + Behavioral Training	Produced largest reductions in ADHD behaviors as well as other externalizing and internalizing behaviors	Growth suppression due to medication and possible deviancy training	Very unlikely to be available to general public, low levels of compliance
Community Control	Community care did manage to produce minimal positive results	No noted negative effects	Problems with compliance and acceptability

With regard to practicality it seemed that the likelihood of a child receiving the MedMgt, Comb, or Beh treatment packages is remote, if not completely nonexistent. Thus, each of these loses a point for accessibility and a point for complexity. Furthermore, the MTA MedMgt lost a point for acceptability due to observed refusals and lower ratings of satisfaction. The CC condition, by definition, was accessed by the public and therefore should be regarded as a minimally practical intervention, with perhaps one point deducted for acceptability and one point deducted for tolerability and compliance problems.

SUMMARY OF EFFICACY, SAFETY AND PRACTICALITY

The summary ratings of the various interventions that have longitudinal data are given in Table 7. We should note that these studies refer to that small subset of longitudinal studies. Different efficacy, safety, and practicality ratings might be reached when considering the far more numerous short-term studies. Nevertheless, our conclusions are generally consistent with others (e.g., Pelham et al., 1998), but may be unstable due to the small number of studies of psychosocial treatments.

Table 7: Overall Efficacy, Safety, and Practicality Ratings

Treatment	Efficacy	Safety	Practicality	Combined ESP Score	Comment
Parent Training Groups	1	3	2	5	With young children
Multisystemic Family Therapy	2	3	2	7	Only one study
Parenting plus child-focused intervention	1	2	2	5	No added benefit of child intervention
Intensive Classroom	0	1	1	2	Only one study
Social Skills Training	0	2	2	4	Only one study
Community Stimulant Medication	2	2	1	5	A common treatment
Intensive medication management	3	2	0	5	Not generally available
Intensive Multimodal Behavioral Treatment	2	2	1	5	Very unlikely to be available
Intensive Medication and Behavioral Intervention	3	2	1	6	Very unlikely to be available

The highest rated interventions in terms of efficacy were the medication management (MedMgt) and combined treatments (i.e., MedMgt combined with intensive behavioral treatment) from the MTA study. A version of the multisystemic therapy (MST) intervention from the Wilmshurst (2002) study was also very promising, but was only given an efficacy score of 2 due to lack of replication of MST with an ADHD population. It is noteworthy, however, that long-term positive effects of MST have been observed with other clinical populations. Considering that the MTA interventions have not been specifically replicated in terms of long-term effects, one might argue that the MedMgt and Comb interventions should also have an efficacy score of 2. Thus, there is a virtual tie between the MedMgt, Comb, and MST interventions for the most efficacious intervention.

The putative tie between MedMgt, Comb, and MST for best treatment in terms of long-term results ratings is broken when the safety and efficacy considerations are added. Even when MST has an efficacy score of 2 and MedMgt and Comb have efficacy scores of 3, the combined ESP score is 7 for MST. This compares to a combined ESP score of 6 for Comb and 5 for MedMgt. Thus, we recommend more widespread use of MST type therapies and continued research and development of this intervention approach.

The second highest total ESP score was for the Comb treatment from the MTA. Unfortunately, the stunning intensity of the behavioral intervention in this study makes it very hard to replicate outside of heavily funded research studies. It would be worth investigating if lower doses of psychosocial intervention could achieve the same results. Until such modifications are possible, it is likely that few will receive this treatment in its fullest form.

In terms of total ESP ratings, the third tier of treatments were (a) medication, and (b) parent training. The efficacy of parent training is very well established in short-term studies, but it did not fare well in terms of efficacy in the few available long-term studies (i.e., efficacy scores of only 1). Nevertheless, such approaches are theoretically sound, generally safe, and have the potential to be much more efficacious if the dose is increased from the meager 10 to 12 weeks typically allocated to treat ADHD. This is a paltry dose to treat a chronic condition.

Medication will remain a controversial treatment for ADHD. It clearly works for some individuals, but many do not respond positively, and is less effective for individuals who develop ADHD as a result of a brain injury. Most estimate the no-response rate at about 30%, but higher response rates are typically seen in intensive medication management protocols (Smith et al., 2006). Furthermore, many parents refuse to put their children on medication. Moreover, compliance is a major issue and there are declining rates of use with increasing age. Overall, medication is neither necessary nor sufficient for treating ADHD and non-pharmacological approaches are in great need of development and long-term research.

Based on the current long-term studies, we would not recommend social skills training, intensive classrooms, or other child-focused interventions at this time. Of note, most of these child-focused studies were with younger children. It will be interesting to see if interventions such as cognitive behavioral therapy are more effective with older children with ADHD, who have more of the mental capacity needed to benefit from treatment.

Methodological Considerations

We present four major methodological considerations that, if addressed, should substantially improve understanding of the long-term results of treatment for ADHD. The four topics were selected because they impacted our effort to summarize the literature on long-term treatment for ADHD. These issues, in no particular order of importance, are (a) the need to conduct more long-term studies of treatments for ADHD, (b) the need to include "treatment as usual" or "community care" control groups, (c) the need to include objective measures of functioning, and (d) the need to test a "chronic care" versus "acute care" approach to treating ADHD.

By our count, only 9 different interventions for ADHD have been subjected to long-term outcome studies. Moreover, long-term may be a misnomer. The longest outcome studies were only two years and we had to substantially reduce the length of follow-up to four months to get the nine interventions we reviewed. Given that ADHD is a chronic disorder and should have lasting effects across the life span, a two-year follow-up provides scant information. There needs to be a major increase in funding for prospective treatment studies with very long follow-up periods. Agencies such as the National Institute of Mental Health routinely provide funding for five-year periods. Moreover, they also allow for competitive renewals of promising projects. Investigators should work with NIMH (and other funding agencies) to undertake reasonably long-term outcomes studies of treatments for ADHD.

Many studies in the review were hard to interpret because they did not have a treatment as usual control group. If all long-term studies of treatment for ADHD had such a control condition, then it would be much easier to compute effect sizes and compare treatments. No treatment control groups would allow for comparison of effect sizes. However, given that there are treatments known to be effective for ADHD, it would be unethical to withhold treatment. In the MTA study, parents were clearly able to get reasonably effective (but not necessarily the very best) services for their children. This lead to meaningful comparisons between innovative interventions and standard care in an ethical and informative manner.

Notably lacking were objective and ecologically valid measures of functioning. A few studies have some direct observation by observers blind to treatment condition. Such measures are worthwhile if they are ecologically valid. For instance, if observed peer aggression correlates with school discipline referrals and related consequences, measuring peer aggression may be a helpful outcome measure. Unfortunately, almost no psychometric data about the validity of measures was reported. Studies were rife with reports of parent and teacher measures, but clearly more work needs to be done in the area of validity and collecting meaningful data from unbiased observers. Currently, the field is precariously depending on parent

ratings, usually of ADHD symptoms, that could be biased (see Table 8).

Although reducing the severity of ADHD symptoms seems to be a sensitive measure of treatment for ADHD, it does not really make sense to focus on eliminating ADHD symptoms if ADHD is, indeed, a chronic disorder. Given ADHD is a chronic disorder and is not expected to be cured by treatment, measures in treatment studies should focus on ADHD-related impairments. These impair-ments might include strained peer relations, poor academic functioning, conflict with adults, accidents, vocational functioning, and other relevant outcomes. As mentioned above, if measures can be collected objectively or through multi-informant methods, validity should improve. Further-more, as mentioned above, the measures should be calibrated with important life outcomes such as grades, suspensions, job performance, automobile accidents, etc.

The final, and perhaps most important methodological consideration, is that the long-term follow-up studies have addressed an acute care model of treating ADHD. This acute care model provides a time-limited intervention of varying intensity presumably with the expectation that the time-limited provision of services will result in a lasting change in the target behavior. A not so surprising finding in the studies is that treatment effect sizes tend to diminish following the acute phase of intervention (see Table 8). In the MTA study, for example, the effect sizes in the year after the active treatment ended were about one half less then they were when treatment was still active. Indeed, Pelham (1999) noted that the MTA probably underestimated the effects of the intensive behavioral intervention because treatment was faded well-before the first major (i.e., 14 month) follow-up.

Despite the fact that every major researcher on ADHD would acknowledge that treatment is not expected to cure ADHD,

Table 8. ADHD outcome measures administered at follow-up

Study	Parent	Teacher	Clinician	Child
Horn et al., 1990	CBCL, CPRS Hyperkinesis Index	CTRS Total, Hyperkinesis Index		
Fehlings et al., 1991	BCP-AP subscale, WWAS, SCRS	SCRS, BPC-AP subscale		Revised MFFT
Strayhorn and Weidman, 1991	Behar, DSM-III-R Criteria Checklist, CBCL	Behar, DSM-III-R criteria		
Pfiffner and McBurnett, 1997	SSRS, CBCL, UCISSS	SSRS, TRF		
Shelton et al., 2000	CBCL, HSQ	CBCL, SSQ, SCRS, SSRS	Restricted Academic Situation Coding System, DISC-P	CPT
Wilmshurst, 2002	SSRS, SCIS	SCIS, SSRS		
MTA Cooperative Group, 2004	SNAP ADHD Sx	SNAP ADHD Sx		
Abikoff, 2004	CPRS Hyperkinesis Index, HSQ		Classroom Observation Code, CTRS Hyperkinesis Index, IOWA CTRS	
Springer, 2004	CBCL, CPRS	TRF, SSRS, CTRS		
Hauch, 2005	Conner's Parent short form, HSQ-R			
BCP-AP=Revised Behavior Problem Checklist-Attention Problem subscale; Behar-Behar Preschool Behavior Questionnaire; CBCL=Child Behavior Checklist; CPRS=Connors' Parent Rating Scale; CPT=Continuous Performance Test; CTRS=Connors' Teacher Rating Scale; MMFT=Matching Familiar Figures Task; SCIS=Standardized Client Information System; SCRS=Self-Control Rating Scale; SSQ=School Symptoms Questionnaire; SSRS=Social Skills Rating System; TRF=Teacher Rating Form; UCISSS=University of California Irvine Social Skills Scale; WWAS=Werry Weiss Activity Scale				

researchers have tended to favor randomized clinical trails that have a pre-test, post-test, and follow-up. We submit that this is not an appropriate model for evaluating treatment for ADHD when active treatment ends prior to post-test. Ending treatment for ADHD is akin to having an acute treatment phase for Type 1 diabetes then terminating care at the start of the follow-up period.

We are well aware that there is some preparation and training of participants in the ADHD treatments designed to promote ongoing use of intervention techniques beyond the active intervention period. This is true with diabetes care too. Nevertheless, it is generally expected with diabetes, ADHD, and other chronic conditions that some sort of professional involvement is needed beyond the acute care period to ensure proper implementation of the aforementioned methods. Thus, there needs to be studies of approaches other than the acute care approach to treating ADHD that focus on fidelity.

A plausible alternative approach to the acute care approach to treating ADHD is the chronic care model. In such a model there should be the expectation of continuous management of the disorder. Dental care provides a suitable metaphor. There needs to be some sort of daily intervention akin to flossing and brushing. In the case of ADHD, this may include taking medication and having active, ongoing behavioral intervention. There also needs to be some sort of regular reviews of progress, akin to a bi-annual tooth cleaning. The bi-annual ADHD Check-Up can be conducted by a professional such as a case manager, school psychologist, or pediatrician (see Smith et al., for a recommended ADHD Check-Up protocol).

The results of the check-ups in the chronic care model guide decisions about the appropriate level and type of care in the near future. The chronic care model dictates that there need to be provisions to provide higher level care when needed. This is akin to having occasional brief interventions provided by experts. In the dental analogy, this would involve having a cavity filled. In ADHD, this may involve an adjustment in medication. Sometimes more intensive, protracted interventions might be needed. In the dental analogy, this might involve services such as braces. In the case of ADHD this may involve participation in parent training, teacher consultation to deal with school issues, medication titration to improve desired effects or ameliorate undesired effects, or even more intensive interventions such as MST.

Concluding Comments

An ample number of studies have been conducted to date that focus on various treatments of ADHD from several theoretical perspectives. Unfortunately, most of these studies lack an adequate follow-up period to ensure effects of the intervention are maintained. ADHD is a chronic disorder that can impair an individual's ability to function throughout their lifespan. Although specific areas affected may change from childhood to adolescence to adulthood, impairments continue to exist. Thus, there is a dire need for a continuum of care treatment approach that focuses on teaching children with ADHD and their families effective methods for controlling and preventing impairments due to ADHD symptoms.

Studies identified for this review attempted to add to the literature by showing long term effects of treatment on ADHD symptoms. Most of these studies failed to find strong positive results at follow-up. The interventions that showed the largest reductions in impairments related to ADHD behaviors (Wilmshurst, MTA) were labor intensive, expensive, and implemented for longer periods of time than other treatments reviewed. These studies at a minimum focused on involving the parents and the children in treatment in order to have multiple levels of intervention, consistent with the beginnings of a continuum of care treatment approach. Research needs to continue to follow this approach and attempt to develop treatments that will teach skills to combat impairments caused by ADHD for life, and not with a quick fix approach.

Concerns for Discussion

As many as 87 percent of clinically diagnosed ADHD children may have at least one other disorder and 67% have at least two other disorders (Kadesjo and Gillberg, 2001). As noted earlier, children with AD/HD are more likely to have co-existing oppositional defiant and conduct disorder symptoms than children who do not have AD/HD (Angold et al., 1999). Depression and juvenile onset bipolar disorder also appear to be more common in children with ADHD than would be expected in the general population (Biederman et al., 1996; Jensen et al., 1993), especially where conduct disorder is present with ADHD (Angold et al., 1999). There is a modest increase in risk for anxiety disorder as well (Angold et al., 1999; Tannock, 2000). The severity of the ADHD symptoms may in part predict the severity of and risk for these comorbid conditions (Gabel et al., 1996). Thus, these disorders need to be taken into account when designing treatments for children with ADHD who suffer from multiple mental health diagnoses.

REFERENCES

Abikoff H, Hechtman L, Klein RG, Weiss G, Fleiss K, Etcovitch J, Cousins L, Greenfield B. (2004) Symptomatic improvement in children with ADHD treated with long-term methylphenidate and multimodal psychosocial treatment. J Am Acad Child Adolesc Psychiatr 43(7): 802-811.

Barkley RA. (1998) Attention-Deficit Hyperactivity Disorder: A Handbook for Diagnosis and Treatment (2nd ed.). New York, NY: The Guilford Press.

Barkley RA, Edwards G, Laneri M, Fletcher K, Metevia L. (2001) The efficacy of problem-solving communication training alone, behavior management training alone, and their combination for parent-adolescent conflict in teenagers with ADHD and ODD. J Consult Clin Psychol 69(6): 926-941.

Barkley RA, McMurray MB, Edelbrock CS, Robbins K. (1990) Side effects of methylphenidate in children with attention-deficit hyperactivity disorder. Pediatrics 86: 184-192.

Biglan A, Mrazek P, Carnine D, Flay B. (2003) The integration of research and practice in the prevention of youth problems behaviors. Am Psychol 58: 433-440.

Chambless DL, Sanderson WC, Shoham V, Johnson SB, Pope KS, Crits-Christoph P. (1996) An update on empirically validated treatments. Clin Psychol 49: 5-18.

Dishion TJ, McCord J, Poulin F. (1999) When interventions harm: Peer groups and problem behavior. Am Psychol 54(9): 755-764.

Dodge KA, Dishion TD, Lansford JE. (2006) Deviant Peer Influences in programs for youth: Problems and Solutions. New York: Guilford Press.

Fehlings DL, Roberts W, Humphries T, Dawe G. (1991) Attention deficit hyperactivity disorder: Does cognitive behavioral therapy improve home behavior? Devel Beh Pediat 12 (4): 223-228.

Hauch Y. (2005) A multimodal treatment program for children with ADHD: A 16-month follow-up (Doctoral dissertation, Farleigh Dickinson University, 2005). Diss Abstracts Intern 66: 1719.

Hengeller SW, Melton GB, Brondino MJ, Scherer DG, Hanley JH. (1997) Multisystemic Therapy with Violent and Chronic Juvenile Offenders and Their Families: The role of treatment fidelity in successful dissemination. J Consult Clin Psychol 65(5): 821-833.

Henggeler SW, Melton GB, Smith LA. (1992) Family preservation using multisystemic therapy: An effective alternative to incarcerating serious juvenile offenders. J Consult Clin Psychol 60(6): 953-961.

Henggeler SW, Schoenwald SK, Borduin C M, Rowland MD, Cunningham PB. (1998) Multisystemic treatment of antisocial behavior in children and adolescents. New York: The Guilford Press.

Horn WF, Ialongo N, Greenberg G, Packard T, Smith-Winberry C. (1990) Additive effects of behavioral parent training and self-control therapy with attention deficit hyperactivity disordered children. J Clin Child Psychol 19(2): 98-110.

Huey Jr. SJ, Henggeler SW, Brondino MJ, Pickrel SG. (2000) Mechanisms of change in multisystemic therapy: Reducing delinquent behavior through therapist adherence and improved family and peer functioning. J Consult Clin Psychol 68(3): 451-467.

Jensen PS, Arnold LE, Severe JB, Vitiello B, Hoagwood K. (2004) National Institute of Mental Health Multimodal Treatment Study of ADHD follow-up: Changes in effectiveness and growth after the end of treatment. Pediatrics 113(4): 762-769.

Jensen PS, Kettle L, Roper M, Sloan M, Dulcan, M, Hoven C, et al. (1998) Suffer the restless children: Attention Deficit Hyperactivity Disorder and its treatment in 4 U.S. Communities. J Am Acad Child Adolesc Psychiatry 1(1): 1-2.

Kupfer DJ, Baltimore RS, Berry DA, Breslau, N, Ellinwood, EH, Ferre J, et al. (2000) National Institutes of Health Consensus Development Conference Statement: Diagnosis and treatment of attention-deficit/hyperactivity disorder (ADHD). J Am Acad Child Adolesc Psychiatry 39(2): 182-193.

Lipsey MW, Wilson DB. (1993) The efficacy of psychological, educational, and behavioral treatment: Confirmation from meta-analysis. Am Psychol 48(2): 1181-1209.

Lonigan CJ, Elbert JC, Johnson SB. (1998) Empirically supported psychosocial interventions for children: An overview. J Clin Child Psychol 27(2): 138-145.

McFall RM. (2000) Elaborate reflections on a simple manifesto. Appl Prev Psychol 9: 5-21.

McKay MM, McCadam K, Gonzales JJ. (1996) Addressing the barriers to mental health services for inner city children and their caretakers. Community Ment Health J 32(4): 353-361.

MTA Collaborative Group. (1999) A 14-Month Randomized Clinical Trial of Treatment Strategies for Attention-Deficit/Hyperactivity Disorder. Arch Gen Psychiatry 56: 1073-1086.

National Education Association. (2007) 2006 Special Education and the Individuals with Disabilities Education Act. Retrieved August 22, 2007, from http://www.nea.org/specialed/index.html

Olfson M, Gameroff MJ, Marcus SC, Jensen PS. (2003) National trends in the treatment of attention deficit hyperactivity disorder. Am J Psychiatr 160(6): 1071-1077.

Pelham WE Jr. (1999) The NIMH Multimodal Treatment Study for attention-deficit hyperactivity disorder: Just say yes to drugs alone? Can J Psychiatry 44(10): 981-990.

Pelham WE, Foster EM, Robb JA. (2007) The economic impact of attention-deficit/ hyperactivity disorder in children and adolescents. Ambulatory Pediatrics 7(1): 121-131.

Pelham Jr. WE, Gnagy EM. (1999) Psychosocial and combined treatments for ADHD. Ment Retard Dev Disabil Res Rev 5(3): 225-236.

Pelham Jr. WE, Wheeler T, Chronis A. (1998) Empirically Supported Psychosocial Treatments for Attention Deficit Hyperactivity Disorder. J Clin Child Psychol 27(2): 190-205.

Pfiffner LJ, McBurnett K. (1997) Social skills training with parent generalization: Treatment effects for children with attention deficit disorder. J Consult Clin Psychol 65(5): 749-757.

Rhule DM. (2005) Take care to do no harm: Harmful interventions for youth problem behavior. Prof Psychol Res Prac 36(6): 618-625.

Sanders, M. (1999). Triple-P positive parenting program: Towards an empirically validated multi-level parenting and family support strategy for the prevention of behavioral and emotional problems in children. Clin Child Fam Psychol Rev 2: 71-90.

Shelton TL, Barkley RA, Crosswait C, Moorehouse M, Fletcher K, Barrett S., Jenkins L, Metevia L. (2000) Multi-method psychoeducational intervention for preschool children with disruptive behavior:Two-year post-treatment follow-up. J Abnor Child Psychol 28(3): 253-266.

Smith BH, Barkley RA, Shapiro CJ. (2006) Attention-Deficit/Hyperactivity Disorder. In EJ Mash and RA Barkley (eds.) Treatment of Childhood Disorders, 3rd edition (pp. 65-136). New York: The Guilford Press.

Smith BH, Barkley RA, Shapiro CJ. (in press) Attention-Deficit/Hyperactivity Disorder. In E.J. Mash and R. A. Barkley (eds.) Assessment of Childhood Disorders, 4rd edition. New York: The Guilford Press.

Smith BH, Pelham WE, Evans S, Gnagy E, Molina B, Bukstein O, et al. (1998) Dosage effects of methylphenidate on the social behavior of adolescents diagnosed with Attention-Deficit Hyperactivity Disorder. Experimental Clin Psycho-pharmacol 6(2): 187-204.

Smith BH, Waschbusch DA, Willoughby M, T, Evans S. (2000) The efficacy, safety, and practicality of treatments for adolescents with attention deficit/hyper-activity disorder (ADHD). Clin Child Fam Psychol Rev 3(4): 243-267.

Springer C. (2004) Treatment adherence in an early intervention program for children with attention deficit hyperactivity disorder (Doctoral dissertation, Farleigh Dickinson University, 2004). Diss Abstracts Intern 65: 453.

Strayhorn JM, Weidman CS. (1991) Follow-up one year after parent-child interaction training: Effects on behavior of preschool children. J Am Acad Child Adolesc Psychiatry 30(1): 138-144.

Weiss B, Caron A, Ball S, Tapp J, Johnson M, Weisz JR. (2005) Iatrogenic effects of group treatment for antisocial youth. J of Consul Clin Psychol 73(6): 1036-1044.

Weisz JR, Hawley KM. (1998) Finding, evaluating, refining, and applying empirically supported treatments for children and adolescents. J Clin Child Psychol 27(2): 206-216.

Weisz JR, Hawley KM, Doss AJ. (2004) Empirically tested psychotherapies for youth internalizing and externalizing problems and disorders. Child Adol Psychiatr Clin N Am 13(4): 729-.

Weisz JR, Weiss B, Alicke MD, Klotz ML. (1987) Effectiveness of Psychotherapy with children and adolescents: A meta-analysis for clinicians. J Consult Clin Psychol 55(4): 542-549.

Wilmshurst LA. (2002) Treatment programs for youth with emotional and behavioral disorders: an outcome study of two alternate approaches. Ment Health Serv Res 4(2): 85-95.

Zuvekas SH, Vitiello B, Norquist GS. (2006) Recent trends in stimulant medication use among US children. Am J Psychiatry 163(4): 579-585.

EMPIRICALLY SUPPORTED TREATMENTS FOR CONDUCT DISORDERS IN CHILDREN AND ADOLESCENTS

Dustin A. Pardini

INTRODUCTION

Conduct disorders (i.e., oppositional defiant disorder, conduct disorder) represent a common clinical referral problem in child and adolescent treatment services. Research suggests that children with conduct disorders and their families have significantly more contact with educational and social services agencies than children with other psychiatric disorders (Vostanis et al., 2003). The behaviors characteristic of severe conduct disorder (e.g., assault with a weapon, robbery, burglary) also result in serious economic costs, with estimates suggesting that the average adult offender who initiates criminal behavior in childhood costs society approximately 1.3-1.5 million dollars (1997 dollars; Cohen, 1998). Given the prevalence and economic burden of conduct disorders, it is not surprising that interventionists have spent considerable time and energy developing empirically supported treatments for these disorders. Emerging research suggests that several contemporary interventions are not only efficacious in reducing the seriousness of conduct problems in youth, but also produce considerable reductions in economic costs to society when compared to historically used methods to address antisocial behavior in youth, such as punitive legal sanctions (Welsh, 2001). The goal of the current chapter is to outline contemporary research on the conceptualization, development, and treatment of conduct disorders in children and adolescents, as well as propose future directions for the successful treatment of these disorders.

Diagnostic Criteria

The most recent version of the Diagnostic and Statistical Manual of Mental Disorders, 4th Edition, Text Revision (DSM-IV-TR), distinguishes between two primary conduct disorders in children and adolescents (American Psychiatric Association, 2000). The disorders are hierarchical in nature, with the less severe and subordinate of the two being Oppositional Defiant Disorder (ODD).

Oppositional Defiant Disorder

ODD describes a persistent pattern of negativistic, hostile, defiant, and disobedient behaviors towards others, particularly parents and teachers. ODD was initially recognized as a diagnosable condition in third edition of the DSM, with the diagnosis requiring two of five symptoms: violations of minor rules, temper tantrums, argumentativeness, provocative behavior, and stubbornness (American Psychiatric Association, 1980). Since its initial conceptualization, the diagnostic criteria for ODD have been revised with each new version of the DSM manual. Currently, a DSM-IV diagnosis of ODD requires four of eight symptoms: a frequent loss of temper, argumentativeness, defiance, deliberate annoyance of others, blaming others, being touchy/easily annoyed, angry/resentful, and spiteful/vindictive (see Table 1). To meet diagnostic threshold, the symptoms must cause clinically significant impairment, occur "often" over a six month period, and occur more frequently than what is considered typical given the child's age or developmental level. However, the interpretation of what constitutes "typical" is not specified and is therefore under the discretion of the clinical professional making the diagnosis. Youth who meet criteria for Conduct Disorder cannot be diagnosed with ODD under the

Table 1: DSM-IV-TR Criteria for Oppositional Defiant Disorder (American Psychiatric Association, 2000)

Four or more of the following symptoms that last at least 6 months, cause clinically significant impairment, and occur more frequently than what is considered typical for individuals of the same age or developmental level:

1. Loses temper
2. Argues with adults
3. Defies adult requests or rules
4. Purposefully annoys others
5. Blames others for mistakes or misbehavior
6. Easily annoyed by others
7. Angry and resentful
8. Spiteful or vindictive

*If criteria for conduct disorder (prior to age 18 years) or antisocial personality disorder (age 18 years and older) are not met, then the diagnosis is not given.

current DSM-IV framework, because it is generally believed that "all of the features of Oppositional Defiant Disorder are usually present in Conduct Disorder" (pp. 102; American Psychiatric Association, 2000).

Conduct Disorder

Conduct Disorder (CD) is characterized by a persistent pattern of behavior that involves significant violations of the rights of others and/or major societal norms. Definitions of CD have also changed with each revision of the DSM, especially in regards to the methods used to identify subtypes of the disorder. Initially, there were four sub-categories of CD based on whether the youth exhibited aggressive (e.g., assault, rape) or nonaggressive (e.g., lying, stealing) conduct problems and whether the youth was socialized (e.g., has lasting friendships, feels guilt/remorse) or unsocialized (e.g., no close friendships, lacks gilt/remorse). The utility of this subtyping schema for understanding the heterogeneity among youth with CD was controversial even when first proposed. Currently, a DSM-IV diagnosis of CD requires at least three of fifteen symptoms to be present in the past year, with at least one of these symptoms being present within the last month (see Table 2). Symptoms fall into one of four broad domains: Aggression (7 symptoms), destruction of property (2 symptoms), deceitfulness/theft (3 symptoms), and serious violations of rules (3 symptoms). The diagnostic criteria stipulate that the less severe symptoms have to occur "often" in order to meet threshold (e.g., starting physical fights, truant from school before age 13), but no frequency requirement is given for more severe symptoms (e.g., forced sex, breaking into a house, building, or car).

Once diagnosed with CD, youth can be classified into one of two subtypes based on the developmental timing of their first CD symptom: the childhood-onset subtype (first symptom present prior to age 10) or the adolescent-onset subtype (first symptom present at age 10 or later). This developmental timing classification was based on work suggesting that childhood-onset CD was more persistent and more likely to develop into Antisocial Personality Disorder than the adolescent-onset subtype (Moffitt, 1993). The importance of considering the aggressive symptoms of CD as a particularly malignant form of CD remains implicit in the severity

Table 2: DSM-IV-TR Criteria for Conduct Disorder (American Psychiatric Association, 2000)

Three or more of the following symptoms in the past 12 months, with at least one occurring over the past 6 months, that result in clinically significant impairment:

Aggression
1. Often bullies, threatens or intimates others
2. Often initiates physical fights
3. Used a weapon when fighting
4. Physically cruel to people
5. Physically cruel to animals
6. Stolen while confronting a victim

Destruction of property
7. Set fires with the intention of causing damage
8. Purposefully destroyed others' property without using fire

Deceitfulness/theft
9. Burglarized a house, building or car
10. Lies to obtain things or avoid obligations
11. Stolen items of non-trivial value (without burglary or robbery)

Serious rule violations
12. Often breaks curfew at night, beginning before age 13
13. Has run away from home overnight twice (or once for an extended period)
14. Often skips school, beginning before age 13

Specify Onset: Childhood-Onset Type diagnosed when at least one symptom first occurred prior to age 10, otherwise Adolescent-Onset Type is diagnosed.

Specify Severity: Can be mild (few symptoms and causes minor harm to others), moderate (between mild and severe in terms of symptoms and harm to others) or severe (many symptoms or causes considerable harm to others).

*If criteria for Antisocial Personality Disorder (age 18 years and older) are met, then the diagnosis is not given.

specification for the disorder, with youth exhibiting either significant violent behavior or many CD symptoms being classified as "severe." However, characteristics of being undersocialized (e.g., few close friends, lacking guilt, empathy, remorse) are presently only included only as associated features of CD.

Given the variations in the diagnostic criteria for ODD and CD, as well as varying methods for assessing the disorder in different populations, prevalence rates differ across studies. The National Comorbidity Study

Replication conducted from 2001-2003 with a large representative sample of adults found that the lifetime prevalence of ODD was 8.5% (median age of onset 8.5), while the prevalence of CD was 9.5% (median age of onset 11.6 years old) with approximately 10% of individuals with a history of CD reporting an onset to their symptoms prior to age 10 (Kessler et al., 2005). In comparison adults who did not meet criteria for a lifetime diagnosis of CD, individuals with a lifetime CD diagnosis were 12 times more likely to have also met lifetime criteria for ODD (Nock et al., 2006). The onset of ODD either temporally preceded or co-occurred with the onset of CD in 76% of individuals who meet criteria for both disorders (Nock et al., 2006). Because retrospective reports may systematically underestimate the prevalence of disorders, these estimates are likely conservative (Nock, 2006). Consistent with prior studies, Kessler et al. (2005) found the prevalence of CD was higher in males (12.0%) than females (7.1%). While there was some initial suggestion in the DSM-IV field trials that this gender disparity may be primarily associated with childhood-onset CD, later studies have found the gender disparity occurs across both childhood and adolescent onset groups (Lahey et al., 1998). However, relatively little is known about the early developmental precursors to significant antisocial behavior in females because many longitudinal studies on conduct disorders have focused on predominately male samples (for an exception see Hipwell et al., 2002).

As evidenced by the continual changes in diagnostic criteria for ODD/CD, there are ongoing debates about the key characteristics of these disorders in youth. Some suggested improvements to the current classification system include lowering the symptom count threshold for an ODD diagnosis (Angold and Costello, 1996) and including a broader array of problem behaviors in the symptoms for CD (Burke et al., 2002). A more substantial criticism of the current classification system is the utility of treating ODD and CD as mutually exclusive and hierarchical diagnostic categories (Lahey et al., 1992; Loeber et al., 1991). Evidence for this conceptualization comes from factor analytic studies indicating that symptoms of ODD and CD represent two separate clusters of interrelated problem behaviors (Frick et al., 1991; Frick et al., 1994), and longitudinal research indicating that CD symptoms are more strongly related to the development of antisocial personality disorder than ODD symptoms

(Lahey et al., 2005; Loeber et al., 2002). However, some have argued that even when a diagnosis of CD is present, it is important to take into account individual differences in levels of ODD symptoms. For example, longitudinal research indicates that ODD symptoms are associated with increases in anxiety, depression, and CD symptoms across adolescence (Burke et al., 2005). As a result, the practice of implicitly ignoring co-occurring ODD symptoms in the presence of a CD diagnosis may eliminate important prognostic information about the course of emotional and behavioral problems in youth.

Another issue often debated is the abandonment of the undersocialized subtype of CD as a clinically meaningful subgroup. A growing body of longitudinal evidence suggests that the callous interpersonal features (e.g., lack of guilt and empathy) historically associated with the undersocialized subgroup may identify a particularly severe and recalcitrant form of CD in children and adolescents with unique etiological origins (Frick et al., 2003; Hawes and Dadds, 2005; Pardini, 2006; Pardini et al., 2006). These issues, as well as others, will likely be debated in the DSM-V workgroup for disorders first diagnosed in infancy, childhood or adolescence in the coming years.

Comorbid Conditions

An overwhelming body of evidence suggests that youth with ODD/CD often present with co-occurring mental disorders. One of the most common comorbid conditions is attention-deficit/hyperactivity disorder (ADHD). A review of existing community studies suggests that youth with ODD/CD are approximately 10.7 times (95% confidence interval = 7.7 – 14.8) more likely to be diagnosed with ADHD than youth without ODD/CD (Angold and Costello, 2001). Studies suggest that the symptoms of ADHD tend to precede the development of both ODD and CD in youth. For example, longitudinal research indicates that ADHD symptoms are associated with increases in ODD symptoms across adolescence, with the association being primarily driven by the hyperactive/impulsive symptoms of ADHD (Burke et al., 2005; Burns and Walsh, 2002). While ODD symptoms uniquely predicted increases in CD symptoms across the same developmental period, ADHD symptoms did not predict increases in CD symptoms independent of their association with ODD. This suggests a developmental progression where ADHD symptoms place youth at risk for developing ODD, which then places them at risk for developing significant CD symptoms. While comorbid CD and ADHD has been associated with persistent antisocial behavior (Lynam, 1996), a growing body of longitudinal research suggests that this increased risk for persistent antisocial behavior is primarily due to increased levels of conduct problems in the comorbid group, not the influence of ADHD per se (Broidy et al., 2003; Lahey et al., 2002; Loeber et al., 1995; Pardini et al., 2006). Moreover, emerging evidence indicates that children with co-occurring ODD/CD and ADHD are responsive to cognitive-behavioral treatments (Beauchaine et al., 2005; Jensen et al., 2001), with the most effective treatments consisting of a combination of medication management for ADHD symptoms and cognitive-behavioral intervention for ODD/CD symptoms (MTA Cooperative Group, 1999).

Internalizing problems (e.g. depression, anxiety) are also common among children with ODD/CD (Angold and Costello, 2001). In terms of temporal ordering, recent research suggests that ODD and CD symptoms place youth at risk for developing depression, whereas depression does not predict increases in CD symptoms across time (Burke et al., 2005). There is also some evidence suggesting that CD is related to the development of later depression because it leads to increased social conflicts, peer rejection, and academic failure (Burke et al., 2005). However, research suggests that children with CD and significant depressive symptoms may be at particular risk for developing substance use problems (Whitemore et al., 1997; Marmorstein and Iacono, 2001; Pardini et al., 2007) and exhibit a severe form of depression that often includes suicidal behaviors (Dadds et al., 1992; Marmorstein and Iacono, 2001). Depressive symptoms may also increase the likelihood that adolescent boys with CD will exhibit antisocial personality disorder in adulthood (Loeber et al., 2002). Research on the association between ODD/CD and anxiety disorders is more complex. While children with ODD/CD are more likely to be diagnosed with anxiety disorders, the co-occurrence is not as common as that found for CD/ODD and depression (Angold and Costello, 2001), and seems to be primarily driven by ODD symptoms leading to an increased risk for anxiety problems (Burke et al., 2005). Further complicating the issue is research suggesting that low levels of anxiety and fearfulness are associated with a particularly severe form of CD (Hinshaw et al., 1993; Walker et al., 1991) that is characterized by high levels of callous and unemotional behaviors (Pardini, 2006). Clearly the association between ODD/CD and anxiety is complex and is in need of further study.

The comorbidity between ODD/CD and substance use disorders during adolescence has also been well documented (Weinberg et al., 1998). Longitudinal evidence suggests that adolescent CD symptoms and substance using behaviors represent two distinct dimensions of behavior (Mason and Windle, 2002) that have at least some unique predictive factors (White et al., 1987). Behaviors consistent with ODD/CD symptoms tend to predict the onset of alcohol use (Clark et al., 1999), escalations in substance using behaviors across time (Mason and Windle, 2002), and the development of substance use disorders by early adulthood (Pardini et al., 2007). The presence of CD with a substance use disorder has been associated with poor outcomes following inpatient drug treatment (Myers et al., 1995), and an increased number of suicide attempts (Young et al., 1995). Adolescents with CD who have high levels of substance use are also at increased risk for developing antisocial personality disorder (Loeber et al., 2002), even after receiving intensive treatment for their substance abuse problems (Myers et al., 1998).

It is also apparent that children with ODD/CD tend to have significant learning problems and cognitive impairments (for reviews see Hinshaw, 1992a; 1992b; Moffitt, 1990). In general, ODD/CD symptoms seem to be more strongly associated with lower levels of both intellectual (particularly verbal) and academic abilities (particularly reading), as opposed to a substantial discrepancy between IQ and achievement as found in children with learning disabilities (Hinshaw, 1992b). Moreover, several studies have found that the significant association between ODD/CD and lower levels of academic achievement can be primarily accounted for by co-occurring ADHD symptoms and low intellectual abilities (Hinshaw, 1992b; Fergusson and Horwood, 1995; Moffitt, 1990). While some studies with clinic-referred youth have found that lower IQ scores may not be related to ODD/CD symptoms in children with high levels of callous-unemotional traits (Barry et al., 2000; Christian et al., 1997; Loney et al., 1998), studies with children recruited from the community have failed to replicate this finding or produce contradictory results (Frick et al., 2003; Loney et al., 2006). In addition, longitudinal research suggests that cognitive deficits may be primarily associated with the early initiation of conduct problems (Fergusson and Horwood, 1995; Hinshaw 1992b), not the persistence of these problems

into late adolescence and early adulthood (Raine et al., 2005; Loeber et al., in press).

Etiology of Conduct Disorders

Although there are several developmental theories that attempt to explain the development of childhood antisocial behavior, few investigators have attempted to document separate etiological pathways to the development of ODD as opposed to CD (Rey, 1993). Many studies either cluster ODD and CD symptoms together into a single index of antisocial behavior or examine symptoms of only one disorder, making it difficult to discern the relative importance of various etiological factors in the development of these two disorders. Despite this limitation, investigators have made significant advances in understanding the development of ODD/CD symptoms across childhood and adolescence. In addition, attempts have been made to differentiate risk factors for general psychopathology from those that are unique to the development of ODD/CD. Because psychosocial treatments for ODD/CD are predominately based upon research indicating that dysfunctional parenting, difficulties with social information processing, and a lack of positive peer relationships place children at risk for antisocial behavior, a brief overview of research documenting the role of these factors in the development of ODD/CD will be reviewed here.

Familial Influences on Conduct Disorders

There is a large body of literature that has linked dysfunctional parenting practices to the development of significant conduct problems in children and adolescents. Longitudinal research indicates that a supportive parent-child relationship characterized by reciprocal cooperation and shared positive affect promotes the internalization of prosocial behavior in early childhood (Fowles and Kochanska, 2000; Kochanska, 1997; Kochanska and Murray, 2000; Laible and Thompson,

2002). Similarly, high levels of parental warmth and positive reinforcement have been shown to buffer children from developing significant antisocial and violent behavior (Brendgen et al., 2001; Loeber and Farrington, 2000; Rey and Plapp, 1990). On the other hand, high levels of parent-child conflict and a harsh and critical parenting style are related to escalating and chronic forms of conduct problems in youth (Burke et al., 2002; Burt et al., 2003; Morrell and Murray, 2003). There is also evidence indicating that parents who inconsistently enforce rules tend to have children who exhibit increases in antisocial behavior over time (Lengua and Kovacs, 2005), including higher levels of ODD/CD symptoms (Frick et al., 1999b). Studies have also found that poor parental monitoring is related to increases in conduct problems (Brendgen et al., 2001), particularly in unsafe neighborhoods (Pettit et al., 1999). Similarly, low levels of parental involvement have been associated with an increased risk for early behavior problems (Shaw and Vondra, 1995), as well as the initiation and escalation of serious antisocial behavior (Frick et al., 1999a; Loeber et al., 2005). Given these findings, it is not surprising that the most effective interventions for ODD/CD attempt to change the manner in which parents interact with their children.

In addition to parenting practices and parent-child relationship characteristics, a large body of literature indicates that parental antisocial behavior is related to the development of conduct problems in youth. Specifically, studies have repeatedly found that parents with a history of antisocial or criminal behavior are more likely to have children who develop severe conduct problems (Frick et al., 1992; Laub and Sampson, 1988). Along these lines, evidence from a meta-analysis of twin and adoptions studies by Rhee and Waldman (2002) suggests that genetic factors explain approximately 40% of the variance in antisocial behaviors among children ($a^2 = .46$)

and adolescents ($a^2 = .43$). However, this raises questions about whether genetic transmission, rather than environmental influence, can account for the observed associations between dysfunctional parenting and the development of conduct problems over time. Along these lines, some studies have found that after controlling for parental antisocial behavior, the association between dysfunctional parenting and CD is reduced to non-significance (Frick et al., 1992), while other studies have found that dysfunctional parenting practices mediate the relation between parental criminality and child antisocial behavior (Johnson et al., 2004; Laub and Sampson, 1988). Genetically informed twin studies have produced convincing evidence that parenting factors such as low parental warmth and high parental negativity, parent-child conflict, and physical maltreatment can influence the development of childhood conduct problems, and this association can not be completely accounted for by genetic factors (Burt et al., 2003; Caspi et al., 2004; Jaffee et al., 2004, 2005). Moreover, twin and adoption studies estimate that shared environmental influences, which include exposure to the same parenting practices, account for 16-20% of the variance in antisocial behavior among youth (Rhee and Waldman, 2002). In sum, the development of conduct problems is influenced by a combination of genetic and environmental factors, with dysfunctional parenting practices playing an important role in shaping the development of early antisocial behavior.

A process that is often overlooked in research on the development of conduct problems is the bidirectional association between child characteristics and parenting behaviors across time. Thomas and Chess (1977) suggested that a "goodness of fit" model best explains the development of behavior problems in children, where temperamental characteristics only produce maladaptive outcomes for youth when they are combined with particular environmental conditions. Building on this theoretical framework, some investigators have hypothesized that emotionally and behaviorally dysregulated children may impact, and respond to, parenting behaviors differently than other children (Dishion et al., 1988; Patterson et al., 1992). For example, longitudinal evidence suggests that preschool children with a difficult temperament tend to elicit harsh punishment and negative treatment from their parents, and this poor parenting accounts for incremental increases in the child's behavior problems (Wong et al., 1999). Longitudinal studies have also found that children with signs of temperamental unmanageability in infancy exhibit greater levels of childhood externalizing problems (i.e. aggression, oppositional behavior, defiance) when they are exposed to low levels of maternal control in comparison to unmanageable children exposed to high levels of maternal control (Bates et al., 1998). More recently, twin studies have found that the effect of childhood maltreatment on conduct problems is more pronounced among children who have a high genetic risk for conduct problems in comparison to those with a low genetic risk (Jaffee et al., 2005). These studies indicate that certain child characteristics may not only influence the development of dysfunctional parenting practices over time, but also influence how children respond to certain parenting practices. Eventually, research in this area may be used to identify those families who are most in need of intervention services, as well as promote the implementation of more targeted interventions for children with ODD/CD that are designed to optimally fit the constellation of child and parent characteristics present within a family.

Social Information Processing and Conduct Disorders

Children and adolescents exhibiting significant conduct problems often have difficulties with social-information processing and interpersonal problem-solving. Contemporary social-cognitive models have attempted to outline the fundamental processing steps associated with encoding and interpreting social information, as well as generating and enacting solutions during social conflicts, as a means of understanding the potential drivers of significant conduct problems. Dodge and colleagues developed one of the most influential and comprehensive social information processing models relevant for understanding and treating ODD/CD (1993; Crick and Dodge, 1994). This model proposes that children exhibiting conduct problems can have difficulties at six different stages of social-information processing, including: 1) encoding social cues; 2) making interpretations and attributions about social information; 3) identifying personal social goals during interpersonal conflicts; 4) generating possible solutions to interpersonal problems;5) deciding which plan to enact based on the perceived consequences; and 6) enacting the chosen plan.

In support of Dodge's theory, several studies have linked childhood aggression and conduct problems to maladaptive social-cognitive processing. For example, children with conduct problems tend to recall fewer relevant cues about events (Lochman and Dodge, 1994) and over-attend to hostile cues (Gouze, 1987; Milich and Dodge, 1984) in comparison to non-aggressive children. Perhaps the most common finding is that youth with significant conduct problems (particularly individuals exhibiting angry and defensive forms of aggression) are more likely to infer that others are acting in an aggressive or hostile manner during ambiguous conflict situations, a cognitive distortion referred to as a "hostile attributional bias" (Burgess et al., 2006; Dodge et al., 1986). When identifying social goals in conflict situations, antisocial youth also tend to focus on dominance and self-centered rewards, and are less concerned with avoiding punishment and the suffering of others (Lochman et al., 1993; Pardini et al., 2003). Aggressive and disruptive children also have difficulties generating appropriate solutions in conflict situations, including offering fewer verbal assertions (Asarnow and Callan, 1985; Loch-man and Lampron, 1988) and compromise solutions (Lochman and Dodge, 1994), and generating more physically aggressive solutions (Pepler et al., 1998; Waas and French, 1989). When evaluating possible responses to social conflicts, children with conduct problems rate aggressive solutions more positively than children without these difficulties (Crick and Werner, 1998), and are less adept at enacting prosocial solutions (Dodge et al., 1986).

While the aforementioned studies on social information processing focused on children with elevated levels of antisocial behavior, rather than those who meet criteria diagnostic for ODD/CD, similar processing problems have been observed in children with conduct disorders. For example, children with ODD/CD tend to encode fewer social cues, generate fewer solutions to problems, and are more confident in their ability to enact aggressive responses across a variety of problematic social situations in comparison to non-disruptive children (Mattys et al., 1999). When given the opportunity to choose from various responses in problem situations, children with ODD/CD are more likely to select an aggressive response, and less likely select a prosocial response, in comparison to non-disruptive controls. Webster-Stratton and Lindsay (1999) found that children with ODD/CD were more likely to attribute hostile intentions to others in hypothetical social situations, and generate fewer positive problem-solving strategies to resolve imaginary conflicts in comparison to normal controls. During their play interactions with peers, children with ODD/CD also displayed fewer positive social skills and exhibited aggressive

problem-solving skills more often than non-problem children. Longitudinal evidence also suggests that the tendency for ODD children to generate aggressive solutions to social problems tends to remain fairly stable over time (Coy et al., 2001). Some research also indicates that there may be subtle differences between children diagnosed with ODD as opposed to CD in terms of their social problem-solving skills when involved in conflicts with peers, parents, and teachers (Dunn et al., 1997). While ODD and CD children do not differ in the total number of solutions generated or the number of aggressive solutions generated in peer conflict situations, youth with CD proposed more aggressive solutions to teacher and parent conflicts in comparison to youth with ODD.

Despite having difficulties with social information processing and social problem solving, it is important to recognize that children with ODD/CD often do not differ from controls in terms of their perceived social competence (Webster-Stratton and Lindsay, 1999). In fact, it is relatively common for children exhibiting significant conduct problems to overestimate their competencies across a wide variety of domains relative to information from other sources (Hymel et al., 1993; Patterson et al., 1990). Moreover, children with conduct problems who overestimate their social competence tend to engage in more bullying behavior than conduct problem youth who hold accurate views of their social compe-tence (Edens et al., 1999; Hughes et al., 2001; Salmivalli et al., 1999). Addressing inaccur-ate perceptions of social competence in children with ODD/CD can be difficult because these youth may be prone to aggressive outbursts when their positive self-perception is threatened or questioned (Baumeister et al., 1996; Salmivalli et al., 1999). As a result, interventions that target dysfunctional social information processing in children with ODD/CD need to establish a supportive environment where children can safely disclose interpersonal problems (Hughes et al., 1997) and help these children recognize how their behavior affects others (Webster-Stratton and Lindsay, 1999).

When examining the social information processing of children with ODD/CD it is also important to recognize the role that heightened negative affect can play in perpetuating social cognitive distortions and dysfunctional social problem-solving. Emotions serve as an adaptive system that motivates individuals to solve their perceived problems (Smith and Lazarus, 1990), and may mediate the relation between attributions and behavior (Weiner, 1990). For example, when a child attributes blame for a social conflict to a peer's hostility, the child will tend to experience frustration or anger, and this attribution-emotion linkage can influence subsequent decisions about appropriate social goals (e.g., revenge) and behavioral responses (e.g., aggression). Along these lines, studies have found that children with conduct problems tend to exhibit increased physiological arousal during experimentally induced provocation situations in comparison to non-disruptive controls (Hubbard et al., 2002). This emotional arousal in the early stages of interactions can persist across time and negatively influence social attributions and response styles throughout an extended social exchange (Dodge and Somberg, 1987; Lochman, 1987; Williams et al., 2003). Importantly, having aggressive boys monitor and regulate their emotional reactions to peer provocation before deciding on a solution to the conflict can reduce the aggressiveness of their chosen response (Orobi de Castro et al., 2003). As a result, interventions targeting dysfunctional social information processing in children with ODD/CD often include training sessions designed to help youth identify and regulate negative emotions (particularly anger) in conflict situations prior to generating and enacting solutions.

Peer Influences and Conduct Disorders

Children with ODD/CD often have difficulties with peer social interactions and these problems can perpetuate and escalate their antisocial behavior over time. For instance, there is substantial evidence indicating that children who exhibit conduct problems are at risk for early rejection by their peers (Coie et al., 1982; Gresham and Little, 1993). Once these children are rejected they are at even greater risk for further negative outcomes, including serious delinquency, academic difficulties, and severe internalizing and externalizing problems (Coie et al., 1995; Miller-Johnson et al, 1999; Parker and Asher, 1987). While there has been some speculation that peer rejection may only be related to the development of serious conduct problems because it serves as a marker for children's early externalizing problems, several longitudinal studies have discounted this theory. Specifically, both peer rejection and conduct problems in early elementary school are independently associated with later externalizing problems (Laird et al., 2001), felony assault (Miller-Johnson et al., 1999) and the development of ODD/CD (Miller-Johnson et al., 2002). One longitudinal study found that children who are rejected in kindergarten are at risk for exhibiting stable levels of mother-reported externalizing problems across an 8-year follow-up period, while non-rejected children tend to exhibit lower initial levels of externalizing problems in kindergarten and greater decreases in externalizing problems over time (Keiley et al., 2000). These findings support the notion that children with significant conduct problems are at risk for early peer rejection, and this social rejection then contributes to the maintenance and escalation of antisocial behavior over time.

While children with conduct disorders are at risk for being rejected by their larger peer group in elementary school, this does not mean antisocial children fail to develop friendships. Aggressive and conduct problem youth do tend to be part of a social network of friends despite their lack of general popularity and likeability among peers (Cairns et al., 1988). However, their friendships tend to be characterized by high levels of conflict and lower levels of emotional intimacy, closeness, and support (Cillessen et al., 2005; Grotpeter and Crick, 1996) and often involve other anti-social youth (Adams et al., 2005; Cillessen et al., 2005). This latter tendency is particularly problematic because evidence indicates that affiliating with other deviant peers tends to escalate adolescent antisocial behavior. Longitudinal studies indicate that deviant peer affiliation is associated with increases in aggression (Capaldi et al., 2001), self-reported delinquency (Vitaro et al., 2000), arrests (Patterson et al., 2000), and the initiation of substance use (Dishion et al., 1995). Moreover, aggressive youth with an aggressive best friend have been shown to exhibit a more persistent form of antisocial behavior than aggressive youth with a non-aggressive best friend (Adams et al., 2005). Even more concerning is evidence from a recent longitudinal investigation indicating that high levels of deviant peer group affiliation is associated with an increased risk for homicide in boys (Loeber et al., 2005).

One mechanism through which deviant peers are believed to influence future anti-social behavior is by reinforcing values that are tolerant of delinquency. Longitudinal research has shown that increased peer delinquency is related to changes in beliefs about the legitimacy of delinquent behavior across adolescence (Pardini et al., 2005). In addition, several studies suggest that adolescents who affiliate with deviant peers are at increased risk for delinquency because they begin adopting beliefs that are more accepting of illegal and aggressive acts (Akers et al., 1979; Henry et al., 2000; Matsueda and Heimer, 1987). In a series of studies, Dishion and colleagues documented a process through which deviant peers subtly communicate messages about the acceptability of delinquent actions: a process they referred to as "deviancy training" (Dishion et al., 1999). Specifically, antisocial peers engage in discussions about rule-breaking behavior and these discussions form the basis for positive affective exchanges, such as shared laughter (Capaldi et al., 2001). This type of peer reinforcement of delinquent values during early adolescence has been shown to influence subsequent escalations in drug use (Dishion et al., 1995), violence (Dishion et al., 1997), and serious delinquency (Dishion et al., 1996). In fact, findings suggested that group interventions for antisocial adolescents may produce iatrogenic effects if this type of deviancy training is allowed to occur (Dishion et al., 1999).

Empirically Supported Interventions for ODD and CD

Substantial efforts have been made to identify empirically supported treatments for a variety of problems in children and adolescents, including externalizing problems (Farmer et al., 2002). Because the current chapter is focused on treatments for children with conduct disorders, this review will focus on interventions that have been implemented with children who meet criteria for ODD/CD or exhibit antisocial behavior severe enough to warrant criminal justice involvement. While empirically supported preventative-interventions for children at risk for developing disruptive behaviors disorders will not be reviewed here (e.g., Nurse Home Visitation, Coping Power Program, Montreal Delinquency Prevention), these interventions have been discussed extensively elsewhere (Brestan and Eyberg, 1998; Greenwood, 2004; Pardini and Lochman, 2003). Nearly all of the treatments that will be reviewed have the empirical support necessary to be deemed "well-established" or "probably efficacious" treatments for conduct disorders in children and adolescents according to criteria outlined by the Clinical Psychology Task Force on Promotion and Dissemination of Psychological Procedures (for details on criteria see Brestan and Eyberg, 1998). Two additional programs that have received growing empirical support in recent reviews of successful treatments for serious juvenile offenders (e.g., Functional Family Therapy, Mutidimensional Foster Care) will also be reviewed (Greenwood, 2004; Nock, 2003). These treatments have been designed to address conduct disorders in youth at different developmental levels, from pre-school to late adolescence. For continuity purposes the treatments will be reviewed in order of the age group typically served and will include Parent-Child Interaction Therapy, The Incredible Years Program, Problem Solving Skills Training with Parent Management Training, Functional Family Therapy, Multidimensional Treatment Foster Care, and Multisystemic Therapy.

Parent-Child Interaction Therapy

Parent-Child Interaction Therapy (PCIT) was originally tailored for pre-school aged children (ages 2-6) exhibiting significant behavioral problems, particularly children meeting diagnostic criteria for ODD (Gallagher, 2003). Treatment sessions typically occur an hour per week and continue for 10-16 sessions, or until the child no longer meets criteria for ODD. All treatment sessions are implemented in the context of naturalistic play settings, and consist of two phases: Child-Directed Interaction (CDI) and Parent-Directed Interaction (PDI; Herschell et al., 2002). The CDI phase is designed to strengthen the parent-child relationship and extinguish maladaptive behaviors that are reinforced by parental attention. Parents are taught to use specific skills when engaging their child in free-play, such as reflecting the child's statements and describing and praising the child's behavior, while ignoring undesir-

able behaviors and avoiding the tendency to question, direct, or criticize the child. Parents practice these skills in session with their child as the therapist provides feedback and suggestions for improvement, and they are asked to practice the skills at home on a daily basis. Once parents master the skills in the CDI phase, they begin the PDI component of treatment. The PDI phase is designed to increase low-rate positive behaviors and decrease maladaptive behaviors that are unresponsive to extinction procedures or are too harmful to be ignored. Skills imparted during this treatment phase include using clear and direct commands, providing consistent and specific reinforcement (i.e. labeled praise) for compliant behavior, and using time out as a way to deal with noncompliance. Parents demonstrate these skills in session with their child, while the therapist offers suggestions and feedback.

A recent 2003 review of 17 studies that used PCIT to treat disruptive behavioral disorders in children found strong evidence of statistically and clinically significant improvements in children's behavioral functioning (Gallagher, 2003). For example, clinic-referred families who received PCIT showed lower levels of clinically significant child conduct problems and increased levels of child compliance following treatment in comparison to waitlist controls (Schuhmann et al., 1998). In addition, parents receiving treatment reported lower levels of personal distress. Evidence also suggests that PCIT can reduce the reoccurrence of physically abusive parenting behaviors (Chaffin et al., 2004), which have consistently been related to conduct disorders in youth. In a long-term follow-up of families who participated in PCIT, Hood and Eyberg (2003) found that treatment gains in child behavioral problems and parental locus of control (i.e., the degree to which parents believe that have control over their child's behavior) are maintained at 3-6 years after treatment, with three fourths of the children who exhibited clinically significant treatment gains at post-treatment maintaining this improvement. One investigation examining the relative effectiveness of the two components of PCIT found that families who received the PDI component first showed faster behavioral improvements and lower levels of parent reported conduct problems at post-treatment than families who received the CDI training first (Eisenstadt et al., 1993). In addition, an abbreviated version of the program that primarily taught parents the PCIT skills through an instructional videotape with minimal in-person sessions, produced improvements in conduct problems and parenting abilities in comparison to a waitlist control by post-treatment at 6-month follow-up (Nixon et al., 2003). Many of the treatment gains were maintained at 1- and two-year follow-ups (Nixon et al., 2004). The program has also been recently been adapted to address cultural issues associated with implementing PCIT in Latino families (Matos et al., 2006; Mcab et al., 2005).

The Incredible Years Program

This program consists of a parent and child component and is designed for children ages 4 to 7 who have conduct problems significant enough to warrant a diagnosis of either ODD or CD. The child component, which is referred to as "Dinosaur School," consists of groups of six or seven children who attend weekly 2-hour sessions for approximately 17 weeks (Webster-Stratton et al., 2004). The intervention uses videotapes and life-size puppets to model ways of successfully dealing with interpersonal problems that are typically experienced by pre-school and young school-aged children. The topics addressed include making friends, emotionally empathizing with others, using perspective-taking skills, resolving conflicts successfully, cooperating with others, coping with teasing, and controlling feelings of anger. During the group sessions, children discuss and practice the social skills that are modeled in the videotaped vignettes and collaborate with one another on acceptable solutions to hypothetical problems. Children are rewarded for using positive social skills while interacting with other members of the group. Weekly letters are sent to parents and teachers explaining the issues being discussed for the week and encouraging them to reward the child for using positive social skills at home or school.

The Parent Training intervention consists of groups of 10-12 parents who meet with a therapist on a weekly basis for approximately 22 sessions, each lasting 2 hours. Similar to the child component, parents watch approximately 17 different videotapes containing vignettes modeling appropriate ways for dealing with problematic parent-child interactions. Two group therapists lead discussions pertaining to the topics addressed in the videos, which include effective play techniques, limit setting, handling misbehavior, and the communication of emotions (Webster-Stratton, 1981). Parents are initially encouraged to initiate non-threatening play sessions with their child in a manner that shows a genuine interest and appreciation for their ideas. Next, parents are taught to use positive attention and praise to reward compliant behaviors, while simultaneously employing consistent limit setting and strategies like ignoring and time out to extinguish misbehavior. Parents are also shown ways in which they can verbally and non-verbally express acceptance, warmth, and caring toward their child. Examples are used to depict how critical and demanding parents can elicit rebelliousness in children, while parents who are accepting and enthusiastic tend to have children who are confident and creative.

Research findings regarding the effectiveness of the Dinosaur School and Parent Training interventions alone and in combination are convincing. The parent training component has produced significant behavioral gains in comparison to wait-list controls across a number of different studies, even when the parenting videotapes were self-administered without the aid of a therapist (Webster-Stratton, 1984; Webster-Stratton and Hammond, 1997; Webster-Stratton et al., 1988). In addition, overall improvements in parent reports of their children's behavior were still present at three-year follow-up, with the intervention combining videotaped modeling with therapist-lead discussion showing stable improvements (Webster-Stratton, 1990). The Incredible Years child intervention has also been shown to produce significant reductions in the amount of conduct problems children exhibit at home and school, as well as produce increases in social problem solving skills in comparison to waitlist control conditions (Webster-Stratton and Hammond, 1997; Webster-Stratton et al., 2004). There is also evidence indicating that at 1-year follow-up approximately two-thirds of children who participated in the intervention have parent ratings of behavioral problems in the normal rather than clinically significant range (Webster-Stratton and Hammond, 1997). This finding indicated that the Incredible Years child component could be used in isolation to reduce disruptive behavior problems in youth when parents are unwilling or unable to participate in treatment.

Problem-Solving Skills Training with Parent Management Training

Kazdin's problem-solving skills training (PSST) with parent management training (PMT) are two of the most extensively researched cognitive-behavioral treatments for conduct problems in middle childhood (Kazdin et al., 1987, 1989, 1992). Although the program is designed for children from 7-13 years of age with a wide variety of antisocial behaviors, research on its effectiveness has included a nearly equal number of children with either ODD or CD. The primary

focus of the child component is teaching and reinforcing prosocial problem-solving skills in order to promote a child's ability to effectively manage potentially volatile interpersonal situations. The children attend 25 individually administered sessions once per week, with each session lasting approximately 50 minutes. During treatment, children are presented with potentially volatile interpersonal situations that are congruent with the environment in which they are having problems (e.g., home, school, peers, siblings). The therapist then assists the child in objectively evaluating the situation, developing prosocial goals, and generating alternative solutions to meet these goals. These problem-solving skills are practiced and refined in session through the use of modeling, role-plays, corrective feedback, and reinforcement. In order to promote the generalization of these skills to settings outside of therapy, children are assigned "super-solver" tasks in which they apply newly learned skills to real-life interpersonal situations of increasing complexity. Moreover, parents are taught to cue and assist the child in the use of these problem-solving strategies at home and in the community.

The parent management component of this program consists of 16 individual treatment sessions that occur over the course of 6 to 8 months, with each session lasting approximately two hours. In general, the program is designed to instruct parents how to apply various behavioral principles like reinforcement and shaping when identifying and modifying problematic behavior in their children. During the sessions, the therapist uses a combination of didactic instruction, modeling, and role-plays to teach parenting skills like the appropriate use of time-out, verbal reprimands, negotiation, and behavioral contracting. After a home behavioral program is started, the therapist works with parents to begin a school-based reinforcement program to help improve their child's academic and behavioral compliance. The school program consists of negotiating certain school goals and monitoring the child's progress in meeting these goals through the use of a home-school behavioral report card. At both home and school, the child is given reinforcement (e.g., special activities, privileges) for achieving specific goals, and the child is frequently given feedback regarding his/her behavioral progress.

Several research studies have provided support for the effectiveness of the problem-solving training and parent management training independently, as well as a combination of the two treatments for oppositional and defiant behaviors. Specifically, the child component was shown to be superior to nondirective relationship therapy and control conditions in reducing global externalizing and internalizing problems, increasing social activities, and improving overall school adjustment (Kazdin et al., 1987). In addition, problem-solving skills training was effective in reducing disruptive behaviors and increasing prosocial activities at both home and school in comparison to non-directive behavior therapy, and these effects remained at 1-year follow-up (Kazdin et al., 1989). Another randomized study indicated that both PSST and PMT in isolation produce significant improvements in global dysfunction, social competence, and deviant behavior at 1–year follow-up, but PSST was superior to PMT alone in terms of improving children's social competence at school and reducing self-reports of aggression and delinquency (Kazdin et al., 1992). However, the combination of PSST and PMT produced the largest improvements in parent and child reported antisocial and delinquent behavior at 1-year follow-up in comparison to either treatment in isolation. More recently a brief (less than one hour) participation enhanced intervention (PEI) has been added to the typically administered PMT, in order to encourage parental motivation and overcome barriers to treatment. Findings from a randomized controlled trial indicate that adding the PEI to PMT resulted in greater treatment motivation, treatment attendance, and greater adherence to treatment among parents in comparison to PMT alone (Nock and Kazdin, 2005).

Multisystemic Therapy

Multisystemic therapy (MST) was originally designed as an individualized and intensive family-focused treatment for seriously antisocial adolescents (ages 11-17) referred to the juvenile justice system (Henggeler et al., 1998). The intervention emphasizes the importance of family preservation as well as the interaction between adolescents and the multiple environmental systems that influence their antisocial behavior, including their peers, family, school, and community (Henggler et al., 1992). Strategies for changing the adolescent's behavior are developed in close collaboration with family members by identifying the major environmental drivers that help maintain the adolescent's deviant behavior, as well as identifying and over-coming barriers to successful treatment outcomes. Services are delivered in the family's natural environment and can include a variety of treatment approaches including parent training, family therapy, school consultation, marital therapy, and individual therapy. Although the techniques used within these treatment strategies can vary, many of them are either behavioral or cognitive-behavioral in nature (e.g., contingency management, behavioral contracting). Often, targets include promoting effective discipline, improving family communication, decreasing the youth's association with deviant peers, and increasing collaborations between the school and family. Clinicians are guided by a set of nine MST principles which include concepts such as focusing on systems strengths, delivering developmentally appropriate treatments, and improving effective family functioning. Throughout the intervention, clinician adherence to these treatment principles is closely monitored through weekly consultation with MST experts. MST therapists typically carry caseloads of four to six families and are available to families 24 hours a day, seven days a week. Families receive approximately 40 to 60 hours of direct clinical contact during the course of treatment, with initial sessions taking place on up to a daily basis and later sessions occurring about once a week. Interventions typically last three to five months. MST therapists require extensive and ongoing training, including an initial five day training, weekly MST clinical consultation, quarterly booster trainings, and continual monitoring of treatment fidelity and adherence. Treatment teams typically consist of a doctoral level supervisor and three master's level clinicians who deliver services to families.

Several published evaluations of the effectiveness of MST with chronic and violent juvenile offenders have produced impressive results. Investigations have shown that families who receive MST report lower levels of adolescent behavior problems and improvements in family functioning at post-treatment in comparison to alternative treatment conditions (Borduin et al., 1995; Henggeler et al., 1992; Henggeler et al., 1986). In the first randomized clinical trial, MST was compared to treatment as usual with a sample of 84 serious juvenile offenders. Juveniles in the MST condition had significantly fewer arrests (means = .87 vs. 1.52) and weeks of incarceration (means = 5.8 vs. 16.2) at a 59-week follow-up (Henggeler et al., 1992), and showed reduced recidivism at a 2-year follow-up (Henggler et al., 1993) in comparison to youths receiving treatment as usual. Results from the longest follow-up evaluation of MST to date found that serious and violent juvenile offenders randomly

assigned to MST had lower arrest rates and were sentenced to fewer days of incarceration than offenders who completed individual therapy approximately 13 years after the end of treatment (Schaefer and Borduin, 2005). However, results from a comprehensive meta-analytic review of randomized MST studies suggest that intervention may not be any more effective than treatment as usual or alternative treatments in reducing youth-reported anti-social behavior, out of home placements, or official arrests and convictions (Littell, 2006; Littell et al., 2005). For example, a randomized study of 407 Canadian juvenile offenders failed to find any significant differences between youth assigned to MST versus treatment as usual in terms of recidivism, days until reconviction, days sentenced to custody, and number of convictions during a 3-year follow-up (Center for Children and Families in the Justice System, 2006; Leschied and Cunningham, 2002). While the MST developers suggest that these non-significant findings may be partially due to difficulties adhering to the MST treatment principles (Henggeler et al., 1997; Henggeler et al., 1999; Henggeler et al., 2006), the fact that poor adherence to MST occurs in stringently controlled research trials, and this significantly impairs the treatment's effectiveness, suggests that the widespread dissemination of the program in its current form may be problematic.

Functional Family Therapy

Functional Family Therapy (FFT) combines principles from both family systems theory and cognitive-behavioral approaches to intervene with antisocial adolescents (ages 11-17) and their families (Sexton and Alexander, 2000). The clinical practice of FFT has evolved over the past 30 years through the development of a systematic approach to training therapists and the institution of outcome assessments to promote therapist accountability (Klein et al., 1977).

A recent version of FFT consists of three intervention phases: (1) engagement and motivation, (2) behavior change, and (3) generalization. During the engagement and motivation phase, the therapist addresses maladaptive beliefs within the family system in order to increase expectations for change, reduce negativity and blaming, build respect for individual differences, and develop a strong alliance between the family and therapist. The behavior change phase is then used to implement concrete behavioral interventions designed to improve family functioning by building relational skills, enhancing positive parenting, improving conflict management skills, and reducing maladaptive interaction patterns. These behavioral interventions are individualized to fit the characteristics of each family member and the family relational system as a whole. Finally, the generalization phase of the intervention is used to improve the family's ability to competently influence the systems in which it is embedded (e.g., school, community, juvenile justice system) to help maintain positive change.

Early examinations of the effectiveness of FFT with adolescent offenders were promising. An early version of the FFT program was evaluated using a sample of 86 adolescents charged with status offenses and their families (Klein et al., 1977). Families were randomly assigned to FFT treatment, client-centered therapy, psychodynamic therapy, or no treatment. Following treatment, families who received FFT exhibited better communication patterns than families in the other three conditions. Moreover, court records indicated that adolescents assigned to FFT had lower rates of recidivism 6-18 months following treatment, while their siblings had fewer court contacts at 2.5 to 3.5 years post-treatment, in comparison to all other groups. A more recent investigation with repeat adolescent offenders found that youth who participated in FFT showed reduced recidivism and a lower number of new offenses during a 15-month follow-up period in comparison to youth assigned to a group home condition (Barton et al., 1985). Other studies have shown that repeat juvenile offenders who received FFT had lower levels of recidivism at 2.5-year (Gordon et al., 1988) and 5.5-year (Gordon et al., 1995) follow-ups in comparison to a probation-only group consisting of lower risk delinquents. However, similar to research on the MST program, emerging research suggests that the program's ability to reduce re-offending in comparison to treatment as usual may be minimal when implemented on a larger scale. Specially, the state of Washington recently conducted an evaluation of 700 moderate to high-risk adolescent offenders that were assigned to either FFT or treatment as usual. After adjusting for pre-existing differences between the groups due to non-random assignment, results indicated that there was no difference in 18-month recidivism rates between offenders who received FFT versus those who received usual care (Barnoski, 2004). However, when the analysis was limited to therapists who were judged to competent in FFT, the results showed that FFT was effective in reducing 18-month felony recidivism rates in comparison to treatment as usual. Taken together, this suggests that therapist difficulties adhering to the FFT protocol may eliminate any advantages that the program has in reducing recidivism over treatment as usual in adolescent offenders.

Multidimensional Treatment Foster Care

Multidimensional Treatment Foster Care (MTFC) is an alternative to traditional group care settings for antisocial adolescents (ages 12-17) who are removed from the care of their parents or guardians. MTFC temporarily places antisocial youth with a community-based foster family where contingencies governing the youth's behavior are systematically modified through consultation with a comprehensive treatment team (Fisher and Chamberlain, 2000). As the youth's behavior improves, a gradual transition is made from the MTFC setting back to their parent's or guardian's home. Each foster family is assigned a behavioral support specialist, youth therapist, family therapist, consulting psychiatrist, parent daily report caller, and case manager/clinical team manager to assist with program implementation. Foster parents, who are informally screened for program participation, engage in a 20-hour pre-service training which provides an overview of the treatment model and teaches techniques for monitoring and modifying adolescent behavior. Adolescents are able to earn privileges within the foster home by following a daily program of scheduled activities and fulfilling behavioral expectations. The youth's biological parents or guardians assist in the treatment planning, engage in family therapy to learn effective parenting skills, and begin applying newly learned skills during short home visits. As the family's functioning improves, the visits are extended until complete reunification occurs. Family therapists continue to follow the case for 1 to 3 months following reunification to assist in the successful resolution of problems that arise.

Initial research on the effectiveness of MTFC has provided some encouraging results. An early version of MTFC was compared to placement in community-based group care (GC) facilities for adjudicated delinquent adolescents using a matched control design (Chamberlain, 1990). Results from this investigation indicated that juveniles in MTFC condition were more likely than GC youth to complete their placement and had fewer days of incarceration two years following treatment. Another matched control designed involving younger abused boys in the juvenile justice system revealed that youth in MTFC had significantly fewer arrests, less self-reported criminal activities, and fewer

days incarcerated one year following treatment in comparison to GC controls (Fisher and Chamberlain, 2000). At two years post-discharge MTFC boys reported using drugs less often than GC controls. A subsequent randomized clinical trial compared MTFC to placement in GC facilities with 79 adolescent boys, many of whom had been previously charged with several serious criminal offenses and had a history of running away from previous placements (Eddy and Chamberlain, 2000). In comparison to GC, boys in the MTFC condition were more likely to complete their program and spent 60% fewer days incarcerated a year following their referral to the program. MTFC boys also had fewer criminal referrals and less self-reported delinquency in comparison to boys in GC one year following program completion. Boys who received MTFC were also less likely to have a criminal referral for violence and had lower levels of self-reported violence in comparisons to GC across a two-year follow-up (Eddy et al., 2004). A more recent randomized trial of 81 chronically delinquent girls found that MTFC resulted in significantly fewer days spent in locked facilities and lower parent-reported delinquency by 12-month follow-up in comparison to typical GC, but no significant group differences were found for the number of criminal referrals or level of self-reported delinquency (Leve et al., 2005).

DISCUSSION
Moderators of Treatment Effectiveness

While several treatments have been shown to reduce disruptive behavior disorders in youth, there remains a large portion of youth who do not seem to benefit from psychosocial interventions. This has led investigators to focus on factors that may moderate or influence individual outcomes in empirically supported inventions (Kazdin, 2003). Some researchers have emphasized therapist competence and characteristics of the client-therapist relationship as important moderators of treatment. While there is some evidence that a therapist's ability to adhere to an intervention's core components and implement the treatment in a competent manner is associated with positive outcomes (Henggeler et al., 1997), some investigators have pointed out that studies on treatment adherence often result in counterintuitive or non-significant findings (Forgatch et al., 2005). More recent studies have focused on the parent-therapist alliance as an important predictor of treatment outcome, including agreement on the tasks, goals, and outcomes in therapy, as well as positive perceptions of the relationship (Kazdin and Whiteley, 2006). In a recent meta-analysis, Shirk and Karver (2003) found evidence that characteristics of the therapeutic alliance are modestly associated with positive outcomes for treatments targeting child externalizing problems (mean $r = .30$), and this association was typically stronger when measures of the relationship were collected later as opposed to early in treatment. However, there remains no convincing evidence that a positive therapeutic alliance or increased treatment fidelity actually precedes positive behavioral changes in children with disruptive behavior disorders. For example, it is likely that positive behavioral change in the target child actually causes parents and therapists to rate their alliance more positively and makes it easier for therapists to adhere to the core intervention components.

A large body of evidence has also examined parent and child characteristics that may moderate the efficacy of treatments for conduct disorders. There is some evidence indicating that children with higher academic dysfunction and more global psychiatric impairment are less likely to benefit from cognitive behavioral therapies (Kazdin and Crowley, 1997; Kazdin and Wassell, 1999). While lower socioeconomic status and increased parental psychopathology and stress have been associated with poorer treatment

outcomes in some studies (Dumas and Wahler, 1983; Kazdin and Wassell, 1999; Webster-Stratton and Hammond, 1990), other researchers have failed to find this association (Beauchaine et al., 2005; Hartman et al., 2003). One of the largest and most comprehensive examinations of treatment moderators was conducted using 514 children who participated in six randomized trials of the Incredible Years program (Beauchaine et al., 2005). In this study, children with co-occurring problems with anxiety/depression and those who had parents with a history of substance abuse showed greater behavioral improvements one year following treatment. Children of parents who exhibited lower levels of critical, harsh, and ineffective discipline at baseline also exhibited greater behavioral improvements following treatment. In contrast to some theoretical models (Lynam, 1996), the intervention was equally effective in reducing conduct problems among children with elevated levels of ADHD symptoms in comparison to those without these problems (Beauchaine et al., 2005; Hartman et al., 2003). While these studies have begun providing insights into possible moderators of treatment efficacy, there remains a lack of understanding about why these factors lead to differential responses to treatment (Nock, 2003). This issue seems particularly important for future research given that findings in this area are often counterintuitive.

Mediators of Treatment Efficacy

A significantly understudied area involves examining the mechanisms through which empirically supported interventions influence reductions in child and adolescent conduct problems (i.e., mediators). Many of the studies in this area have reported that changes in parenting practices and peer group affiliation may be the strongest mediators of treatment efficacy. For example, Eddy and Chamberlain (2000) found that the positive impact of MTFC on antisocial behavior in delinquent adolescents is mediated by improvements in family management skills and reductions in deviant peer associations. Similarly, Huey et al. (2000) found the beneficial effects of MST on antisocial behavior were mediated by improvements in family relationship and decreases in deviant peer group affiliation. Research on the Incredible Years Program has found that reductions in critical, harsh, and ineffective parenting practices tend to parallel improvements in externalizing behavior problems at post-treatment and 1-year follow-up (Beauchaine et al., 2005). Despite these advances, research supporting the assertion that modifying maladaptive or deficient social cognitions in children can lead to subsequent changes in their problem behavior has been limited (Lochman and Wells, 2002).

Summary and Future Directions for Treatment of ODD/CD

Although each of the empirically supported treatments discussed differed in terms of factors such as the target age group, length of treatment, and method of instruction, there are substantial common factors across these interventions. For example, the parent training component of these interventions typically focus on teaching parents how to use the behavioral principles of positive reinforcement and shaping to increase the frequency of prosocial behaviors in their children, while using various extinction procedures like timeout and selective ignoring to reduce the occurrence of conduct problems. In addition, parents are instructed in how to be firm, yet flexible, in their discipline, and they are encouraged to actively monitor their child's peer group interactions and spend quality time with their child on a regular basis. For programs with a child component, there is a focus on teaching children methods for solving interpersonal problems by identifying the intentions of others, generating prosocial solutions, evaluating the consequences of their behavior, and practicing the implementation of prosocial solutions through the use of role-plays in session. Moreover, many of the child programs seek to generalize the skills learned by having teachers and parents reinforce their use and assigning behavioral homework. Another common factor across many treatment studies is that parent training alone seems to produce more beneficial effects than child training alone, while a combination of the two seems optimal.

Identifying the common factors across successful interventions is important for several reasons. First, it gives practicing clinicians a firm theoretical and empirical base from which to build when treating children with ODD/CD in the community. Some prominent professionals have gone so far as to argue that if an empirically supported treatment for a certain disorder exists, it is unethical to initially offer treatments that do not have empirical support (Chambless, 1996; Meehl, 1997). This assertion is validated by studies indicating that newly developed or untested treatments for children with behavioral problems can produce negative, rather than positive, outcomes (Dishion and Andrews, 1995). While many practicing clinicians seem to support the use of empirically supported treatments, they do not routinely use them in their practice (Plante et al., 1999). It seems that clinical practitioners may view manualized treatments as too rigid to be implemented in the "real-world" setting, but it is important to recognize that many of the techniques used in these treatments can be used in clinical practice with minimal modification. Along these lines, a major area of future study will involve isolating the "active ingredients" of empirically supported interventions, as well as identifying the range of appropriate modification that can be made to these treatments without reducing their efficacy. In addition, it will be important to examine the most effective means through which these treatments can be disseminated within communities on a larger scale. As evidenced by the recent evaluations of large scale implementations of FFT and MST, transporting these interventions into the community may prove difficult. Lastly, one of the greatest problems associated with treating conduct disorders in youth is that positive changes in behavior tend to erode over time. One solution to this problem that has shown some early promise involves using booster interventions in the years following an intervention to help maintain positive improvements over time (Lochman, 1992). Given the stability of antisocial behavior in youth, it may be necessary for families to have regularly scheduled check-ups following a circumscribed intervention to prevent problem behaviors from re-occurring. Because these interventions will prove costly, studies demonstrating the cost-effectiveness of these approaches in terms of reducing criminal justice involvement will be important. Given the rising costs associated with adult incarceration, convincing policy makers to make the successful treatment of ODD/CD in children and adolescents a notional priority will hopefully become less difficult in the coming years.

REFERENCES

Adams RE, Bukwski WM, Bagwell C. (2005) Stability of aggression during early adolescence as moderated by reciprocated friendship status and friend's aggression. Int J Behavior Develop 29: 139-145.

Akers RL, Krohn MD, Lanza-Kaduce L, Radosevich M. (1979) Social learning and deviant behavior: A specific test of a general theory. Am Sociol Rev 44: 636-655.

American Psychiatric Association (1980) Diagnostic and Statistical Manual of Mental Disorders, 3rd edition (DSM-III). Washington, DC: American Psychiatric Association.

American Psychiatric Association (1987). Diagnostic and Statistical Manual of Mental Disorders, 3rd edition – revised (DSM-III-R). Washington, DC: American Psychiatric Association.

American Psychiatric Association (1994) Diagnostic and Statistical Manual of Mental Disorders, 4th edition (DSM-IV). Washington, DC: American Psychiatric Association.

Angold, A., and Costello, J. (1996). Toward establishing an empirical basis for the diagnosis of oppositional defiant disorder. J Am Acad Child Adolescent Psychiatr 35: 1205-1212.

Asarnow JR, Callan JW. (1985) Boys with peer adjustment problems: Social cognitive processes. J Consult Clin Psychol 53: 80-87.

Barry CT, Frick PJ, DeShazo TM, McCoy MG, Ellis M, Loney BR. (2000) The importance of callous-unemotional traits for extending the concept of psychopathy to children. J Abnormal Psychol 109: 335-340.

Barnoski R. (2004) Outcome evaluation of Washington State's research-based programs for juvenile offenders. Washington State Institute for Public Policy, January 2004, #04-01-1201.

Barton C, Alexander JF, Waldron H, Turner CW, Warburton J. (1985) Generalizing treatment effects of Functional Family Therapy: Three replications. Am J Family Therapy 13: 16-26.

Bates JE, Pettit GS, Dodge KA, Ridge B. (1998) Interaction of temperamental resistance to control and restrictive parenting in the development of externalizing behavior. Dev Psychol 34: 982-995.

Baumeister RF, Smart L, Boden JM. (1996) Relation between egotism to violence and aggression: The dark side of high self-esteem. Psychol Rev 103: 5-33.

Beauchaine TP, Webster-Stratton C, Reid MJ.

(2005) Mediators, moderators, and predictors of 1-year outcomes among children treated for early-onset conduct problems: A latent growth curve analysis. J Consul Clin Psychol 73,:371-388.

Borduin CM, Mann BJ, Cone LT, Henggeler SW, Fucci BR, Blask DM, Williams RA. (1995) Multisystemic treatment of serious juvenile offenders: Long-term prevention of criminality and violence. J Consult Clin Psychol 63: 569-578.

Brendgen M, Vitaro F, Tremblay RE, Francine L. (2001) Reactive and proactive aggression: Predictions to physical violence in difference contexts and moderating effects of parental monitoring and caregiving behavior. J Abnormal Child Psychol 29: 293-304.

Brestan EV, Eyberg SM. (1998) Effective psychosocial treatments of conduct-disordered children and adolescents: 29 years, 82 studies, and 5,272 kids. J Clin Child Psychol 27: 180-189.

Broidy LM, Nagin DS, Tremblay RE, Bates JE, Brame B, Dodge KA, Fergusson D, Horwood JL, Loeber R, Laird R, Lynam D, Moffitt TE, Pettit GS, Vitaro F. (2003) Developmental trajectories of childhood disruptive behaviors and adolescent delinquency: A six-site, cross-national study. Dev Psychol 39: 222-245.

Burgess KB, Wojslawowicz JC, Rubin KH, Rose-Krasnor L, Booth-LaForce C. (2006) Social information processing and coping strategies of shy/withdrawn and aggressive children: Does friendship matter? Child Dev 77: 371-383.

Burke JD, Loeber R, Lahey BB, Rathouz PJ. (2005) Developmental transitions among affective and behavioral disorders in adolescent boys. J Child Psychol Psychiatr 46: 1200-1210.

Burke JD, Loeber R, Mutchka JS, Lahey BB. (2002) A question for DSM-V: Which better predicts persistent conduct disorder – delinquent acts or conduct symptoms?

Criminal Behav Mental Health 12: 37-52.

Burns GL, Walsh JA. (2002) The influence of ADHD-hyperactivity/ impulsivity symptoms on the development of oppositional defiant disorder symptoms in a 2-year longitudinal study. J Abnormal Child Psychol 30: 245-256.

Burt SA, Kruger RF, McGue M, Iacono W. (2003) Parent-child conflict and the comorbidity among childhood externalizing disorders. Arch Gen Psychiatr 60: 505-513.

Cairns RB, Cairns BD, Neckerman HJ, Gest SD, Gariépy J. (1988) Social networks and aggressive behavior: Peer support or peer rejection? Dev Psychol 24: 815-823.

Capaldi DM, Dishion TJ, Stoolmiller M, Yoerger K. (2001) Aggression toward female partners by at-risk men: The contribution of male adolescent friendships. Dev Psychol 37: 61-73.

Caspi A, Moffitt TE, Morgan J, Rutter M, Taylor A, Arseneault Tully L, Jacobs C, Kim-Cohen J, Polo-Tomas M. (2004) Maternal expressed emotion predicts children's antisocial behavior problems: Using MZ-twin differences to identify environmental effects on behavioral development. Dev Psychol 40: 149–161.

Center for Children and Families in the Justice System (2006) Randomized study of MST in Ontario, Canada: Final results. Retrieved August 22, 2006, from http://www.lfcc.on.ca/mst_final_results.html.

Chaffin M, Silovsky JF, Funderburk B, Valle LA, Brestan EV, Balachova T, Jackson S, Lensgraf J, Bonner BL. (2004) Parent-child interaction therapy with physically abusive parents: Efficacy for reducing future abuse reports. J Consult Clin Psychol 72: 500-510.

Chamberlain P. (1990) Comparative evaluation of specialized foster care for seriously delinquent youths: A first step. Community Alternatives: Int J Family

Care 2: 21-36.

Chamberlain P, Reid JB. (1998) Comparison of two community alternatives to incarceration for chronic juvenile offenders. J Consult Clin Psychol 66: 624-633.

Chambless DL. (1996) In defense of dissemination of empirically supported psychological interventions. Clin Psychol: Sci Practice 3: 230-235.

Christian RE, Frick PJ, Hill NL, Tyler L, Frazer DR. (1997) Psychopathy and conduct problems in children: II. Implications for subtyping children with conduct problems. J Am Acad Child Adolescent Psychiatr 36: 233- 241.

Cillessen AH, Jiang XL, West TV, Laszkowski DK. (2005) Predictors of dyadic friendship quality in adolescence. Int J Behav Dev 29: 165-172.

Clark DB, Parker AM, Lynch KG. (1999) Psychopathology and substance-related problems during early adolescence: A survival analysis. J Clin Child Psychol 28: 333-341.

Cohen MA. (1998) The monetary value of saving a high-risk youth. J Quantitative Criminol 14: 5-33.

Coie JD, Dodge KA, Coppotelli H. (1982) Dimensions and types of social status: A cross-age perspective. Development Psychol 18: 557-570.

Coie JD, Terry R, Lenox K, Lochman J, Hyman C. (1995) Predicting early adolescent disorders from childhood aggression and peer rejection. J Consult Clin Psychol 60: 783-792.

Coy K, Speltz ML, DeKlyen M, Jones K. (2001) Social-cognitive processes in preschool boys with and without Oppositional Defiant Disorder. J Abnormal Child Psychol 29: 107-119.

Crick NR, Dodge KA. (1994) A review and reformulation of social information-processing mechanisms in children's social adjustment. Psych Bull 115: 74-101.

Crick NR, Werner NE. (1998) Response decision processes in relational and overt aggression. Child Dev 69: 1630-1639.

Dadds MR, Sanders MR, Morrison M, Rebgetz M. (1992) Childhood depression and conduct disorder: II. An analysis of family interaction patterns in the home. J Abnormal Psychol 101: 505-513

Dishion TJ, Andrews DW. (1995) Preventing escalation in problem behaviors with high-risk young adolescents: Immediate and 1-year outcomes. J Consult Clin Psychol 63: 538-548.

Dishion TJ, Capaldi DM, Spracklen KM, Li F. (1995) Peer ecology of male adolescent drug use. Dev Psychopathol 7: 803-824.

Dishion TJ, Eddy JM, Haas E, Li F, Spracklen K. (1997) Friendships and violent behavior during adolescence. Social Dev 6: 207-223.

Dishion TJ, McCord J, Poulin F. (1999) When interventions harm: Peer groups and problem behavior. Am Psychol 54: 755-764.

Dishion T, Patterson GR, Reid J. (1988) Parent and peer factors associated with early onset drug use: Implications for treatment. In E. Rahdert and J. Grabowski (Eds.), Adolescent drug abuse: Analyses of treatment research, NIDA Research Monograph 77 (pp.69-93). Washington, DC: U.S. Government Printing Office.

Dishion TJ, Spracklen KM, Andrews DW, Patterson GR. (1996) Deviancy training in male adolescent friendships. Behavior Therapy 27; 373-390.

Dodge KA. (1993) Social cognitive mechanisms in the development of conduct disorder and depression. Ann Rev Psychol 44: 558-584.

Dodge KA, Pettit GS, McClaskey CL, Brown MM. (1986) Social competence in children. Monographs Soc Res Child Dev 51: (2, Serial No. 213).

Dodge KA, Somberg DR. (1987) Hostile attributional biases among aggressive boys are exacerbated under conditions of threats to the self. Child Dev 58: 213-24.

Dumas JE, Wahler RG. (1983) Predictors of treatment outcome in parent training: Mother insularity and socioeconomic disadvantage. Behav Assess 5: 301-313.

Dunn SE, Lochman JE, Colder CR. (1997) Social problem-solving skills in boys with conduct and oppositional defiant disorder. Aggressive Behav 23: 457-469.

Eddy JM, Chamberlain P. (2000) Family management and deviant peer association as mediators of the impact of treatment condition on youth antisocial behavior. J Consult Clin Psychol 68: 857-863.

Eddy JM, Whaley RB, Chamberlain P. (2004) The prevention of violent behavior by chronic and serious male juvenile offenders: A two-year follow-up of a randomized clinical trial. J Emotion Behav Disord 12: 2-8.

Edens JF, Cavell TA, Hughes JN. (1999) The self-systems of aggressive children: A cluster-analytic investigation. J Child Psychol Psychiatr Allied Disciplin 40: 441-453.

Eisenstadt TH, Eyberg S, McNeil CB, Newcomb K, Funderburk B. (1993) Parent-child interaction therapy with behavior problem children: Relative effectiveness of two stages and overall treatment outcome. J Child Clin Psychol 22: 42-51.

Farmer EMZ, Compton SN, Burns B, Robertson E. (2002) Review of evidence base for treatment of childhood psychopathology: Externalizing disorders. J Consult Clin Psychol 70: 1267-1302.

Fergusson DM, Horwood LJ. (1995) Early disruptive behavior, IQ, and later school achievement and delinquent behavior. J Abnormal Child Psychol 23; 183-199.

Fisher PA, Chamberlain P. (2000) Multidimensional Treatment Foster Care: A program for intensive parenting, family support, and skill building. J Emotion Behavior Disord 8: 155-164.

Forgatch MS, Patterson GR, DeGarmo DS. (2005) Evaluating fidelity: Predictive validity for a measure of competent adherence to the Oregon model of parent management training. Behav Therapy 36: 3-13.

Fowles DC, Kochanska G. (2000) Temperament as a moderator of pathways to conscience in children: The contribution of electrodermal activity. Psychophysiol 37: 788-795.

Frick PJ, Christian RE, Wootton JM. (1999a) Age trends in the association between parenting practices and conduct problems. Behav Modification 23: 106-128.

Frick PJ, Cornell AH, Bodin SD, Dane HE, Barry CT, Loney BR. (2003) Callous-unemotional traits and developmental pathways to severe conduct problems. Dev Psychol 39: 246-260.

Frick PJ, Lahey BB, Applegate B, Kerdyk L, Ollendick T, Hynd GW, Garfinkel B, Greenhill L, Biederman J, Barkley RA, McBurnett K, Newcorn J, Waldman I. (1994) DSM-IV field trials for the disruptive and attention deficit disorders: Diagnostic utility of symptoms. J Am Acad Child Adolescent Psychiatr 33: 529-539.

Frick PJ, Lahey BB, Loeber R, Stouthamer-Loeber M, Christ MAG, Hanson K. (1992) Familial risk factors to oppositional defiant disorder and conduct disorder: Parental psychopathology and maternal parenting. J Consult Clin Psychol 60: 49-53.

Frick PJ, Lahey BB, Loeber R, Stouthamer-Loeber M, Green S, Hart EL, Christ MAG. (1991) Oppositional defiant disorder and conduct disorder in boys: Patterns of behavioral covariation. J Clin Child Psychol 20: 202-208.

Frick PJ, Lilienfeld SO, Ellis M, Loney B, Silverthorn P. (1999b) The association between anxiety and psychopathy dimensions in children. J Abnormal Child 27: 383-392.

Gallagher N. (2003) Effects of parent-child interaction therapy on young children with disruptive behavior disorders. Bridges 1: 1-17.

Gordon DA, Arbuthnot J, Gustafson KE, McGreen P. (1988) Home-based behavioral-systems family therapy with disadvantaged juvenile delinquents. Am J Family Therapy 16: 243-255.

Gordon DA, Graves K, Arbuthnot J. (1995) The effect of functional family therapy for delinquents on adult criminal behavior. Criminal Justice Behav 22: 60-73.

Gouze KR. (1987) Attention and social problem solving as correlates of aggression in preschool males. J Abnormal Child Psychol 15 181-197.

Greenwood PW. (2004) Cost-effective violence prevention through targeted family interventions. Annals New York Acad Sci 1036: 201-214.

Gresham FM, Little SG. (1993) Peer-referenced assessment strategies. In TH Ollendick and M Hersen (Eds.), Handbook of child and adolescent assessment: General psychology series, Vol. 167. (pp. 165-179). Needham Heights, MA: Allyn and Bacon.

Grotpeter JK, Crick NR. (1996) Relational aggression, overt aggression, and friendship. Child Dev 67 2328-2338.

Hartman RR, Stage SA, Webster-Stratton C. (2003) A growth curve analysis of parent training outcomes: Examining the influence of child risk factors (inattention, impulsivity, and hyperactivity problems), parental and family risk factors. J Child Psychol Psychiatr 44: 388-398.

Hawes DJ, Dadds MR. (2005) The treatment of conduct problems in children with callous-unemotional traits. J Consult Clin Psychol 73: 737-741.

Henggeler SW, Melton GB, Brondino MJ, Scherer DG, Hanley JH. (1997) Multisystemic therapy with violent and chronic juvenile offenders and their families: The role of treatment fidelity in successful dissemination. J Consult Clin Psychol 65: 821-833.

Henggler SW, Melton GB, Smith LA. (1992) Family preservation using multisystemic therapy: An effective alternative to incarcerating serious juvenile offenders. J Consult Clin Psychol 60: 953-961.

Henggler SW, Melton GB, Smith LA, Schoenwald SK, Hanley JH. (1993) Family preservation using multisystemic treatment: Long-term follow-up to a clinical trial with serious juvenile offenders. J Family Child Stud 2: 283-293.

Henggeler SW, Pickrel SG, Brondino MJ. (1999) Multisystemic treatment of substance-abusing and -dependent delinquents: Outcomes, treatment fidelity, and transportability. Ment Health Serv Res 1: 171-184.

Henggeler SW, Rodick JD, Hanson CL, Watson SM, Borduin CM, Urey JR. (1986) Multisystemic treatment of juvenile offenders: Effects on adolescent behavior and family interaction. Dev Psychol 22: 132-141.

Henggeler SW, Schoenwald SK, Borduin CM, Rowland MD, Cunningham P. (1998) Multisystemic treatment of antisocial behavior in children and adolescents. New York, NY: Guilford Press.

Henggeler SW, Schoenwald SK, Borduin CM, Swenson CC. (2006) Methodological critique and meta-analysis as a Trojan horse. Children Youth Serv Rev 28: 447-457.

Henry D, Guerra N, Huesmann R, Tolan P, Van Acker R, Eron L. (2000) Normative influences on aggression in urban elementary school classrooms. Am J Commun Psychol 28: 59-81.

Herschell AD, Calzada EJ, Eyberg SM, McNeil CB. (2002) Parent-child interaction therapy: New directions in research. Cog Behav Practice 9: 9-16.

Hinshaw SP. (1992a) Academic under-achievement, attention deficits, and aggression: Comorbidity and implications for intervention. J Consult Clin Psychol 60: 893-903.

Hinshaw SP. (1992a) Externalizing behavior problems and academic underachievement in childhood and adolescence: Causal relationships and underlying mechanisms. Psychol Bull 111: 127-155.

Hinshaw SP, Lahey BB, Hart EL. (1993) Issues of taxonomy and comorbidity in the development of conduct disorder. Dev Psychopathol 5: 31-49.

Hipwell AE, Loeber R, Stouthamer-Loeber M, Keenan K, White HR, Kroneman L. (2002) Charecteristics of girls with early onset disruptive and antisocial behavior. Criminal Behav Ment Health 12: 99-118.

Hood KK, Eyberg SM. (2003) Outcomes of parent-child interaction therapy: Mothers' reports of maintenance three to six years after treatment. J Clin Child Adolescent Psychol 32: 419-439.

Hubbard JA, Smithmyer CM, Ramsden SR, Parker EH, Flanagan KD, Dearing KF, Relyea N, Simons RF. (2002) Observational, physiological, and self-report measures of children's anger: Relations to reactive versus proactive aggression. Child Dev 73: 1101-1119.

Huey SJ, Henggeler SW, Brondino MJ, Pickrel SG. (2000) Mechanisms of change in multisystemic therapy: reducing delinquent behavior through therapist adherence and improved family and peer functioning. J Consult Clin Psychol 68: 451-467.

Hughes JN, Cavell TA, Grossman PB. (1997) A positive view of self: Risk or protection for aggressive children? Dev Psychopathol 9: 75-94.

Hughes JN, Cavell TA, Prasad-Gaur A. (2001) A positive view of peer acceptance in aggressive youth risk for future peer acceptance. J School Psychol 39: 239-252.

Hymel S, Bowker A, Woody E, (1993) Aggressive versus withdrawn unpopular children: Variations in peer and self-perceptions in multiple domains. Child Dev 64: 879-896.

Jaffee SR, Caspi A, Moffitt TE, Taylor A. (2004) Physical maltreatment victim to antisocial child: Evidence of an environmentally-mediated process. J Abnormal Psychol 113: 44–55.

Jaffee SR, Caspi A, Moffitt TE, Dodge KA, Rutter M, Taylor A, Tully LA. (2005) Nature × nurture: Genetic vulnerabilities interact with physical maltreatment to promote conduct problems. Dev Psychopathol 17: 67-84.

Johnson JG, Smailes E, Cohen P, Kasen S, Brook JS. (2004) Anti-social parental behaviour, problematic parenting and aggressive offspring behaviour during adulthood: A 25-year longitudinal investigation. Brit J Criminol 44: 915-930.

Kazdin AE. (2003) Psychotherapy for children and adolescents. Ann Rev Psychol 54: 253-276.

Kazdin AE, Bass D, Siegal T, Christopher T. (1989) Cognitive-behavioral therapy and relationship therapy in the treatment of children referred for antisocial behavior. J Consult Clin Psychol 57: 522-535.

Kazdin AE, Crowley M. (1997) Moderators of treatment outcome in cognitively based treatment of antisocial children. Cog Therapy Res 21: 185-207.

Kazdin AE, Esveldt-Dawson K, French NH, Unis AS. (1987) Problem-solving skills training and relationship therapy in the treatment of antisocial child behavior. J Consult Clin Psychol 55: 76-85.

Kazdin AE, Siegel TC, Bass D. (1992) Cognitive problem soling skills training and parent management training in the treatment of antisocial behavior in children. J Consult Clin Psychol 60: 733-

747.

Kazdin AE, Wassell G. (1999) Barriers to treatment participation and therapeutic change among children referred for conduct disorder. J Clin Child Psychol 28: 160-172.

Kazdi AE, Whitley MK. (2006) Pretreatment social relations, therapeutic alliance, and improvements in parenting practices in parent management training. J Consult Clin Psychol 74: 346-355.

Keiley MK, Bates JE, Dodge KA, Pettit GS. (2000) A cross-domain growth analysis: Externalizing and internalizing behaviors during 8 years of childhood. J Abnormal Child Psychol 28: 161-179.

Kessler RC, Berglund P, Demler O, Jin R, Merikangas K, Walters EE. (2005) Lifetime prevalence and age-of-onset distributions of DSM-IV Disorders in the National Comorbidity Survey Replication. Arch Gen Psychiatr 62: 593-602.

Klein NC, Alexander JF, Parsons BV. (1977) Impact of family systems intervention on recidivism and sibling delinquency: A model of primary prevention and program evaluation. J Consult Clin Psychol 45: 469-474.

Kochanska G. (1997) Mutually responsive orientation between mothers and their young children: Implications for early socialization. Child Dev 68: 94-112.

Kochanska G, Murray KT. (2000) Mother-child mutually responsive orientation and conscience development: From toddler to early school age. Child Dev 71: 417-431.

Lahey BB, Loeber R, Burke JD, Applegate B. (2005) Predicting future antisocial personality disorder in males from a clinical assessment in childhood. J Consult Clin Psychol 73: 389-399.

Lahey BB, Loeber R, Burke J, Rathouz PJ. (2002) Adolescent outcomes of childhood conduct disorder among clinic-referred boys: Predictors of improvement. J Abnormal Child Psychol 30: 333-348.

Lahey BB, Loeber R, Burke J, Rathouz PJ, McBurnett K. (2002) Waxing and waning in concert: Dynamic comorbidity of conduct disorder with other disruptive and emotional problems over 7 years among clinic-referred boys. J Abnormal Psychol 111: 556-567.

Lahey B, Loeber R, Quay HC, Applegate B, Shaffer D, Waldman I, Hart HL, McBurnett K, Frick PJ, Jensen PS, Dulcan MK, Canino G, Bird HR. (1998) Validity of DSM-IV subtypes of conduct disorder based on age of onset. J Am Acad Child Adolescent Psychiatr 37: 435-443.

Lahey BB, Loeber R, Quay HC, Frick PJ, Grimm J. (1992) Oppositional defiant disorder and conduct disorder: Issues to be resolved for DSM-IV. J Am Acad Child Adolescent Psychiatr 31; 539-546.

Laible DJ, Thompson RA. (2002) Mother-child conflict in the toddler years: Lessons in emotion, morality, and relationships. Child Dev 73:1187-1203.

Laird RD, Jordan KY, Dodge KA, Pettit GS, Bates JE. (2001) Peer rejection in childhood, involvement with antisocial peers in early adolescence, and the development of externalizing behavior problems. Dev Psychopathol, 13: 337-354.

Laub JH, Sampson RJ. (1988) Unraveling families and delinquency: A reanalysis of the Gluecks' data. Criminol 26: 355-380.

Leschied A, Cunningham A. (2002) Seeking effective interventions for serious young offenders: Interim results of a four-year randomized study of multisystemic therapy in Ontario, Canada. London, Canada: London Family Court Clinic.

Leve LD, Chamberlain P. (2005) Association with delinquent peers: Intervention effects for youth in the juvenile justice system. J Abnormal Child Psychol 3: 339-347.

Leve LD, Chamberlain P, Reid JB. (2005) Intervention outcomes for girls referred from juvenile justice: Effects on delinquency. J Consult Clin Psychol 73: 1181-1185.

Littell JH. (2006) The case for Multisystemic Therapy: Evidence of orthodoxy. Child Youth Serv Rev 28: 458-472.

Littell JH, Popa M, Forsythe B. (2005) Multisystemic Therapy for social, emotional, and behavioral problems in youth aged 10-17. The Cochrane Database of Systematic Reviews, Issue 4. Art. No.: CD004797. pub4. DOI: 10.1002/14651858.CD004797.pub4.

Lochman JE. (1987) Self and peer perceptions and attributional biases of aggressive and non-aggressive boys in dyadic inter-actions. J Consult Clin Psychol 55: 404-410.

Lochman JE. (1992) Cognitive-behavioral interventions with aggressive boys: Three-year follow-up and preventive effects. J Consult Clin Psychol 60: 426-432.

Lochman JE, Dodge KA. (1994) Social-cognitive processes of severely violent, moderately aggressive, and nonaggressive boys. J Consult Clin Psychol 62: 366-374.

Lochman JE, Lampron LB. (1988) Cognitive behavioral intervention for aggressive boys: Seven month follow-up effects. J Child Adolescent Psychotherapy 5: 15-23.

Lochman JE, Wayland KK, White KK. (1993) Social goals: Relationship to adolescent adjustment and to social problem solving. J Abnormal Child Psychol 21: 135-151.

Lochman JE, Wells KC. (2002) Contextual social-cognitive mediators and child outcome: A test of the theoretical model in the Coping Power program. Dev Psychopathol 14: 945-967.

Loeber R, Burke JD, Lahey BB. (2002) What are adolescent antecedents to antisocial personality disorder? Criminal Behav Ment Health 12: 24-36.

Loeber R, Farrington DP. (2001) Child delinquents: Development, intervention and service needs. Thousand Oaks, CA: Sage.

Loeber R, Green SR, Keenan K, Lahey BB. (1995) Which boys will fare worse? Early predictors of the onset of conduct disorder in a six-year longitudinal study. J Am Acad Child Adolescent Psychiatr 34: 499-510.

Loeber R, Lahey BB, Thomas C. (1991) Diagnostic conundrum of oppositional defiant disorder and conduct disorder. J Abnormal Psychol 100: 379-390.

Loeber R, Pardini DA, Homish DL, Wei EH, Crawford AM, Farrington DP, Stout-hamer-Loeber M, Creemers J, Koehler SA, Rosenfeld R. (2005) The prediction of violence and homicide in young males. J Consult Clin Psychol 73: 1074–1088.

Loeber R, Pardini DA, Stouthamer-Loeber M, Raine A. (in press) Do neurocognitive and psycho-social risk and protective factors predict desistance from delinquency in males? Dev Psychopathol

Loney BR, Butler MA, Lima EN, Counts CA, Eckel LA. (2006) The relation between salivary cortisol, callous-unemotional traits, and conduct problems in an adolescent non-referred sample. J Child Psychol Psychiatr 47: 30-36.

Loney BR, Frick PJ, Ellis M, McCoy MG. (1998) Intelligence, callous-unemotional traits, and antisocial behavior. J Psychopathol Behav Assessment 20: 231-247.

Lynam DR. (1996) Early identification of chronic offenders: Who is the fledgling psychopath? Psych Bull 120: 209-234.

Marmorstein NR, Iacono WG. (2003) Major depression and conduct disorder in a twin sample: Gender, functioning, and risk for future psychopathology. J Am Acad Child Adolescent Psychiatr 42: 225-233.

Mason WA, Windle M. (2002) Reciprocal relations between adolescent substance use and delinquency: A longitudinal latent variable analysis. J Abnormal Psychol

111; 63-76.

Matos M, Torres R, Santiago R, Jurado M, Rodrigues I. (2006) Adaptation of parent-child interaction therapy for Puerto Rican families: A preliminary study. Family Process 45: 205-222.

Matsueda RL, Heimer K. (1987) Race, family structure, and delinquency: A test of differential association and social control theories. Am Sociol Rev 52; 826-840.

Matthys W, Cuperus JM, Van Engeland H. (1999) Deficient social problem-solving with ODD/CD, with ADHD, and with both disorders. J Am Acad Child Adolescent Psychiatr 38: 311-321.

McCabe KM, Yeh M, Garland AF, Lau AS, Chavez G. (2005) The GANA program: A tailoring approach to adapting parent child interaction therapy for Mexican Americans. Education Treat Children 28: 111-129.

Meehl P. (1997) Credentialed persons, credentialed knowledge. Clin Psychol: Res Practice 4: 91-98.

Milich R, Dodge KA. (1984) Social information processing in child psychiatric populations. J Abnormal Child Psychol 12: 471-490.

Miller-Johnson S, Coie JD, Maumary-Gremaud A, Bierman K, and the Conduct Problems Prevention Research Group (2002) Peer rejection and aggression and early starter models of Conduct Disorder. J Abnormal Child Psychol 30: 217-230.

Miller-Johnson S, Coie JD, Maumary-Gremaud A, Lochman J, Terry R. (1999) Relationship between childhood peer rejection and aggression and adolescent delinquency severity and type among African American youth. J Emotion Behav Disord 7: 137-146.

Moffitt TE. (1990) The neuropsychology of juvenile delinquency: A critical review. Crime Justice 12: 99-169.

Moffitt TE. (1993) Adolescence-limited and life-cycle-persistent antisocial behavior: A developmental taxonomy. Psychol Rev 100: 674-701.

Morrell J, Murrary L. (2003) Parenting and the development of conduct disorder and hyperactive symptoms in childhood: A prospective longitudinal study from 2 months to 8 years. J Child Psychol Psychiatr 44: 489-508.

MTA Cooperative Group (1999) 14-Month randomized clinical trial of treatment strategies for attention deficit hyper-activity disorder. Arch Gen Psychiatr 56: 1073-1086.

Myers MG, Brown SA, Mott MA. (1995) Preadolescent conduct disorder behaviors predict relapse and progression of addiction for adolescent alcohol and drug abusers. Alcoholism: Clin Exp Res 19: 1528-1536

Myers MG, Stewart DG, Brown SA. (1998) Progression from conduct disorder to antisocial personality disorder following treatment for adolescent substance abuse. Am J Psychiatr 155; 479-485.

Nixon RDV, Sweeney L, Erickson DB, Touyz SW. (2003) Parent-child interaction therapy: A comparison of standard and abbreviated treatments for oppositional defiant preschoolers. J Consult Clin Psychol 71: 251-260.

Nixon RDV, Sweeney L, Erickson DB, Touyz SW. (2004) Parent-child interaction therapy: One- and two-year follow-up of standard and abbreviated treatments for oppositional preschoolers. J Abnormal Child Psychol 32: 263-271.

Nock MK. (2003) Progress review of the psychosocial treatment of child conduct problems. Clin Psychol: Sci Pract 10: 1-28.

Nock MK, Kazdin AE. (2005) Randomized controlled trial of a brief intervention for increasing participation in parent manage-ment training. J Consult Clin Psychol 73: 872-879.

Nock MK, Kazdin AE, Hiripi E, Kessler RC

(2006) Prevalence, subtypes, and correlates of DSM-IV conduct disorder in the National Comorbidity Survey Replication. Psych Med 36: 699-710.

Orobio de Castrol B, Bosch JD, Veerman JW, Koops W. (2003) The effects of emotion regulation, attribution, and delay prompts on aggressive boys' social problem solving. J Cog Therapy Res 27: 153-166.

Pardini DA. (2006) The callousness pathway to severe violent delinquency. Aggressive Behav 32: 590-598.

Pardini DA, Lochman JE. (2003) Treatment for Oppositional Defiant Disorder. In M.A. Reinecke, F.M. Dattilio, and A. Freeman (Eds.), Cognitive therapy with children and adolescents -2nd edition (pp. 43-69). New York: Guilford.

Pardini DA, Lochman JE, Frick PJ. (2003) Callous/unemotional traits and social cognitive processes in adjudicated youth. J Am Acad Child Adolescent Psychiatr 42: 364-371.

Pardini D, Loeber R, Stouthamer-Loeber M. (2005) Developmental shifts in parent and peer influences on boys' beliefs about delinquent behavior. J Res Adolescence 15: 299-323.

Pardini D, Obradovic J, Loeber R. (2006) Interpersonal callousness, hyperactivity/ impulsivity, inattention, and conduct problems as precursors to delinquency persistence in boys: A comparison of three grade-based cohorts. J Clin Child Adolescent Psychol 35: 46-59.

Pardini DA, White HR, Stouthamer-Loeber M. (2007) Early adolescent psycho-pathology as a predictor of alcohol use disorders by young adulthood. Drug Alcohol Depend 88S: S38–S49.

Parker JG, Asher SR. (1987) Peer relations and later personal adjustment: Are low-accepted children at risk? Psych Bull 102: 357-389.

Patterson GR, Dishion TJ, Yoerger K. (2000) Adolescent growth in new forms of problem behavior: Macro- and micro-peer dynamics. Prevention Sci 1: 3-13.

Patterson CJ, Kupersmidt JB, Griesler PC. (1990) Children's perceptions of self and of relationships with others as a function of sociometric status. Child Dev 61: 1335-1349.

Patterson GR, Reid JB, Dishion TJ. (1992) Antisocial boys. Eugene, OR: Castalia.

Pepler DJ, Craig WM, Roverts WI. (1998) Observations of aggressive and nonaggressive children on the school playground. Merrill Palmer Quart 44: 55-76.

Pettit GS, Bates JF, Dodge KA, Meece DW. (1999) The impact of after-school peer contact on early adolescent externalzing problems is moderated by parental monitoring, perceived neighborhood safety and, and prior adjustment. Child Dev 70: 768-778.

Plante TG, Andersen EN, Boccaccini MT. (1999) Empirically supported treatments and related contemporary changes in psychotherapy practice: What do clinical ABPPs think? Clin Psychologist 52: 23-31.

Raine A, Moffitt E, Caspi A, Loeber R, Stouthamer-Loeber M, Lynam D. (2005) Neurocognitive impairments in boys on the life-course persistent antisocial path. J Abnormal Psychol 114: 38-49.

Rey JM. (1993) Oppositional defiant disorder. Am J Psychiatr 150; 1769-1778.

Rey JM, Plapp JM. (1990) Quality of perceived parenting in oppositional and conduct disordered adolescents. J Am Acad Child Adolescent Psychiatr 29: 157-162.

Rhee SH, Waldman, ID (2002) Genetic and environmental influences on antisocial behavior: A meta-analysis of twin and adoption studies. Psychol Bull 128: 490-529.

Salmivalli C, Kaukianinen A, Kaistaniemi L, Lagerspetz KMJ. (1999) Self-evaluated self-esteem, peer-evaluated self-esteem, and defensive egotism as predictors of adolescents' participation in bullying situations. Personality Social Psychol Bull 25: 1268-1278.

Schaeffer CM, Borduin CM. (2005) Long-term follow-up to a randomized clinical trial of multisystemic therapy with serious and violent juvenile offenders. J Consult Clin Psychol 73: 445-453.

Schuhmann EM, Foote R, Eyberg SM, Boggs SR, Algina J. (1998) Efficacy of parent-child interaction therapy: Interim report of a randomized trail with short-term maintenance. J Child Clin Psychol 27: 34-45.

Sexton TL, Alexander JF. (December, 2000) Functional Family Therapy. Office of Juvenile Justice and Delinquency Programs: Juvenile Justice Bulletin.

Shaw DS, Vondra JI. (1995) Infant attachment security and maternal predictors of early behavior problems: A longitudinal study of low-income families. J Abnormal Child Psychol 23: 335-357.

Shirk SR, Karver M. (2003) Prediction of treatment outcome from relationship variables in child and adolescent therapy: A meta-analytic review. J Consult Clin Psychol 71: 452-464.

Smith CA, Lazarus RW. (1990) Emotion and adaptation. In L Previn (Ed.), Handbook of personality: Theory and research (pp. 609-637). New York: Guilford.

Thomas A, Chess S. (1977) Temperament and Development. New York: Brunner/Mazel.

Vitaro F, Brendgen M, Tremblay RE. (2000) Influence of deviant friends on delinquency: Searching for moderator variables. J Abnormal Child Psychol 28: 313-325.

Vontanis P, Meltzer H, Goodman R, Ford T. (2003) Service utilization by children with conduct disorders: Findings from the GB National Study. Eur Child Adolescent Psychiatr 12: 231-238.

Waas GA, French DC. (1989) Children's social problem solving: Comparison of the open middle interview and children's assertive behavior scale. Behav Assess 11: 219-230.

Walker JL, Lahey BB, Russo MF, Frick PJ, et al. (1991) Anxiety, inhibition, and conduct disorder in children: I. Relations to social impairment. J Am Acad Child Adolescent Psychiatr 30: 187-191.

Webster-Stratton C. (1984) Randomized trial of two parent-training programs for families with conduct-disordered children. J Consult Clin Psychol 52: 666-678.

Webster-Stratton C. (1990) Long-term follow-up of families with young conduct-problems children: From preschool to grade school. J Consult Clin Psychol 19: 1344-1349.

Webster-Stratton C, Hammond M. (1997) Treating children with early-onset conduct problems: A comparison of child and parent training interventions. J Consult Clin Psychol 65: 93-109.

Webster-Stratton C, Kolpacoff M, Hollinsworth T. (1988) Self-administered videotape therapy for families with conduct problem children: Comparison with two-cost effective treatments and a control group. J Consult Clin Psychol 56: 558-566.

Webster-Stratton C, Lindsay DW. (1999) Social competence and conduct problems in young children: Issues and assessment. J Clin Child Psychol 28: 25-43.

Webster-Stratton C, Reid MJ, Hammond M. (2004) Treating children with early-onset conduct problems: Intervention outcomes for parent, child and teacher training. J Clin Child Adolescent Psychol 33:105-124.

Weinberg NZ, Rahdert E, Colliver JD, Myer GD. (1998) Adolescent substance abuse: A review of the past 10 years. J Am Acad Child Adolescent Psychiatr 37: 252-261.

Weiner B. (1990) Attribution in personality psychology. In L Pervin (Ed.), Handbook of personality: Theory and research (pp. 609-637). New York: Guilford.

Welsh BC, (2001) Economic costs and benefits of early developmental prevention. In R Loeber and DP Farrington (Eds.), Child delinquents: Development, inter-vention, and service needs (pp. 339-358). Thousand Oaks, CA: Sage Publications.

White HR, Pandina RJ, LaGrange RL. (1987) Longitudinal predictors of serious substance use and delinquency. Criminol 25: 715-739.

Whitemore EA, Mikulich SK, Thompson LL, Riggs LL, Aarons G A, Crowley TJ. (1997) Influences on adolescent substance dependence: Conduct disorder, depresssion, and attention deficit hyperactivity disorder, and gender. Drug Alcohol Dependence 47: 87-97.

Williams SC, Lochman JE, Phillips NC, Barry TD. (2003) Aggressive and non-aggressive boys' physiological and cognitive processes in response to peer provocations. J Clin Child Adolescent Psychol 32: 568-576.

Wong MA, Zucker RA, Puttler LI, Fitzgerald HE. (1999) Heterogeneity of risk aggregation for alcohol problems between early and middle childhood: Nesting structure variations. J Dev Psychopathol 11: 727-744.

PREVENTION OF YOUTH SMOKING

Alessandra N. Kazura and Raymond Niaura

INTRODUCTION

Recent survey data demonstrate a promising decline in youth smoking rates, and prevention efforts need to be optimized to continue this trend. According to the Monitoring the Future Survey, daily smoking by high school seniors in 2002 has decreased to 16.9% from an all time high of 28.8% in 1976 (Johnston et al, 2002b). Additionally, the annual incidence of new smokers among 12-17 year olds has decreased from 1.1 million in 1997 to 747,000 in 2000 (USDHHS, 2002). Later age of onset of smoking experimentation has also been reported, with initial use by grade 6 declining from 20% for the class of 1986 to 15% for the class of 2001 (Johnston et al., 2002a). In this chapter, we summarize youth tobacco use trends and then highlight successful, evidence-based prevention programs. We comment on risk profiles that may signal resilience or vulnerability to smoking uptake and we discuss gaps in our knowledge of prevention efficacy and effectiveness in youth subpopulations. Finally, we identify promising examples of new strategies for preventing youth tobacco use.

Tobacco Use Trends

A comprehensive understanding of youth tobacco use requires attention to patterns of use by age and cohort, gender, ethnicity, location, and other sociodemographic factors. While smoking rates have declined across the majority of subgroups measured by the Monitoring the Future Survey (Johnston et al., 2002b), variation in prevalence rates can be observed among these subgroups. For example, last 30-day prevalence rates of 12.0% and 12.7% were observed for White and Hispanic eighth grade students, but only 7.7% for Black students. Thirty-day smoking rates in

eighth grade students were lowest in the West, at 7.5%, and highest in the South of the United States, at 13.0%. Even more striking differences were noted between students with parents in the highest and lowest educational levels, with 30-day prevalence rates of 5.8% and 20.5%, respectively. Declines in smoking have been attributed to increases in youth perception of risk and disapproval of smoking, anti-smoking media campaigns, and increases in cigarette prices (Johnston et al., 2002b).

Cigarettes remain the most common tobacco product used by youth, but other tobacco products are important to address and may contribute to unique morbidity and mortality concerns. For ninth through twelfth grade students, the last 30-day prevalence of smokeless tobacco use was 8.2% in 2001, while the cigar smoking rate was 15.2% (Grunbaum et al., 2002). Bidis, which are hand rolled cigarettes imported from India, may find favor with some youth; nicotine concentrations are typically higher in bidis than standard cigarettes (NIDA, 2000). Embalming fluid dipped cigarettes (street names include "illy", "wets", and "fry" and may also refer to marijuana based products), have made appearances in some communities and are particularly of concern because of acute toxicity associated with the chemical additives (Modesto-Lowe, 2002; Weiner, 2000: Moriarity, 1996).

Although the delivery of nicotine, and therefore risk of nicotine dependence, is common to all forms of tobacco products, prevention and cessation efforts may need to be tailored to the specific types of tobacco used by youth. For example, only 45% of high school seniors perceive great health risk from regular use of smokeless tobacco compared to 73% endorsing great risk from smoking a pack or more of cigarettes per day

(Johnston et al, 2002c). In addition, different forms of tobacco are likely to be associated with different youth subcultures, such as the association of chewing tobacco with sports such as baseball.

Development of Smoking and Nicotine Dependence

The progression from initial use of cigarettes to nicotine dependence can be conceptualized as a series of stages (USDHHS, 1994). *Preparation* is the stage prior to actual use of cigarettes during which attitudes about smoking are shaped positively toward smoking. The "Trying Stage" is defined as the smoking of the first few cigarettes and is the point of smoking initiation. Experimentation incorporates a range of repeated, but still irregular smoking, while the rate of smoking picks up and becomes established over a range of situations at the "Regular Use" stage. In this model, the final stage is "Addicted or Dependent" and follows a period of regular use of cigarettes. As defined by DSM-IV criteria, nicotine dependent smokers are characterized by at least three of the following symptoms occurring in the same 12-month period: 1) tolerance, 2) withdrawal, 3) use of larger amounts or over a longer time period than intended, 4) persistent desire or unsuccessful attempts to control use, 5) spending considerable time in activities needed to obtain, use or recover from the effects of use (e.g. chain-smoking), 6) reduced time in important activities because of use; and 7) use despite knowledge of having a physical or psychological problem related to use (American Psychiatric Association 1994). The duration and quantity of use necessary for dependence symptoms to develop remains incompletely characterized, but may occur very early---within weeks--- for at least some adolescent smokers (DiFranza et al., 2000). Craving, or a strong desire to smoke during conditions of deprivation, is also considered a typical feature of nicotine dependence (American Psychiatric Association 1994). While adolescent nicotine dependence is generally recognized by researchers and clinicians, the evidence base is considerably lagging behind that for adult dependent smokers (for a comprehensive review of this topic, see Shadel et al., 2000).

The first few experiences inhaling cigarette smoke are thought to be typically unpleasant, but with repeated use, tolerance to aversive effects and increasing experience of pleasurable effects may manifest rapidly (Pomerleau, 1995). As nicotine intake rates increase, symptoms of nicotine dependence are reported by some youth before daily smoking patterns begin. While specific developmental processes of dependence are not well described, the occurrence of nicotine dependence in adolescents is supported by a preponderance of evidence. This evidence includes youth reports of feeling addicted, feeling subjective effects and reasons for sustained smoking, consumption of substantial levels of nicotine, experience of withdrawal symptoms, and difficulty in quitting tobacco use (Lynch et al., 1994). Withdrawal symptoms in adolescents include strong urges to smoke, nervousness, tension, irritability, hunger, concentration difficulties, dysphoria, and insomnia (Rojas et al., 1998; Killen et al., 2001; Prokhorov et al., 2001) Of course, progression is not inevitable, and the majority of youth who try and experiment with cigarettes do not become addicted to them (Pomerleau, 1995).

Risk Profiles

A variety of intrinsic and extrinsic factors are associated with risk of smoking uptake. Factors such as sociodemographic characteristics and environmental characteristics are primarily associated with smoking initiation, while peer smoking influences, and personal characteristics such as tobacco use attitudes and mental health

Table 1: Risk Factors for Youth Smoking Uptake

Risk Factors	Initiation	Regular use/dependence
Sociodemographic factors		
Low socioeconomic status	X	X
Developmental stage	X	
Male gender	X	
Environmental factors		
High accessibility	X	X
High advertising	X	X
Parental tobacco use	X	X
Sibling tobacco use	X	
Peer tobacco use	X	X
High normative expectations	X	
Low social support	X	X
Parenting factors	X	X
Behavioral factors		
Low academic achievement	X	X
Presence of other problem behaviors	X	X
Low tobacco refusal skills	X	X
High intentions to smoke	X	
Experimentation	X	X
Personal factors		
High knowledge of consequences	X	
Functional meanings of tobacco use	X	X
Low subjective expected utility	X	X
Low self-esteem/self-image	X	X
Low self-efficacy	X	X
Personality factors	X	X
Psychological well-being	X	X
Presence of mood disorders	X	X
Presence of externalizing disorders	X	X
Biological factors		
Genetic	X	X
In utero exposure		X

Adapted from: Centers for Disease Control and Prevention. *Preventing Tobacco Use Among Young People. A Report of the Surgeon General.* Washington, DC: U.S. Government Printing Office, 1994. 123.

problems, also predict progression of smoking. A number of family factors have been associated with youth risk for smoking uptake. In a prospective study of 808 ethnically diverse children followed from age 10-11 to age 21, Guo et al. found that baseline parental smoking status, family monitoring and rules, and family bonding were all significant predictors of smoking initiation (Guo, 2000). Higher levels of family bonding and monitoring were protective against daily smoking, even in the presence of parental smoking.

Genetic risk factors have been identified over the last decade, although the biological mechanisms for these are still unknown (Sullivan and Kendler, 1999). Based on reviews of twin, family, and adoption studies, Sullivan and Kendler estimate the genetic liability to smoking initiation to be about 60% and to nicotine dependence to be about 70% Common genes are thought to be the causal mechanism behind the strong associations found between lifetime smoking and lifetime depression; this has been modeled in a population-based register of adult female twins (Kendler et al., 1993). At this time, genetic profiling does not have a role in evidence-based prevention strategies.

Evidence-based Prevention Strategies
School-Based Prevention

A summary of selected school-based prevention interventions can be found in Table 2. For reviews of youth tobacco prevention strategies through the early 1990's, readers are referred to the 1994 report of the Institute of Medicine, Growing Up Tobacco Free, and the 1995 Report of the Surgeon General, Preventing Tobacco Use in Young People (Lynch, 1994; USDHHS, 1994). Reviews of school-based prevention strategies based on information-deficit and affective education models found them to be ineffective in decreasing tobacco uptake; furthermore, concerns were raised about possible inadvertent promotion of interest in tobacco use (Lynch, 1994). On the other hand, efficacy has been demonstrated for many social-influences based general drug prevention programs, with small to moderate effect sizes reported (Sussman et al., 2001).

In 1994, the Centers for Disease Control and Prevention published recommendations for school-based prevention programs, drawing upon current research of protective and risk factors, as well as on results of school intervention studies conducted in previous years (CDC, 1994).

Table 2: Longitudinal Randomized Controlled Interventions for Prevention of Youth Tobacco Use

Social Influences Smoking Prevention Program Cameron et al., 1999.	N = 4466 6th- 8th grade students in 100 schools (Ontario, Canada).	This study compared the effects of nurse versus teacher delivered prevention interventions and workshop versus self-preparation of the intervention providers. The program was based on a social influences model. The intervention was delivered across the study years.	Smoking rates were lower in high-risk intervention schools (16.0%) versus control (26.9%) among students followed from Grade 6 to Grade 8 (about 2.5 years). No significant differences were found for low risk schools, and no significant differences found for teacher versus nurse delivered interventions, or by interventionist training method.

Good Behavior Game and Mastery Learning Curriculum Kellam et al., 1998.	N = 2311 1st grade students in 19 urban public schools.	Three group design with 2 cohorts: 1) Good Behavior Game – teacher delivered classroom management intervention designed to reduce aggressive and disruptive behaviors; 2) Mastery Learning Curriculum – an enriched curriculum to raise reading achievement; 3) control.	At the 7 year follow-up, smoking initiation was lower for the "best behaving" tertile of boys in the Good Behavior Game group compared to control (RR = 0.13; 95% CI – 0.03, 0.62). There was a non-statistically significant trend for all boys (RR = 0.58 (95% CI = 0.33, 1.00) in cohort 1, RR= 0.62 (95% CI = 0.29, 1.29). Girls' smoking was not reduced.
Hutchinson Smoking Prevention Project Peterson et al.2000.	N = 8388 3rd grade students in 40 school districts (state of Washington).	Social learning theory/social influences based intervention vs. observation control. "Best practices" included observational learning, self-efficacy enhancement, refusal skills, family support building over 65 sessions.	There was no significant intervention effect for daily smoking rates at either the 12th grade, or 2-years post high school follow-up periods. No significant intervention effects were found for other measured smoking outcomes or for subgroups determined a priori.
Family-Based			
Family Matters Study Bauman et al, 2001.	N = 1326 12-14 year olds plus parent recruited by random digit dialing, representative of US population with phone (48 states)	This was based on value expectancy theory, Health Belief Model, social learning theory, social inoculation theory. Two group study: 1) 4 mailings plus follow-up phone counseling with parent provided by a health educator; 2) untreated control.	Follow-up rate was 86.2% at 12 months. Smoking onset decreased in the treatment group with OR = 1.30, p = .037; after control for design effect OR = 1.27, p = .059. Program effect positive for non-Hispanic Whites but not other racial/ethnic groups with effect size of 0.25.
Iowa Brief Family Intervention Study Spoth et al., 2001.	N = 667 6th grade students plus parents, 30 rural Iowa schools	Three group design: 1) Preparing for the Drug Free Years (PDFY) based on pro-social bonding model; 2) Iowa Strengthening Family Program (ISFP) based on resiliency and social-ecological theories of adolescent development; 3) control.	At the10th grade follow-up (about 4 years), a significant reduction in smoking initiation was found for ISFP compared to control with a relative reduction of 34.8% (p < .01).

Family-School Partnership and Classroom-Centered intervention Storr et al., 2002.	N = 678 1st grade students Predominately African American.	Three group design: 1) Classroom-Centered (CC) targeted teacher management of child behavioral risks for substance use - aggression, shyness and inattention; 2) Family-School Partnership added parent-teacher communication and parent management of child behaviors to CC; 3) control.	At the 6 year follow-up, smoking was reduced in both intervention conditions compared to control: OR for CC = 0.55 (95% CI = 0.34-0.96); OR for FSP = 0.69 (95% CI = 0.50-0.97).
Project Toward No Drug Abuse Sussman et al., 2002.	N = 2468 High school students in 42 schools.	Three field trials, 2 with alternative high schools. The intervention consisted of twelve 40-minute classroom delivered sessions based on motivation-skills-decision-making model. Delivery was by project health educators and by students was compared in one of the trials.	No reduction was found for last 30-day cigarette smoking in 2 of 3 trials, but a 27% relative reduction of smoking was found in the health educator led condition compared to control in 3rd trial (p< .05). A baseline smoking rate of 57% was observed in this study. Follow-up was at 1 year for all 3 trials.
Community-Based			
Mass media and school intervention Flynn et al., 1994.	N = 5458 4th-6th grade students in 4 communities	A four-year mass media campaign plus school-based intervention was compared to a school-based intervention alone.	At two years post-intervention, daily smoking rates were lower in the media plus school group, OR = 0.62, 95% CI = 0.49, 0.78 (absolute smoking rates not provided). Only 38% of the original sample received "full exposure" to interventions and were included in this outcome analysis.

School-Based			
Computer-based out-of-school intervention Ausems et al., 2002.	N = 3, 349 11 – 12 year old students in 156 schools (The Netherlands)	This was based on a social influence model. Four conditions were compared: 1) a seven lesson in-school program; 2) three computer-tailored letters sent to the students' homes; 3) in-school plus computer-tailored letters; 4) control.	The tailored letters resulted in the lowest level of smoking initiation compared to control (10.4% versus 18.1%) and continuation (13.1% versus 23.5%), at the 6 month follow-up. No significant effects were found for the in-school program alone, or for the combined interventions versus the letters alone.
Life Skills Training Botvin et al., 1995.	N = 5954 7th grade students in 56 schools	This was a three group design based on a social influences model: 1) active intervention with teachers trained with workshops and consultations; 2) active intervention with teachers trained with videotapes; 3) "treatment as usual" control. Active intervention was delivered over 15 classes in 7th grade and 10 booster sessions in 9th grade and involved teaching skills for resisting drugs.	The 12th grade follow-up rate (5 years) was 60.4%. Weekly and monthly smoking rates were lower in the two experimental groups compared to control. For monthly smoking, rates were 27% and 26% for the intervention conditions versus 33% for control; for weekly, 23% and 21% versus 27% ($p < .05$). Stronger effects were found for the high fidelity to program groups.

These recommendations are as follows:

1. Develop and enforce a school policy on tobacco use.

2. Provide instruction about the short- and long-term negative physiologic and social consequences of tobacco use, social influences on tobacco use, peer norms regarding tobacco use, and refusal skills.

3. Provide tobacco-use prevention education in kindergarten through 12th grade; this instruction should be especially intensive in junior high or middle school and should be reinforced in high school.

4. Provide program-specific training for teachers.

5. Involve parents or families in support of school-based programs to prevent tobacco use.

6. Support cessation efforts among students and all school staff who use tobacco.

7. Assess the tobacco-use prevention program at regular intervals.

The details for each of these elements are provided at http://www.cdc.gov/nccdphp/dash/healthtopics/tobacco/guidelines/index.htm.

The Hutchinson Smoking Prevention Project rigorously tested a state-of-the-art social influences approach for schools that was recommended by panels of experts at the

Centers for Disease Control and Prevention and the National Cancer Institute (Peterson et al., 2000). Over 8300 students were enrolled in the study in grade 3, and then followed through grade 12. Schools were randomly assigned to intervention and control conditions (20 schools each), with matching for school district size, location, and smoking prevalence. The intervention was grounded in social learning theory, and built upon previously tested social influences interventions. Intervention elements included observational learning, correction of erroneous perceptions of social norms of smoking, self-efficacy enhancement, reinforcement of nonsmoking behavior, skills for identification of advertising and other social influences, refusal skills building, and enlisting family support for nonsmoking (Peterson et al., 2000). The intervention was initiated with third grade students, with follow-up sessions over 7 years. Intervention content and process was matched to age-specific interests and developmental capabilities of the students. Trained classroom teachers implemented the intervention and maintained a high rate of delivery of key intervention components. A 94% retention rate was achieved at the final assessment point. Despite sufficient statistical power to detect even small differences, no differences in smoking behaviors were detected between intervention and control schools. Daily smoking rates at grade 12 were 24.7% and 24.4% for girls at control and experimental schools; rates for boys were 26.7% and 26.3%. While these results were disappointing, a number of prevention scientists have cautioned against concluding that the social influences model is ineffective. Specific criticisms have been directed at the absence of important elements of social-influences strategies, such as communication and decision-making skills development, as well as questions about the setting issues, such as school-level risk for smoking (Cameron et al., 2001; Sussman et al., 2001).

A school-based multi-drug prevention program, Life Skills Training (LST), was tested in over 56 public schools in the state of New York (Botvin et al., 1995). The intervention was based on specific drug refusal skill development in a context of a general competence enhancement approach that emphasized development of self-management and social skills. LST involved classroom instruction and rehearsals of decision-making, problem-solving, personal control, assertiveness and social skills, peer interaction skills, and drug refusal skills. General skills such as assertiveness were applied to specific drug related situations, such as peer pressure to use drugs. Self-esteem enhancement was also part of the curriculum. These lessons were provided in 15 sessions in the 7th grade, 10 sessions in 8th grade, and 5 sessions in 9th grade. Six thousand 7th grade students were randomized at the level of the school to one of three study conditions. Two experimental groups were compared to a control group. The two experimental groups delivered LST; however, teachers received formal one-day training and implementation feedback in the first group, while teachers in the second group received two hours of videotape training and no implementation feedback. At the follow-up in the 12th grade, smoking, alcohol, and marijuana use were all found to be significantly lower in the intervention group. Sixty percent of the original sample completed the 12th grade follow-up assessment (62%). Monthly smoking rates were 27% in the experimental group in which teachers received formal training and feedback compared to 33% in the control group (p < 0.05). Weekly smoking rates were also lower in the first experimental group (23% vs. 27%; p < 0.05). Smoking rates were also lower in the videotape trained teachers group compared to control, with monthly smoking rates of 26% vs. 33% (p < 0.01) and weekly smoking rates of 21% vs. 27% (p < 0.05). Outcomes varied considerably across schools, with better outcomes observed in schools delivering the intervention with higher fidelity to intervention component delivery, based on secondary analyses of the sub sample that received 60% or more of the intervention during grades 7 through 9.

Kellam et al. (1998) report on two early elementary school prevention interventions, the Good Behavior Game and the Mastery Learning curriculum. These interventions were designed to decrease aggressive and disruptive behaviors, which are associated with increased rates of tobacco use. Teachers in classrooms assigned to the Good Behavior Game intervention were instructed in behavior management strategies to reduce aggressive and disruptive behaviors such as fighting, shouting out of turn, and teasing. Children were placed in teams, and teams were rewarded with points when no member exhibited the proscribed behaviors during the game sessions. The Mastery Learning intervention consisted of an enriched academic curriculum designed to raise reading achievement scores. It included setting of high expectations, small instructional units, use of formative testing, and individualized correction methods. Schools were randomly assigned to either of the two intervention or control conditions and 2311 1st grade students were enrolled. At the seven-year post-intervention follow-up, a significant delay in smoking uptake was found for boys in the Good Behavior game condition compared to control (RR = 0.62, 95% confidence interval = 0.40; p = .04). Furthermore, results were better for well-behaved boys. A trend towards delays in smoking was also observed for the Mastery Learning group, but the difference was not significant compared to control.

School smoking risk level may be a determinant of intervention efficacy. Cameron et al. (1999) found that students at Canadian public elementary schools defined as "high risk" on the basis of 6th grade student smoking rates were responsive to a social influences program compared to control schools (end of 8th grade smoking rate of 16.0% versus 26.9%), while smoking rates in low risk schools did not significantly differ from control. A model-based estimated odds ratio for smoking by study condition suggested that a smoking rate of 20% or more predicted response to the intervention. Of note, in this study, results did not significantly differ based on the interventionist role (teachers versus nurses) or training method (self-preparation versus workshop training).

Although smoking uptake continues to occur throughout adolescence, the majority of randomized clinical prevention trials have targeted pre-adolescents. Project Towards No Drug Abuse is a motivation-skills-decision-making intervention model that was developed and tested in three separate field trials, involving 2468 students (Sussman et al., 2002). Multiple risk behaviors were addressed in this study, including tobacco use, use of alcohol, marijuana and other drugs, weapon carrying and victimization. The active intervention consisted of twelve 40-minute sessions delivered in the classroom. These lessons were systematically organized to address content derived from the theoretical model, including correction of myths about drug use, introduction to smoking cessation materials, and decision-making skills development. Sessions were designed to be interactive. Project Toward No Drug Abuse has been tested in the field in a variety of settings, with different combinations of content delivery channels. Sessions delivered by a study health educator were compared to those delivered by a combination school staff and a study health educator and to a student self-instruction condition, as well as to non-intervention controls. Two of the field trials involved "continuation" schools that provided service to high-risk students; 30-day cigarette use was more than twice the rate of that in the traditional high schools. While several other targeted risk behaviors were reduced in all three field trials, cigarette use was not affected in two of the field trials. In the third trial that involved continuation schools, students receiving health educator delivered sessions experienced lower rates of smoking compared with self-instruction and control classrooms (relative reduction of 27%). The follow-up period for each trial was 1 year.

Storr et al. (2002) tested a combined family and school-based approach in a prevention program with first grade students in a predominately African American public school system. This program was universal in its design, that is, it was delivered to all children, not just subsets of children at high risk for tobacco use initiation. Children were randomly assigned to one of three interventions: the Family –School Partnership classroom (FSP), classroom-centered intervention only (CC), and a control classroom. Early child behavioral risk factors for later substance use--problems with aggression, shyness, and attention--were targeted through enhancing teacher management skills in the CC intervention. The FSP intervention added teacher-parent communications and enhancement of parent management skills to the CC intervention components. Both the CC and FSP program resulted in lower rates of smoking at the 6 year follow-up: the CC intervention had an adjusted relative risk of 0.57 (95% CI = 0.34 – 0.96), and the FSP intervention had an adjusted relative risk of 0.69 (95% CI = 0.50 – 0.97).

Individualized, computer-tailored letters mailed to students at home resulted in lower six month smoking initiation and continuation rates in a study conducted in The Netherlands (Ausems et al., 2002). In this study, 3349 11-12 year old students were randomized to one of four conditions: 1) an in-school, 7 lesson prevention program implemented by teachers; 2) an out-of-school intervention consisting of 3 weekly tailored letters to students that were mailed to students' homes; 3) the in-school plus the out-of-school intervention; 4) control condition. Intervention content was based on a social influences program. The letters were computer-tailored based on student responses to a baseline questionnaire on smoking intention, behavior, attitudes, refusal self-efficacy, and social norms. At the 6 month outcome, self-reported smoking initiation and continuation rates were significantly lower in the out-of-school letter condition compared to control: 10.4% versus 18.1% and 13.1% versus 23.5%, respectively. The in-school program did not outperform the control condition, and it did not significantly reduce smoking in the combined condition when compared to the letters condition alone.

Few cost-effectiveness analyses of successful interventions have been published. Wang et al. (2001) report a saving of $13, 316 per life-year saved and $8,482 per quality-adjusted life year saved for the Project Toward No Tobacco Use (TNT) intervention cost of $16, 403 ($13.29 per student). TNT consisted of a 2-year efficacy trial of a 10-lesson school-based tobacco prevention curriculum for junior high students (Dent et al., 1995). Standard economic evaluation techniques included measurement of program implementation costs, estimation of the numbers of life years and quality adjusted life years saved, estimation of the lifetime medical costs for smokers versus nonsmokers, selection of costs in 1990 dollars to correspond with the intervention period, and discounting costs at a 3% annual rate in keeping with recommendations from the Panel on Cost-effectiveness in Health and Medicine (Gold et al., 1996). An intermediate outcome of number of established smokers that were prevented was used, and then this was translated into the number of life years and quality adjusted life years saved by the intervention. Life years saved was based upon Rogers and Powell-Griner's estimates that never smokers have a life expectancy of 2.1 years more than former smokers, 3.5 years more than light smokers, and 14.2 years longer than heavy smokers (Rogers and Powell-Griner 1991) In this analysis, Wang et al. (2001) started with 14 year olds, and modeled their smoking status at 26 years, with and without the TNT intervention at 26 years. Intervention costs included health educator training costs, health educator salaries, and manuals for the health educators and the students. The savings modeled in these analyses compare quite favorably to cost-effectiveness analyses of breast cancer screening and smoking cessation programs for adults.

Family-Based Interventions

Results are very promising for several recently published outcomes of family-based interventions. The Iowa Brief Family Intervention Study demonstrated significantly reduced rates of cigarette use in family-based interventions compared to control (Spoth et al., 2001). Both of the interventions, the Preparing for Drug Free Years and the Iowa Strengthening Families Program, addressed prevention of alcohol and marijuana use, in addition to tobacco use. Families were recruited from 33 randomly assigned school sites: 667 6th grade students were followed through grade 10.

The Preparing for Drug Free Years (PDFY) intervention condition was based on social control theory, and emphasized prosocial bonding as a key intervention component. Parent groups attended five weekly 2-hour sessions, with children joining parents for one of these sessions. Content focused on educating parents about risk factors for substance abuse, and building skills for establishing behavior guidelines, monitoring compliance and consequences,

managing conflict, enhancing parent-child bonds, and enhancing child participation in family tasks. Children were taught to resist peer influences for drug use, supported by parents.

The Iowa Strengthening Families Program (ISFP) was based on resiliency and social ecological models of adolescent development. Parents and children attended seven 2-hour sessions, the first hour of which parents and children met separately in groups, followed by joint parent-child groups. Parents were instructed in clarification of expectations, use of appropriate discipline, management of emotions and communications, and peer resistance. Skills were practiced in the parent-child sessions. Both intervention groups used videotapes to standardize content.

Overall attendance rates were high for both intervention conditions: 94% attended three or more sessions and 61% attended all five sessions for the PDFY intervention, and 94% attended five or more sessions and 62% attended all seven sessions for the ISFP intervention. Substance use was lower in both intervention conditions compared to control. The relative reduction in "ever" use of cigarettes compared to the control condition was 12.5% for the PDFY intervention and 34.8% for the ISFP intervention (the later was statistically significant at the $p < .01$). Increased emphasis on family interactions, with skills rehearsals within sessions, is hypothesized as the likely source for the better outcome of ISFP compared to PDFY.

The Family Matters Study, conducted by Bauman and colleagues (Bauman et al., 2001), is a population-based experimental study designed to prevent both alcohol and tobacco use. The intervention was based on the Health Belief Model, social learning theory, and value expectancy theory. Adolescents, ages 12 to 14 years, and their families (N = 1316) were recruited by a random digit dial procedure and randomized to intervention versus control condition. The intervention consisted of 4 successive mailed booklets followed by telephone contact by a health educator. Booklets focused on 1) motivation and engagement; 2) education about general family characteristics associated with risk and protection from substance use; 3) focus on tobacco and alcohol specific factors; and 4) resistance to pro-tobacco and alcohol peer and media influences At the 12-month follow-up, smoking initiation rates were 16.4% lower in adolescents in the intervention condition compared to controls. This effect was moderated by race/ethnicity, with an effect size of 0.25 for non-Hispanic White youth and 0.15 for the whole sample. The program did not have a statistically significant effect on alcohol use. Of note, this intervention is relatively inexpensive, with a delivery cost of about $140 per parent-adolescent dyad, and could be widely disseminated with important public health value in reducing smoking uptake.

Wakefield et al. (2000) examined the impact of smoking restrictions on adolescent smoking in a cross-sectional survey study of 17, 287 high school students. Bans on smoking in the home were protective against smoking, even after controlling for the smoking status of the parents; students endorsing home smoking bans had a lower 30 day smoking prevalence rate (OR = 0.79; 95% CI = 0.67-0.91, p <0.001). Although the effect size was lower than with home smoking bans, community restrictions in public places were also protective (OR = 0.91; 95% CI = 0.83 – 0.99, p = 0.03). School smoking bans were only protective if the ban was perceived as being enforced (OR = 0.86; 95% CI = 0.77 – 0.94, p < 0.001).

Community-Based Prevention

Media campaigns and tobacco control policy interventions are the two major community-based strategies for reducing adolescent smoking. Youth appear to be particularly sensitive to increases in cigarette costs, with reductions of 7% per price increase of 10% modeled in econometric analyses, although studies of changes in trajectory of uptake are much needed (Chaloupka et al., 1998).

Flay et al. reviewed media research and added behavioral science constructs to generate recommendations for successful prevention campaigns (Flay et al., 1980). Elements judged to be critical to successful communication and behavior change included generation of motivation and interest, targeting of specific issues, repetition of messages across time and media sources, provision of specific information to support behavioral change, and provision of contacts for further information and help.

Although often conceptualized as universal interventions, media campaigns can also be targeted to high risk populations. Flynn et al. (1997) tested a media campaign addition to a school smoking campaign. The media component was specifically developed to reach youth at high risk. The sample consisted of 2718 4th – 6th grade students in 4 communities: the two communities receiving the media intervention plus the school-based intervention were matched to two communities receiving the school-based intervention only. Students were assessed prior to the interventions, with post-intervention follow-up five years later. High-risk students were characterized as having either personal smoking experience and/or the presence of regular smokers among family or peers (Worden et al., 1988). In addition, high-risk students were subdivided into "rebels" and "conformists," based on their attitudes about smoking. The media intervention provided television and radio messages that were developed with the input from focus groups conducted with students and from consultation with experts in mass media communications, psychologists, and health educators. Additional input from survey data and from showings of the prepared spots to students and a panel of experts were used to guide the final selection. The spots were aired with purchased time during high appeal programs, and they deliberately did not contain any unifying logos to prevent association with an authority source. The spots gave educational messages that were coordinated with the school intervention, and they were tailored for the range of developmental levels of the sample. The communities received an average of 540 television spots and 350 radio spots each of the four intervention years. Among high risk students, the combined media and school intervention resulted in lower smoking rates at follow-up (Odds Ratio = 0.71; Confidence Interval = 0.56, 0.90). As predicted, the higher risk youth also reported more television and radio use than the lower risk youth. Although smoking rates were lower in both high and low risk youth in the media intervention communities, the effect of the intervention was larger for the high-risk youth. Study limitations include problems with matching communities across regions of the country and missing data that resulted in loss of 52% of the sample in the final outcome analyses. Nonetheless, this study introduced a novel method for combining intervention channels with universal reach but with messages targeted to a high-risk population.

Health Care-Based Prevention

Preventive care guidelines have promoted smoking prevention in pediatric health care for over a decade (Glynn, 1989). Smoking cessation interventions by internists and other adult health care providers effectively increase adult smoking cessation rates, but prevention of smoking in pediatric settings has not been demonstrated (Fiore et al., 1996). Our knowledge of guideline implementation is largely based on cross-sectional surveys of physicians and patients.

Tobacco control counseling does not appear to be routine. Only 25% of adolescents and young adults in a large, nationally representative sample recalled any health care provider comments about smoking (Baker, 1995). Less than half of the adolescents surveyed in a large longitudinal study of smoking risk factors in Memphis reported recall of physician advice not to smoke, and only 43.2% recalled physician screening for smoking status (Alfano et al., 2002). Physician self-report surveys tend to result in higher counseling rates. Thorndike et al. (1999) analyzed data from the 1991-1996 National Ambulatory Medical care Surveys (5087 MDs; 16,648 visits), and found screening rates of 72.4% and counseling rates of only 1.6% for all adolescents aged 11-21. Screening and counseling rates did not increase across the survey years. The counseling rate for adolescents who were known to be smokers was also quite low, at 16.9% of visits. In a 1999 survey of pediatricians and family practitioners in western New York state, physicians reported asking most adolescents about smoking status (91%) and reinforcing abstinence with most nonsmokers (84%), but inquiries about parental and peer smoking status were lower (56% and 41%, respectively) (Klein et al., 2001). Zapka et al. (1999) found that the majority of pediatricians in her Massachusetts sample endorsed prevention counseling with children and adolescents, although counseling rates were not independently validated. However, other studies of pediatric health care provider screening and counseling practices report much lower rates, e.g. tobacco counseling was provided during only 1.5% of all visits and 4.1% of well child visits included in the National Ambulatory Medical Care Survey and the National Hospital Ambulatory Medical Care Survey (Tanski et al., 2003).

Tailoring

Most of the prevention studies that have been discussed are intended as universal reach and intervention strategies. Siddiqui et al. (1996) examined characteristics of study participants in a number of longitudinal prevention programs and reported that study dropouts were more likely to be smokers. Dropouts were more likely to have lower academic achievement, to have lower levels of resistance skills, and to have lower levels of tobacco and health knowledge. Among ethnic groups, Black youth were more likely to be missing at follow-up.

Can tailoring of prevention programs improve prevention outcomes? In addition to concerns raised by differential attrition rates in studies, the need for tailoring is suggested by the variation in tobacco use rates and trends across sociodemographic groups as well as our knowledge of other risk and protective factors.

Through the early 1990s, our knowledge of smoking uptake processes has been largely based on studies of White, suburban populations. Similarly, effective interventions were typically tested with White majority samples. Focus groups conducted by Parker and colleagues with African American and Latino adolescents did not find differences in reasons for smoking or for youth identified ideas for prevention programming compared to those described by White youth in prior studies (Parker et al., 1996). In contrast, other investigators have described different smoking uptake patterns when modeling ethnicity and family influences as predictors, and family influences may play a stronger role relative to peer influences in some minority populations (Kegler et al., 2002; Robinson and Klesges, 1997; Sussman et al., 1987).

Botvin et al. demonstrated effectiveness for a social resistance/competence enhancement intervention in a predominately Hispanic, urban sample of 7th grade students (Botvin et al., 1992). The intervention, previously tested with White, suburban students, was revised with modifications in reading level, illustrative examples, and situations used for skills training (Botvin et al., 1989b). There was no direct comparison of the efficacy of the intervention between ethnic groups, but a mediating model suggested that the same processes were active in this predominately Hispanic sample as were active in the earlier White samples. Botvin et al. (1989) also demonstrated feasibility and acceptability of a similar intervention in a predominately Black, urban sample.

Sussman et al. (1995) tested smoking prevention videotapes developed to target African American adolescents. Two videotapes were compared to each other in one study, and both videotapes were compared to discussion groups led by an African American graduate student in the second study. One videotape was designed to be for generic appeal, and the other was designed for target audience appeal. The storyline was similar in both of the tapes, but clothing, music, setting, and language differed. Based on pre- and post-test assessments, both videotapes were well received, but neither appeared to have a differential effect on short-term smoking outcomes than the discussion groups. As in the previously described study, comparisons were not made across ethnic groups.

Direct comparisons of targeted versus universal school-based programs for high-risk youth are needed, but universal programs have been demonstrated to be effective in reducing smoking. Griffin et al. (2003) reported on an analysis of a subset of high risk youth (N = 802) included in a randomized clinical trial of the Life Skills Training Program for prevention of multiple drugs of abuse (program previously described). Risk was defined in two ways: "social risk" on the basis of number of friends who use, and "academic risk" on the basis of school performance. At baseline in 7th grade, the rate of smoking was 10%, with no significant difference between experimental and control groups. Attrition from the study was predicted from pre-intervention lifetime smoking history. The outcome analysis was based on a composite smoking behavior score; a significant effect was observed for the intervention condition compared to control.

Although gender-based differences in smoking patterns have been observed, literature searches did not identify interventions that were specifically tailored to these differences. Similarly, our literature searches did not identify tobacco-specific interventions targeted and tailored to families at high-risk for child tobacco uptake, although risk factors such as parent smoking behaviors and parenting styles have been incorporated into the universal family-based interventions that have been described.

SUMMARY AND CONCLUSION

The field of youth smoking prevention has benefited from important advances over the last decade. Experimental testing of theory driven interventions have provided promising strategies for reduction of youth smoking. Progress has been made in the development of promising strategies for reaching minority youth. Several studies have begun the process of testing interventions targeted to youth at high risk for smoking due to behavioral concerns, as well as analyzing the efficacy of universal programs in a subset of high risk youth. While the preponderance of evidence-based studies continues to use the school as the intervention delivery channel, interventions have moved beyond the classroom, to family and community, with encouraging results. In addition, interventions that combine delivery channels have been added to the list of prevention strategies.

Despite the successes of the last two decades, considerable room remains for innovation in this field. The exploration of targeted interventions is incomplete and may become particularly salient for catching the youth who continue to smoke despite implementation of the best universal strategies. Even universal strategies have not exhausted theoretical approaches, such as identification and intervention with "hot" (affective) and "cold" (rational decision-making) processes involved in risk behaviors, as suggested by Clayton and others (Clayton et al., 2000). Psychiatric symptoms such as depressed mood, stress, attention problems, and conduct problems are known to be associated with smoking in studies of adolescents as well as adults, yet few prevention or early intervention strategies have measured these factors and compared them in smoking versus nonsmoking youth (Upadhyaya et al., 2002). Advances in our understanding of genetic processes of youth smoking uptake are anticipated in the near future, and these will likely require innovations in intervention approaches, including careful attention to the ethics of clinical communication and policy associated with behavioral genetics.

Improved strategies are needed to disseminate and sustain successful interventions. Some of the solutions for this may require a shift in thinking from short term to long term planning, even as interventions are initially conceptualized and developed. Swisher (2000) has proposed guidelines for sustainability of prevention programs that include systematic planning for institutionalization of successful interventions, professional development for practitioners and researchers, long term and early planning for sustainability, less crisis orientation, and community specific adaptations of interventions. Given the number and range of evidence-based interventions for smoking prevention, this shift is well justified.

REFERENCES

Alfano CM, Zbikowski SM, Robinson LA, Klesges RC, Scarinci IC (2002) Adolescent reports of physician counseling for smoking. Pediatrics 109:E47.

American Psychiatric Association (1994). Diagnostic and Statistical Manual of Mental Disorders, Fourth Edition [DSM-IV]. Washington, DC: American Psychiatric Press.

Ausems M, Mesters I, van Breukelen G, De Vries H (2002) Short-term effects of a randomized computer-based out-of-school smoking prevention trial aimed at elementary schoolchildren. Prev Med 34:581-9.

Baker L (1995) Health-care provider advice on tobacco use to persons aged 10-22 Years- United States, 1993. MMWR 44:826-30.

Bauman KE, Foshee VA, Ennett ST, Pemberton M, Hicks KA, King TS, Koch GG (2001) The influence of a family program on adolescent tobacco and alcohol use. Am J Public Health 91:604-10.

Botvin GJ, Baker E, Dusenbury L, Botvin EM, Diaz T (1995) Long-term follow-up results of a randomized drug abuse prevention trial in a white middle-class population. JAMA 273:1106-12.

Botvin GJ, Batson HW, Witts-Vitale S, Bess V, Baker E, Dusenbury L (1989a) A psychosocial approach to smoking prevention for urban black youth. Public Health Rep 104:573-82.

Botvin GJ, Dusenbury L, Baker E, James-Ortiz S, Botvin EM, Kerner J (1992) Smoking prevention among urban minority youth: assessing effects on outcome and mediating variables. Health Psychol 11:290-9.

Botvin GJ, Dusenbury L, Baker E, James-Ortiz S, Kerner J (1989b) A skills training approach to smoking prevention among Hispanic youth. J Behav Med 12:279-96.

Cameron R, Best JA, Brown KS (2001) Re: Hutchinson Smoking Prevention Project: long-term randomized trial in school-based tobacco use prevention--results on smoking. J Natl Cancer Inst 93:1267-8; discussion 1269-71.

Cameron R, Brown KS, Best JA, Pelkman CL, Madill CL, Manske SR, Payne ME (1999) Effectiveness of a social influences smoking prevention program as a function of provider type, training method, and school risk. Am J Public Health 89:1827-31.

Centers for Disease Control and Prevention (1994) Guidelines for school health programs to prevent tobacco use and addiction. J Sch Health 64:353-60.

Chaloupka FJ (1998) Economics. Addicted to Nicotine: A National Research Forum, pp 39-41.

Clayton RR, Scutchfield FD, Wyatt SW (2000) Hutchinson Smoking Prevention Project: a new gold standard in prevention science requires new transdisciplinary thinking. J Natl Cancer Inst 92:1964-5.

Dent CW, Sussman S, Stacy AW, Craig S, Burton D, Flay BR (1995) Two-year behavior outcomes of project towards no tobacco use. J Consult Clin Psychol 63:676-7.

DiFranza JR, Rigotti NA, McNeill AD, Ockene JK, Savageau JA, St Cyr D, Coleman M (2000) Initial symptoms of nicotine dependence in adolescents. Tob Control 9:313-9.

Fiore M, Bailey W, Cohen S, Dorfman S, Goldstein M, Gritz E, Heyman R, Hollbrook J, Jaen C, Kottke T, Lando H, Mecklenbrg R, Mullen P, Nett L, Robinson L, Stitzer M, Tommasello A, Villejo L, Wewers M (1996) Smoking Cessation: Clinical Practice Guideline No.

18. Rockville, MD: Agency for Health Care Policy and Research, Public Health Service, U.S. Department of Health And Human Services.

Flay BR, DiTecco D, Schlegel RP (1980) Mass media in health promotion: an analysis using an extended information-processing model. Health Educ Q 7:127-47.

Flynn BS, Worden JK, Secker-Walker RH, Pirie PL, Badger GJ, Carpenter JH (1997) Long-term responses of higher and lower risk youths to smoking prevention interventions. Prev Med 26:389-94.

Glynn TJ, Manley MW (1989) How to Help Your Patients Stop Smoking. A National Cancer Institute Manual for Physicians. Bethesda, Maryland: Smoking, Tobacco and Cancer Program, Division of Cancer Prevention and Control, National Cancer Institute.

Gold MR, Gold SR, Weinstein MC, eds. (1996) Cost-effectiveness in health and medicine. New York, NY: Oxford University Press.

Griffin KW, Botvin GJ, Nichols TR, Doyle MM (2003) Effectiveness of a universal drug abuse prevention approach for youth at high risk for substance use initiation. Prev Med 36:1-7.

Grunbaum JA, Kann L, Kinchen SA, Williams B, Ross JG, Lowry R, Kolbe L (2002) Youth risk behavior surveillance--United States, 2001. J Sch Health 72:313-28.

Guo (2000) Family Influences on the Risk of Daily Smoking Initiation from Adolescence to Young Adulthood. Boston, MA: NIDA.

Johnston L, O'Malley P, Bachman J (2002a) Monitoring the Future National Survey Results on Drug Use, 1975-2001. Bethesda, MD: National Institute on Drug Abuse.

Johnston L, O'Malley P, Bachman J (2002b) Teen smoking declines sharply in 2002, more than offsetting large increases in the early 1990s. Ann Arbor, MI: University of Michigan News and Information Services.

Johnston LD, O'Malley PM, Bachman JG (2002c) Monitoring the Future National Results on Adolescent Drug Use: Overview of Key Findings, 2001. Bethesda, MD: National Institute on Drug Abuse.

Kegler MC, McCormick L, Crawford M, Allen P, Spigner C, Ureda J (2002) An exploration of family influences on smoking among ethnically diverse adolescents. Health Educ Behav 29:473-90.

Kellam SG, Anthony JC (1998) Targeting early antecedents to prevent tobacco smoking: findings from an epidemiologically based randomized field trial. Am J Public Health 88:1490-5.

Kendler KS, Neale MC, MacLean CJ, Heath AC, Eaves LJ, Kessler RC (1993) Smoking and major depression. A causal analysis. Arch Gen Psychiatry 50:36-43.

Killen, JD, Ammerman S, Rojas N, Varady J, Haydel F, Robinson TN (2001). Do adolescent smokers experience withdrawal effects when deprived of nicotine? Exp Clin Psychopharmacol 9(2): 172-82.

Klein JD, Levine LJ, Allan MJ (2001) Delivery of smoking prevention and cessation services to adolescents. Arch Pediatr Adolesc Med 155:597-602.

Lynch B, Bonnie R, Committee on Preventing Nicotine Addiction in Children and Youths, Institute of Medicine (1994) Growing Up Tobacco Free: Preventing Nicotine Addiction in Children and Youth. Washington, D.C.: National Academy Press.

Modesto-Lowe V (2002) Illy users in Connecticut: two case reports. Subst Abus 23:255-7.

Moriarty AL (1996) What's "new" in street drugs: "illy". J Pediatr Health Care 10:41-3.

National Institute on Drug Abuse (2000) Bulletin Board, NIDA Notes, 15(1).

Parker VC, Sussman S, Crippens DL, Scholl D, Elder P (1996) Qualitative development of smoking prevention programming for minority youth. Addict Behav 21:521-5.

Peterson AV, Jr., Kealey KA, Mann SL, Marek PM, Sarason IG (2000) Hutchinson Smoking Prevention Project: long-term randomized trial in school-based tobacco use prevention--results on smoking. J Natl Cancer Inst 92:1979-91.

Pomerleau OF (1995) Individual differences in sensitivity to nicotine: implications for genetic research on nicotine dependence. Behav Genet 25:161-77.

Prokhorov AV, Hudmon KS, de Moor, CA, Kelder SH, COnroy JL, Ordway N (2001). Nicotine dependence, withdrawal symptoms, and adolescents' readiness to quit smoking. Nicotine Tob Res 3(2): 151-5.

Robinson LA, Klesges RC (1997) Ethnic and gender differences in risk factors for smoking onset. Health Psychol 16: 499-505.

Rogers RG, Powell-Griner E (1991) Life expectancies of cigarette smokers and nonsmokers in the United States. Soc Sci Med 32(10): 1151-9.

Rojas NL, Killen JD, Haydel KF, Robinson TN (1998) Nicotine dependence among adolescent smokers. Arch Pediatr Adolesc Med 152(2): 151-6.

Shadel, WG, Shiffman S, Niaura R, Nichter M, Abrams DA (2000) Current models of nicotine dependence: what is known and what is needed to advance understanding of tobacco etiology among youth. Drug Alcohol Depend 59 Suppl 1: S9-22.

Siddiqui O, Flay BR, Hu FB (1996) Factors affecting attrition in a longitudinal smoking prevention study. Prev Med 25:554-60.

Spoth RL, Redmond C, Shin C (2001) Randomized trial of brief family interventions for general populations: adolescent substance use outcomes 4 years following baseline. J Consult Clin Psychol 69:627-42.

Storr CL, Ialongo NS, Kellam SG, Anthony JC (2002) A randomized controlled trial of two primary school intervention strategies to prevent early onset tobacco smoking. Drug Alcohol Depend 66:51-60.

Sullivan PF, Kendler KS (1999) The genetic epidemiology of smoking. Nicotine Tob Res 1:S51-7; discussion S69-70.

Sussman S, Dent CW, Flay BR, Hansen WB, Johnson CA (1987) Psychosocial predictors of cigarette smoking onset by white, black, Hispanic, and Asian adolescents in Southern California. MMWR Morb Mortal Wkly Rep 36 (Suppl 4):11S-16S.

Sussman S, Dent CW, Stacy AW (2002) Project towards no drug abuse: a review of the findings and future directions. Am J Health Behav 26:354-65.

Sussman S, Hansen WB, Flay BR, Botvin GJ (2001) Re: Hutchinson Smoking Prevention Project: long-term randomized trial in school-based tobacco use prevention--results on smoking. J Natl Cancer Inst 93:1267; discussion 1269-71.

Sussman S, Parker VC, Lopes C, Crippens DL, Elder P, Scholl D (1995) Empirical development of brief smoking prevention videotapes which target African-American adolescents. Int J Addict 30:1141-64.

Swisher JD (2000) Sustainability of prevention. Addictive Behaviors 25:965-73.

Tanski SE, Klein JD, Winickoff JP, Auinger P, Weitzman M (2003) Tobacco counseling at well-child and tobacco-influenced illness visits: opportunities for improvement. Pediatrics 111:E162-7.

Thorndike AN, Ferris TG, Stafford RS, Rigotti NA (1999) Rates of U.S.

physicians counseling adolescents about smoking. J Natl Cancer Inst 91:1857-62.

Upadhyaya HP, Deas D, Brady KT, Kruesi M (2002). Cigarette smoking and psychiatric

comorbidity in children and adolescents. J Am Acad Child Adolesc Psychaitry 41(11): 1294-305.

U.S. Department of Health and Human Services (1994) <u>Preventing Tobacco Use Among Young People: A Report of the Surgeon General</u>. Atlanta, GA: U.S.Department of Health and Human Services, Public Health Service, Centers for Disease Control and Prevention, National Center for Chronic Disease Prevention and Health Promotion, Office on Smoking and Health.

U.S. Department of Health and Human Services, Substance Abuse and Mental Health Services Administration (2002) Results from the 2001 National Household Survey on Drug Abuse: Volume I. Summary of National Findings: NHSDA Series H-17. Rockville, MD: Office of Applied Studies.

Wakefield M, Banham D, Martin J, Ruffin R, McCaul K, Badcock N (2000) Restrictions on smoking at home and urinary cotinine levels among children with asthma. Am J Prev Med 19:188-92.

Wang LY, Crossett LS, Lowry R, Sussman S, Dent CW (2001) Cost-effectiveness of a school-based tobacco-use prevention program. Arch Pediatr Adolesc Med 155:1043-50.

Weiner AL (2000) Emerging drugs of abuse in Connecticut. Conn Med 64:19-23.

Worden JK, Flynn BS, Geller BM, Chen M, Shelton LG, Secker-Walker RH, Solomon DS, Solomon LJ, Couchey S, Costanza MC (1988) Development of a smoking prevention mass media program using diagnostic and formative research. Prev Med 17:531-58.

Zapka JG, Fletcher K, Pbert L, Druker SK, Ockene JK, Chen L (1999) The perceptions and practices of pediatricians: tobacco intervention. Pediatrics 103:e65.

ALCOHOL AND DRUG USE AMONG YOUTH: ADVANCES IN PREVENTION

Elizabeth J. D'Amico and Stefanie A. Stern

INTRODUCTION

Prevalence and consequences

It is well known that alcohol and other drug use increases during adolescence (D'Amico et al., 2005a; Johnston et al., 2006) and is often associated with a host of problems, including school drop out (Muthén and Muthén, 2000), delinquency (Bui et al., 2000), psychological distress (Hansell and White, 1991), and accidents or injury (Hingson et al., 2000). Surveys conducted in middle school settings in the United States indicated substantial increases in use of alcohol and marijuana as youth transition from 6th to 8th grade (D'Amico et al., 2005a; Ellickson and Hays, 1992; Simons-Morton and Haynie, 2003). Similar increases in alcohol and drug use are seen as youth enter the high school setting such that by 12th grade, 20% of seniors report using marijuana in the past 30 days, 11% report using illicit drugs other than marijuana, and 48% report drinking alcohol, with 29% reporting an episode of heavy drinking (e.g., 5 or more drinks in a row) in the last two weeks (Johnston et al., 2005).

Longitudinal data from the general population indicate that adolescents who drink typically begin experimenting with beer or wine, followed by hard liquor or cigarettes. For most adolescents, the risk period for the first full drink of alcohol begins at age 11 and peaks between age 16 and 18. The risk period for onset of regular alcohol use begins around age 14 and peaks at age 19 (DeWit et al., 1997). If other drug use occurs, marijuana use tends to follow alcohol use, which is then followed by other illicit drug use (Kandel and Faust, 1975; Kandel et al., 1992). Initiation of marijuana use typically peaks at age 15 (Gfroerer et al., 2002; Labouvie and White,

2002), with risk of initiation continuing throughout adolescence (Kosterman et al., 2000) and leveling off at age 22 (DeWit et al., 1997). Youth also engage in other risk behaviors related to alcohol and drug use, such as driving after using marijuana or alcohol, or riding with a driver who may be under the influence (O'Malley and Johnston, 2003). Data from our research have shown that approximately 28% of 6th, 7th and 8th graders report that at least once in their lifetime they have ridden with a driver who had been drinking alcohol (D'Amico, 2004). Furthermore, many high school aged teens who use alcohol and drugs report enough problems from use to meet diagnostic criteria for a substance abuse disorder (13.8% and 22.7% in grades 9 and 12, respectively) (Dukes et al., 1997); and many of these youth may go on to have a substance abuse or dependence disorder in late young adulthood (D'Amico et al., 2005b).

The age at which one first uses substances seems to impact risk of later dependence. For example, among adults in 2006 who first tried marijuana before age 14, 12.9% developed abuse or dependence of illicit drugs compared to 2.2% of adults who first tried marijuana after age 18. Similarly, 9.6% of adults who first used alcohol before age 21 developed alcohol abuse or dependence compared to 2.4% who initiated use after age 21 (Substance Abuse and Mental Health Services Administration, 2007).

Alcohol and drug use during this important developmental period can adversely impact functioning across several different areas. For example, the adolescent brain is still developing (Sowell et al., 1999) and alcohol and drug use may disrupt this maturation process and impair brain function over the long term (Chambers et al., 2003; Tapert et al., 2004-2005). Work by Tapert and colleagues has found that adolescents who report using alcohol and marijuana at high levels for an extended period of time exhibit modest but significant neurocognitive deficits by late adolescence (Brown et al., 2000; Schweinsburg et al., 2005; Tapert and Brown, 2000; Tapert et al., 1999). Heavy drinking during this time period can affect working memory function and may also impair the growth and integrity of certain brain structures such as the hippocampus and prefrontal cortex (De Bellis et al., 2000; Tapert et al., 2004-2005).

Substance use during this period may also impact interpersonal, occupational and educational functioning (Brown et al., 2001; Ellickson et al., 1998). For example, early initiation of marijuana and frequent use during this time period is associated with lower grades, dropping out of school, lower life satisfaction and earning less money in young adulthood (Brook et al., 1999; Ellickson et al., 2004). Following a cohort of youth at ages 15-16, 24-25, 28-29, and 34-35, Kandel and Chen found that adolescents who both initiated marijuana use early and engaged in heavy use were more likely to meet criteria for alcohol dependence at age 34-35, report higher rates of illicit drug use and marijuana-related problems, and have had a psychiatric problem compared with teens who reported early onset-light use, mid onset-heavy use, and late onset-light use (Kandel and Chen, 2000).

Heavy alcohol use during adolescence is also associated with problems; specifically, teens who drink heavily during this time period report neurobehavioral and cognitive problems in young adulthood (Brook et al., 2002) and are more likely to report substance abuse and/or dependence problems in late young adulthood (age 29) (D'Amico et al., 2005b). A recent study examined developmental trajectories of smoking, binge drink-

ing, and marijuana from age 13 to age 23 and assessed how these patterns related to several psychosocial and behavioral outcomes in young adulthood at age 23. There were two groups at high risk for poorer outcomes (e.g. more substance use problems, poorer physical health) at age 23 compared to abstainers: those who were using at relatively high levels by ages 13; and those who started at low levels of use at age 13, but steadily increased their use over time (Tucker et al., 2005). Thus, early initiation and frequent alcohol and drug use during this important developmental time can have significant ramifications on the adolescent's potential as an adult.

In addition to personal ramifications, alcohol and drug use incur a substantial economic cost to society, including health costs, lost productivity, legal costs, and early mortality. A National Institute of Alcohol Abuse and Alcoholism report estimated the annual cost of alcohol abuse at $185 billion in 1998 (Harwood, 2000). A separate Department of Justice report estimated underage drinking alone cost $58 billion, or about $200 per capita, in 1996 (US Department of Justice, 1999). Illicit substance use adds to this burden. The Office of National Drug Control Policy estimated the cost of illicit substance use to the US at $180.9 billion dollars, or about $630 per capita in 2002 (Office of National Drug Control Policy, 2004).

Developmental factors

Adolescence is a unique developmental period marked by many biological, social, and cognitive changes, which can play a large role in the initiation and maintenance of alcohol and drug use (Lanza and Collins, 2002; Tarter, 2002; Tschann et al., 1994). For example, norm breaking behavior may become more common (Hurrelmann, 1990; Spear, 2000), which may partially account for the increased experimentation with alcohol and drugs that occurs during adolescence (Alsaker, 1995; Baumrind, 1987; Tarter,

2002).

Some experimentation with alcohol and/or drugs is considered to be normal during adolescence (Chassin and DeLucia, 1996; Guilamo-Ramos et al., 2004; Hurrelmann, 1990). For example, popularity among youth is associated with minor levels of substance use and delinquency (Allen et al., 2005). There is evidence, however, that abstaining youth have better health outcomes and fewer alcohol and drug problems in young adulthood than youth who experiment with substances during this time (Tucker et al., 2005). For example, youth who begin drinking before the age of 14 are more likely to become alcohol dependent compared with those who begin drinking at age 20 or older (Grant, 1998; Hingson et al., 2006). As approximately one-quarter of high school students (28%) report that they have consumed alcohol before 13 years of age (Center for Disease Control and Prevention, 2004), this suggests that many youth may be at risk for developing future alcohol-related problems.

Table 1 highlights risk and protective factors associated with alcohol and drug use during this time period. There are different theories that attempt to explain adolescent alcohol and drug use, many of which focus on social learning and intrapersonal processes (e.g., Petraitis et al., 1995). This section will focus on those processes that are particularly salient during this developmental period and are amenable to change and can therefore be targeted in prevention programming. For example, social processes, such as friends' use of alcohol and drugs, and intrapersonal processes, such as beliefs about substances, are both associated with alcohol and drug use and have been targeted in different prevention efforts.

There is a great deal of empirical evidence that emphasizes the influence that role models can have on adolescents' alcohol and drug use. For example, peer influence increases substantially during this time period (Simons-Morton et al., 1999). Beliefs about peer use of substances can impact both initiation of alcohol and marijuana use and escalation of use (D'Amico and McCarthy, 2006). Recent research has shown that peers may play a more important role than parents in contributing to initiation and escalation of substance use during early adolescence (Beal et al., 2001; Crawford and Novak, 2002; Petraitis et al., 1998; Windle, 2000). Cross-sectional studies have found that peer social influence is the only measure independently associated with abstinence from alcohol and marijuana use (Beal et al., 2001). In addition, modeling of use by best friends and perceived prevalence of use among same aged peers are more strongly related to initiation and experimentation of alcohol than parental modeling of use (Jackson, 1997). Longitudinal work has supported these cross-sectional findings and shown that peer alcohol use is more strongly related to adolescent alcohol use than parental alcohol use (Windle, 2000; Zhang et al., 1997). Thus, many prevention programs incorporate a discussion of peer alcohol and drug use in their programming content and provide normative feedback aimed at changing adolescents' perceptions about peer substance use (e.g., Brown et al., 2005; D'Amico and Fromme, 2002; Hansen and Graham, 1991).

Although the effect of family may be diminished during this time period, it is still an important influence on youth involvement in risk behaviors (Baumrind, 1987; Kandel, 1996). For example, parental behaviors, such as monitoring and disapproval of heavy drinking are significantly negatively associated with adolescent drinking, even after controlling for the impact of peer influence (Wood et al., 2004). In addition, parental involvement in their child's activities is negatively related to adolescent drinking (Simons-Morton and Chen, 2005). Parents are also able to positively influence their teens

Table 1. Risk and Protective Factors for Alcohol and Other Drug (AOD) Use

Domain	Risk Factors	Protective Factors
Individual	• Biological and psychological dispositions • Positive beliefs about alcohol and other drug (AOD) use • Early initiation of AOD use • Negative relationships with adults • Risk-taking propensity/impulsivity	• Opportunities for prosocial involvement • Rewards/recognition for prosocial involvement • Healthy beliefs and clear standards for behavior • Positive sense of self • Negative beliefs about AOD • Positive relationships with adults
Peer	• Association with peers who use or value AOD use • Association with peers who reject mainstream activities and pursuits • Susceptibility to negative peer pressure • Easily influenced by peers	• Association with peers who are involved in school, recreation service, religion, or other organized activities • Resistance to negative peer pressure • Not easily influenced by peers
Family	• Family history of AOD use • Family management problems • Family conflict • Parental beliefs about AOD	• Bonding (positive attachments) • Healthy beliefs and clear standards for behavior • High parental expectations • A sense of basic trust • Positive family dynamics
School	• Academic failure beginning in elementary school • Low commitment to school	• Opportunities for prosocial involvement • Rewards/recognition for prosocial involvement • Healthy beliefs and clear standards for behavior • Caring and support from teachers and staff • Positive instructional climate
Community	• Availability of AOD • Community laws, norms favorable toward AOD • Extreme economic and social deprivation • Transition and mobility • Low neighborhood attachment and community disorganization	• Opportunities for participation as active members of the community • Decreasing AOD accessibility • Cultural norms that set high expectations for youth • Social networks and support systems within the community
Society	• Impoverishment • Unemployment and underemployment • Discrimination • Pro-AOD-use messages in the media	• Media literacy (resistance to pro-use messages) • Decreased accessibility • Increased pricing through taxation • Raised purchasing age and enforcement • Stricter driving-under-the-influence laws

Table 1 is adapted from:
1. SAMHSA (2001). *Science-based substance abuse prevention: A guide.* DMMS Publication No. (SMA)d-3505. Rockville: MD.
2. Chinman M, Imm P, Wandersman A. (2004) *Getting to Outcomes 2004: Promoting Accountability Through Methods and Tools for Planning, Implementation, and Evaluation.* Santa Monica, CA: RAND Corporation, TR-TR101. Available at http://www.rand.org/publications/TR/TR101/.

substance use indirectly. For example, Simons-Morton et al. (Simons-Morton et al., 2004), found that parental involvement, monitoring, and expectations were protective against smoking behavior by limiting the number of the adolescent's peers who smoked cigarettes. Parental modeling of alcohol and drug use is also strongly related to whether or not adolescents choose to use substances (Johnson and Johnson, 2001; Li et al., 2002). For example, non-using parents have a protective effect on peer influence to use alcohol and drugs (Li et al., 2002). In contrast, parental drinking is strongly associated with adolescent drinking (Chassin et al., 1993; Rose et al., 1999), and youth who report that their parents use marijuana are twice as likely to smoke cigarettes, drink alcohol, and use marijuana (Li et al., 2002). Of note, siblings are also an important influence on adolescent alcohol and drug use. Studies have consistently shown that perception of sibling alcohol and drug use is associated with drinking behavior and positive beliefs about drugs (Ary et al., 1993; D'Amico and Fromme, 1997; Windle, 2000). Thus, the impact of family behavior may also be incorporated into prevention programming content for this age group.

Cognitive factors, especially alcohol outcome expectancies, have been strongly and consistently linked to adolescent alcohol, cigarette, and marijuana use in both cross-sectional and longitudinal research (Aarons et al., 2001; Aas et al., 1998; Fromme and D'Amico, 2000; Jones et al., 1999; Leigh and Stacy, 2004; Wahl et al., 2005). Specifically, positive alcohol and drug outcome expect-ancies, or the positive beliefs that one holds about the effects of alcohol and drugs, are typically associated with both increased drinking (Smith et al., 1995) and drug use (Aarons et al., 2001; Ames et al., 1999). In contrast, negative expectancies are typically linked with less alcohol (Jones and McMahon, 1993) and drug use (Aarons et al.,

2001; Galen and Henderson, 1999).

Both peers and adults can influence the development of adolescents' expectancies. For example, Martino and colleagues found that more alcohol use by peers and among important adults predicted increased positive alcohol expectancies among adolescents (Martino et al., 2006). Some examples of positive expectancies are: "I will be more social" or "I will be brave and daring" (Fromme et al., 1993). Some examples of negative expectancies are, "I would feel dizzy" or "I would act aggressively" (Fromme et al., 1993). Because of the strong associa-tion between outcome expectancies and subsequent drinking and drug use, several prevention programs discuss these beliefs and the influence that these beliefs may have on alcohol and drug use (e.g., D'Amico and Fromme, 2002; Darkes and Goldman, 1993; Fromme and Corbin, 2004).

Evidence based prevention and intervention strategies

In the field of prevention, drug and alcohol programs are classified as universal, designed for the general population; selective, designed for subgroups at risk for substance use, such as youth who have parents who abuse substances or who are already experimenting with substance use themselves; or indicated, designed for youth who have been treated but are at high risk for relapse (Institute of Medicine, 1994; NIDA, 1997).

Universal or primary prevention oriented activities remain the most frequently used approach with young people. Most universal prevention programs have been based in middle and high schools and have relied on classroom-based methods delivered through teachers or other authority figures such as police.

Few adolescents may actually seek out help or treatment if they have substance-related problems. This may be because traditional intervention approaches are not well suited for this age group (D'Amico et al., 2005a; Deas et al., 2000). In fact, many intervention efforts for adolescents have been developed from adult or child models (Lonigan et al., 1998; Weisz and Hawley, 2002).

It is important to address the many biological, social, and cognitive changes that take place during adolescence in prevention programming content. Unfortunately, many prevention program evaluations occur *after* the entire curriculum is developed instead of while it is being developed (Sussman et al., 1996). Thus, program content and/or materials may not be developmentally appropriate for youth and there may be significant gaps in coverage of specific adolescent problems and concerns. More effort is needed to study adolescent development, risk, and resilience as the basis for programming content rather than adapting programs originally designed for other age groups (Weisz and Hawley, 2002). It is therefore crucial to build curriculum content and materials with youth collaboration and input (Brown, 2001; D'Amico et al., 2005a; Sussman et al., 1996). For example, because the frontal lobes are still maturing during adolescence, emotional regulation, planning, and organization are continuing to develop (Sowell et al., 1999). This maturation process will therefore impact an adolescent's ability to think ahead and to plan for higher risk situations. Thus, for many youth, focusing on the long-term consequences of alcohol and drug use is not as relevant as discussing other issues more salient for this developmental stage (e.g., social comparison).

Another important aspect of adolescence that should be considered in the development of program content is the substantial increase in peer influence. Because peers play such a large role in adolescents' decisions to use alcohol and drugs, providing prevention programming in a group context is an effective way to reach youth and provide an opportunity for teens to receive peer feedback (D'Amico and Fromme, 2002). Although some research has suggested that this group feedback can sometimes "backfire," and adolescents' deviant behavior may increase (Arnold and Hughes, 1999; Dishion et al., 2002), a recent meta-analytic review of over 66 studies of adolescent group programs targeting substance use found little evidence to support this hypothesis (Weiss et al., 2005). Because the group context is a cost-effective approach to reach youth, many adolescent prevention programs disseminate the information in a group setting.

Meta-analytic research has shown that successful programs for this age group typically use an interactive method (Tobler and Stratton, 1997) and therefore emphasize an active exchange among teens (Ennett et al., 2003). More recently, programs have begun to incorporate motivational interviewing techniques (Miller and Rollnick, 2002) into their programming content. The tone of motivational interviewing is nonjudgmental and encouraging (Resnicow et al., 2002). Motivational interviewing is well suited to adolescents as it is a nonconfrontational approach and emphasizes self-responsibility in decision-making. There are four general principals of motivational interviewing: express empathy (e.g., acceptance facilitates change), develop discrepancy (e.g., let the client present arguments for change), roll with resistance (e.g., avoid arguing), and support self-efficacy (e.g., a person's belief in the possibility of change is an important motivator) (Miller and Rollnick, 2002). Motivational interviewing is effective in helping adolescents reduce substance use (Barnett et al., 2001; Colby et al., 1998; D'Amico and Fromme, 2002; Monti et al., 1999; Stern et al., 2007). Because motivational interviewing emphasizes an interactive process in which people are active participants, this approach increases the probability that program materials will be both culturally appropriate and acceptable to this age group.

Finally, successful programs tend to focus on social influences and comprehensive life skills (Stern et al., 2007; Tobler and Stratton, 1997). For example, social influence programs tend to focus on drug refusal skills and also include information on either media influences or normative information. Comprehensive life skills programs focus on information included in social influence programs *and* add intrapersonal skills, such as self-esteem, decision-making, and goal-setting. Social influence and comprehensive life skill programs tend to have the largest effect sizes in comparison to programs that are knowledge- or affective-based (Tobler and Stratton, 1997). In addition, these types of programs are also more likely to be delivered through an interactive process. Overall, findings highlight the importance of skill-based training during adolescence because, as discussed above, the adolescent brain is still maturing and thus teens may need help in planning ahead more efficiently so that they can make healthier choices.

School-based prevention programs

There are many prevention-related school-based programs available for teens. Some are designed for middle school youth and some are designed for high school students. Some were developed to reach all students, whereas others were developed for more high-risk youth. A recent meta-analysis examined the characteristics of 94 school-based prevention programs to determine what features of these programs were associated with more positive program outcomes (Gottfredson and Wilson, 2003). Results suggest that targeting younger adolescents, such as middle school youth, will increase program effectiveness. In addition, for programs that teach competency skills, it appears that targeting higher risk youth may produce stronger positive outcomes than targeting the general population. There was no relation between program duration and effect size; thus longer programs were not more effective than shorter programs (Gottfredson and Wilson, 2003).

Table 2 provides information on several school-based prevention programs that have published *at least* a one year follow-up and have been shown to be efficacious. We highlight some of these programs below.

Project ALERT is a school-based prevention program for middle school youth that focuses on helping youth understand how drug use affects them, identify pro-drug use pressures, and acquire skills for resisting those pressures (Ellickson and Bell, 1990). Eleven 45-minute sessions were conducted across both 7th (8 sessions) and 8th grade (3 sessions). The study involved a multi-site, longitudinal test of the program for 7th and 8th grade students (Ellickson and Bell, 1990). Thirty control and treatment schools from California and Oregon were chosen to reflect a diverse range of school and community environments, including urban, suburban, and rural areas. Nine of the schools had a minority population of 50% or more and 18 drew from neighborhoods with household incomes below the median for their state. At a 15 month follow-up, students who had participated in Project ALERT were less likely to initiate cigarette and marijuana use, and had lower current use of these substances than students in the control schools. Although intervention effects were found for alcohol use at the 3 month follow-up, these were no longer significant at the 15 month follow-up (Ellickson and Bell, 1990). The curriculum was revised to put more emphasis on curbing alcohol misuse and tested in a large scale randomized trial with 55 schools in South Dakota (Ellickson et al., 2003). Three additional lessons were added in 7th grade. The program continued to curb marijuana and cigarette use. It also decreased alcohol misuse and alcohol-related problems at an 18 month follow-up (Ellickson et al., 2003).

Of note, in this trial, as in almost all

Table 2: School-based interventions with at least one year of follow-up data

Study Name	Study Type and Population	Intervention Description	Major Outcomes
Adolescent Alcohol Prevention Trial Hansen and Graham, 1991	7th grade students in 12 junior high schools in Los Angeles and Orange Counties, California N=3,011 (at time 1)	Four intervention programs were implemented: 1) 4 sessions of 45-minute length about the social and health consequences of using alcohol and drugs (Information only). 2) 4 lessons about consequences of using substances and 5 lessons helping to identify and resist peer and advertising pressure (Information and Resistance Training). 3) 4 information lessons and 4 lessons correcting erroneous perceptions on prevalence and acceptability (Information and Normative Education). 4) 3 lessons about information, 3 ½ lessons on resistance skills; and 3 ½ lessons on establishing conservative norms (Resistance Training and Normative Education).	<u>1 year follow-up</u> Reduced use of alcohol, marijuana, and cigarettes for all students who received normative education (NE) (e.g., information and NE; resistance training and NE) compared to students who did not receive NE (e.g., information; information and resistance training). Incidence of drunkenness increased only 4.2% in the two groups that received NE compared to 11.1% in non-NE groups. No effects for resistance skills training.
Taylor et al., 2000	Follow up with 11th graders N=3,027	Same curriculum as 1991 study.	<u>4 year follow-up</u> Rate of growth of lifetime and recent cigarette smoking, alcohol use, and lifetime drunkenness were all lower for NE group compared to the information only group.

Study Name	Study Type and Population	Intervention Description	Major Outcomes
Alcohol Misuse Prevention Study (AMPS) Shope et al., 1992	5th and 6th grade students at 49 schools in southeastern Michigan N=5,356	AMPS program of 4 sessions and 3 booster sessions of 45 minutes each emphasizing social pressures resistance training, immediate effects of alcohol, risks of alcohol misuse and social pressures to misuse alcohol.	26 month follow-up The program did not affect overall rates of change in alcohol use or alcohol misuse. Means (SD) for alcohol use and misuse among 5th grade students <table><tr><td></td><td>Intervention + Booster</td><td>Intervention</td><td>Control</td><td>p-value</td></tr><tr><td>Use</td><td>0.62 (1.04)</td><td>0.59 (1.03)</td><td>0.68 (1.25)</td><td>p<.001</td></tr><tr><td>Misuse</td><td>0.85 (1.50)</td><td>0.79 (1.47)</td><td>0.80 (1.52)</td><td>p<.001</td></tr></table> Means (SD) for alcohol use and misuse among 6th grade students <table><tr><td></td><td>Intervention</td><td>Control</td><td>p-value</td></tr><tr><td>Use</td><td>0.89 (1.28)</td><td>0.94 (1.45)</td><td>p<.001</td></tr><tr><td>Misuse</td><td>1.17 (1.71)</td><td>1.27 (1.87)</td><td>p<.001</td></tr></table>
Wynn et al., 2000	6th-10th grade students N=232 (6th-7th) N=332 (7th-8th) N=371 (8th-10th)	Same as 1992 study.	AMPS contributed to increased refusal skills and knowledge of appropriate norms. From 8th to 10th grade, knowledge of appropriate norms mediated the effects of AMPS on alcohol misuse such that youth who reported more accurate norms were less likely to misuse alcohol.
Shope et al., 2001	10th grade students in 6 school districts in southeastern Michigan, after receiving driver's license. N=4,635	Same as 1992 study.	Tested the effectiveness of AMPS on 10th grade students through 7.6 years after they received their driver's license (approximately at age 24 years). For the whole sample, no significant treatment effects were found for crash outcomes. Rates of 1st year serious offenses (e.g., involved use of alcohol, resulted in 3 or more points assigned to driver) were reduced slightly among students who consumed less than 1 drink per week; however, the treatment effects disappeared after the first year of licensure.

Study Name	Study Type and Population	Intervention Description	Major Outcomes
keepin' it R.E.A.L. Hecht et al., 2003	7th and 8th grade urban middle school students in 35 schools in Arizona N=6,035	keepin' it R.E.A.L. The resistance strategy forms the acronym Refuse/Rechasa, Explain/Explica, Avoid/Apártate, and Leave/Levántate 10-lesson culturally grounded school-based prevention intervention promoting anti-drug norms and attitudes; teaching life skills to combat negative peer and other influences; and developing risk assessment, decision making, and resistance skills. Sessions were bolstered by booster activities and a media campaign. Three parallel versions were delivered: Mexican American, combined African American and European American, and Multicultural.	<u>14 month follow-up</u> Less increase of alcohol and marijuana use among intervention participants. Little support for matching the content of the program to the culture/ethnicity of the student.

Study Name	Study Type and Population	Intervention Description	Major Outcomes
Life Skills Training Program (LST) Botvin et al., 1990	7th grade students in 56 schools (suburban and rural) in New York N=4,466	15 class sessions of 12 curriculum units designed for 7th grade; 10 booster sessions in 8th grade; 5 booster sessions in 9th grade. Two prevention conditions: teacher training by workshop and feedback (E1) or teacher training via videotape and no feedback (E2). Focus on drug resistance skills, norms against substance use, and development of personal and social skills.	3 year follow-up Reduced cigarette use and marijuana use in both treatment conditions compared to control group. No significant effects for drinking frequency (never [1 to more than once a day [9]) or amount of drinking (don't drink [1] to more than 6 drinks [6]) Substance use means and standard errors (SE) for prevention and control conditions Table below
Botvin et al., 1995	Follow up with 12th graders in 56 schools N=3,597	Same as 1990 study.	6 year follow-up Reduced cigarette, alcohol, and marijuana use in both treatment conditions compared to control group for individuals who received at least 60% of the intervention. Follow up means are adjusted for baseline prevalence.
Botvin et al., 2001	7th grade students in 29 schools (urban, public) in New York N=3,621	LST for minority youth which included new graphics, language, and role-play scenarios appropriate for target population, adjusting the reading level for youth. The overall prevention strategy remained the same with 15 sessions in the 7th grade; 10 booster sessions in the 8th grade, taught by a classroom teacher. Teachers were taught via video material and a one-day workshop.	1 year follow-up LST participants reduced cigarette, alcohol, marijuana, polydrug use compared to control group. Adjusted means and standard errors (SE) at one-year follow up for substance use Table below

Substance use means and standard errors (SE) for prevention and control conditions (Botvin et al., 1990):

	E1	E2	Control	p-value
Smoking	1.46 (0.04)	1.50 (0.04)	1.63 (0.03)	p<.01
Drinking freq.	3.17 (0.05)	3.10 (0.05)	3.15 (0.05)	ns
Drinking amt.	2.65 (0.05)	2.55 (0.05)	2.65 (0.04)	ns
Drunkenness	2.31 (0.04)	2.19 (0.04)	2.32 (0.04)	p=.04
Marijuana Use	1.51 (0.04)	1.54 (0.04)	1.66 (0.04)	p=.02

Adjusted means and standard errors (SE) at one-year follow up for substance use (Botvin et al., 2001):

	Intervention	Control	p-value
Smoking frequency	1.73 (.04)	1.94 (.05)	p<.01
Smoking quantity	1.19 (.02)	1.32 (.02)	p<.01
Drinking frequency	1.77 (.03)	1.99 (.04)	p<.01
Drunkenness freq.	1.17 (.02)	1.26 (.03)	p<.01
Drinking quantity	1.51 (.02)	1.68 (.03)	p<.01
Marijuana frequency	1.41 (.03)	1.51 (.04)	p<.05
Getting "high" freq.	1.26 (.03)	1.34 (.04)	ns
Lifetime polydrug use	0.78 (.02)	0.96 (.03)	p<.01
Current polydrug use	0.24 (.02)	0.33 (.02)	p<.01

Note: GLM p-value

Study Name	Study Type and Population	Intervention Description	Major Outcomes
Life Skills Training Program (cont.) Griffin et al., 2003	7th and 8th grade students identi-fied as high risk either socially (e.g., had friends that smoked or drank) or aca-demically (grades of C or less) from 29 inner-city middle schools N=802	Same as 2001 study except examined effects for youth at high social and academic risk.	1 year follow-up LST students reported less cigarette, alcohol, inhalant and polydrug use compared to control condition Adjusted substance use means and standard errors (SE) at one-year follow up 		Intervention	Control	p-value
Smoking	1.79 (.08)	2.13 (.09)	p<.01
Drinking	1.82 (.08)	2.11 (.08)	p<.01
Marijuana	1.69 (.10)	1.87 (.11)	ns
Polydrug use	0.42 (.05)	0.61 (.05)	p<.01 | Note: GEE p-value
Stay SMART St. Pierre et al., 1992	Youth aged 13 years from 10 Boys and Girls Clubs across the nation; results reported only for youth who participated in all four testing occasions N=161	Lessons based on Botvin's LST (see above) plus additional lessons discussing sexual activity; 2 booster sessions were provided which reinforced knowledge and skills that were taught in the initial program.	27 month follow-up Less recent marijuana use among youth who participated in the program AND received the boosters. Marginally significant results for reduced alcohol and cigarette use among program participants. Adjusted means for prevention and control conditions at the 27 month follow-up |	Program only	Program + Boosters	Control	p-value
---	---	---	---	---
Alcohol	1.89	1.87	2.04	p=.10
Marijuana	1.22	1.25	1.38	p=.05
Cigarette	1.46	1.48	1.63	p=.12	

Study Name	Study Type and Population	Intervention Description	Major Outcomes
Project ALERT Ellickson and Bell, 1990	7th grade students in 30 schools (urban, suburban, and rural in California and Oregon) N=6,527	Curriculum of 8 sessions in 7th grade and 3 lessons in 8th grade. Half of the treatment schools were taught solely by health educators; the other half also utilized teen leaders. Focus on reasons not to use drugs, identifying pressures to use them, counter pro-drug messages, learn how to say no to external and internal pressures, understand that most people do not use drugs, and recognize the benefits of resistance.	<u>15 month follow-up</u> Effects for three levels of users were examined: Nonusers, experimenters, and users. No effects on alcohol use. Decreased smoking among experimenters. For baseline smokers, negative results were found for users, with smokers increasing use by 20%. Project ALERT curbed marijuana initiation rates by 1/3. Marijuana or cigarette abstainers before baseline had substantially lower rates of initiation and current marijuana use compared to the control group. There were early significant reductions in drinking levels amongst nonusers, experimenters, and users, but effects were not sustained over time. Involvement of teen leaders did not show any significant effects.
Ellickson et al., 2003	7th and 8th grade students at 55 South Dakota middle schools N=4,276	Revised Project ALERT curriculum to address alcohol misuse: 11 lessons in 7th grade (3 new lessons) and 3 lessons in 8th grade. The additional sessions focused on smoking cessation and alcohol use via a video of former teenage smokers talking about why and how they quit. New home learning opportunities included parents in prevention activities.	<u>18 month follow-up</u> Three levels: low risk, moderate risk, and high risk. Reduced proportion of new smokers by 19%. Reduced proportion of new marijuana users by 39%; however, no effect on current marijuana use. High-risk participants had lower alcohol misuse scores compared to control students; however, there were no effects on alcohol initiation or current alcohol use. Effects for the low-risk group, 18 months after baseline Effects for the moderate-risk group, 18 months after baseline

Effects for the low-risk group, 18 months after baseline

	Intervention	Control	p-value
Past month cigarette use	8.6%	11.1%	ns
Marijuana initiation	5.0%	8.0%	$p<.01$
Alcohol overall misuse (mean score)	0.22	0.30	ns

Effects for the moderate-risk group, 18 months after baseline

	Intervention	Control	p-value
Past month cigarette use	28.9%	36.6%	$p<.05$
Marijuana initiation	27.2%	36.8%	$p<.05$
Alcohol overall misuse (mean score	0.64	0.65	ns

Study Name	Study Type and Population	Intervention Description	Major Outcomes
Project ALERT Cont.			Effects for the high-risk group, 18 months after baseline 		Intervention	Control	p-value	 	---	---	---	---	 	Past month cigarette use	56.8%	70.8%	p<.05	 	Marijuana initiation	N/A	N/A	N/A	 	Alcohol overall misuse (mean score)	1.78	2.23	p<.05	
Project Towards No Drug Abuse (Project TND) Sussman et al., 1998	Continuation high school students in 21 schools in southern California N=1,074	9 lessons covered in 3 sessions per week for 3 consecutive weeks. Two experimental conditions were tested: 1) classroom program and 2) classroom program plus school-as-community component. Classroom sessions provided motivation-skills-decision-making material targeting the use of cigarettes, alcohol, marijuana, hard drug, and violence-related behavior. School-as-community events included job training, field trips, and sports competitions.	1 year follow-up Reductions in alcohol use and hard drug use among users in the two experimental conditions compared to control students. No effects on cigarette or marijuana use. Mean levels of use in the past 30 days, one year follow up 		Group 1	Group 2	Control	p-value	 |---|---|---|---|---| | Cigarettes	34.53	33.08	30.71	.64	 | Alcohol	8.15	7.16	8.61	.02	 | Marijuana	12.31	13.02	11.21	.75	 | Hard drugs	2.74	2.87	5.03	p<.000	
Sussman et al., 2003	Continuation high school students in 18 schools in southern California N=1,037	Comparison of a health educator delivered program and a self-instruction curriculum.	2 year follow-up The health educator condition significantly lowered the probability of 30-day tobacco and hard drug use. No effects were found for the self-instruction curriculum.

Study Name	Study Type and Population	Intervention Description	Major Outcomes
School Health and Alcohol Harm Reduction Project (SHAHRP) McBride et al., 2004	8th grade students in 14 schools in Perth, Western Australia N=2,343	Conducted in two phases over a 2-year period: phase I conducted when students were 13 years old comprised 17 skills based activities conducted over 8-10 lessons (40-60 minutes each); Phase II conducted when youth were 14 years old comprised 12 activities delivered over 5-7 weeks. Activities included delivery of utility information, skill rehearsal, individual and small group decision-making, and discussions based on scenarios suggested by students.	<u>32 month follow-up</u> Reductions were seen in alcohol use at 8 month and 20 month follow-ups compared to youth who received regular alcohol education classes; however, use rates were not different between these groups at the 32 month follow-up. % consumed alcohol at least once per week <table><tr><td></td><td>Intervention</td><td>Control</td><td>p-value</td></tr><tr><td>Baseline</td><td>12.3</td><td>14.9</td><td>p=.06</td></tr><tr><td>8 months</td><td>16.6</td><td>19.7</td><td>p=.03</td></tr><tr><td>20 months</td><td>23.6</td><td>30.5</td><td>p<.0001</td></tr><tr><td>32 months</td><td>31.8</td><td>36.8</td><td>p=.o7</td></tr></table>
Start Taking Alcohol Risks Seriously (STARS) Werch et al., 2003	6th grade students from two urban middle schools in Jacksonville, Florida N=650	2-year multi-component intervention: brief 20 minute one-on-one health consultation from nurse in 6th grade and prevention postcards to parents; follow up nurse consultation in 7th grade with 4 take home lessons.	<u>1 year follow-up</u> STARS students reported fewer intentions to drink in the future, greater motivation to avoid alcohol use, and fewer total risk factors than control students. No significant differences were found between groups for actual alcohol use. Mean (SD) for alcohol use and risk factor measures at 1 year follow up <table><tr><td></td><td>Intervention</td><td>Control</td><td>p-value</td></tr><tr><td>Intentions</td><td>5.56 (2.75)</td><td>6.70 (3.77)</td><td>p>0.01</td></tr><tr><td>Alcohol frequency</td><td>0.37 (1.13)</td><td>0.57 (1.62)</td><td>ns</td></tr><tr><td>Alcohol quantity</td><td>0.27 (0.92)</td><td>0.47 (1.26)</td><td>ns</td></tr><tr><td>Heavy alcohol use</td><td>0.28 (n/a)</td><td>0.11 (n/a)</td><td>ns</td></tr><tr><td>Motivation to avoid</td><td>2.49 (1.17)</td><td>3.00 (1.79)</td><td>p>0.01</td></tr><tr><td>Total alcohol risk</td><td>7.73 (1.83)</td><td>8.26 (1.96)</td><td>p>0.01</td></tr></table>

Note: When possible, we provided means and standard deviations associated with the findings that are reported in each study.

prevention and treatment trials, measurement of substance use was by self-report. This is not necessarily a limitation; many self-report methodologies have been validated and are the best available measurement of substance use over long-periods. Under appropriate conditions, subjects self-report their substance use with high reliability. Methods should be designed to minimize social desirability of a particular response, fear of reprisal as a result of admitting use, and the cognitive demands of the report (i.e. participants must be able to remember and accurately describe the behavior) (Brener et al., 2003). For example, adolescent self-report obtained by a teacher, parent, school counselor, parole officer, or treating clinician should not be considered reliable, because there may be consequences tied to the subjects' responses, or pressure to report favorable behavior. Assessment must also be conducted privately and with strict confidentiality.

Drug testing, although objective, is a poor measure of substance use in non-drug dependent populations. Drug screening methods generally only detect substance use that has occurred in the last 1-3 days at best. Therefore, drug tesing only reliably detects substance use that occurs every day, such as in substance dependent individuals (Goldstein and Brown, 2003). Drug testing methodologies will not detect the vast majority of sporadic use and thus they are of little value in prevention trials, where detection of initiation, experimentation, and occassional binge use of alcohol and drugs is important.

The Life Skills Training Program (LST) was developed to target drug-related expect-ancies, teach skills to resist influences to use drugs, and promote the development of self-management and social skills for middle school students (Botvin, 1996). LST consists of fifteen 45-minute sessions. In addition, there are ten booster sessions in 8th grade and five booster sessions in 9th grade. Several studies have examined the long-term effects of this program. Among mostly white students, there were fewer smokers, drinkers, and marijuana users by 12th grade among those who had received the LST curriculum relative to control students (Botvin et al., 1995). The program was also successful among minority youth: at a one year follow-up, those youth who had received LST reported less smoking, drinking, and polydrug use relative to those in the control group (Botvin et al., 2001).

The Start Taking Alcohol Risks Seriously (STARS) for families program is different from other school-based programs in that it is very brief. The program provides a single 20-minute one-on-one health consultation by a nurse for youth in the 6th grade. During 6th grade, these youth also receive a series of prevention postcards that are mailed to parents/guardians and provide key facts about alcohol and tips on how to discuss these facts with their children. In the 7th grade, STARS youth receive a follow-up nurse consultation and four family take-home lessons to encourage parent-child communication about prevention skills and knowledge (Werch et al., 2003). At one-year follow-up, students who received the STARS intervention reported weaker intentions to drink in the future and greater motivation to avoid alcohol use than control students. Alcohol use was lower for STARS youth compared to control students; however, these differences were not statistically significant (Werch et al., 2003).

The Adolescent Alcohol Prevention Trial (AAPT) (Hansen and Graham, 1991) was designed to examine how different inter-vention components may impact subsequent alcohol and drug use. The AAPT included an information only group, a resistance training plus information group, a normative educa-tion plus information group, and a group that combined resistance training, normative education, and information in four to nine 45-minute lessons (Taylor et al., 2000).

Information only included four lessons about the social and health consequences of using alcohol and other drugs. Normative education provided four information sessions and five lessons that corrected misperceptions concerning the prevalence and acceptability of alcohol and other drug use among peers and established conservative norms. Resistance skills training prepared the adolescent for rejecting potential pressure for alcohol and drug use in four lessons (Taylor et al., 2000). A recent assessment of the efficacy of the AAPT utilized five waves of longitudinal data. Students were in the 7th grade when they received the program and final follow-up took place in the 11th grade. Findings indicated that only the normative education program had consistent beneficial effects on alcohol and drug use when compared to the information only program. Specifically, average use levels over the four years were lower for youth in the norm program. In addition, the rate of growth of drug use for adolescents who received the normative education program was significantly slower compared to youth who received the information only program (Taylor et al., 2000).

One of the few culturally grounded school-based prevention programs is Keepin' it R.E.A.L. (Gosin et al., 2003), a drug resistance curriculum tailored for Mexican-American youth in the southwest. The curriculum focuses on testing the effectiveness of providing culturally grounded prevention messages. Keepin' it R.E.A.L. is comprised of ten 40-45 minute lessons with five videos. The program teaches cognitive and communication skills for use with four "REAL" resistance strategies: refuse, explain, avoid, and leave (Gosin et al., 2003). Three curriculum versions were developed: one targeting Latino students (Mexican-American version), another targeting non-Latino students (African-American and European version), and a multicultural version combining the previous two versions. The program

was effective: increases in alcohol, marijuana, and cigarette use were less substantial among intervention students compared to control students. The Latino version of the program generated more positive outcomes overall; however, there was little evidence that matching the message to the ethnicity of participants enhanced the program's effectiveness. Specifically, when analyses limited the sample to those youth who reported Mexican/Mexican American ethnic identity, the Latino version did not generate better outcomes than the non-Latino version, suggesting that it may not be necessary to tailor prevention messages to each specific cultural group (Hecht et al., 2003; Kulis et al., 2005).

Successful selective prevention approaches also exist for adolescents (SAMHSA, 2005), although there are far fewer of these types of programs (Brown and D'Amico, 2003). Greater emphasis on selective prevention approaches is warranted for adolescents with mild to moderate substance use problems than has been heretofore provided, as these youth are the least likely to receive attention or help for such problems (Larimer et al., 1998; Shakeshaft et al., 1997).

Sussman and colleagues developed Project Towards No Drug Abuse (TND), which was tailored for high-risk youth in continuation school settings (Sussman, 1996). Curriculum content was developed with the input of high-risk youth (Sussman et al., 2002; Sussman et al., 1998) and includes lessons which focus on active listening, stereotyping, confronting myths about substance use, providing information on chemical dependency, understanding the negative consequences of drug abuse, providing alternatives, learning self-control, and decision-making (Sussman, 1996). In comparison to previous prevention programs, which focus on providing normative information, Sussman found that normative information was not well-received by high-risk youth and was not associated with any change in perceptions of use (Sussman,

1996). Instead, the TND curriculum focuses on how stereotyping may impact behavior. For example, many of these high-risk teens felt that others perceived them as deviant and as drug abusers. Thus, instead of focusing on providing normative feedback, one of the lessons focuses on how these students may be more at risk if they give into this self-fulfilling prophecy that others think they are drug abusers. TND is taught in either a 9 or 12 session curriculum with each lesson approximately 50 minutes (Sussman et al., 2002; Sussman et al., 1998). Studies of the curriculum have indicated that the same types of lessons are applicable to both Latino and Non-Latino white adolescents (Sussman et al., 2003). In one study, high-risk youth who participated in TND decreased their hard drug use by 25% at a one year follow-up compared to a control group, but no reductions were found for tobacco and marijuana use (Sussman et al., 1998). In another study that implemented a 12 session curriculum led by health educators, reductions were seen for involvement with hard drugs and alcohol compared to a control condition at one year follow-up (Sussman et al., 2002). A two year follow-up indicated positive effects for tobacco and hard drug use (Sussman et al., 2003). Thus, this school-based curriculum appears effective in reaching this higher risk population.

Similar to TND, Project SUCCESS (Morehouse and Tobler, 2000) targeted at-risk teens in alternative school settings. There is a prevention education series (8 sessions) and a group counseling module (8 sessions). Project SUCCESS activities include the following goals: increase students' knowledge about the negative effects of substance use; decrease favorable attitudes towards use; correct misperceptions about prevalence and accept-ability of use; increase students' knowledge of and comfort with resistance skills; and decrease unhealthy alcohol and drug use behaviors. A pre-test was conducted at the beginning of the school year and a post-test occurred at the end of the school year. Findings indicated that the intervention decreased alcohol, tobacco, and other drug use by 23% at a post-test among participants compared to non-program youth (Morehouse and Tobler, 2000).

Reconnecting Youth (RY) is another school-based program focused on youth at risk for dropping out of school (Eggert et al., 2001). The RY framework is based on a social-network-support model and has four components: an RY daily class; school bonding activities; parent involvement; and a school-based crisis response plan (Eggert et al., 1995). Students participate in a semester long class that involves skills training and interpersonal communication techniques. At a 10-month follow-up, relative to controls, participants reported increased grades and decreased hard drug use (Eggert et al., 1994). However, a recent randomized trial of RY in two urban school districts was unable to replicate these positive effects at a 6-month follow-up (Cho et al., 2005).

Of note, the programs discussed above take place in the school setting during school time. Most programs, with the exception of STARS, take approximately nine or more weeks to complete and youth who are in the classroom on the day the program is offered during that week receive the intervention if they have parental permission. Thus, the program is part of the classroom curriculum and therefore required, and the majority of youth in the school receive the program. We note, however, that the need for parental permission may cause differences between the populations that do and do not receive the program (e.g., Frissell et al., 2004), and this caveat should be considered when interpreting results.

In contrast to the many mandated preven-tion programs targeting alcohol and drug use during class time, very few voluntary programs are available for adolescents, for example, taking place during "out of school time" (Little and Harris, 2003). Therefore, the potential impact of school-based intervention programs that teens may *choose* to attend has not been extensively examined. Because these programs are voluntary, they must be designed to capture the attention of youth as there are many other competing activities during "out-of-school time", such as sports, band, being in the school play, or simply being with friends. These programs also need to be brief as most students will not choose, for example, to attend fifteen 45-minute sessions. Involving the school community, particularly school staff, students, and par-ents, in the development of the program is key to successful implementation (Brown, 2001; D'Amico et al., 2005a; Masterman and Kelly, 2003; Wagner et al., 2004). Only three studies to date have examined the impact of a voluntary intervention program on adolescent alcohol and drug use, and only two examined outcomes over at least a one-year period. The first study utilized a voluntary intervention strategy for teens who participated in Boys and Girls Clubs by extending an invitation to all youth to participate in the Stay SMART program (St. Pierre et al., 1992). Once youth voluntarily enrolled, however, they were required to attend 9 of the 12 sessions. Thus, initial involvement was voluntary, but subsequent attendance at these sessions was mandated. The Stay SMART program is a component of SMART Moves, which is the national prevention program adapted for Boys and Girls Clubs from Botvin's LST (Botvin, 1996). It includes the original topics discussed in the LST curriculum, with the additional topics designed to addressed early sexual activity (St. Pierre et al., 1992). They also provide booster sessions that are designed to build upon the skills and knowledge presented in Stay SMART. At a 27 month post-test, youth who continued their participation in the Stay SMART program and booster sessions reported less involvement with marijuana compared to a control group (St. Pierre et al., 1992).

The second study evaluated the effects of a voluntary intervention, implemented in several high schools, on alcohol use and self-change efforts (Brown et al., 2005). Project Options was available via individual (four sessions), group (six sessions) or website (unlimited access) format. Individual and group sessions took place either during lunch or after school. Curriculum content across all three options focused on coping, behavioral management, communication, outcome expectancies, and normative feedback. One important component of this research was to better understand which students would voluntarily choose the different intervention formats. Findings indicated that 5 out of 6 participants chose the group format for participation and that youth from minority populations and mixed racial/ethnic back-grounds disproportionately sought the individual context for services (D'Amico et al., 2006). Results based on a one-semester follow-up indicated that the heaviest drinking students who reported attending at least one session of the intervention (individual, group, or web format) also reported more attempts to cut down or quit drinking than heavy drinking adolescents who did not attend the program (Brown et al., 2005).

The third non-randomized trial involved middle school youth. D'Amico and colleagues implemented Project CHOICE in one middle school, which did not have any other school prevention programming occurring at the time of this study. Project CHOICE took place for a half hour after school and had a total of five sessions, which focused on providing normative feedback, challenging unrealistic positive beliefs about substances, resisting pressure to use substances through the use of role plays, discussion of the potential benefits of both continuing use and cutting down or stopping use, and discussion of risky situations and coping strategies, such as getting social support or learning how to avoid certain high-risk situations (D'Amico et al., 2005a). Approximately 13% of students in the intervention school chose to attend Project CHOICE over an academic year and participants did not differ from non-participants on demographic characteristics, deviance, and self-esteem. Of most importance, these youth did not differ on their baseline rates of alcohol and drug use, thus youth who utilized the program ranged from abstainers to higher risk youth who reported regularly using substances (D'Amico et al., 2005a). Longitudinal evaluation of Project CHOICE examined whether this voluntary program would impact both individual *and* school-wide alcohol and drug use, even though not all students had attended (D'Amico and Edelen, in press). Findings indicated that teens who attended Project CHOICE reported less alcohol use and lower perceptions of alcohol, marijuana, and cigarette use than a matched sample of control students. In addition, comparison of the Project CHOICE school to a control school over a two-year period indicated that alcohol and marijuana use, and perceptions of friends' use of alcohol and marijuana, increased more sharply among students in the control school relative to students in the Project CHOICE school. Effect sizes ranged from 0.21 to 0.52 (small to moderate) (D'Amico and Edelen, in press).

Brief interventions

With shrinking health care budgets, the potential effectiveness of brief interventions on adolescent risk-taking behavior has recently been examined. Because these interventions are shorter and less extensive than more traditional interventions, the goal of many brief interventions is to address and enhance motivation to change (Tevyaw and Monti, 2004). Brief interventions typically comprise from one to five sessions (Bien et al., 1993). The majority of brief interventions discussed in this section focus on those that incorporate motivational interviewing techniques described earlier under *"Evidence-based prevention and intervention strategies."* Long-term efficacy research (e.g., one year or more follow-up periods) on brief motivational interventions for adolescents is scarce (Tait and Hulse, 2003), in part, because motivational interviewing is a relatively new technique. For example, Tait and Hulse's recent meta-analytic review of brief interventions identified only 11 studies that were not provided in a classroom setting, of which only 2 had at least a one-year follow-up (Baer et al., 1992).

We present these studies in Table 3 and highlight some of the work here. Evidence has been building for brief interventions since the early 1990's when Baer and colleagues found that providing a single session of professional advice was as effective as a 6-week version of an alcohol skills training program in substantially reducing young adult drinking (Dimeff et al., 1998). This led to the development of the Brief Alcohol Screening and Intervention for College Students (BASICS; (Dimeff et al., 1998)) in the late 90's. BASICS is intended for heavy drinking youth who have either experienced problems due to their consumption or are at high risk of experiencing problems. It is conducted over two 50-minute sessions and provides cognitive-behavioral strategies to encourage moderate, low-risk drinking. BASICS also provides personalized feedback on the youth's consumption pattern and advice about ways to reduce risks related to alcohol use in the future (Dimeff et al., 1998). The BASICS program is typically utilized in college settings for adolescents who are entering as freshmen. BASICS involves an assessment of drinking and related problems and one 50-minute session of advice and normative feedback. In one study, adolescents who were high-risk drinkers were offered BASICS

Table 3: Brief interventions

Study Name	Study Type and Population	Intervention Description	Major Outcomes
College Student Drinkers Borsari et al., 2000	College students from an East Coast university reporting binge drinking 2 or more times in the last 30 days N=60	Brief 1-session intervention conducted by a clinical graduate student consisting of 5 parts: 1) personal alcohol use measured and compared to campus and national norms; 2) personal negative consequences; 3) positive and negative expectancies; 4) challenge misconceptions about drinking with accurate information; and 5) provided options to facilitate a decrease in use and recognize high-risk drinking situations.	6 week follow-up Reductions were found for number of drinks per week, number of times drinking per day in the past month, and frequency of heavy drinking. Means (SD) at baseline and 6-week follow up (see table below)
Hospital Setting/ Adolescent Smoking Colby et al., 1998	Patients at two urban Rhode Island hospitals age 14-17 who were also teen smokers N=40 (20 motivational interview/20 brief advice)	Motivational interview consisted of likes and dislikes about smoking; four videotaped vignettes to stimulate discussion about health, social, and addiction consequences, and financial cost; feed-back to increase motiva-tion to change; relation-ship between smoking and other personal ill-ness; an informational handout; and goals for be-havior change and bar-riers to change. This was compared to 5 min. of advice to stop smoking.	3 month follow-up No significant differences between groups. Both groups decreased smoking and made quit attempts. (see table below)

Major Outcomes — Borsari et al., 2000 (Means (SD) at baseline and 6-week follow up):

	Baseline		Follow up		
	Interven-tion	Control	Interven-tion	Control	p-value
# drinks per week	17.57 (8.20)	18.56 (12.48)	11.40 (7.03)	15.78 (8.17)	p<.017
# times consumed alcohol, past month	4.41 (0.62)	4.53 (0.90)	3.83 (0.89)	4.57 (1.07)	p<.017
Frequency of binge drinking, past month	3.20 (0.90)	3.50 (0.90)	2.55 (1.40)	3.37 (1.25)	p<.017

Major Outcomes — Colby et al., 1998:

	Baseline		3 month follow-up	
	Intervention	Control	Intervention	Control
Cigarettes per day	11.0 (9.9)	9.5(10.1)	9.2(12.5)	8.8(10.8)
Smoking days/week	6.2(1.7)	5.4 (2.7)	5.2(2.8)	5.4(2.7)

Study Name	Study Type and Population	Intervention Description	Major Outcomes
Community Dental Care/ Adolescent Smoking Kentala et al., 1999	12-year olds at their annual routine dental examination at a community dental clinic in Finland N=2,586	Dentist inquires with teen about smoking. If teen does not smoke, positive feedback is given regarding abstaining from smoking. After the examination all teens, whether or not they smoke, are shown a set of photographs of harmful discolorations of the teeth caused by smoking and invited to use a mirror to observe if they have any such discolorations.	2 year follow-up No significant differences were found between groups. Prevalence of smoking was 18.1% in intervention group and 20.8% in the control group.
Hospital Emergency Department/Alcohol-Positive Older Adolescents Monti et al., 1999	Emergency department patients at an East Coast hospital age 18-19 who had a positive blood alcohol concentration or a report of drinking alcohol prior to event that precipitated treatment N=94	Motivational interview: 1) introduction and review of event circumstances; 2) pros and cons of motivation; 3) personalized and computerized assessment feedback; 4) imagining the future; and 5) goal setting. All patients, whether or not they were in the intervention, received a set of handouts on avoiding drinking and driving and a referral to local treatment agencies.	6 month follow-up No differences in drinking. Motivational interview group reported fewer alcohol related problems at 6 month follow-up compared to standard care (ES = .23).

Study Name	Study Type and Population	Intervention Description	Major Outcomes
Fraternities/ Alcohol Intervention Larimer et al., 2001	Pledge class members from 12 fraternities at a large West Coast university N=159	1-hour feedback session addressing: 1) evaluation of typical drinking patterns; 2) training in estimation of blood alcohol content; 3) college normative feedback; 4) biphasic effects of alcohol; 5) alcohol-related expectancies; 6) personalized drinking-related consequences; and 7) strategies for more moderate drinking. Intervention fraternity houses also received a 1-hour house-wide feed-back session similar to the individual-ized feed-back session attended by 80% of the house. Control houses received a 1-hour didactic presentation with some skills training, but no motivational feedback components.	**1 year follow-up** Students in the intervention condition reported significantly fewer average drinks per week than the control group (effect size=.42) and greater reductions in typical peak BACs. Means and standard deviations (SD) for alcohol use <table><tr><td></td><td colspan="2">Baseline</td><td colspan="2">1 year follow-up</td></tr><tr><td></td><td>Interven-tion</td><td>Control</td><td>Interven-tion</td><td>Control</td></tr><tr><td>Total average use (# of drinks)</td><td>15.42 (12.05)</td><td>15.56 (10.59)</td><td>12.27 (10.85)</td><td>17.51 (16.96)</td></tr><tr><td>Typical peak BACs</td><td>0.10 (0.08)</td><td>0.09 (0.06)</td><td>0.07 (0.05)</td><td>0.08 (0.07)</td></tr></table>
BASICS/ College Student Drinkers Murphy et al., 2001	High-risk undergraduates at Auburn University, Alabama N=99	50-min motivational interview-ing session referring to a person-alized feed-back sheet. Informa-tion covered included normative college drinking feed-back, BACs, alcohol-related problems, and risk factors. Goals focused on reducing drinking and un-toward consequences. This was compared to an education condi-tion, with those participants watching a 30-min video called "Eddie Talks" and receiving a 20-min generic discussion with a graduate clinician. A control condition received assessments only.	**3 and 9 month follow-up** No significant multivariate effect of group at 9 months. Among heavier drinking students (> 25 drinks per week), BASICS participants showed greater reductions at 3 month follow-up (ES = .99 within group compared to ES = .24 for control and ES = .19 for education) and they maintained these large reductions at the 9 month follow-up. Of note, this was a small sample of drinkers (e.g., n≈14 per group).

Study Name	Study Type and Population	Intervention Description	Major Outcomes
High-Risk College Student Drinkers Marlatt et al., 1998 Bear et al., 2001	College freshman at a large West Coast university identified high-risk N=348 Two year follow-up Same as 1998 study Four year follow-up	Motivational interview during freshman year of college with review of alcohol self-monitoring cards and individualized feedback about drinking patterns, risks, and beliefs about alcohol effects.Norm-ative feedback, perceived risks for future problems, placebo effects, biphasic effects, and risk reduction were reviewed. During year 2, participants were mailed graphic personalized feedback about baseline, 6- and 12-month drinking quantity, frequency, and problems. Individualized feedback about risk, referrals, and the opporunity to have an additional follow-up interview were offered.	2 and 4 year follow-up Quantity of drinking and negative consequences were significantly reduced for intervention participants.

Mean standardized factor scores and (SD)

	Baseline	1-year	2-year	3-year	4-year	Group x time
Frequency, control	0.74 (0.88)	0.80 (0.92)	0.62 (0.84)	0.88 (1.02)	0.71 (0.99)	ns
Frequency, prevention	0.78 (0.88)	0.60 (0.89)	0.52 (0.88)	0.75 (0.93)	0.64 (1.04)	
Quantity, control	0.73 (0.90)	0.76 (0.82)	0.59 (0.85)	0.51 (0.81)	0.38 (0.77)	p<.001
Quantity, prevention	0.91 (0.92)	0.60 (0.89)	0.46 (0.93)	0.48 (0.84)	0.27 (0.78)	
Negative consequences, control	1.46 (1.27)	1.23 (1.37)	0.95 (1.22)	0.80 (1.26)	0.72 (1.25)	p<.05
Negative consequences, prevention	1.39 (1.26)	0.79 (1.24)	0.53 (1.06)	0.52 (1.10)	0.40 (1.06)	

Note: When possible, we provided means and standard deviations associated with the findings that are reported in each study.

during their freshmen year of college. In contrast to students who did not receive the program, BASICS participants showed consistent reductions in both drinking rates and negative consequences experienced at a 2-year follow-up (Marlatt et al., 1998) and continued decreases in negative consequences at a 4-year follow-up (Johnston et al., 2006). This is quite significant as drinking typically tends to escalate during the college years (Johnston et al., 2006). Larimer and colleagues also conducted a brief motivational intervention for first year fraternity members at a large West Coast university (Larimer et al., 2001). Intervention participants received a 1-hour individual tailored feedback session based on information they provided in an assessment. Each interview addressed: evaluation of typical drinking patterns, training in estimating blood alcohol concentration (BAC), comparisons of typical patterns of alcohol use and perceived norms to actual college-wide norms, review of the biphasic effects of alcohol, identification and challenge of alcohol-related expectancies, and a review of strategies to encourage moderate drinking. At a one-year follow-up assessment, students who received the intervention reported a greater reduction in average drinks per week and greater reductions in typical peak BACs (Monti et al., 1999).

Finally, Monti and his colleagues have utilized brief motivational intervention approaches targeting alcohol and cigarettes in both emergency room settings and clinic settings with successful results (Colby et al., 1998). Colby et al. implemented a brief motivational interven-tion targeting smoking for 14 to 17 year olds who were treated in an emergency room, outpatient clinic, or inpatient unit. Each session began with an open-ended exploration of the adolescent's likes and dislikes about smoking. Teens also watched four videotaped vignettes used to stimulate discus-sion on health effects, social consequences, addiction, and financial cost of

smoking. Teens were also provided with feedback on an individual assessment. This intervention was compared to five minutes of brief advice. Findings at a 3-month follow-up indicated support for both the intervention and the brief advice conditions as 2/3 of the sample reported having made a serious quit attempt (Barnett et al., 2001). Monti's group also conducted a similar brief motivational intervention for older adolescents (18-19) targeting alcohol use (Monti et al., 1999). Youth who were treated in an emergency room for an alcohol-related injury received either a brief motivational intervention or standard care. Findings at 6-month follow-up indicated that teens who received the brief motivational intervention were less likely to report driving after drinking and alcohol-related problems than those who received standard care (Komro et al., 1994).

Community based interventions

Because there are so many factors that can impact adolescent drinking, some interventions have utilized a community-based approach to implement changes in both the individual and the environment. Typically, these types of programs involve not only the individual teen, but also the parents, schools and school staff, and the surrounding community. Table 4 provides information on several community-based prevention programs that have published *at least* a one year follow-up and have been shown to be efficacious. We highlight some of these programs below.

Project Northland is a multilevel, multi-year program that targeted 6th to 12th graders from 1991-1998 in 24 school districts in northeastern Minnesota. Phase I consisted of 3 years of social-behavioral curricula in the classroom, parent involvement programs, and community task forces. During 9th and 10th grade, there was an interim phase in which 9th graders received a brief five-session class-room program. No programming was conducted in 10th grade. During Phase II, a six

Table 4: Community-based programs

Study Name	Study Type and Population	Intervention Description	Major Outcomes
Communities Mobilizing for Change on Alcohol (CMCA) Wagenaar et al., 2000	Socially and geographically diverse communities in Minnesota and Wisconsin (ave. pop. = 20,000) N=15	Mobilizing the entire community as a vehicle for change, not just as a site for an intervention. To reduce the accessibility of alcoholic beverages to underage youth by changing: 1) the influences on policies and practices (e.g. parents, youth, alcohol merchants); 2) policies and practices themselves (e.g. institutional policies, local ordinances, enforcement of existing laws, and volunteer efforts); 3) youth access to alcohol; 4) levels of youth alcohol consumption; and 5) youth alcohol problems.	3 year follow-up Several trends emerged. Alcohol merchants in the intervention community increased ID checks and reduced alcohol sales to minors. 18-20 year olds reduced their likelihood of trying to buy alcohol and fewer 18-20 year olds in the intervention community reported 30 day drinking. (see tables below)

% alcohol merchants ID checks at on-sale establishments

	Intervention	Control	p-value
1992	60.2	49.1	p=.06
1995	78.1	56.5	

% 18-20 year olds trying to buy alcohol

	Intervention	Control	p-value
1992	10.4	10.9	p=.06
1995	7.5	10.7	

% 18-20 year olds 30-day drinking prevalence

	Intervention	Control	p-value
1992	56.3	55.7	p=.07
1995	59.5	62.5	

Study Name	Study Type and Population	Intervention Description	Major Outcomes
Community Trials Intervention to Reduce High-Risk Drinking (RHRD) Grube, 1997	Intervention and comparison communities in northern California, southern California, and South Carolina (pop. = ~100,000 ea.) N=6	The Underage Access Component of RHRD tested three types of interventions: 1) enforcement of underage alcohol sales laws (warning letters to sales outlets, decoy underage sales attempts, citations for violations); 2) responsible beverage service (RBS) training for off-sale clerks, managers, and owners; and 3) media advocacy (newspapers, TV, and other news events) designed for awareness of enforcement and increased public support for intervention activities.	10 month follow-up More citations were given to beverage outlets in the intervention communities. Of 148 outlets, 22 citations were given during the 10 months of the intervention versus 4 during the previous non-intervention year. Sales of alcohol to minors were significantly reduced after the intervention. Intervention communities had fewer sales of alcohol to minors compared to the control communities at post-test. % outlets selling alcohol to underage buyers, all communities combined <table><tr><td></td><td>All 3 interventions</td><td>Control</td><td>p-value</td></tr><tr><td>1995</td><td>45</td><td>47</td><td>p<.0001</td></tr><tr><td>1996</td><td>16</td><td>35</td><td></td></tr></table>
Holder et al., 2000	Same as 1997 study	Interventions for all ages consisting of community mobilization; full enforcement of activities related to drinking and driving (e.g. roadside checkpoints); restricting access to alcohol; and RBS training.	5 year follow-up Traffic data for the intervention communities showed a decline in nighttime injury crashes (10%), crashes in which the driver had been drinking (6%), and assault injuries observed in emergency departments (43%). Population surveys showed a decline in alcohol consumption per drinking occasion and driving after drinking versus the comparison communities (p-values and control group means not reported in study). Self-reported # of drinks of alcohol consumed per drinking occasion <table><tr><td></td><td>Intervention</td></tr><tr><td>1992</td><td>M= 1.37</td></tr><tr><td>1996</td><td>M= 1.29</td></tr></table> Self-reported rate of driving after too much to drink, # times per 6-month period <table><tr><td></td><td>Intervention</td></tr><tr><td>1992</td><td>M= 0.43</td></tr><tr><td>1996</td><td>M= 0.22</td></tr></table>

Study Name	Study Type and Population	Intervention Description	Major Outcomes
Community Trials Intervention to Reduce High-Risk Drinking (RHRD) cont.			Self-reported driving when over the legal limit, # times per 6-month period Intervention 1992 — M=0.77 1996 — M=0.38
Saving Lives Program Hingson et al., 1996	Massachusetts communities varying in population size and geographic location within the state N=6	Community driven initiatives to reduce drunk driving and speeding ($70,000 per community for 5 years). City departments and private citizens implemented a community program that included media campaigns, business information programs, speeding and drunk driving awareness days, telephone hotlines, police training, high school peer-led education, Students Against Drunk Driving chapters, college prevention programs, alcohol-free prom nights, beer keg registration, and increased surveillance for liquor stores.	9 year follow-up Compared with the rest of Massachusetts (the control group), program cities had a decline in fatal crashes (25%), fatal crashes involving alcohol (42%), visible injuries per 100 crashes (5%), proportion of vehicles observed speeding (50%), proportion of teenagers who drove after drinking (50%), and number of fatal crashes involving drivers 15 to 25 years of age (39%). Among teenagers, the proportion who believed the license of a person caught drinking and driving could be suspended before a trial increased (from 61% to 76%) while it did not change statewide. **# of fatal crashes** |	Intervention	Control	p-value
1984	M=178	M=3030	p=.02
1993	M=120	M=2707	| **# of alcohol-involved fatal crashes** |	Intervention	Control	p-value
1984	M=69	M=1162	p=.01
1993	M=36	M=1039	| Note: A log scale was used to compare percentage changes between the intervention area and control area.

Study Name	Study Type and Population	Intervention Description	Major Outcomes
Project Northland Perry et al., 1996	School districts and adjacent rural Minnesota communities targeting those students who were the class of 1998 (6th graders in 1991) N=24	School-based intervention programs in 6th, 7th, and 8th grade (see below) and in intervention communities during these same years. Each year's program was unique and tailored to students' developmental level. Intervention included parent involvement, behavioral curricula, peer led activities, and participation of a community task force (e.g. government officials, law enforcement, health professionals, school personnel, youth workers, clergy, parents, and adolescents). Foci by grade level: 6th grade – "Slick Tracy" (5 sessions), skills to communicate with their parents about alcohol. 7th grade – "Amazing Alternatives!" (8 sessions), peer influence and normative expectations. 8th grade – "PowerLines" (8 sessions), bringing about community-level changes in alcohol-related programs and policies.	3 year follow-up Students in intervention districts had statistically significant lower scores on likelihood of drinking, onset of alcohol use, and prevalence of alcohol use (shown) than students who did not participate in Project Northland. Students in the intervention showed lower scores on prevalence of cigarette and marijuana use. % past month alcohol use for all students % cigarette use for all students % marijuana use for all students The project was more successful with those students who were non-users at baseline compared with those who had already initiated use.

% past month alcohol use for all students

	Intervention	Control	p-value
1991	M= 6.9	M= 3.9	
1994	M= 23.6	M= 29.2	p<.05

% cigarette use for all students

	Intervention	Control	p-value
1991	M= 6.9	M= 4.7	
1994	M= 24.8	M= 30.7	ns

% marijuana use for all students

	Intervention	Control	p-value
1991	M= 0.7	M= 0.4	
1994	M= 7.4	M= 8.6	ns

Study Name	Study Type and Population	Intervention Description	Major Outcomes
Project Northland Perry et al., 2002	Same cohort as in 1996 study, now in 11th and 12th grades (minimal intervention in years 9 and 10). N=24	Phase II (1996-1998) of Project Northland implemented in grades 11 and 12. Included classroom curricula (see below), parent education, print media campaigns, youth development and community organizing via peer action and community action teams. 11th grade – "Class Action" (6 sessions), social and legal consequences and community responsibilities. 12th grade – none.	During the interim phase (grades 9 and 10) alcohol use rates increased among students in the intervention schools. During Phase II (grades 11 and 12), there was a reduced tendency to use alcohol, binge drinking, and ability to obtain alcohol.

Changes in past month alcohol use

	Intervention	Control	p-value
1996	M=1.96 (0.07)	M=1.83 (0.07)	p=.08
Growth rate	0.13	0.20	p=.07

Changes in binge drinking (5+ drinks)

	Intervention	Control	p-value
1996	M=1.60 (0.06)	M=1.45 (0.05)	p=.02
Growth rate	0.09	0.18	p=.02

Mean success rates for ability to obtain alcohol, all outlets (analyzed at community level)

	Intervention	Control	p-value
1991	M=42.3	M=47.9	p=.57
1998	M=13.6	M=25.4	p=.05

Study Name	Study Type and Population	Intervention Description	Major Outcomes
Raising Healthy Children Project (RHC) Brown et al., 2005	Suburban public schools north of Seattle, Washington, comprising 959 1st and 2nd grade students N=10	Prevention strategies addressing risk and protective factors in four key domains: 1) School: teacher/staff development workshops for elementary school and first year middle school teachers in proactive classroom management techniques; cooperative learning methods; and strategies to promote student motivation, participation, reading, and interpersonal and problem-solving skills 2) Student: volunteer participation in after-school tutoring sessions and study clubs during grades 4-6 and individualized booster sessions and group-based work-shops during middle and high school 3) Peer: through classroom instruction and summer camps during elementary school and social skills booster retreats in middle school students learned and practiced social, emotional, and problem-solving skills 4) Family: multiple session parenting workshops and in-home services for selected families during grades 1-8 covering specific risk areas (e.g. transition to high school, peer influences, family expectations, family conflict)	5 - 9 year follow-up in grades 6 - 10 Findings indicated greater linear declines for frequency of alcohol and marijuana use during grades 8-10 for the intervention group relative to the controls

Note: When possible, we provided means and standard deviations associated with the findings that are reported in each study.

session classroom curriculum was implemented in 11th grade, parents received behavioral tips through postcards, print media campaigns occurred, peer leaders and teams were created at each high school to develop and promote alcohol-free activities, and community action teams were formed to help reduce commercial and social access to alcohol among minors (Komro et al., 1994; Perry et al., 2000). Briefly, results from Phase I indicated that youth in the intervention schools were less likely to report a tendency to use alcohol and also had lower rates of past month alcohol use and binge drinking than the control schools. In contrast, during the interim phase when little programming occurred, adolescents in the intervention schools increased their tendency to use alcohol, past month alcohol use, past week alcohol use, and binge drinking. However, Phase II results indicated that the intervention was again successful in reducing binge drinking and adolescents' tendency to use alcohol. Phase II results also indicated a large reduction in underage alcohol purchases in the intervention communities. Perry and colleagues emphasize the importance of continuing prevention programming throughout the period of adolescence (Perry et al., 2002).

Communities Mobilizing for Change on Alcohol (CMCA) is a community-based program designed to reduce youth access to alcohol by changing community policies and practices. Data were collected through surveys of high school students and youth age 18-20, surveys of alcohol retailers, alcohol purchase attempts, content analysis of media coverage, arrest and crash indicators, surveys of strategy team members, and process records (Wagenaar et al., 1999; Wagenaar et al., 1994). The program worked with local public officials, enforcement agencies, alcohol merchants, the media, schools, and other community institutions that influence the environment. The target of this intervention was the entire community rather than individual adolescents. Seven communities were randomly assigned to receive the intervention and eight communities served as a control. Baseline surveys were conducted in each community and again three years later. Findings indicated that in the intervention communities, establishments which sold alcohol (e.g., bars, restaurants) were more likely to check ID and less likely to sell to underage buyers. In addition, surveys of 18-20 year olds indicated a decrease in the number of youth attempting to buy alcoholic beverages. There was no effect of the intervention on high school seniors (Wagenaar et al., 2000).

The Community Trials Intervention to Reduce High-Risk Drinking (RHRD) is a community-based program that targeted all ages and comprised responsible beverage service (e.g., reduce the likelihood of customer intoxication at licensed establishments), increasing restrictions on access to alcohol, enforcement (e.g., reduce underage drinking and drunk driving), and community mobilization (e.g., increase community awareness) (Holder et al., 1997). The project took place over five years from 1992-1996 in three intervention communities. The intervention and comparison communities were not randomized, but they were matched on the basis of similar local geographic area characteristics, industrial/agricultural bases and minority compositions (Holder et al., 1997). Outcomes were assessed by conducting 120 general population telephone surveys of randomly selected individuals per month for 66 months, examining traffic data on motor vehicle crashes, and conducting emergency department surveys in one intervention and one control site (Holder et al., 2000). Findings indicated that people in the intervention communities reported less heavy drinking. In addition, there were declines in night time crashes (from 8pm to 4am), driving after drinking crashes, and assault injuries observed in the emergency departments (Holder et al., 2000). The impact of the

RHRD intervention on youth substance use was not reported; thus the program is promising, but its effectiveness among youth has not been established.

Cognitive behavioral therapy

Cognitive behavioral therapy (CBT) approaches for alcohol and drug use have previously been neglected in adolescent intervention outcome research (Brown and D'Amico, 2003; Waldron and Kaminer, 2004). A recent review article, however, has shown that current work in this area has begun to support this approach (Waldron and Kaminer, 2004).

Typically, CBT approaches emphasize that alcohol and drug use are learned behaviors that are impacted by environmental factors. These approaches tend to include components such as self-monitoring, avoidance of stimulus cues, altering reinforcement, and coping-skills training to avoid using (Kaminer and Slesnick, 2005; Waldron and Kaminer, 2004). The CBT interventions discussed in this section are utilized for youth who are already using and/or abusing substances; thus, they are considered to be selective or indicated prevention approaches. Because of the methodological problems with early studies, it is only within the last decade that rigorous clinical trials of CBT have been conducted (Waldron and Kaminer, 2004). Thus, Table 5 provides examples of randomized trials of these interventions that have *at least* a 6-month follow-up. We highlight some of these programs below.

Kaminer and colleagues have tested CBT for adolescent substance abusers in several studies (Kaminer and Burleson, 1999; Kaminer et al., 1998; Kaminer et al., 2002). In a recent evaluation, they compared 8 weeks of CBT to 8 weeks of psychoeducational therapy (PET) among 88 dually diagnosed (substance use and depression) adolescents. PET core components included either a didactic or videotaped presentation about the immediate

and delayed multidimensional problems associated with adolescent substance use disorders (Kaminer et al., 2002). Despite lower relapse rates at a 3-month follow-up for CBT youth, findings from the 9-month follow-up found no differences on relapse rates between the CBT and PET groups (Kaminer et al., 2002). They also found that youth who had a diagnosis of conduct disorder (in addition to substance abuse and/or dependence) were less likely to complete treatment and follow-up assessments, highlighting that dually diagnosed youth are often at increased risk (Kaminer et al., 2002).

More recent models of CBT have begun to include both behavioral strategies and family therapy to treat adolescent substance abuse as this approach may provide better outcomes over either individual approach (Waldron et al., 2001). Waldron and colleagues conducted a randomized clinical trial of individual CBT, functional family therapy (FFT), combined individual and family therapy, and a peer group intervention for 114 substance-abusing youth (Waldron et al., 2001). Teens received 12 hours of therapy in the FFT, CBT, and group intervention and 24 hours of therapy in the combined condition. The CBT skills-training program was designed to teach youth self-control and coping skills and consisted of a two-session motivational intervention and 10 skills modules, including communication training, problem solving, peer refusal, negative mood management, social support, work- and school-related skills, and relapse prevention. Overall, findings indicated that youth in the combined therapy condition maintained a reduction in days using marijuana at the 7-month follow-up compared to pre-treatment. In addition, youth in the group condition reduced their substance use from pre-treatment to the 7-month follow-up. FFT and CBT youth did not change their use rates significantly from pre-treatment (Waldron et al., 2001). Further research is needed in this area to determine the long-term

Table 5: Cognitive Behavior Therapy (CBT) Interventions

Study Name	Study Type and Population	Intervention Description	Major Outcomes
Cognitive Behavioral Therapy (CBT) Azrin et al., 1996	Psychoactive substance abusers (DSM-III R diagnosis) N=57 adults N=17 youth	Supportive discussion counseling was compared to a directive behavioral program (average treatment 8 months or 17 sessions). The behavioral program consisted of: stimulus and urge control and behavioral contracting, especially between youth and parents.	<u>9 month follow-up</u> Supportive discussion subjects (both adolescents and adults) did not show change in use. Behavioral subjects (both adolescents and adults) decreased drug use 63% by end of treatment and 73% at follow-up.
Kaminer et al., 1998	Dually diagnosed (depression and substance use) consenting adolescents aged 13 to 18 N=32	Participants were randomized into one of two outpatient group psychotherapies: 1) CBT 2) Interactional Treatment (IT) (e.g., explore interpersonal relationships, foster insight) 12-week manually guided program.	<u>3 month follow-up</u> CBT adolescents showed a significant reduction on the ASI (Addiction Severity Index) as compared with the IT group. Mean (SD) ASI substance use scores <table><tr><td></td><td>CBT</td><td>IT</td><td>p-value</td></tr><tr><td>Baseline</td><td>3.50 (1.83)</td><td>4.33 (1.67)</td><td></td></tr><tr><td>Follow up</td><td>1.50 (1.08)</td><td>3.13 (2.64)</td><td>p=.04</td></tr></table>
Kaminer et al., 1999	Same as 1998 study.	Same as 1998 study.	<u>15 month follow-up</u> No differential improvements as a function of therapy type. CBT and IT maintained treatment gains from the 3 month follow-up in substance abuse, family function, and psychiatric status on the ASI.

Study Name	Study Type and Population	Intervention Description	Major Outcomes
Waldron et al., 2001	Substance abusing adolescents aged 13 to 17 in New Mexico referred from the juvenile justice system, public school system, self or parent, and other treatment agencies N=114	Participants were randomly assigned to one of four treatment conditions: 1) Functional Family Therapy (FFT) 2) Individual CBT 3) Combination of FFT and CBT 4) A psychoeducational group Three treatment conditions consisted of 12 total hours of therapy (FFT, CBT, and group) while the joint FFT and CBT involved 24 hours of therapy. Sessions were led by trained therapists (doctoral and masters level).	**4 month follow-up** Significantly fewer days of marijuana use for FFT and combination FFT and CBT. **7 month follow-up** Significant reduction in percentage of days of marijuana use for combination FFT and CBT and psychoeducational groups. **% mean days of use for adolescent marijuana use (SD)**
Kaminer et al., 2002	Adolescents aged 13 to 18 consecutively referred to an outpatient program for psychoactive substance use disorder N=88	Participants were randomized into one of two group conditions: 1) CBT 2) Psychoeducational Therapy (PET) Each therapy curriculum consisted of 8 weekly sessions of 75-90 minutes conducted by a pair of trained therapists (doctoral and masters level).	**9 month follow-up** Addiction Severity Index (ASI) scores improved regardless of condition.

% mean days of use for adolescent marijuana use (SD)

	FFT	CBT	Combo	Group
Pre-treatment	54.88 (32.71)	52.19 (32.37)	56.73 (34.96)	66.21 (27.02)
4 month follow up	24.95 (26.96)	52.09 (40.10)	38.08 (36.49)	55.73 (34.86)
7 month follow-up	40.10 (40.07)	51.13 (37.35)	36.44 (37.24)	41.88 (40.06)

Study Name	Study Type and Population	Intervention Description	Major Outcomes
Latimer et al., 2003	Youth mainly aged 14 to 17 who met diagnostic criteria for one or more psychoactive substance use disorders N=43	A randomized control trial of two treatment conditions: 1) Integrated Family and Cognitive-Behavioral Therapy (IFCBT) 2) Drugs Harm Psychoeducation curriculum (DHPE) IFCBT consisted of 16 weekly individual family therapy sessions and 32 peer group cognitive-behavioral sessions that met twice a week. The DHPE control group consisted of adolescents meeting for 16 90-minute weekly sessions.	6 month follow-up IFCBT adolescents showed significantly lower average number of days per month using alcohol (2.03 vs. 6.06 days) and marijuana (5.67 vs. 13.83 days) as compared to the DHPE group.
Dennis et al., 2004	Adolescents aged 12 to 18 with cannabis related disorders appropriate for outpatient or intensive outpatient treatment N=600	Adolescents were randomized into four short-term outpatient interventions: 1) Motivational Enhancement Therapy (MET) plus CBT (5-sessions) (MET/CBT) 2) MET plus CBT (12 sessions) (MET/CBT12) 3) MET/CBT12 plus family education and therapy components (22 sessions) (Family Support Network [FSN]) 4) Adolescent Community Reinforcement Approach (14 sessions) (ACRA) 5) Multidimensional Family Therapy (12-15 sessions) (MDFT)	12 month follow-up Total days abstinent did not differ for the five programs. Cost-effectiveness analyses indicated that MET/CBTS was more cost effective than FSN and MDFT.

Note: When possible, we provided means and standard deviations associated with the findings that are reported in each study.

effects of CBT and to better understand the impact of integrating family therapy and individual behavioral therapy for youth.

Family oriented interventions

Interventions that involve the family to a greater degree tend to target youth who are at higher risk, such as juvenile delinquents (Dembo et al., 2002; Henggeler et al., 2002), youth who have parents who use substances or who are already using substances themselves (Liddle and Hogue, 2000), and youth whose families have immigrated to the United States (Spoth et al., 1999). There are a few exceptions, such as the Strengthening Families Program (Kumpfer et al., 1996; Spoth et al., 1999) and the "Families in Action" program (Abbey et al., 2000), which have been used in school settings as universal prevention programs. On the whole, however, family interventions tend to be more intensive and are typically considered to be indicated prevention approaches. Compared to universal and selective prevention approaches, indicated approaches require substantial resources in multiple contexts to provoke and sustain lifestyle changes (Kumpfer et al., 2003; Winters, 2001).

Table 6 provides information on several family-based prevention programs that have published *at least* a one-year follow-up and have been shown to be efficacious. We highlight some of these programs below.

Overall, research in this area has found that cognitive behavioral family-focused programs appear to be more effective than didactic parent education programs, which tend to provide knowledge-only sessions (Kumpfer et al., 2003). This finding emphasizes what has also been shown in individual and group programs for youth: disseminating information in an interactive versus didactic style is associated with greater positive change.

Family-based interventions are conceptually based on family systems theory (Hoffman, 2002; Nichols and Schwartz,

1998), which emphasizes the relational and contextual nature of human behavior (Ozechowski and Liddle, 2000). This perspective therefore focuses on how adolescent functioning is associated with parental, sibling, and extended-family functioning and how these systems communicate together. Specifically, a family systems orientation views adolescent alcohol and drug use behavior in the context of the family environment: how do levels of emotional connection and separation, harmony, and conflict among family members contribute to adolescent substance use and how does adolescent substance use contribute to these same factors? (Ozechowski and Liddle, 2000).

The Strengthening Families Program (SFP) has been used as a universal, selective, and indicated program (Kumpfer et al., 2003). A seven session version of the SFP, called the Iowa SFP (ISFP) was developed for use in middle schools. The ISFP focuses on enhancing family protective processes and reducing family risk factors and includes seven 2-hour sessions conducted once per week for seven consecutive weeks (Spoth et al., 1999). Parent training sessions focus on clarifying expectations based on child development norms, using appropriate disciplinary practices, managing strong emotions, and communicating more effectively with teens (Spoth et al., 1999). Adolescent sessions focus on similar content as the parent sessions, and also include skills training for coping with peer pressure (e.g., refusal skills), as well as other personal and social skills training (e.g., how to manage stress; Spoth et al., 1999). During the first six sessions, parents and youth jointly participate in a family session (1 hour) after they have practiced the skills they had learned in their separate sessions (1 hour). The seventh session includes only the family session.

A longitudinal study of the ISFP was conducted with 446 families from 22 rural school districts in the Midwest. Analyses

Table 6: Family Oriented Interventions

Study Name	Study Type and Population	Intervention Description	Major Outcomes
Brief Strategic Family Therapy (BSFT) Santisteban et al., 2003	Hispanic families in Miami (largely immigrant) from poor to middle class backgrounds having an adolescent (age 12-18 years) with reported behavior problem; self- or school counselor referred N=85	The BSFT condition consisted of between 4 and 20 weekly sessions of therapy (M=11.2, SD = 3.8) of approximately 1 hour. All family members who lived with the adolescent were invited to partici-pate. Major therapeutic techni-ques were the therapist: 1) "joining" the family to support the family structure and track its patterns; 2) "diagnosing" repetitive patterns in the family interactions; and 3) "restructuring" or change-produc-ing strategies to create new family patterns. The control condition consisted of between 6 and 16 weekly sessions (M=8.8; SD = 2.6) of approximately 90 minutes. The control group participated in group therapy sessions that did not include a family functioning focus.	Comparisons were made between intake (pre) scores and termination (post) scores. In the BSFT condition, parents reported improvement in adolescent conduct problems and delinquency. Observer ratings and self-reports of family functioning also improved. Adolescent marijuana use decreased for BSFT youth compared to control youth. The groups did not significantly differ in alcohol use at termination.

Means of drug use

	BSFT		Control		
	Intake	Post	Pre	Post	p-value
Days using alcohol, past month	2.24	1.43	0.77	0.04	ns
Days using marijuana, past month	2.24	1.10	0.64	0.73	p<.05

Study Name	Study Type and Population	Intervention Description	Major Outcomes
Familias Unidas Pantin et al., 2003	Hispanic families of 6th and 7th grade students from 3 public middle schools in low-income areas of Miami N=167	Intervention parents attended weekly group sessions for approximately 9 months (M = 24 sessions; SD = 13.9) of approximately 1 hour. Groups consisted of one parent from each family for a total of 10-12 parents per group. The three stages of intervention were: 1) engaging parents in intervention and creating social support among parents; 2) promoting parental investment by introducing three adolescent "worlds" – family, peers, and school; and 3) fostering parenting skills to decrease problem behavior. In the last stage, parent-adolescent discussions were facilitated in home-based family sessions. The control group did not participate in any contact with intervention staff outside of completing assessments.	Familias Unidas participation resulted in increased parental investment and decreased adolescent behavior problems. There was a sharp increase in adolescent behavior problems between 3 and 6 months for the control group coinciding with summer vacation. Conversely, intervention adolescents showed a steady decline in behavior problems. However, by 12 month follow-up, there was a similar pattern of decline for both groups. Mean adolescent behavior problems <table><tr><td>Months</td><td>Intervention</td><td>Control</td></tr><tr><td>0</td><td>1.03</td><td>2.12</td></tr><tr><td>3</td><td>0.51</td><td>0.34</td></tr><tr><td>6</td><td>0.53</td><td>2.43</td></tr><tr><td>9</td><td>-0.67</td><td>0.37</td></tr><tr><td>12</td><td>-2.00</td><td>-1.91</td></tr></table> Note: numbers represent mean standardized scores.

Study Name	Study Type and Population	Intervention Description	Major Outcomes
Families in Action (FIA) Pilgrim et al., 1998	Families of middle or junior high school students in 4 largely rural schools N=58 students N=61 parents	Parents and youth in the FIA program together voluntarily attended 6 weekly 2 ½ hour sessions with approximately 5-12 other families. Sessions focused on: 1) positive thinking to reach behavioral goals; 2) positive communication skills and consequences for actions; and 3) school success and avoidance of alcohol and other substances. The sessions targeted individual, family, peer, school, and community domains. The control group was comprised of those who did not volunteer for the program and did not receive any intervention.	1 year follow-up Effects were only significant for boys. FIA boys scored higher than control group boys on appropriate attitude toward alcohol, age reported "ok" to drink alcohol, school attainment, and peer attachment.

Alcohol use and attitudes, by gender, at 1 year follow-up

	Girls		Boys		p-value (boys only)
	Inter-vention	Con-trol	Inter-vention	Con-trol	
Appropriate alcohol attitudes	2.35	2.51	2.74	2.43	p <.01
Age OK to drink alcohol	17.48	18.33	19.96	16.27	p<.03
School Attachment	.59	.56	.68	.49	p<.03
Peer Attachment	.87	.83	.89	.70	p<.05

1 year follow-up
Parents in FIA reported more involvement in school activities and more involvement in family counseling activities than control group parents.

Parental involvement

	Intervention	Control	p-value
School activities	M=.65	M=.54	p<.002
Family counseling	M=.52	M=.32	p<.001

Study Name	Study Type and Population	Intervention Description	Major Outcomes
Families in Action (FIA) Abbey et al., 2000	Families of middle or junior high school students in 4 schools in a rural county in northeastern Michigan N=29 students N=28 parents	Same as 1998 study.	<u>1 year follow-up</u> FIA students reported greater family cohesion, less family fighting, greater school attachment, higher self-esteem, and higher age "ok" to drink alcohol than control group students. Students: _(see table below)_ FIA parents reported stronger attitudes in opposition to alcohol use by minors and that alcohol should not be consumed until an older age compared to control group parents. Parents: _(see table below)_
Family Empowerment Intervention (FEI) Dembo, Seeberger et al., 2000	Juvenile offenders aged 11-18 years at the Hillsborough County Juvenile Assessment Center, FL N=272	FEI families received three 1-hour home-based meetings per week for 10 weeks with a clinician-trained paraprofessional. The control group received monthly phone contacts and referral information.	<u>1 year follow-up</u> FEI participants reported 1) fewer drug sales, 2) less marijuana use, and 3) a lower frequency of getting drunk on alcohol compared to the control group.
Dembo, Ramirez-Garnica et al., 2000	Same as above	Same as above	<u>1 year follow-up</u> FEI participants and control group did not differ on arrest charges or total number of arrests.
Dembo et al., 2002	Same as above	Same as above	<u>36 month follow-up</u> There were no significant differences in self-reported heavy drinking between the FEI group and the control group.

Students:

	Intervention	Control	p-value
Family cohesion	.74	.63	p=.03
Family fighting	1.32	2.48	p=.002
School attachment	.75	.62	p=.01
Self-esteem	.87	.77	p=.003
Age OK to drink alcohol	18.08	17.16	p=.04

Parents:

	Intervention	Control	p-value
Attitudes opposed to minor's alcohol use	3.51	3.33	p=.04
Age OK to drink alcohol	20.84	19.82	p=.05

Study Name	Study Type and Population	Intervention Description	Major Outcomes
Iowa Strengthening Families Program (ISFP) Spoth et al., 1999	Families of all 6th graders from 22 rural school districts in a Midwestern state N=446	The ISFP program is 7 weekly sessions of approximately 2 hours in a group of 3-15 families. Both parents and youth attend separate concurrent sessions for the first hour of skills-building followed by a joint family session where they practice skills learned in their separate sessions. The parent curriculum teaches clarifying expectations based on child development norms, appropriate disciplinary practices, managing strong emotions, and communicating effectively. The youth sessions are similar but additionally teach skills for dealing with peer pressure and social and personal skills. Together, parents and youth practice conflict resolution and communication. There was a minimal contact control group.	(see below)

1 year follow-up

Alcohol Initiation Index (AII) scores were lower for ISFP participants at both the 1- and 2-year follow ups.

% of users and relative reduction of new user rates, at 1-year follow up

	Pre-test		1-year follow up			
	Int user	Cntl user	Int user	Cntl user	Int new user	Cntl new user
Ever used alcohol	12.4	16.1	26.7	36.1	16.3	23.8
Ever used alcohol w/0 permission	2.5	4.5	8.7	20.0	6.4	16.2
Ever drunk	1.9	1.9	6.8	9.0	5.1	7.2

Note: no p values reported. N=155 (control) and 161 (ISFP). New users = new users at 1 year follow-up.

2 year follow-up

% of users and relative reduction of new user rates, at 2-year follow up

	Pre-test		1-year follow up			
	Int user	Cntl user	Int user	Cntl user	Int new user	Cntl new user
Ever used alcohol	12.4	16.3	35.3	56.0	26.1	47.5
Ever used alcohol w/0 permission	2.0	4.3	19.0	41.8	17.3	39.3
Ever drunk	2.0	1.4	9.8	19.1	8.0	18.0

Note: no p values reported. N=141 (control) and 153 (ISFP).

Study Name	Study Type and Population	Intervention Description	Major Outcomes
Iowa Strengthening Families Program (ISFP) Spoth et al., 2001	Families of all 6th graders from 33 rural schools in a Midwestern state N=667	Participation in the above ISFP program or the Preparing for the Drug Free Years Program (PDFY). The PDFY program was a weekly 5-session program of approximately 2 hours (4 program sessions are for parents only) with an average of 10 total families. Parent sessions taught risk factors for substance use, developing clear guidelines for substance use behaviors, enhancing parent-child bonding, and providing appropriate consequences. Youth were instructed on peer resistance skills. A control group was mailed 4 leaflets on adolescent development.	4 year follow-up Follow up data collected in 10th grade showed more significant differences between ISFP and the control group than on PDFY-control-SP comparisons. Lifetime substance use behavior, 10th grade follow up

Lifetime substance use behavior, 10th grade follow up

	New user proportion			Relative reduction	
	PDFY	ISFP	Cntl	PDFY vs. cntl (%)	ISFP vs. cntl (%)
Ever drank alcohol	.60	.50	.68	11.3	26.4**
Ever drank alcohol w/o permission	.51	.40	.59	12.3	32.0**
Ever drunk	.36	.26	.44	19.4	40.1**
Ever smoked cigarettes	.44	.33	.50	12.5	34.8**
Ever used marijuana	.11	.07	.17	36.6	55.7*

*p < .05, **p < .01

Study Name	Study Type and Population	Intervention Description	Major Outcomes
Spoth et al., 2004	Same as 2001 study at 12th grade follow up	Same as 2001 study	6 year follow-up Lifetime use of alcohol, lifetime cigarette use, and lifetime use of marijuana among those in the ISFP group showed significantly slower overall growth compared with the control group. PDFY only showed delayed growth effects in tobacco use.

Study Name	Study Type and Population	Intervention Description	Major Outcomes
Multidimensional Family Therapy (MDFT) Liddle et al., 2001	Clinically referred marijuana- and alcohol-abusing adolescents aged 13 to 18 years N=182	Youth were randomly assigned to receive Multidimensional Family Therapy (MDFT), Multifamily Educational Intervention (MEI), or Adolescent Group Therapy (AGT). Each treatment consisted of between 14 -16 weekly sessions over 5-6 months in a clinic setting. MDFT was a comprehensive, multi-systemic approach whereby each area of the adolescent's life is assessed. The three phases are: building social competence; promoting new areas of functioning; and bridging ideas, skills, and behaviors begun in treatment into real-world environments by focusing on generalization maintenance of change.	1 year follow-up Improvements in all three groups, with MDFT showing the most improvement.

% of youth who reported a clinically significant reduction in drug use

	MDFT Intervention	MEI Intervention	AGT Intervention
At termination	42	32	25
1 year follow-up	45 p=.672	26	32

Study Name	Study Type and Population	Intervention Description	Major Outcomes
Multisystemic Therapy (MST) Henggeler et al., 1992	Serious juvenile offenders (mean age 15.2 years; average previous arrests = 3.5; including 1 violent crime) referred by the Department of Youth Services in SC, N=84	Multisystemic therapy (MST) of an average of 13.4 weeks (SD = 4.2; mode = 16.0; range = 5 to 23) for a total of 33 hours (SD = 29) of direct contact. MST is a problem-focused intervention that targets multiple systems, including the family, peer, school, and other systems as needed. The control group received usual services.	MST participants reported fewer arrests and spent an average of 10 fewer weeks incarcerated. 59 weeks post-referral <table><tr><td></td><td>Intervention</td><td>Control</td><td>p-value</td></tr><tr><td>Arrests</td><td>0.87 (1.34)</td><td>1.52 (1.55)</td><td>p=.05</td></tr><tr><td>Incarceration (in weeks)</td><td>5.8 (13.9)</td><td>16.2 (19.1)</td><td>p=.006</td></tr></table>
Henggeler et al., 2002	Substance-abusing juvenile offenders (mean age 19.6 years) of those above, 4 year follow up N=80	Same as 1992 study.	Self reported drug use did not differ at 4-year follow up between MST and control participants. Differences were found on biological indicators of marijuana use with MST participants showing higher rates of abstinence than control participants. 4 year follow-up (%) Illicit drug use – biological indicators <table><tr><td></td><td>Intervention</td><td>Control</td><td></td></tr><tr><td>Abstinent from marijuana</td><td>55</td><td>28</td><td>X2 = 4.09</td></tr><tr><td>Abstinent from cocaine</td><td>53</td><td>40</td><td>ns</td></tr></table>
Schaeffer et al., 2005	Serious adolescent offenders aged 12-17 years in Missouri N=176	Youth received either MST or individual therapy (IT) in a randomized clinical trial; follow-up data were obtained 13.7 years later.	Youth who participated in MST were less likely to be rearrested for any type of offense, including drug offenses. % likelihood of re-arrest for different types of crime and therapy condition <table><tr><td></td><td>MST</td><td>IT</td><td>p-value</td></tr><tr><td>Any offence</td><td>50.0</td><td>81.0</td><td>p=.001</td></tr><tr><td>Any drug offense</td><td>13.0</td><td>33.3</td><td>p=.001</td></tr></table>

Note: When possible, we provided means and standard deviations associated with the findings that are reported in each study.

focused on alcohol initiation. At both follow-up time points, rates of alcohol initiation and drunkenness due to alcohol were lower for the ISPF youth than control youth. For example, the percent of ISFP youth who reported ever using alcohol at the 2-year follow-up was 35% compared to 56% of control youth. (Spoth et al., 1999).

A 4-year (Spoth et al., 2004) and 6-year follow-up (Spoth et al., 2004) of the ISFP were also conducted. Thus, students who were originally in the 6th grade were followed up in the 10th and 12th grades. The 4- and 6-year follow-up studies also evaluated another family-based intervention, Preparing for the Drug Free Years (PDFY). Of note, the PDFY program intervenes more exclusively with the parent than jointly with the family, as it comprises five 2-hour sessions, four of which are attended by parents only. Only one session is attended by both parents and youth (Spoth et al., 2001). PDFY focuses on enhancing protective parent-child interactions and reducing family-based risk factors for substance use initiation. Parents are provided information on risk factors for substance use, developing clear guidelines on substance-related behaviors, enhancing child-parent bonding, monitoring compliance with their guidelines and providing appropriate consequences, managing anger and family conflict, and enhancing positive child involvement in family tasks. Children are instructed on peer resistance skills (Spoth et al., 2001).

Results from these long-term studies indicate that new user proportions were lower for the ISFP condition compared to the control condition at a 4-year follow-up for the following behaviors: ever drank alcohol, ever drank alcohol without permission, ever been drunk, ever smoked cigarettes, ever used marijuana. For example, 7% of ISFP youth reported using marijuana compared to 17% of control youth (Spoth et al., 2001). In addition, fewer PDFY and ISFP students reported past month alcohol use compared to the control students. At the 6-year follow-up, differences were seen in the rates of growth for lifetime alcohol, cigarette, and marijuana use whereby youth in the ISFP had slower overall growth in substance use relative to control youth. The PDFY program only showed effects on tobacco use growth rates (Spoth et al., 2004). Spoth and colleagues speculate that the ISFP may have been more effective in the long term due to the greater number of sessions of the ISFP, along with the greater focus on parent and teen involvement in the sessions (Spoth et al., 2004).

The ISFP has been revised and is now called the Strengthening Families Program: For Parents and Youth 10-14 (SFP 10-14). A recent trial compared a control group to the Life Skills Training Program (LST) or the LST + SFP 10-14. Findings 2.5 years after the program indicated that youth in the LST + SFP 10-14 program had a slower rate of growth on a substance use initiation index and a slower rate of growth on weekly drunkenness compared to a control group. No effects were found for regular alcohol use (Spoth et al., 2005).

The "Families in Action" (FIA) curriculum is adapted from Dr. Michael Popkin's program, "Active Parenting of Teens" (Popkin, 1990). Because Dr. Popkin's program was designed only for parents, FIA program staff developed a student curriculum and student handbook to include youth in the program (Pilgrim et al., 1998). An audiotaped version of the parent handbook was also developed. The focus of the FIA curriculum is to reduce alcohol and drug use among younger adolescents by increasing resiliency and protective factors within youth and parents (Abbey et al., 2000). This program is unique in that it is voluntary. It comprises six 2.5 hour sessions, offered once a week for six consecutive weeks. Through the use of video-taped vignettes, family management and communication strategies were emphasized.

Skills were taught through role-play and discussion. Each session included time in which parents and youth met in separate groups and time in which all family members met together (Abbey et al., 2000).

FIA was introduced into eight schools. One study reports on the impact of FIA in the first four schools in which it was introduced (Pilgrim et al., 1998) and a second study reports on the impact of FIA in the second set of four schools (Abbey et al., 2000). Because FIA was voluntary, comparisons were made between students and parents who chose to participate in the program and those who did not. Depending on the study, baseline differences were found among students and parents who chose to participate (e.g., students who voluntarily participated in the program had lower scores on family cohesion than students who did not participate, and parents who voluntarily participated had higher rates of talking to counselors compared to parents who did not participate). Because of these initial differences, they used one-way analysis of covariance (ANCOVA) to control for baseline scores. However, controlling for measured initial differences is not likely to fully account for differences due to self-selection, as other important factors related to the choice to participate may not have been measured. Thus, lack of randomization limits conclusions from this study. Of note, they did not measure alcohol and drug use behavior, but instead focused on attitudes towards alcohol and drugs. Findings at a one-year follow-up from the first study (initial four schools) indicated that program participants were more likely to talk to a counselor than non-participants. Three of the four program effects were moderated by gender. Specifically boy participants scored higher on appropriate attitudes towards alcohol, age reported that it is "ok" to drink alcohol, and school and peer attachment. In addition, parent participants reported more involvement in school activities and more involvement in

family counseling than non-participants (Pilgrim et al., 1998).

Findings from the second study (second set of four schools) at one-year follow-up indicated that youth who participated in the program reported greater family cohesion, less family fighting, greater school attachment, higher self-esteem, and believed that alcohol should not be consumed until an older age. Parent participants reported stronger attitudes in opposition to alcohol use by minors and that alcohol should not be consumed until an older age compared to non participants (Abbey et al., 2000). Thus, the program appears to influence attitudes; however, they have not examined whether this program impacts substance use.

Familias Unidas (FU) is a family-based intervention designed to focus on drug abuse and HIV-risk for Hispanic immigrant adolescents and their families (Tapia et al., 2006). FU consists of nine 90-minute parent support group sessions, four 1-hour family visits, and four 1-hour parent-adolescent discussion circles. Parent group sessions focus on practicing parenting skills (e.g., discussing behavior management, peer supervision issues, and homework) and how to become more involved in their child's life. Once a new skill has been taught in the group, parents practice this skill during the family visit. In the parent-adolescent discussion circle, youth and parents sit on opposite sides of the room and the parents ask the youth about life as a teenager in the United States. Youth talk about the risks they perceive in their environment, plans they have, and how parents can help them achieve their goals (Tapia et al., 2006). In one longitudinal study, 167 families from three schools were randomly assigned to intervention or control conditions and followed up at 3, 6, 9, and 12 months. The intervention was delivered through family-centered, multi-parent groups that met weekly for approximately 9 months, with parents attending a mean of 24 group sessions (Pantin et al., 2003). Of note, there were baseline differences between the FU adolescents and a comparison group of youth. Specifically FU adolescents reported lower mean levels of behavior problems than the comparison group; thus, baseline scores were covaried in the analyses. Briefly, results indicated that problem behaviors, such as aggression and hostility, steadily declined among FU adolescents over the 12-month period. In contrast, control youth evidenced a substantial increase in problem behaviors between 3- and 6-months (during summer break) but then also decreased their involvement in these behaviors by the 12 month follow-up (Pantin et al., 2003). They did not report any specific results for substance use.

Multisystemic Therapy (MST) was designed to treat antisocial and delinquent adolescents who are chronic juvenile offenders. It is a family and community based treatment that has served as a cost-effective alternative to out-of-home placements, such as incarceration or psychiatric hospitalization (Henggeler, 1999). MST targets the social networks of adolescents and families that may be related to subsequent antisocial behavior (Henggeler, 1999; Huey and Henggeler, 2001). For example, MST interventions are directed toward the individual, family relations, peer relations, school performance, and other social systems that may be associated with the problem behavior (Henggeler, 1999). The average hours of therapist contact range from 24-33 over a 13-17 week period (Henggeler et al., 1997) and therapy is provided in the home or community setting by a therapist who is available to the family 24 hours a day, 7 days a week (Henggeler et al., 1986).

Several randomized studies have shown the effectiveness of MST. Specifically, MST produced greater improvements in family relations (Brunk et al., 1987), problematic parent-child relations (Borduin et al., 1995), and reduction in recidivism for violent crimes (Henggeler et al., 2002; Henggeler et al.,

1999) when compared to community training, parent training, and individual therapy. In a 1999 study, Henggeler and colleagues examined the potential of MST to reduce drug use by treating substance abusing juvenile offenders. No significant treatment effects were found (Henggeler et al., 1999). A 4-year follow-up demonstrated some positive long-term effects of the program, with MST participants having fewer convictions related to aggressive criminal activity and higher rates of marijuana abstinence based on a biological measure. However, no long-term treatment effects were found for self-reported drug use (Henggeler et al., 2002). The authors indicated that these mixed findings may be due to treatment fidelity, which was relatively low in this study. The authors believe that outcomes could be improved by focusing more intensely on drug use and the promotion of treatment integrity (Henggeler et al., 2002). A recent meta-analysis assessed MST trials from 1985 to 2003 and identified 35 unique studies (Little et al., 2005). Although the direction of effects did tend to favor MST, the meta-analysis did not find any evidence that MST was consistently more effective than usual services in reducing arrests and convictions. They did not report on substance use outcomes in this meta-analysis (Littel et al., 2005).

Similar to MST, Multidimensional Family Therapy (MDFT) also targets multiple systems; however, MDFT more exclusively targets adolescent substance abuse versus antisocial behavior. MDFT focuses on the adolescent, the parent (e.g., parenting practices), and other family members (e.g., drug-using adults in the home). Thus, MDFT incorporates numerous social systems into the therapeutic context (Liddle and Hogue, 2001). MDFT is also intensive in that counselors make an average of three substantive contacts per week for every case and the family receives 10-25 sessions (lasting from 30-90 minutes each) during a 3-6 month period. In addition, counselors make 5-10 in-person additional contacts with community agencies for the family (Liddle et al., 2001). A randomized clinical trial compared MDFT with adolescent group therapy and a multifamily educational intervention. All participants showed decreased drug use and acting out behaviors over time; however, teens who received MDFT showed the most improvement. Specifically, at the one year follow-up, 45% of the youth in MDFT reported decreases in drug use compared with 32% in adolescent group therapy and 26% in the multifamily educational intervention (Dennis et al., 2004). MDFT was also utilized in the Cannabis Youth Treatment (CYT) study as one of the five comparison treatments. At the 12-month follow-up, 19% of adolescents who had received MDFT were still abstinent (Dennis et al., 2004).

The goal of the Family Empowerment Intervention (FEI) (Dembo and Walters, 2003) is to improve family functioning by empowering parents. In FEI, a paraprofessional meets with the family of a juvenile offender in the home three times a week for 10 weeks. The focus is on restoring the family hierarchy, enhancing parenting skills, encouraging parents to take greater responsibility for family functioning, and improving communication and problem solving skills (Dembo et al., 2000). Results from a 12-month follow-up indicated that FEI youth reported fewer drug sales, less marijuana use, and less drinking to intoxication than youth who received extended services at 12-month follow-up (Dembo et al., 2000). Long-term results at a 36-month follow-up showed that youth who participated in the FEI *and completed all of the FEI sessions* reported fewer occasions of getting intoxicated from alcohol than youth who received extended services or youth who did not complete all of the FEI sessions (Dembo et al., 2000). In addition, adolescents who participated in the FEI and *completed all of the FEI sessions* reported fewer arrests

compared to youth who did not complete all FEI sessions. No overall differences for recidivism were found between FEI youth and those youth who received an extended services intervention (Dembo et al., 2000).

SUMMARY

Prevention for alcohol and drug use among youth has benefited from important advances over the past two decades. There is evidence of effectiveness for a variety of types of intervention: School-based interventions have reduced alcohol, marijuana and cigarette use; brief interventions have reduced alcohol use and alcohol-related problems; community-based interventions have reduced alcohol use and alcohol-related harm; cognitive behavioral therapies have reduced alcohol, marijuana, and drug use in youth in treatment for substance use problems; and family oriented interventions have reduced marijuana use, alcohol initiation and drunkenness. It is exciting that there are so many promising strategies for reducing alcohol and drug use among this population. While the majority of prevention programs tend to be school-based, delivery has moved beyond the individual and the school, to the family and the community, with encouraging results. In addition, the success of brief interventions is particularly significant as attendance across programs with more sessions may be sporadic and thus teens may not receive all of the sessions. With current budget cuts and time limitations, it is noteworthy that providing one or two sessions of prevention programming can decrease adolescents' subsequent alcohol and drug use. It is also notable that research has begun to explore adolescents' self-selection into different types of prevention formats (e.g., group, individual, and website) and has begun to address the potential impact of voluntary interventions on subsequent alcohol and drug use. Further research is needed, however, to assess the long-term outcomes of brief interventions and voluntary types of programs.

It is also encouraging that many of the programs that have been created for this age group have developed the curriculum with youth input. In doing so, these programs have attempted to account for factors associated with this developmental period, for example, by discussing the importance of peer influence and norms and focusing on teaching decision-making strategies for future high risk situations. In addition, the utilization of motivational interviewing as a strategy for reaching this age group is likely an important contributor to the success of many of the curricula that have been developed.

It is important to note that many of the studies discussed in the current chapter had limitations, such as small sample sizes, limited follow-up, attrition, or very small effects on substance use behavior. Furthermore, despite the successes of the last two decades, considerable room remains for innovation in this field. For example, more work is needed to understand adolescent voluntary help-seeking behavior and the barriers and facilitative factors that may influence whether or not youth will choose to utilize available prevention services (e.g., D'Amico, 2005). In addition, understanding how changes in risk factors occur is important because the mechanisms of change are not well understood for many programs that find reductions in alcohol and drug use: Was the reduction in substance use related to youth making more self-change efforts, decreasing their association with peers who use, or other factors? For example, one recent study found that Project ALERT achieved its effects on alcohol and drug use in part through strengthening resistance self-efficacy (Orlando et al., 2005). A better understanding of the mechanisms of change can help clarify which factors are more likely to impact alcohol and drug use, perhaps highlighting components of an intervention that are particularly significant for the targeted population. Additionally, as the world continues to change and technology (e.g., cell phones, internet) evolves, adolescents' lifestyles will become even more complex, and opportunities to become involved with alcohol and drugs may present themselves in new ways, which will require new and innovative prevention approaches. Lastly, it will be important to confirm that interventions that reduce alcohol and drug use during the teenage years actually prevent rather than just postpone alcohol and substance use disorders in adulthood. Thus, we encourage longitudinal follow-up of trial cohorts into adulthood. We must continue to involve youth in the development of programs so that we can address their concerns and therefore increase the likelihood that they will make healthier choices in the future.

REFERENCES

Aarons G, Brown SA, Stice E, Coe M. (2001) Psychometric evaluation of the marijuana and stimulant effect expectancy questionnaire for youth. Addict Behav 26: 219-236.

Aas HN, Leigh BC, Anderssen N, Jakobsen R. (1998) Two-year longitudinal study of alcohol expectancies and drinking among Norwegian adolescents. Addiction 93(3): 373-384.

Abbey A, Pilgrim C, Hendrickson P, Buresh S. (2000) Evaluation of a family-based substance abuse prevention program targeted for the middle school years. J Drug Educ 30: 213-228.

Allen JP, Porter MR, McFarland FC, McElhaney KB, Marsh P. (2005) The two faces of adolescents' success with peers: Adolescent popularity, social adaptation, and deviant behavior. Child Dev 76: 747-760.

Alsaker FD. (1995) Is puberty a critical period for socialization? J Adolesc 18(4): 427-444.

Ames S, Sussman S, Dent CW. (1999) Pro-drug-use myths and competing constructs in the prediction of substance use among youth at continuation schools: A one-year prospective study. Personality and Individual Differences 26: 987-1003.

Arnold ME, Hughes JN. (1999) First do no harm: Adverse effects of grouping deviant youth for skills training. J School Psychol 37: 99-115.

Ary DV, Tildesley E, Hops H, Andrews J. (1993) The influence of parent, sibling, and peer modeling and attitudes on adolescent use of alcohol. Int J Addict 28: 853-880.

Baer JS, Marlatt GA, Kivlahan DR, Fromme K, Larimer ME, Williams E. (1992) An experimental test of three methods of alcohol risk reduction with young adults. J Consulti Clin Psychol 60(6), 974-979.

Barnett NP, Monti PM, Wood MD. (2001) Motivational interviewing for alcohol-involved adolescents in the emergency room. In E. F. Wagner and H. B. Waldron (Eds.), Innovations in adolescent substance abuse interventions (pp. 143-168) Amsterdam, Netherlands: Pergamon/ Elsevier Science Inc.

Baumrind D. (1987) A developmental perspective on adolescent risk taking in contemporary America. New Dir Child Dev 37, 93-125.

Beal AC, Ausiello J, Perrin JM. (2001) Social influences on health risk behaviors among minority middle school students. J Adoles Health 28: 474-480.

Bien TH, Miller WR, Tonigan JS. (1993) Brief interventions for alcohol problems. Addiction 88: 315-336.

Borduin CM, Cone LT, Fucci BR, Blaske DM, Williams RA, Mann BJ, et al. (1995) Multisystemic treatment of serious juvenile offenders: Long-term prevention of criminality and violence. J Consult Clin Psychol 63: 569-578.

Botvin GJ. (1996) Substance abuse prevention through life skills training. In R. D. Peters and R. J. McMahon (Eds.), Preventing childhood disorders, substance abuse, and delinquency (pp. 215-240) Newbury Park, CA: Sage.

Botvin GJ, Baker E, Dusenbury L, Botvin EM, Diaz T. (1995) Long-term follow-up results of a randomized drug abuse prevention trial in a White middle-class population. JAMA 273: 1106-1112.

Botvin GJ, Griffin KW, Diaz T., Ifill-Williams M. (2001) Drug abuse prevention among minority adolescents: posttest and one-year follow-up of a school based preventive intervention. Prev Sci 2: 1-13.

Brener ND, Billy JO, Grady WR. (2003) Assessment of factors affecting the validity of self-reported health-risk behavior among adolescents: evidence from the scientific literature. J Adolesc Health 33(6):436-57.

Brook JS, Balka EB, Whiteman M. (1999) The risks for late adolescence of early adolescent marijuana use. Am J Public Health 89: 1549-1554.

Brook JS, Finch SJ, Whiteman M, Brook DW. (2002) Drug use and neuro-behavioral, respiratory, and cognitive problems: Precursors and mediators. J Adolesc Health 30(6): 433-441.

Brown SA. (2001) Facilitating change for adolescent alcohol problems: A multiple options approach. In EF Wagner and HB Waldron (Eds.), Innovations in adolescent substance abuse intervention (pp. 169-187) Oxford: Elsevier Science.

Brown SA, Anderson K, Schulte MT, Sintov ND, Frissell KC. (2005) Facilitating youth self-change through school-based intervention. Addict Behav 30: 1797-1810.

Brown SA, D'Amico EJ. (2003) Outcomes of alcohol treatment for adolescents. In M Galanter (Ed.), Recent Developments in Alcoholism: Volume XVI: Selected Treatment Topics (Vol. XVI, pp. 289-312) New York: Kluwer Academic/ Plenum Publishers.

Brown SA, D'Amico EJ, McCarthy DM, Tapert SF. (2001) Four year outcomes from adolescent alcohol and drug treatment. J Stud Alcohol 62: 381-388.

Brown SA, Tapert SF, Granholm E, Delis DC. (2000) Neurocognitive functioning of adolescents: Effects of protracted alcohol use. Alcohol Clin Exp Res 24: 164-171.

Brunk M, Henggeler SW, Whelan JP. (1987) A comparison of multisystemic therapy and parent training in the brief treatment of child abuse and neglect. J Consult Clin Psychol 55: 311-318.

Bui KVT, Ellickson PL, Bell RM. (2000) Cross-lagged relationships among adolescent problem drug use, delinquent behavior, and emotional distress. J Drug Issues 30(2): 283-303.

Center for Disease Control and Prevention. (2004) CDC surveillance summaries Vol. MMWR 53, No SS-2, pp. 1-96.

Chambers RA, Taylor JR, Potenza MN. (2003) Developmental neurocircuitry of motivation in adolescence: A critical period of addiction vulnerability. Am J Psychiatr 160: 1041-1052.

Chassin L, DeLucia C. (1996) Drinking during adolescence. Alcohol Health Res, 20: 175-180

Chassin L, Pillow DR, Curran PJ, Molina BSG, Barrera M. (1993) Relation of parental alcoholism to early adolescent substance use: A test of three mediating mechanisms. J Abnormal Psychol 102: 3-19.

Cho H, Hallfors DD, Sanchez V. (2005) Evaluation of a high school peer group intervention for at-risk youth. J Abnormal Child Psychol 33: 363-374.

Colby SM, Monti PM, Barnett NP, Rohsenow DJ, Weissman K, Spirito A, et al. (1998) Brief motivational interviewing in a hospital setting for adolescent smoking: A preliminary study. J Consult Clin Psychol 66: 574-578.

Crawford LA, Novak KB. (2002) Parental and peer influences on adolescent drinking: The relative impact of attachment and opportunity. J Child Adolesc Subst Abuse 12: 1-26.

D'Amico EJ. (2005) Factors that impact adolescents' intentions to utilize alcohol-related prevention services. J Behav Health Serv Res 32: 332-340.

D'Amico EJ, Anderson KG, Metrik J, Frissell KC, Ellingstad T, Brown SA. (2006) Adolescent self-selection of service formats: Implications for secondary interventions targeting alcohol use. Am J Addict 15: 58-66.

D'Amico EJ, Edelen MO. (in press) Pilot test of Project CHOICE: A voluntary after school intervention for middle school youth. Psychol Addict Behav.

D'Amico EJ, Ellickson PL, Collins RL, Martino SC, Klein DJ. (2005b) Processes linking adolescent problems to substance use problems in late young adulthood. J Stud Alcohol 66: 766-775.

D'Amico EJ, Ellickson PL, Wagner EF, Turrisi R, Fromme K, Ghosh-Dastidar B, et al. (2005a) Developmental considerations for substance use interventions from middle school through college. Alcohol Clin Exp Res 29: 474-483.

D'Amico EJ, Fromme K. (1997) Health risk behaviors of adolescent and young adult siblings. Health Psychol 16(5): 426-432.

D'Amico EJ, Fromme K. (2002) Brief prevention for adolescent risk-taking behavior. Addiction 97: 563-574.

D'Amico EJ. (2004) Self-selected brief alcohol intervention for adolescents (R21AA13284-01) Rockville, MD: National Institute on Alcohol Abuse and Alcoholism, National Institutes of Health.

D'Amico EJ, McCarthy DM. (2006) Escalation and initiation of younger adolescents' substance use: The impact of perceived peer use. J Adolesc Health 39: 481-487.

Darkes J, Goldman MS. (1993) Expectancy

challenge and drinking reduction: Experimental evidence for a mediational process. J Consult Clin Psychol 61: 344-353.

De Bellis MD, Clark DB, Beers SR, Soloff PH, Hall JH, Kersch A, et al. (2000) Hippocampal volume in adolescent-onset alcohol use disorders. Am J Psychiatry 157: 737-744.

Deas D, Riggs P, Langenbucher J, Goldman M, Brown S. (2000) Adolescents are not adults: Developmental considerations in alcohol users. Alcohol Clin Exp Res 24: 232-237.

Dembo R, Ramirez-Garnica G, Rollie M, Schmeidler J, Livingston S, Hartsfield A. (2000) Youth recidivism twelve months after a family empowerment intervention: Final report. J Offender Rehab 31: 29-65.

Dembo R, Seeberger W, Shemwell M, Klein L, Rollie M, Pacheco K, et al. (2000) Psychosocial functioning among juvenile offenders 12 months after a family empowerment intervention. J Offender Rehab 32: 1-56.

Dembo R, Walters W. (2003) Innovative approaches to identifying and responding to the needs of high risk youth. Subst Use Misuse 38: 1713-1738.

Dembo R, Wothke W, Livingston S, Schmeidler J. (2002) The impact of a family empowerment intervention on juvenile offender heavy drinking: A latent growth model analysis. Subst Use Misuse, 37: 1359-1390.

Dennis M, Godley SH, Diamond G, Tims FM, Babor T, Donaldson J, et al. (2004) The cannabis youth treatment (CYT) study: Main findings from two random-ized trials. J Subst Abuse Treat 27: 197-213.

DeWit DJ, Offord DR, Wong M. (1997) Patterns of onset and cessation of drug use over the early part of the life course. Health Ed Behavior 24: 746-758.

Dimeff LA, Baer JS, Kivlahan DR, Marlatt GA. (1998) Brief alcohol screening and intervention for college students. New York: Guilford Press.

Dishion TJ, Bullock BM, Granic I. (2002) Pragmatism in modeling peer influence: Dynamics, outcomes, and change processes. Dev Psychopathol 14: 969-981.

Dukes RL, Marinex RO, Stein JA. (1997) Precursors and consequences of gang membership and delinquency. Youth and Society 29: 139-165.

Eggert LL, Nicholas LJ, Owen L. (1995) Reconnecting Youth: A peer group approach to building life skills. Bloomington, IN: National Educational Service.

Eggert LL, Thompson EA, Herting JR, Nicholas LJ. (1994) Preventing adolescent drug abuse and high school dropout through an intensive school-based social network development program. Am J Health Promotion 8: 202-214.

Eggert LL, Thompson EA, Herting JR, Randell BP. (2001) Reconnecting youth to prevent drug abuse, school dropout, and suicidal behaviors among high risk youth. In E. F. Wagner and H. B. Waldron (Eds.), Innovations in adolescent substance abuse interventions (pp. 51-84) Oxford: Elsevier Science.

Ellickson PL, Bell RM. (1990) Drug prevention in junior high: A multi-site, longitudinal test. Science 247: 1299-1305.

Ellickson PL, Bui K, Bell R, McGuigan KA. (1998) Does early drug use increase the risk of dropping out of high school? J Drug Issues 28: 357-380.

Ellickson PL, Hays RD. (1992) On becoming involved with drugs: Modeling adolescent drug use over time. Health Psychol 11(6): 377-385.

Ellickson PL, Martino SC, Collins RL. (2004) Marijuana use from adolescence to young adulthood: Multiple developmental trajec-tories and their associated outcomes. Health Psychol 23: 299-307.

Ellickson PL, McCaffrey DF, Ghosh-Dastidar B, Longshore DL. (2003) New inroads in preventing adolescent drug use: Results from a large-scale trial of project ALERT in middle schools. Am J Public Health 93: 1830-1836.

Ennett ST, Ringwalt CL, Thorne J, Rohrbach LA, Vincus A, Simons-Rudolph A, et al. (2003) A comparison of current practice in school-based substance use prevention programs with meta-analysis findings. Prev Sci 4(1): 1-14.

Frissell KC, McCarthy DM, D'Amico EJ, Metrik J, Ellingstad TP, Brown SA. (2004) The impact of consent procedures on reported levels of adolescent alcohol use. Psychol Addict Behav 14: 307-315.

Fromme K, Corbin W. (2004) Prevention of heavy drinking and associated negative consequences among mandated and voluntary college students. J Consult Clin Psychol 72: 1038-1049

Fromme K, D'Amico EJ. (2000) Measuring adolescent alcohol outcome expectancies. Psychol Addict Behav 14: 206-212.

Fromme K, Stroot E, Kaplan D. (1993) Comprehensive effects of alcohol: Development and psychometric assessment of a new expectancy questionnaire. Psychol Assess 5(1): 19-26.

Galen LW, Henderson MJ. (1999) Validation of cocaine and marijuana effect expectancies in a treatment setting. Addict Behav 24: 719-724.

Gfroerer JC, Wu L-T, Penne MA. (2002) Initiation of marijuana use: Trends, patterns, and implications (No. Analytic Series: A-17, DHHS Publication No. SMA 02-3711) Rockville, MD: Substance Abuse and Mental Health Services Administration, Office of Applied Studies.

Goldstein A, Brown BW. (2003) Urine testing in methadone maintenance treatment: applications and limitations. J Subst Abuse Treat 25(2):61-3.

Gosin M, Marsiglia FF, Hecht ML. (2003) Keepin' it R.E.A.L.: A drug resistance curriculum tailored to the strengths and needs of pre-adolescents of the southwest. J Drug Educ 33: 119-142.

Gottfredson DC, Wilson DB. (2003) Characteristics of effective school-based substance abuse prevention. Prev Sci 4: 27-38.

Grant BF. (1998) The impact of family history of alcoholism on the relationship between age of onset of alcohol use and DSM-IV alcohol dependence. Alcohol Health and Research World 22: 144-147.

Guilamo-Ramos V, Turrisi R, Jaccard J, Gonzalez B. (2004) Progressing from light experimentation to heavy episodic drinking in early and middle adolescence. J Stud Alcohol 65: 494-500.

Hansell S, White HR. (1991) Adolescent drug use, psychological distress, and physical symptoms. J Health Social Behav 32: 288-301.

Hansen WB, Graham JW. (1991) Preventing alcohol, marijuana, and cigarette use among adolescents: Peer pressure resistance training versus establishing conservative norms. Prev Med 20: 414-430.

Harwood, H. (2000) Updating Estimates of the Economic Costs of Alcohol Abuse in the United States: Estimates, Update Methods, and Data. Report prepared by The Lewin Group for the National Institute on Alcohol Abuse and Alcoholism. NIH Publication No. 98-4327. Rockville, MD: National Institutes of Health.

Hecht ML, Marsiglia FF, Elek E, Wagstaff DA, Kulis S, Dustman P, et al. (2003) Culturally grounded substance use prevention: An evaluation of the keepin' it R.E.A.L. curriculum. Prev Sci 4: 233-248.

Henggeler SW. (1999) Multisystemic therapy: An overview of clinical procedures, outcomes, and policy implications. Child Psychol Psychiatr Rev 4(1): 2-10.

Henggeler SW, Clingempeel WG, Glenn W, Brondino MJ, Pickrel SG. (2002) Four-

394

year follow-up of multisystemic therapy with substance-abusing and substance-dependent juvenile offenders. J Am Acad Child Adolesc Psychiatr 41: 868-874.

Henggeler SW, Pickrel SG, Brondino MJ. (1999) Multisystemic treatment of Substance-Abusing and Dependent Delinquents: Outcomes, treatment, fidelity, and transportability. Mental Health Serv Res 1: 171-184.

Henggeler SW, Rodick JD, Borduin CM, Hanson CL, Watson SM, Urey JR. (1986) Multisystemic treatment of juvenile offenders: Effects on adolescent behavior and family interactions. Dev Psychol 22: 132-141.

Henggeler SW, Rowland MD, Pickrel SG, Miller SL, Cunningham PB, Santos AB, et al. (1997) Investigating family-based alternatives to institution-based mental health services for youth: Lessons learned from the pilot study of a randomized field trial. J Clin Child Psychol 26: 226-233.

Hingson RW, Heeren T, Jamanka A, Howland J. (2000) Age of drinking onset and unintentional injury involvement after drinking. JAMA 284: 1527-1533.

Hingson RW, Heeren T, Winter MR. (2006) Age at drinking onset and alcohol dependence. Arch Pediatr Adolesc Med 160: 739-746.

Hoffman L. (2002) Family therapy: An intimate history. New York, NY: W.W. Norton and Co.

Holder HD, Gruenewald PJ, Ponicki WR, Treno AJ, Grube JW, Saltz RF, et al. (2000) Effect of community-based interventions on high-risk drinking and alcohol related injuries. JAMA 284: 2341-2347.

Holder HD, Saltz RF, Grube JW, Voas RB, Gruenewald PJ, Treno AJ. (1997) A community prevention trial to reduce alcohol-involved accidental injury and death: Overview. Addiction 92: S155-S171.

Huey SJ, Henggeler SW. (2001) Effective community-based interventions for antisocial and delinquent adolescents. In J. N. Hughes, A. M. L. Greca and J. C. Conoley (Eds.), Handbook of psychological services for children and adolescents. London: Oxford University Press.

Hurrelmann K. (1990) Health promotion for adolescents: Preventive and corrective strategies against problem behavior. Adolesc 13(3): 231-250.

Institute of Medicine. (1994) Reducing risks for mental disorders: Frontiers for preventive intervention research. Washington DC: Academy Press.

Jackson C. (1997) Initial and experimental stages of tobacco and alcohol use during late childhood: relation to peer, parent, and personal risk factors. Addict Behav 22(5): 685-698.

Johnson PB, Johnson HL. (2001) Reaffirming the power of parental influence on adolescent smoking and drinking decisions. Adolesc Fam Health 2: 37-43.

Johnston LD, O'Malley PM, Bachman JG, Schulenberg JE. (2005) Monitoring the Future national survey results on drug use, 1975-2004. Volume I: Secondary school students Bethesda, MD: National Institute on Drug Abuse.

Johnston LD, O'Malley PM, Bachman JG, Schulenberg JE. (2006) Monitoring the Future national survey results on drug use, 1975-2005. Volume I: Secondary school students. Bethesda, MD: National Institute on Drug Abuse.

Jones B, Corbin W, Fromme K. (1999) Half full or half empty, the glass still does not satisfactorily quench the thirst for knowledge on alcohol expectancies as a mechanism of change. Addiction 16: 57-72.

Jones BT, McMahon J. (1993) Alcohol motivations as outcome expectancies. In W. R. Miller and N. Heather (Eds.), Treating addictive behaviors (pp. 75-91)

New York: Plenum Press.

Kaminer Y, Burleson JA. (1999) Psychotherapies for adolescent substance abusers: 15-month follow-up of a pilot study. Am J Addict 8: 114-119.

Kaminer Y, Burleson JA, Blitz C, Sussman J, Rounsaville BJ. (1998) Psychotherapies for adolescent substance abusers: A pilot study. J Nervous Mental Dis 186: 684-690.

Kaminer Y, Burleson JA, Goldberger R. (2002) Cognitive-behavioral coping skills and psychoeducation therapies for adolescent substance abuse. J Nervous Mental Dis 190: 737-745.

Kaminer Y, Slesnick N. (2005) Evidence-based cognitive-behavioral and family therapies for adolescent alcohol and other substance use disorders. In M. Galanger (Ed.), Recent developments in alcoholism: Volume 17. Alcohol problems in adolescents and young adults. Epidemiology and prevention (pp. 383-405) New York, NY: Kluwer Academic/ Plenum Publishers.

Kandel D, Faust R. (1975) Sequence and stages in patterns of adolescent drug use. Arch Gen Psychiatry 32: 923-932.

Kandel DB. (1996) The parental and peer contexts of adolescent deviance: An algebra of interpersonal influence. J Drug Issues 26: 289-315.

Kandel DB, Chen K. (2000) Types of marijuana users by longitudinal course. J Stud Alcohol 61: 367-378.

Kandel DB, Yamaguchi K, Chen K. (1992) Stages of progression in drug involvement from adolescence to adulthood: Further evidence for the gateway theory. J Stud Alcohol 53: 447-457.

Komro KA, Perry CL, Veblen-Mortenson S, Williams CL. (1994) Peer participation in Project Northland: A community-wide alcohol use prevention project. J School Health 64: 318-322.

Kosterman R, Hawkins JD, Guo J, Catalano RF. (2000) The dynamics of alcohol and marijuana initiation: Patterns and predictors of first use in adolescence. Am J Public Health 90: 360-366.

Kulis S, Marsiglia FF, Elek E, Dustman P, Wagstaff DA, Hecht ML. (2005) Mexican/Mexican American Adolescents and keepin' it REAL: An Evidence-Based Substance Use Prevention Program. Children and Schools 27(3):133-145.

Kumpfer KL, Alvarado R, Whiteside HO. (2003) Family-based interventions for substance use and misuse prevention. Subst Use Misuse 38: 1759-1787.

Kumpfer KL, Molgaard V, Spoth R. (1996) The Strengthening Families Program for the prevention of delinquency and drug use. In R. D. Peters and R. J. McMahon (Eds.), Preventing childhood disorders, substance abuse, and delinquency (pp. 241-267) Thousand Oaks, CA: Sage Publications.

Labouvie E, White HR. (2002) Drug sequences, age of onset, and use trajectories as predictors of drug abuse/ dependence in young adulthood. In D. B. Kandel (Ed.), Stages and pathways of drug involvement: Examining the gateway hypothesis (pp. 19-41) Cambridge, United Kingdom: Cambridge University Press.

Lanza ST, Collins LM. (2002) Pubertal timing and the onset of substance use in females during early adolescence. Prev Sci 3: 69-82.

Larimer ME, Marlatt GA, Baer JS, Quigley LA, Blume AW, Hawkins EH. (1998) Harm reduction for alcohol problems: Expanding access to and acceptability of prevention and treatment services. In G. A. Marlatt (Ed.), Harm reduction: Pragmatic strategies for managing high-risk behaviors (pp. 69-121) New York: Guilford Press.

Larimer ME, Turner AP, Anderson BK, Fader JS, Kilmer JR, Palmer RS, et al. (2001) Evaluating a brief alcohol intervention with fraternities. J Stud Alcohol 62: 370-

380.

Leigh BC, Stacy AW. (2004) Alcohol expectancies and drinking in different age groups. Addiction 99: 215-227.

Li C, Pentz MA, Chou C-P. (2002) Parental substance use as a modifier of adolescent substance use risk. Addiction 97: 1537-1550.

Liddle HA, Dakof GA, Parker K, Diamond GS, Barrett K, Tejeda M. (2001) Multidimensional family therapy for adolescent drug abuse: Results of a randomized clinical trial. Am J Drug Alcohol Abuse 27: 651-688.

Liddle HA, Hogue A. (2000) A family-based developmental-ecological preventive intervention for high risk adolescents. J Marital Fam Ther 26: 265-279.

Liddle HA, Hogue A. (2001) Multidimensional family therapy for adolescent substance abuse. In E. F. Wagner and H. B. Waldron (Eds.), Innovations in adolescent substance abuse interventions (pp. 229-261) New York: Pergamon.

Little JH, Popa M, Forsythe B. (2005) Mulitsystemic therapy for social, emotional, and behavioral problems in youth aged 10-17 (Review) The Cochrane Library (4): 1-42.

Little PMD, Harris E. (2003) A review of out-of-school time program quasi-experimental and experimental evaluation results. In Harvard Family Research Project (Ed.), Out-of-school time evaluation snapshot (Vol. 1, pp. 1-12) Cambridge: Harvard Graduate School of Education.

Lonigan CJ, Elbert JC, Johnson SB. (1998) Empirically supported psychosocial interventions for children: An overview. J Clin Child Psychol 27: 138-145.

Marlatt GA, Baer JS, Kivlahan DR, Dimeff LA, Larimer ME, Quigley LA, et al. (1998) Screening and brief intervention for high-risk college student drinkers: Results from a 2-year follow-up

assessment. J Consult Clin Psychol 66: 604-615.

Martino SC, Collins LM, Ellickson PL, Schell TL, McCaffrey D. (2006) Socio-environmental influences on adolescents' alcohol outcome expectancies: A prospective analysis. Addiction 101: 971-983.

Masterman PW, Kelly AB. (2003) Reaching adolescents who drink harmfully: Fitting intervention to developmental reality. J Subst Abuse Treat 24(4): 347-355.

Miller WR, Rollnick S. (2002) Motivational interviewing: Preparing people for change (2nd ed.) New York, NY: Guilford Press.

Monti PM, Colby SM, Barnett NP, Spirito A, Rohsenow DJ, Myers M, et al. (1999) Brief intervention for harm reduction with alcohol-positive older adolescents in a hospital emergency department. J Consult Clin Psychol 67: 989-994.

Morehouse ER, Tobler NS. (2000) Project SUCCESS final report. Rockville, MD: Center for Substance Abuse Prevention.

Muthén BO, Muthén LK. (2000) The development of heavy drinking and alcohol-related problems from ages 18 to 37 in a U. S. national sample. J Stud Alcohol 61: 290-300.

Nichols MP, Schwartz RC. (1998) Family therapy: Concepts and methods (4th ed.) Needham Heights, MA: Allyn and Bacon.

NIDA. (1997) Drug abuse prevention: for at risk groups. Rockville: MD: DHHS: National Institutes of Health, National Institute on Drug Abuse, Office of Science Policy and Communications.

Office of National Drug Control Policy (2004). The Economic Costs of Drug Abuse in the United States, 1992-2002. Washington, DC: Executive Office of the President (Publication No. 207303)

O'Malley PM, Johnston LD. (2003) Unsafe driving by high school seniors: National trends from 1976 to 2001 in tickets and accidents after use of alcohol, marijuana, and other illegal drug. J Stud Alcohol 64:

305-312.

Orlando M, Ellickson PL, McCaffrey DF, Longshore DL. (2005) Mediation analysis of a school-based drug prevention program: Effects of Project ALERT. Prev Sci 6: 35-46.

Ozechowski TJ, Liddle HA. (2000) Family-based therapy for adolescent drug abuse: Knowns and unknowns. Clin Child Fam Psychol Rev 3: 269-298.

Pantin H, Coatsworth JD, Feaster DJ, Newman FL, Briones E, Prado G, et al. (2003) Familias Unidas: The efficacy of an intervention to promote parental investment in Hispanic immigrant families. Prev Sci 4: 189-201.

Perry CL, Williams CL, Komro KA, Veblen-Mortenson S, Forster JL, Bernstein-Lachter R, et al. (2000) Project Northland high school interventions: Community action to reduce adolescent alcohol use. Health Educ Behav 27: 29-49.

Perry CL, Williams CL, Komro KA, Veblen-Mortenson S, Stigler MH, Munson KA, et al. (2002) Project Northland: Long-term outcomes of community action to reduce adolescent alcohol use. Health Educ Res 17: 117-132.

Petraitis J, Flay BR, Miller TQ. (1995) Reviewing theories of adolescent substance use: organizing pieces in the puzzle. Psych Bull 117(1): 67-86.

Petraitis J, Flay BR, Miller TQ, Torpy EJ, Greiner B. (1998) Illicit substance use among adolescents: A matrix of prospective predictors. Subst Use Misuse 33: 2561-2604.

Pilgrim C, Abbey A, Hendrickson P, Lorenz S. (1998) Implementation and impact of a family-based substance abuse prevention program in rural communities. J Primary Prev 18: 341-361.

Popkin M. (1990) Active parenting for teens. Marietta, Georgia: Active Parenting Inc.

Resnicow K, DiIorio C, Soet JE, Borrelli B, Hecht J, Ernst D. (2002) Motivational interviewing in health promotion: It sounds like something is changing. Health Psychol 21: 444-451.

Rose RJ, Kaprio J, Winter T, Koskenvuo M, Viken RJ. (1999) Familial and socioregional environmental effects on abstinence from alcohol at age sixteen. J Stud Alcohol Supp 13: 63-74.

SAMHSA. (2005) SAMHSA model programs: Effective substance abuse and mental health programs for every community. Retrieved July 21, 2005 from http://www.modelprograms.samhsa.gov/template_cf.cfm?page=model_list

Substance Abuse and Mental Health Services Administration. (2007) Results from the 2006 National Survey on Drug Use and Health: National Findings (Office of Applied Studies, NSDUH Series H-32, DHHS Publication No. SMA 07-4293). Rockville, MD.

Schweinsburg AD, Schweinsburg BC, Cheung EH, Brown GG, Brown SA, Tapert SF. (2005) fMRI response to spatial working memory in adolescents with comorbid marijuana and alcohol use disorders. Drug Alcohol Depend 79: 201-210.

Shakeshaft AP, Bowman JA, Sanson-Fisher RW. (1997) Behavioural alcohol research: New directions or more of the same? Addiction 92: 1411-1422.

Simons-Morton B, Abroms L, Haynie DL, Chen R. (2004) Latent growth curve analyses of peer and parent influences on smoking progression among early adolescents. Health Psychol 23: 612-621.

Simons-Morton B, Chen R. (2005) Latent growth curve analyses of parent influences on drinking progression among early adolescents. J Stud Alcohol 66: 5-13.

Simons-Morton B, Haynie DL, Crump AD, Saylor KE, Eitel P, Yu K. (1999) Expectancies and other psychosocial factors associated with alcohol use among early adolescent boys and girls. Addict Behav 24(2): 229-238.

Simons-Morton BG, Haynie DL. (2003) Psychosocial predictors of increased smoking stage among sixth graders. Am J Health Behav 27: 592-602.

Smith GT, Goldman MS, Greenbaum PE, Christiansen BA. (1995) Expectancy for social facilitation from drinking: The divergent paths of high-expectancy and low-expectancy adolescents. J Abnormal Psychol 104: 32-40.

Sowell ER, Thompson PM, Holmes CJ, Jernigan TL, Toga AW. (1999) In vivo evidence for post-adolescent brain maturation in frontal and striatal regions. Nature Neurosci 2: 859-861.

Spear LP. (2000) The adolescent brain and age-related behavioral manifestations Neuroscience Biobehavioral Rev 24: 417-463.

Spoth R, Randall GK, Shin C, Redmond C. (2005) Randomized study of combined universal family and school preventive interventions: Patterns of long-term effects on initiation, regular use, and weekly drunkenness. Psychol Addictive Behav 19: 372-381.

Spoth R, Redmond C, Lepper H. (1999) Alcohol initiation outcomes of universal family-focused preventive interventions: One- and two-year follow-ups of a controlled study. J Stud Alcohol 13: 103-111.

Spoth R, Redmond C, Shin C, Azevedo K. (2004) Brief family intervention effects on adolescent substance use initiation: School-level growth curve analyses 6 years following baseline. J Consult Clin Psychol 72: 535-542.

Spoth RL, Redmond C, Shin C. (2001) Randomized trial of brief family interventions for general populations: Adolescent substance use outcomes 4 years following baseline. J Consult Clin Psychol 69: 627-642.

St. Pierre TL, Kaltreider DL, Mark MM, Aikin KJ. (1992) Drug prevention in a community setting: A longitudinal study of the relative effectiveness of a three-year primary prevention program in Boys and Girls Clubs across the nation. Am J Community Psychol 20: 673-706.

Stern SA, Meredith LS, Gholson J, Gore P, D'Amico EJ. (2007) Project CHAT: A brief motivational substance abuse intervention for teens in primary care. J Subst Abuse Treat 32:153-165.

Sussman S. (1996) Development of a school-based curriculum for high-risk youths. J Psychoactive Drugs 28: 169-182.

Sussman S, Dent CW, Stacy AW. (2002) Project Towards No Drug Abuse: A review of the findings and future directions. Am J Health Behav 26: 354-364.

Sussman S, Dent CW, Stacy AW, Craig S. (1998) One-year outcomes of Project Towards No Drug Abuse. Prev Med 27: 632-642.

Sussman S, Petosa R, Clarke P. (1996) The use of empirical curriculum development to improve prevention research. American Behavioral Scientist 39: 838-852.

Sussman S, Sun P, McCuller WJ, Dent CW. (2003) Project Towards No Drug Abuse: Two-year outcomes of a trial that compares health educator delivery to self-instruction. Prev Med 37: 155-162.

Sussman S, Yang D, Baezconde-Garbanati L, Dent CW. (2003) Drug abuse prevention program development: Results among Latino and non-Latino white adolescents. Eval Health Prof 26(4): 355-379.

Tait RJ, Hulse GK. (2003) A systematic review of the effectiveness of brief interventions with substance using adolescents by type of drug. Drug Alcohol Rev 22: 337-346.

Tapert SF, Brown SA. (2000) Substance dependence, family history of alcohol dependence and neuropsychological functioning in adolescence. Addiction

95(7): 1043-1053.

Tapert SF, Brown SA, Myers MG, Granholm E. (1999) The role of neurocognitive abilities with adolescent relapse to alcohol and drug use. J Stud Alcohol 4: 500-508.

Tapert SF, Caldwell L, Burke MA. (2004-2005) Alcohol and the adolescent brain--Human studies. Alcohol Res Health 28: 205-212.

Tapia MI, Schwartz SJ, Prado G, Lopez B, Pantin H. (2006) Parent-centered intervention: A practical approach for preventing drug abuse in Hispanic adolescents. Res Social Work Practice 16: 146-165.

Tarter RE. (2002) Etiology of adolescent substance abuse: A developmental perspective. Am J Addict 11(3): 171-191.

Taylor BJ, Graham JW, Cumsille P, Hansen WB. (2000) Modeling prevention program effects on growth in substance use: analysis of five years of data from the Adolescent Alcohol Prevention Trial. Prev Sci 1(4): 183-197.

Tevyaw TO, Monti PM. (2004) Motivational enhancement and other brief interventions for adolescent substance abuse: Foundations, applications, and evaluations. Addiction 99: 63-75.

Tobler NS, Stratton HH. (1997) Effectiveness of school-based drug prevention programs: A meta-analysis of the research. J Primary Prev 18: 71-128.

Tschann JM, Adler NE, Irwin CE, Jr, Millstein SG, Turner RA, Kegeles SM. (1994) Initiation of substance use in early adolescence: The roles of pubertal timing and emotional distress. Health Psychol 13: 326-333.

Tucker JS, Ellickson PL, Orlando M, Martino SC, Klein DJ. (2005) Substance use trajectories from early adolescence to emerging adulthood: A comparison of smoking, binge drinking, and marijuana use. J Drug Issues 35: 307-332.

U.S. Department of Justice. (1999) Costs of Underage Drinking. Report by the Pacific Institute for Research and Evaluation for the Office of Juvenile Justice and Delinquency Prevention. Available at: http://www.udetc.org/documents/costunde ragedrinking.pdf

Wagenaar AC, Gehan JP, Jones-Webb R, Toomey TL, Forster JL, Wolfson M, et al. (1999) Communities mobilizing for change on alcohol: Lessons and results from a 15-community randomized trial. J Community Psychol 27: 315-326.

Wagenaar AC, Murray DM, Gehan JP, Wolfson M, Forster JL, Toomey TL, et al. (2000) Communities mobilizing for change on alcohol: Outcomes from a randomized community trial. J Stud Alcohol 61: 85-94.

Wagenaar AC, Murray DM, Wolfson M, Forster JL, Finnegan JR. (1994) Communities mobilizing for change on alcohol: Design of a randomized community trial. J Consult Psychol 22(CSAP Special Issue): 79-101.

Wagner EF, Tubman JG, Gil AG. (2004) Implementing school-based substance abuse interventions: Methodological dilemmas and recommended solutions. Addiction 99(Suppl2): 106-119.

Wahl SK, Turner LR, Mermelstein RJ, Flay BR. (2005) Adolescents' smoking expectancies: Psychometric properties and prediction of behavior change. Nicotine Tob Res 7: 613-623.

Waldron HB, Brody JL, Slesnick N. (2001) Integrative behavioral and family therapy for adolescent substance abuse. In P. M. Monti, S. M. Colby and T. A. O'Leary (Eds.), Adolescents, alcohol, and substance abuse: Reaching teens through brief interventions (pp. 216-243) New York, NY: The Guilford Press.

Waldron HB, Kaminer Y. (2004) On the learning curve: The emerging evidence supporting cognitive-behavioral therapies for adolescent substance abuse. Addiction 99: 93-105.

Waldron HB, Slesnick N, Brody JL, Peterson TR. (2001) Treatment outcomes for adolescent substance abuse 4- and 7-month assessments. J Consult Clin Psychol 69: 802-813.

Weiss B, Caron A, Ball S, Tapp J, Johnson M, Weisz JR. (2005) Iatrogenic effects of group treatment for antisocial youth. J Consult Clin Psychol 73: 1036-1044.

Weisz JR, Hawley KM. (2002) Developmental factors in the treatment on adolescents. J Consult Clin Psychol 70: 21-43.

Werch CE, Owen DM, Carlson JM, DiClemente CC, Edgemon P, Moore M. (2003) One-year follow-up results of the STARS for families alcohol prevention program. Health Educ Res 18: 74-87.

Windle M. (2000) Parental, sibling, and peer influences on adolescent substance use and alcohol problems. Applied Developmental Science Special Issue: Familial and peer influences on adolescent substance use 4: 98-110.

Winters K. (2001) Assessing adolescent substance use problems and other areas of functioning: State of the art. In P. M. Monti, S. M. Colby and T. A. O'Leary (Eds.), Adolescents, alcohol and substance abuse (pp. 80-108) New York: Guilford.

Wood MD, Read JP, Mitchell RE, Brand NH. (2004) Do parents still matter? Parent and peer influences on alcohol involve-ment among recent high school graduates. Psychol Addictive Behaviors 18: 19-30.

Zhang L, Welte JW, Wieczorek WF. (1997) Peer and parental influences on male adolescent drinking. Subst Use Misuse 32(14): 2121-2136.

INTERVENTIONS TO REDUCE RISKY SEXUAL BEHAVIOR, PREGNANCY AND SEXUALLY TRANSMITTED DISEASE IN TEENS

Douglas Kirby, and B.A. Laris

BACKGROUND

In this chapter, we present the scope of the problem of risky sexual behavior in teens and review interventions to reduce teenage pregnancy and sexually transmitted disease.

Adolescent Sexual Risk-Taking and Its Consequences

Teen Pregnancy and Childbearing

Despite recent declines, the U.S. teen pregnancy rate remains very high. In 2002, among all females aged 15-19, about 75 per 1,000 became pregnant (Guttmacher Institute, 2006). The rate is higher for 18- to 19-year-olds (126 per 1,000) than for 15- to 17-year-olds (42 per 1,000).

The U.S. teen pregnancy rate in 2002 was much higher than those in other western industrialized countries with available data in the mid-1990s. For example, the U.S. rate of 75 pregnancies per 1,000 females was much higher than rates for Canada (52) and England and Wales (55), three to four times as high as rates in France (23) and Germany (19), and approximately five times the teen pregnancy rates in Italy, Spain, and the Netherlands, all of which had a rate of 14 per 1,000 (Singh and Darroch, 2000; Flanigan, 2001).

Although 75 per 1,000 females aged 15-19 become pregnant each year, the cumulative proportion of any cohort of teens who become pregnant increases during each year of their lives. Thus, 30 percent of females in the United States become pregnant before they reach 20 years of age, and many become pregnant a second time before their twentieth birthday (National Campaign to Prevent Teen Pregnancy, 2006). In 2001, about 82 percent of teenage pregnancies were unintended (Finer, 2006).

The U.S. teen pregnancy rate varies considerably by race and ethnicity. The pregnancy rate in 2002 for 15- to 19-year-old females was 48 per 1,000 among non-Hispanic whites, 134 per 1,000 among African-Americans, and 132 per 1,000 among Hispanics (Guttmacher Institute, 2006).

Consistent with the very high U.S. teen pregnancy rate is its very high teen birth rate. The birth rate in the United States in 2005 was 40 births per 1,000 15- to 19-year-old females (Martin, 2006). It is higher for 18- to 19-years-olds (70 per 1,000) than for 15- to 17-year-olds (21 per 1,000). All of these figures are much higher than those in other Western industrialized countries.

Poverty and its related social consequences are related to teen childbearing. In addition, teen childbearing has negative consequences for those involved. When adolescents, especially 15- to 17-year-old females, give birth, their future prospects decline in a number of ways (Hoffman, 2006). They become less likely to complete high school, less likely to attend college, more likely to have large families, and more likely to be single parents. They work as much as women who delay childbearing for several years, but their earnings must provide for a larger number of children (Maynard, 1997; Hoffman, 2006).

It is the children of teen mothers, however, who tend to exhibit the most serious consequences of teen childbearing. Compared to children born to mothers aged 20-21, children born to mothers aged 15-17 have less supportive and stimulating home environments, lower cognitive development, worse educational outcomes, higher rates of behavior problems, higher rates of incarceration (sons) and higher rates of adolescent childbearing themselves (Maynard, 1997; Hoffman, 2006). The effects are much smaller for children born to mothers aged 18-19.

Finally, there are significant public costs associated with adolescent childbearing. After adjusting for other factors related to teen parenthood, the estimated annual cost to taxpayers of births to young women who became mothers when they were 19 or younger, instead of 20-21, was at least $9 billion in 2004. This estimate includes only five categories of costs: lost tax revenues, public assistance, health care for the children, child welfare, and the criminal justice system (Hoffman, 2006). It is important to note that the costs to taxpayers of births to women who became mothers at the age of 17 or younger ($4,080/year) are much higher than the costs to taxpayers of births to women who became mothers at the age of 18-19 ($1,430/year).

Sexually Transmitted Diseases

Teen sexual activity also leads to high rates of sexually transmitted diseases (STDs). While young people aged 15-24 represent 25 percent of the sexually active population, they account for about half of all new cases of STDs (Weinstock, 2004). This means that nearly four million STDs occur annually among teens and over six million among people aged 20 to 24 (Kaiser Family Foundation, 1998). In some geographic areas, rates are much higher. For example, in one community, 40 percent of 14- to 19-year-old females who came to a teen clinic had an STD (Bunnell, 1999). In addition, about one-third of all sexually active young people become infected by an STD by age 24 (Kaiser Family

Foundation, 1998). Of course, many have been treated and cured, but others have not. Furthermore, approximately one-quarter of all reported cases of STDs occur among adolescents, and about another one-third occur among young adults aged 20-24 (Eng, 1997).

Rates of STDs are typically much higher for African-American and Native American teens than white teens. Rates of STDs are usually also slightly higher for Hispanic teens than white teens. For example, in 2004, the rates of both gonorrhea and syphilis among African-American 15- to 19-year-olds was about 17 times higher than the rate among white teens (Centers for Disease Control and Prevention, 2005). In part, these higher rates reflect greater poverty, less access to health services, larger numbers of sexual partners, and possibly differences in reporting by clinics serving low-income minority youth (Santelli, 1999).

Adolescents have very high age-specific rates for some STDs, such as chlamydia and gonorrhea. When 2004 data were analyzed by gender, female teens had the highest rates of chlamydia and gonorrhea, while the rates for male teens were only slightly lower than the rates for men in their twenties (Centers for Disease Control and Prevention, 2005).

Such high rates of STDs among teenagers are caused, in part, by the fact that they are less likely to be married than older sexually active people and therefore have more sexual partners. In addition, they may have sex with other partners at higher risk and may be less likely to receive health care for curable STDs. For some STDs, such as chlamydia, adolescent women may also be more physiologically susceptible to infection than older women (Centers for Disease Control and Prevention, 2005).

Rates of some curable STDs that have been targeted by STD prevention programs have been reduced among adolescents, just as they have been reduced among adults. For example, gonorrhea rates among both genders declined until 2005 when they increased slightly and syphilis rates declined among female teens (rates among male teens are low and remain relatively unchanged) (Centers for Disease Control and Prevention, 2005).

These declines have occurred among all three major racial/ethnic groups with the exception of syphilis rates among Hispanic and white teens (Centers for Disease Control and Prevention, 2005). There has been a particularly dramatic decrease in syphilis rates among African American teens. These data demonstrate that it is possible to reduce STDs among teens. On the other hand, the prevalence of some incurable STDs has increased among teens. For example, the prevalence of herpes simplex virus type 2 increased substantially through the 1980s and remained constant through the 1990s (Weinstock, 2004).

HIV prevalence among young adults in general is quite low. An estimate based upon a nationally representative sample of young men and women aged 18-26 was 1 per 1,000 (Morris et al., 2006). The rate was dramatically greater for non-Hispanic black young adults (5 per 1,000) than for other young adults.

Despite the low prevalence rate, between 2001 and 2005, the estimated number of HIV/AIDS cases increased among teens aged 15-19. By the end of 2005, an estimated 6,324 AIDS cases among 13- to 19-year-old teenagers had been reported in the United States (Centers for Disease Control and Prevention, 2006a). In addition, in the 33 areas with confidential HIV infection reporting, an estimated 5,322 teenagers were reported to be living with HIV/AIDS in 2005. Because of the long and variable time between HIV infection and AIDS, rates of HIV infection provide a more accurate picture of current trends in the epidemic than rates of AIDS. Among younger teenagers (13-15 years), the

majority of HIV diagnoses occur among females (77 percent), while among older teenagers (16-19 years) slightly more than half of HIV diagnoses occurred among males (52 percent). For females, the most common mode of transmission was heterosexual contact, and for males it was male-to-male sex (Rangel, 2006). In 2003, approximately three-quarters of newly diagnosed HIV infections occurred among black youth.

The human and monetary costs of STDs are very high. STDs other than HIV can lead to infertility, ectopic pregnancy, cancer, and other health problems, as well as cause long-term emotional suffering and stress. STDs can also increase the likelihood of HIV transmission. A 1998 study estimated that curable STDs cost a total of $8.4 billion per year in direct costs for sexually active people of all ages (American School Health Association, 1998).

Adolescent Sexual Activity

Among female teens, the median age of menarche is 12.6 years while the median age of marriage is 25.3 (The Alan Guttmacher Institute, 2002; U.S. Census Bureau, 2004). For males, the median age for spermarche is 14.0 years while the median age of marriage is 27.1 years (The Alan Guttmacher Institute, 2002; U.S. Census Bureau, 2004). Therefore, about 13 years elapse on average between the time when adolescents become fertile and their sexual feelings intensify and the time when they marry, creating a long period during which they need to avoid unintended premarital pregnancy and STDs either through abstinence from sex or the use of condoms or other forms of contraception.

About half of all teens report that they have ever had sex (Abma, 2004), and the proportion of teens who have ever had sexual intercourse increases steadily with age. In 2002, the proportion of teens who ever had sex by age 15 was 16% of males and 14% of females. The proportion of teens who ever had sex by age 19 was 70% of males and 75% of females (Flanigan, 2006). Among students in grades 9-12 across the U.S. in 2005, 47 percent reported ever having had sexual intercourse. This ranged from 34% among 9th graders to 63% among 12 graders (Centers for Disease Control and Prevention, 2006b).

Rates of sexual activity also vary with race and ethnicity, although much of this variation disappears if one controls for poverty and other forms of disadvantage. In 2005, among high school students, 68 percent of African-American teens, 51 percent of Hispanic teens, and 43 percent of white teens had ever had sex (Centers for Disease Control and Prevention, 2006b).

When very young females do have sex, many report that it was either involuntary or unwanted. For example, in 2002, among sexually experienced female teens who were 14 years old or younger when they first had sex, 18 percent reported their first sexual experience was involuntary, and 27 percent indicated it was unwanted (Abma, 2004).

Teens who have sex tend to do so sporadically. Of all sexually experienced females, only 43% report that they had sex at all during the 12 months prior to the interview and only 36% report having sex during the previous three months (Abma, 2004). Among high school students in 2005, 47% had ever had sex, but only 34% had sex during the previous three months (Centers for Disease Control and Prevention, 2006b). Because of this sporadic sexual activity, adolescents often do not plan to have sex on a particular occasion, but sometimes do so anyway.

Most sexually experienced teenagers do not have sexual intercourse with more than one sexual partner during any given period of time; they most commonly practice premarital serial monogamy (Alan Guttmacher Institute, 1994). Furthermore, in 2002, about 70% of sexually experienced female teens and 60% of sexually experienced male teens had either zero or one sexual partner in the past year. However, 16% of sexually experienced males and females had two or more partners in the past year and, therefore, are at greater risk, especially of STDs (Abma, 2004). In part because sexually active teens generally accumulate more partners over time, teens who initiate intercourse at younger ages have a greater number of sexual partners.

While most sexually active teens have sexual partners close to their own ages, some have partners that are much older. For instance, among sexually experienced female teens, 22% had their first sexual experience with a male four or more years older, and only 19% first had sex with a partner who was the same age or younger (Abma, 2004). When female teens have sex at a young age with much older males, the chances are greater that their first sexual experiences are involuntary or unwanted, and that they will become a teen parent (Manlove, 2006).

Most sexually experienced teenagers report that they use contraception, at least some of the time. About 74% of female teens used contraception the first time they had sex, and 83% reported using contraception the last time they had sex (Suellentrop, 2006). Reports from males are slightly higher: among male teens, approximately 82% used some form of contraception the first time they had sex, and 90% reported using contraception the last time they had sex (Suellentrop, 2006).

Non-Hispanic white female teens are more likely than both African-American and Hispanic female teens to use contraception the last time they had sex. According to the 2002 National Survey of Family Growth, 89% of white teen females, 74% of African-American teen females, and 63% of Hispanic teen females used one or more methods of contraception the last time they had sexual intercourse (Suellentrop, 2006). For all three racial/ethnic groups, the proportion of teen-age females who used a contraceptive method the last time they had sex increased between 1995 and 2002.

Condoms and oral contraceptives are the two most commonly used methods of contra-ception. In 2005, 69% of African-American, 63% of white, and 58% of Hispanic sexually active high school students used a condom the last time they had sex (Centers for Disease Control and Prevention, 2006b). Since the mid-1980s, the use of condoms has increased, in part because of the HIV epidemic (Darroch and Singh, 1999). In addition, small but increasing percentages of teens use hormonal contraceptives such as Depo-Provera. These long-acting methods were not available before the 1990s, but, by 2002, they accounted for 10% of contraceptive use at last sex, and 21% of teens reported that they had ever used an injectable hormonal method (Abma, 2004).

Condoms are the most commonly used method of contraception at first sex. In 2002, 66% of sexually experienced female teens and 71% of sexually experienced male teens used a condom the first time they had sex (Suellentrop, 2006). More than nine in ten sexually experienced female teens reported that they had ever used a condom (Suellentrop, 2006).

However, the use of condoms declines with age and sexual experience. In 2002, condom use at last sex decreased from 83% among sexually active male teens aged 15-17 to 64% among sexually active male teens aged 18-19 (Suellentrop, 2006). Condoms are used disproportionately with casual partners and less commonly with close romantic partners (Pleck et al., 1988). Furthermore, the longer a sexual relationship between two people lasts, the less likely they are to use condoms (Ku et al., 1994).

Like adults, many teenagers do not carefully and consistently use contraceptives, thereby exposing themselves to risks of

pregnancy or STDs. For example, among 15- to 19-year-old females relying upon oral contraceptives as their main contraceptive, only 70% took a pill every day (Abma et al., 1997). Among never-married female teens who had sex in the past year, only 28% used a condom every time they had sex. Similarly, among never-married sexually experienced male teens, only 48% used a condom during every act of intercourse in the last year (Abma, 2004).

When adolescents were asked why they did not use contraception when they had sex, one of the most frequent responses is that they did not expect or plan to have sex and, therefore, were not prepared (Kirby et al., 1989; Princeton Survey Research Associates, 1996; Kirby et al., 1999). When adolescents fail to use contraception, become pregnant, and go to term, they are far more likely to say that they failed to use contraception because they were not concerned about becoming pregnant (Stevens-Simon et al., 1996). Adolescents say far less frequently that they can't afford birth control, don't know where to get it, can't get it, or don't know how to use it. Among teens who reported that they stopped using a method of contraception, 53% reported that they stopped using that method because of side effects while only 2% indicated that it was too expensive and 7% said it was too hard to obtain (Suellentrop, 2006).

In sum, a large majority of teens initiate sex during their teen years, but fail to use condoms or other forms of contraception consistently and correctly. Consequently, despite large declines, teen pregnancy rates, birth rates and some STD rates remain far too high, both in comparison with other develop-ed countries and in terms of the human costs to the teens and especially their children.

Accordingly, many people concerned with adolescent reproductive health and many schools and other youth serving organizations have developed and implemented programs to reduce unintended pregnancy and sexually transmitted disease among young people. Typically, these programs strive to delay the initiation of sex, increase the return to abstinence, reduce the number of sexual partners, or increase condom or other contraceptive use. More than 100 of these programs have been evaluated. This review summarizes the results of those studies meeting specified criteria.

METHODS

Search for and Identification of Evaluation Studies Meeting Specified Criteria

Except where noted, this review focuses *only* on those studies meeting certain programmatic and methodological criteria. To be included in this review, each study had to meet the following criteria:

- The program had to:
  o Focus on adolescents of middle school or high school age (roughly 12-18) or parents of children up to age 18.
  o Not focus on pregnant or parenting teens.
  o Be implemented in the United States.
- The research methods had to:
  o Include a reasonably strong experimental design with both intervention and comparison groups and both pretest and posttest data collection.
  o Have a sample size of at least 100.
  o Measure program impact upon one or more of the following sexual behaviors (initiation of sex, frequency of sex, and number of sexual partners); use of condoms or contraception more generally; composite measures of sexual risk (e.g., frequency of unprotected sex); pregnancy rates; birth rates and STD rates.
  o Measure impact on those behaviors that can change quickly (i.e., frequency of sex, number of sexual partners, use of condoms, use of contraception or sexual risk-taking) for at least 3 months or measure

impact on those behaviors or outcomes that change less quickly (i.e., initiation of sex, pregnancy rates or STD rates) for at least 6 months.
  o Employ proper statistical analyses.
- The study had to be completed or published in 1990 or thereafter.

To be as inclusive as possible, studies did not have to be published in peer-reviewed journals to be included in the review.

Studies meeting these criteria were identified through searches of 10 databases (PubMed, PsychInfo, Popline, Sociological Abstracts, Psychological Abstracts, Bireme, Dissertation Abstracts, ERIC, CHID, and Biologic Abstracts) through December 2004 and searches of three databases (PubMed, PsychoInfo and Popline) through December 2005. In addition, relevant studies were identified through reviews of past issues of 16 journals through December 2006; contacts with researchers at professional meetings and those in the process of completing studies; a review of reports, training materials, and process evaluation reports; and previous literature reviews from various authors.

Analysis of Study Results

All identified studies meeting these criteria were reviewed and specific information from each study was summarized on a one-page summary sheet that included key data such as characteristics of the sample, the characteristics of the intervention, research methods and effects on both sexual risk behaviors and mediating factors (e.g. relevant knowledge and attitudes). All of these one-page summaries are available from the author. Because each of the effects of each study was coded, each study that measured multiple outcomes was counted multiple times.

All effects on behaviors or mediating factors were considered significant if they met two conditions. First, they were statistically significant at the p<0.05 level or p<0.01 level.

Second, this significance level was based on either the total study sample or a large sub-group (e.g., males or females, one of the three major racial/ethnic groups in the U.S., or sexually experienced or inexperienced youth).

Studies sometimes reported results for multiple measures of each behavior, for different time periods, for different sub-populations, or for various combinations of the above. Thus, some studies reported one or a very small number of positive effects on behavior but also reported a large majority of results that were not significant. To avoid presenting only the positive results and to provide a more balanced overview of the results, the following rules for summarizing results were adopted.

- Regarding *different measures of the same outcome behavior*, all measures across all the studies were rank-ordered according to their probable impact on prevalence. For example, use of condoms over 12 months was ranked higher than was condom use at first sex. Only the results from the highest ranked measure reported in each study were included in tables.

- Regarding *different time periods,* because very *short-term effects on behaviors* would have had little impact on pregnancy or STD rates or HIV prevalence, only those results for at least three months or six months (depending on the behavior) or longer were included in tables.

- Regarding *different sub-samples,* the results had to describe a sub-sample representing roughly one-third of the sample or more in order to be included.

Even these rules for summarizing results provided a more positive picture than all the results from all studies. However, this positive bias was at least partly offset by a different negative bias; many results presented in the studies were based on samples with insufficient power. At least half of the studies reviewed lacked statistical power to detect meaningful program effects on behavior. For example, if a program reduced the percentage of young people who initiated sex (or who had sex without a condom) from 30 percent to 20 percent, this reduction would be programmatically meaningful. However, to have an 80% chance of finding a 10 percentage point change in a dichotomous outcome to be statistically significant at the $p<.05$ level, a completed pretest-posttest sample size of close to 600 is needed. Half the studies had a sample size smaller than 600.

Moreover, the problem of insufficient power was further aggravated by the fact that studies typically had to divide their samples into various sub-samples. For example, to measure the impact of the program on sexual initiation, the samples were typically restricted to those who were sexually inexperienced at baseline, and to measure impact on condom or contraceptive use, the studies were commonly restricted to those who were sexually active. In addition, in some studies, data were further analyzed separately by sex or by age. Despite the fact that many studies were underpowered, if their results were not significant, we coded them as not significant in the tables.

RESULTS
A Typology of Programs that May Reduce Teen Pregnancy and STDs

This review identified 63 studies meeting the criteria above and measuring the impact of programs on adolescent sexual behavior. They are described individually in Figure 1 and summarized in Tables 1–10. This review also identified 50 additional studies that employed strong quasi-experimental designs, but only occasionally are any of those studies reviewed here.

Those programs in the 63 studies were found in schools; in health, family planning, and STD clinics; and in community organizations working with youth (including faith communities). Some are designed to support and encourage abstinence; others to improve knowledge, attitudes, and skills about condoms and other forms of contraception; some to improve access to condoms and other forms of contraception; and still others to improve education, life skills, and life opportunities more generally. Some focus on preventing pregnancy and others concentrate on STDs, particularly HIV. Some target adolescents, while others target parents of adolescents or even parents of younger children. Some focus on sexually inexperienced youth, others on the sexually experienced. Some use structured curricula with groups of youth, others provide one-on-one instruction or counseling, and still others use interactive videos or community-wide media approaches.

Some programs are implemented by adults; others are led by the peers of adolescents. Given all these important differences and dimensions, it is very difficult to create any single typology to organize programs to prevent teen pregnancy.

However, one useful way to categorize prevention programs is by the behavioral risk and protective factors that they target. Accordingly, this review first divides programs and their respective evaluations into those that focus primarily on sexual risk and protective factors affecting adolescent sexual and condom/contraceptive behavior, those that focus primarily upon non-sexual risk and protective factors, and those that address both. Within these three broad categories, programs are divided into seven major groups and several sub-groups (see Box #1 below).

Box 1: Organization of study reviews

Programs Focusing Primarily on Sexual Risk & Protective Factors	Table
Curriculum-based sexuality education programs in any setting	1
Sex and HIV education programs for parents and their families	2
Stand-alone video-based and computer-based interventions	3
Clinic based programs to provide reproductive health care or contraceptive access	4
· Protocols for clinic appointments and supportive activities	4
· Advance provision of emergency contraception	4
Community-wide pregnancy or STD/HIV prevention initiatives with multiple components	5
Programs Focusing Primarily on Non-Sexual Factors	
Early childhood programs	6
Youth development programs for adolescents	7
· Service-learning programs	7
· Vocational education and employment programs	7
· Other youth development programs	7
Programs Focusing on Both Sexual and Non-Sexual Factors	
Programs to address substance abuse, violence, and sexual risk	8
· Client-centered programs	9
Very Intensive Long-Term Programs	10

Figure 1: Experimental Studies[1]

| Curriculum based sex/HIV education | | | |
Study	Design	Intervention	Results
Aarons, Jenkins 2000 Postponing Sexual Involvement	N=422 14 months	Middle and junior high schools 16 sessions 12 hours	Initiation of sex: M=0 F=+ Contraceptive use at last sex: M=0 F=+
Blake, Ledsky 2000	N=930 6 months	High school 17 sessions 14 hours	Initiation of sex: 0 Frequency of sex: 0 Consistency of condom use: 0
Borawski, Trapl unpublished Be Proud! Be Responsible! adapted	N=1252 12 months	High schools 6 sessions 5 hours	Initiation of sex: 0 Sex in past 3 months: 0 Refused sex because did not have condom: 0
Boyer, Shafer 2005	N=1381 14 months	Marine Corps recruit training 4 sessions 8 hours	Sexually transmitted infection: + Unintended pregnancy: 0 Multiple sex partners: - Condom use: +
Bryan, Aiken 1996 Condom Promotion	N=145 6 months	University students 1 session .75 hours	Condom use at last intercourse: +
Coyle, Basen-Enquist 2001, 2004 Safer Choices	N=3058 31 months	High school 20 sessions 16.5 hours	Initiation of intercourse: + Frequency of sex: 0 Number of sex partners: 0 Use of condoms at last sex: + Use of contraception at last sex: + Number of sex partners without condoms: +
Coyle, Kirby 2000, 2004 Draw the Line	N=1811 36 months	Middle school 20 sessions 16.5 hours	Initiation of sex: M=+ F=0 Sexual intercourse in past 12 months: M=+ F=0 Freq of sex in past 12 months: M=+ F=0 Number of sex partners in past 12 months: M=+ F=0 Condom use at last intercourse: M=0 F=0
DiClemente, Wingwood 2004	N=460 12 months	Community health agencies 4 sessions 16 hours	Condom use: + New sex partner in past 30 days: + Pregnancy: + Unprotected sex in past 30 days: + STD incidence: +

[1]Impact on behavior: no significant change = 0; significant desirable change = +; significant undesirable change = -.

410

Figure 1: Experimental Studies[1]

Curriculum based sex/HIV education			
Study	Design	Intervention	Results
Eisen, Zellman 1990 Teen Talk	N=888 12 months	Six family planning service agencies and one school district with 2 programs 10 hours	Initiation of intercourse: M=+ F=0 Use of contraception: 0
Gillmore, Morrison 1997	N=314 6 months	Urban public health clinics and an urban county juvenile detention facility 2 sessions 8 hours	Condom use: 0 Number of sex partners: 0 Refused sex without a condom: 0
Jemmott, Jemmott 1992 Be Proud! Be Responsible!	N=150 3 months	A school on Saturdays 1 session 5 hours	Frequency of sex: + Number of partners: + Condom use: +
Jemmott, Jemmott 1998 Making a Difference! A Sexual Abstinence Curriculum	N=610 12 months	A school on Saturdays 2 sessions 8 hours	Initiation of sex: + Frequency of sex 0 Condom Use: 0 Sexual risk: 0
Jemmott, Jemmott 1998 Making Proud Choices! A Safer Sex Curriculum	N=610 12 months	A school on Saturdays 2 sessions 8 hours	Initiation of sex: 0 Frequency of sex 0 Condom Use: + Sexual risk: +
Jemmott, Jemmott 1999	N=460 6 months	Community 1 session 5 hours	Number of partners: 0 Frequency of sex: 0 Sexual risk: +
Jemmott, Jemmott 2005	N=604 12 months	Adolescent clinic in a hospital 1 session 4 hours	Number of partners: + Sexual Risk: + STD: +
Kirby, Korpi 1997 ENABL	N=7340 17 months	Mixed middle school and community 5 sessions 5 hours	Initiation of intercourse: 0 Frequency of sex: 0 Number of sexual partners: 0 Use of condoms:0 Use of birth control pills: 0 Pregnancy: - STD diagnosis (ever): -

[1]Impact on behavior: no significant change = 0; significant desirable change = +; significant undesirable change = -.

Figure 1: Experimental Studies[1]

Curriculum based sex/HIV education

Study	Design	Intervention	Results
Kirby, Korpi 1997 SNAP	N=1616 17 months	Middle school 8 sessions 6.5 hours	Initiation of sex: 0 Frequency of sex: 0 Number of partners: 0 Condom use: 0 Birth control pill use: - Pregnancy: 0 STD: 0
Koniak-Griffin 2003	N=497 12 months	School district programs for pregnant adolescents or young mothers 4 sessions, 8 hours	Number of partners: + Number of unprotected sex:+
LaChausse 2006	N=287 6 months	High schools 6 sessions	Initiation of sex: + Frequency of sex: + Condom use: 0
Levy, Perhats 1995, 1997 Youth AIDS Prevention Project	N=1229 24 months	Junior high school 15 sessions 12.5 hours	Initiation of intercourse: 0 Frequency of sex: 0 Number of partners: 0 Condom use: 0
Rotheram-Borus, Gwadz 1998 Project Light	N=127 3 months	Social service agency 10.5 hours	Number of partners: + Sexual risk: +
Rotheram-Borus, Lee 2001 Project TLC	N=154 15 months	Adolescent clinic 23 sessions 46 hours	Number of partners: 0 Sexual risk: + Condom use: +
Rotheram-Borus, Murphy 1998 Project Light 2 months	N=102 3 months	Social service agency 3 sessions 11 hours	Frequency of sex: 0 Number of partners: 0 Condom use: 0 Sexual risk: 0
Slonim-Nevo, Auslander 1996	N=218 12 months	Residential center for youth 9 sessions 13.5 hours	Sex with unknown partner: 0 Sex without condom: 0
St. Lawrence, Brasfield 1995 Becoming a Responsible Teen	N=225 14 months	Clinic	Initiation of sex: + Frequency of sex: + Condom use: + Sexual risk: +

[1]Impact on behavior: no significant change = 0; significant desirable change = +; significant undesirable change = -.

Figure 1: Experimental Studies[1]

Curriculum based sex/HIV education

Study	Design	Intervention	Results
St. Lawrence, Crosby 1999 Becoming a Responsible Teen (modified)	N=312 6 months	Juvenile reformatory 8 sessions 14 hours	Number of partners: 0 Condom use: 0 Sexual risk: 0
St. Lawrence, Crosby 2002 Becoming a Responsible Teen (modified)	N=142 12 months	Adolescent residential drug treatment 12 sessions 18 hours	Abstinence: + Number of partners: + Condom use: + Sexual risk: +
Stanton, Guo 2005 Focus on Kids, WV	N=810 9 months	Mixed secondary school and community 8 sessions, 12 hours	Frequency of sex: 0 Used condom at last sex: 0
Stanton 1996, 1996, 2002 Focus on Kids	N=178 36 months	Housing developments 8 sessions 18.5 hours	Condom use: + Initiation of sex: 0
Villarruel, Jemmott, Jemmott 2006 ¡Cuádate! The Latino Youth Health Promotion Program	N=553 12 months	School on Saturday 2 sessions 8 hours	Initiation of sex: 0 Frequency of sex: + Number of partners: + Condom use: + Sexual risk: +
Wenger, Greenberg 1992	N=370 6 months	University health center 1 session 1 hour	Frequency of sex: 0 Number of partners: 0 Condom use: 0

Parent Programs

Study	Design	Intervention	Results
Diiorio, Resnicow, McCarty 2006 Keepin' It R.E.A.L.!	N=525 24 months	Boys and Girls Clubs 7 sessions 14 hours	Initiation of sex: 0 Condom use: +
Miller, Norton 1993 Facts and Feelings	N=503 12 months	home 6 sessions 2 hours	Initiation of sex: 0
Stanton, Cole 2004, 2003 Focus on Kids plus ImPACT	N=494 24 months	Community housing developments 8 sessions plus boosters 12 hours +	Frequency of sex: + Birth control use: 0 Condom use: + Sexual risk: 0 Pregnancy: +

[1]Impact on behavior: no significant change = 0; significant desirable change = +; significant undesirable change = -.

Figure 1: Experimental Studies[1]

Video

Study	Design	Intervention	Results
DeLamater, Wagstaff 2000	N=562 6 months	STD clinic 1 sessions 0.25 hour	Number of partners: 0 Frequency of sex: 0 Condom use: 0
Downs, Murray, de Bruin, 2004 Interactive video intervention	N=258 6 months	clinic 4 sessions 1.25 hours	Frequency of sex: + Condom use: 0 STD: +

Advance provision of emergency contraception

Study	Design	Intervention	Results
Belzer, Sanchez 2005	N=91 12 months	Community Given education and one packet of EC	Birth control use: 0 Condom use: 0 Sexual risk: -
Gold, Wolford 2004	N=192 6 months	Hospital based teen clinic Given written and verbal information and one packet of EC	Birth control use:0 Condom use: + Sexual risk: 0 STD: 0
Raine, Harper 2000	N=213 4 months	Family planning clinic Given education and one packet of EC	Condom use: 0 Sexual risk: 0 Birth control use: -
Raine, Harper 2005	N=1950 6 months	Family planning clinic Given education and three packets of EC	Frequency of sex: 0 Number of partners: 0 Condom use: 0 Sexual risk: 0 Pregnancy: 0 STD: 0
Raymond, Stewart 2006	N=1412 12 months	Family planning clinic Given education and two packets of EC	Frequency of sex: 0 Contraceptive use: 0 Condom use: 0 Pregnancy: 0; STD: 0

Other Clinic Characteristics

Study	Design	Intervention	Results
Hercog-Baron, Furstenberg 1986	N=358 15 months	Clinics 6 sessions	Contraceptive use: 0 Pregnancy: 0

[1]Impact on behavior: no significant change = 0; significant desirable change = +; significant undesirable change = -.

Figure 1: Experimental Studies[1]

Clinic protocols

Study	Design	Intervention	Results
Boekeloo, Schamus 1999 ASSESS	N=197 9 months	Clinic 1 session 0.5 hour	Initiation: - Frequency of sex: 0 Number of partners: 0 Condom use: + STD: 0 Sexual risk: 0
Danielson, Marcy 1990	N=971 12 months	Clinic 1 session 1 hour	Frequency of sex: 0 Contraceptive use: +
Metzler, Biglan, Noell, 2000 MAC-Choice (Monogamy, Abstinence, Condoms)	N=105 12 months	Public health clinic 5 sessions 6.25 hours	Number of partners: + Condom use: 0 Frequency of sex: + Sexual risk: + STD: 0
Orr, Langefeld 1996	N=105 6 months	Family planning and STD clinic 1 session, 0.25 hour	Condom use: +
Roye, C, Silverman, PB, Krauss, B 2006 Project RESPECT, adapted	N=187 12 months	Clinic 1 session of Video + counseling 0.75 hour	Condom use: + STI: 0

Community wide initiatives

Study	Design	Intervention	Results
Sikkema, Anderson, Kelly, 2005	N=763 12 months	Community housing developments Workshop plus leadership council and activities	Initiation of sex: + Condom use: +

Early Childhood

Study	Design	Intervention	Results
Campbell 1999 Abecedarian Project	N=104 216 months	Preschool and elementary schools 8 years of program activities	Birth rates: +

[1]Impact on behavior: no significant change = 0; significant desirable change = +; significant undesirable change = -.

Figure 1: Experimental Studies[1]

Other youth development

Study	Design	Intervention	Results
Hahn, Leavitt 1994 Quantum Opportunities Program	N=149 48 months	Community	Birth rates: 0
Wolchik, Sandler, Millsap 2002 New Beginnings Program	N=218 72 months	community 11 sessions 19.25 hours	Number of partners: +

Service learning

Study	Design	Intervention	Results
Allen, Philliber 1997 TOP	N=695 8 months	mixed school and community Weekly sessions 46 hours	Pregnancy: +
O'Donnell, Stueve 2002, 1999 Reach for Health CYS	N=195 40 months	Middle school 30 weeks 90 hours+	Initiation of sex: + Frequency of sex: + Sexual risk: 0

Vocational education

Study	Design	Intervention	Results
Cave, Bos 1993 JOBSTART	N=1941 48 months	Mixed school and community 400 hours of activities	Pregnancy: - Birth rates: -
Grossman, Snipes 1992, 1992 STEP	N=4800 60 months	Mixed school and community over 2 summers 36 hours	Frequency of sex: 0 Contraceptive use: 0 Births: 0
Jastrzab, Masker 1997 Conservation and Youth Service Corps	N= 15 months	Community 4-5 months	Pregnancy: +
Schochet, Burghardt 2000 Job Corps	N=11787 30 months	Community 8 months 1,000+ hours	Birth rate: 0

Client centered programs

[1]Impact on behavior: no significant change = 0; significant desirable change = +; significant undesirable change = -.

Figure 1: Experimental Studies[1]

Study	Design	Intervention	Results
McBride, Gienapp 2000	N=690 9 months	Mixed – clinic, school and community 27 hours	Initiation of sex: 0 Frequency of sex: + Contraceptive use: 0

Substance abuse, etc programs

Study	Design	Intervention	Results
Clark, Miller, Nagy, 2005 project AIM	N=156 12 months	Middle school 10 sessions	Initiation of sex: +
Flay, Graumlich, Segawa, 2004 Social Development Curriculum (SDC) & School/ Community Intervention	N=1153 44 months	High school 72 sessions	Frequency of sex: + Condom use: +
Harrington, Giles 2001 All Stars	N=1887 20 months	Middle school	Sexual risk: 0
Moberg, Piper 1998 Healthy for Life	N=1386 48 months	Middle school 58 sessions	Initiation of sex: - Frequency of sex: - Condom use: 0

Very intensive youth development

Study	Design	Intervention	Results
Kirby, Rhodes, Campe, 2005 Carrera Program, replication (WAGES)	N=328 31 months	Community 7 program components	Initiation of sex: 0 Number of partners: 0 Frequency of sex: 0 Contraception use: 0 Condom use: 0 Sexual risk: 0 Pregnancy: -
Philliber, Kaye, Herrling, 2002 Carrera Program	N=485 36 months	Community 7 component program	Initiation of sex: + Condom use: 0 Pregnancy: + Childbirth: +

[1]Impact on behavior: no significant change = 0; significant desirable change = +; significant undesirable change = -.

Programs Focusing Primarily on Sexual Risk & Protective Factors

Curriculum-Based STD/HIV Education Programs

During the last two decades, professionals concerned with teen pregnancy and STD have viewed curriculum-based sex and STD/HIV education programs as a partial solution to these problems. Indeed, sex and STD/HIV education programs that are based on a written curriculum and that are implemented among groups of youth in school, clinic, or community settings are a promising type of intervention to reduce adolescent sexual risk behaviors.

Characteristics of the Studies Reviewed

Thirty studies of curriculum-based programs were found that met the criteria described above (Eisen et al., 1990; Jemmott III et al., 1992; Wenger et al., 1992; Levy et al., 1995; St. Lawrence et al., 1995; Slonim-Nevo et al., 1996; Stanton et al., 1996; Gillmore et al., 1997; Kirby et al., 1997b; Kirby et al., 1997a; Jemmott III et al., 1998b; Rotheram-Borus et al., 1998b; Rotheram-Borus et al., 1998a; Jemmott III et al., 1999; St. Lawrence et al., 1999; Aarons et al., 2000; Blake et al., 2000; Coyle et al., 2000; Coyle et al., 2001; Rotheram-Borus et al., 2001a; Rotheram-Borus et al., 2001b; St. Lawrence et al., 2002; Koniak-Griffin et al., 2003; DiClemente et al., 2004; Boyer et al., 2005; Jemmott III et al., 2005; Stanton et al., 2005; Villarruel et al., 2006; Borawski et al., Unpublished). Because there is considerable diversity even among these curriculum-based sex and HIV education programs, the communities in which they are implemented, and their evaluations, some of their important characteristics are summarized below.

About three-fourths of the studies were implemented in urban areas and most were implemented in communities at high risk of STD/HIV. Most commonly they were imple-mented in communities, schools and clinics, in that order.

Despite the fact that these programs were implemented throughout the country and among different age groups, the programs, themselves, had numerous qualities in common and many of them incorporated many of the characteristics of programs previously found to be associated with effectiveness (Kirby, 1997). The majority focused on preventing STD/HIV, but some also focused on preventing pregnancy and a couple focused only on preventing pregnancy. This greater emphasis on STD/HIV undoubt-edly reflects concern about young people contracting HIV and the funds and other resources devoted to reducing STD/HIV transmission.

Virtually all the programs encouraged specific behaviors. Virtually all the programs encouraged abstinence, but also discussed or promoted the use of condoms and/or other forms of contraception if young people chose to be sexually active. Only one was an abstinence-only program.

Almost all the programs identified one or more theories that formed the basis for their programs and often specified particular psychosocial mediating factors to be changed. Nearly all the interventions included at least two different interactive activities designed to involve youth and help them personalize the information (e.g., role playing, simulations or individual worksheets that applied lessons to their lives).

The one area of greatest variation in these programs was length. While one was as short as one class period and another as long as 46 class periods, 80% were between 5 and 17 class periods.

To be included in this review, studies had to measure impact on actual behavior. All measures of sexual and contraceptive behavior relied on self-reports. Although some under- and over-reporting of these behaviors undoubtedly occurred, these data are generally believed to be reasonably reliable and valid, and usually, biases are similar in both the intervention and control groups, especially when the data are collected confidentially by data collectors months after the end of the intervention (Sonenstein, 1996).

Pregnancy and STD can be measured with laboratory tests and thereby overcome many of the problems of self-reported data. Of the four studies that measured impact on pregnancy, only one used pregnancy tests; of the five studies that measured impact on STD, two used a laboratory test. The rest relied on self-reports.

Impact of Programs on Important Sexual Behaviors

These studies demonstrate very clearly that a substantial percentage of sex and STD/HIV education programs significantly decreased one or more types of sexual behavior. Additionally, programs did not increase sexual behavior, as some people have feared (Table 1). More specifically, of those studies that measured impact on one or more sexual behaviors, 43% delayed the initiation of sex, 27% decreased the frequency of sex (which includes returning to abstinence) and 42% reduced the number of sexual partners. In contrast, none of them hastened the initiation of sex, and only 5% or 6% (one program) increased the frequency of sex or number of sexual partners. Given the large number of coefficients, the increase found with this one program could have occurred by chance.

In the studies that measured condom and contraceptive use, half the programs increased condom use and 60% increased contraceptive use (Table 1). Some studies recognized that STD/HIV transmission and pregnancy can be reduced either by decreasing sexual activity or by increasing condom or contraceptive use and developed composite measures of sexual

Table 1: Curriculum-Based Sex and STD/HIV Education Programs: Number of Studies Reporting Effects on Sexual Outcomes

Outcomes Measured	All Studies (N=30)	
Delay sex	(n=14)	
Hastened Initiation	0	0%
No Significant Results	8	57%
Delayed Initiation	6	43%
Reduce Frequency of Sex	(n=15)	
Increased Frequency	1	6%
No Significant Results	10	67%
Reduced Frequency	4	27%
Reduce Number of Partners	(n=19)	
Increased Numbers	1	5%
No Significant Results	10	53%
Reduced Number	8	42%
Increase Condom Use	(n=24)	
Reduced Use	0	0%
No Significant Results	12	50%
Increased Use	12	50%
Increase Contraceptive Use	(n=5)	
Reduced Use	1	20%
No Significant Results	1	20%
Increased Use	3	60%
Reduce Sexual Risk Taking	(n=18)	
Increased Risk	0	0%
No Significant Results	5	28%
Reduced Risk	13	72%
Reduce Pregnancy: Self-Report	(n=3)	
Increased Number	1	33%
No Significant Results	1	33%
Reduced Number	1	33%
Reduce Pregnancy: Laboratory Test	(n=1)	
Increased Number	0	0%
No Significant Results	1	100%
Reduced Number	0	0%
Reduce STDs: Self-Report	(n=2)	
Increased Number	1	50%
No Significant Results	1	50%
Reduced Number	0	0%
Reduce STDs: Laboratory Test	(n=3)	
Increased Number	0	0%
No Significant Results	1	33%
Reduced Number	2	66%

activity and condom use, such as "frequency of unprotected sex" or "number of unprotected sexual partners." These measures are strongly related to STD/HIV transmission and pregnancy. Seventy-two percent reduced these measures of sexual risk-taking.

Only four studies measured impact on pregnancy rate. Two found no significant impact, one found a decrease and one found an increase. Overall, these results suggest these programs did not have an impact on pregnancy.

One of two studies using self-reports found a significant increase in STD rates. This may have been caused by the fact that the intervention encouraged youth to be tested for STD and thus they may have been more likely to report being told they had an STD, even if they were not more likely to actually have an STD. When all study participants were tested and biomarkers were used as the outcome, two of the three studies found significant decreases in STD. These studies were less subject to bias that could result from self report. Therefore, this is an encouraging finding.

Overall, these studies strongly indicate that these programs were far more likely to have a positive impact on behavior than a negative impact. Across all 30 studies, two-thirds (67%) had a significant positive impact on one or more of these sexual behaviors or outcomes, while only 3% had a significant negative impact on one or more of these behaviors or outcomes (a percent roughly equal to or less than what is expected to occur by chance).

In addition, 47% had positive impact on two or more behaviors, but none had a negative impact on two or more behaviors. For example, *Becoming a Responsible Teen* increased abstinence, reduced the number of sexual partners, increased condom use and reduced unprotected sex (St. Lawrence et al., 1995). Similarly, the *Safer Choices* interven-

tion delayed the initiation of sex among Hispanic youth, and increased both condom and contraceptive use among both males and females of all races/ethnicities (Kirby et al., 2004). More generally, studies indicate that it is possible both to reduce sexual behavior and to increase condom or contraceptive use.

While the positive effects of some curriculum-based programs lasted only a few months, the effects of other programs lasted for years. For example, *Safer Choices* (Coyle et al., 2001) found positive behavioral effects over a 31-month period.

Robustness of Findings

These findings were remarkably robust. The patterns of findings remained the same regardless of the type of experimental design used. The results were also very similar for the studies using quasi-experimental designs. In regard to the programs themselves, different programs were effective in different communities and cultures throughout the country. Programs have been found to be effective with low and middle-income youth in low and middle income communities and in rural and urban areas.

These sex and HIV education programs were effective in school, clinic and community settings. A few of the community programs that were effective were actually implemented on school grounds on Saturdays. Because they were not implemented during the school day, they may have been able to include condom-related activities that might not have been allowed in school classes and these activities may have contributed to the success of these programs.

Programs were also effective with both males and females. It is encouraging that programs can increase reported condom use, even among females who have less direct control over condom use. Programs were also effective with both younger and older youth.

Although these findings indicate that these

curriculum-based programs are quite robust, this does not mean that the same program can be effective with all these groups. Rather it means that different programs appropriately designed for each group of youth in each community can be effective.

This robustness should not be confused with magnitude of impact. In general, these programs did not dramatically reduce sexual risk-taking, or STD or pregnancy rates. *Typically, the most effective programs tended to reduce the amount of sexual risk-taking by about a third or less.* Thus, these programs are not a complete solution to the problems of unintended pregnancy, HIV, or other STDs, but they can be an effective component in a larger effort.

Consistency of Results from Replications

A critically important question is whether or not a program that has been found to be effective when designed, implemented and evaluated by a well-funded and highly skilled research team will subsequently be effective when implemented by others in other communities.

Four interventions have now been replicated and evaluated. For three of the four interventions, the majority of the replications also produced positive behavior change. *Be Proud! Be Responsible!* or variations of it have now been evaluated seven times (Jemmott III et al., 1992, 1998a; Jemmott III et al., 1999; Koniak-Griffin et al., 2003; Jemmott III, 2005; Villarruel et al., 2006). All of these studies were randomized trials and one even involved the broad-scale replication of *Be Proud! Be Responsible!* in 86 community-based organizations. In all six studies where it was implemented in the community, *Be Proud! Be Responsible!* had significant positive effects on behavior. However, when the program was implemented in the school class room during the school day, it did not have a significant impact on any sexual behavior (Borawski et al., Unpublished).

Similarly, *Reducing the Risk* was evaluated in four different studies in different parts of the country by three different research teams (Kirby et al., 1991; Hubbard et al., 1998; Zimmerman et al., unpublished-b; Zimmerman et al., Unpublished-a). All of these studies used quasi-experimental designs and are not included in Table 1. However, in all four studies *Reducing the Risk* significantly delayed the initiation of sex and in two studies it also significantly increased condom or contraceptive use among some groups of youth. Replications of other curricula have also demonstrated that curricula can often be effective when they are implemented with fidelity by others in different communities. It is less clear if effective programs will remain effective if *1) they are shortened considerably, 2) activities that focus on increasing condom use are omitted, or 3) they are designed for and evaluated in community settings, but are subsequently implemented in classroom settings.*

Impact of Programs on Risk and Protective Factors that Affect Sexual Risk Behaviors

Although the review of the studies above provides strong evidence that some programs had an impact on sexual risk behaviors, without the results of the impact on risk and protective factors, it does not specify how or why these programs had an impact. Those questions can be partially answered by examining programmatic impact on the risk and protective factors that programs attempted to change in order to change behavior. About half or more of the studies that had either experimental or quasi-experimental designs and measured impact on the following risk and protective factors found a statistically significant impact on these factors:

• *Knowledge about HIV and STDs*

(including methods of preventing STD/ HIV and pregnancy).

- *Perceived risk of HIV or STD.*
- *Values and attitudes regarding any sexual topic e.g., abstinence and condoms.*
- *Self-efficacy to refuse sex, to obtain and use condoms, and to avoid risk.*
- *Motivation to avoid sex or restrict the number of sex partners.*
- *Intention to use a condom*
- *Intention to avoid risk.*
- *Communication with partner*
- *Communication with parents.*
- *Avoiding places that could lead to sex.*

In sum, the evidence was strong that many programs had positive effects on relevant knowledge, awareness of risk, values and attitudes, self-efficacy, and intentions, the very factors specified by many psychosocial theories as being the determinants of behavior. Furthermore, all of these factors have been demonstrated empirically to be related to their respective sexual behaviors (Kirby et al., 2005a). Thus, it appears highly likely that changes in these factors contributed to the changes in sexual risk-taking behaviors.

Common Characteristics of the Curriculum-Based Programs that Had an Impact

The analysis of these effective curricula led to the identification of 17 common characteristics of the curricula, including their development, content and implementation. The methods used to identify these characteristics are described elsewhere (Kirby et al., 2006). The large majority of the effective programs incorporated most of the 17 characteristics of successful curriculum-based programs identified in this analysis. Also, programs that incorporated these characteristics were much more likely to change behavior positively than programs that did not.

The 17 characteristics are described more fully elsewhere (Kirby et al., 2006; Kirby et al., 2007), but are presented in Box 2. A tool to assess whether or not curricula incorporate these characteristics has also been developed (Kirby et al., 2007).

Conclusions about Curriculum-Based Sex and STD/HIV Education Programs

Many of the studies of the impact of sex and STD/HIV education programs had significant limitations. For example, few described their respective programs adequately; none studied programs for youth engaging in same-sex behavior; some had problems with implementation; an unknown number had measurement problems; many were statistically underpowered; most did not adjust for multiple tests of significance; few measured impact on either STD or pregnancy rates; and still fewer measured impact on STD or pregnancy rates with biomarkers. And, of course, there are inherent publication biases that affect the publication of studies: researchers are more likely to try to publish articles if positive results support their theories and programs and journals are more likely to accept articles for publication if results are positive. Fortunately, some of these biases counteract each other.

Despite these limitations, the evidence for the positive impact on behavior of curriculum-based sex and HIV education programs for adolescents is quite strong and encouraging. Most important, 30 studies meeting the criteria described were identified and two-thirds of the programs had a significant positive impact on behavior. Many either delayed or reduced sexual activity or increased condom or contraceptive use or both. The evidence is also strong that these programs in general did not have negative effects. In particular, they did not increase sexual behavior, as some people feared. At least 14 studies found their respective programs had long term behavioral effects lasting one or more years; some lasted

Box 2: The 17 Characteristics of Effective Curriculum-Based Sex and STD/HIV Education Programs

The Process of Developing the Curriculum	The Contents of the Curriculum Itself	The Implementation of the Curriculum
1. Involved multiple people with different backgrounds in theory, research and sex and STD/HIV education to develop the curriculum	*Curriculum Goals and Objectives* 1. Focused on clear health goals – the prevention of STD/HIV and/or pregnancy	1. Secured at least minimal support from appropriate authorities such as departments of health or education, school districts or community organizations
2. Assessed relevant needs and assets of target group	2. Focused narrowly on specific behaviors leading to these health goals (e.g., abstaining from sex or using condoms or other contraceptives), gave clear messages about these behaviors, and addressed situations that might lead to them and how to avoid them	2. Selected educators with desired characteristics (whenever possible), trained them and provided monitoring, supervision and support
3. Used a logic model approach to develop the curriculum that specified the health goals, the behaviors affecting those health goals, the risk and protective factors affecting those behaviors, and the activities addressing those risk and protective factors	3. Addressed multiple sexual psychosocial risk and protective factors affecting sexual behavior (e.g., knowledge, perceived risks, values, attitudes, perceived norms and self-efficacy) *Activities and Teaching Methodologies* 4. Created a safe social environment for youth to participate	3. If needed, implemented activities to recruit and retain youth and overcome barriers to their involvement, e.g., publicized the program, offered food or obtained consent
4. Designed activities consistent with community values and available resources (e.g., staff time, staff skills, facility space and supplies)	5. Included multiple activities to change each of the targeted risk and protective factors 6. Employed instructionally sound teaching methods that actively involved the participants, that helped participants personalize the information, and that were designed to change each group of risk and protective factors	4. Implemented virtually all activities with reasonable fidelity
5. Pilot-tested the program	7. Employed activities, instructional methods and behavioral messages that were appropriate to the youths' culture, developmental age and sexual experience 8. Covered topics in a logical sequence	

close to three or more years, as long as the effects were measured. Most programs also increased psychosocial mediating factors that are known to be related to sexual behavior. These studies help explain how or why these programs are effective.

Given that many programs reduced sexual behavior and/or also increased condom or contraceptive use, they logically would reduce both sexually transmitted disease and pregnancy. The results of the few studies that measured impact on STD or pregnancy were mixed, but those for STD were more encouraging. The lack of consistent positive effects may have been caused, in part, by sample sizes that were too small, by possible negative biases in self-reported STD rates, by significant changes in behavior that were too small or too short term to produce marked changes in STD or pregnancy, by possible failure to change those behaviors that have the strongest impact on STD or pregnancy rates and by other methodological limitations.

Thus, while these programs alone cannot solve the problems of STD, HIV and unintended pregnancy, many of them can change sexual and protective behaviors in desired directions and they can be an important component in larger more comprehensive initiatives.

Sex and HIV/AIDS Education Programs for Parents and Their Families

Most parents and their children have remarkably few conversations about sexual topics, often because both parents and their teens feel so uncomfortable doing so. To help alleviate this problem, many educational programs have been designed to increase parent/child communication. These include programs for parents only, programs for parents and their children together, homework assignments in school sex education classes requiring communication with parents, and

video programs with written materials to be completed at home.

The first study used a clustered randomized design to measure the impact of two different interventions held within the Boys and Girls Clubs (Dilorio et al., 2006). Both programs were intensive: they included seven sessions, two hours each, for mothers and their adolescent daughters. In some of the sessions, mothers and daughters were in the same groups; in others they were not. Both of the programs included the kinds of activities that have been found to be effective in programs for adolescents alone, e.g., they were interactive and skill-based. One of the two programs focused primarily on HIV and its prevention, while the other focused much more broadly on a variety of risk behaviors. The control group met relatively briefly. Neither program had a significant impact on intimate sexual behaviors or on abstinence, but both programs did increase condom use.

Note that another intensive program for mothers and daughters also found an impact on sexual behavior of adolescent females (Dancy et al., 2006). While the study had a cluster experimental design, it measured impact on sexual behavior for only two months, and not three, and thus technically does not meet the criteria for this review and is not included in Table 2. Notably, mothers were trained during six two-hour sessions to teach a course of the same length to their own daughters. Thus, the program was about twice as long for the mothers than for the daughters. The program for the daughters was equally effective, regardless of whether it was taught by their mothers (the first intervention group) or by health experts (a second intervention group), suggesting that it was the instructional content of the program, rather than the communication with the parent that made the difference. Once again, the content of the material for the adolescent daughters may have included some of the qualities of effective curriculum-based programs for teens.

Table 2: Sex and HIV/AIDS Education Programs for Parents and Their Families: Number of Studies Reporting Effects on Different Sexual Outcomes

Outcomes Measured	Parent Programs (N=3)
Delay sex	(n=3)
Hastened Initiation	0
No Significant Results	2
Delayed Initiation	1
Reduce Frequency of Sex	(n=1)
Increased Frequency	0
No Significant Results	0
Reduced Frequency	1
Increase Condom Use	(n=2)
Reduced Use	0
No Significant Results	0
Increased Use	2
Increase Contraceptive Use	(n=1)
Reduced Use	0
No Significant Results	1
Increased Use	0
Reduce Sexual Risk Taking	(n=1)
Increased Risk	0
No Significant Results	0
Reduced Risk	1
Reduce Pregnancy: Self-Report	(n=1)
Increased Number	0
No Significant Results	0
Reduced Number	1

Recognizing that it is often very difficult to get parents to participate in multi-session programs in the community, two studies measured the impact of programs to be delivered in the parents' own homes. The first of these used a rigorous experimental design to measure the impact of a well-designed video and written materials to be used at home (Miller et al., 1993). It increased parent/child communication but failed to delay the onset of intercourse significantly, in part because very few youth in either the intervention or control group initiated sex in the conservative community where it was implemented.

The second study measured the impact of adding a program designed to increase parental monitoring to an effective curriculum for youth alone (Wu et al., 2003). The study measured the impact of the youth program with and without the program for parents to increase parental monitoring. The program for parents in their homes was short. It included a 20-minute video emphasizing parental monitoring and communication about sex, two instructor-led role-plays that involved the parents and youths, and a condom demonstration. At 6 months, but not at 12 months, the youth whose parents received the in-home parent session were less likely to have sex and less likely to have unprotected sex.

Discussion

There are too few studies to reach strong conclusions. However, overall, these results are encouraging. While the results were mixed, two of the three studies did find significant effects on behavior, either abstinence or condom use, and the study that failed to find significant results may have had methodological limitations that contributed to its lack of significant findings. *Notably, those programs that included intensive programs for adolescents as well as their parents were especially likely to be effective.* This result is not surprising because the programs for adolescents by themselves might have been effective even without the parent component. Finally, one study suggests that increasing parental monitoring may also have an impact. While a single study is insufficient to demonstrate the effectiveness of an approach, multiple studies have demonstrated that parental monitoring does affect adolescent sexual risk-taking behavior.

Stand-Alone Video-Based and Computer-Based Interventions

For decades videos have been incorporated into facilitator-led group sessions, either to provide accurate information or to serve as "teasers" to generate group discussion. However, with the rapid changes in media and computer technology during the last decade, people have developed stand-alone video or computer programs.

These programs eliminate the requirements of facilitator-led group sessions and can be implemented nearly anywhere the necessary video or computer equipment is available (e.g., in classrooms, health clinics or the adolescents' own homes). Once developed, the videos or computer programs can be relatively inexpensively disseminated to others. Although adolescent users have some control over how they view interactive videos or computer programs, the basic videos and programs can be replicated with fidelity.

Two different studies have measured the impact of videos, interactive videos, or computer-based interventions on behavior. The first study compared the relative effects of 1) STD/AIDS material presented in a 14-minute non-interactive video tape in an STD clinic, 2) the same material presented by a health educator in the clinic and 3) standard clinic care (DeLamater et al., 2000). The videotape included a number of qualities to enhance its success. For example, it was based on both theory and formative research in the community. It used dialogue, music, images and stories that would appeal to adolescents. It was made by members of the target group (African-American males). It was designed to elicit social responsibility with the message "We got to keep the brothers alive." It was also designed to increase perceived risk of STDs/AIDS and to improve perceptions of peer norms about condom use. It modeled African-American youth discussing condoms and proper methods to use condoms. Finally, it presented information in an authoritative manner. Despite these important qualities, the videotape was too modest an intervention to have a significant impact on behavior. It was short and it was not interactive.

The second study examined the impact of a stand-alone video in health care sites (Downs et al., 2004). The video included a section on sexual situations (negotiation behaviors to reduce STD risk), risk reduction (condom efficacy, getting and using condoms), reproductive health (pelvic exams, female anatomy, physiological responses to infections), and sexually transmitted disease (general information on viral and bacterial STD and eight specific diseases). The video covered this content using vignettes and explicit choice points and behavioral alternatives. Thus, the video was interactive in two ways: users chose which sections to watch and which behaviors the actors should engage in. Users performed cognitive rehearsals, imagining what they would say or do, and then practiced in their heads while the video froze for 30 seconds. Overall, patients spent about 30 minutes with the video during the first visit and at least 15 minutes both three and six months later. The study used an experimental design to compare the impact of the stand-alone video with the impact of the same content in book form or in brochures with the same content. Results over six months indicated that the video reduced the percent of females who had sex during the first three months after the first exposure to the video. It also reduced the reported STD rate at six months.

A different computer-based interactive program was designed for college students (Kiene and Barta, 2006). It was based on the information-motivation-behavioral skills model of health behavior change and also motivational interviewing. A randomized trial measured its impact for only one month and found that it increased condom use during that month.

Finally, video-based interventions have been found to be effective with adults. For example, in an STD clinic a video-based intervention provided information about STDs and their prevention, portrayed positive attitudes about condom use, and modeled appropriate situations for condom use (O'Donnell et al., 1998). After an average of 17 months the intervention group had a lower STD rate than the control group.

Table 3:Stand-Alone Video-Based and Computer-Based Interventions: Number of Studies Reporting Effects on Sexual Outcomes

Outcomes Measured	All Programs (N=2)
Reduce Frequency of Sex	(n=2)
Increased Frequency	0
No Significant Results	1
Reduced Frequency	1
Reduce Number of Partners	(n=1)
Increased Numbers	0
No Significant Results	1
Reduced Number	0
Increase Condom Use	(n=2)
Reduced Use	0
No Significant Results	2
Increased Use	0
Reduce STDs: Self-Report	(n=1)
Increased Number	0
No Significant Results	0
Reduced Number	1

Discussion

In sum, there are too few studies, especially involving adolescents, to reach any strong conclusions. However, these studies suggest that short non-interactive videos alone may not have behavioral effects. *However, when the videos are longer and interactive and when youth view them multiple times, they may have an impact on some behaviors, possibly for as long as six months.*

Family Planning Services

The primary objective of family planning services is to provide clients with contraception and other reproductive health services and the knowledge and skills to use them. According to a 1995 national survey of publicly funded family planning agencies, these agencies typically provided special services for teens (Frost and Bolzan, 1997). About 87% encouraged counselors to spend more time with teenagers than with other clients, and 69% had at least one special program serving teens. According to the 2002 National Survey of Family Growth, an estimated 3.9 million 15- to 19-year-old females (or nearly 40% of all females in that age group) made one or more visits to a clinic or private medical source for a family planning service in a single year (Martinez et al., 2005).

Unfortunately, the research on the impact of family planning services is limited and this review did not uncover any studies that met criteria for inclusion and examined the impact of simply providing services. There were, however, eleven studies that measured the impact of changes in the protocols in the clinic. They studied the impact of modifying what happens during a clinic visit, including the counseling and instruction that takes place between a medical provider and a teen patient and the other materials and activities that can support and reinforce that counseling. These protocol changes are different than group-delivered, curriculum-based sex and STD/ HIV education programs that are sometimes implemented in clinics. These were summarized above and typically have been found to be effective in clinic settings. The programs discussed here involve one-on-one interactions and/or changes in clinics protocols.

Among the eleven studies that examined family planning services, the first five measured the impact of changes in protocols for clinic appointments (Table 4). The first of these five studies evaluated a very modest intervention for female patients with chlamydia (Orr et al., 1996). A nurse spent about 10 to 20 minutes discussing chlamydia with the aid of a pamphlet, demonstrated how to put a condom on a banana and got the patient to practice, and engaged the patient in a brief role-play involving a woman getting her partner to use a condom. An experimental design was used to measure the impact at six months and found that those youth who received the special instruction were substantially more likely to use condoms than those youth who received the standard intervention.

The second study evaluated a program for males that included two parts: (1) a slide-tape program that focused on anatomy, STDs, contraception, couple communication, and access to health services and (2) a visit with a health care practitioner who focused on contraception, reproductive health goals, health risks, and the patient's related interests. Both parts emphasized abstinence and the use of contraception if sexually active. A strong experimental design and questionnaire data collected a year later indicated that the program did not significantly affect sexual activity but did increase use of contraception, especially by the males' partners and by program participants who were not sexually experienced at baseline (Danielson et al., 1990).

The third study evaluated a program that was somewhat similar to the second. (Roye et al., 2006). It included a 21-minute video and 15 to 20 minutes of one-on-one counseling based on a previously successful counseling approach (Project RESPECT). The counseling sessions were client-focused and interactive and one of the primary goals was

Table 4: Clinic-Based Interventions: Number of Studies Reporting Effects

Outcomes Measured	Protocols for Clinic Appointments (N=5)	Advance Provision of Emergency Contraception (N=5)
Delay sex	(n=1)	(n=0)
Hastened Initiation	1	0
No Significant Results	0	0
Delayed Initiation	0	0
Reduce Frequency of Sex	(n=3)	(n=2)
Increased Frequency	0	0
No Significant Results	2	2
Reduced Frequency	1	0
Reduce Number of Partners	(n=2)	(n=1)
Increased Numbers	0	0
No Significant Results	1	1
Reduced Number	1	0
Increase Condom Use	(n=4)	(n=5)
Reduced Use	0	0
No Significant Results	1	4
Increased Use	3	1
Increase Contraceptive Use	(n=1)	(n=4)
Reduced Use	0	1
No Significant Results	0	3
Increased Use	1	0
Reduce Sexual Risk Taking	(n=1)	(n=4)
Increased Risk	0	1
No Significant Results	0	3
Reduced Risk	1	0
Reduce Pregnancy: Self-Report	(n=0)	(n=1)
Increased Number	0	0
No Significant Results	0	1
Reduced Number	0	0
Reduce Pregnancy: Lab	(n=0)	(n=2)
Increased Number	0	0
No Significant Results	0	2
Reduced Number	0	0
Reduce STDs: Self-Report	(n=2)	(n=0)
Increased Number	0	0
No Significant Results	2	0
Reduced Number	0	0
Reduce STDs: Lab	(n=0)	(n=2)
Increased Number	0	0
No Significant Results	0	2
Reduced Number	0	0
Reduce Childbirth	(n=0)	(n=1)
Increased Number	0	0
No Significant Results	0	1
Reduced Number	0	0

to develop a realistic plan for the patient to reduce STD risk. Using an experimental design, the study found that the combination of the video and the counseling (but not either separately) significantly increased condom use at 3 months, but not at 12 months.

The fourth program focused on HIV/STD prevention and served equal percentages of males and females (Boekeloo et al., 1999). It included a 15-minute audio-taped risk assessment and education program, a discussion icebreaker, two brochures on skills and ways to avoid unprotected sex, a brochure on community resources, and parent brochures. On a one-to-one basis, the patient's physician then reviewed the risk assessment with the patient and discussed concerns and methods of avoiding unprotected sex. An experimental design indicated that the program increased use of condoms during the three months after the intervention. It *might* also have increased the chances of having sex but not the frequency of sex during the following three months, but the results were mixed depending upon the type of analysis. However, both results were not significant by nine months after the intervention.

The last study was by far the most intensive (Metzler et al., 2000). Teens attending an STD clinic met individually with counselors for five weekly 60-90 minute sessions. The individual sessions included three primary components designed to 1) prompt a decision to reduce risky sexual behavior and set a safer-sex goal, 2) increase social skills in handling difficult sexual situations, and 3) increase willingness to experience unpleasant reactions to changes in behavior. In a strong randomized trial measuring impact over six months, the intervention reduced the number of partners, reduced the number of non-monogamous partners, reduced the number of sexual contacts with strangers, reduced the frequency of sex, and reduced the use of marijuana before or during sex.

Discussion

The fact that all five of these family planning studies found positive effects on behavior is most encouraging, and the fact that several of them were effective, even with brief, modest interventions is also very encouraging. All five of the interventions focused on sexual and contraceptive behavior, gave clear messages about appropriate sexual and contraceptive behavior, and included one-on-one consultation about the client's own behavior. At the very least, these studies suggest that such approaches should be further developed and rigorously evaluated. These results should also encourage medical providers to review their instructional protocols with youth and to spend more time talking with individual adolescent patients about their sexual and contraceptive activity.

Advance Provision of Emergency Contraception

One of the most common reasons that teens say they didn't use contraception is that they didn't expect to have sex. This situation is far too common among young people who have sex sporadically. Emergency contraception is the only method of contraception that can be used up to 72 hours after sex and can dramatically reduce the chances of pregnancy. Thus, it has the potential to significantly reduce teen pregnancy.

Five studies measured the impact of providing emergency contraception in advance to adolescents (Table 4). However, it should be noted that some of these studies included young women up through age 24. These studies are included in this review, because there are no studies that have measured the impact of advance provision of emergency contraception on only high-school-aged teens and these can provide evidence for the impact of emergency contraception on young people's behavior.

All five studies found that providing

emergency contraception in advance significantly increased the use of emergency contraception. This is consistent with studies of advance provision of emergency contraception to adults in this country (Jackson et al., 2003) and in other countries (Abbott et al., 2004).

The first study was a randomized trial measuring impact of giving one regimen of emergency contraception in advance. It measured impact among young people aged 16-24 over four months (Raine et al., 2000). Providing emergency contraception in advance increased use of emergency contraception by a factor of three. Although the treatment group did not report higher frequencies of unprotected sex than the control group, women in the treatment group were more likely than those in the control group to report using less effective contraception at follow-up compared with enrollment. Further, although the proportion of women in both groups who reported consistent pill use increased from enrollment to follow-up, the control group became more likely than the treatment group to report consistent pill use at follow-up.

The second study involved predominantly minority, low income, sexually active young women aged 15-20 (Gold et al., 2004). The randomized trial compared instruction about how to obtain and use emergency contraception with instruction about emergency contraception in combination with one regimen of emergency contraception. One month after receiving emergency contraception, the advance provision group was about twice as likely to have used emergency contraception as the control group; by six months the difference was no longer significant. In this study, the advance provision of emergency contraception had no impact on unprotected sex or on hormonal contraceptive use measured either at one or six months. However, at six months, those young women who received emergency contraception were more likely to have used a condom during the last month than the control group. Although the intervention group reported only 13 pregnancies in comparison with 18 pregnancies for the control group, this difference was not statistically significant.

In the third study, 15 to 24 year old women were randomly assigned to receive three regimens of emergency contraception in advance, to have access to emergency contraception through a pharmacy, or to have access to emergency contraception through the clinic (the control condition) (Raine et al., 2005). There were no significant differences in emergency contraceptive use or other contraceptive use between the pharmacy group and the control group. However, the group given the three packs of emergency contraception was almost twice as likely to have used emergency contraception by six months as the control group. There were no significant differences in unprotected sex, nor were there significant differences in either pregnancy or STD rates.

The fourth study of adolescents involved adolescent mothers ages 13 to 20 (Belzer et al., 2005). The trial measured the impact of giving one regimen of emergency contraception in advance. Both groups received education about emergency contraception. Those receiving emergency contraception in advance were far more likely to have used emergency contraception at both 6 and 12 months. Although those in the intervention group did not significantly change their methods of contraception, they were more likely to have unprotected sex at 12 months (but not 6 months) than the control group.

Finally, the last study involved sexually active young women ages 14 to 24 (Raymond et al., 2006). The study compared increased access (two regimens of pills provided in advance with unlimited resupply at no charge) with normal access to emergency contraception (pills dispensed when needed at usual charges). After one year, the intervention group was significantly more likely to have used emergency contraception, but was not significantly less likely to have become pregnant. Similarly, there were no significant differences in self-reported sexual behavior, contraceptive use or in STD rates measured with biomarkers.

Discussion

In sum, all five studies, in combination with studies of older women in this country and women in other countries, demonstrate that providing emergency contraception in advance does markedly increase its use, at least in the short term. Furthermore, these studies of teens and young adults found few significant effects on use of other forms of contraceptive or unprotected sex and the few results that were significant were mixed, both positive and negative on use of other forms of contraception or unprotected sex. Although these mixed effects might be further studied, it appears likely that providing emergency contraception to teens does not have negative effects overall, just as it does not have negative effects among adult women.

Only two of the studies measured the impact of the advance provision of emergency on pregnancy rates. Neither found a statistically significant result, although one of the two reported a programmatically meaningful impact; specifically, they observed a trend in the right direction (13 versus 18 pregnancies) that did not reach statistical significance. Because emergency contraception is not designed to be used repeatedly, any given individual is likely to use it only a couple of times a year to protect against previously unprotected sex. Given that the chances of pregnancy resulting from one or two acts of unprotected sex are quite small, the use of emergency contraception once or twice over an entire year will only reduce the chance of

becoming pregnant during that year by a small amount. Thus, very large samples sizes would be needed to detect an impact on pregnancy and these are rare in intervention trials.

Community-Wide Pregnancy or STD/HIV Prevention Initiatives with Multiple Components

During the last two decades, there has been a growing recognition that it might take more than just single programs focusing on discrete populations of teens to change teen pregnancy or STD/HIV rates markedly. Thus, many communities have developed community-wide collaboratives or initiatives with the goal of reducing teen pregnancy or STD.

One study was particularly well designed to measure the impact of the addition of community activities to a workshop intervention (Sikkema et al., 2005) (Table 5). Fifteen low-income housing developments were randomly assigned to three conditions: 1) a control group intervention that included discussion of a videotape and both free condoms and brochures about condoms, 2) a workshop intervention that included two three-hour workshops for younger and older males and females separately (four different workshops), and 3) a community intervention that included the same two three-hour workshops plus follow-up sessions, participation of opinion leaders in a "Teen Health Project Leadership Council," a few community-wide events sponsored by the council and HIV/AIDS workshops for parents.

Its effects were mixed. Regarding delay in initiation of sex, at 18 months the community intervention (that included the workshops) significantly delayed the initiation of sex in comparison with the minimal control group intervention, and almost significantly delayed the initiation of sex in comparison with the two workshops. The two workshops did not affect delay. These results suggest the addition of the community-level activities had an impact beyond the workshops in delaying the initiation of sex. Regarding condom use, at three months, the two workshops, but not the community intervention (which included the workshops) had a significant impact on condom use. This was counter-intuitive. However, at 18 months, both the two workshops and the community intervention, which included the two workshops, had about an equal and significant impact on increasing condom use. Despite the rigorous evaluation design, these overall conflicting results make it unclear whether the community activities above and beyond the workshops had an impact on sexual behavior. The community activities may have had a positive impact on delaying the initiation of sex, but they did not increase condom use significantly more than workshops alone.

Table 5: Community-Wide Initiatives with Multiple Components: Number of Studies Reporting Effects on Sexual Outcomes

Outcomes Measured	Community Based Initiatives (N=1)
Delay sex	(n=1)
Hastened Initiation	0
No Significant Results	0
Delayed Initiation	1
Increase Condom Use	(n=1)
Reduced Use	0
No Significant Results	0
Increased Use	1

Programs that Focus Primarily on Non-Sexual Risk and Protective Factors

Research clearly suggests that improving young women's performance in school, their plans for their futures and their connection to their families, schools, and faith communities all reduce their pregnancy and birth rates (Kirby et al., 2005a). In many countries throughout the world, as young women's educational levels and employment opportunities increased, their fertility rates declined. In this country, between the mid-1950s and the mid-1970s, increasingly large percentages of young women pursued higher education and more challenging professional careers and postponed marriage and child-bearing. During these years, the teen birth rate declined markedly (Alan Guttmacher Institute, 1994). Researchers have found that multiple risk behaviors are related to one another, and others have advocated for an integrated approach that focuses on the whole individual rather than separate programs that focus on specific aspects of each individual.

Observing these trends, some professionals working with youth believe that *two of the most promising approaches to reducing teen pregnancy are to improve educational and career opportunities through youth development programs and to increase the connection between youth and responsible adults and institutions, such as the family, schools, and community organizations.* Whereas the programs summarized above focused primarily on changing the *sexual* factors affecting adolescent sexual behavior (e.g., the knowledge, attitudes, norms, and skills involving sexual and contraceptive behavior), the youth development programs included in this review focused primarily on *non-sexual* factors affecting adolescent sexual behavior (e.g., involvement with other adults, attachment to school, educational goals, and community employment opportunity). They were designed to improve the participants' education, life-skills, and employment options. The first of these groups of youth development programs was designed for very young children. The second was designed for adolescents.

Early Childhood Programs

Only one study meeting the criteria for this review evaluated an early childhood program, the *Abecedarian Project,* in relation to teen pregnancy and child-bearing (Campbell, 1999) (Table 6). Infants in low-income families were randomly assigned either to participate in a full-time, year-around day care program that focused on improving the children's intellectual and cognitive development or to receive whatever day care the families and communities could provide. Then, in elementary school, all the study participants were again randomly assigned to receive either the normal school environment or a three-year program to involve parents and improve parent-school communication about the child. All youth were tracked until age 21. Although the sample size was small (n=104), the children who received the pre-school program delayed childbearing by more than a year in comparison with the control group. Notably, they also performed higher on a number of intellectual and academic measures and received more years of education than the control group. The children who participated in the elementary school program (as opposed to the pre-school day care program) also performed significantly better on all of these outcomes, but the results were not quite as strong. The *Abecedarian* program's impact on educational attainment may partially explain why the program participants delayed childbearing.

Table 6: Early Childhood Interventions: Number of Studies Reporting Effects on Sexual Outcomes

Outcomes Measured	Early Childhood (N=1)
Reduce Childbirth: Self-Report	(n=1)
Increased Number	0
No Significant Results	0
Reduced Number	1

It should be noted that the results of the *Abecedarian* study are consistent with the pregnancy results for females of the *High/Scope Perry Preschool Study*, which measured the long-term impact of a high quality, active-learning preschool program and found a significant reduction in teen pregnancy (Schweinhart et al., 1993). However, the *High/Scope* study is not included in the tables because of its small sample size (n=49).

Discussion

Because there are only two studies measuring the impact on teen sexual behaviors (pregnancy or childbearing) and also because of the very small sample sizes, little can be concluded from these studies. Nevertheless, the results are encouraging and suggest that other studies of early childhood programs should measure long-term impact on teen pregnancy and childbearing.

Youth Development Programs for Adolescents
Service-Learning Programs

By definition, service learning programs include (1) voluntary or unpaid service in the community (e.g., tutoring, working as a teacher's aide, working in nursing homes, or helping fix up parks and recreation areas) and (2) structured time for preparation and reflection before, during, and after service (e.g., group discussions, journal writing, or papers). Sometimes the service is voluntary, but other times it is prearranged as part of a class. Often the service is linked to academic instruction in the classroom.

There is strong evidence that Service Learning Programs reduce actual teen pregnancy rates while youth are in the programs. Three different studies, two with experimental designs and all three with multiple sites, have consistently indicated that service learning reduces either sexual activity or teen pregnancy (Philliber and Allen, 1992; Allen et al., 1997; Melchior, 1998; O'Donnell et al., 1999; O'Donnell et al., 2002) (Table 7).

Table 7: Youth Development Interventions: Number of Studies Reporting Effects on Sexual Outcomes

Outcomes Measured	Service Learning (N=2)	Vocational Education (N=4)	Other Youth Development (N=2)
Delay sex	(n=1)	(n=0)	(n=0)
Hastened Initiation	0	0	0
No Significant Results	0	0	0
Delayed Initiation	1	0	0
Reduce Frequency of Sex	(n=1)	(n=1)	(n=0)
Increased Frequency	0	0	0
No Significant Results	0	1	0
Reduced Frequency	1	0	0
Reduce Number of Partners	(n=0)	(n=0)	(n=1)
Increased Numbers	0	0	0
No Significant Results	0	0	0
Reduced Number	0	0	1
Increase Contraceptive Use	(n=0)	(n=1)	(n=0)
Reduced Use	0	0	0
No Significant Results	0	1	0
Increased Use	0	0	0
Reduce Sexual Risk Taking	(n=1)	(n=0)	(n=0)
Increased Risk	0	0	0
No Significant Results	0	0	0
Reduced Risk	1	0	0
Reduce Pregnancy: Self-Report	(n=1)	(n=2)	(n=0)
Increased Number	0	1	0
No Significant Results	0	0	0
Reduced Number	1	1	0
Reduce Childbirth: Self-Report	(n=0)	(n=3)	(n=1)
Increased Number	0	1	0
No Significant Results	0	2	1
Reduced Number	0	0	0

The first study of a service learning program used a quasi-experimental design to measure the impact of the *Teen Outreach Program* (TOP) in multiple sites (Philliber and Allen, 1992). It found that youth were less likely to report becoming pregnant during the school year in which they participated in TOP. Because the comparison group consisted of youth identified by participants as similar to themselves, there was a clear potential for self-selection effects. Consequently, a second study was completed, this time with an experimental design, including random assignment of youth to participate in TOP or not to participate (Allen et al., 1997). Again, this study evaluated the impact of TOP in multiple sites around the country. On the average, these TOP participants spent about 46 hours doing service. TOP participants again reported lower pregnancy rates during the school year in which they participated in TOP than did controls. It should also be noted that TOP participants also had lower rates of school failure than the control group.

Finally, a pair of studies measured the impact of a health education curriculum alone and the combined impact of the same health education curriculum and service learning (O'Donnell et al., 1999; O'Donnell et al., 2002). Results indicated that the health education curriculum alone did not significantly decrease recent sexual activity, but the addition of service learning did significantly reduce sexual activity. In the short term, it delayed the onset of sex while, more than three years later, it both delayed the onset of sex and reduced the percentage of students who had sex the previous month. These studies suggest that service learning may reduce teen pregnancy rates in part by reducing sexual activity.

It is not known for sure why service learning has positive effects on pregnancy, but several explanations have been suggested: participants developed on-going relationships with caring program facilitators; some may have developed greater autonomy and felt more competent in their relationships with peers and adults; some may have been heartened by the realization that they could make a difference in the lives of others. These effects may have increased motivation to avoid pregnancy.The volunteer experiences also encouraged youth to think more about their futures. It may also be that both supervision and alternative activities simply reduced the opportunity for participants to engage in problem behaviors, including unprotected sex. These programs were time intensive: the mean numbers of hours that youth spent in TOP and *Learn and Serve* programs during the academic year were 46 hours and 77 hours respectively. The study of TOP found that the kinds of volunteer service varied considerably from site to site, but TOP appeared to be most effective when young people had some control over where they volunteered (Allen et al., 1997). The effectiveness of TOP was *not* dependent upon the fidelity of the implementation of the TOP curriculum (Allen et al., 1990), which suggests that the service itself is the most

important component of the programs.

Vocational Education and Employment Programs

Vocational education and employment programs typically include academic instruction or an educational requirement and either vocational education or actual jobs. Four different studies evaluated such programs, all in multiple sites (Table 7).

The first study evaluated the impact of the *Summer Training and Education Program* (STEP) (Allen et al., 1990; Grossman and Sipe, 1992; Walker and Vilella-Velez, 1992). Youth in the treatment group received 90 hours of academic remediation and half-time summer employment. They also received other support services, including 36 sessions of life skills education and 5-15 hours of other support during the school years. By contrast, the control group received full-time summer employment. Thus, in comparison with the control group, the intervention group received less summer employment but did receive the academic remediation, life skills education, and personal support. A very strong experimental design revealed that the program did not have a consistent and significant impact on either sexual activity or use of contraception.

The remaining three programs, the *Conservation and Youth Service Corps*, the *Job Corps*, and *JOBSTART*, were all implemented in the late 1980s or 1990s and were targeted toward somewhat older youth. In the *Job Corps* and *JOBSTART* programs, about 73% of the participants were 16- to 19-years-olds; the other 27% were older. These programs combined remedial, academic, and vocational education (Cave et al., 1993; Jastrzab et al., 1997; Schochet et al., 2000). To varying degrees, these programs also provided other support services, including life skills education, health education, health care, child care, and job placement assistance. While all three programs focused on disadvantaged youth, only *JOBSTART* was restricted to school dropouts. *Job Corps* was mostly residential; *JOBSTART* and the *Conservation and Youth Service Corps* were for the most part not residential. All three studies incorporated strong experimental designs with random assignment of individual youth, large sample sizes, long-term measurement (15-48 months), and measurement of either pregnancy or childbearing (but not sexual behavior). Results from these three studies demonstrate that the programs did not affect overall pregnancy or birth rates. There was no significant impact of the *Conservation and Youth Service Corps* on unmarried pregnancy rates measured 15 months later; no impact of *Job Corps* on birth rates measured 30 months later; and no impact of *JOBSTART* on pregnancy or birth rates measured 48 months later among women not residing with any of their own children at baseline. There were, however, two small exceptions to the general finding of no effects. Among African-American women in the *Conservation and Youth Service Corps* study, participants were significantly less likely to experience an unmarried pregnancy than the control group, and, in the *JOBSTART* study, among teen mothers residing with their children, participants were *more* likely to experience a pregnancy or birth than non-participants. Overall, these studies provide rather strong evidence that these programs did not have significant positive overall effects on pregnancy or childbearing.

Other Youth Development Programs

Two other studies have examined the impact of youth development programs for adolescents. The programs differed considerably from each other (see Table 7). The first study evaluated the impact of a very comprehensive program called the *Quantum Opportunities Program* (Hahn et al., 1994), which was implemented among high school students from families receiving public

assistance. The program included educational activities (e.g., tutoring and computer-based instruction), community service activities, and development activities (e.g., arts, career and college planning). It focused on academic achievement but gave considerable attention to social competence as well. Participants received small stipends and bonus payments for participation and completion of activities and matching funds for approved activities after the school day. Although the evaluation had a strong research design, its sample size was small (n=156 for analyses of birth rates), and the quality of the program implementation was questionable. The program participants tended toward a lower birth rate than the control group (p=.10).

The second study used a randomized controlled design to measure the six year impact of a program to prevent mental health problems among children of divorced parents (Wolchik et al., 2002). The program had two versions, one for only divorced mothers and a second for both divorced mothers and their adolescent children. The program for mothers focused on methods of improving the quality of the mother-child relationship, using effective discipline, accessing the father and preventing inter-parent conflict. The program for mothers and their children also focused on effective coping strategies, improving parent-child relationships and addressing stressors related to divorce. Groups met for 11 sessions. The programs had significant positive effects on a number of mental health and behavioral outcomes. Both versions of the intervention had significant positive effects on mental health problems, substance use and number of sexual partners. Other sexual behaviors were not measured.

Discussion

These studies of different types of youth development programs support several conclusions. *Service learning, which combines community service with reflection on those experiences, appears to reduce teen pregnancy during the academic year in which youth complete the service. It appears to be effective even without addressing sexuality directly. In contrast, vocational education programs that include academic remediation, vocational education, and a few support services do not significantly reduce teen pregnancy or birth rates in the long run.* Other youth development programs, such as very comprehensive and intensive youth development programs and programs for divorced parents with their adolescent children have produced encouraging results, but there are too few studies and too many important study limitations to reach any strong conclusions.

At this point, it is not clear why some youth development programs (i.e., service learning) reduce teen pregnancy and others with similar characteristics (i.e., vocational education programs) do not. This is an important area for further research.

Programs that Focus on Both Sexual and Non-Sexual Risk and Protective Factors

A number of studies have examined programs that focused on *both* sexual and non-sexual factors affecting teen pregnancy. Specifically, they had components addressing both sexuality and youth development more broadly.

Character Education and Other Programs to Address Substance Abuse, Violence, and Sexual Risk Behaviors

Character education programs are much broader than sexuality education programs. Typically they strive to infuse a wide range of positive values in young people with the expectation that these values will guide and discourage them from engaging in a variety of anti-social or risk behaviors.

Teen Star was a character education program designed to reduce adolescent drug use, violent behavior and sexual behavior (Table 8) (Harrington et al., 2001). It attempted to help students identify their ideal desired lifestyle and understand how drug use, violence and sex can conflict with that lifestyle. It also attempted to improve students' perceptions of peer norms regarding these three topics, to make commitments to avoid these behaviors and to become more attached to school. According to the results from the well-designed study, Teen Star did not have an overall impact on substance use, violence or sexual activity.

Healthy for Life targeted multiple health behaviors including nutrition, marijuana, tobacco use, drinking and driving, and sexuality (Moberg and Piper, 1998). Taught in middle school, it was based on social learning theory and social influence theory. For example, it was taught by college students who were designed to serve as role models and helped conduct role-plays. It provided information about peer behavior in order to improve perception of peer norms. It also emphasized short-term effects of risk behaviors. It was supplemented with parent, peer and community components. In a large randomized trial, the intervention appeared to increase the initiation of sex at one time period (but not two other time periods) and frequency of sex again at one time period (but not two other time periods). It did not affect condom use. Despite an otherwise strong study design, the study was not able to measure sexual behavior before the intervention nor to rule out preexisting differences in the schools.

Project AIM (Adult Identity Mentoring) is based on the theory that motivation to engage in various behaviors, including sexual behaviors, is affected by people's "mental images of possible future selves" (Clark et al., 2005). If their views of possible future selves are too negative, they may not plan for the future and may not be motivated to delay gratification. If their views are too positive, they may not accurately gage possible set-backs or obstacles. Project AIM was designed to get young people to develop positive adult professional identities and to consider how their current behaviors might affect their futures. The program incorporated small groups and role models to encourage norms favoring delaying or abstaining from sex and other behaviors, such as using drugs, engaging in violence or dropping out of school. In a randomized trial, the study found that Project AIM reduced sexual activity at 19 weeks for males and females combined and reduced sexual activity for males at one year.

Table 8: Programs to Address Substance Abuse, Violence, and Sexual Risk Behaviors: Number of Studies Reporting Effects on Sexual Outcomes

Outcomes Measured	Programs Addressing Substance Abuse, etc. (N=4)
Delay sex	(n=2)
Hastened Initiation	1
No Significant Results	0
Delayed Initiation	1
Reduce Frequency of Sex	(n=2)
Increased Frequency	1
No Significant Results	0
Reduced Frequency	1
Increase Condom Use	(n=2)
Reduced Use	0
No Significant Results	1
Increased Use	1
Reduce Sexual Risk Taking	(n=1)
Increased Risk	0
No Significant Results	1
Reduced Risk	0

The *Aban Aya Youth Project* developed two programs, a social development curriculum and a school-community initiative (Flay et al., 2004). The social development curriculum included 16 to 21 lessons per year for youth in grades 5 through 8. The lessons focused on social competence skills needed to manage situations that might lead to high-risk behaviors such as drug use, violence and unprotected sex (e.g., skills to build self-esteem and empathy, manage stress, improve relationships, resist pressure, set goals, make better decisions and resolve conflicts). The curriculum also strove to increase African-American cultural values and pride. The school-community intervention included this curriculum plus reinforcements through parental support, school-wide activities and community linkages among the students, parents, schools and local businesses. *The long-term results of the randomized trial indicated that among males the curriculum alone reduced violence and substance use, while the curriculum in combination with the parental, school-wide and community activities significantly reduced violence, provoking behavior, school delinquency, substance use and recent sexual activity and increased condom use. In contrast, among females there were no significant effects.*

Discussion

As a group, these programs designed to reduce substance use, violence and sexual risk had very mixed results: two had positive effects for males only, one had no significant effects, and one even appeared to have two negative effects. It is not clear why two interventions may have been effective when the other two were not, nor why they had significant positive effects on males only.

Client-Centered Programs

A single study evaluated the impact of three programs in Washington state (McBride and Gienapp, 2000) (Table 9). All three programs started with the premise that many adolescents, especially high-risk adolescents, have a variety of emotional needs and problems that affect their sexual behavior. These three programs implemented a "client-centered" approach that was based on the service providers' understanding of why the teens they were working with were involved in sexual risk-taking. The service providers generally believed that their teen clients lacked one or more of the following: (1) information about sex, (2) a variety of coping skills, (3) emotional support, (4) positive guidance, and (5) adults they could trust and talk to about sensitive issues. The programs tried to address these problems and others by providing small group and individualized education and skill-building sessions, as well as several other individualized services, such as counseling, mentoring, referrals, and advocacy, which were tailored for each teen. Results indicated that the programs did not delay sex nor increase contraceptive use, but did decrease the frequency of sex.

Table 9: Client Centered Programs: Number of Studies Reporting Effects on Sexual Outcomes

Outcomes Measured	Client Centered Programs (N=1)
Delay sex	(n=1)
Hastened Initiation	0
No Significant Results	1
Delayed Initiation	0
Reduce Frequency of Sex	(n=1)
Increased Frequency	0
No Significant Results	0
Reduced Frequency	1
Increase Contraceptive Use	(n=1)
Reduced Use	0
No Significant Results	1
Increased Use	0

Very Intensive Long-Term Programs with a Strong Reproductive Health Component

Perhaps the most intensive and long-term program was the *Children's Aid Society-Carrera Program* (CAS-Carrera Program) (Table 10) (Philliber et al., 2002). It recruited youth when they were about 13 to15 years old and encouraged them to participate through-

out high school. During those school years, it operated 5 days a week. Some programs had regularly scheduled special events, education programs, and entrepreneurial activities. During the summer months, paid employment, including entrepreneurial activities, was emphasized, along with evening maintenance programs. Participants spent an average of 16 hours per month in the program during the first three years; many spent more time in the program. The *CAS-Carrera Program* used a holistic approach, providing multiple services: (1) family life and sex education, (2) an education component that included individual academic assessment, tutoring, help with homework, preparation for standardized exams, and assistance with college entrance, (3) a work-related intervention that included a job club, stipends, individual bank accounts, employment, and career awareness, (4) self-expression through the arts, and (5) individual sports. In addition, the program provided mental health care and comprehensive medical care, including reproductive health and contraception when needed. In all these areas, staff tried to create close caring relationships with the participants. Although the program focused on youth, it also provided services for the participants' parents and other adults in the community.

The evaluation study of the *CAS-Carrera Program* was a very rigorous one. It included multiple sites in New York City and elsewhere in the country, random assignment, a large sample size, long-term measurement including behavior, and proper statistical analyses. *The study found that, after three years and among females in the New York City sites, the program significantly delayed the onset of sexual intercourse, increased the use of condoms as a secondary method with another highly effective method of contraception, and reduced pregnancy rates. Among males in the New York City sties, the program did not have significant positive behavioral effects, but the study did have one unexpected finding; males in the programs were significantly less likely to report using both condoms and another highly effective contraception method at last sex than males in the control group.* Among females in sites outside of New York City, the program did not have significant behavioral effects on either females or males (Scher and Maynard, 2006).

While studies of other programs have found significant impact on pregnancy rates, this study of the *CAS-Carrera Program* remains the only evaluation to date using random assignment, multiple sites, and a large sample size that found a positive impact on sexual and contraceptive behavior and pregnancy rates among females *for three years in an urban area. The pregnancy rate among females in the intervention group was less than half the rate among the control group (10 percent versus 22 percent).*

This is a complex program to implement, requiring significant financial and staff resources, and sites that do not implement all the components or that do not fully engage young people over time cannot expect to achieve these positive results.

Some of the challenges of implementing the *CAS-Carrera Program* were manifested in a serious attempt to replicate the program in three communities in Florida (Kirby et al., 2005b). The Florida staff earnestly tried to implement all the *CAS-Carrera Program* components, but they did so without the benefit of the training, materials and support from the CAS-Carrera staff. They faced challenges in recruiting youth, keeping them involved and retaining excellent staff. Youth participated less frequently and for shorter periods of time in these programs than in the original CAS-Carrera program in New York City and those youth who were assigned to the control group ended up participating in other somewhat similar activities (e.g., school sports) offered by the communities. In part because of the control group's partici-

Table 10: Very Intensive Long-Term Youth Development Programs: Number of Studies Reporting Effects on Sexual Outcomes

Outcomes Measured	Very Intensive Youth Development (N=2)
Delay sex	(n=2)
Hastened Initiation	0
No Significant Results	1
Delayed Initiation	1
Reduce Frequency of Sex	(n=1)
Increased Frequency	0
No Significant Results	1
Reduced Frequency	0
Reduce Number of Partners	(n=1)
Increased Numbers	0
No Significant Results	1
Reduced Number	0
Increase Condom Use	(n=2)
Reduced Use	0
No Significant Results	2
Increased Use	0
Increase Contraceptive Use	(n=1)
Reduced Use	0
No Significant Results	1
Increased Use	0
Reduce Sexual Risk Taking	(n=1)
Increased Risk	0
No Significant Results	1
Reduced Risk	0
Reduce Pregnancy: Self-Report	(n=2)
Increased Number	1
No Significant Results	0
Reduced Number	1
Reduce Childbirth: Self-Report	(n=1)
Increased Number	0
No Significant Results	0
Reduced Number	1

pation in other programs, there were no significant positive effects on the large majority of outcomes including sexual behaviors. These results suggest that when 1) the *CAS-Carrera Program* is implemented without the imple-mentation manuals, the training and the oversight by the CAS-Carrera staff, 2) excellent staff are not retained for long periods of time, and 3) other community programs serve youth, the program may not produce the positive effects on sexual outcomes for females that were observed in the original CAS-Carrera study.

Why was the *CAS-Carrera Program* successful in New York City where other programs with some similar components (*JOBSTART*, *Job Corps*, and the *Conservation and Youth Service Corps*) were not? There are several possible explanations: (1) the vocational education programs targeted somewhat older youth and tracked them into their early twenties when childbearing is more normative and less costly; (2) the *CAS-Carrera Program* included a strong sexuality education component in combination with improved access to reproductive health and other health services, as well as the intensive youth development components; (3) staff in the *CAS-Carrera Program* may have developed closer relationships with the young people they served and (4) these staff gave a much stronger message about avoiding pregnancy than did the vocational education programs.

Discussion

Of all the programs identified in this review, the program that was the most intensive, comprehensive and long lasting, the CAS Carrera program, provided evidence for the largest and longest term impact on behavior and even pregnancy in its New York City sites (but not elsewhere). It had at least four important characteristics that may have contributed to this success: *1) it incorporated many youth development activities that may have increased motivation to avoid pregnancy; 2) the on-going and intensive components of the program provided the opportunity for staff to create close connections with the youth and to express clear messages; 3) the program continually reinforced a strong and clear message about avoiding pregnancy; 4) and the program*

provided access to reproductive health services to help females obtain and use contraception to avoid pregnancy. In addition, other components addressed other emotional and mental health needs of the youth.

However, the CAS-Carrera program did not have a significant positive impact on any male sexual behavior. Furthermore, it did not have significant effects on behavior when implemented outside of New York City, either in the original study by the original research team or in a subsequent serious attempt to replicate it without the benefit of training, materials or supervision from the CAS-Carrera program staff.

CONCLUSIONS
Research Limitations

At least four factors limit the conclusions that can be drawn from the many studies reviewed in this report. First, although 63 studies with experimental designs have examined the impact of programs on sexual risk behaviors, pregnancy, childbearing, or STD, there are many different approaches to reducing sexual risk-taking that have not been evaluated sufficiently, if at all. Consequently, it is not appropriate to reach conclusions about an entire approach to pregnancy or STD prevention on the basis of one or even a small handful of studies. This is especially true when programs are implemented in different settings because their success may vary by the setting and group targeted.

Second, there have been replications of evaluations of only a few specific programs. While the replications of sex and STD/HIV education programs are very encouraging, an attempted replication of one youth development program did not reproduce the desired effects and only a few programs have multiple studies conducted by independent research teams demonstrating effectiveness. Our ability to make general statements about the effectiveness of some types of programs based on results from non-replicated studies is questionable.

Third, many of these studies were limited by methodological problems or constraints. Many studies had sample sizes that were too small (and therefore failed to detect programmatically important outcomes, produced anomalous results, or had very large confidence intervals); used exploratory analytic techniques instead of confirmatory techniques (i.e., searched for positive results, rather than stating hypotheses first and then reporting results); failed to control for the clustering of youth in schools or agencies (and thereby may have exaggerated the statistical significance of results); or failed to report and publish negative results. Accordingly, the results that are published are undoubtedly biased in multiple unknown ways. Fortunately, some of these biases tend to cancel each other in aggregate (e.g., the bias caused by the studies often being underpowered would partially offset the bias caused by failure to adjust for multiple tests of significance).

Fourth, some studies have produced inconsistent results. Some programs appeared to affect behavior, while other seemingly similar programs did not. When these inconsistencies occur, it is difficult to know whether the results varied because of methodological differences, whether the programs were implemented differently, or whether the programs were effective with only specific groups of youth in selected settings at specific time periods.

Suggestions for future research

To produce more definitive conclusions about what works, the research community needs to:

- Continue to identify and evaluate those programs that appear promising but that have not been well-evaluated, including abstinence-only programs, clinic outreach efforts, pre-school interventions, additional types of youth development programs, mass media programs for youth, and programs to encourage testing and treatment for STD.

- Conduct more replication studies by independently evaluating the impact of programs found to be effective with different youth at different times in different communities.

- Conduct basic research on other topics that may help to develop new approaches to reducing teen pregnancy. Such topics include, for example: approaches to preventing and dealing with sexual abuse, methods for discouraging romantic relationships with much older partners, methods for addressing other factors affecting early voluntary sexual activity, methods of reducing numbers of sexual partners, the role of concurrent versus sequential sexual partners in STD transmission, the role of sexual networks in STD transmission and how to change them, approaches to increasing contraceptive continuation, ways to involve males in programs, important characteristics of effective youth development programs, and approaches to improving the life options of young people, especially those who are poor or otherwise disadvantaged.

- Identify rigorous intervention studies in other fields (e.g., substance abuse prevention, violence prevention, and youth development programs) that may have data on fertility or STD outcomes, and encourage new studies in these fields to add measures of fertility or STD outcomes to the outcomes they are already tracking in order to expand the range of program types evaluated that may help to reduce teen pregnancy and STD.

- Improve the quality and rigor of each research study in several ways:
  - Use experimental designs with random assignment.
  - Involve much larger samples that have sufficient statistical power to

conduct needed analyses among important subgroups (e.g., those who have had sex and those who have not, or males and females).

- Track youth for at least a year and preferably longer.
- Measure actual sexual and contraceptive behavior as opposed to only risk and protective factors.
- Measure impact on pregnancy and STD whenever appropriate (e.g., when there is sufficient statistical power) and use laboratory tests, as opposed to self-reports, to measure pregnancy and STD when possible.
- State primary hypotheses ahead of time and report the results for those hypotheses regardless of whether they are positive or negative.
- Conduct proper statistical analyses that adjust for covariates as necessary, clustering if necessary, and multiple tests of significance as appropriate.
- When possible, have independent parties complete these evaluations.

- Include mediational analyses to better determine which risk and protective factors are affected by effective programs and in turn change behavior.
- In published articles, provide much more complete descriptions of the programs, as well as more informative process evaluations, so that reviewers can better ascertain why some programs were effective and others were not. If these descriptions are too long for professional journals, then make them readily available upon request for interested parties.
- Conduct evaluations of effective programs specifically to identify which components or characteristics of these programs are the critical to their success.
- Conduct research to improve our understanding of how to replicate with fidelity those programs that are found to

be effective in two or more studies.
- Conduct research to determine to what extent and how effective programs can be changed without significantly reducing their impact.

Conclusions about the Effectiveness of Programs

Despite the important caveats expressed above, the patterns of results among existing studies do warrant several general conclusions about the effectiveness of particular types of programs:

- There are no single, simple approaches that will dramatically reduce adolescent pregnancy and STD across the country. While there are a number of effective programs, there are no "magic bullets."
- There are, however, multiple and markedly different approaches that can help reduce sexual behaviors that place youth at risk of pregnancy or sexually transmitted disease. This review identified 13 different types or sub-types of programs and every one of them had at least one study demonstrating that a program had a positive impact on some sexual behavior. Thus, there are no single answers; there are multiple answers to the problems of pregnancy and STD.
- *The programs that reduce sexual risk-taking, pregnancy, childbearing or sexually transmitted disease fall into three different large groups. The first group includes those programs that address the sexual antecedents of sexual risk-taking (e.g., school- or community-based sex and STD/AIDS education programs and some health clinic programs). The second group primarily addresses non-sexual risk and protective factors (e.g., service learning programs). The third group addresses both groups of factors.*
- Abstinence and use of condoms and other forms of contraception are compatible

goals and topics. There are two ideas behind this simple statement. First, the overwhelming weight of the evidence demonstrates that *programs that focus on sexuality and discuss contraception, including sex and STD/HIV education programs, school-based clinics, and condom-availability programs, do not increase sexual activity.* Furthermore, a number of programs that discussed condoms or other forms of contraception and encouraged their use among sexually active youth also delayed or reduced the frequency of sexual intercourse. Second, programs that emphasized abstinence, that gave it clear prominence, and that presented it as the safest and best approach, while also emphasizing condoms or contraceptives for sexually active youth, did not decrease condom or other contraceptive use, and sometimes increased their use. *Thus, giving appropriate emphasis to both abstinence and condoms or other contraceptives does not have the negative effects that people sometimes fear, and it can, in fact, have many positive effects.*

- *Studies of some sex and STD/HIV education programs have produced strong evidence that they reduce sexual risk-taking either by delaying the onset of sex, reducing the frequency of sex, reducing the number of sexual partners, or increasing the use of condoms or other forms of contraception.* Some, but not most, programs have positive effects on more than one behavior. Some studies found these positive effects to endure for as long as 31 months. These programs have been demonstrated to be quite robust. Multiple studies also indicated that when these programs are implemented and evaluated by others in other communities or even states, they continue to have positive effects provided they are implemented with fidelity in similar

settings with similar populations. *When sex and STD/HIV education programs have incorporated the 17 characteristics of effective programs, they are especially likely to be effective.*

- *Programs for parents and their children sometimes reduce sexual risk-taking, either by delaying sex or increasing condom use, especially when they include educational components for youth that incorporate many of the 17 characteristics of effective curriculum-based programs for youth.* However, there is too little evidence for the impact of programs for parents alone to reach any conclusions. Also, getting parents and families to participate in parent or parent/child programs remains a challenge.

- While short non-interactive videos may be too modest a stand-alone intervention to have a significant impact on behavior, videos that are longer and interactive and that are viewed multiple times sometimes have an impact on behaviors, possibly for as long as six months. However, there is too little evidence on the impact of videos to reach any firm conclusions.

- *Several studies have consistently indicated that when clinics provide improved educational materials, discuss the adolescent patient's sexual and condom or contraceptive behavior one-on-one, give a clear message about that behavior, and incorporate other components into the clinic visit, clinics can increase condom or contraceptive use, although not always for a prolonged period of time.*

- *When clinics provide emergency contraception to young people in advance, they are not more likely to have sex, but they are more likely to use emergency contraception if they have unprotected sex.*

- In schools, clinic settings and community programs, in groups and one-on-one counseling sessions and with individual interactive media programs, it is possible to increase knowledge about sexual behavior and its consequences, increase perception of risk or pregnancy and STD, change values and attitudes about abstaining from sex and using condoms or other forms of contraception, change perception of peer norms about sex and contraceptive use, increase self-efficacy to avoid sex or use protection, or increase intentions to abstain from sex or use protection, and thereby actually change sexual and contraceptive behavior.

- *Effective programs that addressed sexual risk and protective factors shared two common attributes: they focused clearly on sexual behavior and condom or contraceptive use, and they gave clear messages about abstaining from sex or using protection against STDs and pregnancy. Those programs that addressed sexual risk and protective factors but did not give clear messages about abstinence and the use of protection appeared to be less effective.*

- *Service learning programs have strong evidence that they actually reduce teen pregnancy rates.* However, it is unclear whether these programs reduce teen pregnancy beyond the academic year in which the students are involved in the programs. Notably, these programs did not focus on sexual risk and protective factors for unprotected sex, and some were not even designed to reduce teen pregnancy. However, they were intensive in that youth participated in them for many hours and often for prolonged periods of time. In addition to their success in reducing teen pregnancy, some of these programs had other positive results, such as reducing school failure.

- Some other youth development programs (e.g., vocational education programs) that addressed non-sexual factors did not reduce teen pregnancy or childbearing even though they addressed seemingly important factors (such as basic reading, writing, and math skills and preparation for employment), were relatively intensive, and were long-lasting.

- One more comprehensive and intensive youth development program with a strong reproductive health component for females did provide strong evidence of impact on both pregnancy for three years. However, it did not affect males and the positive results were not replicated outside of New York City .

- Intensity, quality and continuity may be factors that help programs to have long-term effects on pregnancy rates. The programs that had long-term effects tended to be more intensive, have multiple components and to last multiple years.

These conclusions indicate that programs may be effective both when they focus clearly on sexual behavior and when they don't address sexuality at all. Moreover, it is apparent that if programs target sexual factors, they must do so directly and must give a clear message. For example, they may discuss realistic situations that might lead to unprotected sex and methods for avoiding those situations, for remaining abstinent, and for using protection. If programs target non-sexual factors, then they need to intervene sufficiently intensively in the lives of youth so that youth become more motivated to avoid pregnancy and childbearing or simply have less opportunity to engage in unprotected sex.

REFERENCES

Aarons SJ, Jenkins RR, Raine TR, El-Khorazaty MN, Woodward KM, Williams RL, Clark MC, Wingrove BK. (2000) Postponing sexual intercourse among urban junior high school students: A randomized controlled evaluation. J Adolesc Health 27:236-247.

Abbott J, Feldhaus KM, Houry D, Lowenstein SR. (2004) Emergency contraception:

what do our patients know? Ann Emerg Med 43:376-381.

Abma J, Chandra A, Mosher W, Peterson L, Piccinino L. (1997) Fertility, family planning, and women's health: New data from the 1995 National Survey of Family Growth. Vital and Health Statistics 23.

Abma JC, Martinez GM, Mosher WD, Dawson BS. (2004) Teenagers in the United States: Sexual activity, contraceptive use, and childbearing, 2002. Vital Health Statistics 23 24: 1-48.

Alan Guttmacher Institute. (1994) Sex and America's teenagers. In. New York: Alan Guttmacher Institute.

Allen JP, Philliber S, Hoggson N. (1990) School-based prevention of teen-age pregnancy and school dropout: Process evaluation of the national replication of the Teen Outreach Program. Am J Community Psychol 18:505-524.

Allen JP, Philliber S, Herrling S, Kuperminc GP. (1997) Preventing teen pregnancy and academic failure: Experimental evaluation of a developmentally-based approach. Child Dev 64:729-742.

American School Health Association. (1998) Sexually transmitted diseases in America: How many and at what cost. In: (Alexander LL, Cates JR, Herndon N, Ratcliffe JF, eds). Research Triangle Park: American School Health Association.

Belzer M, Sanchez K, Olson J, Jacobs AM, Tucker D. (2005) Advance supply of emergency contraception: a randomized trial in adolescent mothers. J Pediatr Adolesc Gynecol 18:347-354.

Blake SM, Ledsky R, Lohrmann D, Bechhofer L, Nichols P, Windsor R, Banspach S, Jones S. (2000) Overall and differential impact of an HIV/STD prevention curriculum for adolescents. Washington, D.C.: Academy for Educational Development.

Boekeloo BO, Schamus LA, Simmens SJ, Cheng TL, O'Connor K, D'Angelo LJ.

(1999) A STD/HIV prevention trial among adolescents in managed care. Pediatr 103:107-115.

Borawski EA, Trapl ES, Goodwin M, Adams-Tufts K, Hayman L, Cole ML, Lovegreen LD. (Unpublished) Taking Be Proud! Be Responsible! To The Suburbs: A Replication Study. In. Cleveland: Case Western Reserve University School of Medicine.

Boyer C, Shafer M, Shaffer R, Brodine S, Pollack L, Betsinger K, Chang Y, Kraft H, Schachter J. (2005) Evaluation of a cognitive-behavioral, group, randomized controlled intervention trial to prevent sexually transmitted infections and unintended pregnancies in young women. Prev Med 40: 420-431.

Bunnell RE, Dahlberg L, Rolfs R, Ransom R, Gershman K, Fashy C, Newall W, Schmid S, Stone K. (1999) High prevalence and incidence of sexually transmitted diseases in urban adolescent females despite moderate risk behaviors. J Infect Dis 180: 1624-1631.

Campbell FA. (1999) Long-term outcomes from the Abecedarian study. In: Biennial Meeting of the Society for Research in Child Development. Albuquerque, NM.

Cave G, Bos H, Doolittle F, Toussaint C. (1993) JOBSTART: Final report on a program for school dropouts. In: Centers for Disease Control and Prevention (2005) Sexually Transmitted Disease Surveillance, 2004. Atlanta, GA: U.S. Department of Health and Human Services.

Centers for Disease Control and Prevention (2005) Sexually Transmitted Disease Surveillance, 2004. In. Atlanta, GA: U.S. Department of Health and Human Services.

Centers for Disease Control and Prevention. (2006a) HIV/AIDS Surveillance Report, 2005. In. Atlanta, GA: U.S. Department of Health and Human Services, Centers for Disease Control and Prevention.

Centers for Disease Control and Prevention (2006b) Youth Risk Behavior Surveillance - United States 2005. In: Surveillance Summaries, MMWR.

Clark L, Miller K, Nagy S, Avery J, Roth D, Liddon N, Mukherjee S. (2005) Adult identity mentoring: reducing sexual risk for African-American seventh grade students. J Adolesc Health 37:337.e331-337.e310.

Coyle KK, Kirby D, Marin B, Gomez C, Gregorich S. (2000) Effect of Draw the Line/Respect the Line on sexual behavior in middle schools.

Coyle KK, Basen-Enquist KM, Kirby DB, Parcel GS, Banspach SW, Collins JL, Baumler ER, Caravajal S, Harrist RB. (2001) Safer Choices: Reducing Teen Pregnancy, HIV and STDs. Pub Health Rep 1:82-93.

Dancy B, Crittenden K, Talashek M. (2006) Mothers' effectiveness as HIV risk reduction educators for adolescent daughters. J Health Care Poor Underserved 17:218-239.

Danielson R, Marcy S, Plunkett A, Wiest W, Greenlick MR. (1990) Reproductive health counseling for young men: What does it do? Fam Planning Perspect 22: 115-121.

Darroch JE, Singh S. (1999) Why is teenage pregnancy declining? The roles of abstinence, sexual activity and contraceptive use. New York: Alan Guttmacher Institute.

DeLamater J, Wagstaff DA, Havens KK. (2000) The impact of a culturally appropriate STD/AIDS education intervention on black male adolescents' sexual and condom use behavior. Health Edu Behav 27:453-469.

DiClemente RJ, Wingood GM, Harrington KF, Lang DL, Davies SL, Hook EW, Oh KM, Crosby RA, Hertzberg VS, Gordon AB, Hardin JW, Parker S, Robillard A. (2004) Efficacy of an HIV Prevention Intervention for African American Adolescent Girls: A Randomized Controlled Trial. JAMA 292:171-179.

Dilorio C, Resnicow K, McCarty F, De AK, Dudley WN, Wang DT, Denzmore P. (2006) Keepin' It R.E.A.L.! Results of a mother-adolescent HIV prevention program. Nurs Res 55:43-51.

Downs JS, Murray PJ, Bruine de Bruin W, Penrose J, Palmgren C, Fischhoff B. (2004) Interactive video behavioral intervention to reduce adolescent females' STD risk: a randomized controlled trial. Social Sci Med 59:1561-1572.

Eisen M, Zellman GL, McAlister AL. (1990) Evaluating the impact of a theory-based sexuality and contraceptive education program. Fam Planning Perspect 22:261-271.

Eng TR, Bulter WD. (eds) (1997) The hidden epidemic: Confronting Sexually Transmitted Diseases. Washington, DC: National Academy Press.

Finer LBHSK. (2006) Disparities in Rates of Unintended Pregnancy In the United States, 1994 and 2001. Perspect Sex Reproduct Health 38:90-96.

Flanigan C. (2001) What's Behind the Good News: The decline in teen pregnancy rates during the 1990s. Washington, DC: National Campaign to Prevent Teen Pregnancy.

Flanigan C, Suellentrop K, Whitehead M, Smith J. (2006) Teens Sexual Experience, 1995-2002. Science Says 22.

Flay BR, Graumlich S, Segawa E, Burns JL. (2004) Effects of 2 Prevention Programs on High-Risk Behaviors Among African American Youth. Arch Pediatr Adolesc Med 158:377-384.

Frost J, Bolzan M. (1997) The Provision of Public-Sector Services By Family Planning Agencies in 1995. Fam Planning Perspect 29:6-14.

Gillmore MR, Morrison DM, Richey CA, Balassone ML, Gutierrez L, Farris M.

(1997) Effects of a skill-based intervention to encourage condom use among high-risk heterosexually active adolescents. AIDS Prev Edu 9:22-43.

Gold M, Wolford J, Smith K, Parker A. (2004) The effects of advance provision of emergency contraception on adolescent women's sexual and contraceptive behaviors. J Pediatr Adolesc Gynecol 17:87-96.

Grossman JB, Sipe CL. (1992) Summer Training and Education Program (STEP): Report on long-term impacts. Philadelphia: Public/Private Ventures.

Guttmacher Institute. (2006) U.S. Teenage Pregnancy Statistics National and State Trends and Trends by Race and Ethnicity. New York, NY: Guttmacher Institute.

Hahn A, Leavitt T, Aaron P. (1994) Evaluation of the Quantum Opportunities Program (QOP): Did the program work? In. Waltham, MA: Brandeis University, Center for Human Resources.

Harrington NG, Giles SM, Hoyle RH, Feeney GJ, Yungbluth SC. (2001) Evaluation of the All Stars Character Education and Problem Behavior Prevention Program: Effects on mediator and outcome variables for middle school students. Health Educ Behav 28:533-546.

Hoffman SD. (2006) By the Numbers: The Public Costs of Adolescent Childbearing. Washington, DC: The National Campaign to Prevent Teen Pregnancy.

Hubbard BM, M.L. G, Rainey J. (1998) A replication of Reducing the Risk, a theory-based sexuality curriculum for adolescents. J School Health 68:243-247.

Jackson RA, Schwarz EB, Freedman L, Darney P. (2003) Advance supply of emergency contraception: effect on use and usual contraception—a randomized trial. Obstetr Gynecol 102:1-213.

Jastrzab J, Masker J, Blomquist J, Orr L. (1997) Youth corps: Promising strategies for young people and their communities.

Cambridge, MA: Abt Associates, Inc.

Jemmott III J. (2005) Effectiveness of an HIV/STD risk- reduction intervention implemented by nongovernmental organizations: A randomized controlled trial among adolescents. Am Psychol Assoc Annual Conference.

Jemmott III J, Jemmott L, Fong G. (1992) Reductions in HIV risk-associated sexual behaviors among black male adolescents: Effects of an AIDS prevention intervention. Am J Public Health 82:372-377.

Jemmott III J, Jemmott L, Fong G. (1998) Abstinence and safer sex: HIV risk-reduction interventions for African-American adolescents: A randomized controlled trial. JAMA 279:1529-1536.

Jemmott III J, Jemmott L, Fong G, McCaffree K. (1999) Reducing HIV risk-associated sexual behaviors among African American adolescents: Testing the generality of intervention effects. Am J Commun Psychol 27:161-187.

Jemmott III J, Jemmott L, Braverman P, Fong G. (2005) HIV/STD risk reduction interventions for African American and Latino adolescent girls at an adolescent medicine clinic. Arch Pediatr Adolesc Med 159: 440-449.

Kaiser Family Foundation ASHA. (1998) Sexually Transmitted Diseases in America: How Many and at What Cost? Menlo Park, CA: The Foundation.

Kiene S, Barta W. (2006) A brief individualized computer-delivered sexual risk reduction intervention increases HIV/AIDS preventive behavior. J Adolesc Health 39: 404-410.

Kirby D .(1997) No Easy Answers: Research Findings on Programs to Reduce Teen Pregnancy. Washington, DC: National Campaign to Prevent Teen Pregnanc.

Kirby D, Waszak C, Ziegler J. (1989) An assessment of six school-based clinics: Services, impact, and potential. Washington D.C.: Center for Population Options.

Kirby D, Lepore G, Ryan J. (2005) Sexual risk and protective factors: Factors affecting teen sexual behavior, pregnancy, childbearing and sexually transmitted disease: Which are important? Which can you change? Washington DC: National Campaign to Prevent Teen Pregnancy.

Kirby D, Laris B, Rolleri L. (2006) Sex and HIV Education Programs for Youth: Their Impact and Important Characteristics. Scotts Valley, California: ETR Associates.

Kirby D, Rolleri L, Wilson MM. (2007) Tool to Assess the Characteristics of Effective Sex and STD/HIV Education Programs. Washington DC: Healthy Teen Network.

Kirby D, Barth R, Leland N, Fetro J. (1991) Reducing the Risk: Impact of a new curriculum on sexual risk-taking. Fam Planning Perspec 23:253-263.

Kirby D, Korpi M, Adivi C, Weissman J. (1997a) An impact evaluation of Project SNAPP: An AIDS and pregnancy prevention middle school program. AIDS Educ Prev 9:44-61.

Kirby D, Korpi M, Barth RP, Cagampang HH. (1997b) The impact of the Postponing Sexual Involvement curriculum among youths in California. Fam Planning Perspec 29:100-108.

Kirby D, Brener ND, Brown NL, Peterfreund N, Hillard P, Harrist R. (1999) The impact of condom distribution in Seattle schools on sexual behavior and condom use. Am J Pub Health 89:182-187.

Kirby D, Baumler E, Coyle K, Basen-Enquist K, Parcel G, Harrist R, Banspach S. (2004) The "Safer Choices" intervention: It's impact on the sexual behaviors of different subgroups of high school students. J Adolesc Health 35:442-452.

Kirby DB, Rhodes T, Campe S. (2005b) The Implementation of Multi-Component Youth Programs to Prevent Teen Pregnancy Modeled after the Children's Aid Society Carrera Program. Scotts Valley: ETR Associates.

Koniak-Griffin D, Lesser J, Nyamathi A, Uman G, Stein J, Cumberland W. (2003) Project CHARM: an HIV prevention program for adolescent mothers. Fam Commun Health 26:94-107.

Ku L, Sonenstein FL, Pleck JH. (1994) The dynamics of young men's condom use during and across relationships. Fam Planning Perspec 26:246-251.

Levy SR, Perhats C, Weeks K, Handler A, Zhu C, Flay BR. (1995) Impact of a school-based AIDS prevention program on risk and protective behavior for newly sexually active students. J School Health 65:145-151.

Manlove JS, Terry-Humen E, Ikramullah EN. (2006) Young Teenagers and Older Sexual Partners: Correlates and Consequences for Males and Females. Perspec Sex Reproduc Health 38:197-207.

Martin JA, Hamilton BE, Ventura SJ, Menacker F, Kirmeyer S. (2006) Births: Final Data for 2004. Nat Vital Stat Rep 55: 1-101.

Maynard RA. (1997) Kids having kids: Economic costs and social consequences of teen pregnancy. Washington D.C.: National Campaign to Prevent Teen Pregnancy.

McBride D, Gienapp A. (2000) Using randomized designs to evaluate a client-centered program to prevent adolescent pregnancy. Fam Planning Perspec 32:227-235.

Melchior A. (1998) National evaluation of Learn and Serve America school and community-based programs. Waltham, MA: Center for Human Resources, Brandeis University.

Metzler CW, Biglan A, Noell J, Ary DV, Ochs L. (2000) A Randomized Controlled Trial of a Behavioral Intervention to Reduce High-Risk Sexual Behavior Among Adolescents. Behav Ther 31:27-54.

Miller BC, Norton MC, Jenson GO, Lee TR,

Christopherson C, King PK. (1993) Impact evaluation of FACTS and feelings: A home-based video. Fam Relat 42:392-400.

Moberg DP, Piper DL. (1998) The Healthy for Life Project: Sexual risk behavior outcomes. AIDS Educ Prev 10:128-148.

Morris M, Handcock MS, Miller WC, Ford CA, Schmitz JL, Hobbs MM, Cohen MS, Harris KM, Udry JR. (2006) Prevalence of HIV Infection Among Young Adults in the United States: Results From the Add Health Study. Am J Pub Health 96:1091-1097.

National Campaign to Prevent Teen Pregnancy. (2006) How is the 3 in 10 Statistic Calculated? Washington, DC: Author.

O'Donnell C, O'Donnell L, San Doval A, Duran R, Labes K. (1998) Reductions in STD infections subsequent to an STD clinic visit. Using video-based patient education to supplement provider interactions. Sex Transm Dis 25:161-168.

O'Donnell L, Stueve A, O'Donnell C, Duran R, Doval AS, Wilson RF, Haber D, Perry E, Pleck JH. (2002) Long-term reduction in sexual initiation and sexual activity among urban middle school participants in the Reach for Health community youth service learning HIV prevention program. J Adolesc Health 31:93-100.

O'Donnell L, Stueve A, Doval AS, Duran R, Haber D, Atnafou R, Johnson N, Grant U, Murray H, Juhn G, Tang J, Piessens P (1999) The effectiveness of the Reach for Health community youth service learning program in reducing early and unprotected sex among urban middle school students. Am J Pub Health 89:176-181.

Orr DP, Langefeld CD, Katz BP, Caine VA. (1996) Behavioral intervention to increase condom use among high-risk female adolescents. J Pediatr 128:288-295.

Philliber S, Allen JP, eds. (1992) Life options and community service: Teen Outreach Program. Newbury Park, CA: Sage Publications.

Philliber S, Kaye JW, Herring S, West E. (2002) Preventing pregnancy and improving health care access among teenagers: An evaluation of the Children's Aid Society--Carrera program. Perspec Sex Reproduc Health 34:244-251.

Pleck JH, Sonenstein FL, Swain SO. (1988) Adolescent males' sexual behavior and contraceptive use: Implications for male responsibility. J Adolesc Res 3:275-284.

Princeton Survey Research Associates. (1996) Kaiser Family Foundation survey on teens and sex: What they say teens today need to know and who they listen to. Menlo Park, CA: Kaiser Family Foundation.

Raine T, Harper C, Leon K, Darney P. (2000) Emergency contraception: advance provision in a young, high-risk clinic population. Obstetr Gynecol 96:1-7.

Raine T, Harper C, Rocca C, Fischer R, Padian N, Klausner J, Darney P. (2005) Direct access to emergency contraception through pharmacies and effect on unintended pregnancy and STIs: a randomized controlled trial. JAMA 293:54-62.

Rangel MC, Gavin L, Reed C, Fowler MG, Lee LM. (2006) Epidemiology of HIV and AIDS among Adolescent and Young Adults in the United States. J Adolesc Health 39:156-163.

Raymond E, Stewart F, Weaver M, Monteith C, Van Der Pol B. (2006) Impact of increased access to emergency contraceptive pills: A randomized controlled trial. Obstet Gynecol 108: 98-106.

Rotheram-Borus M, Murphy D, Fernandez M, Srinivasan S. (1998a) A brief HIV intervention for adolescents and young adults. Am J Orthopsychiatr 68:553-564.

Rotheram-Borus M, Gwadz M, Fernandez M, Srinivasan S. (1998b) Timing of HIV interventions on reductions in sexual risk among adolescents. Am J Commun Psychol 26:73-96.

Rotheram-Borus M, Lee M, Murphy D, Futterman D, Dwan N, Birnbaum J,

Lightfoot M, Consortium TLtC. (2001) Efficacy of a prevention intervention for youths living with HIV. Am J Pub Health 91:400-405.

Roye C, Silverman P, Krauss B (2006) A Brief, Low-Cost, Theory-Based Intervention to Promote Dual Method Use by Black and Latina Female Adolescents: A Randomized Clinical Trial. Health Educ Behav 34: 608-621.

Santelli JS, DiClemente RJ, Miller KS, Kirby D. (1999) Sexually transmitted diseases, unintended pregnancy, and adolescent health promotion. Adolesc Med 10:87-108.

Schochet PZ, Burghardt J, Glazerman S. (2000) National Job Corps study: The short-term impacts of Job Corps on participants' employment and related outcomes. In: Report and Evaluation Report Series 00-A. Washington, DC: U.S. Department of Labor, Employment and Training Administration.

Schweinhart LJ, Barnes HV, Weikart DP. (1993) Significant benefits: The High/Scope Perry Preschool study through age 27. In: Monographs of the High/Scope Educational Research Foundation. Ypsilanti, MI: The High/Scope Press.

Sikkema K, Anderson E, Kelly J, Winett R, Gore-Felton C, Roffman R, Heckman T, Graves K, Hoffmann R, Brondino M. (2005) Outcomes of a randomized, controlled community-level HIV prevention intervention for adolescents in low-income housing developments. AIDS 19: 1509-1516.

Singh S, Darroch JE. (2000) Adolescent pregnancy and childbearing: Levels and trends in developed countries. Fam Planning Perspec 32:14-23.

Slonim-Nevo V, Auslander WF, Ozawa MN, Jung KG. (1996) The long-term impact of AIDS-preventive interventions for delinquent and abused adolescents. Adolesc 31:409-421.

Sonenstein F. (1996) Measuring sexual risk behaviors. Washington DC: American Enterprise Institute.

St. Lawrence J, Crosby R, Brasfield T, O'Bannon III R. (2002) Reducing STD and HIV risk behavior of substance-dependent adolescents: A randomized controlled trial. J Consult Clin Psychol 70: 1010-1021.

St. Lawrence J, Crosby R, Belcher L, Yazdani N, Brasfield T. (1999) Sexual risk reduction and anger management interventions for incarcerated male adolescents: A randomized controlled trial of two interventions. J Sex Educ Ther 24:9-17.

St. Lawrence JS, Jefferson KW, Alleyne E, Brasfield TL, O'Bannon RE, III, Shirley A. (1995) Cognitive-behavioral intervention to reduce African American adolescents' risk for HIV infection. J Consult Clin Psychol 63:221-237.

Stanton B, Li X, Galbraith J, Feigelman S, Kaljee L. (1996) Sexually transmitted diseases, human immunodeficiency virus and pregnancy prevention. Arch Pediatr Adolesc Med 150:17-24.

Stanton B, Guo J, Cottrell L, Galbraith J, Li X, Gibson C, Pack R, Cole M, Marshall S, Harris C. (2005) The complex business of adapting effective interventions to new populations, An urban to rural transfer. J Adolesc Health 37:17-26.

Stevens-Simon C, Kelly L, Singer D, Cox A. (1996) Why pregnant adolescents say they did not use contraceptives prior to conception. J Adolesc Health 19:1-79.

Suellentrop K. (2006) Teen Contraceptive Use. In: Science Says. Washington, DC: The National Campaign to Prevent Teen Pregnancy.

The Alan Guttmacher Institute. (2002) In Their Own Right: Addressing the Sexual and Reproductive Health Needs of American Men. In. New York, NY: AGI.

U.S. Census Bureau. (2004) Annual Social and Economic Supplement: 2003 Current

Population Survey - Table MS-2. Current Population Reports P20-553.

Villarruel A, Jemmott III J, Jemmott L. (2006) A Randomized Controlled Trial Testing an HIV Prevention Intervention for Latino Youth. Arch Pediatr Adoles Med 160:772-777.

Walker G, Vilella-Velez F. (1992) Anatomy of a demonstration. In. Philadelphia, PA: Public/Private Ventures.

Weinstock H, Berman S, Cates W. (2004) Sexually Transmitted Diseases Among American Youth: Incidence and Prevalence Estimates. Perspec Sex Reproduc Health 36: 6-10.

Wenger N, Greenberg J, Hilbourne L, Kusseling F, Mangotich M, Shapiro M. (1992) Effect of HIV antibody testing and AIDS education on communication about HIV risk and sexual behavior: A randomized, controlled trial in college students. Ann Intern Med 117:905-911.

Wolchik S, Sandler I, Millsap R, Plummer B, Greene S, Anderson E, Dawson-McClure S, Hipke K, Haine R. (2002) Six-year follow-up of preventive interventions for children of divorce: a randomized controlled trial. JAMA 288:1874-1881.

Wu Y, Stanton B, Galbraith J, Kaljee L, Cottrell L, Li X, Harris C, D'Alessandri D, Burns J. (2003) Sustaining and broadening intervention impact: a longitudinal randomized trial of 3 adolescent risk reduction approaches. Pediatr 111:e32-38.

Zimmerman R, Donohew L, Sionéan C, Cupp P, Feist-Price S, Helme D. (Unpublished-a) Effects of a school-based, theory driven HIV and pregnancy prevention curriculum.

Zimmerman R, Cupp P, Hansen G, Donohew R, Roberto A, Abner E, Dekhtyar O. (unpublished-b) The effects of a school-based HIV and pregnancy prevention program in rural Kentucky.

BEHAVIORAL INTERVENTIONS TO REDUCE YOUTH EXPOSURE TO UNHEALTHFUL MEDIA

Leonard A. Jason and William T. O'Donnell, Jr.

"American youth spend more time with media than with any single activity other than sleeping"
--Kaiser Family Foundation, 1999

INTRODUCTION

Children in the United States are exposed to many hours of media and a wide variety of media content. In order to guide recommendations for media use by children, it is necessary to 1) understand the potential harms of media exposure on health and psychosocial development, and 2) identify interventions that minimize harms related to media use. Here, we describe media use patterns of children in the United States, examine the range of negative effects of media exposure, and then discuss interventions that have been tested to reduce the negative impact of media exposure.

Media Use in Children in the United States

As the century came to a close, 99% of children aged two to 18 years old lived in homes with a television set (60% lived in homes with three or more TV's, and over half the children had a TV in their bedroom), 70% had video game consoles, and 69% lived in homes with a personal computer (Roberts et al, 1999; Roberts and Foehr, 2004). As of 2004, children spent nearly six and a half hours per day using media, during which time they were exposed to eight and a half hours of media messages, a result of some using two or more media sources simultaneously (Roberts et al., 2005). Five hours of that media time was spent in front of a screen (Roberts et al., 2005). By age 18, the average child has watched 22,000 hours of TV, exceeding the time spent in a classroom (Jason and Hanaway, 1997). In addition, children are spending increasing amounts of time devoted to other electronic pursuits, such as video games and the Internet. For many children, these activities result in high and inappropriate levels of electronic media use.

The 2005 Kaiser Family Foundation study on media in the lives of eight to 18 year olds provided findings on media use by children (Table 1) (Roberts et al., 2005).

Table 1: Average time per day spent using media (Hours: Minutes)

Age	TV	Video-games	Music	Computer
8-10	3:17	1:05	0:59	0:37
11-14	3:16	0:52	1:42	1:02
15-18	2:36	0:33	2:24	1:22

Today's youth spend more time with media than any generation before them, and there is no reason to think the time spent with media will not continue to increase (Roberts et al., 1999).

Over the past five years, more media outlets have become available to children. Media today include broadcast, cable, and satellite television, offered in high-resolution (HDTV); home viewing and recording capabilities (VHS, DVD, TiVo, DVR); music players (tape, CD, AM/FM radio, iPod, MP3, and satellite radio); video games (xBox, PlayStation, PlayStation Portable (PSP) and Game Boy Advance); personal computers with Internet access; cellular phones; and books, magazines and movie theaters.

In a society where media are widely accessible, concern is growing over the issue of "media multitasking", using two or more media at the same time. As of 2004, children were spending 26% of their total media time multitasking, up 10% from 1999 (Roberts et al., 2005). The media experience is becoming more miniaturized, personalized, and privatized. Children with personal possession of any electronic media experienced an average of two hours more per day of overall media exposure (Roberts et al., 2005). Children with a television or computer in their bedroom read significantly less than children without those media (Roberts et al., 2005). Children were making more media choices on their own and without assistance or supervision. One out of every four children lived in a home in which no rules governed the use of television; the television was on "most of the time", and was "usually" playing during meals. In these highly "TV-oriented" homes, children were being exposed to 2.5 hours more daily media than those households without a high TV orientation (Roberts et al., 2005).

It is difficult to assess exactly how this media flood is affecting children. Most studies of the relationship between health and media exposure are correlational, making it difficult to determine whether media use is a cause or consequence of poor health. Thus, randomized controlled trials of interventions to alter media exposure are a focus of this chapter, as they facilitate causal inferences.

DEFINING HEALTHFUL VS. UNHEALTHFUL MEDIA

It is critical to determine what constitutes inappropriate use of media by children. There is mounting evidence that excessive viewing can seriously challenge a child's social, emotional, mental, and physical well-being (Jason and Hanaway, 1997). Villani's (2001) review of the literature concluded that the primary effects of high media exposure are increased violent behavior, accelerated onset of sexual activity, and increased high-risk behaviors such as alcohol and tobacco use. Media content is an additional concern as it includes violence, sex, and stereotyping.

The amount and content of media exposure that is associated with harmful effects may vary depending on the outcome assessed. Several studies indicate that children who are exposed to over six hours of media daily are at risk of developing academic and social problems (Jason and Hanaway, 1997). For example, Fetler's (1984) study of over 10,000 children reported a threshold of television viewing (i.e., more than 6 hours per day) beyond which television was negatively associated with achievement. Studies of obesity risk found that viewing more than four hours per day was associated with weight gain (Anderson et al., 1998), and commercials for unhealthful food were a substantial concern. Studies focusing on mental health and behavioral effects suggested that hours of exposure to violent content were of greatest concern. Considering the broad range of effects that media exposure may have on children's health and well-being, the American Academy of Pediatrics recommends no more than one to two hours of television per day (i.e. less than 12 hours/week) (American Academy of Pediatrics, 2007).

There is currently little research to guide recommendations for healthful Internet use; there are few studies involving the Internet, and most are compromised by self-selected samples without control groups (DeAngeles, 2000). There are published examples of Internet abuse, in which people demonstrated significant impairment to family life resulting from Internet use (Young, 1996). Kandell (1998) defined psychological dependence on the Internet as characterized by an increasing investment of resources on Internet-related activities and unpleasant feelings (e.g., anxiety, depression, emptiness) when offline. Greenfield (1999) found that six percent of the 17,251 persons surveyed met criteria for compulsive Internet use, and over 30% report using the Internet to escape from negative feelings. The vast majority reported experiencing time distortion, accelerated intimacy, and feeling uninhibited when on-line.

Though there are more studies documenting the deleterious effects of media use, it is important to recognize that television, video games, and computer activities are not all harmful. The Internet is frequently used for school-related tasks (LaFerle et al., 2000), and quality programs, games, software, and web sites can serve as an entertaining, informative part of a child's day. Exposure to educational television programs (e.g., Sesame Street, Mr. Roger's Neighborhood) during early childhood was associated with later academic success and imaginative behavior during adolescence (Anderson et al., 2001). Many educational programs on commercial stations have little violence (Jordan et al., 2001). In addition, some children were able to divide their attention between viewing these electronic media and doing other activities without losing control. "E-Learning," an approach to learning inside and outside the classroom through electronic media, is gaining attention from researchers and educators, broadening the possibilities for global scientific and social education (Huffaker and Calvert, 2003). Parents can steer their children toward viewing television series and using computer media that promote positive outcomes (Sanders et al., 2000).

Still, use of media should be appropriately balanced with a mix of social, physical, and imaginative pursuits (Jason et al., 1999). Unfortunately, many children spend a much larger part of their day viewing media programs, which places them at risk for "unhealthful" media exposure. First we examine risk factors for developmental problems associated with high media use in order to choose appropriate behavioral interventions. Next, we discuss research on negative effects of media on social skills development, sexual development, body image, aggression and violence, academic achievement, exercise, and nutrition and obesity.

Social Skills

Children who spent much of their time with electronic media were at risk of failing to develop crucial social skills and strong family ties (Jason and Hanaway, 1997). Children that presented themselves as the least content spent more time with electronic media and less time with printed media than their contented peers (Kunkel et al., 2005). Singer, Slovak, Frierson, and York (1998) found that heavy television use was associated with trauma symptoms and violence. In a survey of third to eighth grade children, self-reported severity of trauma symptoms and violent behaviors was positively correlated with number of hours of television watched per day, with a particularly significant increase in severity in children who watched over five hours per day. Notably, a higher percentage of boys and girls who watched greater than six hours of television per day had symptom severity within the clinically significant range compared to children who watched fewer hours. Children who watched excessive amounts of television engaged in interpersonal play less frequently than those who watched less TV (Bjorkland and Bjorkland, 1989). A longitudinal study of two to seven year old children in low to middle income families examined how young children spent their time based upon periodic time-use interviews with their parents. Time spent in educational activities or reading and socializing was negatively related to time watching animated or general audience television programming, and time spent in play was positively correlated with time spent viewing television (Huston et al., 1999). Heavy viewers were more likely to hold common cultural stereotypes, many of which are emphasized on television. In addition, children who watched large amounts of television and used other electronic media had less time to devote to critical developmental experiences, such as learning to play cooperatively with others.

Sexual Activity

The amount of sexual content in today's media, especially television, can have negative consequences for young viewers. The sexual content shown on television has a significant influence on young people, and the amount of sexual content on television has risen dramatically over recent years (Kunkel et al., 2005). Brown and Newcomer (1991) reported high correlations between watching television high in sexual content and early initiation of sexual intercourse by adolescents. In 2005, researchers found that overall exposure to sexual content was significantly correlated with sexual activity and future sexual intentions of seventh and eighth graders (Pardun et al., 2005). In a recent longitudinal study with a nationally representative sample of 12 – 17 year olds, researchers reported a causal relationship between adolescent exposure to sexual content on television and the acceleration of their own sexual activity (Collins et al., 2004). Messages promoting sexual responsibility and risk issues were effective in sensitizing viewers about sexual health issues; however, the number of these messages on television has leveled off while the amount of sexual content has increased (Kunkel et al., 2005). Greater exposure to sexual content on television has been associated with stronger endorsement of recreational attitudes toward sex by adolescents (Ward and Rivadeneyra, 1999). These changes in attitude and behavior may have serious consequences, including teenage pregnancy and risk of sexually transmitted disease (see Chapter 14).

Body Image

Television and other media contribute to children and adolescents "sense of self" and concern is growing over media's influence on body image, especially for teens. According to Tiggeman (2005) television content, particularly soap operas and music videos, and the motivations for watching have a critical impact on children's sense of body image, more so than the amount of television watched. The main finding of associational studies was that various aspects of television contribute to negative body image in both sexes. Girls became more sensitized to weight and body shape and boys to muscular development. This trend suggests that media exposure may contribute to inappropriate dieting in girls and the use of steroids among male youth. Overall, media presents both boys and girls with stereotyped ideals of beauty, and leads to stereotyping of themselves and others.

Aggression and Violence

A five-year study by the American Psychological Association estimated the average child has watched 100,000 acts of violence and 8,000 acts of murder by the time he or she leaves elementary school (Huston et al., 1992; Villani, 2001). By the end of high school, the average youth has been exposed to 200,000 acts of violence (Huston et al., 1992). According to the American Academy of Pediatrics, exposure to violence in television, movies, and video games is a significant risk to the health of children and adolescents (Media Violence, 2001). Singer and colleagues (1999) examined predictors of self-reported violent behavior in a sample of third through eighth grade students. They found that higher levels of television viewing and favoring action-focused television programming were associated with greater violent behavior after controlling for demographics and parental monitoring. However, television viewing contributed to far less of the variance in students' violent behavior than actual exposure to violence (2% versus 25%).

Wilson et al. (2002) found that programs for children contained more violence than other types of programming (i.e., nearly 70% of children's programs and 60% of non-children's programs contained some physical violence). Sixty-seven percent of prime-time television programming contained graphic violence (Smith et al., 2002). The majority of child-oriented cartoons included violence, but the pain and suffering accompanying the violence was rarely shown (Jason and Hanaway, 1997). In addition, nearly half of the violent perpetrators suffered no consequences for their acts. There were more violent acts per hour on children's programs than on prime time television (i.e. 16 versus 6). Many children observed their aggressive television heroes repeatedly solving problems by using violence. Classic research conducted in the 1980's found a predictive relationship between excessive TV viewing and subsequent aggressive behavior among children (Singer et al., 1984). Similar findings continue to emerge in the scientific literature. For example, in a longitudinal study, Johnson et al. (2002) found a significant association between the amount of time spent watching television during adolescence and early childhood and the likelihood of aggressive acts against others, even when controlling for childhood neglect, family income, neighborhood violence, parental education, and psychiatric disorders. In a longitudinal study, Huesmann et al. (2003) found the amount of self-reported viewing of violent television programming in third and fourth graders predicted aggressive behaviors when these individuals were in their early 20's. Childhood viewing of violent television predicted 3% of variance in aggressive behavior in young adulthood in females and 5% in males after controlling for cohort effects. Children who achieved less in school tended to watch television more often, identify more strongly with aggressive television characters, and believe that aggressive television content was real.

Media exposure includes acts of violence that are witnessed in the form of video games (Roberts, 2000). Whereas viewing television is a fairly passive experience, playing video games and Internet surfing are highly interactive. These new electronic media sources can promote violence and hate (Sher, 2000). Video games often set a child in the role of the aggressor and reward him or her for violent behavior. Griffiths and Hunt (1998) maintain that video games allow the player to rehearse an entire behavioral script, and as a result, video games may produce addiction-like behaviors, specifically compulsive use despite negative consequences, in children and adolescents. Additionally, studies showed that children in grades four through eight preferred video games that awarded points for violence against others (Funk and Buchman, 1996). Interactive media are relatively new, and consequently there has been little time to assess their influence. Nevertheless, several studies indicated that the effects from interactive media may be even more harmful than those of passive media, such as television (Anderson and Dill, 2000; Irwin and Gross, 1995). For example, after playing violent video games, children exhibited measurable decreases in prosocial behaviors and increases in violent retaliation to provocation in a laboratory challenge. In fact, playing violent video games was found to account for a 13% to 22% increase in adolescents' violent behavior (The Impact of Interactive Violence on Children, 2000). For many, the negative effects of childhood exposure to media violence extended into adulthood (Andersen et al., 2003).

Academic Achievement

Children who spend a large amount of time with media often sacrifice reading time, which may affect cognitive development (including verbal, quantitative, and nonverbal skills) and academic achievement (Comstock and Scharrer, 1999; Razel, 2001). Heavy media viewers developed reading and language skills later than lighter viewers, and they achieved less academically (Bjorkland and Bjorkland, 1989; Singer et al., 1998).

Hancox and colleagues (2005) conducted a longitudinal study of the effects of high-level media viewing from birth to adulthood. Higher rates of television viewing in childhood were associated with lower educational achievement by 26 years of age. After controlling for sex, IQ, socioeconomic status, and behavioral problems at age five, relative risk ratios for each one hour increase in the mean hours per weekday spent watching television between ages five and 15 were 1.34 (95% CI: 1.10-1.62) for not graduating from secondary school and 0.85 (95% CI: 0.75-0.98) for attaining a university degree by age 26. Although the results of this study could be affected by unidentified confounding factors, the association suggests that high levels of viewing impair educational achievement and thus may lower socioeconomic status and related well-being (Hancox et al., 2005).

In an extensive examination of the literature over the past two decades, Comstock and Scharrer (1999) concluded that children who watched excessive television performed more poorly on standardized achievement tests. Razel (2001) found that excessive media exposure negatively affected school performance because viewing replaced time that would otherwise be spent reading or participating in other school-related activities. Practice time was lost, and as a result, children (particularly those with learning disabilities) lost fluency and automaticity in skills (Corteen and Williams, 1986). Researchers also found that children's writing was often similar in style to television show scripts (i.e. fragmented and disconnected).

Exercise, Nutrition, and Obesity

Media use has also been associated with reduced exercise and poor eating habits. Eating and drinking regularly accompany television viewing (Van den Bulck, 2000). The Third National Health and Nutrition Examination Survey, conducted in eight to 16 year old children in the US between 1988 and 1994, found that children who watched greater than four hours per day of television had a significantly higher body mass index and significantly more body fat, as measured by trunk skin folds, than children watching less than two hours per day (Anderson et al., 1998).

Children who watched television were exposed to high levels of advertising promoting unhealthful food. In 1995, afternoon and weekend television programming aimed at preschool to elementary school age children presented an average of 21.3 commercials, each averaging 28.6 seconds. Forty-eight percent of these commercials were for food, and 91% of the food advertised was high in fat, salt, or sugar (Taras and Gage, 1995). In 2004, children watched an estimated 40,000 advertisements on television per year. Of the advertisements targeting children, 32% featured candy, 31% cereal, and 9% fast food (Kaiser Family Foundation, 2004). The fast food industry alone spent 3 billion dollars in 2004 for ads aimed at children (Kaiser Family Foundation, 2004). Television viewing was related to the intake of nutrient-poor foods and time spent watching television was linked to the consumption of foods advertised on television (Kotz and Story, 1994). A randomized study of preschool children found that even brief exposure to televised food commercials influenced their food preferences, such that they picked the advertised product when presented a choice of comparable food items (Borzekowski and Robinson, 2001).

Poor eating and nutritional habits increase risk of obesity, and children's food intake has changed dramatically over the past three decades. According to surveys from the US Department of Agriculture, there was an overall decrease in the consumption of milk (-

133%), vegetables (-42%), and eggs (-5%), and an increase in snack foods such as chips (9%), cheese (6%), candy (7%), fried potatoes (9%), and soft drinks (94%) from 1977-1995 (Enns et al., 2002). These types of foods have been linked to childhood obesity (Ludwig et al., 2001) Furthermore, television watching may contribute to higher fat intake. For example, a community survey found that each hour of television viewing was associated with additional consumption of 136 calories per day and a higher percentage of fat intake in low income women (French et al., 2001). Snacking while watching television, and exposure to food advertising were hypothesized to contribute to the associations between television viewing and increased food intake.

Faith et al. (2001) maintained that elevated television viewing and resulting physical inactivity promoted obesity in children. Inactivity was significantly and positively related to total body fat in boys and girls (Crespo et al., 2001). In addition, there was a link between the amount of time children spent watching TV and body weight. Interventions that reduced children's media time resulted in weight loss (Kaiser Family Foundation, 2004, see Chapter 9). The odds of being overweight were 4.6 times greater for a child who watched more than five hours of television per day as compared to a child who watched less than one hour. An estimated 29% of the incidence of obesity could be prevented by limiting television use to under one hour per week. As obese children are at higher risk of developing Type II diabetes, hypertension, asthma, and heart disease (CDC, 2003), it is critical to find ways to decrease the amount of time children spend with media.

Note that in the research cited concerning the negative effects of high levels of media exposure, many of the studies employed cross-sectional, non-longitudinal designs, which are unable to rule out important threats to internal validity, especially selection effects. In addition, the effect sizes of the negative outcomes of media exposure have sometimes been modest. Still, the data are consistent with the hypothesis that adverse nutrition follows excessive media exposure.

PART 3: INTERVENTIONS

This section describes a variety of interventions to limit the amount and effects of media exposure. The effectiveness of various approaches is discussed and directions for future research are presented.

Parents may express concerns that their children are exposed to too much media, but may not be motivated or know how to effectively limit media use by their children (Roberts et al., 2005; Sarlo et al., 1988). Self-monitoring, i.e recording the amount of media use a child engages in daily, is a method that may address low parental motivation to limit media use and has been effective in some families for reducing children's excessive levels of television viewing or use of inappropriate media (Jason et al., 1999, Jason and Fries, 2004).

Parents influence how their children interact with media (Nathanson and Botta, 2003). Valkenburg, Krcmar, Peeters, and Marseille (1999) reviewed studies that have investigated the occurrence of television mediation in the home (how often parents restrict their children's television viewing, how often they discuss television shows with their children, and how often they coview), identified precursors of various styles of mediation, and examined the effects of mediation.

Valkenburg et al. (1999) found that the use of restrictive mediation was higher among parents concerned about television-induced aggression. They also discovered that parents with more education tended to restrict child viewing more often than parents of a lower educational level. For parents attempting to limit the negative impact of television, restricting what their children watch was the most direct way of accomplishing this. Comstock (1990) noted that parents determine whether a child will be a light, moderate, or heavy viewer of these different media sources through rules and structures.

The interventions presented in table 2 and the following sections are representative of the best available studies of interventions designed to reduce harm associated with children's media use. For each main type of intervention, randomized controlled studies of interventions that have shown effectiveness are discussed and the design and results of the study are summarized in Table 2. Four general strategies for reducing media related harm have been studied: 1) restrictive mediation, where interventions attempt to reduce media exposure, 2) factual approaches to active mediation, where interventions attempt to change the impact of media exposure by teaching children to evaluate the source of the information, 3) evaluative approaches to active mediation, where interventions focus on modifying children's evaluation of the social appropriateness of content viewed, and 4) contingency management, where interventions attempt to make media use healthful by making media use dependent on performance of positive health behaviors.

Table 2: Controlled Interventions For Reducing Media Exposure

Study	Participants Per Group	Intervention	Outcome
Restrictive Mediation			
Robinson and Borzekowski (2006) Effects of the SMART Classroom Curriculum to Reduce Child and Family Screen Time	N = 181 3rd and 4th grade students.	Children in one elementary school received an 18-lesson, 6-month classroom curriculum to reduce television, videotape, and video game use.	Boys in treatment group decreased media use by 6 hours/week, compared to 1 hour increase in control. Girls in treatment decreased use by 7 hours/week, compared to 2 hours decrease in control.
Robinson et al. (2003) Dance and Reducing Television Viewing to Prevent Weight Gain in African-American Girls: The Stanford GEMS Pilot Study	N = 61 8-10 year old African American girls and their parents or guardians.	Treatment group participated in after-school dance classes and a 5-lesson intervention designed to reduce television, videotape, and video game use. Control group intervention consisted of health lectures and newsletters.	Girls in treatment group exhibited lower BMI and waist circumference, increased physical activity, reduced television, videotape, and video game use - both personal and in the home, less concern about weight, and improved school grades.
Robinson et al. (2001) Effects of Reducing Children's TV and Video Game Use on Aggression	N = 105 3rd and 4th grade students and their parents or guardians.	Children in one elementary school received an 18-lesson, 6-month classroom curriculum to reduce television, videotape, and video game use.	Children in the intervention group had statistically significant decreases in peer ratings of aggression and observed verbal aggression.

Study	Participants Per Group	Intervention	Outcome
Dennison et al. (2004) An Intervention to Reduce Television Viewing by Preschool Children	N = 91 Children aged 2.6 through 5.5 years.	Children in intervention centers received a 7-session program designed to reduce television viewing as part of a health promotion curriculum.	Children in the intervention group decreased their television/video viewing by 3.1 hours per week.
Gortmaker et al. (1999) Reducing Obesity via a School-Based Interdisciplinary Intervention Among Youth	N = 1295 Ethinically diverse 6th and 7th grade students .	Over 2 years children participated in sessions focused on reducing television viewing, decreasing consumption of high-fat foods, increasing fruit and vegetable intake, and increasing physical activity.	Children in the intervention group reduced TV viewing hours and prevalence of obesity among girls. Reductions in TV viewing predicted obesity change and mediated the inter-vention effect. Among girls, TV reduction predicted reduced obesity.
Epstein et al. (2000) Decreasing Sedentary Behaviors in Treating Pediatric Obesity	N = 90 Families with obese 8 to 12-year old children	Family-based behavioral weight control program, differing in whether sedentary or physically active behaviors were being targeted.	Both approaches were associated with significant decrease in overweight, body fat, and improved aerobic fitness
Factual Approaches to Active Mediation			
Huesmann et al. (1983) Mitigating the Imitation of Aggressive Behaviors by Changing Children's Attitudes About Media Violence	N = 92 1st through 3rd grade students	Group sessions designed to reduce modeling of aggressive behavior (part 1) with elements of counter attitudinal advocacy research (part 2).	Part 1: No significant changes or reductions in aggressive behavior. Part 2: The children's attitudes about television violence being harmful were altered in the desired direction and there was significant reduction in children's propensity to behave violently.
Dorr et al. (1980) Television Literacy for Young Children	N = 88 Kindergarten, 2nd, and 3rd grade students	Intervention: curricula to decrease the perception of TV as "real" and the credibility ascribed to television, and increase children's tendencies to compare TV content with other sources of info.	Children in the intervention groups scored much higher in evaluating television content.

Study	Participants Per Group	Intervention	Outcome
Evaluative Approaches to Active Mediation			
Hicks (1968) Effects of Co-Observer's Sanctions and Adult Presence on Imitative Aggression	N = 84 Boys and girls aged 5 – 8.75 years -old.	Intervention designed to influence children's aggressive behavior through positive and negative evaluative statements, as well as adult's presence, while watching a film depicting aggressive behavior.	Positive and negative comments by experimenter were related to disinhibition and inhibition of imitation response, especially when the experimenter remained present in the playroom.
Corder-Bolz (1980) Comments of a significant other can mediate the effects of television.	Part 1. N = 500 Anglo boys and girls aged 5 –11 years-old. Part 2. N = 75 Anglo boys and girls aged 5 – 10.	Part 1. Active mediation intervention designed to measure whether adult comments during a TV program challenging sex-stereotypes influenced children's attitudes. Part 2. Active mediation intervention designed to measure whether adult comments influenced children's attitudes regarding violence and ethical choices.	Part 1. Children who received mediation were more accepting of non-traditional sex roles. Part 2. Children who received mediation expressed less favorable attitudes regarding violence and unethical behavior.
Nathanson and Cantor (2000) Reducing effects of violent cartoons by increasing empathy with the victim	N = 357 2nd through 6th grade students.	Active mediation intervention designed to encourage children to think about the victim of violence in a cartoon.	Boys who watched the cartoon without mediation were more aggressive afterwards, while boys who received the mediation did not show an increase in aggressive tendencies.
Contingency Management			
Faith et al. (2001) Effects of contingent television on physical activity and television viewing in obese children	N = 10 Obese 8-12 year old children.	TV viewing was contingent on pedaling a stationary bike for intervention group, while control group's TV access wasn't contingent on pedaling.	Intervention group significantly increased pedaling and decreased TV viewing time. Intervention group watched 1.6 hours of TV per week, while control group watched 21 hours per week. Intervention group pedaled 64.4 minutes per week while control group pedaled 8.3 minutes per week.

Restrictive Mediation

Robinson and Borzekowski (2006)

A randomized controlled trial of SMART (Student Media Awareness to Reduce Television), an 18-lesson, theory-based classroom curriculum to reduce screen time among third and fourth grade students, was implemented in two matched public elementary schools. SMART was based upon Bandura's social cognitive model. Bandura's model emphasizes the importance of personal thoughts, feelings, and interpretations in determining behavior (see Volume 1, Chapter 2 for more on self-efficacy, a specific component of this model). This intervention targeted reductions of television viewing, videotape viewing, and video game use, without providing specific alternative activities. Nonselective approaches included (a) budgeting total weekly screen time and (b) limiting access to screen media (e.g., removing TV sets from home, especially kitchens and bedrooms; hiding remote controls; and putting VCR's and video games in cabinets). Selective approaches included (a) limiting screen time to certain days of the week or times of the day (e.g., not until after dinner and/or homework is completed), (b) restricting screen media to specific content (e.g., prohibiting media that is violent or sexually explicit), and (c) limiting screen media use to certain circumstances (e.g, playing video games only with a parent in the room, no television during meals).

The SMART curriculum consisted of four sections, which were delivered by classroom teachers in the following order:

1. *TV awareness.* Lessons intended to increase children's awareness of the roles television, videotapes, and video games play in their lives, as well as promote positive attitudes and motivations for reducing targeted media use.
2. *TV Turnoff.* Children attempted to watch no television or videos, and play no video games for 10 days. Lessons helped children to resist and control targeted media use.
3. *Staying in control.* Lessons designed to help children achieve a goal of less than 7 hours of media use per week.
4. *Helping others.* Final lessons intended to reinforce goals of reduced media use, as well as help peers overcome their "addictions" to television, videotapes, and video games.

At the end of the intervention, third and fourth grade students in the intervention school were spending 14 hours a week using electronic media, while the students in the matched control school were spending about 24 hours per week. Children who were identified at baseline as heavy users and children who were rarely left alone without adult supervision responded most to the intervention. The intervention also reduced television watching by other members of the household. Intervention students' mothers, fathers, siblings and others living in the home watched three to four hours less per week than the control school household members. These results demonstrate the efficacy and validity of the social cognitive model of intervention in influencing screen media use.

Robinson et al. (2003)

A 12 week randomized controlled trial was implemented to test the feasibility of after-school dance classes and a family-based intervention based on Bandura's social cognitive model for reducing television viewing, and thus reducing weight gain, among 61 eight to ten year old African-American girls. The girls were separated into control and treatment groups. Girls in the treatment group were encouraged to attend the dance classes, offered five days a week, as often as possible for the length of the study. Each session lasted two and a half hours, starting with a healthy snack and hour-long homework period, followed by 45-60 minutes of moderate-to-vigorous dance. The sessions ended with 30-minute talks exploring the meaning of dance in the girls' lives and in the African-American culture. Girls in the treatment intervention also participated in START (Sisters Taking Action to Reduce Television). Five lessons were delivered during home visits over the length of the study. The specific behavioral goals included self-monitoring, a two week TV-turnoff, budgeting viewing hours, and "intelligent viewing".

The control intervention consisted of an information-based health education program designed to promote healthful diet and activity patterns. The program included monthly health lectures and newsletters focusing on reducing risks, especially among African-Americans, for obesity, heart disease, diabetes, stroke, and hypertension.

At 12-week follow-up, girls in the treatment group tended to have both lower BMI (Body Mass Index) and lower waist circumference compared to girls in the control group. Girls in the treatment group showed 13% more after-school physical activity than the control group when measured *after* the 12-week trial. The treatment group reported 23% less media use than the control group, and a significant decrease in total household television use. The treatment group reported a 40% decrease in dinners eaten with the television on compared to the control group. Further, girls in the treatment group reported greater liking of physical activities, decreases in weight concerns and body dissatisfaction, and improvements in most recent school grades compared to girls in the control group.

The results of this intervention were promising. The study demonstrates the potential efficacy of using after-school dance classes, coupled with a family-based television reduction program, to prevent excess weight gain in eight to ten year old African American girls.

Robinson et al. (2001)

In a randomized, controlled trial, third and fourth grade students in two different elementary schools rated their peers on aggressive behavior, and reported the degree to which they perceived the world as a "mean and scary place." In addition, 60% of the students were randomly sampled to be observed on the playground for physical and verbal aggression, and parents were interviewed by telephone about their child's aggressive and delinquent behaviors

Students in the treatment group were provided with lessons to reduce television and videotape viewing, and video game playing over the course of six months. Students in the control group received no intervention. At the end of the six months, all children were reassessed. The intervention consisted of eighteen 30 to 50 minute classroom lessons taught by the regular school teacher (trained by the research staff) designed to motivate students to reduce time spent viewing television and playing video games. The lessons were followed by a "TV Turnoff", during which children were challenged to watch no television or play no video games for ten days. After the TV Turnoff, students were encouraged to follow a seven hour per week TV, video, and video game budget.

Based on peer ratings, this intervention to reduce television, videotape, and video-game use decreased aggressive behavior in third and fourth grade students, including a significant reduction in peer rated aggression (adjusted mean difference: -2.4% (95% CI: -4.6%--0.2%) and observed verbal aggression (adjusted mean difference -0.10 act/minute/child (95% CI: -0.18--0.03). Students identified as having medium or higher aggression levels at the beginning of the trial showed larger reductions in aggression. Reductions in observed physical aggression, parental reports of aggressive behavior, and perceptions of a "mean and scary world" were not statistically significant but did favor the treatment group. Note that this intervention sought to reduce media exposure and not violent or aggressive media exposure. Nevertheless, this social cognitive intervention was effective in reducing both screen media use and resultant aggression.

Dennison et al. (2004)

In a randomized controlled study to reduce television viewing among preschoolers, significant results were attained from implementing a media literacy program in the child-care setting. Seven sessions were designed to include components for the child-care center provider, the child, and the parents. Twenty-minute interactive and educational sessions encouraged children to identify alternative activities to watching television, such as reading books. Parents were sent these lists, as well as supplemental materials promoting positive aspects of these alternative activities. Healthy alternatives included improved literacy skills from reading books and improved social skills from eating meals together as a family with the television turned off. Children made "No TV" signs, brought them home to be placed on the television and discussed how they would spend their time when not watching television or videos. Children were encouraged to go a week without watching television and were rewarded with a party, where they discussed what they had done instead of watching TV. Parents were given "No TV" stickers to reward children when they went a day without watching television.

This intervention was well received by children, parents and staff and all seven sessions were implemented successfully at the child-care centers. Based on parental report, the children in the intervention group reduced their television/video viewing by 3.1 hours per week, representing a one third reduction in weekly viewing hours. In contrast, the control group's viewing increased 1.6 hours per week, representing a 4.7 hour per week

difference between those who received the intervention and those who did not. Since television-viewing habits begin to develop and increase during the preschool years, this study illustrates the need for and effectiveness of interventions during these formative years. The preschool or child-care setting, where young children spend increasing amounts of time, might prove to be an opportune milieu for such intervention.

Gortmaker et al. (1999)

In a school-based interdisciplinary intervention to reduce obesity among sixth and seventh graders, students participated in a curriculum focused on decreasing television viewing, decreasing consumption of high-fat foods, increasing fruit and vegetable intake, and increasing moderate and vigorous physical activity. A two week campaign to reduce television viewing in households, called "Power Down," was instituted by Planet Health. The lessons provided teacher resources, behavioral and learning objectives, lesson extension and homework activities, and student resources and handouts.

The intervention reduced television viewing hours among both boys and girls. Reductions in television viewing predicted a reduction in obesity and mediated the intervention effect. Among girls, each hour of reduction in television viewing predicted reduced frequency of obesity. These interventions designed to enhance healthy diet and exercise habits constitute a promising approach to reduce obesity.

Epstein et al. (2000)

The effect of reducing television watching and other sedentary behaviors was evaluated as a component of an obesity treatment program. Ninety families with obese 8 to 12 year old children were provided a family-based behavioral weight control program, differing in whether sedentary or physically active behaviors were targeted. After two years, both approaches were associated with significant decreases in percent overweight (-12.9 +/- 17.0%), percent body fat (-2.9 +/- 4.4%), and improved aerobic fitness as measured by physical work capacity at a heart rate of 150 beats/minute. The findings are consistent with the hypothesis that a reduction of sedentary behaviors associated with media exposure is helpful in reducing the risk of childhood obesity.

Conclusion

These studies indicate that limiting the amount of time a child is allowed to view or interact with media reduces exposure to inappropriate and negative content. Viewing restrictions reduce the sedentary lifestyle that is promoted by heavy television use, and programs that include a focus on reducing television or media use have effectively reduced obesity and improved fitness in children.

Factual Approaches to Active Mediation
Huesmann et al. (1983)

Based on the hypothesis that children act more aggressively after watching violent television because they believe that television violence is (a) realistic, (b) acceptable in the real world, and (c) one should behave like aggressive characters seen on TV, researchers sought to teach children facts about television in an attempt to mitigate the effects. Children were divided into two groups: one that received the factual intervention and another that did not. Children in the intervention group were taught three principles: 1) that the characters in the shows do not behave the way most people do, 2) the camera and special effects create an illusion that the characters can accomplish unrealistic acts, and 3) that the average person uses problem-solving methods differently than the characters in TV shows. The intervention was conducted in two parts. Part one used group sessions designed to reduce modeling of aggressive behavior by

providing factual information. Part two used counter attitudinal advocacy, a technique where persons were asked to make public statements defending a position that they do not hold.

The findings of part one of the intervention were contrary to what the researchers had predicted, as there was no reduction in aggression from the factual approach. However, in part two of the intervention, the children's attitudes about television violence being harmful were altered in the desired direction and there was significant reduction in children's propensity to behave violently. The researchers posited that in the part one intervention, drawing children's attention to the violent content made the violence even more salient, causing children to encode the aggressive behavior they watched as part of the lesson. In part two, the researchers altered their approach, instead focusing on changing the experimental group's attitudes towards the violent content they were viewing. Following part 2, the experimental group showed significantly less increase in aggressiveness and violence, as rated by their peers, than did the control group.

Dorr et al. (1980)

This study tested interventions designed to: 1) decrease the degree to which children perceived the programs they watch as "real"; 2) increase the children's tendencies and abilities to compare television content with information from other sources; and 3) diminish the credibility children ascribed to television through teaching about the industry's economic goals and production methods. The goal of these lessons was to allow children to apply this knowledge to effectively evaluate television content. Three curricula, two interventions, and one control, were designed and randomly assigned to children in grades kindergarten through third. The first intervention curriculum was designed to teach children about the production of entertainment programs and the economic motivation involved. Children were taught eight facts, four regarding television production and four regarding broadcast economics. The eight facts were: 1) Plots are made up, 2) Characters are actors, 3) Incidents are fabricated, 4) Settings are constructed, 5) Programs are broadcast to make money, 6) Money for programs comes from advertisers purchasing air-time, 7) Ads are to sell products to the viewer, and 8) Audience size determines broadcaster income.

The second intervention curriculum was designed to teach children the processes and sources for evaluating television content, with an emphasis on teaching children the resources available to them to evaluate television content. Children were taught four facts: 1) Entertainment programs are made up, 2) Entertainment programs vary in how realistic they are 3) Viewers can decide how realistic they find entertainment programs, and 4) Television content may be evaluated by comparing it to one's own experience, asking other people, and consulting other media sources.

The children in the intervention groups scored much higher than the children in the control group when evaluating television content, including its production goals and realism. Although children who learned more about the medium were able to evaluate it better, there was nothing to suggest that they would make better content choices or their attitudes regarding racial and other stereotypes were influenced. The results of the intervention did show that young children can learn much about the reality of television in a short amount of time, then apply that knowledge in reasoning about the reality of television content.

Evaluative Approaches to Active Mediation
Hicks (1968)
Children (ages 5-9) were assessed for aggression after watching a film of someone kicking, hitting, and throwing a doll. Some children watched the film with an adult present who made either positive (e.g. "Wow, look at him kick Bobo") or negative (e.g. "He shouldn't do that") comments. The other children watched the film without the adult making comments. After watching the film, children were taken to an experimental room containing various play materials, including dolls and instruments similar to those in the film, and their behavior was observed. The adult who co-viewed the film with the child and made the positive/negative comments joined the child in the experimental room on half the occasions.

The children who watched the film with the adult making negative comments exhibited significantly less aggressive behavior in the experimental room than the children who heard the adult make positive comments, particularly when the adult accompanied the child to the playroom. This intervention illustrated that aggressive behavior resulting from viewed violence can be mediated if an adult is present to make comments that discourage such behavior, and aggressive behavior is further mediated when the same adult accompanies the child during his or her play following the viewing.

Corder-Bolz (1980)
Corder-Bolz found that when children watched a television program challenging sex-role stereotypes with an adult providing mediating comments, their acceptance of non-traditional sex-roles increased significantly more than those children who did not receive mediation. The mediation was most effective when both a man and a woman watched with the children.

In a parallel study, Corder-Bolz (1980) found that children who watched "Batman" with an adult providing mediating comments regarding the undesirability of violent and unethical choices were *less* likely to report that other people hit and stole after viewing the program. In contrast, the children who received no mediation were *more* likely to say that other people hit and stole after viewing the program. Both studies illustrate the mediating effect of adults when they actively watch television with children, both in regards to violence and stereotypes.

Nathanson and Cantor (2000)

In a randomized, controlled trial, children in second through sixth grades were divided into two groups. Both groups watched a violent cartoon in which a woodpecker committed various acts of violence against a man. Before watching the cartoon, children in the treatment group were asked to consider the feelings of the man, while children in the control group were not told anything. Afterwards, children in both groups were asked whether they thought the violence was justified, how much they liked the victim and the perpetrator, how mean they thought the victim and the perpetrator were, and how funny they perceived the cartoon to be. Additionally, children's behavior in both groups was evaluated for post-viewing aggressive tendencies.

Children in the treatment group liked the victim significantly better and found him less mean than the children in the control group. The children who were asked to consider the victim's feelings perceived the violence inflicted on him significantly less justified than the children who were not asked to consider the victim's feelings. Although girls' aggressive behavior following viewing was not significantly changed in either group, boys who were asked to consider the victim's feelings were significantly less aggressive than the boys who were not.

Taken together, this study reveals that asking children to consider the victim of violence changed their interpretation of and reaction to the violence. Note that a formal media literacy program was not necessary to

obtain these results. This simple mediation required only two sentences.

Active Mediation Conclusions: Factual versus Evaluative Approaches

Nathanson (2004) compared two approaches to mediation: factual and evaluative. The factual approach aimed to challenge children's interpretations of television and inform them about the medium's technical aspects (special effects, stunts, camera angles) and its "literary devices," such as plotlines and settings. The programs using the factual approach sought to improve children's sense of "factuality", or understanding that television is scripted and produced. The evaluative approach to mediation highlighted the undesirability of violence on television and encouraged children to form negative evaluations of the violent characters and their actions. The evaluative approach has proven effective in a number of experimental studies using different strategies including, Hicks (1968), Horton and Santogrossi (1978), Corder-Bolz (1980), Voojis and van der Voort (1993), and Nathanson and Cantor (2000).

Though some of the factual approaches have been effective in teaching children more about television (Singer et al., 1980; Rapaczynski et al., 1982), others have found no such gain (Nathanson and Yang, 2003). Of concern, one study found that children who were taught the "facts" about television acted more aggressively than children who were not (Dolittle, 1980). In a similar media literacy intervention, Huesmann and colleagues (1983) posited that the factual approach may have made the violence even more salient, causing children to encode the aggressive behaviors they watched as part of the lesson. The factual approach may be too abstract for young children who are not fully developed cognitively, and may bring too much attention to violence for older children, which might make undesirable media effects more likely (Nathanson, 2004).

When compared, the evaluative approach was a superior method to the factual approach. Moreover, the factual approach may produce undesirable media effects (Nathanson, 2004). The evaluative approach may be more accessible and effective for children of all ages. Highlighting negative behaviors and their social consequences (e.g., being disliked, getting into trouble) would seem more relevant and understandable to most children. In contrast, the factual approach of asking young children to analyze violent scenes, implies that the content is worth thinking about and thus increases childrens' vulnerability to the material.

Contingency Management

Contingency management generally involves monitoring and reinforcing desired positive behaviors. In the case of media use, children might be required to engage in particular prosocial behaviors, such as completing homework, performing chores, or playing outside with friends. The completion of these positive activities would earn the children media time. This simple behavior modification system has been used to develop new behaviors as opposed to simply extinguishing media use. The key to implementing this type of behavior modification system is to keep the activities enjoyable for the involved children and family members (Jason and Fries, 2004). One of the side benefits of these contingency management programs is that they provide structured opportunities for parents and children to dialogue with each other. Through regular discussion, families learn better ways to work cooperatively and problem solve. In several studies, after one or two weeks of involvement in a behavioral program, important changes in the children's viewing occurred, and after about eight weeks, the children shifted their interests into more productive activities.

Electronic devices have also been used in contingency management programs to reduce media use (Jason, 1987). As a case example, Jason (1985) had a parent provide her child tokens that were earned for participation in certain positive activities such as reading, doing chores, or playing with friends. The tokens could be used to turn on the television set for a half hour. The child's average TV viewing was decreased from seven hours at baseline to one hour at a nine month follow-up. At the conclusion of the study, the mother said: "It geared her into other areas that she wouldn't have gone into without the program (swimming, musical instruments, interviewer at church). Her grade in science increased from D to A and she recently won the second prize in a science fair."

Another device was designed to require a child to exercise on stationary bicycle in order to view television (Jason and Brackshaw, 1999). Tools of this kind can be applied to reduce media use time, particularly with children who are excessive media users. However, once lower levels of media use are achieved, it is desirable to gradually phase out the use of these external devices.

Faith et al. (2001)

Ten obese 8 to 12 year old children were selected to participate in a randomized 12-week study. For six of the children, television viewing was made contingent on pedaling a stationary bike ("TV Cycle") while for a control group of four children, television viewing was not contingent on any such physical activity. The investigators hypothesized that the children whose television viewing was contingent upon the amount of physical activity they undertook would both watch less television and increase their physical activity over the control group.

Across the ten-week treatment phase, the group of children who rode the "TV Cycle" watched 1.6 hours of television per week, while the control group watched 21 hours per week (at the time of this study, the general population of 2-11 year olds watched 23 hours of television per week). Secondary analyses indicated that the children who rode the stationary bike to activate the television had significantly greater reductions in leg fat and total body fat than the children who did not have to ride the bike to view the television. In fact, the children whose television viewing was not contingent on riding the bike showed a 1% increase in leg fat.

These results indicate that changes in physical activity and sedentary behavior can be driven by contingencies on television and media use. The lack of pedaling by the control group indicates, as supported by behavioral theory, that without incentives a marked behavioral change cannot be expected.

Electronic Devices

Several products are available on the market to aid in managing the problem of childrens' excessive media viewing. For instance, there are computerized channel locks that may be purchased with new televisions. Problematically though, they are often quite expensive and most can be connected to only a small range of television set models. In addition, they cannot be inserted on older sets. Rather than to reduce the amount of TV viewing or help children develop new interests, these systems were built to help block out undesirable channels. Some of the computerized channel blockers are easier to unlock than to lock. Because they rely on a continuous availability of electricity to remain functional, if the set is unplugged, the programming may be cancelled. There are also several products on the market that enclose the prongs on the TV cord into a lock. This effectively prohibits a child from watching any TV at all (Positive Impact, Electro-Lok, Plug-Lok, CPAC). This system holds only limited value though, because instead of helping children to reduce their TV watching, it instead completely prevents it. Further, there are devices on the market to lock computers or to screen the content of the

Internet.

One type of television locking device is called "The Switch". It can be attached to the cord of any TV set, allowing parents to "lock" the television with a key, thereby prohibiting television viewing. Jason, Johnson, and Jurs (1993) assessed the effectiveness of this device using an operant research design, and they found that it decreased the amount of television viewed by the children in the experimental group. In another study, Johnson and Jason (1996) found that a computerized television lock, called "SuperVision," was effective in reducing the number of hours two children spent watching television. The above mentioned devices were limited in that they only prevented TV viewing, and therefore, did not re-structure the socialization activities or social learning experiences of parents and children. In contrast, parent-child behavioral programs using token activated meters do have the potential of creating a context where parents and children learn new behaviors that are encouraged by the device.

PART 4: CONCLUSIONS

Inappropriate media content contributes to adolescents' disengagement from family and community (Schwartz and Greenfield, 1999). Decades of psychological research have shown that violence in media may influence children to be less sensitive to the pain and suffering of others, more fearful of the world around them, and more likely to behave in aggressive and harmful ways toward others (Jason et al., 1999).

To ensure balance between time spent on media and non-media related activities, parents need to play an active role in monitoring the amount of time their children devote to electronic entertainment (Jason and Fries, 2004). Many articles have been written describing the actions parents can take to help their children use media appropriately, and one common feature is active parental supervision (American Academy of Pedia-trics, 2003; Jason et al., 1999; Jason and Hanaway, 1997; National Institute on Media and the Family, 2002). Observing media viewing patterns is a necessary preliminary step in understanding the nature of a child's media use. Unfortunately, Levine's (1996) review of literature indicates that the majority of parents are *not* making an effort to monitor what their children are viewing. Parents need to spend time becoming better acquainted with their children's media viewing patterns (Levine, 1996).

Based on the studies reviewed, there are several simple actions that parents can take to help develop media rules: 1) The amount of inappropriate material reaching a child may be limited by restricting the amount of time a child is allowed to view or interact with media (Jason et al., 1999; National Institute on Media and the Family, 2002; Villani, 2001). The National Institute on Media and the Family (2002) and the American Academy of Pediatrics (American Academy of Pediatrics, 2003) suggest limiting total viewing time to no more than one to two hours per day, however, personal circumstances and conditions should be considered when establishing such guidelines (Jason and Fries, 2004). 2) Parents need to model appropriate media use patterns. In other words, parents should lead by example (Jason and Hanaway, 1997). If parents excessively view media, their children are likely to adopt similar media use styles (Levine, 1996). Moreover, parents need to place less emphasis on the use of media as a solitary endeavor (American Academy of Pediatrics, 2003), and this can be done through parents more actively super-vising their children's media use and engaging in conversation about the media content. 3) Parents can establish ground rules that would limit a child's media viewing. For example, parents can place time limits on media use, determine that use is not permitted one day per week or on school nights, and

allow only certain types of content to be viewed (Jason and Hanaway, 1997). Parents could also allow media use contingent upon completion of other activities, including homework. Additionally, rules can be developed to limit media exposure by requiring that homework not be completed when the television is on, as this interferes with the retention of information (National Institute on Media and the Family, 2002). While remaining firm and consistent in enforcing these types of media rules, parents may need to be flexible when unexpected situations occur, for example, when a child wants to watch a special program that might require several hours of television viewing.

Though establishing clear rules and expectations is a natural start, the better and more enduring part of monitoring involves the use of diversionary tactics, that is, introducing children to pleasures separate from media. These may make media less attractive in the first place. Homes that heartily encourage reading, art, music, storytelling, imaginative play, sports, and nature will find that television and other electronic entertainment naturally play lesser roles in their children's lives. This approach to family life is easiest to institute when children are very young, but even families with older, dedicated viewers will see positive changes if new interests and opportunities are introduced. Parents need to commit to the hard work of monitoring how much time is spent watching television and playing computer games, surfing the Internet, and interacting with other electronic enter-tainment. The issue of content will have been mitigated in part simply by limiting the time of their overall exposure. Yet even with time rules in place, content issues will continue to need monitoring (Jason and Kim, 2006).

FUTURE DIRECTIONS

Interventions designed to reduce unhealthful exposure to media are in an early stage of development. Well-executed, randomized controlled trials of theory-based interventions, including those discussed in this chapter, need to be conducted with longitudinal follow-up of effects on mood, behavior, health, and quality of life over years. Trials such as these will not only delineate the most effective strategies for promoting healthful use of media in children, but also are necessary to determine what negative outcomes are actually caused by media use. Most randomized studies to date have not examined outcomes over the long-term, and most studies with longitudinal outcomes have been observational or not strictly controlled.

Additionally, there are many unexplored issues regarding youth experience with media. We have little understanding of the cumulative effects of using more than one medium simultaneously. "Media-multi-tasking" is a common practice among youth today. About a quarter of the time young people are using one medium, they are doing something else media-related at the same time. For example, they may talk on the phone while playing a video game and listening to music (Roberts et al., 2005). With the portability of media devices, the integration of more than one media within a device (e.g. cellular phones with MP3 players, streaming video, video games), and the accessibility of different media at virtually all times, today's youth are exposed to a near-constant stream of media messages. Though the developmental effects of this experience, both long and short-term, are difficult to measure, they are important to consider for potential research.

Also, there is continued debate regarding the effects of media on the youngest of children. Infants and toddlers are being exposed to television, video and other media, both directly and indirectly, at ages the medical community recommends they not be exposed at all (American Academy of Pediatrics, 2003). Companies are profiting on the marketing of educational media for babies, toddlers, and preschoolers, though they provide little support for their claims of education and enrichment. Though many parents regard media as an educational tool, there is little evidence to support that young children learn from television, videos, or interactive computer games. More likely, what young children are learning is that the screen is somewhere to find stimulation. But, perhaps of more concern is how young children are affected growing up in a media saturated environment, where televisions, computers, music, and video games are on in the background most of the time. Two-thirds of children zero to six-year olds live in homes where the TV is left on at least half the time, even if no one is watching, and one-third live in homes where the TV is on "almost all" the time; children in the latter group of homes read less and are slower to learn to read than other children (Rideout et al., 2003). The impact of this level of media exposure on children's development is relatively unknown, but certainly warrants consideration for future research.

The issue of media violence and how it affects children has long been analyzed. However, video games are becoming increasingly more violent and sexual, with graphic images appearing more and more life-like. Although a rating system has been designed to keep younger children away from games with high levels of violent and sexual content, many parents fail to regulate their children's exposure. Images that would be unsettling to most adults are becoming commonplace in video gaming. The effects on children who spend significant amounts of time playing these types of video games deserve further scrutiny from researchers.

Children are using the Internet with greater frequency, for both schoolwork and pleasure. Most parents do not actively regulate their children's Internet use. The result could be damaging, considering the variety of disturbing images and information that can be found on the Internet. A simple misspelling of an Internet address can connect a child to a website containing graphic and illicit material. A 2003 study revealed that 25% of youth had unwanted exposure to sexual pictures on the Internet, with a quarter of those children reporting they were extremely upset by what they saw (Mitchell et al., 2003). Since the average child spends 48 minutes per day on-line, this issue should be of concern to parents and professionals alike (Roberts et al., 2005).

Surprisingly, it seems that the most common sense of all youth media interventions has yet to be tested, removing the television set from the bedroom. Children with a television set in their bedroom watch almost and hour and a half more television per day than those that do not (Roberts et al., 2005). No studies have measured the outcomes of removing televisions and other media from bedrooms, or reducing the number of screens in a home, on overall youth media use.

Lastly, given the emerging epidemic of obesity and type II diabetes in children and adolescents, further study of the effects of media and advertising exposure on children's activity and diet patterns are warranted.

PART 5: RESOURCES FOR PROFESSIONALS
Center on Media and Child Health
www.cmch.com
This center is dedicated to understanding and responding to the effects of media on the physical, mental, and social health of children through research, production, and education.

Coalition for Quality Children's Media
www.cqcm.org
The Coalition for Quality Children's Media is

a national, non-profit organization founded in 1991. Because they believe that media profoundly affects children, their mission is 1) to teach children critical viewing skills and 2) to increase the visibility and availability of quality children's programs.

Common Sense Media
www.commonsensemedia.org
Common Sense Media exists to give parents, educators and kids a choice and a voice about the media they consume. Their goal is to provide trustworthy information and create a forum where adults and kids can learn from each other, speak out, and participate in creating a responsible and enjoyable media environment for everyone. They are a non-partisan, non-profit organization. Membership is free.

The Lion and The Lamb Project
www.lionlamb.org
The mission of The Lion and Lamb Project is to stop the marketing of violence to children. They do this by helping parents, industry, and government officials recognize that *violence is not child's play* – and by galvanizing concerned adults to take action. The Lion and the Lamb Project works to reduce the marketing of violent toys, games, and entertainment to children in two distinct ways. They work with parents and other concerned adults to reduce demand for violent "entertainment" products, and with industry and government to reduce the supply of such products.

National Institute on Media and the Family
www.mediafamily.org
Their mission is to maximize the benefits and minimize the harm of media on children and families through research, education, and advocacy. Their vision is to build healthy families and communities through the wise use of media.

Parents Television Council
www.parentstv.org
The PTC's primary mission is to promote and restore responsibility and decency to the entertainment industry in answer to America's demand for positive, family-oriented television programming. The PTC does this by fostering changes in TV programming to make the early hours of prime time family-friendly and suitable for viewers of all ages. They seek to serve as the conscience of the entertainment industry and corporate advertisers who sponsor broadcast content.

TV Watch
www.televisionwatch.org
TV Watch is a broad-based coalition that opposes government control of TV programming and promotes the use of tools like content ratings and parental controls. TV Watch educates parents about existing tools to manage their families' TV viewing and gives a voice to Americans who prefer personal responsibility to government regulation.

Federal Communications Commission
www.fcc.gov/parents
The FCC has published a large amount of information that can help parents deal with, decipher, and monitor the communications that their children can access.

REFERENCES

American Academy of Pediatrics. (2003) Understanding the Impact of Media on Children and Teens. Available at: http://www.apa.org/family/mediaimpact.htm, viewed on April 4, 2003.

American Academy of Pediatrics. (2007) Television and the Family. Available at: http://www.aap.org/family/tv1.htm, viewed on June 17, 2007.

Anderson CA, Berkowitz L, Donnerstein E, Huesmann LR, Johnson JD, Linz D, Malamuth NM, Wartella E. (2003) The influence of media violence on youth. Psychological Science in the Public Interest 4: 81-110.

Anderson CA, Dill KE. (2000) Video games and aggressive thoughts, feelings and behavior in the laboratory and in life. J Personality Social Psychol 78: 772-90.

Anderson ER. (1994) Accelerating and maximizing information from short-term longitudinal research. In J. Gottman (Ed.), The analysis of change. Mahwah, NJ: Erlbaum.

Anderson RE, Crespo CJ, Bartlett SJ, Cheskin LJ, Pratt M. (1998) Relationship of physical activity and television watching with body weight and level of fatness among children: Results from the third national health and nutrition examination survey. JAMA 279: 938-42.

Anderson DR, Huston AC, Schmitt L, Linebarger DL, Wright JC. (2001) Early Childhood Television Viewing and Adolescent Behavior. Monographs of the Society for Research in Child Development. (Serial 264): 66(1).

Bjorkland B, Bjorkland B. (1989) A clearer view of television. Parents' Magazine 64: 219-20.

Borzekowski DLG, Robinson TN, Killen JD. (2000) Does the camera add 10 pounds? Media use, perceived importance of appearance, and weight concerns among adolescent girls. J Adolescent Health 26: 36–41.

Borzekowski DLG, Robinson TN. (2001) The 30-second effect: An experiment revealing the impact of television comercials on food preferences of preschoolers. J Am Dietetic Assn 101(1): 42-6.

Brown JD, Newcomer SF. (1991) Television viewing and adolescents' sexual behavior. J Homosexuality 21: 77-91.

Bulck J Van den, Bergh B Van den. (2000) The influence of perceived parental guidance patterns on children's media use: Gender differences and media displacement. J Broadcasting Electronic Media 44: 329-48.

Calvert SL. (1999) Children's journeys through the information age. New York: McGraw-Hill.

Coffey S, Stipp H. (1997) The interactions between computer and television usage. J Advertising Res 37: 61-7.

Collins RL, Elliot MN, Berry SH, Kanouse DE, Kunkel D, Hunter SB, Miu A. (2004) Watching sex on television predicts adolescent initiation of sexual behavior. Pediatrics 114: 280-9.

Comstock G. (1990) Television and the American child. San Diego: Academic Press.

Comstock G, Scharrer E. (1999) Television: What's on, who's watching, and what it means. San Diego, CA: Academic Press.

Corder-Bolz (1980) Mediation: the role of significant others. J Commun 3: 106-18.

Corteen RS, Williams TM. (1986) Television and reading skills. In T.M.Williams (Ed.), The impact of television. Orlando, FL: Academic Press.

Crespo CJ, Smit E, Troiano RP, Bartlett SJ, Macera CA, Andersen RE. (2001) Television watching, energy intake, and obesity in US children: Results from the third National Health and Nutrition Examination Survey, 1988-1994. Arch Pediatrics Adolescent Med 155: 360-5.

DeAngelis T. (2000) Internet addiction. American Psychological Association's Monitor 31: No. 4.

Dennison BA, Russo TJ, Burdick PA, Jenkins PL. (2004) An intervention to reduce television viewing by preschool children. Arch Pediatric Adolescent Med 158: 170-6.

Doolittle JC. (1980) Immunizing children against possible antisocial effects of viewing television violence: A curricular intervention. Perceptual Motor Skills 51: 498.

Dorr A, Graves SB, Phelps E. (1980) Television literacy for young children. J Commun 30(3): 71-83.

Enns CW, Mickle SJ, Goldman JD. (2002) Trends in food and nutrient intakes by children in the United States. Family Econ Nutrition Rev 14(2): 56-68.

Epstein LH, Paluch RA, Gordy CC, Dorn J. (2000) Decreasing sedentary behaviors in treating pediatric obesity. Arch Pediatr Adolesc Med 154: 220-6.

Faith MS, Berman N, Heo M, Pietrobelli A, Gallagher D, Epstein LH, Eiden MT, Allison DB. (2001) Effects of contingent television on physical activity and television viewing in obese children. Pediatrics 107(5): 1043-48.

Fetler M. (1984) Television viewing and school achievement. J Commun 34: 104-18.

French SA, Story M, Jeffery RW. (2001) Environmental influences on eating and physical activity. Ann Rev Public Health 22: 309-35.

Funk JB, Buchman DD. (1996) Playing violent video and computer games and adolescent self-concept. J Commun 46: 19-32.

Gorham BW. (1999) Stereotypes in the media: So what? Howard J Communications 10: 229-47.

Gortmaker SL, Peterson K, Wiecha J, Sobol AM, Dixit S, Fox MK, Laird N. (1999) Reducing obesity via a school-based interdisciplinary intervention among youth. Arch Pediatric Adolescent Med 153: 409-18.

Greenfield DN, (1999, August). The Nature of Internet Addiction: Psychological Factors in Compulsive Internet Use. Paper presented at annual meeting of the American Psychological Association, Boston, Massachusetts.

Griffiths MD, Hunt N. (1998) Dependence on computer games by adolescents. Psychol Rep 82: 475-80.

Hancox RJ, Milne BJ, Poulton R. (2005)

Association of television during childhood with poor educational achievement. Arch Pediatr Adolesc Med 159: 614-8.

Henke LL. (1999) Children, advertising, and the Internet: An exploratory study. Schumann, David W. (Ed); Thorson, Esther (Ed). Advertising and the World Wide Web. Advertising Consumer Psychol: 73-80.

Hicks DJ. (1968) Effects of co-observer's sanctions and adult presence on imitative aggression. Child Dev 39: 303-9.

Horton RW, Santogrossi DA. (1978) The effect of adult commentary on reducing the influence of televised violence. Personality Soc Psychol Bull 4: 337-40.

Huesmann LR, Eron LD, Klein R, Brice P, Fischer P. (1983) Mitigating the imitation of aggressive behaviors by changing children's attitudes about media violence. J Personality Social Psychol 44: 899-910.

Huesmann LR, Moise-Titus J, Podolski C-L, Eron LD. (2003) Longitudinal relations between children's exposure to TV violence and their aggressive and violent behavior in young adulthood: 1977-1992. Dev Psychol 39: 201-21.

Huffaker D, Calvert S. (2003) The new science of learning: Active learning, metacognition and transfer of knowledge in e-learning applications. J Educational Computing Res 29: 325-34.

Huston AC, Donnerstein E, Fairchild H, Feshbach ND, Katz PA, Murray JP, Rubenstein EA, Wilcox BL, Zuckerman D. (1992) Big world, small screen: The role of television in American society. Lincoln: University of Nebraska Press.

Huston AC, Wright JC, Marquis J, Green SB. (1999) How young children spend their time: Television and other activities. Dev Psychol 35: 912-25.

Irwin AR, Gross AM. (1995) Cognitive tempo, violent video games, and aggressive behavior in young boys. J Fam Violence 10: 337-50.

Jason LA. (1983) Self-monitoring in reducing children's excessive television viewing. Psychol Reports 53: 1280.

Jason LA. (1984) Reducing excessive television viewing among seven children in one family. Behav Ther 7: 3-4.

Jason LA. (1985) Using a token-actuated timer to reduce television viewing. J Appl Behav Anal 18: 269-72.

Jason LA. (1987) Reducing children's television viewing and assessing secondary changes. J Clin Child Psychol 16: 245-50.

Jason LA, Fries M. (2004) Helping parents reduce children's TV viewing. Res Social Work Practice 14: 121-31.

Jason LA, Brackshaw E. (1999) Case study: Reducing TV viewing and corresponding increases in physical activity and subsequent weight loss. J Behav Ther Exp Psychiatr 30: 145-51.

Jason LA, Hanaway L. (1997) Remote control: Strategies for parents in a television age. Sarasota, Fl.: Professional Resource Press.

Jason LA, Hanaway L, Brackshaw EA. (1999) Violent behavior and the media. In TP Gullotta and SJ McElhaney (Ed.) Voices in homes and communities (pp. 133-156). Washington, D.C.: National Mental Health Association.

Jason LA, Johnson S, Jurs A. (1993) Reducing children's television viewing with an inexpensive lock. Child Fam Behav Ther 15: 45-54.

Jason LA, Johnson S. (1995) Reducing excessive television viewing while increasing physical activity. Child Fam Behav Ther 17: 35-44.

Jason LA, Kim KL. (2006) Sex, guns, and rock 'n' roll: The influence of media in children's lives. Commissioned by Kathleen Kovner Kline (Ed.). Hardwired to connect—Investigating the social, moral, and spiritual foundations of child well being. A report to the nation from the Commission on Children at Risk. Dartmouth Medical College: Hanover, New Hampshire.

Jason LA, Rooney-Rebeck P. (1984) Reducing excessive television viewing. Child Fam Behav Ther 6: 61-9.

Jason LA, Klich MM. (1982) Use of feedback in reducing television watching. Psychol Reports 51: 812- 4.

Jason LA, Weine AM, Johnson JH, Warren-Sohlberg L, Filippelli LA, Turner EY, Lardon C. (1992) Helping transfer students: Strategies for educational and social readjustment. San Francisco: Jossey-Bass.

Johnson SZ, Jason LA. (1996) Evaluation of a device aimed at reducing children's television viewing. Child Fam Behav Ther 18: 59-61.

Johnson JG, Cohen P, Smailes EM, Kasen S, Brook JS. (2002) Television viewing and aggressive behavior during adolescence and adulthood. Science 295: 2468-71.

Jordan AB, Schmitt KL, Woodard E H. (2001) Developmental implications of commercial broadcasters' educational offerings. J Applied Dev Psychol l22: 87-101.

Kandell J. (1998). Internet addiction on campus: The vulnerability of college students. CyberPsychol Behav 1: 1.

Kayany JM, Yelsma P. (2000) Displacement effects of online media in the socio-technical contexts of households. J Broadcasting Electronic Media 44: 215-29.

Knight JL, Giuliano TA. (2001) He's a Laker; She's a "Looker": The cones-quences of gender-stereotypical portray-als of male and female athletes by the print media. Sex Roles 45(3-4): 217- 29.

Kotz F, Story M. (1994) Food advertisements during children's Saturday morning television programming: Are they consistent with dietary recommendations? J Am Dietetic Assn 94: 1296-1300.

Kunkel D, Eyal K, Finnerty K, Biely E, Donnerstein E. (2005) Sex on TV 4: A biennial report to the Kaiser Family Foundation. Menlo Park, CA: Kaiser Family Foundation.

LaFerle C, Edwards SM, Lee W-N. (2000) Teens' use of traditional media and the Internet. J Advertising Res 40: 55-65.

Levine M. (1996) Viewing Violence: How Media Violence Affects Your Child's and Adolescent's Development. New York: Doubleday Press.

Linzer-Schwartz L. (Ed.). (1999) Psychology and the Media: A Second Look. Washington, D.C.: American Psycho-logical Association.

Ludwig DS, Peterson KE, Gortmaker SL. (2001) Relation between consumption of sugar-sweetened drinks and childhood obesity: a prospective, observational analysis. The Lancet 357: 505-8.

Media Awareness Network (2003). Media Education and Media Violence. Retrieved on April 1, 2003 from http://www.reseaumedias.ce/english/issue s /violence/role_media education.cfm

Media Violence. (2001) Amer Academy Pediatr 108: 1222-6.

Mitchell KM, Finkelhor D, Wolak J. (2003) The exposure of youth to unwanted sexual material on the Internet: A national survey of risk, impact, and prevention. Youth Society 34: 330-358.

Nathanson AI. (1999) Identifying and explaining the relationship between parental mediation and children's aggres-sion. Communication Res 26: 124-43.

Nathanson AI. (2001) Parents versus peers: Exploring the significance of peer mediation of antisocial television. Communication Res 28: 251-74.

Nathanson AI. (2004) Factual and evaluative approaches to modifying children's responses to violent television. J Commun 54: 321-36.

Nathanson AI, Cantor J. (2000) Reducing the

aggression-promoting effect of violent cartoons by increasing children's fictional involvement with the victim: A study of active mediation. J Broadcasting Electronic Media 44: 125-42.

Nathanson AI, Botta RA. (2003) Shaping the effects of television on adolescents' body image disturbance: The role of parental mediation. Communic Res 30: 304-31.

Nathanson AI, Yang M. (2003) The effects of mediation content and form on children's responses to violent television. Human Communication Research 29: 111-34.

National Institute on Media and the Family (2002). What Goes in Must Come Out: Children's Media Violence Consumption at Home and Aggressive Behaviors at School. Retrieved March 26, 2003, from http://www.mediaandthefamily.org

Pardun CJ, L'Engle KL, Brown JD. (2005) Linking exposure to outcomes: Early adolescents' consumption of sexual content in six media. Mass Communication and Society 8: 75-91.

Rapaczynski W, Singer DG, Singer JL. (1982) Teaching television: A curriculum for young children. J Commun 32: 46-54.

Razel M. (2001) The complex model of television viewing and educational achievement. J Educational Res 94: 371-9.

Rice B. (1992) Mixed signals: TVs effect on children continues to stir debate. Am Health 62; 24-30.

Rideout VJ, Vandewater EA, Wartella EA. (2005) Zero to six: Electronic media in the lives of infants, toddlers, and preschoolers. Kaiser Family Foundation, Menlo Park, CA.

Roberts DF. (2000) Media and youth: access, exposure, and privatization. J Adolesc Health 27(suppl):8-11.

Roberts DF, Foehr UG. (2004) Kids and Media in America. Cambridge, United Kingdom: Cambridge University Press.

Roberts DF, Foehr UG, Rideout VJ. (2005) Generation M: Media in the lives of 8-18 year olds, Kaiser Family Foundation, Menlo Park, CA.

Roberts DF, Foehr UG, Rideout VJ, Brodie M. (1999) Kids and media @ the new millennium, Kaiser Family Foundation, Menlo Park, CA.

Robinson TN, Wilde ML, Navracruz LC, Haydel KF, Varady A. (2001) Effects of reducing children's television and video game use on aggressive behavior. Arch Pediatric Adolescent Med 155: 17-23.

Robinson TN, Killen JD, Kraemer HC, Wilson DM, Matheson DM, Haskell WL, Pruitt LA, Powell TM, Owens AS, Thompson NS, Flint-Moore NM, Davis GJ, Emig KA, Brown RT, Rochon J, Green S, Varady A. (2003) Dance and reducing television viewing to prevent weight gain in African-American girls: The Stanford GEMS pilot study. Ethnicity and Disease 13: 65-77.

Robinson TN, Borzekowski DL. (2006) Effects of the SMART classroom curriculum to reduce child and family screen time. J Commun 56: 1-26.

Sanders MR, Montgomery DT, Brechman-Toussaint ML. (2000) The mass media and the prevention of child behavior problems: The evaluation of a television series to promote positive outcome for parents and their children. J Child Psychol Psychiatr Allied Disciplines 41(7): 939-48.

Sarlo G, Jason LA, Lonak C. (1988) Parents' strategies for limiting children's television watching. Psychol Reports 63: 435-8.

Schwartz LL, Greenfield MR. (1999) Tuning into the media: Youth, violence, and incivility. In L.L. Schwartz (Ed.). Psychology and the media: A second look. Psychology and the media. Vol.2 (pp 173-214). Washington, D.C., U.S., American Psychological Association.

Sher L. (2000) The Internet, suicide, and human mental functions. Canadian J Psychiatry 45: 297.

Singer DG, Zuckerman DM, Singer JL. (1980) Helping elementary school children learn about TV. J Commun 30: 84-93.

Singer JL, Singer DG, Rapacynski WS. (1984) Family patterns and television viewing as predictors of children's beliefs and aggression. J Commun 34: 274-8.

Singer MI, Miller DB, Guo S, Flanner DJ, Frierson T, Slovak K. (1999) Contributors to violent behavior among elementary and middle school children. Pediatr 104: 878-4.

Singer MI, Slovak K, Frierson T, York P. (1998) Viewing preferences, symptoms of psychological truama, and violent behaviors among children who watch television. J Amer Academy Child Adoles Psychiatr 37: 1041-8.

Smith SL, Nathanson AI, Wilson BJ. (2002) Prime-time television: Assessing violence during the most popular viewing hours. J Communication 52: 84-111.

Taras HL, Gage M. (1995) Advertised foods on children's television. Arch Pediatr Adolesc Med 149: 649-52.

The Center for Media Literacy (2003) Assignment Media Literacy—Maryland Project. Retrieved on April 2, 2003, from http://www.medialit.org

The Impact of Interactive Violence on Children. (2000) Hearing Before the Senate Committee on Commerce, Science, and Transportation. 106th Cong, 1st Session (2000) (statement of Craig Anderson, Professor, Iowa State University, Department of Psychology)

The Kaiser Family Foundation. (2004) The Role of Media in Childhood Obesity. Report available at: http://www.kff.org/entmedia/loader.cfm?url=/commonspot/security/getfile.cfmandPageID=32022

The Henry J. Kaiser Family Foundation. (1994) Kids and Media at the New Millennium: A Kaiser Family Foundation. Report. Menlo Park, CA: The Henry J. Kaiser Family Foundation.

Tiggeman M. (2005) Television and adolescent body image: The role of program content and viewing motivation. J Social Clin Psychol 24: 361-81.

Villani S. (2001) Impact of media on children and adolescents: A 10-year review of the research. J Amer Acad Child Adolesc Psychiatr 40: 392-401.

Voojis MW, van der Voort THA. (1993) Learning about television violence: The impact of a critical viewing curriculum on children's attitudinal judgments of crime scenes. J Res Dev Educ 26: 133-42.

Young KS. (1996) Addictive use of the Internet. Psychol Reports 79: 899-902.

Valkenburg PM, Krcmar M, Peeters AL, Marseille NM. (1999) Developing a scale to assess three styles of television mediation: "Instructive mediation," "Restrictive mediation," and "Social coviewing". J Broadcasting Electronic Media 43: 52-66.

Van den Bulck J. (2000) Is television bad for your health? Behavior and body image of the adolescent "couch potato." J Youth Adolesc 29: 273-88.

Ward LM, Rivadeneyra R. (1999) Contributions of entertainment television to adolescents' sexual atttitudes and expectations: The role of viewing amount versus viewer involvement. J Sex Res 36: 237-49.

Wartella EA, Jennings N. (2000) Children and computers: New technology—old concerns. The Future of Children 10(2): 31-43.

Wilson BJ, Smith SL, Potter WJ, Kunkel D, Linz D, Colvin CM, Donnerstein E. (2002) Young children's perceptions of television reality: Determinants and developmental differences. Dev Psychol 30: 229-39.

Wright JC, Huston AC, Reitz AL, Piemyat S. (1994) Violence in children's television programming: Assessing the risks. J Commun 52: 5-35.

PREVENTION OF SCHOOL VIOLENCE

Catherine N. Dulmus, Eugene Maguin and Amy R. Manning

INTRODUCTION

School violence refers to various aggressive and antisocial behaviors among students that range from serious physical acts involving the use of lethal weapons (Cantor and Wright, 2002), to less serious physical behaviors like shoving and pushing (Juvonen, 2001). The purpose of this chapter is to review studies focusing on the prevention or reduction of violence in school with emphasis upon a review of randomized controlled studies.

School violence is a national concern in the United States. The shootings at Columbine High School in 1999 captured media attention. However, forty-one school shootings occurred in the United States between 1974 and 2000 (Vossekuil et al., 2002). Findings from the 1999 Youth Risk Behavior Survey (YRBS) revealed that during the 30 days preceding the survey, 7% of students in grades 9 through 12 reported carrying a weapon on school property. In the 12 months preceding the survey, 36% of these students reported being in a physical fight at least once and four percent suffered injuries that required medical treatment. Alarmingly, almost nine percent of students reported being intentionally hit, slapped, or physically hurt by a boyfriend or a girlfriend during the previous 12 months (NCIPC, Youth violence-A national problem).

School-associated violent deaths that occurred between 1994 and 1999 represent less than one percent of all homicides and suicides among school-aged children. During this period, of the 172 student victims, 15 were in elementary school. The rate of school-associated violent death was 14 times higher among students in schools that included grades 9-12 than among students in elementary schools (Anderson et al., 2001). In a 1996 to 1997 survey of U.S. public high schools, it was reported that 60% of violent acts occurred in only four percent of the schools surveyed. Demographic characteristics of schools prone to serious violence included city, urban fringe and town location high schools, schools with higher student enrollment size, and schools who draw students living in neighborhoods with high levels of crime (Miller, 2003).

School Violence: Trends and Incidents

According to the National Center for Educational Statistics and the Bureau of Justice Statistics (DeVoe et al., 2005) fighting, carrying weapons, assault and robbery are forms of violence that occur on school grounds. Boys were more likely than girls to report being in a fight on school grounds. Urban students were 5% more likely to be in a fight than rural students (15% versus 10%). Though fighting on school grounds has dropped from 16% to 13% between the years 1993 and 2003 and weapon carrying on school grounds decreased from 12% in 1993 to 6% in 2003, 6% of students reported being afraid of an 'attack' at school. Students in urban schools were more likely to fear an attack at school than suburban or rural students. Student fears, however, are decreasing. In 1995, 7% of students reported having skipped school or avoided areas in their school because of fear for safety, and in 2003 only 5% of students reported the same behavior/fear. Between 1999 and 2003 there was an increase in school usage of security measures of any kind, and in 2003 99% of students reported being aware of at least one security measure in place at their school. Serious violent crimes in schools were identified as rape, sexual assault, robbery and aggravated assault. These incidents almost doubled between 2002 and 2003 (88,100-154,200), with the number of violent incidents (including 'serious violent' as well as "simple assault") increasing from 658,600 in 2002 to 738,700 in 2003. In 2003, almost 2 million students (age 12-18) were victims of crime at school. Middle school students were victims of these crimes at school at a rate of almost 2 to 1 compared to high school students. Almost 20% of schools reported gang activities within the school (DeVoe et al., 2005).

Risk factors For Aggression In Youth

Risk factors for youth aggressive behaviors include a history of neglect and abuse, poverty, family stress and conflict, and drug and alcohol involvement (Walker et al., 1998). Other risk factors are lack of parent support and involvement, poor anger management skills, lack of academic interest (Hunt et al., 2002), hyperactivity and aggression in early childhood, male gender, and a controlling type of parenting (Stormont, 2002). The strongest risk factors during childhood are involvement in serious criminal behavior, substance abuse, being male, physical aggression, low family socio-economic status, and antisocial parents (U.S. Surgeon General). Child developmental outcomes are worse the greater the length of exposure and the greater the number of risk factors present (Walker et al., 1998). Behavioral manifestations of risk factors include defiance of adults, restlessness and over activity, aggression, disruptive classroom behavior, lack of self-regulation, and poor school readiness (Walker et al., 1998).

A longitudinal study of students from age 10 to 18 investigated how risk factors indicating an adolescent's propensity to participate in violence changed with age during this period (Herrenkohl et al., 2000). Measures were taken at ages 10, 14, 16 and 18. Assessments were taken from students, their parents and their teachers; 94% of participants completed the survey. The study confirmed previously identified risk factors including hyperactivity (teacher and/or parent rating), early initiation of violence, parental violence, poor family management, family conflict, low academic performance, low school commitment, sibling and/or peer delinquency, gang membership, and economic deprivation. New risk factors identified by this study included: drug selling, parental attitudes favorable to violence, residential mobility, low educational aspirations, school transitions, community disorganization, low neighborhood attachment, availability of drugs, neighborhood adults involved in crime, and poor enforcement of existing laws against violence. The study showed that exposure to multiple risk factors put children at a significantly greater likelihood of school-related violence by the age of 18. Students exposed to more than five risk factors at any of the age groups were between 7 and 11 times more likely to be involved in violence by the age of 18 than their peers who were exposed to 2 or less risk factors at their corresponding age. At age 10, antisocial behavior (as assessed by the teacher) was a strong predictor of violence in adolescence. Hyperactivity, as measured by a parent, was a predictor of violence at ages 10, 14, and 16. At age 10, favorable parental attitudes toward violence predicted future violence significantly. Even though family conflict and poor family management at age 10 did not predict violence outcomes, at 14 and 16 years of age these two risk factors were predictors of violence. Low academic performance at all age levels was a predictor of violence by age 18. Antisocial influences within peer groups (including gang involvement) and the community are risk factors at ages 14 and 16.

Thus, risk factors were specific to a given developmental period in youth.

Aggressive and antisocial behaviors in children increase with age (White et al., 2002). Children who become violent before age 13 generally commit more crimes, and exhibit a pattern of escalating violence through childhood (U.S. Surgeon General [n.d.]). Thus, the literature favors early intervention for youth violence to prevent its escalation into adolescence and adulthood (Walker et al., 1998).

METHODS

In this review, we present research on interventions to prevent school violence, including approaches that target both school violence itself and prevention of risk factors for school violence. Our literature review identified robust prevention interventions, as well as interventions without effectiveness, thus allowing us to view the current gaps in knowledge about in-school violence prevention. As described in Gordon's model of prevention (Gordon, 1987; Gordon, 1983), we categorized interventions into three areas: universal, selective and indicated. Universal preventive interventions are targeted to the general public or a whole population group. Selective preventive interventions are targeted to a subgroup of the population who are at high risk of becoming delinquent or violent (Connor, 2002). Indicated prevention interventions are targeted to those identified as having minimal but detectable signs of delinquency or violence. Search terms used to locate studies concerning school-related violence included: violence, school violence, school violence prevention, primary prevention, universal prevention, indicated prevention, elective prevention, prevention in schools, school based programs, violence outcomes, violence measures, school violence outcomes, school violence measures, school violence interventions, school interventions, as well as randomized controlled study paired with previous search terms. Databases searched to locate studies were the Wilson Web (Education Full Text), ERIC Database through EBSCO, Host Research Databases, PsycINFO through Ovid, Ingenta Connect, JSTOR, Science Direct, Taylor and Francis Online Journals, Wiley InterScience Journals, Journals @ Ovid Full Text, MEDLINE, and JAMA. After initial searches were conducted, the same databases were searched for the specific names of programs mentioned in articles that were found. Also, a general search for author names identified in the database search was conducted on both Yahoo and Google. This search strategy identified 13 randomized controlled trials that are reported below and in Table 1.

RESULTS
Universal Prevention Interventions

Universal prevention interventions were educational or addressed reduction of risk factors and/or enhancement of protective factors for prevention of violence among all youth, regardless of risk status. Our literature review identified the following 4 universal prevention intervention programs that have been tested in randomized controlled trials.

SMART Talk

Bosworth, Espelage, DuBay, Daytner, and Karageorge (2000) studied the effectiveness of a multimedia format violence prevention curriculum for students in grades 6, 7 and 8. The SMART Talk program utilizes an interactive computer program that combines games and skill-building activities with resources on anger management, and dispute resolution. The program presentation was designed to reduce differences in instruction that may occur when information is presented by varying instructors. Five hundred sixteen students participated in the study (42% of participants were in 6th grade) and 538 also participated in the follow up. Classrooms were randomly assigned and in the

Table 1: Studies with Randomized Controlled Trial Designs and Violence Outcomes

Study	Participants	Intervention	Measures	Outcome
Bosworth et al., 2000 "SMART Talk", a multimedia violence prevention program for adolescents.	516 6th, 7th, and 8th grade students from a single 'economically diverse' Midwestern middle school. Three preexisting academic teams of randomly assigned students were randomized to intervention (2 teams) or control	Computer-based modules on anger management, perspective taking, and dispute resolution. Modeled on BARN (Body Awareness Resource Network).	Aggressive behavior frequency. Seven items measuring threats of physical aggression, fighting, retaliation, and specific fight behaviors in past 30 days.	Not significant. Effect size (ES) = 0.031
Farrell et al., 2001 "Responding in Peaceful and Positive Ways" (RIPP): A school-based prevention program	27 non-special education, 6th grade classrooms in three middle schools serving a 96% African-American population randomly assigned to intervention (13 classrooms, 305 students) or control (14 classrooms, 321 students).	A social-cognitive problem solving model plus specific violence prevention skills (RIPP) to teach knowledge, attitudes and skills to promote nonviolence.	In- and out of- school suspensions, disciplinary code violations for violent behavior, all from school records. Past 30 days self-report: threatened to harm teacher, brought weapon to school, threatened someone with a weapon, injured in fight and needed medical attention.	Significant effects in spring, grade 6 for violent disciplinary code violations, in-school suspensions, and injured in fight and needed medical attention; in fall, grade 7 for threatened to harm teacher; and in spring, grade 7 (girls only) for threatened to harm teacher.
Schick and Cierpka, 2003 "Faustlos"	21 German elementary schools randomly assigned to treatment (n = 14 schools, 238 children) or control (n = 7 schools, 97 children). A boy and girl in each class were randomly selected for interview. Age range at posttest: 5-6 years, 17%; 7-8 years, 74%, >=9 years, 7%.	Second Step program. Program consists of 51 lessons divided into three units: empathy, impulse control, and anger management.	Parent report aggression and delinquency scales, teacher report aggression, child self-report aggression.	No significant effects for parent, child, or teacher report aggression or delinquency scales.

Study	Participants	Intervention	Measures	Outcome
A) Flannery et al., 2003 B) Krug et al., 1997 "PeaceBuilders" universal school-based violence prevention program.	8 K-5 schools selected for high historical rates of suspension and expulsions from two Southwestern districts. Schools matched and randomly assigned to immediate (1,717 students) or one-year delayed (2,411 students) intervention condition.	PeaceBuilders program. Program intended to change setting characteristics of negative behavior and increase prosocial models. Program elements (rules and practices) implemented by teachers throughout school day.	A) Aggressive behavior. Teacher report and child report. B) School nurse logs of injury visits attributed to a) confirmed fighting, and b) possible fighting.	A) Significant decrease in teacher report aggression in grades 3-5 at Year 1 spring, Year 2 fall and Year 2 spring but not grades K-2 at any follow-up point. No effect for child report aggression in grades 3-5 or in grades K-2 at any follow-up point. B) Significantly lower rates of confirmed fighting injuries in intervention schools but no change for rates of possible fighting injuries.
Simon et al., 2002 "Project Towards No Drug Abuse"	21 California continuation (alternative) high schools matched on substance abuse prevalence, ethnicity, school size, and achievement scores and randomly assigned to control or either of two treatment conditions (seven schools in each condition). Sample was 850 students with complete data (30% of baseline sample) and was 55% male; 49% Latino, 34% white, 16% other; mean age 16.8 years. Sample differed from student population.	Both treatment groups received a 9 session program delivered by health educators to all students in core classes. Sessions addressed health motivation issues, social skills development, and non-drug use decision making skills. Also, one set of intervention schools conducted a school-wide set of activities emphasizing a drug-free focus. Control schools conducted no special programs.	Past 12 months frequency at one year follow-up of any violence perpetration (beat up a person, used a weapon to threaten, or used a weapon to injure), any victimization (same three items), and weapons carrying.	Two treatment conditions did not differ and were combined. Analysis by gender. Control males had significantly higher victimization than treatment males ($OR = 0.64$). No difference for perpetration and weapons carrying ($OR = 1.23$ and 1.50, respectively, NS). Control females did not differ from treatment females ($OR = 0.90$, perpetration; 0.88, victimization; 0.73, weapons carrying).

Study	Participants	Intervention	Measures	Outcome
(A) Flay et al., 2004 (B) Ngwe et al., 2004, (C) Segawa et al., 2005 "Aban Aya Youth Project"	Elementary schools serving inner city and near-suburban areas were ranked on risk criteria. 12 schools with high but similar risk scores were selected and randomly assigned to control or one of two interventions. Participating schools were predominantly African American (91%). All 5th grade students were eligible and 571 boys and 582 girls comprised the dataset.	Three conditions, each consisting of 16-21 lessons per year for the four years of the study. Social development (SD) condition: curriculum of social skills, problem solving and conflict resolution skills. School-Community (SC) condition added parent training workshops and teacher and school development components to the SD components. Health enhancement condition controls primarily taught health behaviors related to nutrition, physical activity and general health but did include some SD lessons.	Child-report violent behavior and child-report school delinquency.	(A) Relative to control boys, boys in both SD and SC had significant decreases in violent behavior (SD: *ES*=-0.40; SC: *ES*=-0.53) and school delinquency (SD: *ES*=-0.33; SC: *ES*=-0.70). Effects for girls were not significant for violent behavior (SD: *ES*= 0.22; SC: *ES*=-0.21) or school delinquency (SD: *ES* =-0.18; SC: *ES*=-0.18). (B) Growth curve model of child-report violence showed significant decrease for SD+SC relative to control for boys. (C) Latent class growth mixture model of child report school violence showed that intervention effect was significant for only the boys who were most violent at pretest. Analysis for girls not reported in B and C.
August et al., 2003 "Early Risers Skills for Success"	Base study: 245 kindergarten children with elevated teacher-reported aggression scores. This article: 143 (of the 245 now-fourth grade children) plus 1,364 of their classmates.	Program consists of a 6 week summer school program providing academic instruction, social skills training, creative and recreational activities; teacher	Aggressive-disruptive score by peer nomination	No significant effect for program.

Study	Participants	Intervention	Measures	Outcome
		consultation and student mentoring; and a tailored program of proactive family support.		
Grossman, et al., 1997 "Second Step",	12 elementary schools from four districts matched on demographics then randomly assigned to treatment or control. 790 2ⁿᵈ and 3ʳᵈ grade students participated.	Second Step program, consisting of 30 lessons teaching empathy training, impulse control, and anger management, implemented by regular class room teachers trained in the program	1) Aggression and delinquency scales completed by teachers and parents. 2) behavioral observation of verbal negative and physical negative behavior in school settings.	At posttest, no effects for parent report of aggressive and delinquent behavior and for teacher report of aggressive behavior, delinquent behavior, antisocial-aggressive behavior, and demanding-disruptive behavior. Significant decrease in direct observation physical negative behavior in classroom at posttest and follow-up and in playground/ cafeteria at posttest only.
Lochman and Wells, 2004 "Coping Power Program"	Boys in 4ᵗʰ and 5ᵗʰ grades were screened by their teacher and parents for aggression and disruptiveness. 183 boys randomly assigned to Child component only (n = 60), Child plus Parent components (n = 60), or control (n = 63).	Coping Power program. Child component consisting of 33 sessions covering awareness of feelings and associated arousal, relaxation and distraction techniques, coping statements. Parent component comprised 16 sessions based on existing parent training programs.	At the 1-year follow-up, child report of overt and covert delinquency.	Covert delinquency compared to control. Child component only: (ES = 0.10, NS). Child plus parent component: (ES = -0.28, p<.05). Overt delinquency compared to control: Child component only: (ES = -.07, NS) Child plus parent component: (ES = -.24, NS).

Study	Participants	Intervention	Measures	Outcome
Webster-Stratton et al., 2004 "Incredible Years Intervention"	121 4 to 7 year old children referred for conduct problems and screened to meet DSM-IV CD or ODD criteria, and 2 SD elevation in parent report behavior problems. Children randomly assigned one of five training conditions: 1) child only ($n = 30$), 2) parent only ($n = 31$), 3) parent + teacher ($n = 24$), 4) child + teacher ($n = 23$), 5) parent, child, and teacher ($n = 25$); or 6) wait-list control ($n = 26$).	Incredible Years program for parents consisting of 17 video-taped programs on parenting and interpersonal skills. Children received18-19 sessions focusing on topics that included social skills, empathy, and compliance. Teachers received 4 days of training on classroom management, relationship development, and social skills strengthening.	Mother report conduct problems, father report conduct problems, teacher report conduct problems	Compared to wait-list control at posttest, significant improvement in mother report conduct problems in 5 of 5 contrasts ($ES = -1.17$ to -0.71), in father report conduct problems in 3 of 5 conditions ($ES = -0.94$ to -0.24, and in teacher report conduct problems in 5 of 5 conditions ($ES = -1.05$ to -0.60).
Shechtman, 2000 "Bibliotherapy"	70 students (20 10-11 year olds and 50 12-15 year olds; 55 males, 15 females) nominated by their teachers for high aggressiveness. Students from special education classes in 10 Israeli schools. Student randomly assigned to wait-list control or treatment	10 45-minute variable format sessions led by counseling and special education graduate students. Sessions consisted of discussion of age appropriate literary works selected to include aggression motivations and dynamics and application of the themes to their lives.	Teacher report and child report of aggressive behavior and delinquent behavior.	Significant decrease in child report aggressive behavior ($ES = -0.64$) and teacher report aggressive behavior ($ES = -0.42$). No significant effect for either child-report ($ES = -0.42$) or teacher report ($ES = 0.03$) delinquent behavior.

Study	Participants	Intervention	Measures	Outcome
Sukhodolsky et al., 2005 Anger control training program	31 boys aged 7-11 years screened for excessive anger intensity, history of verbal and physical aggression, and history of oppositional behavior or conduct problems. Boys averaged 9.7 years of age and were 48% white. Boys matched on age and assigned to either social skills training (SST) or social problem solving training (SPST).	Study compared the SST module to SPST module, both of which are part of the Anger Control Training program. Within each condition, 5-7 person groups received 10 sessions of their assigned module.	Parent report aggression and conduct problems.	Significant decrease in aggression in both groups (SST: *ES* = -0.52; SPST: *ES* = -0.41) and in conduct problems in both groups (SST: *ES* = -0.52, SST; SPST: *ES* = -0.56)
Komro et al., 2004 "D.A.R.E middle school program plus classroom, parent, and community components"	24 rural, suburban, and inner-city Minnesota schools teaching a 7th grade (N = 6,278 7th grade students at baseline). Eight schools each randomly assigned to either the standard D.A.R.E. middle school curriculum, D.A.R.E. middle school curriculum plus additional components (D.A.R.E. Plus), or the schools' usual drug and violence prevention activities.	D.A.R.E. Plus included additional components of peer-led classroom program with homework, postcards sent to parents, student-planned after-school activities, and neighborhood action teams of adults to create better school and neighborhood environments.	Child reported physical violence and weapons carrying scales assessed at baseline and two follow-ups in fall and spring of 7th grade and spring of eighth grade.	Boys: Compared to control students, D.A.R.E. Plus students reported significantly less physical violence but no difference on weapons carrying. Girls: No difference on either physical violence or weapons carrying.

Notes. *ES* = effect size. *OR* = odds ratio. Effect size reported if computable. Unless otherwise noted, effect size computed as (intervention pretest – intervention posttest/follow-up) - (control pretest – control posttest/follow-up) divided by pooled pretest standard deviation. A larger score indicates more of the named measure.

intervention condition, the SMART Talk program was installed on computers accessible to student participants during study halls and open periods. The program was available during the spring semester of the school year, and students accessed the program at their discretion, as there were no set times for participation. The results of the study indicated that students in the intervention group were slightly more likely to report the intent to use nonviolent conflict resolution when compared to the control group who did not receive the intervention. The intervention group also showed slight differences in self-awareness surrounding responses to conflict when compared to the control group. Control and intervention groups did not differ in the use of aggression over time. Survey results indicated that intervention participants as a whole (81%) enjoyed the program and 87% felt that they learned conflict resolution skills from the program.

Responding in Peaceful and Positive Ways

Farrell, Meyer and White (2001) evaluated the Responding in Peaceful and Positive Ways (RIPP) program designed to reduce violence by teaching social-cognitive problem-solving. The intervention curriculum was presented to randomly assigned classrooms in three schools, by 'prevention specialists'. Classrooms assigned to the control group received no intervention. The curriculum was presented to students in intervention classrooms in 25 sessions lasting 50 minutes each and included instruction on positive communication, as well as skills and knowledge to promote nonviolence. Intervention participants had fewer in-school suspensions for violent offences compared to controls. The intervention-related reduction in in-school suspensions was maintained through the 12-month follow-up among boys only. Students who scored high on violent behavior at pretest had significantly lower follow-up

scores when compared to controls, demonstrating that this intervention had a positive impact on higher risk students.

Fastulos: A German Language Violence and Aggression Prevention Program

The German language violence and aggression prevention program Faustlos was evaluated by Schick and Cierpka (2005). It was developed from the Second Step program (Beland, 1988) and is based upon theories of developmental psychology. Faustlos focused on improving empathy, impulse control and anger management, deficits that aggressive children often exhibit. These three areas were covered in 51 lessons taught by classroom teachers who received a one day teacher training. The lessons were taught beginning in first grade and culminating in third grade in 21 elementary schools (in Germany) that were randomly assigned to experimental or control conditions. The intervention program was implemented over 18 months. Parent questionnaires were used to assess outcomes (47% response rate) and structured interviews of students were conducted on a limited basis (one boy and one girl randomly selected per classroom). There was no significant effects found for parent, child, or teacher reported aggression or on delinquency scales.

PeaceBuilders

Outcomes of the implementation of the PeaceBuilders program were reported by Flannery, Vazsonyi, Liau, Guo, Powell and colleagues (2003). The PeaceBuilders program is a universal prevention program designed to be implemented by an entire school (staff and students). The focus of the program is to reduce negative behavior triggers and increase prosocial behaviors. A mediation program is utilized to assist in dealing with negative behaviors, and a reward system is used for recognizing prosocial behaviors. The program includes the introduction of five rules geared toward positive behaviors such as 'notice and correct hurts we cause' and 'praise people'. Students are recognized with principal "preferrals" for doing positive things within the school, and adults are trained to be active in praising prosocial behavior in areas where negative behaviors could be harder to detect/control, such as in the lunchroom or hallway. Eight matched elementary schools (K-5) were randomly assigned to either immediate program implementation (immediate start), or delayed implementation (start the following school year). There was a high rate (93%) of teacher buy-in to the philosophy of PeaceBuilders and 83% felt that the ideas presented in the trainings could be easily implemented. School interaction effects were found after one semester of program implementation. At this time, students in the immediate intervention school were rated higher in social competence and lower in aggression than the students in the delayed intervention school which showed no significant behavior change. This included a lower rate of injury related visits to the school nurse in the immediate intervention school (Krug et al., 1997),

D.A.R.E. Plus

The D.A.R.E. Plus Project was implemented in Minnesota as a universal violence prevention program. Komro, Perry, Mortenson, Stigler, Bosma and colleagues (2004) reported violence-related outcomes among middle school students. Twenty-four schools were randomly assigned to the middle school D.A.R.E. curriculum, the D.A.R.E. Plus multi-component intervention, or control. The total sample size consisted of 4,976 students who were primarily white, although it did include small samples of Hispanic, black, American Indian, and Asian students. The D.A.R.E. Plus intervention provided the normative D.A.R.E. 10-session curriculum taught by trained police officers but added four additional interventions. These

included a four-session peer-led classroom program with four interactive homework assignments, prevention message postcards sent home to parents every 6 to 8 weeks, student-planned after-school activities, and neighborhood action teams composed of adult volunteers who worked to create safer school and community environments for young adolescents. The study cohort completed a self-report questionnaire at baseline and at two follow-ups within the regularly scheduled, required classes with teachers present. Results showed that boys had higher rates of violence and victimization than girls. The D.A.R.E. Plus study demonstrated that a multiple component intervention significantly reduced physical and verbal violence and related psychosocial risk factors among boys. The small behavioral effect that D.A.R.E. Plus demonstrated on physical and verbal violence among boys was entirely mediated by a decrease in norms that support violence, an increase in outcome expectancies about being violence-free, and an increase in parental consequences for fighting.

Selective Prevention

Selective prevention interventions target the reduction of risk factors associated with school violence, and enhance protective factors associated with violence prevention among at-risk youth (U.S. Surgeon General [n.d.],). Selective prevention involves assessment, selection, and treatment of students that have been identified to be at-risk. Such students are often identified by teachers, counselors, staff, and/or peers as aggressive, "trouble-makers" and/or at-risk for school failure. These students need specialized intervention because they are less likely to respond positively to universal interventions than not at-risk students (Sugai et al., 2000). Our literature review identified the following 2 selective prevention intervention programs that were studied in randomized controlled trials, with one showing promising preliminary prevention outcomes for males.

Project Towards No Drug Abuse

Project Towards No Drug Abuse (TND) was evaluated for violence risk outcomes (Simon et al., 2002). TND utilized a curriculum focused on motivation skills and decision-making abilities. The program was specifically geared towards students in alternative school placements in California, called continuation high schools. These 21 high schools were matched on substance abuse prevalence, ethnicity, school size, and achievement scores and randomly assigned to control or either of two treatment conditions (seven schools in each condition). The curriculum was divided into nine, 40-minute lessons and presented within a three week period. Lessons addressed health motivation issues, social skills development, and drug abstinence decision-making skills. In addition, one set of intervention schools conducted a school-wide set of activities emphasizing a drug-free focus. Control schools conducted no special programming. Seventy-five percent of the student body (2,863 students) were eligible to participate. Parental consent was attained for 1,587 students and at follow up (13.5 months) 68% (1,074 students) completed surveys. For the current study 850 students with complete data were analyzed. The only difference reported for intervention participants was a decrease in violence victimization among male participants compared to controls, though there were no differences in participation in violence-related activities between groups.

Aban Aya Youth Project

The Aban Aya Youth Project (Flay et al., 2004; Ngwe et al., 2004; Segawa et al, 2005) compared three interventions with respect to violence prevention. Two experimental programs focusing on violence risk behaviors were combined and compared

to a control intervention that focused on health behaviors. A school-community program (SC) and a social development curriculum (SDC) were used in the experimental programs. These programs were both taught in the classroom, and had a similar focus on risk behaviors (violence, substance abuse, etc.). The SC program had additional components to the classroom intervention, which included a parent program, a school-wide initiative to help students utilize skills learned in the program throughout the school, as well as a community component which linked families with local businesses and agencies. The control group received a health enhancement curriculum (HEC) that included topics such as nutrition and oral health. Students participated in the interventions from fifth through eighth grades, and over the course of four school years, received 71 lessons related to their intervention curriculum. Twelve inner-city and near-suburban elementary schools were matched on school report card characteristics and location (inner-city or near-suburban) and randomly assigned to condition. Study schools were 91% African-American. A total of 1,153 students (582 females, 571 males) participated in all four years of the study. Latent variable growth models of violence and of school delinquency showed no program effects for girls. Relative to the HEC (control) condition, SC boys showed significant reductions in violence and school delinquency while SDC boys showed a significant reduction in violence but only a trend-level ($p < .10$) reduction in school delinquency. Ngwe et al. (2004), in a follow-up study, found that decreases in violence by intervention condition (SDC or SD) boys was mediated by intervention-related changes in hypothesized intermediary processes (behavioral intentions, attitudes towards violence, peer [classmates] behavior, and best friends' behavior). In a second follow-on study, Segawa et al. (2005), using latent class growth mixture modeling, found that intervention boys with high initial violence levels and a greater growth in violence level over the 5th to 8th grade study period had a significantly lower growth in violence than did similar control boys. No intervention effect was noted for boys with low initial violence scores and little growth in violence or for boys with moderate initial violence scores and some growth in violence. Thus significant intervention effects were limited to the most violent boys.

Indicated Prevention Interventions

Indicated school violence prevention are those interventions targeted to specific youth who have been identified on the basis of risk and/or observable negative behaviors (e.g., aggression, impulse control, social skill deficits) but who have not demonstrated violence in school. Our literature review identified the following 6 indicated prevention intervention programs that were evaluated in randomized controlled trials. Findings from these studies are mixed for interventions targeted at this level of prevention.

Early Risers Skills for Success

For the "Early Risers Skills for Success" program, (August et al., 2003) students from 20 schools in Minnesota were screened in Kindergarten utilizing the aggression scale from the Child Behavior Checklist-Teacher Rating Form and followed through fourth grade. Students who were determined to be at risk for aggressive behavior were invited to participate in the original intervention. The intervention was comprised of two components: a summer program and group sessions during the school year. In the six-week summer program, indicated children and "non-aggressive" peers in a mentoring role were paired together for activities. The summer program included educational and social/behavioral supports and a family

program consisting of biweekly group sessions for parents that taught effective parenting, stress management and school engagement. Group sessions were conducted with the children throughout the school year and followed a social skills curriculum emphasizing conflict resolution skill-building. The follow-up results included children who participated in the Early Risers Skills for Success program and their current fourth grade classmates. Students responded to several scales about student likeability and friendship qualities, while parents and teachers also filled out behavioral assessments of the students. One hundred and twenty-five of the original study participants (75 program children and 50 control children) and 1,364 of their classmates participated in the current study. No significant effect of the program was found.

Second Step

Grossman, Neckerman, Koepsell, Liu, Asher and colleagues (1997) reported the effects of use of Second Step with second and third grade students (n=790) at 12 elementary schools in Washington State. Second Step is a 30 lesson curriculum that is presented in 35 minute segments that focus on empathy, impulse control and anger management. Role-playing was a component of the intervention strategy and a photograph was used to set the stage for the topic and activity. A two-day teacher training was required prior to the intervention. The intervention occurred over one semester, and follow-up data were collected six months after the completion of the intervention. At the end of the intervention semester, students in the intervention school decreased negative behaviors, including reductions in physical negative (p=.05) and general negative behaviors (p=.07), as compared to students in control schools. Observed prosocial behaviors also increased in intervention schools.

Coping Power Program

The Coping Power Program was reviewed by Lochman and Wells (2004). The intervention consisted of group sessions for preadolescent aggressive males, group sessions for parents and individual child meetings. The 33 hour-long student group sessions occurred across 15 months and focused on topics such as skill-building, anger management, social problem solving and perspective taking. The 16 parent group sessions followed a social learning theory approach and focused on skill building for parenting and communication. Participants (N=183) were randomly assigned to either the child only intervention, the child and parent intervention or the control condition. Controls received services as usual within the school system. A random sample of non-aggressive boys formed a normative comparison group. Students participating in the program with their parents showed lower rates of delinquent behaviors considered to be covert (e.g. theft, property damage) than control children at the one year follow-up: the child only group did not differ from controls. Child participants in both intervention groups showed improvements in teacher rated behavioral measures (e.g. anger management, problem solving skills) when compared to the control group at follow-up. In addition at follow-up, intervention children did not differ from normative children on either covert delinquency or teacher-rated behavioral measures.

Incredible Years Intervention

Reid, Webster-Stratton, and Hammond (2003) reported on the outcomes of the Incredible Years Intervention. Children between the ages of 4 and 7 years of age with oppositional defiant disorder (ODD) were eligible to participate in the study. One hundred fifty-nine families completed the pre and post assessments and 91% of these families also completed 2-year follow-up

assessments. Families were assigned to one of five treatment conditions:

1. Parent training (PT)
2. Parent training and Teacher training (PT+TT)
3. Child training (CT)
4. Child training and teacher training (CT+TT)
5. Parent training, child training and teacher training (PT+CT+TT)

or to a wait-list control group. PT was provided in 22 two-hour sessions, CT in 18 two-hour sessions and TT consisted of 4 days of training. Participation was high with over 90% of children and parents participating in at least 15 sessions of their respective programs and 100% of teachers completing their program. Attrition rates at the 2-year follow-up were highest for participants in the CT condition. Children who participated in CT showed higher rates of prosocial behaviors with peers at immediate post-intervention than children in the wait-list control condition. According to parent report, 75% of the entire sample were functioning within normal ranges of behavior at home, school or both settings at the two year follow-up.

Bibliotherapy

A bibliotherapy approach was used as part of an experimental intervention to reduce aggression for special education students (Shechtman, 2000). Study participants were from special education classes in 10 urban schools in northern Israel. The students ranged in age from 10-15 and were in elementary and junior high schools. The intervention was conducted in 10 weekly 45 minute sessions which included randomly assigned participants as well as non-indicated students who volunteered to participate in groups (not included in the analysis). The therapist chose the type of treatment (individual, dyadic, or small group) based upon student availability. The intervention included short stories, poems and films that included triggers for aggression, negative behaviors and risks for aggression. After the therapist introduced the piece of literature or film, a game or drawing was completed to clarify the concept and relate it to personal behaviors and attitudes. Participants were asked their opinion with regard to which activity/part of the program was the most meaningful and 44% indicated films, while only 9% indicated the conversation. Teacher and student reports post-intervention differed in their responses. Results indicated a significant decrease in child-report aggressive behavior and teacher-report aggressive behavior, but no significant effect for either child-report or teacher-report delinquent behavior. Students reported that they had fewer instances of social problems and withdrawal instances however this improvement was not confirmed by teacher response. Of note, the current study did not compare effects of the type of treatment received (i.e., individual, group), but did indicate this as an area for further study.

Anger Control Training

"Anger Control Training" (ACT) is comprised of three modules that focus on specific aspects of treatment (Sukhodolsky et al., 2005). Relaxation is the main component addressed in the arousal management module. The experimental components of this study were the other two modules: social problem solving training (SPST) and social skills training (SST). SPST utilized cognitive restructuring and focused on anger mediators. SST utilized behavioral rehearsal and modeling of appropriate behaviors. The study included 31 boys, aged 7-11, who were referred by schools and parental nomination based on significant anger issues. There were three criteria for inclusion in the study:

1. excessive intense anger episodes occurring several times a week (in various settings)
2. history of disciplinary consequences

(school or community) stemming from physical or verbal aggression
3. Oppositional behavior or conduct problems at home.

For inclusion in the study, the duration of these problems had to be a minimum of 6 months. All subjects were matched on age and formed into small groups. There was a 16% attrition rate, however, all remaining participants attended 80% or more of all sessions offered. The interventions were conducted in a 50-minute, weekly group session format for 10 consecutive weeks. Although significant decreases in aggression and conduct problems were found in both groups; the two groups did not differ.

Future Research Directions

This chapter examined the efficacy of 13 school-based prevention programs that were evaluated in randomized controlled trials and examined outcomes that met our definition of school violence. We applaud the researchers who conducted these rigorous studies and the contributions their findings make to the knowledge base. However, interventions developed to date have not utilized the most evidence-based methods for behavior change, nor have they addressed many important risk and protective factors for school violence. Specifically, most interventions tested to date have been strictly psychoeducational. Studies examined how youth get along with others, how they managed differences and conflicts, and how they managed and expressed emotion. While these are important components, they are not necessarily specific to the school setting or the family and ignore structural and dynamic factors that may contribute to the expression of violent behaviors.

Measurement also appears to be problematic. Although the interventions targeted child aggressive/violent behaviors in school, in most studies overt and covert measures of delinquency were measured by parent report of child behavior in the community setting, not the school. Teacher and peer reported behavior (or nomination) in school might better measure school violence problems than community measures of behavior, such as delinquency. Parental reports might actually measure how well the lessons and behavior change have generalized from school to home or to the street, rather than whether behavior change occurred in the school setting.

Sample sizes need to be increased so that multiple hypotheses can be tested with adequate power. Power analyses in current studies guarantee that there is adequate power to determine whether a significant difference in outcomes exists for any one measure. To adequately address the complex problem of school violence, we need to examine multiple outcomes in more sophisticated ways. Expanding the number of outcomes tested in trials will require that sample sizes be increased substantially. Increasing sample size will also allow investigators to examine interactions between levels. For example, do children in the same classroom respond to an intervention more similarly to each other than to children in different classrooms? Similarly, do teachers within a school rate children's behaviors more similarly to each other than to teachers in a different school? These are important considerations as we build prevention science.

Research studies that have identified risk factors related to youth violence have aided efforts to develop programs for the prevention of violence in children and youths. This initial research has led to the development of multiple prevention programs to address youth violence and conduct disordered youth in general. Unfortunately, these programs often fall short, in that their preventive effects diminish over time, fail to prevent violence to a significant degree, or do not change behavior at all (Rapp-Paglicci and Dulmus, 2003). One possible explanation for the lack of effectiveness of current interventions is

that risk and protective factors do not have the same influence on children at different ages (Hawkins et al., 2000). For example, a minimal risk factor for a fifteen year-old may be a serious risk factor for an eight year-old. These findings have critical implications for redirecting our prevention efforts.

Taking into consideration the above methodological recommendations, it is essential that more research be done on programs intended specifically for children at different grade levels. Different age groups have different skills and issues associated with their level of development. Schools should implement efficacious prevention programs that are developmentally appropriate to best meet the students' needs.

SUMMARY AND CONCLUSIONS

Given the level of school violence in the United States, it is startling that more resources and attention have not been given to the development of sophisticated prevention interventions at the universal, selective, and indicated levels. Our review found that only 25% of interventions studied in randomized trials produced significant changes in violence outcomes. This general lack of efficacy could be because most of the interventions consisted only of group psycho-education. These interventions do nothing to alter the environments within the school, home or community that foster violent behavior. Studies of interventions where the environment is changed are needed. For example, schools could vary their procedures, or teachers could be trained in new classroom management techniques and these attempts to alter the school environment could be compared to matched schools that did not receive the intervention. Though we did identify one study that involved some school level change, we were unable to include a small number of other studies where such an intervention was used because there was no control and/or no random assignment. As we seek to prevent school violence, attempting to change the school environment where the expression of aggression and violence occurs is a promising approach to investigate. Similarly, focusing on the expression of aggression and violence rather than the underpinning biology and psychology might be a more fruitful approach to prevention as these behaviors are more likely to be modifiable than underlying biological and personality factors.

The current lack of evidence-based interventions and knowledge on effective methods for altering aggressive behaviors has enormous human and financial consequences. It is imperative for research scientists to design and conduct randomized controlled trials to further develop the prevention science necessary to address this serious societal problem. But to do so policy makers must make school violence prevention research funding a national priority.

USEFUL RESOURCES

http://mentalhealth.samhsa.gov/schoolviolenc e/

This website has numerous fact sheets and prevention resources available at no charge under the heading "Publications". This site also presents information on the SAMHSA Safe Schools/ Healthy Students initiative.

http://www.safeyouth.org/scripts/index.asp

This website is co-sponsored by the Centers for Disease Control and Federal partners working on youth violence. Information specific to health care practitioners is included and contains checklists, warning signs and treatment needs for adolescents dealing with depression, suicide, bullying, dating violence, physical fighting, substance abuse and gangs. Links to federal agencies and their study reports are also available from this website.

http://www.childrenssafetynetwork.org/

This site provides statistical information about multiple forms of violence and injury related to youth and excellent links to research reports and sites. The injury prevention information tab contains multiple links for school violence information.

REFERENCES

Anderson M, Kaufman J, Simon T, Barrios L, Paulozzi L, Ryan G, et al. (2001) School associated violent deaths in the United States, 1994-1999. JAMA 286:2695-2702.

August GJ, Egan EA, Realmuto GM, Hektner JM. (2003) Four years of the Early Risers Early-Age-Targeted Preventive Intervention: Effects on aggressive children's peer relations. Behav Ther 34: 453-470.

Beland K. (1988) Second Step. A violence-prevention curriculum. Grades 1-3. Seattle, Committee on Children.

Bosworth K, Espelage D, DuBay T, Daytner G, Karageorge K. (2000) Preliminary evaluation of a multimedia violence prevention program for adolescents. Am J Health Behav 24:268-280.

Cantor D, Wright MM. (2002) School crime patterns: A national profile of public high schools using rates of crime reported to police. Report on the Study on School Violence and Prevention, Rockville, MD. (ERIC Document Reproduction Service No. 471 867).

Connor D. (2002) Aggression and Antisocial Behavior in Children and Adolescents. New York: Guilford Press.

Farrell AD, Meyer AL, White KS. (2001) Evaluation of Responding in Peaceful and Positive Ways (RIPP): A school-based prevention program for reducing violence among urban adolescents. J Clin Child Psychol 30:451-463.

DeVoe JF, Peter K, Noonan M, Snyder TD, Baum K, Snyder TD. (2005) Indicators of School Crime and Safety: 2005 (NCES 2006-001/NCJ 210697).U.S. Departments of Education and Justice. Washington,

DC: U.S. Government Printing Office. Available online at: www.ojp.usdoj.gov/bjs

Flannery DJ, Vazsonyi AT, Liau AK, Guo S, Powell KE, Atha H, Vesterdal W, Embry D. (2003) Initial behavior outcomes for the PeaceBuilders universal school-based violence prevention program. Dev Psychol 39:292-308.

Flay BR, Graumlich S, Segawa E, Burns JL, Holliday MY. (2004) Effects of 2 prevention programs on high-risk behaviors among African American youth. Arch Pediatr Adoles Med 158: 377-84.

Gordon R. (1983) An operational classification of disease prevention. Public Health Rep 98: 107-109.

Gordon R. (1987) An operational classification of disease prevention. In: Preventing Mental Disorders (Steinberg, J, Silverman, M ,eds), pp. 20-26. Rockville, MD: Department of Health and Human Services.

Grossman DC, Neckerman HJ, Koepsell TD, Liu PY, Asher KN, Beland K, Frey K, Rivara FP. (1997) Effectiveness of a violence prevention curriculum among children in elementary school. A randomized controlled trial. JAMA 277: 1605-11.

Hawkins J, Herrenkohl T, Farrington D, Brewer D, Catalano R, Harachi T, Cothern L. (2000) Predictors of Youth Violence. Juvenile Justice Bulletin:1-11.

Herrenkohl T, Maguin E, Hill K, Hawkins JD, Abbott R, Catalano R. (2000) Developmental risk factors for youth violence. J Adolesc Health 26:176-186.

Hilton N, Harris G, Rice M, Krans T, Lavigne S. (1998) Antiviolence education in high schools. J Interpers Violence 13:726-742.

Hunt MH, Meyers J, Davies G, Meyers B, Grogg K, Neel JA. (2002) Comprehensive needs assessment to facilitate prevention of school drop out and violence. Psychol Sch 39: 399-416.

Institute of Medicine. (1994) Reducing Risks for Mental Disorders: Frontiers for Preventive Intervention Research. Washington, DC: National Academy Press.

Juvonen J. (2001) School violence: Prevalence, fears and prevention. Rand Education Issue Paper. Retrieved October 30, 2003 from http://www.rand.org/publications/IP/IP219/

Komro KA, Perry CL, Veblen-Mortenson S, Stigler MH, Bosma LM, Munson KA, Farbakhsh K. (2004). Violence-related outcomes of the D.A.R.E. Plus Project. Health Educ Behav 31: 335-354.

Krug EG, Brener ND, Dahlberg LL, Ryan GW, Powell KE. (1997). The impact of an elementary school-based violence prevention program on visits to the school nurse. Am J Prev Med 13: 459-463.

Lochman JE, Wells KC. (2004) The Coping Power Program for preadolescent aggressive boys and their parents: Outcome effects at the 1-year follow-up. J Consult Clin Psychol 72:571-578.

Miller AK. (2003) Violence in U.S. public schools: 2000 School Survey on Crime and Safety. Education Statistics Quarterly 5: 2004-2314.

Molina IA, Dulmus CN, Sowers KM. (2005) Secondary prevention for youth violence: A review of selected school-based programs. Brief Treat Crisis Interv 5: 95-127.

Nansel T, Overpeck M, Haynie D, Ruan W, Scheidt P. (2003) Relationships between bullying and violence among US youth. Arch Pediatr Adolesc Med 157:348- 353.

National Center for Injury Prevention and Control [NCIPC] (n.d.). Youth violence facts. Retrieved March 30, 2004, from http://www.cdc.gov/ncipc/factsheets/yvfacts.htm

National Center for Injury Prevention and Control [NCIPC] (n.d.). Youth violence- A national problem. Retrieved April 20, 2004, from http://www.cdc.gov/ncipc/dvp/bestpractices/FactsYV-BP.htm

Ngwe JE, Liu LC, Flay BR, Segawa E. (2004)

Violence prevention among African American adolescent males. Am J Health Behav 28:S24-S37.

Petersen G, Pietrzak D, Speaker KM. (1996) The enemy within: A national study on school violence and prevention. Paper presented at the annual meeting of the Association of Teacher Educators, St. Louis, MO, February 24-28, 1996. (ERIC Document Reproduction Service No. ED 394 907)

Rapp-Paglicci LA, Dulmus CN. (2003) Developmental considerations in youth violence prevention. School Social Work Journal 28:21-35.

Reid MJ, Webster-Stratton C, Hammond M. (2003) Follow-up of children who received the Incredible Years Intervention for Oppositional-Defiant Disorder: Maintenance and prediction of 2-year outcome. Behav Ther 34:471-491.

Schick A, Cierpka M. (2005) Faustlos: Evaluation of a curriculum to prevent violence in elementary schools. Appl Prev Psychol 11:157-165.

Segawa E, Ngwe JE, Liu LC, Flay BR. (2005) Evaluation of the effects of the Aban Aya Youth Project in reducing violence among African American adolescent males using latent class growth mixture modeling techniques. Eval Rev: 128-148.

Shechtman Z. (2000) An innovative intervention for treatment of child and adolescent aggression: An outcome study. Psychol Sch 37:157-167.

Sheehan K, Kim L, Galvin MS. (2004) Urban children's perceptions of violence. Arch Pediatr Adolesc Med 158:74-77.

Simon TR, Sussman S, Dahlberg LL, Dent CW. (2002) Influence of a substance-abuse-prevention curriculum on violence-related behavior. Am J Health Behav 26:103-110.

Stormont M. (2002) Externalizing behavior problems in young children: Contributing factors and early intervention. Psychol Sch 39:127-138.

Sugai G, Sprague JR, Horner RH, Walker HM. (2000) Preventing school violence: The use of office discipline referrals to assess and monitor school-wide discipline interventions. Journal of Emotional and Behavioral Disorders 8: 94-101.

Sukhodolsky DG, Golub A, Stone EC, Orban L. (2005) Dismantling anger control training for children: A randomized pilot study of social problem-solving versus social skills training components. Behav Ther 36: 15-23.

U.S. Surgeon General (n.d.). Youth violence: A report of the Surgeon General (chap. 5). Retrieved April 4, 2004 from http://www.samhsa.gov/cgibin/MsmGo.exe?grab_id=7andEXTRA_ARG=andCFGN

Vossekuil B, Fein RA, Reddy M, Borum R, Modzeleski W. (2002) The final report and findings of the Safe School Initiative: Implications for the prevention of school attacks in the United States. Washington, DC: US Secret Service and U.S. Department of Education.

Walker H, Severson H, Feil E, Stiller B, Golly A. (1998) First step to success: Intervening at the point of school entry to prevent antisocial behavior patterns. Psychol Sch 35:259-268.

White JL, Earls F, Robins L, Silva P. (1990) How early can we tell? Predictors of childhood conduct disorder and adolescent delinquency. Criminol 28: 507-525.

PREVENTION OF CHILDREN & YOUTHS' ACCESS TO AND OPERATION OF FIREARMS: A REVIEW OF INTERVENTIONS

Renee M. Johnson and David Hemenway

INTRODUCTION

Firearms are a significant source of injury among children and youth (defined here as ages 0-18) in the United States (Fingerhut and Christoffel, 2002). From 2000 to 2004 – the most recent years for which data are available – more than 2,000 children and youth died from firearm injuries annually (CDC, 2007). During this same time period, about 10,000 annually were treated for firearm injuries in emergency departments (Eber et al., 2004; CDC, 2007).

Approximately 60% of firearm injury deaths among children and youth are homicides, about 30% are suicides, and less than 10% are unintentional injuries. In contrast, about one-third of the nonfatal gunshot wounds are from assaults and barely one percent are from self-harm; the rest are unintentional firearm injuries or of undetermined cause (Eber et al., 2004; CDC, 2007).

Boys and adolescents are substantially more likely to sustain firearm injuries than girls and younger children (DiScala and Sege, 2004; Eber et al., 2004). In 2004, the firearm injury death rate for boys was five times greater than the death rate for girls (4.4 vs. 0.8 per 100,000, respectively) (CDC, 2007). The 2004 firearm injury death rate for 0-11 year olds was 0.7 per 100,000. For each year after age 11, the death rate increased anywhere from 25%-60%, to a high of 16 per 100,000 for 18 year olds (CDC, 2007).

The home environment has considerable relevance for pediatric firearm injuries, particularly for unintentional injuries and suicides. Whereas guns used by or against youth in assaults and homicides are often acquired through street sources or from older relatives or friends (Ash et al., 1996; Smith, 1996; Webster et al., 2002), firearms used in suicides and unintentional injuries are most frequently obtained from the home of the victim, or from the home of a friend or relative of the victim (Grossman et al., 1999; CDC, 2003). Moreover, homes are the primary setting for firearm-related suicides and unintentional injuries (DiScala and Sege, 2004). Unsupervised child and youth access to guns, including playing with or handling a household gun, is a frequent precipitating circumstance for unintentional firearm injuries (Wintemute et al., 1987; Martin et al., 1991; Ismach et al., 2003; Eber et al., 2004).

Compared to other high-income nations, the U.S. has extraordinarily high rates of pediatric firearm injury (Hemenway, 2004). The firearm death rate for 0-14 year olds in the U.S. is more than double the rate for any other developed nation (Krug et al., 1998; CDC, 1997; Krug et al., 1996). The firearm injury problem seems to result from the fact that the U.S. has the highest rates of household gun ownership, and no national storage requirements (Hemenway, 2004), which sets a context in which young people have substantial access to firearms. This is supported by the fact that, within the U.S., geographic areas with a higher household prevalence of firearms and with less safe storage practices have significantly more pediatric firearm injuries (Miller et al., 2005; Miller et al., 2002).

About one-third of U.S. households with children and youth contain firearms (Schuster et al., 2000; Smith, 2002). Many U.S. children have access to unsafely stored firearms and/or handguns, which are relatively easy to operate compared to long guns (Naureckas et al., 1993). Among households with children and guns, more than half have handguns, 5%-15% report having a firearm stored loaded, about

43% have an unlocked firearm, and 2%-14% have a firearm stored both loaded and unlocked (Stennies et al., 1999; Azrael et al., 2000; Schuster et al., 2000; Johnson et al., 2004; Okoro et al., 2005). A recent study from the Centers for Disease Control and Prevention (CDC) estimated that 1.6 million U.S. children live in homes with loaded, unlocked firearms (Okoro et al., 2005). Even though adolescents are more likely to sustain a firearm injury than younger children, parents are less likely to employ safe storage practices when all their children are 12 years of age or older (Azrael et al., 2000; Johnson et al., 2006).

Having firearms in the home, and having them stored loaded and unlocked in particular, is associated with an increased risk for firearm injury, especially suicide (Brent et al., 1991; Shah et al., 2000; Miller et al., 2002; Shenassa et al., 2003; Grossman et al., 2005; Miller et al., 2005). For example, one case-control study showed that firearms were twice as likely to be found in the home of adolescent suicide decedents as compared to psychiatric controls (Odds Ratio = 2.2, 95% CI 1.4-3.5) (Brent et al.,1991). A recent study found that when firearms were stored loaded or unlocked, they were significantly more likely to have been used by a young person (age<20 years) in a suicide, suicide attempt, or unintentional injury (Grossman et al., 2005).

Different areas for intervention

Because of the possible negative outcomes, it is important to prevent young peoples' access to or operation of firearms in their homes. Many types of interventions have been implemented over the past few decades. At the policy level, several states have passed "Child Access Prevention" (CAP) laws, which make a gun owner criminally liable if his or her gun is not stored safely and is subsequently used by a child to injure him or herself or another person (Hardy, 2002b). Some studies suggest that CAP laws may be

associated with a reduction in pediatric suicide and unintentional firearm injury rates (Cummings et al., 1997; Webster and Starnes, 2000; Hepburn et al., 2006; Webster et al., 2004). However, more research is needed, specifically to assess whether CAP laws are associated with actual storage practices

At the individual and community-levels, educational programs designed to prevent child and youth access or operation of firearms have been undertaken by advocacy groups, medical and public health professionals, law enforcement agencies, gun manufacturers and sporting organizations (Coyne-Beasley et al., 2001; Howard, 2001; Hardy, 2002b; Horn et al., 2003; McGee et al., 2003; Wafer and Carruth, 2003; Sidman et al., 2005; National Shooting Sports Foundation, 2007; NRA, 2007). Some educational programs focus on encouraging children and youth not to play with or handle a firearm in the event that they come into contact with one. These types of programs are frequently based in school or community settings, and are typically directed at younger children (Hardy, 2002b).

In contrast to child gun safety education programs, safe storage programs are focused on parents' behavior. These programs aim to restrict young peoples' access to firearms in the home by encouraging parents to either store firearms safely, or remove them from the household altogether (Grossman et al., 2000; Coyne-Beasley et al., 2001; Hardy, 2002b). Safe storage includes keeping firearms stored locked up, unloaded, and separately from ammunition. It may include use of extrinsic safety devices, such as gun locks, trigger locks, locks boxes, or gun cabinets. Safe storage programs usually take place in clinical or community settings (Grossman et al., 2000; Coyne-Beasley et al., 2001; Hardy, 2002b).

Aim of this review

In this Chapter we review the literature on

evaluations of educational interventions designed to prevent child and youth access to or operation of firearms in their homes, including child gun safety education programs and safe storage programs targeted to parents. Different types of interventions will be described, as well as their impact on behavior. Our aim is to describe the state of the science in terms of programming and evaluation.

METHODS

This review is limited to peer-reviewed, published scientific evaluations of programs, interventions, or experiments that sought to modify individual behavior. A literature search was conducted using PubMed, a service of the U.S. National Library of Medicine that includes over 16 million citations from life sciences, public health, and medical journals. The search was limited to English language articles published from January 1992 through December 2006. Articles containing at least one key word from each of the following three search phrases were examined: (1) firearm or handgun or gun or weapon, (2) child or youth or adolescent or young or children or pediatric, and (3) education or program or intervention or teach or promotion or giveaway or training or evaluation or counseling. The term "giveaway" was included so as to identify articles describing giveaways of gun locks or other extrinsic safety devices for firearms.

The title and abstract of each candidate article was read and reviewed for appropriateness for inclusion. We excluded articles that were solely descriptions of programs and that had no evaluative component, (e.g., Becker et al., 1993; Quist, 1994) evaluations of policy-level interventions (e.g., CAP laws), and evaluations of interventions focused on restricting firearm access to adults. Articles describing interventions that addressed conflict resolution, aggression management, or fighting prevention, and that did not aim to directly prevent youth access to firearms from

their homes and/or directly prevent youth use or handling of the guns they access, were also excluded.

RESULTS

There is a growing body of research that examines the effectiveness of efforts to reduce child access to or operation of firearms. However, this is not a research area involving large randomized controlled trials or long-term follow-up. Many studies included in this review used convenience sampling procedures, had small sample sizes, or used pre- or quasi-experimental study designs. The remainder of this section reviews the literature in three categories: (1) child gun safety education programs, (2) community-based safe storage programs, and (3) clinic-based safe storage programs.

1. Child gun safety educational programs
Introduction

Since the mid-1980s, several programs have been developed to teach elementary school-aged children about firearm safety. The intended participant group for such programs is "universal", meaning participants are recruited regardless of their level of risk. Only a handful of the programs have been evaluated. We did not find any evaluations of gun safety programs for adolescents.

The Eddie Eagle GunSafe ® Program, an initiative of the National Rifle Association, began in 1988 and instructs children from kindergarten through third grade to do the following if they come across a firearm: (1) Stop, (2) Don't touch, (3) Leave the area, and (4) Tell an adult. The Program is publicly available and has been used in several arenas, including classrooms (NRA, 2007). Its behavioral recommendations establish the basis of many of the studies reviewed in this section (Liller et al., 2003; Howard, 2005). Eddie Eagle has been characterized as a program that provides children with information about what they should do, but that does not provide them with effective learning strategies designed to build the skills needed to carry out the recommended behaviors (Hardy, 2002b; Hardy, 2006). For the sake of simplicity, we refer to this type of program as an "Information-Provision" (IP) program.

We found 11 studies that examined the effectiveness of child gun safety education programs – including Eddie Eagle – in terms of their effect on behavior, knowledge, and/or ability to verbalize or role-play the recommended behaviors (Hardy et al., 1996; Gresham et al., 2001; Hardy, 2002a, 2003; Liller et al., 2003; Gatheridge et al., 2004; Miltenberger et al., 2004; Himle et al., 2004a; Himle et al., 2004b; Howard, 2005; Miltenberger et al., 2005). Eight of those studies assessed actual child behavior as an outcome variable (Hardy et al., 1996; Hardy, 2002a, 2003; Gatheridge et al., 2004; Miltenberger et al., 2004; Himle et al., 2004a; Himle et al., 2004b; Miltenberger et al., 2005). The remaining three assessed the effect of a gun safety program on child knowledge of what to do upon coming across a firearm (Gresham et al., 2001; Liller et al., 2003; Howard, 2005).

Studies with child behavior as the outcome variable

A 1996 evaluation of an IP program modeled after Eddie Eagle showed that children in the intervention group were no less likely to handle firearms they came across than those in the control group (see Table 1) (Hardy et al., 1996). For five years after the publication of that evaluation, there were no published evaluations of child gun safety education programs. Then seven articles assessing the potential of child gun safety education programs were published from 2002-2005 (Hardy, 2002a, 2003; Gatheridge et al., 2004; Miltenberger et al., 2004; Himle et al., 2004a; Himle et al., 2004b; Miltenberger et al., 2005).

The five evaluation studies of child gun safety education that employed an experi-mental design are summarized in Table 1 (Hardy, 1996, 2002a, 2003; Gatheridge et al., 2004; Himle et al., 2004b). They described the extent to which brief instruction on gun safety education resulted in children's ability to verbalize, role-play, and demonstrate the recommended gun safety behaviors in a naturalistic setting. One study reviews the effectiveness of an IP program (Hardy, 1996), and one reviews the effectiveness of a program that took a behavioral skills training (BST) approach, meaning that students were taught the recommended messages, but the instruction also included several different learning strategies including: modeling, corrective feedback, and rehearsal (Hardy, 2002a). Two studies compared the effectiveness of a BST program to that of an IP program (Gatheridge, et al., 2004; Himle, et al., 2004b).

Children who received BST and/or IP education were better able to verbalize the recommended behaviors as compared to controls who had not received any form of gun safety education (Gatheridge et al., 2004; Himle et al., 2004b). In terms of the role-play assessment, children who had received a BST program performed significantly better than control participants or than those who received IP education (Gatheridge et al., 2004). However, the studies did not show that children who received education were less likely to engage in gun play (Hardy, 2002a, 2003; Himle et al., 2004b). In the most promising study, 11 of the 15 children who received a BST program performed all three recommended behaviors (i.e., don't touch it, get away, tell an adult), whereas only 2 of the 15 who received only an IP program did (Gatheridge et al., 2004).

Three additional studies included *in situ* training (i.e., "training in the test situation") in addition to a BST program (Miltenberger et al., 2004; Himle et al., 2004a; Miltenberger et al., 2005). In these studies, researchers provided children with a BST program, and

Table 1. Experimental studies assessing the effective of child gun safety education on behavior change, 1992-2006

Lead Author (Pub. Year)

Purpose	Design	Procedures	Sample & Groups	Observations	Key Findings
Hardy (1996)					
Compare children's gun play behavior before and after an information provision intervention.	2 group, before and after design, with random assignment.	*Intervention Group:* Children and their parents listened to presentations by a psychologist and a police officer, and were instructed to never touch guns, and to tell an adult upon finding a gun. *Control Group:* Waitlist: Children received the intervention after observations were completed.	48 children aged 4-6 years (30 boys, 18 girls) recruited from day care centers in a Southern city. Children paired based on age and gender, children from each pair were randomly assigned to a group.	A playroom had toys and guns, children were instructed to play and were told that their parents were outside. Observations took place prior to and one week after the intervention. Behaviors were observed and coded.	Although children in the intervention group exhibited less gun play after the intervention, this difference was not statistically significant in a repeated measures multivariate analysis of variance.
Hardy (2002a)					
Assess whether a behavioral skills training (BST) program prevents gun play.	2 group, after-only design, with random assignment at the pair or individual level.	*BST Group:* 5-day long program with brief lessons on: the dangers of touching firearms, resisting peer pressure, making good choices, and preventing fights. *Control Group: Waitlist:* Children received a similar intervention after observations were completed.	70 4-7 year olds (42 boys, 28 girls) recruited from day care centers. Pairs were matched on age & gender; 9 pairs were assigned to BST, & 10 to control. In 16 pairs, one was randomly assigned to each group. (Control, n= 34;BST, n=36)	Following the intervention, pairs were placed in a playroom containing toys and a hidden gun, and were monitored via a 2-way mirror. Behavior was coded for gun play, telling an adult about a gun, and other behaviors.	53% (37/70) children handled the gun; 33 found but did not touch the gun. Only 1 child alerted an adult. Children in the intervention group were no less likely than those in the control group to handle to the gun.

Lead Author (Pub. Year)

Purpose	Design	Procedures	Sample & Groups	Observations	Key Findings
Hardy (2003)					
Assess whether instructions to not touch or play with guns is associated with gun play.	2 group, before and after design, with random assignment to groups. Boys were randomized to receive a weak or strong admonition.	Participants were in a room with toys and games and were instructed not to touch the gun (or another object, depending on group). Admonitions were either weak ("Please don't touch the ___.), or strong "Do not touch the ___.).	55 9-15 year old boys in a summer sports program at a college. Randomization based on whether boys ranked a gun as the object they would "least like to play with" or not. Those who did not rank the gun lowest at baseline were instructed not to touch the gun (forbidden gun group); those who did were instructed not to touch another object (forbidden object group)	*Pre-Test.* In a room with several toys and games, respondents were asked to rank and rate each for how much they wanted to play with them. *Post-Test.* Participants came in for a second visit, were left alone in the room, and were instructed not to touch the gun or another object (depending on group). Behavior was recorded via a 2-way mirror, and then coded. A research assistant returned to the room and asked participants to rank and rate the objects once more.	23% (7 out of 30 boys) told not to touch the gun did so anyway, whereas none of 25 boys told not to touch the forbidden object did so. 40% (10 out of 25 boys) in the forbidden object group touched the gun. There was no association between strength of admonition and touching the object or gun. Gun admonitions did not result in boys saying they liked the gun more.

Lead Author (Pub. Year)

Purpose	Design	Procedures	Sample & Groups	Observations	Key Findings

Gatheridge (2004)

Purpose	Design	Procedures	Sample & Groups	Observations	Key Findings
Examine whether an information provision (IP) program (i.e., Eddie Eagle) and a behavioral skills training (BST) program effectively teach children specific rules about gun play, examine whether the programs prevent gun play.	3 group (2 intervention, 1 control), after-only design, with random assignment.	*Behavioral Skills Training Intervention.* Education took place in 10-15 minute session daily for 5 days at an after-school program. Included modeling, rehearsal, praise, and corrective feedback to teach children what to do if they came across a firearm (i.e., stop, don't touch, leave the area, tell an adult). *Information Provision Intervention.* Promoted the same message as the BST program, but without a skills-building approach. *Control Group.* Children in the control group received a BST program after data collection was completed.	45 6- and 7- year old children (22 boys, 23 girls); 15 in each group.	*Self-Report.* Children were asked to describe what they would do if they came across a gun. *Role Play.* Children asked to act out what they would do if they came across a gun. *In Situ.* 1-week after training, children were placed in a room with a gun and without adults. Behavior was monitored with a hidden camera. Responses in all three assessments were coded ordinally, with 0 being "touched the gun", and 3 being "didn't touch the gun, left the area, and told an adult".	For the self-report, role play, and in situ assessments, BST participants scored highest followed by IP participants; BST and IP participants scored significantly higher than controls. BST participants performed the recommended behaviors more frequently in situ; 4/15 BST participants did not perform all three recommended behaviors (i.e., don't touch, leave the area, tell an adult), compared to 11/15 IP participants. IP participants did no better than controls on the in situ assessment.

Himle (2004b)				
Compare the effectiveness of an IP program (i.e., Eddie Eagle) and a BST program.	3 group (2 intervention, 1 control), after-only design, with random assignment to groups.	*IP Intervention.* Children were told that if they came across a gun they should: stop, not touch, leave the area and tell an adult. Education included 5 days of 10-15 minute instruction. *BST Intervention.* Children provided with the same safety instructions, and also received multiple learning strategies including: modeling, rehearsal, praise, and corrective feedback. *Control Group.* Children received a BST program after data collection was finished.	31 children aged 4-5 years (20 boys, 11 girls) recruited from local preschools.	*Self-Report.* Children were asked to describe what they would do if they came across a gun. *Role Play.* Children asked to act out what they would do if they came across a gun. *In Situ.* 1-week after the training, students were placed in a room with a gun and without adults. Behavior was monitored with a hidden camera. Behavior was coded in the following categories: (1) handled the gun, (2) did not handle the gun, but did not leave the area or tell an adult, (3) did not handle the gun, but did not tell an adult, (4) did not handle the gun, left the area, and told an adult.	For the self-report assessment, IP and BST participants exhibited more firearm safety skills than controls. For the role-play assessment, IP and BST participants exhibited better skills than the controls, BST participants performed better than IP and control participants. Participants in the three groups were equally unlikely to perform the recommended behaviors in situ. 8 out of 10 experimental group participants touched the gun.

Abbreviations. BST: Behavioral Skills Training; IP: Information Provision.

then applied *in situ* trainings until the child performed all of the recommended behaviors several times. The *in situ* training procedure included having a child being left in a room alone with toys, games, and a gun, and being observed by a researcher. If the child handled the firearm, the researcher entered the room and reinforced the recommended gun safety practices. The child was assessed *in situ* only after performing the appropriate series of behaviors several times. Because of the lack of a standardized number of "doses" of the intervention and small sample sizes (each study had fewer than 10 participants in total), the effectiveness of *in situ* training over and above behavioral skills training is unclear. However, articles describing *in situ* training suggest that children vary in how quickly they adopt the recommended gun safety behaviors. Some children needed five or more *in situ* trainings before they performed the recommended behaviors (Miltenberger et al., 2004; Himle et al., 2004a; Miltenberger et al., 2005).

Studies with child knowledge as the outcome variable

Three studies assessed the effect of classroom-based gun safety programs on children's knowledge of what to do in the event that he or she comes across a firearm (Gresham et al., 2001; Liller et al., 2003; Howard, 2005). Behavioral recommendations for the three programs were similar to Eddie Eagle, i.e., do not touch the gun, leave the area, and tell an adult. The programs targeted children in grades K through 3. Each study concluded that children's knowledge of what to do increased from pre- to post-test (Gresham et al., 2001; Liller et al., 2003; Howard, 2005). One of the three evaluations assessed whether children's knowledge of the recommended behaviors would be higher with BST in addition to IP training. The authors found that post-test scores were highest among students who received a comprehensive BST program compared to an IP program (Howard, 2005).

2. Community-based safe storage programs

There were five published evaluations of community- or population-based programs to promote safe firearm storage (Wafer and Carruth, 2003; Horn et al., 2003; Sidman et al., 2005; Coyne-Beasley et al., 2001; Meyer, et al., 2003). As with the child gun safety education programs, all the community-based safe storage programs enrolled participants regardless of their individual or family level of risk. Only one evaluation restricted the analysis to adults who had children in the home (Sidman et al., 2005). With one exception (Meyer et al., 2003), the community-based safe storage programs assessed behavior change as the primary outcome. The exception was an article by Meyer, in which he described the effect that radio public service announcements had on knowledge about gun safety practices in a Michigan county. The findings indicated that respondents who recalled the campaign were significantly more likely to believe that guns should be stored in a locked compartment (Meyer et al., 2003).

The four community-based safe storage interventions that assessed behavior change are summarized in Table 2 (Wafer and Carruth, 2003; Horn et al., 2003; Sidman et al., 2005; Coyne-Beasley et al., 2001). In terms of intervention strategies, two involved face-to-face safe storage counseling (Coyne-Beasley et al., 2001; Wafer and Carruth, 2003), one involved a mass media campaign (Sidman et al., 2005), and the other focused on distribution of gun safes (Horn et al., 2003). All four programs included distribution of extrinsic safety devices (i.e., lock boxes, trigger locks, gun locks, or gun safes), or coupons for extrinsic safety devices. In addition, all four programs involved collaboration with law enforcement officers or agencies, public health workers, and/or community leaders at

Table 2. Community-based programs promoting safe firearm storage, 1992-2006

Lead Author (Pub. Year)				
Purpose	**Procedures**	**Study Design**	**Setting & Sample**	**Key Findings**
Coyne-Beasley (2001)				
Assess the extent to which a community-based safety counseling program and gun lock giveaway resulted in safe firearm storage practices.	Participants received 10-15 minutes of tailored counseling about safe storage that included strategies for making the home safe against intruders. Were given take-home information about safe storage information, and up to 4 gun locks. Police officers were available to teach participants how to use the gun lock.	1 group, before and after design. Post-test administered approximately 6-12 months after the intervention	City in central North Carolina. 112 adult gun owners recruited through a mass media campaign. 61% had children, 67% were male, 73% (n=82) were contacted for a follow-up survey	Gun safety practices increased following the intervention. The percent who reported keeping the gun in a locked compartment went from 48% to 77% (p<0.05). 72% were using a gun lock at the post-test, whereas none were at the baseline assessment. The proportion of respondents who stored their firearms unlocked and loaded decreased from 18% at baseline to 7% at the post-test (NS).
Wafer (2003)				
Promote use of trigger locks.	One-on-one firearm safety counseling at a booth at a local festival. Trigger locks were distributed free of charge. Real (unloaded) guns were available to teach participants how to secure the trigger locks.	1 group, before and after trial. 135 received trigger locks, completed assessment	Rural parish in Louisiana. 135 adults went through the counseling and received a gun lock. 19 of the 135 were contacted for follow-up.	14/19 reported that they were using trigger locks at the follow-up.

Lead Author (Pub. Year)					
Purpose	**Procedures**	**Study Design**	**Setting & Sample**	**Key Findings**	

Horn (2003)

| Assess whether residents would use gun safes and trigger locks after receiving them free of change. | Gun safes and trigger locks were distributed free of charge. Public safety officers installed the gun safes, explained how to use the trigger locks, and counseled individuals about storing the key in an inaccessible location. | 1 group, before and after design. Gun storage practices were assessed at the home at the time of installation, and again three months later. | Two villages in southwest Alaska, with a population that is 70% Alaska Native. 40 individuals were randomly selected from a list of adult residents who had at least two long guns, and who did not have a gun safe. 33 of the 40 had children; 37 out of 40 completed the post-test. | A higher proportion of participants had the firearms stored in a locked place at the post-test (32 out of 37) as compared to the baseline assessment (6 out of 40). Only 11/37 were using trigger locks. |

Sidman (2005)

| Assess whether a mass media campaign resulted in increases in safe firearm storage, especially use of lock boxes. | Campaign promoted the message that it was dangerous to keep firearms unlocked when children were in the home. Activities included television and radio public service announcements, a telephone hot-line, posters, brochures, fact sheets, mass mailings, a Web site, and distribution of coupons for extrinsic safety devices. | 10 group (1 intervention, 9 control), before and after design. Gun storage practices were assessed from a random sample of adults before and after the intervention. (The baseline and follow-up assessments used separate samples.) | The intervention county was King County, Washington. The control counties were 9 U.S. counties west of the Mississippi River and outside of Washington state. Eligible respondents had to have a handgun in the home and have children living with them. Surveys were completed in 151 intervention and 151 control county households at baseline (1996) and 127 intervention and 128 control households at follow-up (2001). | From 1996-2001, reported storage of all handguns in lock boxes or gun safes increased significantly in households in both the intervention and control counties. The increases were greater among households in the intervention county (from 45% to 53%; OR= 1.71) than in households in the control counties (45% to 49%, OR=1.66). Also during this time period, the percentage with a handgun stored loaded decreased from 20% to 13% (NS). |

the planning and implementation stages.

The results showed modest improvements in firearm storage practices. All four studies reported that participants were more likely to keep firearms locked up after the intervention (Wafer and Carruth, 2003; Horn et al., 2003; Sidman et al., 2005; Coyne-Beasley et al., 2001) (Table 2). However, the evaluations had relatively weak study designs; only one had a control group (Sidman et al., 2005).

In one study, the percentage of respondents who reported storing a firearm locked after the intervention increased significantly to 77% (from 48% at baseline, $p<0.05$) (Coyne-Beasley et al., 2001). However, recruitment was based on self-selection, which may have resulted in a sample of participants who had intentions to change their storage practices, even in the absence of counseling. Similarly, a multi-faceted public education campaign also resulted in a significant increase in the proportion of households in the intervention county who reported that all handguns were secured in a lock box or gun safe (from 45% in 1996 to 53% in 2001, OR= 1.71) (Sidman et al., 2005). All these studies relied on reported behavior rather than observing actual behavior.

3. Clinic-based safe storage programs

There were seven published evaluations of clinic-based interventions to promote removal or safe storage of household firearms (Stevens et al., 2002; Oatis et al., 1999; Albright and Burge, 2003; Carbone et al., 2005; Grossman et al., 2000; Kruesi et al., 1999; Brent et al., 2000). Two programs were targeted to parents whose children were at high-risk for suicide (Kruesi et al., 1999; Brent et al., 2000). In a prospective follow-up study, Kruesi and colleagues assessed whether safe storage education resulted in behavioral changes among a sample of parents of high-risk youth (i.e., youth aged 6-19 years who were being treated in the emergency department (ED) for mental

health problems). Five of the eight parents who received firearm safety education changed their storage practices (3 locked the firearm, 2 removed it from the home), compared to none of the seven parents who did not receive education (Kruesi et al., 1999). The next year Brent and colleagues published a study in which parents of adolescents (aged 13-18 years) with major depression were counseled about removing firearms from their homes; counseling about keeping firearms stored more safely was not a component of the education. Seven out of the 26 gun-owning families removed guns from the home. Interestingly, guns were acquired in 4 of the 73 non-gun-owning households; those parents had not received education about guns in the home (Brent et al., 2000).

The remaining five studies described the effects of clinician counseling on firearm ownership and storage practices with parents whose children had no known risk factors for firearm injury (Stevens et al., 2002; Oatis et al., 1999; Albright and Burge, 2003; Carbone et al., 2005; Grossman et al., 2000). The counseling strategies used in all four of these studies were based on the "Steps to Prevent Firearm Injury" (STOP2) program developed by the American Academy of Pediatrics (AAP) and the Brady Center in 1998 (Brady Center, 2007). STOP2 is an instruction guide for physicians to conduct counseling with adults. It emphasizes that firearms are dangerous in the hands of children and youth. The main message is that it is safest not to have a gun in the home at all, but if there is a gun, it should be stored unloaded and locked. There are pamphlets and brochures that can be distributed to parents.

Results of the five studies are summarized in Table 3. Findings are consistent in that they show that counseling did not have a large effect on parents removing firearms from the home (Stevens et al., 2002; Oatis et al., 1999; Albright and Burge, 2003; Carbone et al., 2005; Grossman et al., 2000). In one study the

Table 3. Clinic-based studies assessing the effectiveness of safe firearm storage counseling on behavior change, 1992-2006

Lead Author (Pub. Year)			
Study Design	**Procedures**	**Sample & Groups**	**Observations**
Oatis (1999)			
1 group, before and after.	Implementation of the AAP's STOP program (Steps to Prevent Firearm Injury in the Home), which included an explanation of the risks involved with firearm owner-ship, and advice to remove firearms from the home or to keep them stored locked up and/or unloaded. Parents completed a baseline survey at one visit, and completed a follow-up survey at a subsequent visit.	Pediatric clinic in an urban hospital in the Midwest (70% of client population was African American), 93% of the sample at baseline (n=1,236) were women. Only 381 were surveyed for the follow-up.	Changes in firearm ownership and storage practices were not statistically significant. The prevalence of having a firearm in the home decreased from 9.4% to 7.0%, the prevalence of having an unlocked firearm remained the same (2.7%), and the percentage of those with a loaded gun at home decreased from 1.6% to 0.5%.
Grossman (2000)			
2 group, before and after, with randomization at the level of the practitioner.	Physicians counseling parents on firearm safety using materials and information from the STOP program. This included a description of the risks involved in firearm ownership, and advice that parents should remove guns from their home or keep them stored more safely. They also described the importance of extrinsic safety devices (e.g., gun safes, lock boxes). Parents were also given take-home materials, and a coupon to purchase a trigger lock or lock box. Parents were contacted before their appointment and asked to complete the baseline survey by mail; a follow-up survey was sent 3 months after the intervention.	9 primary care clinics in urban or suburban communities Washington. Patient population is 90% white. Study participants had to have a physical exam scheduled for a child aged 2 months -18 years. Baseline surveys were collect-ed from 1,673 individuals, 77% of whom also completed the follow-up survey (n=1292). There were 618 in the intervention group (151 had firearms in the home), and 677 in the control group (160 had guns in the home).	There were no statistically significant differences in the proportion of participants who removed a gun from their home, or who purchased an extrinsic safety device. Of those with firearms, 6.7% in the intervention group removed the gun from the home compared to 5.7% in the control group (NS). Also among those with guns, 27.3% of the participants in the intervention group and 21.0% in the control group purchased an extrinsic safety device. Storage practices were not reported.

Lead Author (Pub. Year)			
Study Design	**Procedures**	**Sample & Groups**	**Observations**
Stevens (2002)			
2 group, before and after, with randomization.	Parents received safety counseling along with their children, and were encouraged to talk with each other about the safety issue outside of the clinic. One group received safety counseling focused on prevention alcohol and drug use, the other group received counseling on firearm storage, and use of seatbelts and bicycle helmets. Participants were given take-home materials and sent newsletters about the intervention topics. Parents completed baseline surveys at one visit, and completed follow-up surveys at subsequent visits.	Sample included parents and their 5th or 6th grade children n=2,183), recruited from 12 pediatric practice clinics in New England.	After a year of follow-up, there was no difference in the proportion of children living in homes with unlocked guns across intervention groups and among homes with guns.
Albright (2003)			
3 group (2 intervention, 1 control), before and after design, with randomization.	Participants were enrolled at the clinic by completing a survey; a follow-up survey was administered 60-90 days later over the telephone. Participants were randomized to receive no intervention (control group), a brief message about the risk of guns and advice to store them safely or remove them from the home (intervention group 1), or the brief message and take home materials developed as part of the STOP program (intervention group 2).	Family practice clinic in an urban area in the southwestern region of the U.S. 156 patients at baseline, 127 recontacted for follow-up. About 41% had children, 69% were women, 76% were Hispanic.	At baseline, 36% had their guns locked, or unlocked and "inaccessible to children". In the control group (n=39) 33% made a safe change (e.g., stored a previously unlocked gun locked, or stored a previously loaded gun unloaded), compared to 64% in intervention group 1 (n=36), and 58% in intervention group 2 (n=52). Group differences were statistically significant. Participants in the intervention groups were more likely than controls to make a safe change; OR= 3.04, 95% CI: 1.28- 7.24.

Lead Author (Pub. Year)

Study Design	Procedures	Sample & Groups	Observations
Carbone (2003)			
2 group, before and after design, without randomization.	Control group participants received the usual anticipatory guidance; they completed baseline surveys in the clinic and follow-up surveys 1-month later over the telephone. Intervention group participants completed baseline surveys, and then received counseling messages based on the STOP2 program, a gun lock, and take home materials about gun safety. They completed a telephone-based follow-up survey a month after their counseling session.	Community based public health clinic in Tucson, Arizona. Population was 59% Hispanic, 9% Native American, and 14% white. Inclusion was limited to those with firearms in the home. There were 206 participants, 180 of whom were successfully recontacted for follow-up.	16% of the control group participants and 22% of the intervention group participants removed the gun from the home; this finding was not statistically significant. 25% of intervention group participants, compared to 5% of control group participants reported a greater frequency of locking the firearm after counseling (P<0.05). Intervention group participants were significantly more likely to make an improvement in their firearm safety practices than control group participants (RR = 4.13, 95% CI: 2.06, 8.30), ie, they kept the gun unloaded more often, locked up more often, and/or locked in a more secure way.

prevalence of those with a gun in the home decreased from 9.4% at baseline to 7% at follow-up (Oatis et al., 1999). Another showed that a greater percentage of those in the intervention group removed guns fromtheir homes compared to those in the control group (22% vs. 16%) (Carbone et al., 2005). Neither finding was statistically significant.

Results on the effect that counseling had on changing storage practices were mixed. Two studies showed that a brief counseling session on safe firearm storage was significantly associated with reports of overall improvements in storage practices (Carbone et al., 2005; Albright and Burge, 2003). Three studies assessed change in the reported prevalence of having a locked gun as an outcome. Two found no statistically significant differences either before versus after counseling (Oatis et al., 1999) or across study groups (Stevens et al., 2002). In contrast, Carbone and colleagues (2005) found that those in the intervention group were significantly more likely than those in the control group to report storing firearms locked up following counseling.

The studies provide only modest evidence that counseling was associated with changes in parents' likelihood of storing guns unloaded. Oatis and colleagues' (1999) found that the reported prevalence of having a loaded gun decreased from 1.6% to 0.5%, but the decrease was not statistically significant. Although Carbone and colleagues (2005) found that participants in the intervention group were more likely to make improvements in their firearm storage practices compared to control group participants, the finding was not statistically significant. The other two studies did not measure the prevalence of keeping guns stored loaded as an outcome (Stevens et al., 2002; Grossman et al., 2000).

CONCLUSIONS
Child gun safety education programs

In this chapter, we reviewed the results of 11 programs that taught children not to touch a firearm they come across, and to tell an adult. Although some of the programs demonstrated effectiveness in training children to verbalize and role-play what they *should* do in the event that they come across a firearm, no study has shown that the programs are effective at training children to actually carry out recommended gun safety behaviors in a real-life situation. Compared to behavioral skills training, which includes multiple learning strategies, programs that solely include information provision appear to be particularly ineffective at teaching children to not handle firearms.

In addition to their limited effectiveness, there is concern that child gun safety education programs may increase children's interest in touching firearms (Hardy, 2000b; Hardy, 2003; Dowd et al., 2004). In a review by the National Research Council, authors stated that: "For children, firearm violence education programs may result in increases in the very behaviors they are designed to prevent" (Wellford et al., 2004, p. 9).

Another limitation of these child gun safety education programs is that they train children how to behave in the event that they "by chance" stumble upon a gun. However, this does not appear to be the way most children are exposed to firearms. Rather than occasionally discovering a gun someplace, many children and youth live in homes with firearms and know where they are stored and how to use them. Research suggests that young people frequently handle firearms in the home, sometimes without adult supervision or knowledge (Baxley and Miller, 2006; Bergstein et al., 1996; Miller and Hemenway, 2004, Jackman et al., 2001; Connor and Wesolowski, 2003). The recommended gun safety behaviors (i.e., stop, don't touch, leave the area, tell an adult) may make little sense for young people who live in homes with guns that are always easily accessible to them, for those who know they are going against their parents' wishes in handling a gun, or for those who are acting on suicidal impulse. An improvement in behavioral skills training programs is unlikely to overcome these deficiencies.

In summary, child gun safety education, as currently constructed, can not be recommended as a cost-effective, promising intervention for preventing child handling of firearms. Limited evidence on its effectiveness, as well as the deficiencies described above, suggest that other strategies for preventing child access to firearms should be prioritized over child gun safety education. Many pediatricians and public health advocates worry that child education may focus too much on "gun-proofing" the child at the expense of the more effective action of "child-proofing the home." It is generally considered better for adults to provide a safe environment for children than to rely on children to always behave safely in a dangerous environment.

Safe storage promotion programs

Limiting child and youth access to firearms in the home environment appears to be a more useful strategy for preventing firearm injury. Both the AAP and the Society for Adolescent Medicine have policy statements discouraging parents from keeping guns in the home, and promoting safe storage of household firearms (Borowsky and Resnick, 1998; AAP, Committee on Adolescence, 2000; AAP, Committee on Injury and Poison Prevention, 2000). Limiting youth access to firearms is a particularly important recommendation for young people at high risk for suicide, e.g., those being treated for depression (Brent et al., 2000).

Community-based safe storage promotion programs

The community-based programs reviewed in this chapter involved collaboration with multiple sectors (law enforcement, business, health) and community members in general. As such, they have the potential to be a nice complement to clinic-based counseling in that they can be delivered to individuals who do not have access to health care, and the counseling may not have the time limitations that are present in clinical settings. Unfortunately, there is limited evidence demonstrating that community-based interventions have been successful at changing firearm storage practices. The interventions reviewed here had weak study designs (e.g., no control group) and potentially-biased samples, and some had distribution of safety devices as the main focus rather than safe firearm storage more generally. More research is needed to assess the effect of community-based safe storage promotion programs.

Clinic-based safe storage promotion programs

Clinic-based safe storage promotion programs were the one area in this review that could be divided into those interventions that focus on high-risk populations and those that focus on universal populations. The studies on gun removal in homes with suicidal adolescents suggest that firearm safety counseling may be effective at persuading parents of high-risk youth to remove firearms from their homes. Clinic-based counseling on restricting access to means to self-harm for the parents of youth at high-risk for suicide is an emerging issue for those who do suicide prevention (Mann et al., 2005). Much more research will likely be done in this area in the next few years.

Evaluations of clinic-based programs that involved counseling with parents whose children had no known risk factors for firearm injury indicate that while these programs may be unlikely to influence parents to remove guns from the home altogether, they may result in improvements in storage practices. More research is needed to assess how clinic-based counseling works across differently populations. Specifically, more information is needed about how the efficacy of counseling varies by gender, across race and ethnic groups, and among those in urban versus rural populations.

Future directions for improving safe storage promotion

Much more research is needed to assess the effectiveness of safe storage promotion programs targeted to parents. In order to improve the state of the research, it will be important for experts to come to some agreement on definitions of terms and on which outcomes to measure. While some articles focused on removal of guns from the home, others focused on the prevalence of any loaded guns or the frequency with which guns were stored loaded, and still others focused broadly on "any improvements in safe storage". This lack of consistency greatly complicates comparison across studies.

As described in a separate review paper, there is also disagreement with respect to the definition of "locking" in gun storage research – does it mean keeping firearms secured with an extrinsic device or kept in a lockable container? (Johnson et al., 2005). A large, cross-site study with systematic definitions and outcome variables would help provide better information about the effects of counseling on changes in firearm storage. Such a study should be informed by the growing body of literature examining clinicians' counseling practices and their clients' receptivity to firearm safety messages (Sege et al., 2006; Grossman et al., 1995; Becher and Christakis, 1999; Webster et al., 1992; Solomon et al., 2002; Barkin et al., 1998).

SUMMARY
The literature reviewed in this chapter

shows that child gun safety education programs, which do little more than tell children what they should do in the event that they come across a firearm, are ineffective at preventing children from handling firearms. Adding a behavioral skills training component appears an important improvement, but there is still no convincing evidence that even this type of training can protect most children in real world situations. Changing the child's environment by modifying parents' firearm storage practices is considered a more effective safety strategy.

There is a small but growing body of evaluation research on programs that aim to change parents' firearm ownership and storage practices. These programs have not been successful at getting parents to remove firearms from their homes, especially those parents whose children have no known risk factors for suicide. However, some safe storage promotion programs have had modest success in changing storage practices, including getting adults to use extrinsic safety devices, or store their firearms unloaded and secured in a lockable container. While this research is promising, it is not definitive.

Safe storage practices have the potential to prevent firearm injuries to children and youth by making firearms harder for them to access and operate. The results of this review underscore that more research is needed to determine the extent to which safe firearm storage promotion programs can be effective at getting parents to change their firearm storage practices.

REFERENCES
Albright TL, Burge SK. (2003) Improving firearm storage habits: impact of a brief office counseling by family physicians. J Am Board Fam Pract 16:40-46.
American Academy of Pediatrics (AAP), Committee on Injury and Poison Prevention. (2000) Firearm-related injuries affecting the pediatric population.

Pediatrics 105:888-895.

American Academy of Pediatrics (AAP), Committee on Adolescence. (2000) Policy Statement: Suicide and suicide attempts in adolescents (RE9928). Pediatrics 105: 871-874.

Ash P, Kellermann AL, Fuqua-Whitley D, Johnson A. (1996) Gun acquisition and use by juvenile offenders. JAMA 275: 1754-1758.

Azrael D, Miller M, Hemenway D. (2000) Are household firearms stored safely? It depends on whom you ask. Pediatrics 106:e31.

Barkin S, Duan N, Fink A, Brook RH, Gelberg L. (1998) The smoking gun: do clinicians follow guidelines on firearm safety counseling? Arch Pediatr Adolesc Med 152:749-756.

Baxley F, Miller M. (2006) Parental misperceptions about children and firearms. Arch Pediatr Adolesc Med 160:542-547.

Becher E, Chistakis NA. (1999) Firearm injury prevention counseling: are we missing the mark? Pediatrics 104: 530-535.

Becker TM, Olson LM, Vick J. (1993) Children and firearms: a gunshot injury prevention program in New Mexico. Am J Public Health 83:282-283.

Bergstein JM, Hemenway D, Kennedy B, Quaday S, Ander R. (1996) Guns in young hands: a survey of urban teenagers attitudes and behaviors related to handgun violence. J Trauma 41:794-798.

Borowsky IW, Resnick MD. (1998) Adolescents and firearms: position paper of the Society for Adolescent Medicine. J Adolesc Health 23:117-118.

The Brady Center to Prevention Handgun Violence. (2007) About STOP 2. http://www.bradycenter.org/stop2/ [Accessed February 2007].

Brent DA, Baugher M, Birmaher B, Kolko D, Bridge J. (2000) Compliance with recommendations to remove firearms in families participating in a clinical trial for adolescent depression. J Am Acad Child Adolesc Psychiatry 39:1220-1225.

Brent DA, Perper JA, Allman CJ, Moritz GM, Wartella ME, Zelenak JP. (1991) The presence and accessibility of firearms in the homes of adolescent suicides: a case-control study. JAMA 266:2989-2995.

Brent DA, Perper JA, Goldstein CE, Kolko DJ, Allan MJ, Allman CJ, Zelenak JP. (1988) Risk factors for adolescent suicide: a comparison of adolescent suicide victims with suicidal inpatients. Arch Gen Psychiatry 45:581-588.

Brent DA, Perper JA, Moritz G, Baugher M, Schweers J, Roth C. (1993) Firearms and adolescent suicide: a community case-control study. Am J Dis Child 147:1066-1071.

Bukstein OG, Brent DA, Perper JA, Moritz G, Baugher M, Schweers J, Roth C, Balach L. (1993) Risk factors for completed suicide among adolescents with a lifetime history of substance abuse: a case-control study. Acta Psychiatrica Scandinavica 88:403-408.

Carbone PS, Clemens CJ, Ball TM. (2005) Effectiveness of gun-safety counseling and a gun lock giveaway in a Hispanic community. Arch Pediatr Adolesc Med 159:1049-1054.

Centers for Disease Control and Prevention (CDC). (1997) Rates of homicide, suicide, and firearm-related death among children - 26 industrialized countries. MMWR Morb Mortal Wkly Rep 46:101-105.

Centers for Disease Control and Prevention (CDC). (2003) Source of firearms used by students in school-associated violent deaths--United States,1992-1999. MMWR Morb Mortal Wkly Rep 52:169-172.

Centers for Disease Control and Prevention (CDC). (2007) Web-based Injury Statistics Query and Reporting System (WISQARS) [On-line]. In: Available from: http://www.cdc.gov/ncipc/wisqars. Office of Statistics and Programming,

National Center for Injury Prevention and Control, Centers for Disease Control and Prevention (producer). [Accessed January 2007].

Connor SM, Wesolowski KL. (2003) "They're too smart for that": predicting what children would do in the presence of guns. Pediatrics 111:e109-e114.

Coyne-Beasley T, Schoenbach VJ, Johnson RM. (2001) "Love Our Kids, Lock Your Guns": A community-based firearm safety counseling and gun lock distribution program. Arch Pediatr Adolesc Med 155:659-664.

Cummings P, Grossman DC, Rivara FP, Koepsell TD. (1997) State gun safe storage laws and child mortality due to firearms. JAMA 278:1084-1086.

DiScala C, Sege R. (2004) Outcomes in children and young adults who are hospitalized for firearms-related injuries. Pediatrics 113:1306-1312.

Dowd DM, Sege R, Smith GA, Wright JL. (2004) Firearm injury prevention: failure of gun-safety education. Pediatrics 113.

Eber GB, Annest JL, Mercy JA, Ryan GW. (2004) Nonfatal and fatal firearm-related injuries among children aged 14 years and younger: United States 1993-2000. Pediatrics 113:1686-1692.

Fingerhut LA, Christoffel KK. (2002) Firearm-related death and injury among children and adolescents. Future Child 12:25-37.

Gatheridge BJ, Miltenberger RG, Huneke DF, Satterlund MJ, Mattern AR, Johnson BM, Flessner CA. (2004) Comparison of two programs to teach firearm injury prevention skills to 6- and 7- year-old children. Pediatrics 114:e294-e299.

Gresham LS, Zirkle DL, Tolchin S, Jones C, Maroufi A, Miranda J. (2001) Partnering for injury preveniton: evaluation of a curriculum-based intervention program among elementary school children. J Pediatr Nurs 16:79-87.

Grossman DC, Cummings P, Koepsell TD, Marshall J, D'Ambrosio L, Thompson RS, Mack C. (2000) Firearm safety counseling in primary care pediatrics: a randomized controlled trial. Pediatrics 106:22-26.

Grossman DC, Mang K, Rivara F. (1995) Firearm injury prevention counseling by pediatricians and family physicians: practices and beliefs. Arch Pediatr Adolesc Med 149: 973-977.

Grossman DC, Mueller BA, Riedy C, Dowd DM, Villaveces A, Prodzinski J, Nakagawara J, Howard J, Thiersch N, Haruff R. (2005) Gun storage practices and risk of youth suicide and unintentional firearm injuries. JAMA 293:707-714.

Grossman DC, Reay DT, Baker SA. (1999) Self-inflicted and unintentional firearm injuries among children and adolescents: the source of the firearm. Arch Pediatr Adolesc Med 153:875-878.

Hardy MS. (2002a) Teaching firearm safety to children: failure of a program. Dev Behav Pediatr 23:71-76.

Hardy MS. (2002b) Behavior-oriented approaches to reducing youth gun violence. Future Child 12:101-117.

Hardy MS. (2003) Effects of gun admonitions on the behaviors and attitudes of school-aged boys. Dev Behav Pediatr 24:5.

Hardy MS. (2006) Keeping children safe around firearms: pitfalls and promises. Aggression Violent Behav 11:352-366.

Hardy MS, Armstrong FD, Martin BL, Strawn KN. (1996) A firearm safety program for children: they just can't say no. J Dev Behav Pediatr 17:216-221.

Hemenway D. (2004) Private Guns, Public Health. Ann Arbor, MI: University of Michigan Press.

Hepburn L, Azrael D, Miller M, Hemenway D. (2006) The effect of Child Access Prevention Laws on unintentional child firearm fatalities, 1979-2000. J Trauma 61:423-428.

Himle MB, Miltenberger RG, Flessner C,

Gatheridge B. (2004a) Teaching safety skills to children to prevent gun play. J Appl Behav Anal 37:1-9.

Himle MB, Miltenberger RG, Gatheridge BJ, Flessner CA. (2004b) An evaluation of two procedures for training skills to prevent gun play in children. Pediatrics 113:70-77.

Horn A, Grossman DC, Jones W, Berger LR. (2003) Community based program to improve firearm storage practices in rural Alaska. Inj Prev 9:231-234.

Howard PK. (2001) An overview of a few well-known national children's gun safety programs and ENA's newly developed program. J Emerg Nurs 27:485-488.

Howard PK. (2005) Evaluation of age-appropriate firearm safety interventions. Pediatr Emerg Care 21: 473-479.

Ismach RB, Reza A, Ary R, Sampson TR, Bartolomeos K, Kellerman AL. (2003) Unintended shootings in a large metropolitan area: an incident-based analysis. Annals Emerg Med 41:10-17.

Jackman GA, Farah MM, Kellermann AL, Simon HK. (2001) Seeing is believing: what do boys do when they find a real gun? Pediatrics 107:1247-1250.

Johnson RM, Coyne-Beasley T, Runyan CW. (2004) Firearm ownership and storage practices, U.S. households, 1992-2002: A systematic review. Am J Prev Med 27: 173-182.

Johnson RM, Miller M, Vriniotis M, Azrael D, Hemenway D. (2006) Are household firearms stored less safely in homes with adolescents? Arch Pediatr Adolesc Med 160:788-792.

Kruesi MJ, Grossman J, Pennington JM, Woodward PJ, Duda D, Hirsch JG. (1999) Suicide and violence prevention: parent education in the emergency department. J Am Acad Child Adolesc Psychiatry 38: 250-255.

Krug E, Dablberg LL, Rosenberg ML, Hammond WR. (1998) America: where kids are getting killed. J Pediatr 132:751-755.

Krug EG, Dahlberg LL, Powell KE. (1996) Childhood homicide, suicide, and firearm deaths: an international comparison. World Health Stat Q 49:230-235.

Liller KD, Perrin K, Nearns J, Pesce K, Crane NB, Gonzalez RR. (2003) Evaluation of the "Respect Not Risk" firearm safety lesson for 3rd-graders. J Sch Nurs 19:338-343.

Mann JJ, Apter A, Bertolote J, Beautrais A, Durrier D, Haas A, Hegerl U, Lonnqvist J, Malone K, Marusic A, Mehlum L, Patton G, Phillips M, Rutz W, Rihmer Z, Schmidtke A, Shaffer D, Silverman M, Takahashi Y, Varnik A, Wasserman D, Yip P, Hendin H. (2005). Suicide prevention strategies: a systematic review. JAMA 294:2064-2074.

Martin JR, Sklar DP, McFeeley P. (1991) Accidental firearm fatalities among New Mexico children. Annals Emerg Med 20: 58-61.

McGee KS, Coyne-Beasley T, Johnson RM (2003) Review of evaluations of educational approaches to promote safe storage of firearms. Inj Prev 9:108-111.

McManus B, Kruesi MJP, Dontes AE, Defazio CR, Piotrowski JT, Woodward PJ. (1997) Child and adolescent suicide attempts: an opportunity for emergency departments to provide injury prevention education. Am J Emerg Med 15:357-360.

Meyer G, Roberto AJ, Atkin C. (2003) A radio-based approach to promoting gun safety: process and outcome evaluation implications and insights. Health Commun 15:299-318.

Miller M, Azrael D, Hemenway D. (2002) Firearm availability and unintentional firearm deaths, suicide, and homicide among 5-14 year olds. J Trauma 52:267-275.

Miller M, Azrael D, Hemenway D, Vriniotis M. (2005) Firearm storage practices and rates of unintentional firearm deaths in the

United States. Accident Anal Prev 37:661-667.

Miller M, Hemenway D. (2004) Unsupervised firearm handling by California adolescents. Inj Prev 10:163-168.

Miltenberger RG, Flessner C, Gatheridge B, Johnson B, Satterlund M, Egemo K. (2004) Evaluation of behavioral skills training to prevent gun play in children. J Appl Behav Anal 37:513-516.

Miltenberger RG, Gatheridge B, Satterlund M, Egemo-Helm K, Johnson BM, Jostad C, Kelso P, Flessner CA. (2005) Teaching safety skills to children to prevent gun play: an evaluation of *in situ* training. J Appl Behav Anal 38:395-398.

National Rifle Association. (2007) The Eddie Eagle GunSafe® Program. In. Fairfax, VA: Available from: http://www.nrahq.org/safety/eddie/. National Rifle Association (producer). [Accessed January 2007].

National Shooting Sports Foundation. (2007) Project ChildSafe, Homepage, Available On-line: http://www.projectchildsafe.org. In. Newtown, CT.

Naureckas SM, Galanter C, Naureckas ET, Donovan M, Christoffel KK. (1993) Children's and women's ability to fire handguns. Arch Pediatr Adolesc Med 149:1318-1322.

Oatis PJ, Buderer NMF, Cummings P, Fleitz R. (1999) Pediatric practice based evaluation of the Steps to Prevent Firearm Injury program. Inj Prev 5:48-52.

Okoro CA, Nelson DE, Mercy JA, Balluz LS, Crosby AE, Mokdad AH. (2005) Prevalence of household firearms and firearm-storage practice in the 50 states and the District of Columbia: Findings from the Behavioral Risk Factor Surveillance System, 2002. Pediatrics 116:e370-e376.

Quist S. (1994) The Utah Gun-Wise Program: another emergency nurse makes a difference. J Emerg Nurs 20:330-333.

Schuster M, Franke T, Bastian A, Sor S, Halfon N. (2000) Firearm storage patterns in US homes with children. Am J Public Health 90:588-594.

Sege RD, Hatmaker-Flanigan E, DeVos E, Levin-Goodman, Spivak H. (2006) Anticipatory guidance and violence prevention: results from family and pediatrician focus groups. Pediatrics 117:455-463.

Shah S, Hoffman RE, Wake L, Marine WM. (2000) Adolescent suicide and household access to firearms in Colorado: results of a case-control study. J Adolesc Health 26:157-163.

Shenassa ED, Rogers ML, Spalding KL, Roberts MB. (2003) Safer storage of firearms at home and risk of suicide: a study of protective factors in a nationally representative sample. J Epidemiol Community Health 58:841-848.

Sherman ME, Burns K, Ignelzi J, Raia J, Lofton V, Toland D, Stinson B, Tilley JL, Coon T. (2001) Firearms risk management in psychiatric care. Psychiatr Serv 52:1057-1061.

Sidman E, Grossman DC, Koepsell T, D'Ambrosio L, Britt J, Simpson E, Rivara FP, Bergman AB. (2005) Evaluation of a community-based handgun safe-storage campaign. Pediatrics 115:e654-e661.

Solomon BS, Duggan AK, Webster D, Serwint JR. (2002) Pediatric residents' attitudes and behaviors related to counseling adolescents and their parents about firearm safety. Arch Pediatr Adolesc Med 156:769-775.

Smith DM. (1996) Sources of firearm acquisition among a sample of inner-city youths: research results and policy implications. J Crim Justice 24:361-367.

Smith TW. (2002) 2001 National Gun Policy Survey of the National Opinion Research Center: Research Findings. In. Chicago, IL: National Opinion Research Center, University of Chicago.

Stennies G, Ikeda R, Ledbetter S, Houston B, Sacks J. (1999) Firearm storage practices and children in the home, United States, 1994. Arch Pediatr Adolesc Med 153:586-590.

Stevens MM, Olson AL, Gaffney CA, Tosteson TD, Mott LA, Starr P. (2002) A pediatric, practice-based, randomized trial of drinking and smoking prevention, and bicycle helmet, gun, and seatbelt safety promotion. Pediatrics 109:490-497.

Wafer MS, Carruth A. (2003) "Locks for Life": A gun lock distribution community health intervention program. J Emerg Nurs 29:349-351.

Webster DW, Freed LH, Frattaroli S, Wilson MEH. (2002) How delinquent youths acquire guns: initial versus most recent gun acquisitions. J Urban Health: Bull N Y Acad Med 79:60-69.

Webster DW, Starnes M. (2000) Reexamining the association between child access prevention gun laws and unintentional shooting deaths of children. Pediatrics 106:1466-1469.

Webster DW, Vernick JS, Zeoli AM, Manganello JA. (2004) Association between youth-focused firearm laws and youth suicides. JAMA 292:594-601.

Webster DW, Wilson MEH, Duggan AK, Pakula LC. (1992) Firearm injury prevention counseling: a study of pediatricians' beliefs and practices. Pediatrics 89:902-907.

Wellford CF, Pepper JV, Petrie CV, eds. (2004) Firearms and Violence: A Critical Review. Washington, DC: National Academies Press.

Wintemute GJ, Teret SP, Kraus JF, Wright MA, Bradfield G. (1987) When children shoot children: 88 unintended deaths in California. JAMA 257:3107-3109.

BEHAVIORAL INTERVENTIONS TO REDUCE INTIMATE PARTNER VIOLENCE AGAINST WOMEN

Gene Feder, Marianne Hester, Emma Williamson and Danielle Dunne

In this chapter we review evidence for behavioral interventions to reduce intimate partner violence against women that can either be delivered in a health care setting or can be made available to patients via referral by clinicians.

BACKGROUND

Definition of intimate partner violence

Intimate partner violence is power over a partner or ex-partner to try to harm them, or to exert control that will harm them either immediately or eventually if repeated over time. The abuse may manifest itself in a variety of forms, including physical violence (ranging from slaps, punches and kicks to assaults with a weapon and murder), sexual violence (such as forced sex, or forced participation in degrading sexual acts), emotionally abusive behaviors (such as prohibiting a woman from seeing her family and friends, ongoing belittlement or humiliation, or intimidation), economic restrictions (such as preventing a woman from working, or confiscating her earnings), and other controlling behaviors (Watts and Zimmerman, 2002). Often these different forms of abuse coexist, but they may also present individually (Taft et al., 2001). In this chapter we consider behavioral interventions to reduce all forms of partner violence against women.

Prevalence of partner violence

The prevalence of partner violence varies between societies and with the definition used by investigators, in particular whether the definition includes sexual and emotional as well as physical violence. Crime victimization surveys produce a lower prevalence than community surveys and the highest prevalence is in studies of clinical populations, such as women presenting to primary care (Hegarty, 2006). In a well designed community survey, it was reported that 24.8% of women in the United States have a lifetime experience of sexual or physical assault by their husband or boyfriend and 1.5% have experienced this in the last year (Tjaden and Thoennes, 2000). A study of primary care internal medicine clinic populations in the Baltimore area found that 5.5% of respondents had experienced partner violence in the past year (McCauley et al., 1995). These acts of violence are not isolated events; violence perpetrated against women by their husband or boyfriend is often accompanied by systematic emotional abuse and controlling behavior.

Partner violence can have short-term and long-term negative health consequences, which may persist even after the abuse has ended (Campbell, 2002a). Of the estimated 4.8 million intimate partner rapes perpetrated against women, approximately 2 million will result in injury and over half a million will require medical treatment (Tjaden and Thoennes, 2000). A World Development Report from the United Nations emphasizes that partner violence is a significant cause of death and disability on a world-wide scale and the World Health Organization highlights violence against women as a priority health issue(http://www.int/frh-whd/VAW/infopack/English/VAW_infopack.html).

Physical health of abused women

Partner violence is one of the most common causes of acute injury in women. In a UK cross-sectional study of consecutive women attending family practices, 16% of respondents reported being punched in the face, 20% were punched on the body, arms or legs, and 13% were kicked. Of these women, 50% required medical attention for their injuries (Richardson, 2002). Similar figures emerge from research conducted in hospital emergency rooms (Guth and Pachter, 2000). One in three female homicides are committed by a partner or ex-partner (Paulozzi et al., 2001).

Battered women experience many chronic health problems. The most consistent and largest physical health difference between abused and non-abused women is the incidence of gynecological problems (e.g. sexually-transmitted diseases, vaginal bleeding and infection, genital irritation, chronic pelvic pain, urinary-tract infections (Campbell, 2002b). Other conditions more common in abused women include chronic pain (e.g. headaches, back pain) and central nervous system symptoms (e.g. fainting and seizures), (Diaz-Olavarrieta et al., 1999) self-reported gastrointestinal symptoms (e.g. loss of appetite, eating disorders) (Coker et al., 2000a) and diagnosed functional gastro-intestinal disorders (e.g. irritable bowel syndrome), (Tollestrup et al., 1999) and self-reported cardiovascular conditions (e.g. hypertension, angina) (Coker et al., 2000b).

Health of abused women during pregnancy

Partner violence continues when a woman becomes pregnant; indeed, violence may start or even escalate at this time (Gazmararian et al., 2000). The most serious outcome is the death of the mother (Parsons and Harper, 1999) or the fetus. Partner violence during pregnancy is associated with low birth weight babies, with an odds ratio of 1.4 in a meta-analysis (Murphy et al., 2001), and with premature birth, with an odds ratio of 1.6 in a study of over 3000 pregnant women in Alabama (Neggers et al., 2004).

Psychosocial health of abused women

The impact of partner violence has psychological parallels with the trauma of being taken hostage and subjected to torture (Graham et al., 1998). The most prevalent health sequelae are depression and post-traumatic stress disorder with odds ratios of 2.8 and 3.3 respectively in Golding's meta-analysis (Golding, 2002). Women living in abusive relationships often have feelings of low self-esteem and hopelessness. Abused women are five times more likely to attempt to commit suicide compared with non-abused women. Other signs of emotional distress associated with partner violence are anxiety, insomnia and social dysfunction (Ratner, 1993). In industrialized countries, women who have experienced physical or psycho-logical abuse are fifteen times more likely to abuse alcohol and nine times more likely to abuse drugs than are non-abused women (Golding, 2002). There is evidence that, for many women, substance abuse is directly attributable to partner violence (Golding, 2002).

Impact of partner violence on health service use

Women experiencing partner violence present frequently to health services and require wide-ranging medical care (Campbell, 2002c). They are admitted to hospital more often than are non-abused women and are issued more prescriptions (Koss et al., 1991b; Wisner et al., 1999). There is evidence of a linear relationship between severity of abuse and the use of health services (Koss et al., 1991a).

Health service use by violent male partners

Men who are violent to their female partners may access health services as a consequence of their behavior (Dobash et al., 2000). In a UK study of men on voluntary perpetrator programs, 32 of 45 had accessed their family doctor prior to entering the program. While some explicitly raised their violence in the consultation, others presented with conditions such as depression or non-specific symptoms, such as feeling 'low' or 'down' (Hester et al., 2006).

STRUCTURE OF THE CURRENT REVIEW

Although it has become conventional to restrict evaluations of clinical interventions to randomized controlled trials, these are particularly challenging in the field of domestic violence (Hegarty et al., 2006). The relatively small number of trials of behavioral interventions for women who have experienced partner violence and for male perpetrators of this violence have led us to extend the scope of relevant research on effectiveness to other controlled study designs. We have also included qualitative research, which has a crucial role in informing guidance to clinicians on responding to partner violence and can contribute to our understanding of how and why interventions work.

The evidence we report here is based on (1) a systematic review of qualitative studies of what women want from health care professionals after they disclose partner violence (Feder et al., 2006b), (2) a systematic review of controlled evaluations of behavioral interventions for women survivors of intimate partner violence (Ramsay et al., 2006) and (3) a systematic review of behavioral interventions for perpetrators, which we report here for the first time.

Intimate partner violence is a complex phenomenon and although behavioral interventions have often been assessed separately, a narrowly focused, single intervention approach may be less effective in tackling domestic violence than approaches combining support for survivors and engagement with perpetrators (Hester and Westmarland, 2005).

REVIEW OF QUALITATIVE STUDIES OF WHAT WOMEN DESIRE WHEN THEY DISCLOSE INTIMATE

PARTNER VIOLENCE TO HEALTH CARE PROFESSIONALS

The response of clinicians to disclosure of abuse is not a behavioral intervention *per se*. Nevertheless, we believe that it is a crucial part of what medical and allied health professionals have to offer women experiencing domestic violence. Health care settings, particularly those where there is a potential long-term relationship between women and health professionals (family practice, gynecology, internal medicine, nurse practitioner practice), may be the only places where a woman feels safe to discuss partner abuse. If the experience of partner abuse is akin to being trapped in a war zone, disclosure to a doctor or nurse who knows you and responds compassionately can be, at least, a momentary escape and, at best, a step towards freedom. We know from interviews with survivors of partner abuse in California that women hope that their physicians and, presumably, other clinicians will respond to disclosure with unconditional support and no pressure to act in a particular way (Gerbert et al., 2002). Physicians with expertise in domestic violence validate the experience of abuse that a woman discloses to them, affirm the unacceptability of that experience and express support, before any other response (Gerbert et al., 2000). Even if a woman does not choose to pursue a behavioral intervention or engage with other agencies, validation of her experience by the health care professional and the offer of support is a moral and political act that may in the long run contribute to the woman being able to change her situation.

Much has been written on the experience of survivors and their expectations of health care workers, mostly emphasizing the process of screening and disclosure. In addition to offering support, the health care professional needs to make an assessment of the abused woman's safety. This may be as simple as checking with the woman if it safe for her and her children, if she has any, to return home. A more detailed risk assessment will include questions about escalation of abuse, the content of threats, direct and indirect abuse to the children.

Here we summarize the findings of a meta-analysis of 25 qualitative studies of women's expectations and experiences when they encounter health care professionals (847 informants in total) (Feder et al., 2006a).

Inclusion criteria for the review of qualitative studies

Published articles or reports of studies with a qualitative design investigating abused women's views of health care professionals were reviewed. The informants were 15 years or older with a lifetime experience of intimate partner violence. If the study presented domestic abuse victims as a subset, the abused women's views were discussed separately. There were no demographic or geographic restrictions placed on sample participants or study setting. Only English language articles were included.

Search and identification of studies

We searched for studies on five bibliographic databases from their respective start dates to July 1, 2004: MEDLINE Applied Social Sciences Index and Abstracts (1987), Social Science Citation Index, CINAHL and PsychINFO. For each of the databases, an inclusive search was initiated using subject headings, text words, and keywords; the Boolean logic terms "or" and "and" were also used to combine searches. In the first instance, a search was conducted for articles pertaining to intimate partner violence against women and other related terms (such as domestic violence, battered women, and spouse abuse). Following from this, search terms were used to identify articles that reported studies using a qualitative research design. The specific search terms varied as a function of the bibliographic database but

were comparable across the five databases. We complemented these searches with forward and backward citation tracking and contact with researchers in the field of domestic violence research.

Summary of qualitative study results

We have expressed these as recommendations to health care professionals by stage of interaction with abused women:

- Before disclosure or questioning

1. Have a full understanding of the issue of domestic violence, including knowledge of community services and appropriate referrals.
2. Try to ensure continuity of care.
3. Assure abused women about privacy, safety, and confidentiality issues.
4. Place brochures and posters in the medical setting so that women are aware that domestic violence is an issue that can be broached.
5. Ensure that the clinical environment is supportive, welcoming, and non-threatening.
6. Use verbal and nonverbal communication skills to develop trust.
7. Be compassionate, supportive, and respectful toward abused women.
8. Be alert to the signs of abuse and think about domestic violence along with other possibilities.

- When the issue of domestic violence is raised

1. Raise the issue of domestic violence in the clinical consultation.
2. Be nonjudgmental, compassionate, and caring when questioning about abuse.
3. Be confident and comfortable asking about domestic violence and ask questions in a caring manner.
4. Do not pressure women to disclose.
5. Be aware that simply raising the issue of domestic violence can help women because it raises awareness, abused women may begin to feel validated, and it communicates concern.
6. Ask about abuse several times because this may allow the women to discuss the situation at a later date.

7. Ensure (and reassure the woman) that the environment is private and confidential, and provide time for abused women.

- Immediate response to disclosure

1. Respond in a nonjudgmental way, showing compassion, support, and belief of the women's experiences.
2. Acknowledge the complexity of the issue of domestic violence, be willing to respect the women's unique concerns and decisions, and put patient-identified needs first.
3. Take time to listen to the women, provide information, and offer referrals and specialist help and services.
4. Validate the women's experiences, challenge assumptions, and provide encouragement.
5. Ensure that the women believe that they have control over the situation, and address safety concerns.
6. Make sure that the social and psychological needs (in addition to the medical needs) of the women are addressed.

- Response in later interactions

1. Be patient and supportive, and allow the women to progress at their own therapeutic pace.
2. Understand the chronicity of the problem and provide follow-up and continued support.
3. Respect the women's wishes and do not pressure them into making any decisions about changing the situation.
4. Be nonjudgmental if the abused women do not follow up referrals immediately.
5. Give abused women an opportunity to disclose at a later date.

Strength of evidence

We applied the CASP criteria to the primary studies that we reviewed. These 10 criteria cover the credibility and relevance of the research (available at: http://phru.nhs.uk/casp/qualitat.htm). The conclusions of the review did not differ when only the high quality studies were considered. Moreover, the quality ranking of the studies was stable when the quality criteria were differentially weighted.

REVIEW OF CONTROLLED STUDIES OF BEHAVIORAL INTERVENTIONS FOR WOMEN

Below we discuss interventions that are potentially available to clinicians via referral. We are assuming that they will not deliver these interventions themselves. The initial response to disclosure of intimate partner violence requires training in order that doctors and other clinicians respond effectively and safely (Wong et al., 2006), but that training will not cover the more specialized interventions reviewed below.

Inclusion criteria for studies of interventions

We review studies of interventions targeted directly at abused women with the aim of reducing abuse or improving their health. These include advocacy and psychological interventions, including forms of therapy and counseling. The primary focus of the review was to evaluate the evidence from intervention studies initiated in health care settings. However, evidence from interventions conducted outside of health care systems was included if the studies reported data on health outcomes or levels of abuse from the perspective of abused women and the intervention could potentially be accessed via referral from a health care professional. Outcomes included incidence of abuse of women (physical, sexual, psychological, emotional or financial abuse), physical health of women (deaths, physical injuries - including self-harm, any chronic health disorders - including alcohol or drug abuse, sexual health, any general measures of physical health), psychosocial health of women (depression, anxiety, post-traumatic stress, self-efficacy, self-esteem, quality of life, perceived social support). Study participants were female, aged at least 16 years, and identified as experiencing or having experienced partner violence. There were no restrictions on geographical or national setting. Published peer and non-peer reviewed studies were included. There were no restrictions based on the language in which the study was reported.

Study designs included: fully randomized controlled studies in which participants were randomly allocated to groups, including cluster randomized controlled trials; "Before-and-after" matched parallel groups design, where assignment to groups was not random; studies employing an "after-only" matched parallel groups design, where the process of assignment to groups was not random; before-and-after studies with no parallel control and with different participants before and after the intervention, where women in the "before" group act as the comparison group (historical controls); before-and-after studies with no parallel control and using the same participants before and after the intervention, where the women receiving the intervention acted as their own controls.

Search and identification of studies

We combined searches of 12 electronic databases (Medline, Embase, Cinahl, Database of Abstracts of Reviews for Effectiveness, National Research Register, Cochrane Collaboration Central Register, Campbell Collaboration Library, PsycInfo, BIDS International Bibliography of the Social Sciences, Institute for Scientific Information Proceedings (Social Science and Humanities edition), Social Science Citation Index, Social Trends, Violence and Abuse Abstracts) to September 30th 2004 with citation tracking, personal communications and hand searching of key journals. Independent data extraction and quality assessment were conducted by two reviewers. We assessed the strength of the evidence using pre-defined criteria (Harris, 2001). The review was updated with a search for relevant studies published to December 2006 (new studies are summarized in Tables 1 and 2).

Results

We identified three types of behavioral interventions for women who have experienced intimate partner violence that have been evaluated with controlled studies: advocacy, group support and psychological treatments. We will discuss these separately. The United States Preventative Services Task Force (USPSTF) (Harris, 2001; Briss, 2004) quality appraisal framework was used to assess the primary studies in this review. These criteria assess both the quality of the design and quality of execution of the study. The USPSTF tool rates both internal and external validity. Quality of execution of the study is rated on a three point scale (good, fair or poor), based on the following design specific criteria: for randomized controlled trials, there must be adequate randomization and consideration of confounders; for other study designs, consideration of other potential confounders must be reported; all studies need to maintain comparable groups and no greater loss to follow-up than 20%; all measurements must be equal, reliable and valid; clear definition of interventions; all important outcomes should be considered or a good match of outcomes to goals; and analysis is either intention-to-treat for RCTs, or statistical adjustments are made for confounders if other study designs were used.

Study design is also rated on a three point scale (greatest, moderate and least). Prospective studies with parallel controls are rated greatest suitability, all retrospective studies or multiple assessment before and after studies without parallel controls are given a moderate rating and single before and after measurements and no parallel control, or case studies and series designs are rated as least suitable.

Advocacy

Advocacy generally refers to the provision

Table 1: Study design of new studies of behavioral interventions for women

Study	Setting	Inclusion criteria	Intervention	Assessments	Outcome Measures	Number	Participants
Advocacy Studies							
Bybee and Sullivan, 2005 RCT	USA DV shelter	Abused women who stayed at least 3 night in refuge and intended to stay in area for at least 3 months post-refuge	1) Individual advocacy to help women leaving a DV refuge to devise safety plan and access community resources: 4-6 hours planned contact per week for first 10 weeks after leaving refuge, actually provided mean 7 hours per week contact Control care: 2) Standard shelter services provided to all residents, and then usual after-refuge care (if any)	Baseline, and 10 weeks, 6, 12, 18, 24 months post-intervention, and 3-year post-intervention follow-up for the original sample	Validated: Abuse (CTS–modified) Psychological abuse (IPA, developed for study) Resources (EOR and DOR) Depression (CES-D) Locus of control (I-E) Fear and anxiety (RAST) Self-efficacy (developed for study) Non-validated: Independence from assailant 3–year F/U: Abuse (CTS–modified) Quality of life Social support Resources (DOR)	N eligible: 157 N participants: 146 N completing intervention: 141 (97% of recruited) 1) 71 2) 70 N completing follow-up (% of partici-pants): 6 months 131 (90% of recruited; 93% of (1) who completed 3+ sessions and all (2).	Age range: 17-61; Mean = 28 (Not stated if between group differences for all participant data) Ethnic origin: 42% African American 46% White 7% Latina 2% Asian American 3% other SES: 61% unemployed 81% government aid 64% high school 34% some college Features of abuse: Severe abuse occurring once a month or less Relationship with abuser (at study entry): 77% married or cohabiting and living with assailant 6% involved but not living with assailant 15% single, divorced, separated

Study	Setting	Inclusion criteria	Intervention	Assessments	Outcome Measures	Number	Participants
Constantino et al., 2005 RCT	USA DV shelter	None stated explicitly but women were first-time residents of a DV shelter	A social support intervention provided by a trained nurse to provide resources, information on and time to access resources, and an environment in which to chat with a counselor and friends. Based on theory that there are four separate functions of social support: belonging, evaluation, self-esteem, and tangible support (BEST). Belonging was generated through listening and responding to other abused women. Evaluation or appraisal was incorporated into sessions by helping women to see themselves as others do. Self-esteem was promoted by focusing on each woman's strengths and accomplishments in surviving IPV. Tangible support included discussion of community resources. 90 minutes sessions, once a week for 8 weeks. Control care: Unstructured, free-flowing, group chat session with the PI. They received the standard shelter services.	Baseline and immediate post-intervention	Validated: Social support (ISEL) Distress (BSI) Healthcare utilization (GSQ)	N eligible: Not stated N participants: 30 N completing intervention: 24 (80% of recruited) N completing follow-up (% of participants) : N/A, no post-intervention F/U	Age range: 28-43; Mean = 35 n/s group differences for all participant data Ethnic origin: 71% white 29% black SES: Income 58% <$10000 17% $10-$19999 21% $20-$29999 4% >$30000 Education 12% junior high 67% high school 4% trade school 17% degree Features of abuse: Talks about abuse being the intentional violence or controlling behavior of a current or ex intimate male partner Relationship with abuser at study entry 17% married 21% divorced 17% separated 4% widowed 21% cohabiting 21% single

Study	Setting	Inclusion criteria	Intervention	Assessments	Outcome Measures	Number	Participants
McFarlane et al., 2006 RCT	USA 2 primary care public health clinics and 2 Women, Infants, and Children clinics (WICs).	Women aged 18-44 yrs, English or Spanish speaking, identified by nurse as physically or sexually abused by an intimate partner within last 12 months (AAS)	A nurse case management intervention empowering abused women by increasing independence/ control, based on Dutton's empowerment model: focus on protection/safety, enhanced choice-making/ problem solving. An underlying feature of the model is that each woman knows what is best for her and her children, and the nurse is simply facilitating this (by listening, encouraging discussion), giving anticipatory guidance, and guided referrals tailored to woman's individual needs. All project nurses received a 40-hour training program. Case management sessions lasted for 20 minutes, on average. Control care: A referral card listing a safety plan and sources for IPV services. No counseling, education, referrals or other services were offered.	Baseline, 6, 12, 18 and 24 months	Validated measures: Abuse (SVAWS) Homicide risk (DAS) Harassment at work (EHS) Non-validated: Resource use (CRA) Use of safety behaviors	N eligible: 433 N partici-pants: 360 Intervention 180 Control 180 N completing intervention: N/A, single session N completing follow-up (% of partici-pants) : 319 (89% of recruited)	Age range: Intervention mean: 30 Control mean: 31 (p=0.003) Ethnic origin: Intervention 67% Hispanic; 22% Black; 9% White; 1% other Control 52% Hispanic; 33% Black; 15% White; (p=0.01) SES: Income: 31% <$5000 21% $5-$10000 31% $10-$20000 17% > $20000 Education: 49% < highschool 29% highschool 22% > highschool (n/s differences) Features of abuse: Physical & sexual Relationship with abuser at study entry 65% current spouse 5% former spouse 16% current boyfriend 14% former boyfriend

Study	Setting	Inclusion criteria	Intervention	Assessments	Outcome Measures	Number	Participants
Tiwari et al., 2005 RCT	Hong Kong Public hospital antenatal clinic	Pregnant women aged 18+ yrs, <30 weeks gestation, attending first antenatal appointment, identified as physically, psychologically or sexually abused by an intimate partner within last 12 months	Intervention based on an empowerment protocol to enhance abused women's independence and control: safety advice, choice making, problem solving. Some items in the protocol were modified to ensure cultural congruence. A component of empathic understanding, derived from client-centered therapy, was also added. Empathic understanding emphasized the need to take in and accept the woman's perceptions and feelings. It was designed to help women positively value themselves and their own feelings. Session lasted about 30 minutes, women given a reinforcing brochure at end.

Control care: Standard care: a wallet-sized card with information on community resources, including shelter hotlines, law enforcement, social services and non-government organizations. | Baseline and 6 weeks post delivery | Validated (although not for telephone administration): Abuse (CTS-modified) Depression (EPDS) Quality of life (SF36) | N eligible: 117

N partici-pants: 110

N completing intervention: N/A, single session

N completing follow-up (% of partici-pants): 106 (96% of recruited women) | Age range: Intervention mean= 30 Control mean = 31 (No information on group differences, appear n/s)

Ethnic origin: All Chinese

SES: Income (HK$11000 ave. wage): Intervention 13% <$10000 28% $10-$20000 55% >$20000 Control 19% <$10000 39% $10-$20000 37% >$20000. (No information on group differences, but control group appear somewhat poorer

Features of abuse: Physical, sexual or psychological abuse Relationship with abuser at study entry: All women stayed with their partners for the pre- and post-test period |

Study	Setting	Inclusion criteria	Intervention	Assessments	Outcome Measures	Number	Participants
Support Group Studies							
Fry and Barker, 2002 Case-control study	USA DV shelter	Not reported	"Tell Us Your Story" sessions: women narrated a story about six salient events which she experienced in the last 4 to 6 months. Group facilitator offered encouragement, directed questions, and steered the contents. Sessions ranged from 30 minutes to an hour and a half. Control group: Women attended information-giving support groups at women's shelters.	Baseline and post-intervention (at 4 months)	Validated: Abuse (ISA, modified) Depression (BDI) Self-esteem (SES) Non-validated: Fry's 25-item measure of Global and Domain-Specific Efficacy Scale, the Ego-strength scale	N eligible: Not reported N partici-pants: 39 21 Interven-tion 18 Controls N completing intervention: N/A, single session N completing follow-up (% of partici-pants) : 38 (97.4% of recruited)	Age range: Not reported Ethnic origin: Not reported SES: Not reported Features of abuse: Intervention: "had experienced abuse in the previous 6 months or so" Control: unreported
Psychological Intervention Studies							
Cruz-Almanza et al., 2006 Before and After Study	Mexico Community	Women who had completed at least 6 grades of education, lived with a problem drinker spouse and suffered marital abuse or neglect. Women were excluded if they had been referred to psychiatric treatment due to	Group cognitive-behavioral therapy to promote self-esteem, coping strategies and assertiveness: 3 main components a) identifying and correcting cognitive biases and defective information, b) establishing emotional regulation strategies and c) acquiring assertive interpersonal skills. Women received 18, 150 –	Baseline, 3, 6 and 18 months.	Validated: Assertion (Assertion Inventory) Self-esteem (Self-esteem inventory) Non-validated: Coping (The Birmingham Coping inventory)	N eligible: 18 N partici-pants: 18 N completing intervention: 18 N completing follow-up (% of partici-pants) : 18 at 3 and 6-	Age range: 25-50 Ethnic origin: Not reported SES Ranged from low to middle Education – ranged from completing elementary school to college education Features of abuse: Not reported

Study	Setting	Inclusion criteria	Intervention	Assessments	Outcome Measures	Number	Participants
		depression, were alcohol dependent, participating in support groups or receiving psychological or psychiatric treatment.	minute weekly group sessions.			month follow-ups 15 (83%) at 18-months	Relationship with abuser (at study entry) All women were still living with the abuser
Gilbert et al., 2006 RCT	USA Methadone Maintenance Treatment Programs (MMTPs)	Women aged 18 or older currently enrolled in an out-patient MMTP, who reported using any illicit drug in the past 90 days and reported physical aggression, sexual coercion, abuse related injury or severe psycho-logical IPV by an intimate partner in the past 90 days. Women were excluded if they had a cognitive impairment that would prevent comprehension of the assessment or intervention or did not speak conversational English.	A relapse prevention and relationship safety intervention to help women reduce drug use and IPV: 11 2-hour group sessions and 1 individual session. Sessions were held twice weekly for 6 weeks. Women attended a mean of 11 out of 12 sessions, half of the women attended all 12 sessions and the remaining half attended between 9 and 11 sessions. Control care: An informational session was provided to the control group and consisted of a 1-hour didactic presentation of a wide range of local community services that women in MMTPs can access, tips on help-seeking, and a comprehensive directory of local IPV-related services.	Baseline and 3-month follow-up	Validated: Abuse (CTS2) Depression (BSI) Drug and alcohol use (Drug and alcohol use behavior questionnaire) PTSD (PTSD Checklist-Civilian) Non-validated Sexual risk behavior (SRBQ)	N eligible: 40 N participants: 34 N completing intervention: 31 N completing follow-up (% of participants): 31 (91%)	Age range: Mean 41.8 years (SD = 6.6) Ethnic origin: 59.3% Latina 20.6% White 15.6% Black SES: Education – 54.5% graduated high school Employment – 21.8% currently employed Features of abuse: physical aggression, sexual coercion, injury-related abuse or severe psychological 63% of the interven-tion group and 44% of the control group had severe physical or sexual abuse Relationship with abuser at entry: Not reported

Study	Setting	Inclusion criteria	Intervention	Assessments	Outcome Measures	Number	Participants
Koopman et al., 2005 RCT	USA Community	Women over 18 years, who had experienced IPV. Able to converse and write in English and living in conditions that the women judge as safe from abuse.	Individual expressive writing sessions used to write about the most stressful events of her life, exploring their deepest emotions and feelings Control group: Neutral writing task. Women wrote as objectively as possible about their daily schedule, and how they used their time.	Baseline and post-intervention (at 4 months)	Validated: Pain (Bodily Pain Scale of the SF36 Health Survey) Depression (BDI) PTSD (PCL-S)	N eligible: Not reported N =59 Not known how many in each group N completing intervention: N/A single session N completing follow-up (% of partici-pants) : 47 (80% of recruited women)	Age range: 21-56 Mean:36.5, SD=8.9 Ethnic origin: White 68%, Latina 13%, Mid-Eastern 6%, Black 6%, Asian 2%, other 4% Employment: 43% full time, 21% part time, 36% not employed. 60% household income under US$40K Education ranged from highschool to completing graduate school. Intervention women completed more years (16.8 yrs) than controls (mean 14.8 yrs), but not related to the outcomes. Features of abuse: "quite severe": 83% hit, 79% pushed, 50% choked, 46% kicked, 46% raped and 16% threatened with a weapon. Relationship with abuser: Not living with abuser. On average, left 5 years earlier.

Study	Setting	Inclusion criteria	Intervention	Assessments	Outcome Measures	Number	Participants
Reed and Enright, 2006 RCT	USA Not reported Women were all self-selecting volunteers: 10% responded to recruitment flyers (posted in domestic abuse resource centers) and 90% responded to newspaper advertisements	Women between the ages of 25 and 55 who had experienced spousal psychological abuse but not physical abuse and who had been permanently separated for at least 2 years. Women were excluded if they were currently involved in an abusive relationship, had a history of childhood physical abuse, or had a significant ongoing psychiatric illness, such as suicidal ideation or psychosis.	Forgiveness therapy based on the Enright forgiveness process model. Participants determined the time spent on each topic. Sessions were held weekly. Mean treatment time (one 1 hour/week) was 7.95 months (SD =2.61, Min 5, Max 12). There was no pre-scheduled number of sessions, therapy ended when the woman reported the work was complete. Control care: participants engaged in 1-hr weekly participant-initiated discussion of current life concerns (considering the impact of past abuse) and in intervener facilitated therapeutic discussions about the validity of anger regarding the injustice of past abuse, present strategies for healthy assertive choices, and interpersonal relationship skills. Participants determined the time spent on each participant-initiated concern. Care was designed to match as closely as possible the basic elements of the therapy approach (anger, validation with mourning, assertiveness strategies, and interpersonal skills).	Baseline, post-test and follow-up (the length of the follow-up period was not reported)	Validated: Forgiveness (EFI) Self-esteem (CSEI) Anxiety (STAI) Depression (BDI-II) Environmental Mastery (Environmental Mastery Scale) Finding meaning in suffering (Reed Finding Meaning in Suffering Scale) Post traumatic stress (DSM-IV criteria) Non-validated: Role of the abuse in women's lives (story measure)	N eligible: Not reported N participants: 20 (10 intervention, 10 control) N completing intervention: 20 (10 intervention, 10 control) N completing follow-up (% of participants) : 20 (10 intervention, 10 control) 100%	Age range: 32-54 years Mean 44.95 (SD=7.01) Ethnic origin: 90% Caucasiam 5% Hispanic 5% Native American Education – 20% high school 30% some college or an associate's degree, 20% college 15% some postgraduate degrees Employment – 15% unemployed, 25% part-time, 60% full-time Features of abuse: Psychological abuse without physical abuse. All women had experienced serious emotional abuse. Relationship with abuser (at study entry) Participants had been divorced or separated for at least 2 years from their partner.

Table 2: Results of new studies of behavioral interventions for women

Study	Outcomes including any multivariate analysis / adjustment for confounders
Advocacy Studies	
Bybee and Sullivan, 2005	These results are based on the findings as reported in the 2005 paper (3 year follow up of the original sample recruited in 1992) Contact with original assailant: 19% still involved with the men and 50% had contact in last 6 months. No data by condition. Assault by perpetrator over last year: 19% (n=23). Of these, 65% (n=15) were still in a relationship with the man. Mean severity of assaults = 2.00 (severe abuse occurring once a month or less). No data about if there was any condition effect. Harassment and intimidation over last 6 months: 22% no longer involved reported such behaviour. No significant condition effects. New relationships: 81% had new relationship some time over the 3 years. 19% (n=23) of the total sample had been assaulted by new partner in last 6 months. Mean severity of assaults = 2.13 (severe abuse occurring once a month or less). No data about if any condition effect. Condition effects at 3 years: MANOVA (physical abuse, quality of life, social support, difficulty accessing resources) was significant p=.089 (alpha had been set at >.10 to avoid Type II errors), suggesting that there were modest overall differences between conditions at 3 years. Univariate oneway ANOVAs also conducted and 2 attained significance: quality of life (p=.058), social support (p=.016), the two non-significant findings related to physical abuse (p=.18) and DOR (p=.13). (Race was also added into a second analysis, but there was no main effect for race or any interaction with condition). Physical abuse at 3 yr F/U and change from 2 yr F/U: 36% (n=44) experienced some level of physical abuse by a partner or ex-partner during past 6 months. 28% (n=34) experienced severe physical abuse by a partner or ex-partner during past 6 months. These percentages similar to 2-yr F/U, but a correlation of only .53, so some women improved while others became re-abused. Only 53% (n=66) of the women reported no abuse at either 2 or 3 year F/U. There was a slight increase for women in advocacy intervention (up from 31% to 36%) and a slight decline in the control group (down from 43.55 to 35.5%), but these changes did not differ significantly by condition (p=.44). Continued abuse risk predicted by: prior abuse (last 6 months), difficulties accessing resources, problems with state welfare system, social contacts making life more difficult. Reduced risk predicted by: being employed, higher quality of life, social contacts providing practical help or available to talk.
Constantino et al., 2005	Social support (ISEL): Total score: A trend toward significance (p = .060). Control group pre to post intervention means 19.54 to 29.00. Intervention group pre to post intervention means 20.64 to 21.91. Belonging subscale: Intervention group had a statistically significant greater improvement post treatment than Control group (p = .016). Control group pre to post intervention means of 4.54 to 7.54. Intervention group pre to post intervention means of 6.00 to 4.82. Tangible subscale: A trend toward significance (p = .084). Control group pre to post intervention means 4.31 to 7.23. Intervention group pre to post intervention means 4.82 to 5.55. Appraisal subscale: no trend found. Self-esteem subscale: no trend found. Psychological distress (BSI): Intervention group had statistically significant greater improvement (p = .013). Control group pre to post intervention means of 152.15 to 108.38. Intervention group pre to post means of 159.73 to 151.36. Healthcare utilization (HSQ): Intervention group showed statistically significant less health care utilization (p = .032). Control group pre to post means of 0.36 to 0.29. Intervention group showed pre to post intervention means of 0.82 to 0.21.

Study	Findings
McFarlane et al., 2006	For a like with like analysis, combined 6 and 12 months, and 18 and 24 months. Main finding is that there was no effect for the intervention; all outcomes improved over time, regardless of group allocation: Both groups reported significantly (p<.001) fewer threats of abuse, assaults, danger risks for homicide, events of work harassment. Both groups reported significantly (p<.001) more safety behaviours but community resource declined. Subgroup analyses – abuse scores were stratified into tertiles again there were no differential effect of the intervention (no statistics reported). Adverse effects: none reported by study participants.
Tiwari et al., 2005	The analysis was conducted on 'intention-to-treat' basis. In addition, a per-protocol analysis was conducted on the 106 participants who completed. There were no differences when comparing the results of the two analyses. N.B. It is not reported if they tested for baseline differences between groups for outcome measures and demographic measures, although – with the possible exception of income and there being more sexual abuse in the Control group at baseline - the baseline outcome measures look very similar. Abuse (CTS): Following the intervention, the experimental group reported significantly less psychological abuse (mean difference -1.1, 95% CI -2.2, -0.04, p<.05) and less minor physical violence (mean difference -1.0, 95% CI -1.8, -0.17, p<.05. Severe abuse and sexual abuse did not differ between groups. Quality of life (SF36): Following the intervention, the experimental group had significantly higher physical functioning (mean difference 10, 95% CI 2.5, 18, p<.05) and significantly improved scores on the role limitation measures for both physical (mean difference 19, 95% CI 1.5, 37, p<.05) and emotional problems (mean difference 28, 95% CI 9, 47, p<.05). There was however more bodily pain reported in this group. General health, vitality, social functioning, and mental health did not differ between groups. Depression (EPDS): Significantly fewer women in the intervention group had postnatal depression at follow up. 25 controls scored ≥10 compared with 9 interventions (RR 0.36, 0.15–0.88). Adverse events: At F/U, women asked if the frequency of violence had increased since the last interview, and if so, whether it was the result of their taking part in this study. No adverse events were reported by the women in the experimental or control group as a result of receiving the intervention or standard care.
Support Group Studies	
Fry and Barker, 2002	Main finding is that there was no effect for the intervention; all outcomes improved over time, regardless of group allocation: Depression: Both the intervention group and the control group experienced significant reductions in depression (p<.001), but the reductions in the intervention group were greater. Ego Strength Scale: Both the intervention group and the control group experienced significant improvements in the ability to share feelings, feelings of personal adequacy, and a sense of reality (measured by the ego strength scale) (p<.001), but the improvements in the intervention group were greater. Self-Efficacy: Both the intervention group and the control group experienced significant improvements in global self-efficacy scores (p<.001), but the improvements in the intervention group were much greater. Self-Esteem: Both the intervention group and the control group experienced significant improvements in self-esteem scores (p<.001), but the improvements in the intervention group were greater.

537

Psychological Intervention Studies

Cruz-Almanza et al., 2006	Self-esteem: Increases in self-esteem were significant at all three follow-up periods (3, 6 and 18-months), but there were no significant changes from pre-test to immediate post-test. Coping strategies: Differences were statistically significant from pre-test to all three follow-ups. Non-significant differences were obtained from pre-test to post-test. Assertiveness: The likelihood to act showed statistically significant increases from both pre-test to follow-ups 1 and 2 along with pre-test to 2, but no significant changes were found between pre and post-test, or at the third follow-up. Degree of discomfort differences from pre-test to follow-up 2 revealed only a marginal significance (p<.10). Differences from pre-test to immediate post-test and follow-ups 1 and 3 showed non-significant statistical differences.
Gilbert et al., 2006	Abuse: Women in the intervention group were 7.1 times more likely than women in the information group to report a decrease in experiencing minor physical, sexual and/or injurious IPV in the past 90 days at the follow-up assessment (p = .05). Women in the intervention group were more likely than women in the information group to report a decrease in both minor psychological IPV (OR = 5.3, p= .03) and severe psychological IPV (OR = 6.07, p=.03). Women in the intervention group were 5.3 times more likely than women in the information group to report a decrease in experiencing any physical, sexual and/or injurious IPV at the 3-month follow-up assessment, but this was not significant (p = .10). Compared to women in the information group, women receiving the intervention were also 7.1 times more likely to report a decrease in experiencing severe physical IPV, but this was not significant (p= .07). No significant differences were found between women in the intervention and information group with respect to sexual IPV or injurious IPV outcomes. Substance Use: Women in the intervention group were 3.3 times more likely than women in the control group to report a decrease in any drug use in the past 90 days at follow-up, but the difference was not significant (p = .08). Women in the intervention group were more likely to report a decrease in binge drinking and crack cocaine use, but the difference was not significant. No significant differences were found between the groups with respect to their heroin or marijuana use at follow-up. Depression: Women in the intervention group were 5.7 times more likely than women assigned to the control group to report a decrease in their level of depression at 3 month follow-up (p = .01). PTSD: Women in the intervention group were 4.6 times more likely than women assigned to the control group to report a decrease in avoidance PTSD symptoms, but the difference was not significant (p= .06). No significant differences were found between women in the intervention and control groups with respect to changes in their hyper-arousal or re-experiencing PTSD symptoms at the 3 month follow-up. Sexual HIV Risk Behavior: Women in the intervention group were 6.1 times more likely than women in the control group to report a decrease in having sex while high on illicit drugs (p =.04). Women in the intervention group were also more likely than the control group to report a decrease in having multiple sex partners, but the difference was not significant at a 95% level (OR = 2.77, p= .09). No significant differences were found between groups with respect to changes in the number and proportion of protected sexual acts at the 3-month follow-up. Adverse Events: None of the potential adverse events identified by the authors, or other adverse events were detected.

| Koopman et al., 2005 | Depression and PTSD: At baseline, 40% of women reported significant levels of pain, 53% met criteria for likely PTSD, and 40% met screening criteria for clinical depression. Intervention group had reduced depression at follow-up (difference scores intervention group mean -5.8 (10.3), control group mean -2.6(6.7). The mean difference score for PTSD in the treatment group was -6.6 (10.3) and in the control group 0.3 (2.7). Women who were more severely depressed at baseline and allocated to the intervention fared significantly better in terms of F/U depression scores when compared with their similarly baseline depressed control counterparts (interaction p=0.05). Paradoxically, the reverse was true for bodily pain); here women in greater pain at baseline benefited more if allocated to the control condition (interaction p<0.05). There was no group x time interaction for PTSD.

Adverse Effects: none, as the safety net of referral to the clinical psychologist was not needed. |
|---|---|
| Reed and Enright, 2006 | Comparison of mean change from pretest to posttest: Statistical significance was demonstrated on all the dependent variables, with the exception of state anxiety. Women in the intervention group demonstrated a significantly greater increase in forgiving the former abusive partner p<.001; in self-esteem p<.05, in environmental mastery (everyday decisions), p<.05, in finding meaning in suffering (moral decisions) p<.05, and in new stories (survivor status) p<.01. The intervention group also demonstrated a significantly greater reduction in trait anxiety p<.05, depression p<.05, in posttraumatic stress symptoms p<.05, and in old stories (victim status) p<.001. There was within-group statistical significance (in the intervention group from pretest to posttest) for improvements in state anxiety scores p<.05.

Comparison of mean change from pretest to posttest and from pretest to follow up for intervention: The intervention group had significant improvements in self-esteem, state anxiety and trait anxiety between posttest and follow-up, p<.05. The improvements experienced by the intervention group on forgiveness, depression, environmental mastery (everyday decisions), finding meaning in suffering (moral decisions) and in new stories (survivor status) were maintained at follow-up. |

of support and access to resources in the community. In the UK, advocates tend to be employed outside of the health system and are not qualified professionals. In the United States, advocates may be employed in health and community settings and are often qualified social workers.

Ten studies evaluated the use of advocacy. All but one were conducted in north America (eight from the United States, one from Canada and one from Hong Kong).

Two separate randomized controlled studies (a pilot and a main study) by Sullivan and colleagues (Bybee and Sullivan, 2002; Sullivan and Bybee, 1999; Sullivan et al., 1994; Sullivan et al., 1992; Sullivan and Davidson, 1991) trained undergraduate psychology students to provide 10 weeks of community-based advocacy to severely abused women exiting from refuges. Advocacy was tailored to the individual women's needs to help them to access community resources (such as housing, employment, legal assistance, transportation, and childcare, as well as empowering the women themselves). A number of beneficial outcomes were observed over time. At the end of the advocacy period, there was a significant improvement in the women's perceived effectiveness in obtaining resources, quality of life and perceived social support as compared with baseline and control group scores. At 10 weeks, the women who received advocacy reported improvement in their quality of life and this was maintained at 6 months after the cessation of advocacy. Initial improvements in perceived effectiveness in obtaining resources and perceived social support were no longer statistically significant at 6 months. However, when followed up 2 years after the cessation of advocacy, women in the advocacy group reported significantly less physical abuse and still had a significantly higher quality of life than they did at baseline and in comparison with women from the control arm of the study. A 3-year follow-up (Bybee and Sullivan, 2005) showed that advocacy continued to have a positive impact on women's quality of life and level of social support, although there was no continuing benefit in terms of re-victimization. These studies had the greatest quality design and were executed to a fair standard.

Tutty (Tutty, 1996) considered the effects of advocacy for women leaving domestic violence shelters, using a before-and-after study design where women served as their own historical controls. The intervention program of support and advocacy was of longer duration than the model used by Sullivan (from 3 to 6 months post-refuge) and targeted at abused women who chose to live independently of their abusive partners. The intervention was provided by a graduate social worker, and provided simultaneous counseling and other help for the woman. The main goals of the advocacy were to respond to the individual woman's needs and to coordinate support services so that the woman could remain independent and safe. It therefore included help for the woman to move and settle into a new community, help with responding to the ex-partner, and provision of support on issues such as initiating divorce and child custody proceedings. Tutty found that this program of advocacy resulted in significant improvements over baseline scores for physical abuse and for "appraisal support" (the availability of someone to talk to about one's problems). However, there was no significant improvement for "belonging support" (obtaining support from friends and family) or perceived stress levels. This study had a moderate quality design and a poor standard of execution.

Advocacy and associated services also benefited pregnant abused women who were still in a relationship with the abuser, according to a parallel group intervention study conducted by McFarlane and colleagues (Parker et al., 1999; McFarlane et al., 1998);

McFarlane et al., 1997). The women, attending an antenatal clinic, were offered an intervention of three brief sessions of individual advocacy (not described in any detail), education, referral and safety planning, spread over their pregnancies. Additionally, half of the intervention group was offered three further support group sessions at a local refuge but outcomes for these were not considered separately. The investigators found that women receiving the intervention significantly increased their use of safety behaviors, with most behaviors showing an increase after only one session. Safety behaviors included hiding keys, hiding clothes, asking neighbors to call the police, establishing a danger code with others, and hiding money. When compared with a control group of women who had not received the intervention, it was found at 12-month follow-up that women in the intervention group reported significantly improved resource use but not use of the police. There were also significant reductions in violence, threats of violence, and non-physical abuse against the women receiving the intervention. This study had the greatest quality of design and a poor standard of execution.

The fifth advocacy study was also conducted in an antenatal setting by McFarlane and colleagues (McFarlane et al., 2000). In this cluster randomized controlled trial, abused Hispanic women were allocated to one of three intervention groups: (1) "brief" where women were offered a wallet-sized card with information on community resources and a brochure; (2) "counseling" where for the duration of the pregnancy, women were offered unlimited access during clinic open times to an onsite bilingual domestic violence advocate who was able to provide support, education, referral, and assistance in accessing resources; (3) "outreach" which included all aspects of the "counseling" intervention, plus the additional services of a bilingual trained non-professional mentor

mother who offered support, education, referral, and assistance in accessing resources. There was no inclusion of a no-treatment control group. The investigators found that violence and threats of violence decreased significantly across time for all three intervention groups. At 2 months post-delivery, violence scores for the "outreach" group were significantly lower as compared with the "counseling" only group; but there was no significant difference when the advocacy interventions ("outreach" or "counseling") were compared with the "brief" intervention group women who had only received a resource card and brochure. Subsequent follow-up evaluations at 6, 12 and 18 months found no significant differences between the three intervention groups. Use of resources was low for each of the groups and did not differ significantly by type of intervention at any of the follow-up evaluations. This study had the greatest quality of design and a poor standard of execution.

The sixth advocacy study was also a randomized controlled trial conducted by McFarlane and colleagues; (McFarlane et al. 2002; McFarlane et al., 2004) however, on this occasion, the setting was a family violence unit of a large urban district attorney's office. All women received the usual services of the unit, which included processing of civil protection orders and optional advocacy referral, and the phone number of a caseworker for further assistance. They also received a 15-item Safety-Promoting Behavior checklist. In addition the intervention group received six follow-up phone calls over 8 weeks to reinforce the advice on adopting safety behaviors. The number of safety-promoting behaviors increased significantly in the intervention group, both compared with the control group and up to 18 months later. This study had the greatest quality of design and a poor standard of execution.

The seventh advocacy study (Feighny and Muelleman, 1999) was different from the others reviewed here in that only one session of advocacy was provided and this took place in a hospital's emergency department. The advocate saw the woman within 30 minutes, discussed the incident with her, addressed safety issues, provided education about the cycle of violence, and informed her of community resources. A before-and-after design with historical controls was employed to evaluate outcomes, with data obtained from police/judicial, refuge and medical records. Women receiving advocacy significantly increased their use of refuges and refuge-based counseling services in comparison with pre-intervention controls. However, there was no effect on any of three measures of subsequent experience of abuse: (1) number of repeat visits to the emergency department over a mean follow-up period of 65 weeks; (2) number of police calls made by women after their initial visit to the emergency department; (3) number of women who went on to obtain full protection orders. This study had a moderate quality of design and a poor standard of execution.

Because they were not included in the published meta-analysis, details of the three most recent advocacy studies are summarized in tables 1 and 2.

These include a randomized controlled trial conducted in two primary care public health clinics and two Women, Infants and Children clinics. This study compared a nurse case management intervention with a referral card that listed a safety plan and sources of IPV services (McFarlane et al., 2006). Project nurses received a 40-hour training program based on the March of Dimes protocol prior to study implementation. Advocacy sought to empower the women by increasing independence and control through encouraging the use of a 15-item Safety-Promoting Behavior Checklist supplemented with supportive care and anticipatory guidance by a nurse and guided referrals tailored to the women's individual needs, such as job training. Case management sessions lasted an average of 20 minutes. No effect for the intervention was found at the 24 month follow-up; all outcomes (use of safety behaviors and community resources, threats, assault, homicide risk, and work harassment) improved over time, regardless of group allocation. This study had the greatest quality of design and a fair standard of execution.

Constantino and colleagues conducted a pilot study to evaluate an advocacy intervention with a therapeutic component for first-time residents of an urban domestic violence refuge (Constantino et al., 2005). This individually randomized controlled trial compared a structured nurse-led social support intervention with unstructured discussion sessions. Both groups continued to receive standard refuge services. The intervention comprised eight weekly sessions (each lasting 90 minutes) and sought to empower abused women through the provision of four dimensions of social support: belonging, evaluation, self-esteem, and tangible support (BEST). It provided resources to the women as well as information on further resources, it allowed them time to access resources when these were available, and provided an environment where they could talk with a counselor and friends. Follow-up did not extend beyond the intervention period. At the end of the program the experimental group had significant improvements on the "belonging" function of social support, and had significant reductions in psychological distress and healthcare utilization. This study had the greatest quality of design and a fair standard of execution.

The 10th advocacy study was a randomized controlled trial of advocacy in a public hospital antenatal ward in Hong Kong (Tiwari et al., 2005). Abused women at less than 30 weeks gestation received either a referral card that listed community resources and sources of IPV services, or advice on safety, choice making and problem solving. The intervention sessions lasted about 30 minutes and afterwards women were given a brochure reinforcing the information provided. Follow-up was 6 weeks post delivery, so ranged from 16-34 weeks from the intervention, depending on gestational age at recruitment. At follow-up, the intervention group reported significantly less psychological abuse and less minor physical abuse, however the rate of severe abuse and sexual abuse did not differ between groups. The intervention group had significantly higher physical functioning and significantly improved scores on the role limitation measures for both physical and emotional problems. While women did not report any adverse effects as a result of participation in the study, the intervention group reported more bodily pain than the control group. There were no differences between groups on outcomes of general health, vitality, social functioning and mental health. Significantly fewer women in the intervention group had post-natal depression at follow-up than in the control group. This study had the greatest quality of design and a good standard of execution.

Group support

Two of the primary studies evaluated support groups for abused women, both were conducted in Canada.

The first was a before-and-after Canadian study reported in two papers by Tutty and colleagues (Tutty et al., 1993; Tutty et al., 1996). In total, 12 support groups for battered women, based on a feminist theoretical framework, that were part of a community family violence program, were evaluated. The goals of the groups were to stop violence by educating participants about male/female socialization, building self-esteem and helping group members to develop concrete plans. These goals were uniform and did not

differ as a function of whether or not the woman resided with her abuser. The groups were facilitated by professionals over a 10 to 12 week period. A number of statistically significant benefits were observed immediately after the end of the intervention including improvements in all physical and non-physical abuse measures, perceived support from friends and family, locus of control (i.e. the feeling that you have control over your own environment), self-esteem, and perceived stress and coping. Tangible support, the availability of someone to talk to, and total perceived social support did not improve. At six months follow-up, many of the benefits were still present. Specifically, there were continued reductions in physical abuse and one measure of non-physical abuse, and increases in self-esteem and perceived stress and coping. Improvements in social support and locus of control were sustained. Using multivariate analysis, the investigators showed that groups with two facilitators, rather than one alone, may be more effective in reducing emotional abuse. This study had a moderate quality of design and a poor standard of execution.

The second (see tables 1 and 2 for details of design and outcomes) was a case-control study comparing the effectiveness of a story-telling intervention with information-giving support groups at women's shelters. (Fry and Barker, 2002). The intervention group participated in facilitator-led "Tell Us Your Story" sessions where each woman was given an opportunity to narrate a story about six salient events which she experienced in the last 4 to 6 months and which she believed had the strongest impact on her self-confidence, self-esteem and self-worth. A group facilitator attempted to put relevant structure on the reminiscence process by offering encouragement, directing questions, and steering the contents. Other members of the group were also free to react to the narrative of the storyteller and to respond in terms of asking for clarification and offering support, encouragement, affirmation and validation. These sessions ranged from 30 minutes to an hour and a half. At the 4-month follow-up women in both story-telling and information giving groups had a significant reduction in depression, and significant improvements in self-esteem, global self-efficacy scores, the ability to share feelings, feelings of personal adequacy and a sense of reality. This study had the greatest quality of design and a poor standard of execution.

Psychological interventions

Fifteen studies evaluated the use of psychological interventions. Most studies were conducted in the United States. Six of the fifteen studies reported on the effects of group interventions. One compared a group intervention with a slightly modified version, one included overall findings from 54 different domestic violence programs (which incorporated individual, group, or both individual and group counseling sessions), one compared group and individual therapy, and the remaining five considered the benefits of individual therapy, with two of these also each comparing two different interventions.

In the studies where two types of psychological intervention were compared, both groups tended to have improved out-comes, but there were no statistically reliable differences between the interventions. It is unclear whether this means that (a) neither intervention is effective, as there is spontaneous improvement in these outcomes once a woman has left an abusive situation, or that (b) one intervention is more effective than the other, but with insufficient power to detect the difference or that (c) both inter-ventions are equally effective (i.e. superior to no intervention). Positive outcomes from studies comparing a psychological interven-tion to no intervention suggest that (a) is unlikely. These and the other psychological interventions are described in more detail below.

Group psychological interventions

In a randomized controlled trial in Columbia (Laverde and Laverde, 1987) abused women in the intervention arm were given cognitive behavioral therapy, with lectures and structured exercises. The women were shown models of appropriate and inappropriate behavior in different situations and this was then followed by role play. Twenty 3-hour group sessions were held over a period of 10.5 weeks. Abused women allocated to the control condition attended a support group; these sessions were unstructured and aimed to discuss issues around partner violence and to provide information about the women's legal rights and the availability of services of the Columbian Family Welfare Institute. It was found that the frequency and intensity of abuse decreased markedly in both groups at 15, 30 and 45 days post-intervention, but the numbers were too small for any conclusions to be drawn. Other benefits over time for intervention group participants also were observed. In comparison to their baseline scores, women receiving cognitive behavioral therapy significantly improved on several measures: communication skills, handling of aggression, assertiveness, and their feelings towards their partners and the relationship, such as their feeling less sentimental. These improvements did not extend to the control group and significant between-group differences were observed. This study had the greatest quality of design and a poor standard of execution.

Cognitive-behavioral therapy was also used in a parallel group study by Cox and Stoltenberg (1991). New shelter residents were recruited to a personal and vocational group psychological program that included cognitive therapy, skills building and problem-solving. The Personality Factors instrument (16PF) was administered to half of the intervention group, which was then given full feedback about their answers on the measure, creating two intervention sub-groups. The control group received normal shelter care, which included weekly non-structured counseling sessions. When assessed immediately after the cessation of the intervention, both intervention groups showed significant improvements over base-line levels of self-esteem. However, all other benefits over time, including anxiety, depression, hostility and assertiveness, were limited to those women who received the intervention *without* any feedback from the 16PF. Neither of the two intervention groups improved in terms of locus of control. None of the outcome measures improved over time for women in the control group. This study had the greatest quality of design and a poor standard of execution.

Another group intervention was a parallel group evaluation in Korea by Kim and Kim (2001) and was conducted with battered women residing in a shelter long-term. The intervention group women were given eight weekly sessions of counseling based on an empowerment crisis-intervention model that was problem-focused and goal-directed. Follow-up was restricted to an immediate post-intervention assessment. Women who received counseling had significantly reduced levels of trait anxiety compared to women in the control group. State anxiety and depression scores decreased in both intervention and control group similarly. Self-esteem did not change between or within groups. This study had a moderate quality of design and a poor standard of execution.

A psycho-educational group program was evaluated in a parallel group study by Limandri and May (2002). The content of this program included information about domestic violence, safety planning, stress management, building self-esteem, coming to terms with loss and grief, and developing a number of life skills. Women were recruited primarily

through the victim witness programs of two district attorney offices. Follow-up did not extend beyond the 12-week intervention. At the end of the intervention, self-efficacy scores improved for the women receiving group counseling, but declined slightly for women in the control arm of the study. There was an improvement in women's perception of abuse across time in both groups. There were no between group comparisons, no scores for the outcome measures and no reporting of any statistical analysis. This study had the greatest quality of design and a poor standard of execution.

Variable results were obtained in a randomized controlled trial of group counseling by Melendez and colleagues (2003), where abused and non-abused women recruited from a family planning clinic were offered four or eight group sessions of cognitive-behavioral therapy to prevent HIV/STD infection. This study was somewhat different to the other psychological intervention studies we have reviewed since it focused on improving sexual health rather than mental health outcomes. Two measures were used to test safe sex practices: condom use in general and episodes of unprotected sex. Abused women receiving eight sessions of counseling were significantly more likely to say they used condoms at least sometimes, when compared with controls and women receiving four sessions of counseling, at 1- and 12-months follow-up. On the other hand there was no difference between groups in number of unprotected sex occasions (ie., women receiving eight sessions had more protected sex but the same amount of unprotected sex). Short-term benefits were reported in the use of alternative safer sex strategies in both intervention groups, and negotiation over safer sex after eight sessions of therapy, but these were not maintained to 12-months follow-up. There was no difference in abuse outcomes between the intervention and control groups at any post-intervention assessment. This study had the greatest quality of design and a poor standard of execution.

A before-and-after evaluation conducted by Howard and colleagues (2003) considered counseling delivered by 54 domestic violence providers in Illinois county, USA. These varied in terms of theoretical framework and delivery. Generic counseling significantly improved the well-being and coping of physically abused women who approached support services for help and was of particular benefit to women who had been both physically and sexually assaulted as compared with women who had suffered physical assault alone. This study had the least quality of design and a poor standard of execution.

A parallel group study by Rinfret-Raynor and Cantin (1997) in Canada evaluated feminist-informed therapy for battered women based on a feminist framework. Women were referred to social services, either in individual or group sessions. The intervention was compared with the normal non-structured therapy provided to clients by the agencies. The therapies were administered in a number of settings, including community health centers. When followed up after 12 months, women in all three arms of the study showed similar improvement over time in terms of abuse, self-esteem, and assertiveness. This study had the greatest quality of design and a poor standard of execution.

Gilbert and colleagues (2006) conducted a pilot study using a randomized controlled trial design to test the feasibility, safety and short-term preliminary effects of a relapse prevention and relationship safety (RPRS) intervention in reducing drug use and partner violence among women in methadone maintenance treatment programs (MMTPs). The geographical region was not reported. Details of this and the other most recent group psychological intervention studies are summarized in tables 1 and 2.

The 11 two-hour group sessions and one individual session were tailored to the realities of low-income, African American and Latina women and focused on the enhancement of self-worth, ethnic pride, and risk avoidance in the future. Materials and exercises incorporated social cognitive skill building. The control group received an information session consisting of a one-hour didactic presentation of a wide range of local community services that women in MMTPs can access, tips on help-seeking, and a list of local partner violence services. Women in the intervention group demonstrated reductions in minor physical, sexual and/or injurious partner violence in the past 90 days at the follow-up assessment and were more likely than the information group to report a decrease in both minor and severe psychological partner violence. Women in the intervention group also demonstrated decreases in depression at the 3 month follow-up. Women in the intervention group were more likely than women in the control group to report a decrease in having sex while high on illicit drugs. This study had the greatest quality of design and a fair standard of execution.

A before and after study by Cruz and Sanchez (2006) assessed the effectiveness of a group cognitive-behavioral intervention on promoting self-esteem, coping strategies and assertiveness in abused spouses of problem drinkers. The intervention comprised of three components: (1) identifying and correcting cognitive biases and defective information, (2) establishing emotional regulation strategies, and (3) acquiring assertiveness skills. Women received eighteen 150-minute weekly group sessions. Women's self-esteem was found to have improved significantly from pre-test at the 3, 6 and 18 month follow-ups, but not immediately after the intervention. There were also significant improvements in coping strategies at the 3, 6 and 18 month follow-ups. Women's assertiveness increased significantly from pre-test to the 3 and 6 month follow-up, but this was not sustained at 18 month follow up. This study had the greatest quality of design and a fair standard of execution.

Individual psychological interventions

In a randomized controlled study, women who contacted a battered women's agency were provided with a rapid response crisis intervention (Mancoske et al., 1994). They were then randomly assigned either to feminist-oriented counseling or grief resolution-oriented counseling, both of which were provided over eight weekly sessions by trained social workers, and both of which combined basic problem solving and psycho-education. At the end of counseling, both groups showed improvements over baseline in self-esteem and self-efficacy, and reported more positive attitudes towards feminism. Only the results for the women who received grief resolution-oriented counseling attained statistical significance. This study had the greatest quality of design and a poor standard of execution.

In a parallel group study of women residents in a shelter or getting shelter-associated services, two types of intervention were compared: individual counseling versus case management (McNamara et al., 1998; McNamara et al., 1997). When assessed after three sessions, women in both groups showed significantly improved life satisfaction and coping ability, as compared with baseline values. Additionally, women who had received individual counseling showed a significantly greater increase in global improvement scores than women in the case management group. This study had the least quality of design and a fair standard of execution.

Two individual psychological intervention studies were conducted by Kubany and colleagues and were of similar design (2003; 2004). The intervention was based on cognitive behavioral therapy and was targeted at battered women with post-traumatic stress disorder (PTSD). Specifically, the intervention included elements from existing treatments for PTSD, feminist modules that focused on self-advocacy and empowerment strategies, assertive communication skill-building, the managing of unwanted contacts with former partners, and identifying potential perpetrators to avoid re-victimization. The two evaluation studies, both randomized controlled trials, found a sustained improvement at 3- and 6-months respectively in a range of mental health measures including PTSD, depression, and self esteem. This study had the greatest quality of design and a fair standard of execution.

One of the two most recent studies was a randomized controlled trial by Koopman and colleagues (2005) that compared the effectiveness of an expressive writing intervention with a neutral writing control arm. Women were recruited through fliers, newspaper advertisements and electronic postings. Women in the intervention group were asked to use expressive writing and to write about the most stressful events of their lives, exploring their deepest emotions and feelings. Women in the control group were asked to write about their daily schedule and how they used their time, and were told that the researchers were not interested in emotions or opinions and to write as objectively as possible. Women in the intervention group had significant reductions in depression compared with the control group at the 4-month follow-up. However, the reverse was true for bodily pain: women in greater pain at baseline benefited more if allocated to the control condition. The intervention had no effect on PTSD. This study had the greatest quality of design and a fair standard of execution.

A "matched, yoked and randomized" experimental and control group design was used by Reed and colleagues (2006) in an urban setting to compare the effectiveness of forgiveness therapy against an alternative treatment consisting of discussions about the validity of anger regarding the injustice of past abuse, present strategies for healthy assertive choices, and interpersonal relationship skills. Self-selected volunteer women in the intervention group engaged in weekly one-hour sessions based on the Enright forgiveness process model. Participants determined the time spent on each topic and the intervention finished when each participant reported that she had completed the work of forgiving her former partner. The mean treatment time (one session per week) for the pairs was 8 months, with a range of 5 to 12 months. The intervention group demonstrated a significantly greater increase in forgiving their former abusive partner, self-esteem, environmental mastery (everyday decisions), finding meaning in suffering (moral decisions) and in "new stories" (survivor identity). The intervention group also had significant reductions in trait anxiety, depression, post-traumatic stress symptoms, and in old stories (victim identity). However, they did not have significant decreases in state anxiety scores. This study had the greatest quality of design and a fair standard of execution.

Conclusions: Strength of evidence for interventions targeted at women survivors of partner violence

The strongest evidence for advocacy-based interventions, emerging from Sullivan and colleagues' relatively well-executed randomized controlled trials, is for an intensive advocacy program for women who are leaving a shelter. The evidence for the effectiveness of advocacy with a less intensive intervention or for women identified in pre-natal care or emergency room is less robust, either because study designs were more prone to bias or because the execution of the studies was flawed. Yet all the studies show some benefit of advocacy for some outcomes and therefore this is a legitimate referral option for health care professionals.

As there is only one, poorly executed, study on (non-psychological) group intervention, there is insufficient evidence on which to judge this method's effectiveness. Although there are nine studies of group psychological interventions, all showing improvement in one or more psychological or mental health outcomes, most are poorly executed. In our judgment the effectiveness of this type of intervention remains uncertain, particularly for women who are still experiencing partner violence. Two fairly executed randomized controlled trials of individual cognitive therapy based interventions for women with PTSD who were no longer experiencing violence give reasonable evidence for this intervention, but this should not be extrapolated to women still in an abusive relationship.

Unanswered research questions related to behavioral interventions for survivors of partner violence

Further research on advocacy interventions needs to be focused on their effectiveness for women who disclose to health care professionals and are referred to an advocacy service. The current evidence is weakest for women who are still in an abusive relationship, although in countries where advocacy services are already considered essential, it may be difficult to conduct controlled studies. Future studies will require longer follow-up, as the emotional recovery from partner violence may take years and the benefits of advocacy or other behavioral interventions may not be apparent in the short term. In the areas of psychological interventions, better designed studies for group interventions are required, with clearly described, protocol-based interventions and measurement of valid and reliable quality of life and mental health outcomes. With regard to individual interventions, if these are going to be considered for women still within an abusive relationship or threatened by an ex-partner, the model requires careful consideration of the woman's safety and needs to incorporate understanding of partner violence as a continuing threat to her identity and well-being.

BEHAVIORAL INTERVENTIONS FOR PARTNER VIOLENCE PERPETRATORS

Below we discuss behavioral interventions for male perpetrators that are potentially available to doctors via referral. As in the case of interventions for abused women, we are assuming that doctors will not deliver these interventions themselves. The initial response to disclosure of violent and abusive behavior requires training in order that doctors and other clinicians respond effectively and safely, and so that they may refer to appropriate interventions.

Inclusion criteria for studies of male perpetrator interventions

An initial search of the literature identified two recent meta-analyses of existing studies evaluating "prevention and treatment of violence against women" (MacMillan et al., 2001) and "treatment efficacy for domestically violent males" (Babcock et al., 2004). It was decided due to time and resource constraints to use these existing studies as the basis for the review, and to carry out further searches to see if additional studies had been published since.

The further search included behavioral interventions for perpetrators, focusing on controlled studies and couples interventions where the role and agency of the client as a perpetrator of domestic abuse was explicit. Studies were not limited to randomized controlled trials due to the nature of conducting appropriate and ethical research in this area. Controlled studies had a follow-up of at least 6 months and ideally 1 year or more. Only English language articles were included.

Search and identification of studies

We searched for studies on Medline; Social Science Citations; and Intute: Social Sciences bibliographic databases from their respective start dates to November 24, 2006. In addition, we searched databases relating to both Sage and Taylor and Francis journals. This was particularly important in identifying studies within the various counseling and therapeutic disciplines.

For each of the databases, an inclusive search was initiated using subject headings, text words, and keywords; the Boolean logic terms "or" and "and" were also used to combine searches. In the first instance, a search was conducted for articles pertaining to intimate partner violence against women and other related terms (such as domestic violence, domestic abuse, battered women, and spouse abuse). Secondly, in order to identify articles relating to perpetrators interventions, we searched for reports and articles under the terms: perpetrator, abuser, and batterer. Finally, we combined these searches in order to generate a number of "hits". In order to minimize the risk of missing any articles because the intervention or methodological approach was unusual or secondary to the focus of the article, the corresponding hits were manually sorted as opposed to searching electronically for words such as "intervention".

In addition to the search for articles relating to general interventions with perpetrators of domestic violence, we searched specifically for "anger management" and "couple counseling" within the domestic violence search context. Combining domestic violence terms with the intervention terms often returned zero hits. In these cases we searched solely for the intervention term and manually sorted the responses.

Results of review of behavioral interventions for perpetrators

There was considerable overlap between

the two meta-analyses mentioned above (MacMillan et al., 2001; Babcock et al., 2004). In addition, two further studies about perpetrator programs published since the meta-evaluations that complied with our methodological criteria were also identified (Bowen et al., 2005; Hendricks et al., 2006). Three additional experimental studies focusing on couples counseling were identified within a review by Stith and colleagues (2003). Table 3 combines the two meta-analyses and adds the additional studies, providing a total of 31 studies included.

Perpetrator programs

The meta-evaluation by Babcock et al. (2004) set out to review findings from controlled quasi-experimental and experimental studies "to test the relative impact of Duluth cognitive-behavioral therapy (CBT) and other types of treatment on subsequent recidivism of violence" (p 1023). The Duluth model is a coordinated approach to domestic violence that combines empowering support services for women with programs for violent men (Hester et al., 2007). The model incorporates an inter-agency community response to abuse within which behavioral interventions with perpetrators take place. In practical terms this means that programs are run alongside services for partners, ensuring that the safety of women and children is central to the aims of the intervention with perpetrators. In terms of theoretical underpinnings, the Duluth model uses a feminist psycho-educational approach (Pence et al., 1993).

Twenty-two studies were reviewed. Overall, the review found no differences in effect sizes when comparing Duluth and CBT-type interventions. Effects due to treatment were also found to be in the small range, indicating that the interventions had minimal impact beyond the effect of being arrested. The review by MacMillan and Wathan (2001) focused on the effectiveness of interventions with emphasis on physical and mental health outcomes for women. As the review progressed, the authors decided to revise the inclusion criteria to include batterer treatment programs. The appraisal of studies was carried out using the methodology of the Canadian Task Force on Preventive Health Care. On the basis of the review, the Task Force concluded that there is conflicting evidence regarding the effectiveness of batterer interventions (with or without partner participation) in reducing rates of further domestic violence (MacMillan and Wathan, 2001).

Couple Counseling

The use of couple counseling as an intervention in domestic violence cases has been considered contentious (Barnish, 2004). Concerns have primarily focused on the safety issues that can arise for women whose partners are abusive and controlling. This might include instances where women feel blamed for their partners abuse or where disclosure in a therapeutic setting can result in further abuse.

Beyond the published review conducted by Stith et al. (2003), the review we conducted specifically for couple counseling and domestic violence provided no further studies examining the effectiveness of couple counseling. The review was identified in our domestic violence perpetrator literature search but warrants a specific section because it focuses on research addressing a specific intervention. Stith and colleagues identified six experimental studies examining the effectiveness of various forms of therapeutic couples treatment. Three of these studies were already identified and included in Table 3. The additional three studies (Stith et al. 2002; O'Leary et al., 1999; Fals-Stewart et al., 2002) were also added to table 3.

Although the six studies identified by Stith and colleagues are interesting, the use of different eligibility criteria, outcome measures, and treatment approaches within

Table 3: Perpetrator intervention studies including studies included in the meta-analysis by Babcock et al., 2004 and Canadian task force on preventative medicine, 2001.

Study	Method	Intervention	Sample/Controls	Outcome/Recidivism
Babcock and Steiner (1999) [1]	Quasi-experimental	36 weeks: Multi-site, majority Duluth model, psycho-educational and probation.	Completers = 106; Dropouts = 178; incarcerated = 55.	Completers = 8%; Dropouts = 23%; Incarcerated = 62% [Effect size (d): Completers vs. dropouts = .40].
Bowen et al., (2005)	Quasi-experimental	West Midlands Probation Area's Domestic Violence Perpetrator Programme (DVPP). 24 weekly 2.5 hour group sessions and 5 monthly 2.5 hour follow-up sessions.	86 men assigned to the program	Of the 86 offenders assigned to the intervention, 21% alleged to have re-offended within an 11 month post-treatment period. Completers = 15%; dropouts = 33%. There was a "marginally non-significant association". Completing was not significantly associated with either alleged re-offending or time to first incident [Effect size (w) = 0.20].
Brannen and Rubin (1996) [2]	Quasi-experimental	2 groups of 12 weekly 1.5 hour sessions. (1) Couples group, cognitive-behavioral. (2) Gender-specific used domestic abuse project model.	Referred by Texas County court. 60 couples, 49 agreed to participate. 1)= 26; (2) = 26. Post data available: (1) = 22; (2) = 20.	No non-treatment control. Lack of blinding. 86% completed treatment; data available for 53% at 6 months. No significant difference in recidivism. Suggests couple group more effective where there was a history of alcohol abuse.
Chen et al., (1989) [1, 2]	Quasi-experimental;Design "poor" as they used unvalidated recidivism scale because there were too few charges post treatment to use police records.	8 weeks: Anger management	Mandated to program= 120; not mandated= 101. 37% completed less than 7 sessions.	For those completing 75% + of sessions, a statistically significant effect was found for recidivism reduction. [Effect size (d): = 0.19].

Study	Method	Intervention	Sample/Controls	Outcome/Recidivism
Davis et al., (2000). [Listed in Babcock as 2001 report feb. 2000] [1]	Experimental design: Police and partner report of new incident in past 2 months (50% of sample) at 1 year follow-up.	(1) 26 week Duluth model treatment. (2) 8 week psycho-educational group. (3) 70 hours community service control group.	376 court mandated men. (1) Duluth group (long) = 129; (2) Duluth group (brief) = 61; (3) control = 186.	Police report: (1) = 10%; (2) = 25%; (3) = 26%. Statistically significant reduction in recidivism for long group only. [Effect size (d): (1) = 0.41; (2) = 0.02]. Partner report: (1) = 14%; (2) = 18%; (3) = 22%. When based on partner reports neither intervention had a statistically significant impact on recidivism compared to control group. [Effect size (d): (1) = 0.21; (2) = 0.10].
Dobash et al., (1996) [1,2]	Quasi-experimental Cohort study	(1) 24-28 weekly psycho-educational groups (findings from 2 groups combined) CHANGE and the Lothian Domestic Violence Proba-tion Project [LDVPP] both use a model of reeducation, cognitive behavioral ther-apy, and identified as pro-feminist in content. [See Dobash et al.,; 2000 for further information]. (2) Other criminal justice intervention. Includes partner reports.	(1) Intervention: LDVPP men = 25; partners = 22. CHANGE men = 26; partners = 25. (2) Other criminal justice (OCJ): Probation men = 19; partners = 16. Court men = 41; partners = 64. Prison men = 11; partners = 7.	At 12 months, 7% of (1) and 10% of (2) convicted of similar offences. Partner reports showed rate of violent incidents lower in (1) than (2) at 3 months (30% vs. 62%) and at 12 months (33% vs. 75%). No statistical comparison
Dunford, (2000) [1,2]	Experimental design RCT: Self report, police records and standard measures.	Couples randomly assigned to 4 groups. (1) CBT Men's group weekly 1.5 hour sessions for 30 sessions over 12 months. (2) Conjoint group as (1) but included partners. (3) Rigorous monitoring	San Diego Navy Experiment. Specific population group. 861 couples randomized; 1722 participants (1) men = 160;	Police report: (1) = 4% [effect 0.00]; (2) = 3% [effect 0.05]; (3) = 6% [effect -0.09]; (4) = 4% Partner report: (1) = 29% [effect 0.13] (2) = 30% [effect 0.10]; (3) = 27% [effect 0.17 (4) = 35%.

Study	Method	Intervention	Sample/Controls	Outcome/Recidivism
		group 12 monthly individual counseling sessions. (4) Control group.	partners = 162. (2) men = 146; partners = 158. (3) men = 169; partners = 155. (4) men = 144; partners = 145.	No statistically significant differences were found across 4 groups for prevalence of new or continued abuse from either men or partners reports or from police records.
Dutton et al., (1997) [1] (1986) [2]	Quasi-experimental Cohort study	(1) 16 week court mandated therapy including CBT, anger management and assertiveness. (2) control group.	Men convicted of "wife assault" (1) = 50; (2) = 50.	(1) = 2 out of 50 repeated assaults; (2) = 20 out of 50 [P<.001]. Both self and partner reports showed significant pre- to post intervention decrease in violence but in only 74% [n=37] of intervention group and 37% of entire sample.
Edleson and Syers (1991) [2]	Quasi-experimental Randomized, non-controlled trial	3 group treatment models provided in 2 intensities: (1) Self help model similar to AA. (2) Education model. (3) Combined model. (A) 12 weekly 2.25 hour sessions. (B) 16 weeks of twice weekly 2.25 sessions.	283 Male batterers Compliant with treatment = 153. Follow-up = 70. (1) = 19; (2) = 22; (3) = 29; (A) = 40; (B) = 30. Analysis included men who attended 80% + of sessions.	No statistically significant differences at 18 months across groups (1) = 21.1%; (2) = 36.4%; (3) = 37.9%. No impact of the intensity of groups. Very high attrition rate = 54% completed program and 25% available at follow-up.
Edleson and Grusznski (1988) [1]	Quasi-experimental: Partner report, 6 months	8 weeks psycho-educational +16 weeks. Completers vs. dropouts.	Completers = 84; dropouts = 37. 31% attrition rate.	Re-offending: Completers = 42%; dropouts = 49%. [Effect size (d) 0.14].
Edleson and Grusznski (1988) [1] Study 1	Quasi-experimental:Partner report at 6 months	8 weeks psycho-educational +16 weeks. Completers vs. dropouts.	Completers = 27; dropouts = 30. 47% attrition rate.	Re-offending: Completers = 33%; dropouts = 46%. [Effect size (d) 0.26].

Study	Method	Intervention	Sample/Controls	Outcome/Recidivism
Fals-Stewart et al., (2002) [3]	Experimental design	(1) 56 Individual substance treatment sessions (2) 56 sessions/12 conjoint behavioral couples treatment (BCT)	(1) = 43 individuals; (2) BCT = 43 couples.	Individual = 43% BCT = 18% However, not clear that all of those referred were experiencing violence.
Feder and Forde (1999) [1]	Experimental design	(1) Duluth + probation (2) probation only	(1) = 174; (2) = 230.	Police report: (1) = 4.8%; (2) = 5.7% [Effect size (d) = 0.04]. Partner report: (1) = 32.7%; (2) = 31.6% [Effect size (d) = -0.02].
Flournoy (1993) [1]	Quasi-experimental	(1) CBT intervention; (2) psycho-educational intervention; (3) waitlist control.	(1) = 16; (2) = 13; (3) = 14. Attrition rate (1): 19%; (2): 38%	(1) = 8%; [Effect size (d) = -0.03]. (2) = 0%; [Effect size (d) = 0.33]. (3) = 7%.
Ford and Regoli (1993) [1]	Experimental design	(1) Pre-trial counselling diversion; (2) counselling as condition of trial; (3) other criminal justice (OCJ).	(1) = 127; (2) = 114; (3) = 106. 31% of sample at 6 month follow-up	(1) = 34%; [Effect size (d) = 0.00]. (2) = 45%; [Effect size (d) = -0.22]. (3) = 34%.
Gondolf (1997, 1998, 2000) [1,2]	Quasi-experimental Cohort study	Four Duluth programs of different length. (1) Pittsburgh = 12 weeks with some additional services; (2) Denver = 26 weeks; (3) Houston = 24 weeks; (4) Dallas = 12 weeks with several additional services.	(1) Completers= 158; dropouts=55; (2) Completers= 145; dropouts=64; (3) Completers= 140; dropouts= 75; (4) Completers= 135; dropouts=72. 32% across all sites attended<8 weeks. Attrition: Police reports 57% at 15 mo. Cumulative reports 48% at 30 mo.	Police reports: (1)=17%; dropouts= 41%; [Effect size (d) = 0.58]. (2)=26%; dropouts= 51%; [Effect size (d) = 0.54]. (3) = NA; dropouts = NA (4)=12%; dropouts = 19%; [Effect size (d) = 0.20]. Partner report: (1)=40%; dropout = 50%; [Effect size (d) = 0.20]. (2)=35%; dropouts= 55%; [Effect size (d) =0.41]. (3)=35%; dropouts= 59%; [Effect size (d) = 0.50]. (4) 33%; dropouts = 58%; [Effect size (d) = 0.52].

Study	Method	Intervention	Sample/Controls	Outcome/Recidivism
Hamberger and Hastings (1988) [1]	Quasi-experimental: Combination of police, self, and partner report at 12 months.	15 week CBT group	Completers = 32; dropouts = 36. 53% attrition rate.	Completers = 9%; dropouts = 17%. [Effect size (d) = 0.23].
Harrell (1991) [1]	Quasi-experimental; Perpetrators assigned on the basis of whether or not they were court mandated onto a program.	(1) 8-12 week court mandated CBT (2) no treatment mandated	(1) = 81; (2)= 112. 20% attrition rate.	Police report: Treatment = 43%; Control = 30%. [Effect size (d) = -0.42]. Partner report: Treatment = 43%; Control = 12% [Effect size (d) = -0.76].
Harris et al., (1988) [2]	Experimental design RCT	68 out of 81 eligible couples randomized (1) Group program – 10, 3 hour sessions, (2) Couple counseling, (3) wait list control.	(1) = 23; (2) = 35; (3) = 10 Drop out rate varied: (1)=16%; (2)=67%; (3)=60%. Follow-up rate: 41%	19 out of 20 women still living with their partners reported decrease in violence (29% of the 68). Not enough data to judge effectiveness.
Hawkins and Beauvais (1985) [1]	Quasi-experimental: Police report at 6 months.	1-6 group + 6 couple and individual sessions of cognitive behavioral therapy.	Completers = 52; dropouts = 43.	Completers = 18%; dropouts 18%. [Effect size (d) = 0.00].

Study	Method	Intervention	Sample/Controls	Outcome/Recidivism
Hendricks et al., (2006)	Quasi-experimental: Poor randomization	(1) SAFE program: 14 weekly 2 hour sessions, psycho-educational. (2) RandR program: 13 twice weekly 2 hour sessions including CBT and social functioning training. Referrals only made with high-risk group.	200 court mandated and probation men. All 200 were referred to the SAFE project and 17% were deemed appropriate for referral to RandR project. 17.5% attrition rate.	(1) Completers = 10.6%; dropouts = 38.8%. (2) Completers = 32.4%; dropouts = 14.4%. This represents high-risk group. Poor allocation to the groups makes any conclusions difficult to draw.
Leong et al., (1987) [1]	Quasi-experimental: Police report at 6 months	CBT group; unknown length.	Completers = 33; dropouts = 34.	Completers = 13%; dropout = 29%.
Murphy et al., (1998) [1]	Quasi-experimental: Police records 12-18 months post-prosecution	22 Duluth psycho-educational sessions	Completers = 10; Dropouts = 225.	Completers = 0%; Dropouts = 16%. [Effect size (d) = 0.44].
Newell (1994) [1]	Quasi-experimental: Police reports (re-arrest) at 2 year follow-up	(1) 12 week feminist psycho-educational group (2) Alcoholics Anonymous format couple counseling (3) group dropouts (4) no treatment control	(1) = 155; dropouts = 118; (2) = 83; (3) = 135; (4) = 135. 57% attrition rate.	(1) = 23%; (2) = 16%; (3)=36%; (4) = 22% [Effect size (d): (1) completers vs. (3) = 0.29. (1) completers vs. (4) = -0.02. (2) vs. (4) = 0.15].
O'leary et al., (1999) [3]	Experimental design	(1) 14 weekly sessions of men's/partner CBT group (2) Couples CBT group.	(1) = 30 couples; (2) = 44 couples.	No significant difference identified between the approaches.

Study	Method	Intervention	Sample/Controls	Outcome/Recidivism
Palmer et al., (1992) [1]	Experimental design: Police at 1-2 year follow-up.	(1) 10 week psycho-educational (2) probation only	(1) = 30; (2) = 26. 30% attended more than 7 sessions	(1) = 10%; (2) = 31%; [Effect size (d) = 0.54].
Saunders (1996) [2]	Quasi-experimental Quasi-randomized non-controlled trial	20 weekly 2.5 hour sessions for both interventions (1) Feminist CBT (2) Process psycho-dynamic treatment, similar to standard treatment in center	Not clear which intervention clients referred to. 218 men referred, 178 began treatment, and 136 completed treatment. 107 participated in follow-up.	No differences between groups on recidivism.
Stacey and Shupe (1984) [1]	Quasi-experimental	10-18 weeks, 2 sites CBT and 1 site psycho-dynamic.	Initially 193 men; Intervention at follow-up = 77; dropouts at follow-up = 30.	Completers = 34%; dropouts = 50%. [Effect size (d) = 0.33].
Stith et al., (2002) [3]	Experimental design: 6 month follow-up. Partner reports of any violence.	(1) 18 sessions couple counseling (2) 18 couples group sessions (3) no treatment	(1) = 20; (2) = 22; (3) = 9.	(1) = 43%; (2) = 25%; (3) = 66%. No significant differences found between interventions and control.
Taft et al., (2001) [1]	Quasi-experimental	16 sessions of (1) supportive (2) CBT intervention. Findings based only on those who were retained within either program.	(1) completers= 33; (2) compl-eters=41; dropouts = 12. 18% completed more than 12 weeks.	Police report: (1) = 9.5%; [Effect size (d) = 1.15] (2) = 9.7%; [Effect size (d) = 1.22]; dropouts = 54%. Partner report: (1) = 10%; [Effect size (d) = 0.69] (2) = 18.5%; [Effect size (d) = 0.36]

Study	Method	Intervention	Sample/Controls	Outcome/Recidivism
Waldo (1988) [1]	Quasi-experimental	12 week relationship enhancement group for men.	Completers = 30; dropouts = 30; control = 30. 50% attrition rate.	Completers = 0%; Dropouts = 20%; Controls = 20%. [Effect size (d): Completers vs. dropouts = 0.70; completers vs. control = 0.70].

[1] = Included in Babcock et al. (2004).
[2] = Included in the Canadian taskforce on preventive health care (2001) Prevention and treatment of violence against women. See: http://www.ctfphc.org/Full_Text/CTF_DV_TR_final.pdf
[3] = Included in Stith et al., (2003).

each makes any meta-analysis of the studies impossible. As such, the author's claim that, "despite its controversy, carefully conceptualized and delivered couples treatment appears to be at least as effective as traditional treatment for domestic violence" (Stith et al., 2003) should be treated with caution.

Anger management

While some domestic violence perpetrator programs include anger management within them (see Table 3), we found no literature within our search evaluating the effectiveness of generic anger management provision for this population of men. The use of anger management techniques have been deemed inappropriate as a main focus when working with violent men (Respect, 2004) because they do not address the specifically gendered nature of abuse. As such, there is often confusion among professionals, the judicial system and the general public on the difference between anger management and domestic violence intervention for perpetrators.

Four studies of perpetrator inventions

Below we outline four of the six studies identified where a randomized controlled methodology was employed. The two remaining studies (Harris et al., 1988; Ford and Regoli, 1993) were left out because the study concerned was not deemed to have enough data to establish effectiveness in the meta-evaluation (Ford and Regoli, 1993), or because the study was not designed to assess effects due to treatment (Harris et al., 1988).

The first study, by Davis, Taylor and Maxwell (2000), randomly assigned 376 court-mandated perpetrators in Brooklyn to batterer treatment or to a community service control. All the men assigned to batterer treatment were mandated to complete 39 hours of class time, across 26 weeks or 8 weeks. The program was psycho-educational, based on the Duluth model (see outline of the

Duluth model above). The control group involved 40 hours of community service, including clearing of vacant lots, painting senior citizen centers, etc. For both groups, case interviews were attempted with victims and perpetrators at 6-month and 12-month intervals after the sentence date. In addition, records of criminal justice agencies were checked to determine whether new crime reports or arrests had occurred that involved the same defendant and victim. Completion rates were higher for the 8-week group than the 26-week group. The 26-week group showed significantly lower recidivism at 6-month and 12-month post-sentencing compared to the control, with an effect size (d) of 0.41 standard deviations based on criminal records. The 8-week group showed no difference to the community service control (d=0.21). Neither the 26 nor 8 week interventions had a significant effect on re-assault based on victim report, and consequently the intervention had a small effect size for this outcome (d=0.21). Babcock et al. (2004) point out that the small effect size based on victim report may have been influenced by the particular approach taken to calculate re-assault: "Only new incidents of violence in the 2 months prior to the follow-up contact point were included rather than a cumulative account" (p. 1034). The report authors conclude that "batterer intervention has a significant effect in suppressing violent behavior while batterers are under court control, but may not produce long-term change in behavior" (Davis et al., 2000).

The second study was carried out by Dunford (2000). Babcock et al. (2004) see this as the most methodologically rigorous study with regard to "sample size, length of follow-up, attrition rates, follow-up reporting rates, and assessment of treatment adherence" (p. 1034). Due to its inclusion of couple therapy, this study also appears in the review of couple counseling as an intervention within domestic violence conducted by Stith et al.. (2003). The study involved a large sample of U.S. Navy personnel stationed in San Diego, and examined three different 12-month interventions for servicemen who had been substantiated as having physically assaulted their wives. The 861 couples of the study were randomly assigned to four groups: a 36-week cognitive-behavioral perpetrator group, a 26-week couples therapy group based on similar cognitive-behavioral approaches, a rigorously monitored group where perpetrators were seen monthly for individual counseling, and a control group involving victim safety planning. Outcome data were gathered from male perpetrators and female victims at roughly 6-month intervals over the approximately 18-month experimental period. Four types of outcome measures were used: self-report to assess the number of incidents or episodes in which a victim or perpetrator reported being abused across three different levels of abuse; types of abusive behaviors as reported by respondents using items from the Modified Conflict Tactics Scale; official police and court records for all respondents (both victims and perpetrators) living within the boundaries of San Diego County; and the date of the first instance in which a repeat case of spouse assault occurred as indicated by both official arrest records and victim reports of new physical injuries (Dunford, 2000). Neither the perpetrator program (d=0.13) nor couples therapy (d=0.10) showed any significant impact on recidivism after one year, based on victim report or official records. The author points out that the lack of impact may be due to the particular nature of and context for the sample: "It is possible that the military setting in which the experiment was conducted could, in and of itself, explain the no-difference findings if men in the Navy referred to the Family Advocacy Service (FAC) for assaulting their wives perceived that their Navy careers would be put at risk if they continued to abuse their

wives. The effects of such a perception may have overwhelmed the deterrent effects of the interventions" (Dunford, 2000: 474). There were no statistically significant differences between the experimental groups.

The third study, by Feder and Forde (1999; 2000; Feder and Dugan, 2002) involved 404 male defendants in Broward County Courthouse who were randomly assigned to a one-year probation and court-mandated counseling program following the Duluth model, or a control group involving one-year of probation conditions. The study followed these men for 12 months, collecting information from offenders' self-reports, victims' reports, and official measures of re-arrests. No significant differences were found between the experimental and control groups regarding recidivism as measured by police records (d=0.04) or by victim report (d=0.02). The intervention also did not produce differences in perpetrators' attitudes or beliefs with regard to domestic violence. There was, however, a small but significant effect on recidivism for those men who attended all 26 sessions of the perpetrator program. There were problems in attaining random assignment of the sample, with uneven numbers of men assigned to the treatment and control groups. The study also suffered from high attrition rates of men from the program (60%) and there were low response rates from victims (22%). The authors point out that stake-in-conformity variables (employment and age) appeared to predict both attendance at treatment and re-offending.

Finally, a small-scale study using a block randomized approach was carried out in Canada by Palmer, Brown and Barrera (1992). If a new perpetrator group was to commence within 3 weeks men were assigned to a 10-week psycho-educational program which consisted of "relatively unstructured, client-centered treatment [which] addressed beliefs about violence, responsibility for violent behavior, coping with conflict and anger, self-esteem, and relationships with women" (Babcock et al., 2004). If a new group was not due to start within 3 weeks men were assigned to a probation conditions only control group. In this way 30 men were assigned to the perpetrator program group and 26 to the probation conditions group. Men assigned to the perpetrator program re-offended at a significantly lower rate than men assigned to probation only, yielding a medium effect size (d=0.54). Babcock et al. (2004), however, express concern about the small sample size.

Unanswered research questions related to the topic of perpetrator programs

The meta-evaluations of interventions with male perpetrators of domestic violence focus primarily on outcome measures for recidivism related to physical abuse, based on victim report or criminal justice agency records. Such measures will inevitably provide a very partial picture of the impact of interventions, not least because domestic violence consists of emotional and sexual abuse as well as physical violence. Even where interventions may have an impact on physical violence, perpetrators may continue or possibly increase the use of emotionally controlling behaviors (Dobash et al., 2000). Reliance on criminal justice records is also problematic as the advocacy and support provided to victims alongside perpetrator interventions may in some instances empower and enable victims to contact criminal justice agencies leading to an increase in reports (Gondolf, 2003; Hester and Westmarland, 2005). The existing meta-evaluations leave other questions unanswered regarding broader impacts of perpetrator interventions, motivations of the men concerned, and processes by which successful change may occur (Scott, 2004). There may also be other, methodological and ethical, issues that make it difficult to carry out robust randomized control trials to assess the impact of perpetrator interventions. Instead, to provide data analogous to that obtained in a randomized experiment, Gondolf and colleagues (Gondolf, 1997, 1998, 2000 – study 16 in Table 3) applied propensity score analysis to a three-site quasi-experimental evaluation involving 633 batterers attending programs based on the Duluth model, and their partners. Propensity score analysis takes account of treatment dose. The score was estimated as the probability of completing the program conditional on observable character-istics. Subclassification was used to balance program completers and program dropouts. Based on this approach there was a 33% difference in probability of re-assault between program completers and drop-outs during the 15 month follow-up for the full sample, increasing to nearly 50% where men had been court-ordered. The authors conclude that "program completion reduces the probability of re-assault by an amount that is of practical importance" (Jones et al., 2004). The study also indicated that men with severe psychopathology appear less likely to benefit from perpetrator programs and should be provided with supplemental mental health treatment.

For further material on health care responses to domestic violence, see the health pages of the Family Violence Prevention Fund website:
http://www.endabuse.org/programs/healthcare and the Duluth model website: http://www.duluth-model.org/

REFERENCES

Babcock JC, Steiner R. (1999) The relationship between treatment, incarceration, and recidivism of battering: A program evaluation of Seattle's coordinated community response to domestic violence. J Family Psychology 13: 46-49

Babcock JC, Green CE, Robie C. (2004) Does batterers' treatment work? A meta-analytic review of domestic violence treatment. Clin Psych Review 23: 1023-

1053.

Barnish M. (2004) <u>Domestic Violence: A Literature Review</u>. London: HM Inspectorate of Probation.

Bowen E, Gilchrist EA, Beech AR. (2005) An examination of the impact of community-based rehabilitation on the offending behaviour of male domestic violence offenders and the characteristics associated with recidivism. Legal and Criminological Psychology 10: 189-209.

Brannen SJ, Rubin A. (1996) Comparing the effectiveness of gender-specific and couples groups in a court-mandated spouse abuse treatment program. Res Social Work Pract 6: 405-416.

Briss PA, Brownson RC, Fielding JE, Zaza S (2004). Developing and using the Guide to Community Preventive Services: lessons learned about evidence-based public health. Annu Rev Public Health 25:281-302.

Bybee DI, Sullivan CM. (2002) The process through which an advocacy intervention resulted in positive change for battered women over time. Am J Community Psychol 30(1): 103-132.

Bybee D, Sullivan C. (2005) Predicting Re-Victimization of Battered Women 3 Years After Exiting a Shelter Program. Am J Community Psychol 36(1-2): 85-96.

Campbell JC. (2002). Health consequences of intimate partner violence. Lancet 359(9314): 1331-1336.

Chen H, Bersani S, Myers SC, Denton T. (1989) Evaluating the effectiveness of a court-sponsored abuser treatment program. J Family Violence 4: 309-322.

Coker AL, Smith PH, Bethea L, King MR, McKeown RE. (2000). Physical Health Consequences of Physical and Psychological Intimate Partner Violence. Arch Fam Med 9(5): 451-457.

Constantino R, Kim Y, Crane P. (2005) Effects of a Social Support Intervention on Health Outcomes in Residents of a Domestic Violence Shelter: A Pilot Study. Issues in Mental Health Nursing 26(6): 575-590.

Cox JW, Stoltenberg CD. (1991) Evaluation of a treatment program for battered wives. J Family Violence 6:395.

Cruz AGM, Sanchez S. (2006). Empowering women abused by their problem drinker spouses: effects of a cognitive-behavioral intervention. Salud Mental 29(5):25-31.

Davis R, Taylor B, Maxwell C. (2000). Does batterer treatment reduce violence? A randomized experiment in Brooklyn. Washington, DC: National Institute of Justice.

Diaz-Olavarrieta C, Campbell J, Garcia de la CC, Paz F,Villa AR. (1999) Domestic violence against patients with chronic neurologic disorders. Arch Neurol 56(6): 681-685.

Dobash R, Dobash R, Cavanagh K, Lewis R. (1996) Reeducation programs for violent men – An evaluation. Research Findings, 46: 309-322.

Dobash R, Dobash R, Cavanagh K, Lewis R. (2000) Changing Violent Men. London: Sage

Dunford DG. (2000) The San Diego Navy experiment: An assessment of inter-ventions for men who assault their wives. J Consult Clin Psych 68: 468-476.

Dutton DG. (1986) The outcome of court-mandated treatment for wife assault: a quasi-experimental evaluation. Violence Vic 1(3): 163-175.

Dutton DG, Bodnarchuk M, Kropp R, Hart SD. (1997) Wife assault treatment and criminal recidivism: An 11-year follow-up. Int J Offender Therapy Comparative Criminol 41: 9-23.

Edleson JL, Syers M. (1991) The effects of group treatment for men who batter: An 18 month follow-up study. Res Social Work Pract 1: 227-243.

Edleson J, Grusznski, R. (1988) Treating men who batter: Four years of outcome data from the domestic abuse project. J Social Service Res 12: 3-22.

Fals-Stewart W, Kashdan M, O'Farrell TJ, Birchler GR. (2002) Behavioral couples therapy for drug-abusing patients: Effects on partner violence. J Substance Abuse Treat 22: 87-96.

Feder GS, Hutson M, Ramsay J, Taket AR. (2006) Women exposed to intimate partner violence: expectations and experiences when they encounter health care professionals: a meta-analysis of qualitative studies. Arch Intern Med 166(1): 22-37.

Feder L, Dugan L. (2002) A test of the efficacy of court-mandated counseling for domestic violence offenders: The broward experiment. Justice Quart 19(2):343- 375.

Feder L, Forde D. (1999) A test of the efficacy of court-mandated counseling for convicted misdemeanor domestic violence offenders: Results from the Broward experiment. Paper presented at the International Family Violence Research Conference, Durham, NH.

Feder L, Forde DR. (2000) A Test of the efficacy of court-mandated counselingfor domestic violence offenders: The Broward Experiment (Final report, NIJ-96-WT-NX-0008). Washington, DC: National Institute of Justice.

Feighny KM, Muelleman RL. (1999) The effect of a community-based intimate-partner violence advocacy program in the emergency department on identification rate of intimate-partner violence. Mo Med 96(7): 242-244.

Ford DA, Regoli MJ. (1993) The criminal prosecution of wife batterers: Process, problems, and effects. In Legal responses to wife assault (Hilton, N.Z. ed). Pp. 127-164. Newbury Park, CA: Sage.

Fry P, Barker L. (2002) Female Survivors of Abuse and Violence: The Influence of Storytelling Reminiscence on Perceptions of Self-Efficacy, Ego Strength, and Self-Esteem. Springer Publishing Co, New York, NY:197-217.

Gazmararian JA, Petersen R, Spitz AM, Goodwin MM, Saltzman LE, Marks JS. (2000) Violence and reproductive health: current knowledge and future research directions. Matern Child Health J 4(2): 79-84.

Gerbert B, Caspers N, Milliken N, Berlin M, Bronstone A, Moe J. (2000) Interventions that help victims of domestic violence. A qualitative analysis of physicians' experiences. J Fam Pract 49(10): 889-895.

Gerbert B, Moe J, Caspers N, Salber P, Feldman M, Herzig K, Bronstone A. (2002) Physicians' response to victims of domestic violence: toward a model of care. Women Health 35(2-3): 1-22.

Gilbert L, El-Bassel N, Manuel J, Wu E, Go H, Golder S, Seewald R, Sanders G. (2006) An integrated relapse prevention and relationship safety intervention for women on methadone: testing short-term effects on intimate partner violence and substance use. Violence and Victims 21(5): 657-672.

Golding JM. (2002) Intimate partner violence as a risk factor for mental disorders: a meta-analysis. J Family Violence 14:99-132.

Gondolf EW. (1997) Patterns of reassault in batterer programs. Violence Victims, 12,:373-387.

Gondolf EW. (1998) The victims of court-ordered batterers: Their victimisation, helpseeking, and perceptions. Violence Against Women 4 (6): 659-676.

Gondolf EW. (2000) Reassault at 30-months after batterer programs intake. Int J Offender Therapy Comparative Criminol 44: 111-128.

Gondolf EW. (2003) MCMI results for batterers: Gondolf replies to Dutton's response. J Family Violence 18 (6): 387-389.

Graham DLR, Rawlings E, Rimini N. (1998)

Survivors of terror: battered women, hostages and the Stockholm Syndrome. In Yllo K, Bograd M, eds. Feminist perspectives on wife abuse, London: Sage.

Guth AA, Pachter L. (2000) Domestic violence and the trauma surgeon. Am J Surg 179(2): 134-140.

Hamberger K, Hastings J. (1988) Skills training for treatment of spouse abusers: An outcome study. J Family Violence 3: 121-130.

Harrell A. (1991) Evaluation of court ordered treatment for domestic violence offenders (Final report). Washington, DC: Urban Institute.

Harris R, Helfand M, Woolf S, Lohr K, Mulrow C, Teutsch S, Atkins D. (2001) Current methods of the US Preventive Services Task Force. Am J Prev Med 20(3S), 21-35.

Harris R, Savage S, Jones T, Brooke W. (1988) A comparison of treatments for abusive men and their partners within a family-service agency. Can J Community Mental Health 7(2):147-155.

Hawkins R, Beauvais C. (1985) Evaluation of group therapy with abusive men: The police record. Paper presented at the meeting of the American psychological association, Los Angeles, CA.

Hendricks B, Werner T, Shipway L, Turinetti GJ. (2006) Recidivism among spousal abusers: Predictions and program evaluation. J Interpersonal Violence 21 (6): 703-716.

Harris RP, Helfand M, Woolf SH, Lohr KN, Mulrow CD, Teutsch SM, Atkins D. (2001) Current methods of the US Preventive Services Task Force: a review of the process. Am J Prev Med 20(3 Suppl): 21-35.

Hegarty K. (2006) What is intimate partner abuse and how common is it? In G.Roberts, K.Hegarty, & G.Feder (Eds.), Intimate partner abuse and health professionals:new approaches to domestic violence (pp. 19-40). Edinburgh: Churchill Livingstone Elsevier.

Hegarty K, Feder GS, Roberts G. (2006) Intimate partner abuse research and training: The way forward. In G.Roberts, K.Hegarty, & G.S.Feder (Eds.), Intimate partner abuse and health professional s:new approaches to domestic violence Edinburgh: Churchill Livingstone Elsevier.

Hester M, Westmarland N. (2005) Tackling Domestic Violence: Effective Interventions and Approaches. Home Office Research Study 290, London: Home Office. http://www.homeoffice.gov.uk/rds/pdfs05/hors290.pdf

Hester M, Westmarland N, Gangoli G, Wilkinson M, O'Kelly C, Kent A, Diamond A. (2006) Domestic Violence Perpetrators: Identifying Needs to Inform Early Intervention, Bristol: University of Bristol in association with the Northern Rock Foundation and the Home Office.

Hester M, Pearson C, Harwin N. with Abrahams, H. (2007) Making an Impact - Children and Domestic Violence. A Reader, 2nd Edition. London: Jessica Kingsley.

Howard A, Riger S, Campbell R, Wasco S. (2003) Counseling services for battered women: a comparison of outcomes for physical and sexual assault survivors. J InterpersViolence 18(7): 717-734.

Jones AS, D'Agostino RB Jr, Gondolf EW, Heckert A. (2004) Assessing the effect on batterer program completion on reassault using propensity scores. J Interpersonal Violence 19 (9): 1002-1020.

Kim S, Kim J. (2001) The effects of group intervention for battered women in Korea. Arch Psychiatr Nurs 15(6): 257-264.

Koopman C, Ismailji T, Holmes D, Classen CC, Palesh O, Wales T. (2005) The effects of expressive writing on pain, depression and posttraumatic stress disorder symptoms in survivors of intimate partner violence. J Health Psychol 10: 211-221.

Koss MP, Koss PG, Woodruff WJ. (1991) Deleterious effects of criminal victimization on women's health and medical utilization. Arch Intern Med 151(2):342-347.

Kubany ES, Hill EE, Owens JA. (2003) Cognitive trauma therapy for battered women with PTSD: Preliminary findings. J Traumatic Stress 16:81-91.

Kubany ES, Hill EE, Owens JA, Iannce-Spencer C, McCaig MA, Tremayne KJ et al. (2004) Cognitive trauma therapy for battered women with PTSD (CTT-BW). J Consul Clin Psychol 72:3-18.

Laverde, Laverde DI. (1987) Efectos del tratamiento cognoscitivo-conductal en el maltrato fisico en la pareja. [Effects of cognitive-behavioral therapy in controlling wife abuse.]. Revista de Analisis del Comportamieno 3:193-200.

Leong DJ, Coates CJ, Hoskins J. (1987) Follow-up of batterers treated in a court-ordered treatment program. Paper at the Third National Family Violence Research Coinference, University of New Hampshire, Durham, NH.

Limandri BJ, May BA. (2002) Psychoeducational intervention to enhance self-efficacy of abused women. 35th Annual Communicating Nursing Research Conference/16th Annual WIN Assembly, "Health Disparities: Meeting the Challenge" held April 18-20, 2002, Palm Springs, California. Communicating Nursing Research 35:261

McCauley J, Kern DE, Kolodner K, Dill L, Schroeder AF, DeChant HK, Ryden J, Bass EB, Derogatis LR. (1995) The "battering syndrome": prevalence and clinical characteristics of domestic violence in primary care internal medicine practices. Ann Intern Med 123(10): 737-746.

McFarlane J, Malecha A, Gist J, Watson K, Batten E, Hall I, Smith S. (2002) An intervention to increase safety behaviors of abused women: results of a randomized clinical trial. Nurs Res 51(6): 347-354.

McFarlane J, Malecha A, Gist J, Watson K, Batten E, Hall I, Smith S. (2004) Protection orders and intimate partner violence: an 18-month study of 150 black, Hispanic, and white women. Am J Public Health 94(4): 613-618.

McFarlane J, Parker B, Soeken K, Silva C, Reel S. (1998) Safety behaviors of abused women after an intervention during pregnancy. J Obstet Gynecol Neonatal Nurs 27(1): 64-69.

McFarlane J, Soeken K, Reel S, Parker B, Silva C. (1997) Resource use by abused women following an intervention program: associated severity of abuse and reports of abuse ending. Public Health Nurs 14(4): 244-250.

McFarlane J, Soeken K, Wiist W. (2000) An evaluation of interventions to decrease intimate partner violence to pregnant women. Public Health Nurs 17(6): 443-451.

McFarlane JM, Groff JY, O'Brien JA, Watson K. (2006) Secondary prevention of intimate partner violence: a randomized controlled trial. Nurs Res **55**(1):52-61.

MacMillan HL, Wathan CN, with the Canadian Taskforce on Preventative Health Care. (2001) Prevention and treatment of violence against women: systematic review and recommendations. CTFPHC Technical Report #01-4. London, ON: Canadian Teask Force.

McNamara JR, Ertl M, Neufeld J. (1998) Problem-solving in relation to abuse by a partner. Psychol Rep 83(3 Pt 1):943-946.

McNamara JR, Ertl MA, Marsh S, Walker S. (1997) Short-term response to counseling and case management intervention in a domestic violence shelter. Psychol Rep 81(3 Pt 2): 1243-1251.

Mancoske RJ, Standifer D, Cauley C. (1994) The effectiveness of brief counseling services for battered women. Res Social Work Pract 4:53-63.

Melendez RM, Hoffman S, Exner T, Leu CS, Ehrhardt AA. (2003) Intimate partner violence and safer sex negotiation: effects of a gender-specific intervention. Arch Sex Behav 32(6): 499-511.

Murphy CC, Schei B, Myhr TL, Du MJ. (2001) Abuse: a risk factor for low birth weight? A systematic review and meta-analysis. CMAJ 164(11): 1567-1572.

Murphy CM, Musser PH, Maton KI. (1998) Coordinated community intervention for domestic abusers: Intervention system involvement and criminal recidivism. J Family Violence 13: 263 – 284.

Neggers Y, Goldenberg R, Cliver S, Hauth J. (2004) Effects of domestic violence on preterm birth and low birth weight. Acta Obstet Gynecol Scand 83(5): 455-460.

Newell RG. (1994) The effectiveness of court-mandated counseling for domestic violence: An outcome study. Dissertation Abstracts International Section A: Humanities and Scoial Sciences 53: 1193.

O'Leary KD, Heyman RE, Neidig PH. (1999) Treatment of wife abuse: A comparison of gender-specific and conjoint approaches. Behavior Therapy 30: 475-506.

Palmer SE, Brown RA, Barrera ME. (1992) Group treatment program for abusive husbands: Long term evaluation. Am J Orthopsychiatry 62: 276-283.

Parker B, McFarlane J, Soeken K, Silva C, Reel S. (1999) Testing an intervention to prevent further abuse to pregnant women. Res Nurs Health 22(1): 59-66.

Parsons LH, Harper MA. (1999) Violent maternal deaths in North Carolina. Obstet Gynecol 94(6): 990-993.

Paulozzi LJ, Saltzman LE, Thompson MP, Holmgreen P. (2001) Surveillance for homicide among intimate partners--United States, 1981-1998. MMWR CDC Surveill Summ 50(3): 1-15.

Ramsay J, Feder G, Rivas C. (2006) Interventions to reduce violence and promote the physical and psychosocial well-being of women who experience partner abuse: a systematic review. London, Department of Health. http://www.dh.gov.uk/assetRoot/04/12/74/26/04127426.pdf

Ratner PA. (1993) The incidence of wife abuse and mental health status in abused wives in Edmonton, Alberta. Can J Public Health 84(4): 246-249.

Reed GL, Enright RD. (2006). The effects of forgiveness therapy on depression, anxiety, and posttraumatic stress for women after spousal emotional abuse. J Consult Clin Psychol 74(5): 920-929.

Respect. (2004) <u>Statement of principles and minimum standards of practice for domestic violence perpetrator programs and associated women's services</u>. London: Respect. http://www.respect.uk.net/

Richardson J, Coid J, Petruckevitch A, Chung WS, Moorey S, Feder G. (2002) Identifying domestic violence: cross sectional study in primary care. BMJ 324(7332): 274-278.

Rinfret RM, Cantin S. (1997) Feminist therapy for battered women: An assessment. In Kantor GK, Jasinski JL, eds. Out of the darkness: Contemporary perspectives on family violence, pp 219-34. Thousand Oaks: Sage Publications.

Saunders DG. (1996) Feminist-cognitive-behavioral and process-psychodynamic treatments for men who batter: Interaction of abuser traits and treatment model. Violence and Victims 57393-414.

Stacey WA, Shupe A. (1984) An evaluation of three programs for abusive men in Texas (Research Monograph No. 29). Arlington, TX: Center for Social Research, University of Texas.

Stith SM, McCollum EE, Rosen KH, Locke LD. (2002) Multicouple group treatment for domestic violence. In: Comprehensive textbook of psychotherapy (Vol.4) (Kaslow, F., ed) New York: John Wiley & Sons.

Stith SM, Rosen KH, McCollum EE. (2003) Effectiveness of couple in treatment for spouse abuse. Journal of marital and family therapy 29: 407-426.

Sullivan CM, Bybee DI. (1999) Reducing violence using community-based advocacy for women with abusive partners. J Consult Clin Psychol 67(1): 43-53.

Sullivan CM, Campbell R, Angelique H, Eby KK, Davidson WS. (1994) An advocacy intervention program for women with abusive partners: six-month follow-up. Am J Community Psychol. 22(1), 101-122.

Sullivan CM, Davidson WS. (1991) The provision of advocacy services to women leaving abusive partners: an examination of short-term effects. Am J Community Psychol 19(6): 953-960.

Sullivan CM, Tan C, Basta J, Rumptz M, Davidson WS. (1992) An advocacy intervention program for women with abusive partners: initial evaluation. Am J Community Psychol 20(3): 309-332.

Taft A, Hegarty K, Flood M. (2001) Are men and women equally violent to intimate partners? Aust N Z J Public Health 25(6): 498-500.

Taft CT, Murphy CM, Elliott JD, Morrel TM. (2001) Attendance-enhancing procedures in group counseling for domestic abusers. J Counseling Psychol 48 (1): 51-60.

Tiwari A, Leung WC, Leung TW, Humphreys J, Parker B, Ho PC. (2005) A randomized controlled trial of empowerment training for Chinese abused pregnant women in Hong Kong. BJOG. 1249-1256

Tjaden P, Thoennes N. (2000) Extent, Nature, and Consequences of Intimate Partner Violence. 1-62. Washington: US Dept of Justice.

Tollestrup K, Sklar D, Frost FJ, Olson L, Weybright J, Sandvig J, Larson M. (1999) Health indicators and intimate partner violence among women who are members of a managed care organization. Prev Med 29(5):431-440.

Tutty LM. (1996) Post-shelter services: the efficacy of follow-up programs for abused women. Res Social Work Pract 6:425-41

Tutty LM, Bidgood BA, Rothery MA. (1993) Support groups for battered women - research on their efficacy. J Family Violence 8:325-43.

Tutty LM, Bidgood BA, Rothery MA. (1996) Evaluating the effect of group process and client variables in support groups for battered women. Res Social Work Pract 6:308-24.

Waldo M. (1988) Relationship enhance-ment counseling groups for wife abusers. J Mental Health Counsel 10:37-45.

Watts C, Zimmerman C. (2002) Violence against women: global scope and magnitude. Lancet 359(9313):1232-1237.

Wisner CL, Gilmer TP, Saltzman LE, Zink TM (1999). Intimate partner violence against women: do victims cost health plans more? J Fam.Pract 48(6): 439-443.

Wong SL, Wester F, Mol SS, Lagro-Janssen TL. (2006) Increased awareness of intimate partner abuse after training: a randomized controlled trial. Br J Gen Pract 56(525): 249-257.